Corrections

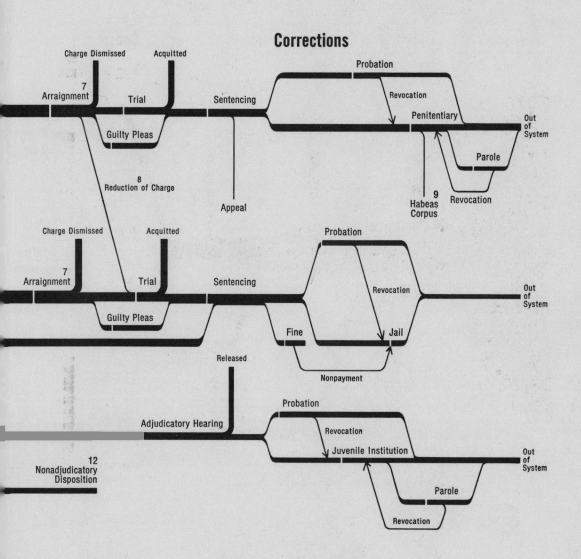

Charge Dismissed   Acquitted

7
Arraignment   Trial   Sentencing   Probation   Revocation   Penitentiary

Guilty Pleas   Out of System

8
Reduction of Charge   Parole

Appeal   **9**
Habeas Corpus   Revocation

Charge Dismissed   Acquitted

7
Arraignment   Trial   Sentencing   Probation   Revocation   Jail

Guilty Pleas   Fine   Out of System

Released   Nonpayment

Adjudicatory Hearing   Probation   Revocation   Juvenile Institution

12
Nonadjudicatory Disposition   Out of System

Parole

Revocation

8   Charge may be reduced at any time prior to trial in return for plea of guilty or for other reasons.

9   Challenge on constitutional grounds to legality of detention. May be sought at any point in process.

10 Police often hold informal hearings, dismiss or adjust many cases without further processing.

11 Probation officer decides desirability of further court action.

12 Welfare agency, social services, counselling, medical care, etc., for cases where adjudicatory handling not needed.

Introduction To
Criminal Justice

Introduction To Criminal Justice

DONALD J. NEWMAN

School of Criminal Justice
State University of
New York at Albany

J. B. Lippincott Company

Philadelphia   New York   Toronto

ISBN 0-397-47324-9

Library of Congress Catalog Card Number 74-18344

Printed in the United States of America

3 5 7 9 8 6 4

Library of Congress Cataloging in Publication Data

Newman, Donald J.
Introduction to criminal justice.

Bibliography: p. 417
1. Criminal justice, Administration of—United
States. 2. Criminal procedure—United States.

I. Title.
KF9223.N5   345'.73'05   74-18344
ISBN 0-397-47324-9

To my wife, Evelyn
and my children
Richard, Bethany Ann, and Kendall

PREFACE

The Field of Criminal Justice

In 1965 President Lyndon B. Johnson declared war on crime. Since that time the crime problem has remained high in public opinion polls concerned with major domestic issues. President Nixon, the Congress, and successive attorneys general have continued and even escalated the war not only with rhetoric, but also with new legislation. Perhaps more significantly, strong budgetary support has been given to federal, state, and local crime control efforts.

Governmental intervention in crime control is not new, of course. What is new is the breadth and intensity of public concern and the stress placed on the need for an integrated, systems approach to the control of the multiple types of offenses in our society. Historically, in our ancestral European, Asian, and African cultures, crime control was largely a matter of private concern, of physical vengeance or monetary forfeiture wreaked upon the perpetrator by the victim or his family. Gradually, in our society, the control of crime became a function of the state, which became defined as the ultimate victim of all serious criminal offenses. Today we have added the requirement that most criminal conduct be defined by statute rather than by common-law precedent.

To fulfill the crime control mandate, various governmental agencies, offices, and courts were created, supported, and staffed, each with separate obligations and functions, yet all united in their ultimate purpose—the control of crime—and by the array of decisions affecting a suspect as he is processed from arrest, through the courts, to prison and parole. As crime control became routinized, a number of occupational specialities were developed to staff the agencies and to run the crime control process. The three major bureaucracies—police, courts, and corrections—for the most part defined their own requirements for recruitment, each reaching into separate manpower pools and providing distinct training or educational preparation. At present, legal education is generally necessary for judges and prosecutors; in-service training is common for most police and custodial personnel in prisons; college degrees in social work or liberal arts are often required for correctional professionals. Though these key personnel work in contiguous agencies and make interlocking determinations about suspects and offenders, their loyalties and identities have tended to bind them to their separate professions rather than to the total criminal justice system, while the agencies they staff have developed operational policies and practices in isolation from each other.

The result of all this has been the development of a criminal justice system composed of a loose federation of agencies and offices, each separately budgeted, each drawing its manpower from separate wells, and each a profession unto itself. That this should be so is, in historical perspective, somewhat dysfunctional, and perhaps part of the blame can be placed on our colleges and universities.

Normally when our society experiences a serious problem or when it is confronted by a major threat, our higher educational resources respond by lending their research experience and expertise to the search for solutions. Every major societal problem—for example, illness, space exploration, poverty—is seen as a mandate for professional researchers to look for solutions and for colleges to train appropriate manpower. Of course, other agencies and institutions also respond to the challenge; but it is important to stress the academic response, since it is a major source of concentrated and sophisticated research efforts. The academic's advantages of distance and detachment help him to see processes and programs objectively and to bring a sense of history and prior experimentation to novel suggestions. Academic search for solutions to economic or social problems has occasionally created new research and teaching disciplines which borrow from traditional fields of knowledge, but which maintain clear and separate identities. For example, university response to the problems of food supply for our increasingly industrial society led to the creation of land-grant agricultural colleges from which came such new disciplines as horticulture and biochemistry. Through the development and use of their extension field services, the agricultural schools made direct and continuous impact on all aspects of farming and other means of food production. Perhaps the time has come for our colleges to respond in kind with involvement in problems of criminal justice.

Criminology and Criminal Justice

When Lyndon Johnson was promising "not only to reduce crime but to banish it," there were few programs or curricula in criminal justice on American campuses. There were some degree-granting departments of police administration and occasionally a program in corrections which was usually attached to a sociology department. Even in law schools, which provide not only prosecutors and judges, but also a good many legislators, there was no clear focus on the total criminal justice process, little attention given to procedures other than trial and appeal, and almost complete lack of attention to such important post-conviction processes as sentencing. However, course offerings in criminology in many undergraduate and graduate curricula were common, and there was professionally conducted research into criminological problems. To what extent can criminology, perhaps allied with police or correctional programs, be taken as the basis of a new and searching academic response to crime control? Certainly there seems to be a clearly felt need to create a new discipline of criminal justice administration as we see colleges and universities offering criminal justice programs at all degree levels up to and including the doctorate. The proliferation of academic programs in criminal justice in the past few years is truly astonishing.[1] But the question must be asked: is there really a new field of criminal justice or simply a shift from basic research to applied administration?

This is not easily answered. Some criminal justice programs have grown out of criminology courses; others have sprung from police or correctional training curricula; still others were created from whole cloth. Whatever the root discipline or the historical origin, the evidence indicates the emergence of a new academic field of scholarship, research, and didactics called criminal justice administration. And as with most such endeavors, the passage is a difficult and stormy one, nowhere completed but in process on literally hundreds of campuses across our nation.

There are some major differences between the traditional academic field of criminology and what is commonly meant by criminal justice. Criminology, usually a subconcentration in a sociology or psychology curriculum, is primarily concerned with the etiology of criminal behavior: why certain persons commit crimes; how criminal roles originate and crystallize. In similar fashion the criminologist attempts, through research, to explain the complex interactions between persons and cultural norms that lead to criminal conduct in our society.[2] The criminologist is also interested in societal response to crime, whether by ostracism or imprisonment, and attempts to measure the effectiveness of such intervention. Some criminologists have worked in parole prediction; others have attempted to measure and evaluate the deterrence claims of death penalty advocates. Still others have attempted to assess offenders' self-concepts as they are apprehended and processed through police, courts, and correctional stages of the criminal justice system. Another important interest of criminologists has been the measurement of the incidence of crime and delinquency in our society by the use of official records and self-reporting devices.

The comparative effectiveness of intervention in criminal matters and the measurement of crime rates come closer to the traditional interest of criminal justice scholars than does etiology. This does not mean that crime causation is irrelevant to criminal justice; quite the contrary. The matter is one of degree and emphasis. Criminal justice is mostly concerned with the decision process in the crime control agencies of police, prosecutors' offices, trial courts, and correctional facilities, and in programs like probation and parole. Thus the effectiveness or dysfunction of criminal justice intervention may be tested against, and in turn test, hypotheses and theories of crime causation proposed by criminologists. Sociologists, for example, are currently much interested in labelling theory, which asserts that deviant roles become hardened and internalized in proportion to the degree and intensity of official intervention. Merely being arrested and booked may convince the minor offender that he is indeed deeply "criminal." This theory is of direct interest to criminal justice and an important factor to be weighed in evaluating the effectiveness of system decisions. There are other ties as well. A study of influence of broken homes on criminal behavior is more likely to be undertaken by a criminologist, but it would also be of interest to the analyst of criminal justice in the use of such criteria for sentencing or for correctional treatment.

The distinction in research focus between the criminological emphasis on causal factors in contrast to research into the operational reality and effectiveness of criminal justice agencies has sometimes been viewed as merely a difference between "pure" and "applied" research, comparable to the relationship of chemistry and the practice of medicine. While there may well be some truth in this analogy, it is an oversimplified one. Criminal justice is not applied criminology; it may test certain theoretical propositions of criminology in terms of court or agency response to them, but it takes its basic building blocks from many sources, and is not limited to criminology or even to such operational specialities as police or correctional administration.

Criminal Justice and Law

The criminal justice scholar must familiarize himself with law and legal process if he is to make a meaningful contribution to the field, for the criminal justice system is a legal entity. Criminal behavior is defined only by statute (though there are a few common-law crimes in some jurisdictions), and in turn these are finally interpreted by courts. All the agencies, offices, and programs in criminal justice exist by law and are controlled by legal process. Of course, it can be said that all systems of state intervention, such as compulsory public education, are legal systems and involve legal processes. Again the matter is one of degree and perspective. Most compulsory programs, whether of schooling or of mental health, are intended to be beneficent, though this may be only partially achieved in practice. The criminal justice process, however, is punitive in origin, deals with a reluctant and litigious population, and in a real sense tests the limits of state intervention into the lives of citizens. Substantive criminal laws form the enabling basis of enforcement and set its limits; offices and agencies are created and controlled by statute. Today most major decisions of participants in the criminal process, from police to parole boards, are extensively governed and controlled by statute and case law.

This does not mean that every action of participants in the process, every policy and each decision, is clearly fixed in statute or case law so that the system is one of automatic imposition of evidentiary standards or legal sanctions with no room for variance or discretion. Quite the contrary. Not only is there ample room for discretion at all stages of the process, but the range and variation for choices and decisions in daily practice are immense. But just as it would be wrong to say that the formal, written law is irrelevant to criminal justice, that what needs to be studied are solely operational practices, there is a danger in reverse, that is, viewing discretion as somehow deviant from absolute norms fixed in statutory law. The system is much more complicated than this, but at a minimum, analysis requires sophisticated awareness of law and legal procedures. A student of criminal justice who ignores this will likely find himself adrift in a world he never made.

Perhaps one of the reasons why criminal justice did not become academically distinct until recently is that the rules and literature of law were assumed to be the exclusive province of lawyers. There are usually separate libraries on university campuses, each with its own collection of legal literature. The separation of law faculty from other departments and schools makes interaction with other faculty and students logistically unlikely. By custom, it would be presumptuous for most scholars untrained in the law to speak authoritatively on legal matters. This does not mean that lawyers and legal scholars were uninterested or reluctant to deal with criminal justice matters. In fact, some very high quality criminal justice programs originated and remain in law schools, but isolation still exacts a price. Here, very often, a different neglect is notice-able; relevant social science materials tend to be overlooked or discounted by lawyer-researchers.

Criminal Justice and Other Disciplines

Basic to criminal justice are important elements from political science, for crim-inal justice studies encompass law-making as well as law-breaking processes, and the total system exists in a political context. Crime control rests ultimately on force. Here, if anywhere, the extremes of the proper use of physical force to control domestic misconduct are tested against our ideological values of fairness, individual liberty, and due process of law.

In addition to its thread of origin in political science, much research and training for the day-by-day operations of various criminal justice agencies rest on concepts and methodology borrowed from the interdisciplinary field of systems analysis of complex organizations. The intricacies of organizational policy making, managerial styles and effectiveness, systems forecasting, and planning for change, as well as sophisticated measures of goal attainment and process effectiveness, are all relevant and applicable to criminal justice issues.

Likewise, techniques borrowed from psychology, psychiatry, and social work are of central importance to the criminal justice task of changing persons and organizations. It is tempting to treat the flow of the criminal justice process as if it were a production line in a factory. Analysis of processes and policies in abstraction from those processed can yield valuable knowledge of the criminal justice system. But carried to an extreme, the people-processing, people-changing objectives of the system become muted. The flow of suspect to defendant to offender to inmate to parolee is not a single-edged task; unlike ketchup bottles, the "product" of the criminal justice process generates input into decision making, reacts to each step of state intervention, and becomes worse or better because of it. In fact, measurement of the impact of processing and programs on the individual is a critical part of criminal justice analysis.

Last but not least, criminal justice borrows from and contributes to a variety of technological fields, devices, and methodologies. The computer is operationally important in practically all agencies from police to parole boards, in addition to being a research tool of major significance. The mapping of the complex criminal justice decision network can only be accomplished by sophisticated electronic techniques. The computer is so much a part of police and correctional work (courts are just discovering it) that it is hard to see how records were kept, decisions made, and programs evaluated in precomputer days. Other electronic devices are also operationally important, with their full potential still to be realized. Electronic eavesdropping is a major and controversial police tool. Television monitoring is currently used in some prisons, particularly in high-security segregation units. Electronic tracking of probationers and parolees, such as substituting a wrist beeper and console for the surveillance of field agents is under development. Chemotherapy is not currently of great significance, but use of chlorpromazine has revolutionized the world of mental hospitals, and similar impact with offenders is possible. Narcotic substitutes (e.g., methadone) for heroin are already in use.

It would be possible to take almost any field of knowledge and relate it to criminal justice, though certain disciplines and methodologies are obviously more directly relevant than others. However, it is abundantly clear that major criminal justice concerns are multidisciplinary in nature, requiring the agency practitioner, the consultant, the researcher, and the informed observer to be aware of knowledge and perspectives from diverse sources. Single-minded viewpoints of the process, or failure to recognize its complexity in origin and operation leads inevitably to simplistic suggestions for change or reform. This is precisely what is *not* needed at the present time. The history of the criminal justice system is littered with discarded, simple, and even weird suggestions for increased effectiveness and reform. Perhaps fear of crime or an equally strong fear of governmental repression leads many otherwise well-informed citizens to advance naive proposals for the improvement of criminal justice. Persons who readily accept the complexity and paradoxes of our economic system, who recognize the subtlety of interpersonal interactions even within a single family, often fail to comprehend the complicated processes and multiple purposes of crime control in our society. Disarm the police, censor comic books, increase or decrease wiretapping, increase or decrease prison sentences, speed up the court process, fingerprint everyone or no one, punish parents for the transgressions of their children, define all criminal conduct as sick, tear down prison walls, legalize marijuana, and make pollution a felony—each has been seriously suggested as a means to control crime or to curb excesses in crime control in our society.

Hopefully the field of criminal justice will become immune to serious advocacy of banal reforms. At the same time, it is only too obvious that there is a real need for improvement in virtually all aspects of crime control. However, realistic assessment and suggestions for fundamental improvements are hard tasks. The interlocking relationships of legislation, court functions, and agency operations are so complex that it is difficult to extract critical themes to improve understanding and evaluation of the entire criminal justice system. Though the field of criminal justice can be broadly defined and circumscribed, there are at present few, if any, *experts* in total systems analysis. Direct participants in the process tend to be certain of their own roles and functions, but relatively unfamiliar with others; distant observers are often too abstract and impractical to achieve operational significance; researchers and experimenters too often focus on minute issues and measure trivia. Hopefully a new generation of persons trained to deal with the total system, to delineate its arteries, to discover central themes and issues, will bring needed expertise. Thus the purpose of this book is *not* to attempt to provide answers for all inquiries about criminal justice, nor even to ask all questions, but rather to assist criminal justice students and practitioners to develop total system perspectives and to make them aware of the tremendous complexity of the system and the hard work that must precede changes for the better.

NOTES

1. See Charles W. Tenney, Jr., *Higher Education Programs in Law Enforcement and Criminal Justice* (Washington, D.C.: U.S. Department of Justice, 1971).

2. See Edwin H. Sutherland and Donald R. Cressey, *Principles of Criminology,* 9th ed. (Philadelphia: J. B. Lippincott, 1974). See also Marvin E. Wolfgang and Franco Ferracuti, *The Subculture of Violence: Towards an Integrated Theory in Criminology* (London: Tavistock, 1967).

ACKNOWLEDGMENTS

No author writes a book without the help and support of others. The stimulation of colleagues is essential and this I have found and deeply appreciate with each of my fellow professors at the School of Criminal Justice. Special thanks are due my two team-teaching partners, Vincent O'Leary and Jack Kress. Thanks go not only to present colleagues, but to those of yesteryear. I wish to express my appreciation to Marshall B. Clinard who introduced me to criminology and to Frank J. Remington who taught me much about criminal justice.

Colleague stimulation is only part of the picture. As with many professors I have learned a great deal from my students. To every student, past and present, I owe a debt of gratitude.

Scott Christianson, my research assistant on this book from first draft to publication, helped immeasurably. His command of the literature, firm grasp of substantive issues, and his fine critiques of writing style were essential.

My secretaries, Helen Stenzel and Kathleen Glebatis did yeoman's work at all stages of manuscript preparation from interpreting my poor handwriting through final draft. Without their dedication and attention to detail, this book would never have seen the light of day.

Editorial assistance has been magnificent. Richard Heffron worked closely with me every step of the way, and his help and guidance is truly appreciated.

In addition, I wish to thank the following authors and publishers for granting permission to reprint material from their publications:

The American Bar Association, *Standards Relating to Sentencing Alternatives and Procedures; Pleas of Guilty;* and *Fair Trial and Free Press,* Copyright © 1968 by the American Bar Association. *Standards Relating to Probation,* Copyright © 1970 by the American Bar Association. *Standards Relating to the Prosecution Function and the Defense Function,* Copyright © 1971 by the American Bar Association. *Standards*

Relating to the Urban Police Function, Copyright © 1973 by the American Bar Association.

The American Law Institute, excerpts from the *Model Penal Code.* Copyright © 1962. Reprinted with permission of the American Law Institute.

The Bobbs-Merrill Company, Inc. for excerpts reprinted from *Criminal Justice Administration* by Frank J. Remington, Donald J. Newman, Edward L. Kimball, Marygold Melli and Herman Goldstein. Copyright © 1969, by The Bobbs-Merrill Company, Inc. Reprinted by permission. All rights reserved.

Ramsey Clark, *Crime in America.* Copyright © 1970 by Ramsey Clark. Reprinted by permission of Simon and Schuster.

The Harvard Law Review, Note "Anthropolemeletry: Dr. Schwitzgebel's Machine," 80 *Harvard Law Review* 403 (1966). Copyright © 1966 by The Harvard Law Review Association.

Little Brown for excerpts reprinted from *Sentencing: The Decision as to Type, Length and Conditions of Sentence* by Robert O. Dawson. Copyright © 1969 by Little Brown and Company. *Conviction: The Determination of Guilt or Innocence Without Trial* by Donald J. Newman. Copyright © 1966 by Little, Brown and Company. *Prosecution: The Decision to Charge a Suspect with a Crime* by Frank W. Miller. Copyright 1970 by Little, Brown and Company. *Detection of Crime: Stopping and Questioning, Search and Seizure, Encouragement and Entrapment* by Lawrence P. Tiffany, Donald M. McIntyre, Jr., and Daniel Rotenberg. Copyright © 1967 by Little, Brown and Company. *The Discovery of the Asylum* by David J. Rothman. Copyright © 1971 by Little, Brown and Company.

The Yale Law Journal Company and Fred B. Rothman & Company, "Police Discretion not to Invoke the Criminal Process" by Joseph D. Goldstein; "Law Enforcement: An Attempt at Social Dissection" by Thurman Arnold; and "Ideology in Criminal Procedure or a Third 'Model' of the Criminal Process" by John Griffiths. Reprinted by permission of The Yale Law Journal Company and Fred B. Rothman & Company from *The Yale Law Journal,* Vol. 69, p. 543, Vol. 42, pp. 17-18, Vol. 79, pp. 374, 376, 389.

Finally, I owe my deepest thanks to my family for putting up with all the traumas and pressures caused by a writer in the house.

Donald J. Newman
Albany, New York
Summer 1974

CONTENTS

Contents

PART THREE CONTEMPORARY ISSUES AND TRENDS IN
CRIMINAL JUSTICE ADMINISTRATION

Part One

The Criminal Justice System

When reference is made to the criminal justice system or to criminal justice administration, what is usually meant is the complex decision network devoted to control of "traditional" crimes in our society. In our statutes, as in those of all large diversified cultures, there is a wide range of conduct defined as criminal. For example, there are nearly 3,000 federal criminal statutes, and any state is likely to have more, for federal crimes are somewhat limited by interstate or federal interest requirements. Some of our crimes existed in common law as far back as history can be traced. These, "evil in themselves" (*mala in se*), were archaic prototypes of such present-day offenses as homicide, robbery, burglary, larceny, sex offenses, and other forms of what has been variously termed traditional, conventional, or "street" crime. Generally these offenses are grouped together in statutes which collectively make up the penal code (or the criminal code) of the jurisdiction. In addition, scores of other legislative proscriptions are scattered throughout the collected laws of any jurisdiction and may have attached to them some of the traditional penal sanctions, like fines or jail terms. These proscriptions may also provide for the use of such sanctions as injunctions, treble damage suits, and the like, which are largely absent from penal codes. Many of these offenses have no exact counterparts in common law (or they may reverse some ancient common-law assumptions), for they are largely legislative creations (*mala prohibita*) necessary to control the intricate commercial and interpersonal relationships that characterize industrial, urban society. Examples of these crimes

1

include antitrust violations of corporations, income tax evasion, price fixing, and various other forms of corporate fraud. American criminologists particularly have invested a good deal of time in research and have made extensive commentary on these "white-collar" crimes. However, the primary focus of criminal justice has been directed toward analysis of the system used to control traditional street offenses.

Special agencies created by legislation to investigate and process white-collar violations, like the Internal Revenue Service or the Food and Drug Administration, are involved in a form of criminal justice administration. And sometimes white-collar violators are investigated, arrested, convicted, and serve sentences in the traditional criminal justice system. Some persons take the position that the kinds of crimes processed through special enforcement and administrative processes (e.g., price fixing) are really the most seriously damaging offenses to the social order and therefore should be the heart of criminal justice study. This is a perfectly legitimate stance, but it leaves the traditional and routine responses to murder and mayhem unanalyzed. Any single criminal justice process, with all of its variations, is complex enough to be worthy of full and exclusive scrutiny without making judgments about the relative importance of other forms of criminal justice processing, whether in our society or in other cultures. In any analytic endeavor, a basic decision about focus must be made. What is meant here by criminal justice is a system that enforces traditional penal laws, analysis of which involves describing the structural interrelationships of legislatures, appellate courts, and enforcement and administrative agencies, as well as their corresponding processes of decision making from arrest of suspects through charging, adjudication, sentencing, imprisonment, and release on parole.

It must be stressed that focus on the routine functioning of police agencies, on the traditional tasks of prosecutors and criminal court judges, and on the standard correctional bureaucracies of probation services, prisons, and parole boards is not meant to denigrate the importance of other enforcement systems in which different deviant behaviors are involved. Nor is it to be inferred that the crime control system is more important than other forms of legal intervention systems like juvenile delinquency processes or procedures for the civil commitment of the mentally ill. However, it is necessary to begin dealing in systemic terms with one major system at a time, though with full awareness that the traditional criminal justice system is neither the only example of state intervention into the lives of citizens, nor the only form of the legitimate use of force. Other systems, whether compulsory education or incarceration of the mentally ill, are important models for comparison wherever and whenever possible.

2

APPROACHES TO CRIMINAL JUSTICE ANALYSIS

Given the traditional criminal justice system as the focus for analysis, a number of questions arise concerning approach. There are, for example, some extreme ideological positions which may be taken about this matter. One of these rests on claims that the present criminal justice system is inherently repressive, a tool of the Establishment to control "the people," the essence of fascism that underlies our pretensions at equality and democracy, and generally no more than a white, chauvinistic, racist system which uses force to maintain the economic and political status quo. On this premise, rather than attempting to analyze or understand the system, we are urged to attack it, to tear it down and build a whole new social order in which crime control is unnecessary, or if this is not possible, to create a different kind of criminal justice system designed to get at the "real criminals" and punish "crimes against the people." The difficulty with this as a starting point for analysis and evaluation is that it is so extreme, so broadly negative, that it is little more than a battle cry. It is virtually impossible to do systematic, sophisticated, and detailed analysis with this type of conclusion already drawn. Selective illustrations from practice in a single agency or in the system as a whole can be used to stereotype the system in any manner the illustrator wishes. Horror stories of corruption, brutality, indifference, and neglect can be assembled and used to characterize the criminal justice system as being itself criminal. Conversely, helpful and even heroic actions of the police, sensible and just decisions of prosecutors and courts, and successful rehabilitation of persons in the correctional system can also be marshalled to demonstrate the beneficence and effectiveness of present crime control efforts. It is a saint-sinner paradox. Both are stereotypic, public relations approaches to criminal justice analysis which distort reality and which are of little help to the objective student of the process or to dedicated persons working in it. Nevertheless it must be recognized that in our society today there are nihilists who view any dispassionate analyses of the present system as not only futile, but as obstacles which delay or prevent change. On balance and given the very real problems and dilemmas of crime control, the present structure of the criminal justice system, and indeed the structure of our social order, it would seem that a candid study, analysis, and evaluation of the system is the best path to valid conclusions about it.

Another commonly advocated analytic approach, somewhat less extreme than total overthrow of the system, would require the major focus of investigation to be on the elimination of corruption and brutality in the system. In contrast to the nihilistic stance, this posture agrees in essence with the objectives of the system but wishes to achieve these in a more effective and more honest fashion. This is not a bad request; there is no doubt that corruption of police, courts, and correctional agencies has been common in the past and may be so at present. The difficulty with this as a central theme of analysis is that by focusing on corruption, the basic and proper functions of the system are ignored, with the result that rather simplistic and specious suggestions for improvement are made. It is an "evil man" approach which calls for replacing the dishonest, incompetent, or brutal with more honest and upright persons. The assumption is that if better people are attracted to system roles, all problems of criminal justice will be solved. This is rather like trying to analyze higher education by focusing on student cheating. Even if victory is total, if honest and upright citizens can be found to run the entire system, such major issues as the range of proper exercises of discretion, the effectiveness of controls and limitations on decision making, or the propriety of various methods of enforcement, prosecution, and corrections remain largely unresolved. A policeman who accepts a bribe from a suspect is not exercising discretion; he is simply corrupt. Yet the important question of when and under what conditions a police officer may *properly not arrest* a suspect, though he has sufficient evidence and authority to do so, remains a central issue in criminal justice analysis.

Rejecting anarchy and corruption as starting points and central themes still leaves the problem of how best to become immersed in criminal justice problems, how to dissect the complex bureaucratic structures and their functional processes so that a meaningful overview of the entire system is developed and a useful basis for analysis is provided. There are a number of potentially valuable approaches to analysis, somewhat overlapping, yet each with enough difference in focus to require some choice. One approach involves concentration on the bureaucracies that operate the criminal justice process, such as the police, prosecutors, courts, and corrections. Essentially this approach divides the system into its component institutions and agencies, studying each independently but with a view toward comparing organizational patterns and similarities and differences in administrative processes. The study might begin, for example, with a description of police organizational response to differential crime patterns dealing with such matters as the functions of detectives in contrast to those of patrolmen; the creation of specializing squads and units (vice, homicide, intelligence, and so on) in police agencies; problems of overlapping jurisdictions among sheriffs, metropolitan police, and state and federal enforcement agencies. Likewise, corrections can be studied in terms of alternative organizational patterns. For example, studies can be made of the advantages and disadvantages of merging or separating probation and parole systems, or of combining adult and juvenile institutions under one agency. Though important and valuable in itself, the organizational approach does not lead to true systems analysis, but rather to parallel descriptions of administrative problems within bureaucracies.

4

Focus on police organization and manpower needs quickly demonstrates that police have many duties which are not directly related to criminal justice. For example, the bulk of police work involves such things as controlling traffic patterns, keeping fire watch while prowling neighborhoods at night, guarding dignitaries, leading parades, and similar functions. Only *part* of police work, though indeed an important part, involves direct participation in the criminal justice process. Likewise, other agencies, offices, and courts are in many instances only part-time participants in crime control. Prosecutors in small rural jurisdictions often devote half or more of their professional activities to the private practice of law; even in jurisdictions with full-time county attorneys, the office may have civil as well as criminal functions. In some places there are specialized criminal trial courts; in others criminal work may fill only a small part of a judge's calendar. Appellate courts and legislatures may devote 90 percent or more of their efforts to noncriminal concerns. Even corrections has part-time personnel in some roles; many parole boards are manned by citizen appointees who serve only part-time; and a number of correctional efforts with juveniles often involve dealing with dependent and neglected children, in addition to processing juvenile delinquents. The bureaucracy approach—studying the organizational problems of police, courts, and corrections—comes closest to criminal justice administration in a *business administration* sense. Stress is on internal structuring of the agencies: on budget, manpower, and operational efficiency.

Another and closely related approach focuses less on the organizational structure of agencies than on the roles of those who run the system. Questions about who police are, where they come from, how prosecutors are selected, how judges are chosen, and the role and functions of prison wardens are all central to this method. Predictably, the usual conclusions from such analysis is that the system needs to become more "professional," although, paradoxically, today there are also suggestions that many criminal justice roles can best be filled by "paraprofessionals," including offenders and ex-offenders.

Combining both approaches, organizational and role, the analysis would conclude with elaborate reports covering the way police organize to meet the crime problem, the way prosecutors' offices are staffed, and on such court problems as overcrowding and delay, and whole treatises on the complex bureaucratic structures of correctional facilities and programs. Probably there would also be information on selection, training, career patterns, and the like, about persons operative in the system. The difficulty with this combined structure and role approach is that, although it has great merit in itself, it is not really systemic. It provides helpful analysis of contiguous agencies and of separate professions and occupations in crime control, but the functional threads of the process are missing.

5

Another way of cutting into criminal justice analysis is to deal with the decision flow of the criminal process and the interaction of policies and practices among the courts and operational agencies. This is essentially a decision-making emphasis which attempts to explain how the system works rather than who runs it. It stresses law enforcement, court and correctional *functions* rather than intraorganizational problems. Working details of the total police task which are not directed to criminal law enforcement, like routine traffic management, are recognized but considered ancillary to police functions in crime investigation, arrest, and in-custody interrogation of suspects. Likewise, whether a trial judge is appointed or elected on a partisan ticket is merely background information for analyzing his decisions in adjudication, sentencing, and probation revocation. This approach to criminal justice analysis will be followed in the remainder of this book.

FUNCTIONAL ANALYSIS OF THE CRIMINAL JUSTICE SYSTEM

A major advantage of the functions approach is that this perspective provides avenues for total systems analysis of problems, issues, and even techniques that are not localized in agencies but that occur repeatedly at various points in the process. For example, when this approach is used, it becomes clear that the functions of interrogation, search, and arrest (taking into custody) are not issues limited to the police bureaucracy. Probation officers, wardens, custodial officers, and parole agents also perform these tasks, though often in contexts different from the police. Likewise, functional practices effecting the rehabilitation or reintegration of offenders are by no means solely the prerogative of correctional agencies. Police, prosecutors, and trial judges all have or can have a *corrective function,* and today this type of function at *preconviction* stages is considered crucially important in criminal justice processing.

The decision-making, functional approach also has the advantage of cutting through the provincialism that has characterized criminal justice planning and programing. For example, when the decision flow of the process is analyzed it becomes clear that police activity (or activity of the prosecutor, the court, or the correctional agency) has major influence on the policies, practices, and decisions of other agencies. Decisions made by police, such as whether or not to invoke the criminal process, and if so, how and how vigorously, are not merely in-house concerns. What the police do, or do not do, has a pervasive effect across the system, as do decisions made in other agencies and offices. This whole approach demonstrates that the criminal justice system is a system not because of bureaucratic structure, for the agencies of crime control are relatively independent, but rather because of the functional relationships among the enforcement efforts of the police, the prosecutory decisions of states' attorneys, the adjudicatory and sentencing functions of trial judges, and the postconviction treatment of offenders in correctional agencies. The cement that binds the system together is the flow of persons who enter as suspects and, if fully processed, leave by parole and eventual discharge from sentence. No single agency or office is in itself a complete criminal justice system; the police serve as the intake agency for correctional populations, and in turn corrections returns to the community ex-inmates who are hoped to be rehabilitated, but who may soon again become police problems. The flow of persons through the system, or diverted from it, measures its parameters and provides the most comprehensive way of dealing with the system in total context.

Maintaining focus on decision points across the entire spectrum of the criminal justice process is a hard task, for each agency and office has its own problems, ranging from budgetary support to the use of new techniques or methods of enforcement, of court processing, or of corrections. The trouble is that the processes and problems of each agency are so fascinating in themselves that it is easy to become immersed in the details of managing a particular agency, to be attracted by the life and times of a prison warden, or to become diverted in other ways so that the overall systemic relationship of roles and functions is lost. It is nearly impossible and perhaps unnecessary to attempt to relate every action or inaction of police, prosecutors, judges, and parole officers to each other and to the total system. Yet awareness of interlocking decision consequences and analysis of large problems of the system are important for accurate analysis, for planned change, and as a basis for any reform that may be necessary or desirable.

THE MULTIPLE GOALS OF THE CRIMINAL JUSTICE PROCESS

The task of criminal justice systems analysis, as complex and difficult as it is, has more profound objectives than the simple description of how the system works. Implicit in the task of analysis is an evaluation mandate, a need to do more than merely study current enforcement, prosecutory, and correctional practices, to go beyond determination of how the system works to evaluation of how well it works. This makes the task not only more difficult, but more important. Criminal justice administration does not occur in an ideological vacuum, nor are its processes and practices value-neutral. The tremendous complexity of the system is compounded many times over by multiple and often divergent expectations assigned to it, not only by legislatures and the general public, but by direct participants in it as well. One fact that seems very difficult to accept in analyzing criminal justice is that the system has multiple purposes, that there is not just one goal or a single objective of either the total system or of any process within it. The multiplicity of purposes, and of hopes, not only makes the system controversial, but often adds a dimension of confusion to any attempt to assess or to evaluate it. It is not unusual for persons who advocate one type of program or one objective to find themselves debating with persons interested in the same problem but with entirely different perspectives and purposes. This is the subtle and insidious issue underlying all attempts at evaluation and all proposals for reform. No matter how carefully phrased, or how effective a single crime control program is, there is bound to be opposition, equally well phrased, which seeks to achieve other, perhaps conflicting objectives. For example, today a rather strong case can be made and documented that maximum-security prisons do not rehabilitate offenders. In fact, persons who spend considerable time in prison often turn out to be worse risks when they are returned to the community than when they entered prison. Assuming strong and objective evidence of this, it could follow that imprisonment should be changed or abandoned altogether, possibly to be replaced by other forms of intervention. However, this position rests on the assumption that the primary purpose of incarceration is rehabilitation so that the prison system fails if it does not meet this goal. Another position, equally credible within the historical purposes of imprisonment in our society, assumes the purpose of imprisonment to be the restraint of offenders, their incapacitation during the period of their sentences. If incapacitation is assumed as a primary goal, a case can be made that prisons are successes rather than failures, for few prisoners escape, and the community *is* protected from offenders while they are behind bars. While it might be possible by means of public opinion polls or other measurements to rank purposes of the criminal justice process, exercises in this vein would likely show that the priority given to any one goal shifts over time or differs between offense categories. Even if attempts to list and rank goals were carefully done, the most it would do would make clear the fact of multiple expectations, multiple objectives, and divergent motives for use of the criminal process. In a way, the criminal justice system is like the elephant to the five blind men, each of whom touched and described the beast from a single vantage point. Likewise, observers and analysts of criminal justice have a tendency to grab hold of certain parts of the system, or certain processes within it, and to define these as paramount concerns. But no matter how worthy single perspectives and the motives of proponents of particular viewpoints, the elephant of criminal justice exists as a whole entity, and before any one position can assume priority over others, it is necessary for the total beast to be described and evaluated.

The chapters in Part I will deal with the criminal justice process in the total system context. The macroorganization of the system, the bases of enforcement authority, and the locus of decisions will all be tied together in the hope of finding a way to meaningfully analyze problems in criminal justice, a way that is neither too abstruse to be useful, nor too detailed to destroy overall perspectives.

Chapter 1

Crime and Crime Control in a Democratic Society

THE CRIME PROBLEM

It is generally accepted that the crime rate in the United States is among the highest, if not *the* highest, of all industrial, urbanized societies in the world.[1] This applies not only to such traditional crimes as homicide, robbery, burglary, and common forms of theft and fraud, but also to white-collar offenses, including corporate crimes and crimes by prominent and trusted government officials. Since all crime statistics are estimates, the true amount of crime in the United States is unknown, and accurate measure is not presently possible. In 1967 a presidential crime commission concluded:

There is much crime in America, more than ever is reported, far more than ever is solved, far too much for the health of the Nation. Every American knows that. Every American is, in a sense, a victim of crime. Violence and thefts have not only injured, often irreparably, hundreds of thousands of citizens, but have directly affected everyone. Some people have been impelled to uproot themselves and find new homes. Some have been made afraid to use public streets and parks. Some have come to doubt the worth of society in which so many people behave so badly. Some have even become distrustful of the Government's ability, or even desire, to protect them. . . .

The most understandable mood in which many Americans have been plunged by crime is one of frustration and bewilderment. For "crime" is not a single simple phenomenon that can be examined, analyzed and described in one place. It occurs in every part of the country and in every stratum of society. Its practitioners and its victims are people of all ages, incomes and

National Crime Rate and Percent Change

CRIME INDEX OFFENSES	ESTIMATED CRIME 1970		PERCENT CHANGE OVER 1969		PERCENT CHANGE OVER 1965		PERCENT CHANGE OVER 1960	
	NUMBER	RATE PER 100,000 INHABITANTS	NUMBER	RATE	NUMBER	RATE	NUMBER	RATE
Total	5,568,200	2,740.5	+11.3	+10.6	+90.0	+81.3	+176.4	+143.9
Violent	731,400	360.0	+11.7	+11.0	+90.0	+82.2	+156.5	+126.4
Property	4,836,800	2,380.5	+11.3	+10.6	+89.9	+81.1	+179.7	+146.8
Murder	15,810	7.8	+8.4	+8.3	+60.5	+52.9	+75.7	+56.0
Forcible rape	37,270	18.3	+2.2	+1.1	+62.3	+53.8	+121.1	+94.7
Robbery	348,380	171.5	+17.1	+16.4	+152.3	+140.5	+224.4	+186.3
Aggravated assault	329,940	162.4	+7.7	+7.0	+55.6	+48.3	+117.1	+91.7
Burglary	2,169,300	1,067.7	+11.3	+10.6	+71.9	+64.0	+141.7	+113.3
Larceny $50 and over	1,746,100	859.4	+14.5	+13.8	+120.4	+110.2	+244.9	+204.4
Auto theft	921,400	453.5	+5.7	+5.0	+86.9	+78.3	+182.9	+149.7

FBI *Uniform Crime Reports*, 1970, p. 6.

backgrounds. Its trends are difficult to ascertain. Its causes are legion. Its cures are speculative and controversial.[2]

For the purpose of cross-cultural or cross-jurisdictional comparisons, whether or not the United States is really the world leader in crime is debatable, since different penal codes often differ in definitions of criminal conduct.[3] Even more confusing is the fact that in a given jurisdiction, changes in statutory definitions of crime make it difficult to determine if a particular kind of crime is increasing or decreasing.[4] For example, in some jurisdictions murder in the first degree once required proof of premeditation, while subsequent law revisions changed this requirement to "intentionally killing another." Although the difference appears small, variations in interpretations of *intentional* and *premeditated* can affect the way homicide offenses are recorded and reported. Likewise, some jurisdictions define burglary to include "breaking and entering," while others permit burglary to be proved without the need to show forcible entry. All this complicates periodic comparative assessment of crime rates, even within a single jurisdiction.

Attempts to Measure Crime

Beyond jurisdictional differences, there are a number of other reasons why crime measures are difficult to obtain. For example, we do not require the police to report to any central source the number or types of crimes which come to their attention. The Federal Bureau of Investigation maintains a central statistical bank on certain crimes reported to municipal and state police which have in turn been reported to the FBI. Various law enforcement agencies throughout the United States are *invited* to send semiannual reports to the FBI, but they are not compelled to do so. The result is that the FBI regularly receives crime data from only about 8,000 of approximately 40,000 police departments. While this return rate encompasses only 20 percent of all police agencies, it does include most of the country's large local and state forces. Thus FBI reports are regularly received from police agencies which serve over 90 percent of the U.S. population.

The FBI *Uniform Crime Reports* are based on data concerning seven "Index" crimes: willful homicide, forcible rape, aggravated assault, robbery, burglary, larceny over fifty dollars, and motor vehicle theft. The basic statistic is the number of crimes "known to the police," that is, those which are reported or discovered but not necessarily solved. In addition, the *UCRs* give the number and percentages of those crimes which have been "cleared by arrest," and in some cases where data are available, the percentage of conviction is also given. For example, in 1971 there were 2,368,400 burglaries known to the police and

11

Percent of Arrests Accounted for by Different Age Groups—1971
(percent of total)

OFFENSE CHARGED	PERSONS 11–17	PERSONS 18–24	PERSONS 25 AND OVER
POPULATION[a]	13.9	12.4	52.3
Willful homicide	10.2	33.9	55.5
Forcible rape	20.5	43.5	36.0
Robbery	31.5	44.6	23.1
Aggravated assault	17.0	30.0	52.5
Burglary	47.8	32.4	16.7
Larceny (includes larceny under $50)	47.1	25.5	22.0
Motor vehicle theft	52.6	31.3	15.7
Willful homicide, rape, robbery, aggravated assault	22.2	36.4	40.8
Larceny, burglary, motor vehicle theft	48.0	29.3	19.6

[a] U.S. Bureau of the Census, *Statistical Abstract of the United States, 1972,* ed. 93 (Washington, 1972).

FBI *Uniform Crime Reports, 1971,* pp. 122-123.

450,000 burglaries solved by arrest, but only 9.5 percent of these cases resulted in trial and conviction.[5]

FBI Index crimes do not include all forms of traditional offenses, but they do provide information about a broad variety of offenses ranging from serious crimes against the person (i.e., murder and rape) to property crimes of varying degrees of seriousness. Furthermore these crimes, while not identically defined in all jurisdictions, show less variation than some others, such as gambling, other vice offenses, and public order crimes. It is widely assumed that Index crimes are more or less routinely reported to the police and that they remain relatively stable over time in both definition and reporting practices. There are some difficulties with this, of course. Studies have indicated forcible rape to be one of the most underreported of serious felonies, and the category of thefts over fifty dollars does not take inflation into account. For example, most bicycle thefts in the United States today would fall within the latter category, whereas they would have remained unreported a few years ago when bicycles were cheaper. It is important to note that the FBI Index does not include such crimes as fraud or forgeries, narcotic offenses, and a number of serious crimes against the person, such as negligent homicide, or sex crimes like child molestation. Nor are crimes of extortion, kidnapping, racketeering, airplane hijacking, or serious misdemeanors reported.

12

Victim Surveys

Despite incomplete coverage and the possibility of distortion, the FBI reports are still probably the best available data covering the nation as a whole.[6] Other attempts to measure more precisely the incidence of crimes have included a technique which relies on household surveys to discover how many persons claim to have been victimized by crime over a specific period of time. Initiated by the President's Commission on Law Enforcement and Administration of Justice, the National Opinion Research Center at the University of Chicago sampled some 10,000 households and asked each person interviewed whether he had been the victim of a crime during the past year, whether any member of his family had been victimized, and if so whether the crime had been reported to the police.[7] There have been similar surveys in Washington, D.C., Boston, Detroit, and other cities by such agencies as the Bureau of Social Research in Washington[8] and the Survey Research Center at the University of Michigan.[9] These studies have demonstrated that the incidence of Index crimes reported by victims was several times greater than that reported by police in the *Uniform Crime Reports*. According to these surveys, the number of forcible rapes was more than 3½ times that reported to the police; robbery was 50 percent greater than the *UCRs* rate.[10] There was some agreement between the surveys and *UCRs* for willful homicide, but this is one of the few crimes that is regularly reported, and that is most likely to be "cleared by arrest"—although not necessarily by conviction. Many non-Index crimes were also routinely mentioned by victims, but there is no simple way to test victim claims against police reports since *UCRs* do not tabulate these offenses.

Despite our sophisticated census measurements and our ability to produce accurate economic and marketing data, the unfortunate fact is that even when measurements are restricted to conventional crimes like homicide, rape, stickups, burglaries, and various snatch and grab thefts, there is no reliable method of counting offenses or offenders. The criminal justice system is operating in a sea of law violations whose tides and depths are not fully known. Thus there is no base from which to measure the effectiveness of different criminal justice interventions, especially when dealing with nonreported and victimless crimes for which no currently available data are reliable. We can only speculate about the incidence of vice offenses like gambling or prostitution, and very little information is available about offenses known only to the perpetrator himself. There is no way of determining, for example, how many Americans carry concealed weapons, though the number surely is far greater than indicated by the number of persons arrested for this offense. In fact, belief in the prevalence of concealed weapons has sometimes generated police sweep searches to confiscate contraband

Percent of Victimizations Reported to the Police, by Type Victimization and City, 1972

TYPE OF VICTIMIZATION	CHICAGO	DETROIT	LOS ANGELES	NEW YORK	PHILADELPHIA
PERSONAL					
Crimes of violence	37	39	33	38	36
Rape and attempted rape	48	51	44	45	47
Robbery	53	55	46	61	55
Robbery and attempted robbery with injury	52	60	48	47	50
Serious assault	69	75	64	50	64
Minor assault	70	72	69	58	70
Robbery and attempted robbery without injury	67	79	57	41	57
Robbery without injury	57	62	51	51	57
Attempted robbery without injury	27	39	27	33	27
Assault	44	42	42	41	44
Aggravated assault	52	53	52	57	51
With injury	72	68	57	73	59
Attempted assault with weapon	41	46	50	44	46
Simple assault	37	28	34	31	36
With injury	54	41	46	45	54
Attempted assault without weapon	31	25	30	27	31
Crimes of theft	30	31	28	33	28
Personal larceny with contact	41	48	37	37	39
Purse snatching	61	74	58	53	57
Attempted purse snatching	19	(B)	(B)	22	(B)
Pocket picking	35	35	26	29	35
Personal larceny without contact	28	29	27	31	27

HOUSEHOLD	48	50	44	49	46
Burglary	53	57	53	52	55
Forcible entry	74	75	75	71	78
Unlawful entry (without force)	40	44	45	52	44
Attempted forcible entry	35	35	30	25	31
Household larceny	26	25	25	24	22
Completed larceny	27	26	25	25	22
Attempted larceny	20	18	31	(B)	25
Auto theft	78	78	69	73	69
Completed theft	93	96	92	92	92
Attempted theft	35	26	26	26	32
COMMERCIAL	75	77	73	80	78
Burglary	71	76	71	79	75
Robbery	91	83	84	82	88
Completed robbery	97	90	95	89	96
Attempted robbery	81	61	50	64	66

NOTE: In general, small differences between any two figures in this table are not statistically significant because of sampling. (B) Percent not shown because estimated number of victimizations in this category was too small to be statistically significant.

Crime in the Nation's Five Largest Cities: National Crime Panel Surveys of Chicago, Detroit, Los Angeles, New York, and Philadelphia—Advance Report (Washington, D.C.: U.S. Department of Justice, April 1974), pp. 28-29.

Reasons Cited by Citizens for Not Reporting a Crime to Police, 1972

	PERSONAL %	HOUSEHOLD %
Nothing could be done; lack of proof	34	37
Not important enough	28	31
Police would not want to be bothered	8	9
Too inconvenient	5	4
Private or personal matter	4	3
Afraid of reprisal	2	1
Reported to someone else	7	3
Other or not available	12	12

Data gathered for individual and household in victimization surveys conducted in 1972 by the National Crime Panel. Adapted from *Crime in the Nation's Five Largest Cities: National Crime Panel Surveys of Chicago, Detroit, Los Angeles, New York, and Philadelphia—Advance Report* (Washington, D.C.: U.S. Department of Justice, April 1974), p. 5.

weapons in the hope of preventing serious assaults and homicides. It is doubtful that this practice can be effective because of the ease with which guns and knives can be obtained. But strong pressures on most police agencies to "do something" to prevent street violence keep the practice from being discontinued.

Counting Criminals

Gross statistical measures of the incidence of crimes in our society, whether obtained from police reports or victim studies, indicate the number of criminal offenders only in a very general way. The frequency of homicides may come closest to revealing the number of murderers, because, except for comparatively rare mass killings, murder is usually a single perpetrator-one victim crime. In contrast, a single thief may be responsible for dozens of robberies, burglaries, or larcenies. Thus crimes "cleared by arrest" in the FBI reports may give only a broad approximation of the number of offenders, and even in these data there is a large discrepancy between crimes reported and crimes cleared. In fact, because so few property crimes are solved by arrest, the major message of these data is that most crimes are unsolved; that in a probability sense, crime does pay.[11]

There have been attempts to measure the number of criminals by self-reporting surveys.[12] Just as victim studies sampled persons as to whether they had been victims of crime, self-report studies ask respondents if they have *committed* crimes. Obviously, the truthfulness of responses to self-incriminating questions is always suspect, even with promises of confidentiality or with anonymous data retrieval methods. Yet a surprisingly high percentage of respondents have anonymously admitted committing undetected crimes, some of them quite serious. For example, in a survey of 1,698 persons in Metropolitan New York, 91 percent of the respondents stated they had committed one or more crimes after the age of 16. If true, 64 percent of the male respondents and 29 percent of the females could have been convicted of felonies. The admitted felonious acts ranged from auto theft to robbery.[13]

Statistics on crime or criminals are normally based on measurement over a period of time, usually a month or a year. It is no doubt useful to tabulate crimes in this way, but the number of criminals accumulates. Last year's murderers are joined by those who kill this year, and to these will be added successive future killers. A particular year may produce 14,000 "nonnegligent" homicides, but since few murderers are executed, the extant number of murderers is much greater. Regular hours, proper nutrition, and state-provided medical care make it possible for homicide offenders to live a full span of years. Crimes other than murder and sentences shorter than life cause criminal populations to accumulate, both in prison and on the street, posing a perplexing question: is a person always a criminal because he once committed a crime? Despite some legislative attempts to expunge criminal records of former offenders who have completed their sentences and remained law-abiding for a number of years,[14] police intelligence units often keep track of known criminals.[15] Round-up investigations are not uncommon, particularly when serious or heinous crimes have been committed. And even those few prisoners who receive pardons may be known as "ex-cons" for the rest of their lives.

There is no accurate census of the number of current and former criminals in our society. Various states and the federal government have compiled fingerprint banks, but these contain prints of suspects released without prosecution, including those arrested by mistake, and prints of others not caught up in the criminal justice system. Retrieval or expungement of fingerprints and other arrest records of those totally innocent or improperly accused is nearly impossible, even upon court order and with a willing police agency.[16]

Systems Analysis and Problems of Cohort Measurement

Deficiencies in measurement of the content of crimes and in estimates of the number of suspects and offenders are only one aspect of the lack of adequate criminal justice statistics. If criminal justice programs and interventions are to be successfully evaluated, there is need for good, easily retrievable data, covering the entire spectrum of the criminal justice process.[17] Important questions are being asked today not only about crimes reported to the police, but also about such subsequent matters as bail-or-jail determinations, indictments, acquittals or convictions, probation and probation revocation decisions, prison and prisoners, and parole and parolees. Adequate population statistics are needed by all criminal justice agencies to support sensible budget and facility forecasts, to accurately assess their present achievements or failures, and are essential for planning innovative projects and for assessing experimental programs. Most operational criminal justice agencies keep some form of summary data on persons processed. However, this is usually a process of simple tabulation, known as "gate keeping" data, similar to that used by a prison when counting the number of prisoners who come in and go out.[18] In fact, it is probable that accurate gate keeping is found only in correctional agencies, where it is both a matter of legal accountability and a necessity for feeding and housing purposes. Reports of the *arrest* activity of police are required as a part of booking procedure, but prearrest contact with citizens and suspects is rarely a matter of record. The largest gap in gate keeping data may be found in prosecutors' offices and in trial courts. In most cases, statistical reports from district attorneys or trial judges are not required annually, and even summary statistics can be retrieved only with great difficulty. Large police and correctional agencies commonly make use of computers, but prosecutors and courts seldom do.

Even if every criminal justice agency could implement adequate summary reporting procedures, such reports would be useless except for workload assessments and for other intra-agency purposes. Tracking cases across agencies through major decision points is not possible with summary statistics, yet the current demand for total systems analysis and evaluation cannot be met without such measurement. Full computerization of the criminal justice processing of persons at all stages in the process is increasingly viewed as the only satisfactory solution to the need for data that are complete and accurate. The *tracking* of specific persons across the entire criminal process spectrum is sometimes known as *cohort analysis*. This technique begins with an input sample of perhaps 10,000 persons arrested for felonies over a period of time in a particular jurisdiction, and follows their paths and branchings as they are processed deeper into the system or are diverted out of it.[19] The technique requires flow data and can answer questions and evaluate alternative processing in ways not possible with only summarized tabulations of the work of various criminal justice agencies. But most criminal justice systems currently lack the facilities required for cohort analysis. During the large-scale research efforts of the 1960s which centered around the task forces of the President's Crime Commission, the deplorable state of criminal justice statistics was fully revealed.[20] Since then high priority has been given to the development of criminal justice reporting systems, but despite strong federal pressures and significant amounts of federal funds granted to the states, data reporting systems in most jurisdictions are still primitive.

Resistance to Crime Reporting

There are all kinds of structural obstacles to the development of even rudimentary baseline data systems. The criminal justice system is composed of relatively independent agencies and offices, each with its own reporting forms, data needs, and traditional ways of doing things. Some agencies are municipal; some are county; and others are statewide, presenting differing research budget requirements and some indifference to gathering information for other than immediate and local use. The entire criminal justice system and each agency in it is not only public, it is politically volatile as well, with the result that most criminal statistics are potentially embarrassing to past claims of effectiveness.[21] Most crimes are not solved by arrest; many prosecutors plea bargain a high proportion of their cases; many judges show statistical disparity in their sentences; and few offenders are rehabilitated in some correctional programs. Inevitably, some agencies, when offered elaborate computer devices that could provide full and accurate statistics, but which would also open their records to public accounting, show little enthusiasm for new reporting systems.

Despite technical difficulties and some resistance to change, the application of computer techniques to criminal justice processing is developing rapidly.[22] Computer potential is both a stick and a carrot; there is little doubt that electronic information systems can be important administrative and enforcement aids to quickly identify suspects, to retrieve records, to make cost accounting more efficient and accurate, and otherwise to smooth and speed the business of the agency, but they are also important research and evaluation tools and initially may present some threat to established policies and practices.

In addition to the application of systems analysis techniques to entire criminal justice jurisdictions, there is also a trend toward standardization of reporting systems so that cross-jurisdictional comparisons can be made. A major program, SEARCH, is funded by the federal government and aims to integrate the reporting systems of all states. This requires a variety of operational and technical modifications ranging from shared definitions of crimes, decision steps, common terms (i.e., "frisk," "arrest," "initial appearance," and so on) and administrative procedures, as well as adoption of common points and techniques of data retrieval.[23]

The emerging stress on acquisition of more accurate crime data, the drive toward improved cohort analysis, and the creation of large, secure, but administratively available, data banks indicate that a much clearer picture of our crime problem and of our methods for coping with it is developing. As with many technological revolutions, there is a danger that too much will be promised, and too much expected from electronic techniques. However elaborate, these devices will simply measure crime and evaluate programs; it is unlikely that they will do much to ameliorate the crime problem. They may be valuable aids in quickly identifying suspects, in suggesting ways to reduce delay in the courts, or in their most sophisticated form, in providing data about associational patterns from which criminal conspiracies can be inferred. But it is unlikely that they will be able to identify specific casual factors in criminality, for our knowledge of the etiology of criminal behavior is so fragmentary that we are unable to formulate many basic questions. The computer can respond only to precise questions; it cannot theorize or conceptualize on its own.

The Differential Seriousness of Types of Crime

Gross crime rate measurements and even sophisticated techniques of offender counting, though important for evaluating operational programs and assessing the effectiveness of crime reduction interventions, do not give any subjective interpretation, nor do they accurately reflect the intensity of our crime problem. Whether statistics show that crime is increasing or decreasing is irrelevant to the actual nature of the crime threat to our society, to its seriousness, or to fears about the safety of life and limb.[24] The FBI Crime Index, for example, is based on the unweighted sum of all reported offenses and is dominated by property crimes. The Science and Technology Task Force of the President's Crime Commission rightly pointed out that the Index is relatively insensitive to changes in serious crimes against persons, since numerically these offenses are comparatively small. Their report notes: "Thus, murders could increase 1,000 percent, but if auto theft fell by 10 percent, the Index would decline."[25] The Task Force goes on to point out that from almost any standpoint, not all crimes are equally undesirable. "Most people would be willing to tolerate a considerable amount of private gambling, or perhaps even shoplifting, if they could know that doing so would reduce the amount of street robberies."[26]

The fact that there are different types of crime, each of which varies by culturally defined seriousness and the intensity of perceived threat, has implications for preventive and control efforts. Certainly police activities are not directed equally toward enforcement of all legislative proscriptions, nor are crime prevention or control resources distributed in proportion to the numerical frequency of different types of law violations. Instead there are differential responses by crime control agencies and by preventive programs to differing forms and patterns of criminal conduct which are ranked, often crudely, according to perceived "seriousness."[27]

Common Law and Modern Crimes

The actual seriousness of any type of crime, the real degree of its threat to our social order, can be endlessly debated with different outcomes depending upon debaters' points of view. Thus, whether murder is a worse crime than embezzlement or whether crimes against persons or "crimes against the people" are more threatening to our social system than are other crimes are questions that have been argued many times. In any case, such questions are unlikely to be resolved by debate, yet the controversy goes on. Proposals are made to "decriminalize" certain crimes, such as possession and sale of soft narcotics, and to "criminalize" or more seriously punish other conduct, like pollution, which until now has not been viewed as a serious threat to our way of life.

The ranking of crimes by degree of seriousness is not simply a debater's exercise. Formal, recognized distinctions in classes of crimes have existed throughout history; our present-day criminal codes and corresponding sentencing structures owe much of their content to origins in common law. We retain in our codes many of the ancient and very serious felonies which outlaw forms of conduct (evil in themselves or *mala in se*).[28] We have added crimes peculiar to different stages in our urban industrial development, crimes that have no exact counterparts in common law. Thus they are offenses created by legislation rather than history (*mala prohibita*).[29] With few exceptions, *mala in se* are considered more serious than *mala prohibita*, and in both categories we retain finer distinctions of seriousness, including major differences between heavily penalized felonies and less severely treated *delicta* or misdemeanors.

Classification of Crimes: Felonies and Misdemeanors

Criminal codes in all jurisdictions make distinctions between felonies and misdemeanors, and sometimes lesser offenses called violations. Felonies are the more serious crimes with correspondingly harsher penalties, including such civil disabilities as loss of voting privilege following conviction. Both felonies and misdemeanors are graded by degrees of seriousness. For example, a criminal code may provide different penalties for the felony of burglary in the first degree (often defined as breaking and entering a dwelling at night while armed and with intent to steal), burglary in the second degree (daytime unarmed breaking and entering a dwelling), burglary in the third degree (unarmed breaking and entering a building other than a dwelling), and so on. Some crimes may cross the felony-misdemeanor line as their contexts or consequences become less serious. Aggravated assault (often defined as assault with a weapon with intent to do great bodily harm) may move through degrees to simple assault, a misdemeanor covering common fistfights. Sometimes the distinction between felony and misdemeanor involving the same criminal conduct is determined by consequences, such as the loss suffered by the victim. Grand larceny is a felony because of the amount of money or property stolen; petty larceny—stealing smaller amounts—is usually a misdemeanor. In some instances, the degree of the crime is determined by the intent of the perpetrator, which is often inferred from his behavior. Thus, whether a homicide is murder, killing by reckless conduct, negligent homicide, or some lesser degree of manslaughter depends upon proof of the mental state of the actor, that is, the extent to which the criminal consequences were intended and willful, or careless and negligent.[30]

There is no single classification of crimes or of penalties that are identical and uniform in all jurisdictions. Only by reference to specific statutory provisions in each jurisdiction can it be determined whether an offense is a felony or misdemeanor, or its ranking or degree of seriousness be measured. While, in general, felonies have more severe penal sanctions than lesser crimes, this is not invariably true. Technically, a felony and its degree of seriousness are defined by statute. However, there are some rules-of-thumb about the relationship of type of crime and severity of penal sanction. Normally, conviction of a felony carries a potential state *prison* sentence of a year or longer, while conviction of a misdemeanor carries a sentence of a year or less in a county *jail*. While probation can be used as an alternative to incarceration in both instances, fines usually are levied more commonly in misdemeanor cases, either as alternatives to incarceration or probation, or in addition to either. The person convicted of a felony experiences more severe collateral consequences, including the loss of certain political rights (i.e., being unable to vote or hold public office), and may also suffer loss or denial of licenses and other franchises. He may also find a wide range of employment closed to him and, if a professional or politician, face disbarment or impeachment. In the past, offenders convicted of serious felonies and sentenced to prison for life or for a long term of years were subject to *civil death* proceedings, an action which terminated many relationships with family and property as if the offender were, in fact, dead. While we no longer brand the faces of criminals, we do "brand" their official records with notation of a felony conviction which can be expected to follow them all their lives.

The determination of relative seriousness of types of crimes is a legislative function.[31] However, except during periods of law revision, legislators rarely review or rerank crimes, and when they do, most changes occur in borderline offenses where proposals to change such crimes as marijuana possession, adult consensual sexual misconduct, abortion, and similar crimes are common. Changes are debated; perhaps some offenses are shifted from felony to misdemeanor, or the reverse, or are removed from the criminal code altogether. Nevertheless, the majority of traditionally serious crimes, such as murder, robbery, rape, and so on, and traditional minor offenses, like petty larceny, simple assault, and other public order crimes are rarely reduced, raised, or omitted, though their statutory definitions may be refined or modified slightly. But generally the rank order of most traditional crimes has remained the same throughout our history. Probably there is a consensus that murder and kidnapping are indeed very serious crimes,[32] that most felonies should remain as defined, and that most misdemeanors are correctly classified. In contrast, for a long time there has been a lack of consensus about so-called victimless crimes, the question being whether such offenses as gambling and prostitution should be crimes at all.[33] And as our society becomes larger and technologically more complex, we encounter new crimes or new forms of old crimes, triggering new legislation which in turn effects changes in the ranking of some offenses. Airplane hijacking is currently viewed with alarm, with resultant hasty modification of laws, procedures, and penal sanctions. But the enduring division between felony and misdemeanor probably reflects widespread agreement about the relative seriousness of major forms of criminal conduct.

Despite this agreement about the seriousness of crimes in abstract, there are intense disputes and controversies about permissible defenses to criminal liability. For example, while there is little doubt that most Americans view the intentional killing of another as one of our most serious crimes, there is a good deal of disagreement about defenses to this crime. Few would deny self-defense, but there is less agreement about insanity and "childhood" (i.e., delinquency). Currently the most controversial defense is *justification,* the legitimate killing of another by one acting properly in the course of his duty as a law-enforcement officer, whether policeman,[34] correctional officer,[35] soldier, or guardsman.[36] Killing *per se* remains a most serious crime, though there continue to be disagreements about the actual use and the circumstances of use of deadly force by the state and about other defenses.

Ordinary versus Dangerous Crimes and Criminals

Classifying crimes as felonies or misdemeanors helps to facilitate and to set limits to enforcement efforts. Evidentiary standards for arrest, the range of permissible use of force, limits to booking, and similar operational standards are defined by this basic classification of crimes. However, it is generally conceded that the felony-misdemeanor dichotomy by itself is insufficient for other criminal justice determinations—for example, determining the actual length of sentence within legislative limits—or for effectively achieving broader goals of crime control, such as protecting the public from dangerous acts and violent persons. In recent years there have been attempts to develop additional classifications of offenses and offenders along some sort of "dangerousness" continuum. These efforts aim to provide enabling legislation that will permit criminal justice agencies, from police to prisons, to distinguish between degrees of dangerous conduct and to deal more severely and perhaps more effectively with truly dangerous persons. In these attempts the close relationship between specific criminal conduct and the total personality of individual offenders sometimes tends to blur distinctions. But efforts to define and isolate dangerous *conduct* by providing extended prison sentences for certain classes of crimes continue to be separate from attempts to define and identify dangerous or violence-prone *persons* by psychiatric and other "personality" criteria.

Major efforts to develop classifications based on criteria of dangerousness have centered largely on the sentencing decision. Within the past few years, a number of model sentencing codes have been drafted, among which the best known is the *Model Penal Code* proposed by the American Law Institute.[37] Two other major efforts are the *Model Sentencing Act* of the National Council on Crime and Delinquency[38] and the *Sentencing Alternatives* of the American Bar Association.[39] Additionally, about half the states and the federal system have revised their criminal codes in the past decade, many relying heavily on one or more of these model sentencing proposals. Both in model provisions and in most new codes, serious attention has been given to separating dangerous cases from more routine, nonthreatening conduct and persons. The *Model Penal Code* provides extended terms of imprisonment for persistent offenders, professional criminals, multiple offenders, and those found to be "dangerous and mentally abnormal" whose extended commitment is "necessary for protection of the public."[40] The *Model Sentencing Act* distinguishes "atrocious" crimes from felonies in general, making extended sentences possible for such offenses as second-degree murder, arson, forcible rape, armed robbery, mayhem, and bombing.[41] The *MSA* also attempts to distinguish dangerous offenders from run-of-the-mill felons, basing the distinction in part on the criminal act, that is, a felony where the "defendant inflicted or attempted to inflict serious bodily harm" and, as a necessary correlate, on a clinical diagnosis that the offender is suffering from a severe personality disorder "indicating a propensity toward criminal activity." In addition, the *Model Penal Code* and the *Model Sentencing Act* (as well as some current state and federal revisions) also provide extended terms for the organized criminal, sometimes called the professional or the racketeer.[42]

Though the most extensive efforts to develop classification of crimes and offenders around "dangerous" criteria have been concentrated on the sentencing decision, interest in this form of classification has not been limited to this stage of the process. There have been a number of recent proposals to apply such criteria at some preconviction stages as well. "Stop-and-frisk" laws are designed to protect police officers from potential violence in situations of routine, on-the-street stopping and questioning.[43] Criteria prescribed in this legislation enable police to conduct "pat-down" searches of suspects in order to confiscate any weapons which might be used to jeopardize the officer's safety.[44] Likewise, there is continuing interest in the drafting of constitutionally permissible "preventive detention" legislation that would deny bail to suspects shown to have potential for violent crimes if released before trial.[45] The preventive detention provisions of the District of Columbia Crime Act of 1970 are good examples of this kind of legislation.[46] Though very sparingly used and still of dubious constitutional validity,[47] the District of Columbia Act illustrates the dilemma: whether it is possible to build a system of crime and offender classification that will maintain basic procedural safeguards, that will not violate standards of due process, and that will establish reliable and useful criteria of dangerousness in contrast to routine, ordinary, and nonphysically threatening criminal conduct.

The slowly emerging division of the criminal justice system into two parallel processes built around dangerous-nondangerous classifications remains one of the major challenges of our time. All efforts to distinguish and to treat differentially persons who are guilty of the same criminal acts, but who differ in *propensity* to violence, impinge on constitutional protections ranging from the First to the Fourteenth Amendment. Appellate court determinations of the constitutionality of various "dangerous" programs or provisions, such as preventive detention, sex psychopath laws, statutes defining conspiracies to incite riots as crimes, "maxi-maxi" prisons, selective use of the death penalty, airport searches to prevent skyjacking, have been mixed. The potential conflict between rigid adherence to the personal freedoms guaranteed by the Constitution and effective means of detecting dangerous crimes and processing violent offenders is not easily resolved. Professor Sidney Hook, long known as a respected and articulate civil libertarian, recently said:

I submit that at the present juncture of events, because our American cities have become more dangerous to life and limb than the darkest jungle, we must give priority to the rights of potential victims. I am prepared to weaken the guarantees and privileges to which I am entitled as a potential criminal, or as a defendant, in order to strengthen my rights and safeguards as a potential victim. Purely on the basis of probabilities, I am convinced that I run a greater danger of suffering disaster as a potential victim than as a potential criminal or defendant. It is these probabilities that shift from one historical period to another that must be the guide of wise, prudent, and just administration of law.[48]

Criminological Classification of Criminals

Law enforcement is enabled, while at the same time intervention of criminal justice officials is limited, by legal classification of criminal offenses and by distinguishing atrocious crimes and dangerous offenders from "ordinary" crimes and nonthreatening violators. Such classification is critical for crime control efforts, including law enforcement, prosecution, conviction, sentencing, and the extent and type of postsentencing control over offenders. But many observers and criminological researchers believe that classification in this legalistic manner is insufficient either to accurately describe our crime problem, or to ameliorate or prevent crime.[49] Instead, criminologists, most of whom have been trained as sociologists or psychologists, argue for "behavioral" classification schemes. They assert that this method will identify causal factors in criminal conduct so that prevention and control interventions can be more effectively and more selectively directed to changing individual offenders, to modifying crime related group behavior, and to changing crime producing environment patterns.

In recent years, while attempting to refine and test various theories of crime causation, American criminologists and other students of deviant behavior have conducted research into so-called behavior systems among criminal offenders.[50] It is increasingly evident that any single explanation of crime causation is not valid for the entire range of conduct covered by the spectrum of penal laws. Professors Clinard and Quinney explain the need for behavioral typology:

. . . efforts are being made to delineate categories of crime and criminal behavior which are homogenous with respect to a specific explanation. In criminology, considering the wide range of phenomena subsumed under the concept of crime, an adequate general theory may be formulated after specific types of crime have been established.[51]

In the search for causes of crime, it is readily apparent that certain factors in offenders' personalities and other conditions in the social order may be sufficient to explain in a general way the crime of murder, but that these same factors, no matter how carefully measured, may be quite insufficient to account for more rational crimes, such as bank robbery or racketeering. To the extent that certain *types* of criminal behavior—indicated by clusters of similar offense patterns, common criminal career pathways, similar demographic and environmental histories of offenders—can be identified and verified by research, appropriate forms of intervention for control or prevention can be developed to cope with the causal patterns that underlie these behaviors. For example, if it were found that the most violent crimes, such as murder and forcible rape, were products of deep-seated, measurable emotional patterns in offenders, it may be that the traditional system response to such offenses of imposing severe penalties may fail in its secondary purpose, that of deterring other potential violators. Nevertheless, similar deterrent efforts with bank robbers, professional thieves, and other more rational and calculating offenders might prove more successful. Likewise, rehabilitative efforts with offenders who are inept even at crime, personally inadequate, educationally and vocationally deprived, but not yet deeply advanced into a criminal career might succeed quite well. Similar techniques may prove fruitless with professional, hardened offenders who are personally adequate though legally deviant.

Some criminologists have isolated gross criminal behavior systems that depend for their identity on the motives, skills, career patterns, self-concepts, and similar behavioral indices of the criminal himself, rather than on legal classifications of crime.[52] Thus it is quite clear that intrafamily homicides committed after extended periods of mutual aggravation and in the heat of passion are quite different from murders committed by hired killers for insurance, for revenge, or to support the organized crime system. And the hulking alley-way mugger, though indeed a robber, differs in significant ways from the cool and calculating heister who disdains bank or store stickups that are likely to net less than fifty thousand dollars. The behavioral criminologist thus asserts that the classification of murder, robbery, or other crimes by title alone, even if modified by relevant "dangerous" criteria, does not accurately describe the criminal population or the crime problem generally, nor is it helpful in suggesting ways to curb or prevent crime.

Although experts do not fully agree on the details of different behavioral types, criminologists have distinguished a number of separate *criminal behavior systems* as follows:

1. *violent personal offenders* (exhibiting chronic patterns of assault, sometimes including homicides);
2. *professional criminals* (with two subtypes, one including confidence men, shoplifters . . . "boosters," . . . pickpockets, and various flim-flam artists and the second covering "heavies," including big-time armored car and bank robbers, safecrackers, jewelry and fur thieves, operators of massive auto theft rings and the like);

3. *organized criminals* (highly systematized sellers of vice and protection, variously referred to as gangsters, racketeers, or collectively, the mafia or the syndicate);

4. *occasional property crime violators* (amateur thieves and vandals whose criminal activity is sporadic and opportunistic and who neither make large profits from their crimes nor progress into full-time criminal careers);

5. *conventional criminals* (the thieves, burglars, robbers, check writers, forgers, and lower echelon narcotic pushers who occupy the major time of police enforcement efforts and fill our jails and prisons. Unlike the occasional offender, these violators define themselves as criminals, tend to progress from simple thefts for thrills to more complex and serious ways of stealing for profit, and try to make crime their major occupation);

6. *sex offenders* (including all violators whose major deviation is some form of sexual perversion or compulsion but who often are not "criminal" in other ways; that is, they neither progress to more sophisticated forms of crime, they do not steal, and they define themselves and are defined by others as sick rather than criminal. This category includes a wide range of deviant conduct from nonviolent forms of voyeurism, exhibitionism, and obscene phone calls to much more dangerous behavior like violent child molestation and forcible rape of random victims);

7. *white-collar criminals* (encompassing law violations of corporations as well as persons and including forms of theft and fraud committed in the course of the offender's occupation, including crimes such as embezzlement, price fixing, and the formation of illegal trusts and cartels);

8. *political criminals,* for example, draft resisters, Weathermen, and;

9. *public order violators,* like vagrants and chronic down-and-out inebriates.[53]

In addition to these gross categories, there also have been attempts to distinguish subtypes within categories. For example, research may reveal a number of distinct patterns, different motivational sets, and variable career paths within an overall category of organized criminal, occasional property violator, vandal, child molester, or murderer.

While there is no firm consensus on these definitions and though typologies may occasionally be misapplied to certain individual offenders, their use in suggesting etiological patterns of criminal behavior is a significant development. For it has been unfortunately true that the criminal justice system in our society has long assumed that the causes of all crime are similar and that all crime can be prevented or controlled by common techniques of apprehension, conviction, and punishment.[54] Though often unspoken, certain assumptions about crime causation are held by legislators, courts, police, prosecutors, and correctional personnel who continue to legislate or to react to criminal behavior as if the same sanctions and enforcement methods will work for all crime.

Despite some fuzziness and weaknesses in a number of theories of crime causation, the classification of criminal conduct by behavioral syndromes offers some promise of a more effective way of understanding, measuring, and perhaps preventing or controlling crime than simply classifying felonies and misdemeanors and assigning a hierarchy of penal sanctions to them. Obviously we have had little success with many laws forbidding particular conduct and penalizing violators who are caught. One difficulty is that despite the vagaries and politics of legislatures, lawmaking is basically a rational process. Common sense would seem to dictate that the death penalty would deter potential murderers; and it can be argued that it does, for the number of those who would kill but refrain because of capital punishment is unknown. However, there is ample evidence to show that severe penalties do not deter all killers,[55] and conversely that the abolition of severe penalties does not seem to lead to dramatic increases in serious personal crimes.[56]

The isolation of these clusters of conduct and motivational patterns suggests the need for differential modes of prevention, deterrence, enforcement, and effective rehabilitation or reintegration of offenders. The task of identifying and delineating behavioral types of crime and criminals is difficult and is only a first step in identifying and assigning comparative weights to factors in individuals' personalities and in cultural inequities that combine to produce crime.[57] Whether it is sociologists interested in deviant behavior, criminologists researching behavioral crime types, or informed observers of the criminal justice system who offer crime causation theories, there is general agreement that basic causes flow ultimately from the way we organize our social order and from the disparity between our ideological goals and actual opportunities for their achievement.[58] Following his term as U.S. Attorney General, Ramsey Clark commented:

Crime reflects more than the character of the pitiful few who commit it. It reflects the character of the entire society.
. . . .
If we are to deal meaningfully with crime, what must be seen is the dehumanizing effect on the individual of slums, racism, ignorance and violence, of corruption and impotence to fulfill rights, of poverty and unemployment and idleness, of generations of malnutrition, of congenital brain damage and prenatal neglect, of sickness and disease, of pollution, of decrepit, dirty, ugly, unsafe overcrowded housing, of alcoholism and narcotic addiction, of avarice, anxiety, fear, hatred, hopelessness and injustice. These are the fountainheads of crime.
. . . .
We are clearly afflicted with crime because we have failed to care for ourselves and for our character. We are guilty of immense neglect. Neglect, not permissiveness, is the culprit.[59]

If valid, the implications of this statement for the criminal justice system are broad and deep. For if every variable from poverty and discrimination to pollution and economic exploitation is a factor in underlying causes of criminal behavior, the immediate, daily task of the criminal justice system in enforcing, controlling, and processing offenders—the "banishment" of crimes—is endless, frustrating, and perhaps hopeless.[60] At best enforcement is a holding operation, a method of containment, with the criminal justice system merely a conglomeration of agencies and programs designed to meet immediate crises in street crime. In cultural perspective it is only one among many systems and institutions which must change and improve if crime is to be significantly reduced or eradicated.

It is easy to be pessimistic about truly effective crime control, for both the problem and the pessimism have existed since Cain killed Abel. But even if it is conceded that the roots of crime rest in basic flaws in our social order and that crime will not be alleviated until the entire social system is changed, there remains a vital need for a sincere, dedicated crime control effort. Understanding the cultural and personality pressures leading to murder, whether these flow from a "subculture of violence"[61] or explode from fundamental emotional instability, may lead ultimately to realistic murder prevention or to murder control programs.[62] The immediacy of murder, however, cannot wait. It is a police, court, and correctional problem of the first rank. Similar urgency applies to all crimes from the most serious and threatening—armed robbery, rape, and kidnapping—to lesser public order offenses such as public intoxication. Speaking of the latter offense, which occupies a heavy proportion of police time and often results only in the "revolving door" of jail drunk tanks, Mr. Justice Marshall said:

Faced with this unpleasant reality, we are unable to assert that the use of the criminal process as a means of dealing with the public aspects of problem drinking can never be defended as rational. The picture of the penniless drunk propelled aimlessly and endlessly through the law's "revolving door" of arrest, incarceration, release and re-arrest is not a pretty one. But before we condemn the present practice across-the-board, perhaps we ought to be able to point to some clear promise of a better world for these unfortunate people. Unfortunately, no such promise has yet been forthcoming.[63]

VALUES AND VALUE CONFLICTS OF CRIME CONTROL

The Ideological Basis of Crime Control

Observers inside and outside the criminal justice system have often found reason to denounce it as ineffective, unjust, or corrupt. It is easy to point to a high, and perhaps increasing, crime rate to show that despite slogans to the contrary, crime does pay, and to ridicule the clumsiness and inefficiency of many of our crime control programs and agencies. Examples of cruelty, indifference, incompetence, and sometimes corruption are comparatively easy to gather. This kind of criticism becomes particularly intense when certain crimes or crime patterns are highly publicized, as when a so-called crime wave is proclaimed or when particularly infamous crimes remain unsolved.[64]

Vigorous demands for quicker and more certain law enforcement, for fewer courtroom "charades," or for more severe punishment often appear to rest on the assumption that effectiveness of crime control is the only purpose underlying our crime control efforts. This is a superficial point of view, of course, for our philosophy as well as our techniques of crime control reside within a much more complex ordering of ideological values. If efficiency and effectiveness were the sole objective of our crime control effort, subject to no checks or balances, law enforcement followed by severe punishment could be accomplished with relative ease. Wide and unrestrained use of electronic eavesdropping could provide law enforcement officials with a much longer list of suspects. Mandatory use of the lie detector or truth serum would convict many more of these suspects, thus tending to eliminate the necessity for jury trials and their uncertainty. Experiments with chemotherapy or psychosurgery might prove more effective than present methods of probation, jail, and prison in restraining or even rehabilitating offenders. However, even the strongest advocate of greater efficiency, of "law and order," is likely to retreat in the face of the full implications of unrestrained wiretrapping, sweep searches, widespread preventive detention, long sentences, chemical or surgical manipulation of offenders, and dungeonlike prisons. For most of us will accept the fact that there are certain techniques, procedures, and devices which are more repugnant to our national ideals than inefficiency in law enforcement.[65] Cruel enforcement devices are not peculiar to totalitarian regimes such as the Third Reich, for we can find in our system techniques which, as Mr. Justice Frankfurter put it, "shock the conscience."[66] To curb and control such potential state power, we have a series of complex checks and balances in our criminal justice system. Its complexity is not accidental, nor does its bureaucracy result from mere historical drift. Rather, the tap roots of our criminal justice system are deep in an ideology based on personal freedom and the fundamental dignity of man.

The origins of our political order, expressed in the Declaration of Independence, the Bill of Rights, the Constitutional Amendments, and the other great documents of our history, rest mainly upon the desire to build safeguards which would control and limit the power of the state to intervene in the life of citizens.

31

Virtually every statement in the Bill of Rights and in later amendments to the Constitution relate directly to major aspects of our criminal justice process.[67] Historically, a relatively high proportion of appellate court decisions, including decisions of the U.S. Supreme Court, apply constitutional restraints to unfettered and uncontrolled crime control efforts. It is thus fundamental to our ideals and our system of government that higher allegiance to principles of individual liberty, fairness, and due process of law must check and control law-enforcement efforts, trial court functions, and correctional interventions. Improper methods of catching criminals, no matter how effective, must not threaten the freedom of society at large.[68] Though much of our criminal justice ideology has gradually accrued from interpretation of broad principles which are usually only indirectly related to police work or prisons (e.g., First Amendment guarantees of free speech and freedom of religion), other constitutional clauses set quite specific standards for criminal justice administration. The Fourth Amendment forbids unreasonable searches and seizures; the Fifth protects citizens from self-incrimination; the Sixth guarantees the right to trial by jury; and the Eighth prohibits cruel and unusual punishment. Though court interpretation of each of these Amendments is necessary to apply broad constitutional protections to day-to-day situations, it is clear that many of the foundation blocks of our political ideology are directly applicable to crime control efforts.[69]

We will not attempt to provide here an exhaustive list of relevant ideological principles, but it is important to note some of the most fundamental of these, for they are applied in one way or another at every step of the decision network of the criminal justice process. Some of our ideological principles appear to overlap, some merge in the manner of the due process elements of the Fifth and the Fourteenth Amendments to the Constitution, but all simultaneously apply to crime control. Most expressions of our basic values, constitutional or otherwise, are phrased in necessarily broad terms, often vague in language, but firm in intent.[70] Each requires careful judicial interpretation and application to situations arising from the daily activities of the criminal justice process. "Thou shalt not kill" is fine as a biblical commandment, but it would make poor legislation, and would require careful interpretation as to killing who, what, by whom, and when. The continuous honing of the law, the sifting and winnowing of standards and general principles from myriad variations in cases brought before our criminal courts, shapes the criminal justice system. This process sometimes curbs enforcement vigor, or it may give impetus to new programs and proposals, as in the series of Supreme Court decisions expanding the right of indigent offenders to assistance of counsel.[71] Some of the more important of these principles in terms of current applicability to criminal justice issues include the following:

1. DUE PROCESS OF LAW. This general principle states that no person shall be deprived of his liberty, his life, or his property without due process of law. The scope of due process is broad, and necessarily and continuously interpreted and refined by appellate court decisions.[72] Currently, though its parameters are not fixed, it means that the state cannot intervene arbitrarily or capriciously into the lives of citizens, even those properly convicted and sentenced for crimes.[73] Officials must have some appropriate degree and proper kind of evidence before a suspect can be arrested, charged with a crime, convicted, sentenced, and punished or rehabilitated.[74] The fullest measure of due process is required and given at trial, and specific procedural requirements are more firmly demanded before conviction, rather than after. A citizen accused of a crime is accorded rights that include notice of specific charges, reminder of his right to silence and to trial, the effective assistance of counsel, and at the apex, a trial by a jury of peers. Due process also includes the right of a defendant to confront his accusers, to rebut evidence, to be taken before neutral judicial authority for consideration of bail, to be publicly tried, and to be treated fairly and humanely, with strict observance to rules and procedures defined in statute, in constitutional principle, and in court interpretation. The full dimensions of due process continue to be litigated, though the trend in recent years has been to expand both the limits and the locus of applicability of due process requirements.[75] For example, currently there is uncertainty and litigation about the applicability of procedural due process at postconviction stages of the process, from sentencing to parole revocation. Recent court decisions, even those of the Burger "strict constructionist" court, have tended to expand due process requirements for prison and parole decisions.[76]

2. FUNDAMENTAL FAIRNESS. In general, our ideology rests on a strong belief that crime control efforts must be fair even if enforcement efficiency is impaired or guilty persons are freed. At various points in the system, fairness is specifically mandated by statute or constitution, while at others it may be decided case-by-case by appellate litigation. Though the limits to fairness are presently flexible like those of due process, the principle is clear. Accused persons are entitled not only to a trial, but specifically to a *fair* trial; confessions may be used to convict a person by his own words, but these confessions must be obtained in a fair manner.[77] A suspect may be placed in a police lineup, but he must be exhibited fairly; for example, he cannot be the only one handcuffed.[78] A defendant is even entitled to a fair guilty plea with a standard requirement that the judge explain the maximum possible criminal sentence before accepting the plea.[79] The *accuracy* of the plea in terms of the individual's actual guilt or innocence is not affected; the requirement is purely one of fairness.

33

Fairness extends also to postconviction stages, though in such matters as prisoner's rights there are many and varied new developments. Until recently appellate courts took a hands-off posture regarding the treatment of prison inmates by their keepers (and also with probationers and parolees), but this doctrine of disdain is undergoing change.[80] Now a whole new set of due process requirements applies to in-custody treatment of prisoners.[81] Due process and procedural regularity in decision making are themselves a measure of fairness, but there are signs that the fairness issue with regard to prisoners may be expanding to cover more subtle issues than freedom from excessively cruel or unusual punishments, and that it may go beyond simple requirements for hearings and opportunity for defense before loss of prison privileges or movement to solitary confinement.[82] In a recent federal district case regarding mail censorship, the court castigated "abrasive conditions" in prison life, defining these as rules and regulations beyond those needed to preserve order. Judge James Doyle argued that the burden of proof should be on the state to show a "compelling governmental interest" when prisoners are treated differently from other citizens.[83] This case was reversed on appeal on a number of grounds, including the compelling interest test. The Court of Appeals substituted a requirement that actions by correctional authorities must be "related both reasonably and necessarily to the advancement of a justifiable purpose of imprisonment."[84]

Balance of advantage between state and accused is an aspect of fairness in the operation of the criminal justice system that is an important perspective for analysis of the system.[85] It is evident that the police and the prosecutor have tremendous resources for investigation and evidence accumulation which are not available to most suspects and defendants. One major trend of recent constitutional interpretation has been toward balancing the adversarial system by providing more resources for defendants, particularly for those who are indigent and often friendless and powerless. Various appellate court decisions have extended the right of defense counsel to the poor; other decisions and legislation have allowed the accused greater discovery of state's evidence before trial, and have provided transcripts to assist indigent defendants in appeals. The trend will probably continue to be toward expansion of advantages and assets, material and otherwise, to the accused in criminal matters. Whether equal balance will actually ever be achieved is uncertain, but various programs, from legal aid for indigents to recognizance rather than monetary bail, have been developed to make the system fairer between the state and the accused, and also more equal between wealthy and powerful defendants and their impoverished counterparts.

3. PROPRIETY. Related in some degree to fairness, proper legal intervention also encompasses the issue of appropriate standards of the *quality* of evi-

dence obtained by the state. The quantity of evidence alone is not enough for arrest or conviction; it must also be obtained in proper fashion.[86] Propriety issues include such things as the trustworthiness of confessions, the form and process of search and seizure, the accuracy of guilty pleas, and procedures for humane treatment of the guilty in prisons or elsewhere. In our society we place restrictions on the way crimes can be solved, the way evidence can be gathered, and the manner in which offenders are treated. Our belief in the need for a proper and an efficient criminal justice system is reflected in now universally applicable *exclusionary rules*.[87] These rules prohibit the use of improperly obtained evidence, whether from search or interrogation, at a trial where the state is seeking conviction of defendants.

4. FREEDOM FROM CRUEL AND UNUSUAL PUNISHMENT. This is a guarantee of the Eighth Amendment to the Constitution and an expression of limitation on the way we treat even the worst among us. Though it is true that the courts have traditionally held that any sentence which falls within statutory provisions in a particular jurisdiction is presumed not to be cruel or unusual,[88] there seems to be a trend toward increasing review and reversals not only of sentences generally,[89] but of their lengths and the conditions of servitude as well.[90] For the most part we have eliminated corporal punishment in our society.[91] At least officially we no longer beat, brand, maim, or publicly ridicule offenders. Recently the U.S. Supreme Court, in an unusual and complex decision, held the death penalty to be unconstitutional under Eighth Amendment provisions.[92] There were, however, sufficient differences among the opinions of the justices to possibly allow states to attempt to rephrase statutes or to reapply methods of invoking the death penalty to conform to constitutional requirements.[93]

Today there are emerging a number of law suits which challenge the whole idea of the prison itself as cruel and unusual, though imprisonment within appropriate limits continues to be permitted everywhere.[94] However, appellate courts no longer refrain from deciding prison issues on the ground that correctional administrators have been delegated sole power to set prison rules and conditions. It is acknowledged that certain fundamental rights are retained by prisoners, and their effective demand for these rights has become one of the most important and most controversial issues in criminal justice administration.

5. EQUAL PROTECTION. It is a constitutionally sanctioned principle that the law be applied equally and impartially to all, rich and poor, black and white, powerful or helpless.[95] This ideal has often been violated in the past (the use of monetary basis for bail is a clear example of economic discrimination),[96] and it is currently the basis of a great deal of litigation. The propriety of this principle has been affirmed often in recent years by legislatures and appellate courts in issues ranging from representative and fair jury selection[97] to racial disparity in prison populations.[98]

6. RULE OF LAW. The principle that our system is one ruled by the letter of the law, not by the whims of men, is closely related to issues of equal protection.[99] In theory, statutes forbid specific criminal conduct, courts interpret and apply these laws, and the operational agencies—the police, prosecutors, trial judges, juries, and correctional personnel—carry out the legislative mandate without further interpretation or selection. In fact, however, the criminal justice system does not, and probably cannot, work in such automatic fashion. All criminal justice agencies and agents exercise discretion in applying the law.[100] Often, as with prosecutor and correctional authorities, such discretion—the authority to choose among alternative actions or not to act at all—is recognized by tradition or by legislative delegation. In other instances, as with police agencies, no such formal discretionary authority exists. Nevertheless, no police agency has sufficient resources to investigate all criminal activities, to detect and to arrest violators of all laws, nor is this actually desired in daily operation. Police have literally thousands of citizen contacts in which arrests could be made, but in which for a variety of reasons, they are not.[101] Likewise, prosecutors often choose among many different but possible charges to level against a defendant or decide in certain cases not to initiate charges at all.[102] Also, not all persons who are actually guilty are so found by judges or juries, and, in his sentencing capacity, the judge usually has a number of alternatives from fines to imprisonment among which to choose.[103] In actual operation, the criminal justice system is largely one of men, that is, one of choices for action within prescribed limits, rather than automatic implementation of all legislative proscriptions. Given the nature of the crime problem, the resources available for crime control, and the multiple and often conflicting purposes of criminal justice administration, discretion in the application of criminal sanctions is inevitable. Perhaps it is also desirable. Full enforcement of all laws would in the words of Judge Charles Breitel, be "ordered but intolerable."[104]

Currently there are various proposals to curb and to control agency discretion and in some cases, as with mandatory sentences, to eliminate it altogether.[105] The effective control of discretion and attempts to define and monitor its proper use are other issues of great importance in criminal justice administration.

7. PRESUMPTION OF INNOCENCE. If a number of ordinary citizens were asked to express in a single phrase the basic underlying philosophy of our criminal justice system, a common response would no doubt be that a person is presumed innocent until proven guilty. There is little question that this is a very strong ideological stance, and yet, in actual operation it presents the system with a paradox. The criminal justice process is invoked and works on an increasing belief in a person's guilt.[106] When police arrest a suspect they may indeed have in mind the fundamental principle of *ultimate* innocence (i.e., acquittal at trial), but their function in arrest depends upon a *reasonable* belief that the suspect has committed a crime. Likewise, as the arrestee proceeds through the system, evidence of guilt against him is accumulated and tested by the grand jury or at the preliminary hearing. The fullest adherence to the principle of presumption of innocence occurs during the trial, when both a rigid format and strict rules place the burden of proof of guilt on the state. A number of recent developments in procedural law, such as that requiring the *Miranda*[107] warning to be given immediately after arrest (notifying the suspect of his right to remain silent and to have assistance of counsel), reinforce the presumption of innocence until trial can be had. Nevertheless, the presumption is primarily an ideal that applies most strictly at the trial; initial steps in the process necessarily rely not on assumption of innocence, but upon belief of guilt.[108]

The list of ideological principles which are fundamental to our criminal justice system and which act to curb simple efficiency in crime control could be expanded and elaborated to fill a number of treatises. It will be clear from those listed above that our process of criminal justice exists within a complex set of values, expectations, and desires that preclude simplistic solutions to crime control efforts. Merely to demand greater police efficiency, to call for a "get tough" policy of enforcement, or to suggest that technological innovations turned loose will cut crime is to ignore the complexity of the problem. Demands for greater efficiency and effectiveness of police, prosecutors, courts, and correctional agencies are appropriate, but it must be clearly understood that there are other demands for fairness, propriety, and equal protection which also must be met if we are to retain our identity as a free and humane society.

The Multiple Objectives of Crime Control

One of the reasons why comparisons of the criminal justice system with other large complex organizations, such as the army or giant industrial corporations, are inappropriate is that the basic purposes and objectives of the criminal justice system are many and varied, and conflicts are not unusual. While common corporate endeavor may have multiple purposes, there usually is some consensus and congruence of objectives such as profits, growth, and perhaps public service. No such consensus exists about the specific purposes or techniques of the criminal justice system. It has varied purposes, and there is some incongruity concerning both long-range and short-range objectives. There are, of course, some commonly understood and accepted, but very broad, objectives shared in all criminal justice activity under the somewhat vague headings of crime control and prevention. These account for the existence of the system and form the terms under which the budget is given to agencies and for which resources are deployed in particular ways. However, the criminal justice system is made up of a federation of structurally distinct agencies having no line-staff relationship.[109] Intra-agency objectives may not be as clearly articulated as basic overall purposes, but they are nonetheless important in daily operations. These are the purposes and goals that relate to system maintenance and to the survival of individual bureaucracies like the police, courts, and corrections in the competition for funds and resources. The police may require a short-range objective of increasing arrests; corrections may wish to rehabilitate more offenders. Sometimes agency goals are directed toward objectives smaller than overall crime prevention, such as holding certain crimes to an "irreducible minimum."

Whether short-range or long-range, whether articulated or mute, the overall objectives of the criminal justice system fall into two general sets of purposes: the control of crime by solving offenses, arresting suspects, and processing and incapacitating offenders, and the prevention of crime through this processing or by other means. The crime control objective deals with the immediate situation and rests on discovery of past criminal behavior, whereas prevention is forward looking, forecasting and forestalling future crimes by present interventions. It is necessary to be aware of both control and prevention purposes, for only by such awareness can we explain certain legislative, court, and administrative agency activity.

It can be argued, of course, that control and prevention are so closely related as to be indistinguishable. For example, the purpose of arrest, conviction, and correctional processing of an offender may be to rehabilitate him, and thereby to prevent future crimes, or the use of marked police prowl cars in high crime incidence neighborhoods may be designed to deter and therefore prevent criminal acts. Obviously the two purposes become intertwined, though one or the other is usually given priority. The use of force by the police is primarily a control issue, but the *show* of force by police is future directed and to this extent is preventive.[110]

A number of major goals of the criminal justice system overlap, each having some elements of prevention and some of control. Yet they are distinct enough in purpose and in implementation to warrant extraction and separate attention when one is analyzing the system. Each of these major goals has within it subsidiary objectives that often come to be considered goals in themselves. Some major purposes follow:

1. TO DETECT, APPREHEND, CONVICT, AND INCAPACITATE CRIMINALS.

This is the most immediate, most direct, and most traditional purpose of criminal justice processing. The question of how best to do this, and to know when it has been done, is the source of many value conflicts about the criminal justice system.[111] In this respect, there are two major operational stances that can be taken, each of which generates disagreements about its worth and creates problems about how to implement and measure success.[112] One position holds that the criminal justice process should be invoked often, vigorously, and fully against criminals in our society. The opposing stance is that a better and more effective criminal justice system can be achieved when it acts reluctantly and when its purpose is the diversion of as many suspects as possible from criminal justice processing; or, if arrest and conviction must occur, to remove offenders from the system as rapidly as possible. Measures of effectiveness of the first position include high arrest rates, the charging of the highest crimes possible with available evidence, the convicting of offenders as charged, and the sentencing of violators to maximum terms. Its reciprocal is to arrest only under extreme conditions, to divert violators to other available agencies, but when processing defendants to charge only according to what seems best for the individual and after conviction to put him on probation or in a community correctional facility for a short period of time. Which approach is better or more effective is open to question,[113] and generates some strong conflicts about the basic nature of crime control in our society. For example, there is the question of whether a "good" police department is one which makes many arrests, or whether it is one which keeps the streets "cool" by adjusting issues and conflicts and by using arrest only as a last resort. There is also the question of whether the presumption under which the sentencing judge operates following conviction should be to incarcerate the offender unless he has a good record, or whether he should consider probation first, incarcerating only if he has a bad record. Probably the most common test of the effectiveness of each approach is to measure recidivism, to determine whether the frequency and rate of offenders who commit new crimes increases or decreases depending upon the way in which they are processed through the system.[114] This is difficult to determine with accuracy, but even if it can be measured, the issue remains of how to achieve low recidivism. While the use of punishment such as long prison sentences is often applied for the purpose of deterring other potential violators, imprisonment is also intended to change the offender into a law-abiding citizen. Sometimes long prison terms are imposed with the stated objective of "teaching the offender a lesson."[115] Whether he will be reformed by the penal sanction or personally deterred from committing more crimes out of fear makes little difference.

Punishment has long been accepted as a way of changing behavior, of forcing conformity.[116] The punitive ideal is still very much alive and its proponents often argue that punishment is a much better way to "reform" bad persons than are social work techniques or other forms of rehabilitation.[117] Besides imposing punitive sanctions to condition the offender to conformity, the use of imprisonment and the incapacitation of offenders have other objectives which are important historically.[118] These rest on certain religious principles, partly on the matter of vengeance—an eye for an eye—and also on the value of reflection and repentance.[119] The word "penitentiary" indicates this objective, as does the use of cells and the spartan fixtures that tend to give prisons a monastic aura.[120] Thus incarceration to punish and to force repentence was important in the development of our criminal justice system and continues to exert some influence.[121]

A different position about how to effectively change law breakers is prominent today, coequal with the punitive ideal. This involves use of the justice system much like a process of hospitalization (including out-patient care, i.e., probation) with goals of treatment, rehabilitation, and return of offenders to conforming behavioral patterns in the community. In this approach the punitive theme is muted, though physical control of offenders is maintained. However, the major purpose is to meet the adjustment needs of offenders in ways that will enable them to lead law-abiding lives once they have been paroled or discharged. Thus we have the anomaly of offenders who are locked in walled maximum-security prisons, outlawed from society and physically incapacitated, but who are engaged in individual and group counselling, educational programs, self-help groups, and other "treatment modalities" designed to modify their identifications with crime so that they are able to function and to achieve acceptable cultural goals in a law-abiding manner.

2. TO DETER POTENTIAL OFFENDERS.

Another largely preventive goal of the criminal justice system is to use it in a way that will effectively deter crime by stopping or frightening off potential lawbreakers. While it is generally recognized that permanent prevention of crime, if attainable at all, will require basic modification of cultural values, revision of opportunity structures, reorganization of social class structures, and elimination of economic imbalance, in general, actors in the criminal justice process see their preventive task in more modest terms, although it can be argued that the ultimate aim of the criminal justice system should be to reorder societal values to eradicate the *need* for crime. Even if such marked cultural changes could be agreed upon, the criminal justice system is not powerful or persuasive enough to achieve this goal. For the most part, prevention in the crime control context means short-range deterrence of potential violators or rehabilitation of previous offenders. These are closely related, and rehabilitation may imply nothing more than deterrence of a particular person processed through the system. For example, arguments that long prison sentences deter potential violators also claim effectiveness from the fact that the offender is restrained and unable to commit new crimes while he is held in prison. Likewise, the death penalty aims not only to deter other potential offenders, but in a gruesome manner "deals effectively" with the person executed. Whether general deterrence is actually possible is a moot question, for inference about its effectiveness is essentially negative; how many people would commit crimes if they were not deterred is not known.[122] There have been limited studies of certain offenses where a deterrent function has been observed. Emotional crimes and crimes of passion, such as murder or child molestation, are difficult and perhaps impossible to deter, for ultimately deterrence rests on rationality, on a fear of apprehension and a belief in the certainty of penal sanctions.[123] But in cases of more rational offenses like stealing, posting a police officer near the apple barrel is likely to reduce the number of apples stolen.

Two major approaches to deterrence are employed in the criminal justice system and both generate controversies about their effectiveness and their appropriateness in our society. The first engenders a belief in the certainty of criminal justice processing and a hope that the severity of official reactions when offenders are caught will deter people from initiating criminal activities.[124] To this end there is a desire to make the criminal justice system omnipresent, visible, certain, and swift, but there is disagreement on how to achieve this. At the police agency level this involves such issues as the use of clearly marked prowl cars, uniformed officers with side arms, techniques of frequent, random patrolling, and so on. It is expected that courts will be somber and dignified, with the raised bench and the black robes of the judge indicating seriousness of purpose in court proceedings—a posture critics feel is diminished by the more casual, juvenile court form of processing. Likewise, prisons should look like prisons to those on the outside as well as to those incarcerated. The wall and the gun turrets of the maximum-security prison have dual functions: to control the inmates within and to demonstrate the severe price of crime to potential offenders on the outside.

An opposing position, though also designed to create an aura of certain apprehension and stern punishment, is that the system should be nearly invisible while nurturing the belief that it is operating efficiently. Police activities should be primarily undercover, like those of narcotics officers who infiltrate the drug subculture in disguise to make arrests. Statistics on the effectiveness of law enforcement efforts should be kept confidential, and a sort of Dick Tracy,

"Crime Does Not Pay" posture should be maintained. At the same time, and seemingly inconsistent with this position is recognition of the danger of overkill: too severe punishment may lead to revolt, as in prison riots. Furthermore, making big-time prisons mysterious can cause them to be attractive to offenders who see them as a route to status not provided by other forms of correctional intervention.

In addition to apprehension and stern and sure punishment, another form of deterrence currently in vogue involves taking actions which prevent *opportunities* for crimes to occur or which assure quick discovery of violators. Devices used range from television cameras in banks to exact-fare requirements on public transportation. In New York City a public announcement that many off-duty policemen were driving taxicabs reduced markedly the incidence of taxi holdups for a period of time. Airplane hijacking is a serious problem that has elicited a strong demand for prevention. In addition to using a constructed "profile" of a skyjacker to screen passengers, federal law now requires that passengers be subject to luggage search and metal detection screening before boarding aircraft.[125] New statutes have made skyjacking subject to stringent punishment. Experiments with other techniques designed to deter range from the relatively simple and noncontroversial placing of "ghost" (unmanned) police cars distantly visible along superhighways to control traffic, to the use of police dogs in surveillance and park patrol. One problem with all deterrence techniques is the extent of the noncriminal population's willingness to put up with such inconveniences as exact change rules, searches upon entering public transportation, or the saturation of neighborhoods with armed police.

3. TO CREATE AN ORDERED SOCIETY. It has been said that if criminals did not exist they would have to be created, for they provide a necessary common enemy, a group of scapegoats, against which we can measure our own righteousness.[126] This is more than a matter of an abstract hated class, for any form of deviation—physical, mental, moral, or social—could serve the same purpose. In idealized form, the existence of criminals and the reaction of the criminal justice system to them exemplifies the apparently necessary belief in justice which we espouse and which helps to hold our society together. The efficiency and the vengeance elements of the criminal justice system are reinforced by other elements which are more symbolic and ceremonial. The pomp and rituals of the criminal court, the starkness of prisons, and the presence of the police with side arms are all visible embodiments of "justice" which serve to assure order and protection from disorder in our daily lives. Criminal justice agencies are indeed the agents of the status quo, of the Establishment, and attempts to change, reform, or otherwise modify them require more than proof of their inefficiency or ineffectiveness; tradition and symbolism are not only important parts of the system, but occasionally may be impediments to what appear to be rational and sensible reforms. There is a tendency, particularly among professional people within the criminal justice system, to attribute to it a high degree of rationality, and to assume that logic and research evidence will bring about desired and needed changes. This is rarely the case. It can be demonstrated, for example, that small, modern prisons with rooms instead of cells, with only a fence for perimeter security, with inmates dressed in civilian clothing, free to move about the institution and eligible for work release and furloughs, are not only more effective, but much cheaper than warehousing inmates in walled maximum-security prisons. But whenever such correctional facilities have been proposed, there has been a good deal of opposition on the grounds that prisons are not supposed to be this way, that such quarters are too pleasant to be prisons, and that they weaken the deterrent function of imprisonment. Most of us have deeply ingrained opinions about the way prisons should be, the way policemen should dress, and about the way judges should act when on the bench. The dispassionate proponent of change may be frustrated by what appear to be illogical components of the criminal justice system if he fails to take into account its essentially symbolic nature.

The desire for an ordered and safe society implies more than that the agencies of justice be visibly present, and give an appearance of law and order. There is also a demand that the system be effective, that somehow the police, courts, and other agencies operate to protect citizens from criminal predators, to make our streets and neighborhoods safe, and to create an environment where both the business and pleasure of our people can take place freely and safely. If indeed this is expected of our criminal justice system, it has failed ruefully in its task, particularly in the heart of our metropolitan areas.[127] Despite a federally declared "war on crime," the Safe Streets Act, the Omnibus Crime Control Act, the intensive and extensive establishment of experimental crime control programs, and the pouring of federal and state monies into law-enforcement efforts, many of our streets, neighborhoods, parks, and schools are neither safe nor orderly. It has been both easy and popular to blame these failures of crime control efforts on liberal court decisions, which over the past few decades have greatly expanded the rights of suspects and defendants at virtually all stages of criminal processing.[128] In fact, this argument was a major platform issue in the presidential election campaign of 1968 (a year which saw street rioting, looting, and burning in over a hundred different cities) and has influenced presidential appointments to the Supreme Court in the years since.[129]

The problem, however, is much more difficult and will not be ameliorated by merely strengthening the "peace forces" of our nation. A number of exceedingly complex forces have joined to create in our social order what the French sociologist Emile Durkheim long ago termed *anomie*,[130] a state of norm-lessness, of uncertainty of goals, purposes, identities, roles, procedures, and norms necessary for a properly ordered society to function. The frustrations, rage, and increasing political awareness of the poor which have culminated in a resurgence of a revolutionary, even anarchist, ethic, the widespread use of demonstrations and civil disobedience in reaction to racial inequalities and to war, the spread of a drug contraculture,[131] generation gaps, and the deteriora-tion of our environment have all combined to make law and order a far more complex and controversial matter than ever before in our history. The constable of yesterday has become the "pig" of today. This epithet reflects a widely held negative attitude toward law enforcement as symbolizing repression and defense of the status quo and opposing all demands for change.[132]

The safe-streets function of the criminal justice system has been greatly complicated by what many authorities believe to be a true epidemic of heroin addiction in our cities.[133] For example, it is estimated from addict registry lists and overdose deaths reported by the coroner, that there are as many as 500,000 heroin addicts in New York City alone and that these addicts account for up to 85 percent of all robberies, muggings, and other street crimes.[134] Given the chronic and intense nature of addiction, as well as the other antilaw and order pressures, the hope seems dim for immediate effectiveness in policing, prosecution, ad-judication, sentencing, and correctional treatment. To establish and maintain an ordered society is perhaps the major challenge of our time and certainly the most pressing and difficult task facing the criminal justice system.

The Resources of the Criminal Justice System

A factor often overlooked by proponents of effectiveness or of reform of the criminal justice system is the amount of support in terms of operating budgets, manpower, and other resources that it receives. As with all governmental agencies and programs, there are basic budgetary restrictions in crime control which limit agency activity and act to modify some long-range objectives. Even though today crime control is a high-priority domestic issue, there is a limitation on the amount of public monies we as a people are willing to spend in crime control efforts. The criminal justice system must compete with all other public systems and institutions for its share of tax funds; it must compete for the public dollar with education, health, welfare, and various other public endeavors. It can be argued that if hundreds more psychiatrists were employed by prisons, increased effectiveness in rehabilitating certain types of inmates would result. And if uniform patrol forces in police departments were doubled or tripled, the deterrent effect of visible police power would be much greater. Whether expansion of these and similar programs would achieve desired results may be questionable.[135] But to permit such expansion, the tax base would have to be expanded, or larger proportions of public budgets would have to be allotted to crime control efforts with smaller budgets for health, education, and welfare. These real and pervasive monetary concerns are powerful levelers of innovative and costly reform proposals. Every agency of crime control must modify its objectives and shape its ideal hopes to the basic feasibility of monetary support.

While the restriction of agency programs to actual and feasible budget is a factor which compels choices in the deployment of scarce resources, there is danger that budgetary restrictions can be wrongfully used to rationalize failure. Since all criminal justice agencies fail to achieve ideal objectives (if all were achieved we would have no crime problem), there is a tendency to blame lack of funds for shortcomings. Certainly there is some truth in this; there are few criminal justice agencies today which are satisfied with their resources and which could not do better jobs if they were more liberally funded. However, there is danger in supporting particular enforcement objectives or treatment modalities which may be subject to chronic failure regardless of the extent of their resources. The number of demonstrably effective crime control programs is limited indeed. Any warden can claim that he could do a much better job of rehabilitating inmates if he had a large staff of psychiatrists, but there is serious doubt that psychiatric services for most inmate populations would make much difference,[136] because the great bulk of prisoners are not insane or emotionally disturbed and are probably not an appropriate target population for effective clinical psychiatry. Similarly, police saturation of a community is as likely to engender hostility as to deter potential offenders. An actual embarrassment of riches has been the fate of some agencies which have received increased budgets and more resources. A number of police agencies, for example, have been retooled, receiving new pieces of equipment ranging from stun-guns to helicopters which have long been demanded for the purpose of increasing effectiveness. Yet when put into operation there is very little evidence that such equipment has affected the nature or extent of the community crime problem or the efficiency of the enforcement agency. Despite this experience, there is little doubt that criminal justice has failed to get its share of public monies in proportion to its importance in the social order. There are some areas of neglect that could be improved by more funds for training, equipment, and the recruitment of manpower, and overall there continue to be glaring inequities in the support of criminal justice programs in contrast to other public endeavors.

Not long ago a Committee to Revise the Children's Code in Wisconsin discovered that some house parents in youthful correctional institutions were resigning to seek employment in a neighboring zoo. As zoo keepers these persons received more money and had much less responsibility. And for reasons that make little sense, police salaries in many communities have been linked with the salaries of firemen, with both agencies commonly under control of a Police and Fire Commission. While there are some similarities in the routines of policemen and firemen—both wear uniforms, work around the clock seven days a week, and have dangerous employment—the tasks, expectations, necessary training, and skills of the two occupations are quite different. Putting out fires is a dangerous but fairly straightforward task involving little or no discretion. But the exercise of judgment, the sensible and proper use of discretion by a policeman is today a most complex, crucial issue, making his job one of the most important in our social order.[137] The linking of salaries and promotional opportunities between essentially disparate occupational groups is evidently largely a historical phenomenon, demonstrating a public judgment of the comparative importance of these jobs, and indicating some common misconceptions about them. Some changes in this relationship are occurring in many communities today.

Most criminal justice agencies try to deploy their limited budgets and resources in the most effective fashion. But because resources are often scarce within as well as between agencies, there is commonly an understandable effort to preserve units or programs within an agency, even including those programs which are demonstrably ineffective. Thus abolition of some crime control efforts can be as difficult as the creation of new ones. Personnel within any agency unit can be expected to have a vested interest in its survival or in its expansion. These *system maintenance* concerns—attempts to retain resources in hand, as well as to compete for additional support—are important factors in understanding the way the criminal justice system operates, and also provide some insight into its resistance to change. At present no criminal justice agency is completely efficient and effective; most crimes, particularly property crimes, reported to the police are never solved; in practice the prosecutory role is often one of negotiation rather than trial, for if enough guilty pleas can be obtained in exchange for concessions of sentence or charge, a prosecutor can maintain a very favorable conviction record; all judges are somewhat unsure of their effectiveness in sentencing and may, upon close examination, discover patterns of disparity in their own sentencing determinations. Finally, correctional programs often fall far short of any rehabilitative or reintegrative objectives.

Because of their chronic ineffectiveness, whether in an abstract sense or in terms of specific claims made to obtain funds, many criminal justice agencies take such protective action as barring review by outsiders to minimize threats to budgets and to ongoing programs. This is a particularly intense issue for a number of reasons: measures of effectiveness are not uniformly agreed upon, and there is no consensus on the primary task of any agency from police to prisons; the nature of the crime problem is so complex that even if acceptable standards of efficiency or effectiveness could be determined, it would be impossible to maintain them with present methods of control and treatment; and sharp budgetary restrictions on many crime control agencies necessitate reduced or improvised programs directed to less than the full achievement of stated purposes, such as *containing* certain crimes within numerical limits or geographical location, or in programs to *improve* offenders without attempting to rehabilitate them.

Despite the uncertainty of objectives, the inherent difficulty of the crime problem itself, and limited resources to cope with it, there are more pressures on criminal justice agencies to measure and evaluate their own activities than on almost any other public system in our society. Educational institutions are not required to pursue former students to see if they are good or bad, sick or well, successful or unsuccessful, happy or unhappy. This is also true of many other agencies in which statistics are kept on performance but in which there is no requirement to measure effectiveness. In some agencies, such as public assistance, effectiveness may be inferred simply from the amount of money given or the amount of money denied and thereby "saved." However, corrections and the other criminal justice agencies have strong mandates not only to report their activities, but to assess their effectiveness, and thus to justify in measurable form their very existence. Normally it is not sufficient for police to report how many crimes they investigated; they must also indicate how many they solved. Prosecutors often feel obligated to give a win-loss report in order to be reelected; judges face the responsibility of appellate reversal of their actions if they are deemed improper by a higher court; and prisons must make effectiveness claims of both security and rehabilitation. The time spent by criminal justice agencies counting and evaluating their activities probably exceeds that of any other public system, yet, as pointed out earlier, the amount and reliability of criminal justice reporting is less than adequate. One consequence of this pressure to report is that illusory improvements or failures can be shown simply by changing methods of record keeping, making rates appear to increase or diminish.[138] This in turn can change the bias of parole boards from liberal to conservative, or vice versa, with predictable effects on the number of prisoners rehabilitated. The absolute sales marketing statistics used in industry to test the effectiveness of advertising or other programs are not readily applicable to criminal justice, since there is no consensus on what ultimate measures should be. In any event, by selective statistics or by other means, there is great pressure within and between criminal justice agencies toward self-maintenance, toward winning a larger share of available tax-based resources with a corresponding need to maintain a facade of success. Thus survival requires practices that may appear dishonest, but that political realities demand.

There are other minor intra-agency objectives that may become important in understanding or evaluating a criminal justice agency or its processes. Because they are public agencies, all criminal justice offices and bureaucracies have public relation needs. Agency image is important not only for receiving budget support, but also for maintaining respect of the public at large, particularly if their cooperation is sought in helping to achieve crime control goals. Image making is not directed outside exclusively, but is equally important for those who work in the agencies, to maintain the morale and *esprit de corps* necessary to attain even limited success in achieving objectives. The Federal Bureau of Investigation is probably as well known for its careful guarding of image and the relatively high morale among its operatives as it is for its successes in solving crimes.

The fact that the criminal justice system has multiple objectives, and that internally it is characterized in part by self-sustaining activities, gives some indication of its complex nature. It is not a simple, unified organization with high consensus. Nevertheless, its existence and the way it operates is of critical importance to our democratic ideology. In our desire for an ordered society, we face a great dilemma: we want quick, effective and efficient means of crime control to protect each of us, but simultaneously we view police power with extreme caution, and for this reason we place stringent controls on the power of the state to intervene in the lives of our citizens. To meet both objectives, we have created a system of criminal justice which is extremely complex in both structure and function, and it is necessary to confront the complexity directly if the processes of the crime control system are to be understood and improved.

NOTES

1. See National Commission on the Causes and Prevention of Violence, *To Establish Justice, to Ensure Domestic Tranquility* (New York: Bantam, 1970), p. xxv.

2. President's Commission on Law Enforcement and Administration of Justice, *The Challenge of Crime in a Free Society* (Washington, D.C.: U.S. Government Printing Office, 1967), p. 1.

3. President's Commission on Law Enforcement and Administration of Justice, *Task Force Report: Crime and Its Impact—An Assessment* (Washington, D.C.: U.S. Government Printing Office, 1967), p. 39. See Walter C. Reckless, *The Crime Problem*, 3rd ed. (New York: Appleton-Century-Crofts, Inc., 1961), pp. 49-72; Terrence Morris, *The Criminal Area* (London: Routledge & Kegan Paul, 1957), pp. 37-64. Statistics published by Interpol, the international police agency, reflect the drastic differences in reported crime rates for such crimes as murder and robbery. In 1965-66, for example, the United States had a reported murder rate (offenders detected by police for murder) of 5.6 per 100,000. This compared to a worldwide high of 27.7 in the Congo and a low of .19 in Indonesia.

4. In light of modern improvements in American crime reporting, the President's Commission concluded in 1966 that it was unable to decide if Americans today were any more or less criminal than their counterparts of previous eras. President's Commission, *Crime and Its Impact—An Assessment*, p. 40.

5. *Uniform Crime Reports for the United States*—1971 (Washington, D.C.: U.S. Government Printing Office, 1972), pp. 18-21.

6. For scholarly evaluation of the *UCRs,* see Marvin E. Wolfgang, "Uniform Crime Reports: A Critical Appraisal," *U. of P. Law Review* 111, 709 (April 1963).

7. Philip H. Ennis, "Criminal Victimization in the United States: A Report of a National Survey," *Field Surveys II,* President's Commission on Law Enforcement and Administration of Justice (Washington, D.C.: U.S. Government Printing Office, 1967).

8. Alfred D. Biderman, Louis A. Johnson, Jennie McIntyre, and Adrianne W. Weir, "Report on a Pilot Study in the District of Columbia on Victimization and Attitudes Toward Law Enforcement," *Field Survey I,* President's Commission on Law Enforcement and Administration of Justice (Washington, D.C.: U.S. Government Printing Office, 1967).

9. Albert J. Reiss Jr., "Studies in Crime and Law Enforcement in Major Metropolitan Areas," *Field Surveys III,* Vol. I, Sec. I, President's Commission on Law Enforcement and Administration of Justice (Washington, D.C.: U.S. Government Printing Office, 1967).

10. President's Commission, *Crime and Its Impact—An Assessment,* p. 17.

11. A major conclusion of the New York City Criminal Justice Plan for 1971 was that "the crime control system in New York poses little threat to the average criminal." American Bar Association Special Committee on Crime Prevention and Control, *New Perspectives on Urban Crime* (Washington, D.C.: American Bar Association, 1972), p. 7.

12. Most self-report surveys, also known as hidden delinquency studies, have been performed with samples of school children and focus on delinquency rather than crime. Some prominent examples include: K. Elmhorn, "Study on Self-Reported Delinquency Among School Children in Stockholm," in K. O. Christiansen, ed., *Scandinavian Studies in Criminology* (London: Tavistock, 1965), pp. 117-46; M. L. Erickson and L. M. Empey, "Court Records, Undetected Delinquency and Decision-Making," *J. Crim. Law, Criminology and Pol. Sci.* 54 (1963); M. Gold, "Undetected Delinquency Behavior," *J. Res. in*

Crime and Delin. 3 (1966): 27-46; R. A. Dentler and L. J. Monroe, "Social Correlates of Early Adolescent Theft," *Amer. Soc. Review* 26 (1961): 733-43; L. M. Empey and M. L. Erickson, "Hidden Delinquency and Social Status," *Soc. Forces* 44 (1966): 546-54.

13. James S. Wallerstein and Clement J. Wyle, "Our Law Abiding Law-Breakers," *Nat. Probation* 25, 107 (1947).

14. The *New York Times,* 9 February 1973, p. 1, reported that the New York City Police Department had purged its intelligence file of the names of more than one million persons, following the filing of a federal court suit alleging the department's intelligence activities had been "overbroad and unconstitutional."

For a leading case on spying by the military on civilians, see Laird v. Tatum, 92 S. Ct. 2318 (1972). Another leading case in the police intelligence area is Anderson v. Sills, 56 N.J. 210, 265 A. 2d 678 (1970). Both of these cases have upheld the power of the police and the military to gather intelligence data.

15. The most common categories of known or suspected criminals compiled by police include the names of alleged gamblers, prostitutes, and narcotics pushers. Specialized police units also frequently maintain lists of reputed organized crime members and alleged political extremists.

16. See, generally, Alan F. Westin, *Privacy and Freedom* (New York: Atheneum, 1967).

17. See, generally, Albert P. Blaustein, "Systems Analysis and the Criminal Justice Systems," *Annals* 374, 92 (1967).

18. See, generally, Donald J. Newman, "The Effect of Accommodations in Justice Administration on Criminal Statistics," *Sociol. and Soc. Res.* 46, 144 (1962).

19. Marvin E. Wolfgang, Robert M. Figlio, and Thorsten Sellin, *Delinquency in a Birth Cohort* (Chicago: University of Chicago Press, 1972) defined as cohort those boys who had been born in Philadelphia in 1945, who resided there from their tenth to their fourteenth birthdays.

20. This theme is evident throughout several of the task force reports prepared by the President's Commission, including *The Challenge of Crime in a Free Society, Crime and Its Impact—An Assessment,* and *Science and Technology.*

21. This organizational interest can take several different forms, depending on the agency's goals, the current political climate, and numerous other factors. Alfred D. Biderman and Albert J. Reiss, Jr., "On Exploring the Dark Figure of Crime," *Annals Amer. Acad. of Pol. and Soc. Sci.* 374 (1967): 1-15, suggest that the police have a vested interest in maintaining an increasing crime rate. Jerome S. Skolnick, however, has noted that in the desire of the police to maintain a good image, they often seek to manipulate crime figures to show a substantial clear-up rate. See Skolnick, *Justice Without Trial* (New York: John Wiley and Sons, 1966), esp. pp. 165-81.

22. Leslie T. Wilkins, "New Thinking in Criminal Statistics," *J. Crim. Law, Criminology and Pol. Sci.* 56, 277 (1965).

23. The System for Electronic Analysis and Retrieval of Criminal Histories (SEARCH) was launched in 1969. It was designed to explore the potentialities and feasibility of an on-line system which would permit interstate exchange of offender history files, as maintained by state and local criminal justice agencies. Funded by the federal Law Enforcement Assistance Administration (LEAA), Project SEARCH has already entered its implementation stage. See LEAA, *Third Annual Report of the Law Enforcement Assistance Administration* (Washington, D.C.: U.S. Government Printing Office, 1972), esp. pp. 93-98. See also *Designing Statewide Criminal Justice Statistics Systems—An Examination*

of the Five State Implementation (Washingon, D.C.: Technical Report No. 5, December 1972).

24. See Richard Harris, *The Fear of Crime* (New York: Praeger, 1969).

25. President's Commission, *Science and Technology*, p. 56.

26. *Ibid.*

27. Some of the more successful attempts to devise this type of "seriousness" index have been made by Thorsten Sellin and Marvin E. Wolfgang, *The Measurement of Delinquency* (New York: John Wiley and Sons, 1964). See also Wilkins, "New Thinking in Criminal Statistics."

28. See Henry M. Hart, "The Aims of the Criminal Law," *Law and Contemp. Prob.* 23, 401 (1958): esp. 419-425; Oliver Wendell Holmes, *The Common Law* (Boston, 1881); H. L. A. Hart, *The Concept of Law* (London: Oxford U. Press, 1961).

29. See Hart, "The Aims of the Criminal Law," esp. pp. 419-425; Graham Hughes, "Criminal Omissions," *Yale Law J.* 67, 590 (1958). A critical examination of malum prohibitum legislation is contained in Troy Duster, *The Legislation of Morality* (New York: The Free Press, 1970).

30. See Hart, "The Aims of the Criminal Law"; Marvin E. Wolfgang, *Patterns in Criminal Homicide* (Philadelphia: U. of P. Press, 1958). For an historical analysis of the concept of guilt and its relation to the law of homicide, see John Biggs Jr., *The Guilty Mind: Psychiatry and the Law of Homicide* (Baltimore: Johns Hopkins Press, 1955). See also, Herbert Wechsler and Jerome Michael, "A Rationale of the Law of Homicide," *Columbia Law Review* 37, 1291 (1937).

31. See Hart, "The Aims of the Criminal Law," for a general discussion of the aims and operation of the criminal law; and Jerome Hall, "Objectives of Federal Criminal Procedural Revision," *Yale Law J.* 51, 723 (1942).

32. See Stuart L. Hills, *Crime, Power, and Morality: The Criminal Law Process in the United States* (Scranton: Chandler Publ. Co., 1971), p. 5.

33. This argument, by no means new, continues to loom as one of the most heated controversies surrounding the criminal law in a free society. Among the most sophisticated champions of the enforcement of morality is Patrick Devlin, *The Enforcement of Morals* (London: Oxford U. Press, 1959). Opposing him in the debate have been H. L. A. Hart, *Law, Liberty, and Morality* (Stanford: Stanford U. Press, 1963); Edwin Schur, *Crimes Without Victims* (Englewood Cliffs, N.J.: Prentice-Hall, 1965); Norval Morris and Gordon Hawkins, *The Honest Politician's Guide to Crime Control* (Chicago: U. of Chicago Press, 1969); Norval Morris, "Crimes Without Victims: The Law is a Busybody," The *New York Times Magazine,* 1 April 1973, p. 10; Sanford Kadish, "The Crisis of Overcriminalization," *Annals Amer. Acad. of Pol. and Soc. Sci.* 374 (November, 1967); Troy Duster, *The Legislation of Morality;* Herbert L. Packer, *The Limits of Criminal Sanction* (Stanford: Stanford U. Press, 1968).

34. It has been estimated that killings by police officers constitute from 2 percent to 5 percent of all intentional violent deaths in the United States; Gerald Robin, "Justifiable Homicide by Police Officers," *J. Crim. Law* 54, 224 (1963).

35. New York State Special Commission on Attica, *Attica* (New York: Bantam, 1972) contains detailed analysis of the 1971 prison uprising which resulted in 43 deaths and although the fatal shots were fired primarily by state police, the Commission report includes considerable material on the use of deadly force by correctional officers as well. See also Russell G. Oswald, *Attica—My Story* (Garden City, N.Y.: Doubleday, 1972).

Also, see Min S. Yee, "Death on the Yard: The Untold Killings at Soledad and San Quentin," *Ramparts* (April 1973): 35-40, 49-55.

36. Perhaps the most famous episode involving the controversial use of deadly force by national guardsmen occurred at Kent State University in May 1970. See James Michener, *Kent State: What Happened and Why* (New York: Random House, 1971). John Hersey, *The Algiers Motel Incident* (New York: Bantam, 1968) provides a journalist's account of similar deadly force during the 1967 Detroit riots.

37. American Law Institute, *Model Penal Code,* proposed official draft (Philadelphia: American Law Institute, 1962).

38. Advisory Council of Judges of the National Council on Crime and Delinquency, *Model Sentencing Act* (1963).

39. Advisory Committee on Sentencing and Review, American Bar Association Project on Minimum Standards for Criminal Justice, *Sentencing Alternatives and Procedures* (New York: Institute of Judicial Administration, 1967).

40. *Model Penal Code,* R.O.D. (1962) Sec. 7.03, 109.

41. *Model Sentencing Act, Optional,* Sec. 8, 21.

42. *Model Sentencing Act,* Sec. 5, 16; *Model Penal Code,* 109.

43. *Model Code of Pre-Arraignment Procedure,* Sec. 2.02, Comment at 95-97 (Tentative Draft No. 1, 1965), in the American Law Institute's Model Code. For an examination of the operational effects of these laws, see Frank J. Remington, Donald J. Newman, Edward L. Kimball, Marygold Melli, and Herman Goldstein, *Criminal Justice Administration: Materials and Cases* (Indianapolis: Bobbs-Merrill, 1969), pp. 151-160.

44. See, for example, Office of the Police Commissioner, "Instructions to Members of the Force Concerning 'Stop and Frisk' (Chap. 86) and 'No Knock' (Chap. 85) Laws," New York City Police Dept., Cir. No. 25, June 26, 1964.

45. Comment, "Preventive Detention Before Trial," *Harvard Law Review* 79, 1489 (1966); Comment, "Preventive Detention," *George Washington Law Review* 36, 178 (1967); Comment, "Preventive Detention: An Empirical Analysis," *Harvard Civ. Rights— Civ. Lib. Law Review* 6, 291 (1971).

46. Vera Institute of Justice, *Preventive Detention in the District of Columbia: The First Ten Months* (New York: Vera Institute, 1972).

47. *Ibid,* p. 69.

48. Sidney Hook, "The Rights of Victims of Crime," *Congressional Record,* 4 March 1972, p. 53943 and 17 February 1972, p. 41268.

49. Richard R. Korn and Lloyd W. McCorkle, *Criminology and Penology* (New York: Holt, Rinehart & Winston, 1959), pp. 142-156, examines many of the disadvantages of this legalistic approach. See also, Marshall B. Clinard and Richard Quinney, *Criminal Behavior Systems: A Typology,* 2nd ed. (New York: Holt, Rinehart & Winston, 1973), p. 3-5.

50. Roebuck, for example, has constructed a typology based on arrest records derived from a sample of 1,115 Washington prisoners. See Julian B. Roebuck, "The Negro Numbers Man as a Criminal Type: The Construction and Application of a Typology," *J. Crim. Law, Criminology and Pol. Sci.* 54, 48 (March 1963); Roebuck and Mervyn L. Cadwallader, "The Negro Armed Robber as a Criminal Type: The Construction and Application of a Typology," *Pacific Soc. Review* 4, 21 (Spring 1961); Roebuck, "The Negro Drug Addict as an Offender Type," *J. Crim. Law, Criminology and Pol. Sci.* 53, 36

(March 1962); Roebuck, *Criminal Typology: The Legalistic, Physical-Constitutional-Heredity, Psychological-Psychiatric and Sociological Approaches* (Springfield, Ill.: Charles C Thomas, 1967). For another discussion about the construction of a typology see Don C. Gibbons and Donald L. Garrity, "Definitions and Analysis of Certain Criminal Types," *J. Crim. Law, Criminology and Pol. Sci.* 53, 27 (1962).

51. Clinard and Quinney, *Criminal Behavior Systems*, p. 3.

52. Alfred R. Lindesmith and H. Warren Dunham, "Some Principles of Criminal Typology," *Soc. Forces* 19 (March 1941): 307-314, constructed a continuum of criminal behavior ranging from the "individual criminal" to the "social criminal." The first type finds little support for his criminal conduct and commits his acts for various personal reasons, such as jealousy or anger. The second type acts criminally in order to achieve status and recognition from peers, and his acts are generally supported by the norms of the group (i.e., gang) to which he belongs. For a typology stressing career patterns, see Reckless, *The Crime Problem*, esp. Chaps. 9 and 10.

53. Clinard and Quinney, *Criminal Behavior Systems*, pp. 16-21.

54. See Frank J. Remington and Victor G. Rosenblum, "The Criminal Law and the Legislative Process," *U. of Ill. Law F.* 1960, 481; Henry M. Hart, "The Aims of the Criminal Law," *Law and Contemp. Prob.* 23, 401 (1958).

55. Hugo Adam Bedau, ed., *The Death Penalty in America* (New York: Anchor, 1967); Thorsten Sellin, ed., *The Death Penalty* (New York: Harper & Row, 1967); Washington Research Project, *The Case Against the Death Penalty* (1971).

56. See, generally, Johannes Andenaes, *Punishment and Deterrence* (Ann Arbor, Mich.: U. of Mich. Press, 1974).

57. David Abrahamsen, *Who Are the Guilty?* (New York: Holt, Rinehart, & Winston, 1952).

58. This thesis is especially prominent in contemporary delinquency theory. See, for example, Richard Cloward and Lloyd Ohlin, *Delinquency and Opportunity* (New York: The Free Press, 1960).

59. Ramsey Clark, *Crime in America: Observations on its Nature, Causes, Prevention and Control* (New York: Simon & Schuster, 1970), pp. 17-18.

60. Diametric opposition to the Ramsey Clark view of crime causation was enunciated by Richard Nixon, before and after his 1968 presidential campaign. For a detailed analysis of the Nixon position, see Richard Harris, *Justice: The Crisis of Law, Order, and Freedom in America* (New York: Dutton, 1970).

61. Marvin E. Wolfgang and Franco Ferracuti, *Subcultures of Violence: Towards an Integrated Theory in Criminology* (London: Tavistock, 1967).

62. Norval Morris and Gordon Hawkins, *The Honest Politician's Guide to Crime Control* (Chicago: U. of Chicago Press, 1969) are among those, however, who have strongly resisted this "seductive notion," holding that man continues to lack the capability of predicting most violence.

63. Powell v. Texas, 392 U.S. 514, 526 (1968).

64. For a revealing look at so-called crime waves, see Fred J. Cook, "There's Always a Crime Wave," The *New York Times Magazine*, 6 October 1968. Lincoln Steffens, the great muckraker, recounted in his *Autobiography* (New York: Harcourt, Brace and Co., 1931), pp. 285-91, how he had "created" several crime waves through his dramatic coverage.

65. See, generally, Herbert L. Packer, "Two Models of the Criminal Process," *U. of P. Law Review* 113, 1 (1964); Fred E. Inbau, "Democratic Restraints Upon the Police," *J. Crim. Law, Criminology and Pol. Sci.* 57, 265 (1966); Jacob Chwatz, "Value Conflicts in Law Enforcement," *Crime and Delin.* 11, 151 (1965).

66. Rochin v. California, 342 U.S. 165 (1952).

67. "It is not without significance that most of the provisions of the Bill of Rights are procedural. It is procedure that spells much of the difference between rule by law and rule by whim or caprice. Steadfast adherence to strict procedural safeguards is our main assurance that there will be equal justice under law." Justice Douglas concurring in Joint Anti-Fascist Refugee Committee v. McGrath, 341 U.S. 123 (1951).

68. "When society acts to deprive one of its members of his life, liberty, or property," wrote former Chief Justice Warren, "it takes its most awesome steps. No general respect for, nor adherence to, the law as a whole can well be expected without judicial recognition of the paramount need for prompt, eminently fair, and sober criminal law procedures. The methods we employ in the enforcement of our criminal law have aptly been called the measures by which the quality of our civilization may be judged," Coppedge v. United States, 369 U.S. 438, 449 (1962).

69. Leo Pfeffer, *The Liberties of an American* (Boston: Beacon Press, 1956), p. 158. "It took centuries to evolve the conception of the fair trial we have today. It was against a background poignant with memories of evil procedures that our Constitution was drawn." William O. Douglas, *We the Judges* (Garden City, N.Y.: Doubleday, 1956), p. 379.

70. Henry M. Hart, "The Aims of the Criminal Law," and Remington and Rosenblum, "The Criminal Law and the Legislative Process."

71. Gideon v. Wainwright, 372 U.S. 335 (1963), held that the states have a duty in all serious criminal cases to provide counsel for those indigent defendants who have not knowingly and intelligently waived their right to counsel. The Court extended the duty to indigent defendants accused of minor crimes, in Argersinger v. Hamlin, 407 U.S. 25 (1972).

72. See, for example, the Supreme Court's continuing attempts to define due process standards for juveniles. Kent v. United States, 383 U.S. 541 (1966); In re Gault, 387 U.S. 1 (1967); In re Winship, 397 U.S. 358 (1970).

Basically, the Due Process Clause has been interpreted as meaning that the accused person must be accorded all the procedural safeguards of "those minimal standards which are of the very essence of a scheme of ordered liberty." Palko v. Connecticut, 302 U.S. 319, at 325 (1937); also, that due process amounts to "those canons of decency and fairness which express the notions of justice," Adamson v. California, 332 U.S. 46, 67 (1947). Justice Jackson has asserted that due process is nothing more or less than a short-hand transcript for the Bill of Rights. Ronald L. Goldfarb, *Ransom: A Critique of the American Bail System* (New York: Harper & Row, 1965), p. 96. The "great generalities of the Constitution have a content and a significance that vary from age to age," wrote Justice Benjamin N. Cardozo, in *The Nature of the Judicial Process* (New Haven: Yale U. Press, 1921), p. 21. Along these lines, Charles Beard, the historian, referred to the Constitution as a "living thing," because it contained so many vague words and broad phrases requiring interpretation by the courts. Beard, "The Living Constitution," *Annals* 185 (May, 1936): 30-31.

73. United States ex rel. Campbell v. Pate, 401 F.2d 55, 57 (7th Cir. 1968), for example, held that at a prisoner's disciplinary hearing the "relevant facts must not be capriciously or unreliably determined."

74. These changing criteria for evidence are examined in Abraham S. Goldstein, "The State and the Accused: Balance of Advantage in Criminal Procedure," *Yale Law J.* 69, 1166 (1960). For detailed discussion of particular evidentiary requirements, see Wayne R. LaFave, *Arrest: The Decision to Take a Suspect into Custody* (Boston: Little, Brown, 1965) (police); Frank W. Miller, *Prosecution: The Decision to Charge a Suspect with a Crime* (Boston: Little, Brown, 1969) (prosecutor); and Robert O. Dawson, *Sentencing: The Decision as to Type, Length, and Conditions of Sentence* (Boston: Little, Brown, 1969).

75. For a highly readable journalistic account of the due process revolution of the Warren Court, see Fred P. Graham, *The Self-Inflicted Wound* (New York: Macmillan, 1970).

76. See Fred Cohen, "A Comment on Morrissey v. Brewer: Due Process and Parole Revocation," *Crim. Law Bull.* 7, 616 (September 1972).

77. Miranda v. Arizona, 384 U.S. 436 (1966); Hoffa v. United States, 385 U.S. 293 (1966).

78. United States v. Wade, 388 U.S. 218 (1967); Kirby v. Illinois, 406, U.S. 682 (1972); Foster v. California, 394 U.S. 440 (1969).

79. People v. Cairns, 4 Mich. App. 633, 145 N.W. 2d 345 (1966); Durant v. United States, 410 F.2d 689 (1st Cir. 1969); Federal Rules of Criminal Procedure (Preliminary Draft of Proposed Amendments, April 1971), Rule 11.

80. See President's Commission on Law Enforcement and Administration of Justice, *Task Force Report: Corrections* (Washington, D.C.: U.S. Government Printing Office, 1967), esp. pp. 32-34; Note, "Beyond the Ken of the Courts: A Critique of Judicial Refusal to Review Complaints of Convicts," *Yale Law J.* 72, 506 (1963); E. N. Barkin, "The Emergence of Correctional Law and the Awareness of the Rights of the Convicted," *Neb. Law Review* 45, 669 (1966); Note, Constitutional Rights of Prisoners: The Developing Law," *U. of P. Law Review* 985 (1962); Donald J. Newman, "Court Intervention in the Parole Process," *Albany Law Review* 36, 257 (1972); Comment, "The Parole System," *U. of P. Law Review* 120, 281 (1971); Note, "Parole: A Critique of Its Legal Foundations and Conditions," *N.Y.U. Law Review,* 38, 702 (1963); Edward L. Kimball and Donald J. Newman, "Judicial Intervention in Correctional Decisions: Threat and Response," *Crime and Delin.* 14, 1 (1968).

81. For a concise but useful compendium of these newfound rights, see David Rudovsky, *The Rights of Prisoners: The Basic ACLU Guide to Prisoner's Rights* (New York: Avon, 1973). See also Sheldon Krantz, Robert Bell, Johnathon Brant, and Michael Magruder, *Model Rules and Regulations on Prisoners' Rights and Responsibilities* (St. Paul: West, 1973).

82. *Ibid;* Fred Cohen, "The Discovery of Prison Reform," *Buffalo Law Review* 21, 855 (1972).

83. Morales v. Schmidt, 340 F. Supp. 544 (W. D. Wis. 1972).

84. Morales v. Schmidt, 494 F. 2d 85, 87 (7th Cir. 1974). See also Mabra v. Schmidt, 356 F. Supp. 620 (W. D. Wis. 1973).

85. Abraham S. Goldstein, "The State and the Accused." A. Amsterdam, B. Segal, and M. Miller, *Trial Manual for the Defense of Criminal Cases;* Jonathan D. Casper, *American Criminal Justice: The Defendant's Perspectives* (Englewood Cliffs, N.J.: Prentice-Hall, 1972).

86. See Hoffa v. United States, 385 U.S. 293 (1966); Rochin v. California, 342 U.S. 165 (1952); Terry v. Ohio, 392 U.S. 1 (1968); Miranda v. Arizona, 384 U.S. 436 (1966).

87. In 1914, the Supreme Court held that the Fourth Amendment required the application of the exclusionary rule in federal prosecutions in Weeks v. United States, 232 U.S. 383 (1914). In Wolf v. Colorado, 338 U.S. 25 (1949), however, the Court was divided on the issue of whether the rule had to be used in state courts where evidence had been obtained by unconstitutional search and seizure. The exclusionary rule was finally extended to state courts in Mapp v. Ohio, 367 U.S. 643 (1961) holding that evidence leading to the conviction of a defendant charged with possession of lewd and obscene material had been obtained illegally, and thus that it must be excluded as evidence.

88. See, for example, Director of Patuxent Institution v. Daniels, 243 Md. 16, 221 A. 2d 397 (1966); Powell v. Texas, 392 U.S. 514 (1968). Judge Charles D. Breitel of the New York State Court of Appeals has estimated that as many as three-quarters of all criminal appeals which came before his court mentioned "excessiveness" in sentence. However, he concluded that "this issue is seriously argued in very few, and . . . even then, little additional work is involved."

89. In Skinner v. Oklahoma, 316 U.S. 535 (1942), the U.S. Supreme Court invalidated a state habitual-criminal law under which persons convicted two or more times of felonies involving "moral turpitude" could be sexually sterilized. (Contrast this decision with Buck v. Bell, 274 U.S. 200 (1972), in which the court upheld involuntary sterilization after determining that due process safeguards provided by the statute had been followed.)

90. In Watson v. United States, 439 F.2d 442 (D.C. Cir. [1970]), the court ruled that a mandatory ten-year prison sentence imposed on a "subsequent" narcotics possessor and addict was cruel and unusual punishment. Also, Workman v. Kentucky, 429 S.W. 2d 374 (1968), which held that sentences of life imprisonment without parole for two juveniles convicted of rape amounted to cruel and unusual punishment.

91. Most states explicitly forbid the use of corporal punishment against prisoners, and the U.S. Court of Appeals for the Eighth Circuit has ruled that any form of such punishment amounts to cruel and unusual punishment under the Eighth Amendment. Jackson v. Bishop, 404 F.2d 571 (1968).

92. Furman v. Georgia, 408 U.S. 238 (1972).

93. For early interpretations of this complex decision, see Hugo Adam Bedau, "Capital Punishment and the Supreme Court," *Jewish Advocate,* Boston (August 10, 1972); Isadore Silver, "Death and the Judges: Cruel and Unusual Punishment?" *Commonweal* (April 14, 1972): 136. Less than a year after the ruling that the death penalty, as currently imposed in most states, was unconstitutional, 13 states had enacted laws to bring back the penalty, and bills were awaiting signature in two other states. The *New York Times,* 10 May 1973.

94. In Holt v. Sarver, 309 F. Supp. 362 (E. D. Ark. 1970), aff'd 442 F.2d 304 (8th Cir. 1971), Chief Judge Henley undertook an extensive review of numerous alleged unconstitutional practices within the Arkansas prison system and held that the cumulative impact of the substandard conditions there amounted to cruel and unusual punishment. In Commonwealth ex rel. Bryand v. Hendrick, 444 Pa. 83 (1971), the Pennsylvania Supreme Court ruled that the general conditions prevailing in a Philadelphia prison constituted cruel and unusual punishment even though the petitioners in the case had not suffered such terrible abuses; in other words, the mere fact that the petitioners were subject to them, was deemed as a sufficient showing of unconstitutionality. Cases ruling that confinement in local jails constituted cruel and unusual punishment include the following: Wayne County Jail Inmates v. Wayne County Board of Commissioners, C. A. No. 173-217 Cir. Ct. Mich., 1971; Jones v. Wittenberg, 323 F. Supp. 93 (N. D. Ohio, 1971).

95. The term "equal protection," like "due process," "justice," and so many others recently litigated, is impossible to define with precision. The clause was designed to protect the rights of newly-freed slaves after the American Civil War. The Slaughterhouse Cases, 16 Wall. 36 (1873). However, the clause was not vigorously applied to the criminal justice area until the middle of the twentieth century. For a leading case in this area, see Baxstrom v. Herold, 388 U.S. 107 (1966).

96. This economic discrimination of bail is explored in Goldfarb, *Ransom: A Critique of the American Bail System*. Perhaps the foremost authority on bail is Caleb B. Foote. See Foote, "The Coming Constitutional Crisis in Bail," *U. of P. Law Review* 113, 1125 (1965); Foote, "The Bail System and Equal Justice," *Fed. Probation* 23 (Sept. 1959): 43-48; Foote, ed., *Studies on Bail* (Philadelphia: U. of P. Press, 1967). See also President's Commission on Law Enforcement and Administration of Justice, *Task Force Report: The Courts* (Washington, D.C.: U.S. Government Printing Office, 1967).

97. In Peters v. Kiff, 407 U.S. 493 (1972), the Supreme Court ruled that any defendant may object to a panel which has been chosen discriminatorily, even if he is not a member of the excluded group. However, the fact remains that whites are generally disproportionately represented on American juries—often over the objection of the minority-member defendant. For a highly critical view of the jury selection process, see Charles R. Garry, "Minimizing Racism in Jury Trials," in Jonathan Black, ed., *Radical Lawyers: Their Role in the Movement and in the Courts* (New York: Avon, 1971).

98. See Montgomery v. Oakley Training School, 426 F.2d (5th Cir. 1970), Washington v. Lee, 263 F. Supp. 327 (M. D. Ala. 1966); Affirmed, pee. curiam, Lee v. Washington, 390 U.S. 333 (1968).

99. Pfeffer, *The Liberties of an American*, p. 156.

100. An excellent treatise on the operation of this recurrent discretion is found in Kenneth Davis, *Discretionary Justice: A Preliminary Inquiry* (Baton Rouge: L.S.U. Press, 1969). Police discretion is examined by Egon Bittner, "Police Discretion in Emergency Apprehension of Mentally Ill Persons," *Soc. Prob.* 14 (1967); 287-292; Herman Goldstein, "Police Discretion: The Ideal versus the Real," *Pub. Admin. Review* 140 (September 1963); Joseph Goldstein, "Police Discretion Not to Invoke the Criminal Process: Low Visibility Decisions in the Administration of Justice," *Yale Law J.* 69, 543 (March 1960); and LaFave, *Arrest*. Prosecutor discretion is discussed in Brian Grosman, *The Prosecutor: An Inquiry into the Exercise of Discretion* (Toronto: U. of Toronto Press, 1969); Norman Abrams, "Internal Policy: Guiding the Exercise of Prosecutorial Discretion," *U.C.L.A. Law Review* 19, 1 (1971); John Kaplan, "The Prosecutorial Discretion—A Comment," *N. W. U. Law Review* 60, 174 (1965); and Miller, *Prosecution*. Judicial discretion in sentencing is explored by Dawson, *Sentencing*. For a study of postconviction discretion, see Note, "Discretionary Revocation of Probation and Parole," *U.S.F. Law Review* 4, 160 (1969). Another prominent contribution to this general area of discretion is Francis Allen, *The Borderland of Criminal Justice* (Chicago: U. of Chicago Press, 1964).

101. Goldstein, "Police Discretion Not to Invoke the Criminal Process."

102. Grosman, *The Prosecutor*. Miller, *Prosecution*. Newman v. United States, 382 F.2d 479 (D.C. Cir. 1967).

103. Edward Green, *Judicial Attitudes in Sentencing* (London: Macmillan, 1961); Dawson, *Sentencing*.

104. Charles D. Breitel, "Controls in Criminal Law Enforcement," *U. of Chicago Law Review* 27, 427 (Spring 1960). A similar remark was made by Dan Dodson, in a speech

at Michigan State University in May 1955. "No policeman enforces all the laws of a community. If he did, we would all be in jail before the end of the first day."

105. See, American Friends Service Committee, *Struggle for Justice: A Report on Crime and Punishment in America* (New York: Hill & Wang, 1971), esp. pp. 124-44.

106. Herbert L. Packer, *The Limits of the Criminal Sanction* (Stanford: Stanford U. Press, 1968), esp. pp. 160-161.

107. Miranda v. Arizona, 384 U.S. 436 (1966).

108. Franz Kafka, the great Austrian fiction writer whose works often have great relevance to criminal justice matters, once put it this way: "My guiding principle is this: guilt is never to be doubted," Nahum N. Glatzer, ed., "In the Penal Colony," in *Franz Kafka: The Complete Stories* (New York: Schocken Books, 1971), p. 145.

109. Remington, Newman, Kimball, Melli, and Goldstein, *Criminal Justice Administration,* esp. pp. 6-17.

110. The show of force pervades the entire criminal justice system, of course, and takes on a variety of manifestations from the somber, robed judge to the stark architecture of the maximum security prison.

111. For an examination of some of these conflicts, see Jacob Chwatz, "Value Conflicts on Law Enforcement," *J. Res. in Crime and Delin.* 11, 151 (1965).

112. See Herbert L. Packer, "Two Models of the Criminal Process," *U. of P. Law Review* 113, 1 (November 1964).

113. John Griffiths has posited a *third* model. "Ideology in Criminal Procedure or a Third 'Model' of the Criminal Process," *Yale Law J.* 79, 359 (1970).

114. Despite years of intensive research into this question, however, we still appear to be at the stage, as Professor Leslie T. Wilkins has said, where "the nature of our ignorance is beginning to be revealed." For a comprehensive treatment of modern attempts to assess the effectiveness of punishments and treatments, see Roger Hood and Richard Sparks, *Key Issues in Criminology* (New York: World U. Lib., 1971), esp. pp. 171-214.

115. See, for example, Judge Holbrook's statement in People v. Cairns, 4 Mich. App. 633 (1966).

116. See, generally, H. L. A. Hart, *Punishment and Responsibility* (Oxford: Clarendon Press, 1968); Nigel Walker, "Aims of Punishment," in Leon Radzinowicz and Marvin E. Wolfgang, eds., *The Criminal in the Arms of the Law* (New York: Basic Books, 1971), pp. 48-65.

117. This rehabilitative ideal is thoroughly explored in Francis Allen, "Legal Values and the Rehabilitative Ideal," *The Borderland of Criminal Justice* (Chicago: U. of Chicago Press, 1965), pp. 25-41. Among the many critics of this philosophy is C. S. Lewis, "The Humanitarian Theory of Punishment," *Res Judicatae* 6, 224 (1953). For an excellent analysis of the outgrowth of the rehabilitative ideal—the therapeutic state—see Nicholas N. Kittrie, *The Right to be Different: Deviance and Enforced Therapy* (Baltimore: Johns Hopkins Press, 1971).

118. Jerome Hall, in "Objectives of Federal Criminal Procedural Revision," *Yale Law J.* 51, 723, 734 (1942), has observed:
   "No reform of criminal procedure may lightly ignore the public 'sense of justice,' the interminable conflict between the conscience and animal desire, or the criminal trial as a vicarious avenue of emotional release which supports the delicate balance of adjustment to social restraint."

119. See, Morris R. Cohen, "Moral Aspects of the Criminal Law," *Yale Law J.* 49, 1009 (1940); A. C. Ewing, *The Morality of Punishment.*

120. The origins of the penitentiary, the insane asylum, and other coercive institutions during the Jacksonian era are examined in David J. Rothman, *The Discovery of the Asylum* (Boston: Little, Brown, 1971).

121. See, Erik Olin Wright, *The Politics of Punishment: A Critical Analysis of Prisons in America* (New York: Harper & Row, 1973).

122. For a leading authority's thoughts on this point, see Johannes Andenaes, "The General Preventive Effects of Punishment," *U. of P. Law Review* 114, 949 (1966).

123. Johannes Andenaes, "General Prevention—Illusion or Reality," *J. Crim. Law, Criminology and Pol. Sci.* 43 (1952), pp. 176-98.

124. Regarding this severity of punishment, a Victorian jurist once remarked that "the fact that men are hung for murder is one great reason why murder is considered so dreadful a crime." Hood and Sparks, *Key Issues in Criminology.*

125. For a case concerning the use of magnetometers in airport security, see United States v. Lopez, 328 F. Supp. 1077 (E.D. N.Y. 1971).

126. Emile Durkheim, the great sociologist, once offered this example:

"Imagine a society of saints, a perfect cloister of exemplary individuals. Crimes, properly so called, will there be unknown; but faults which appear venial to the layman will create there the same scandal that the ordinary offense does in ordinary consciousness. If, then, this society has the power to judge and punish, it will define these acts as criminal and will treat them as such." (Durkheim, *The Rules of the Sociological Method* (New York: The Free Press, 1956), pp. 68-69.

127. For a revealing and disturbing assessment of urban crime control, see American Bar Association Special Committee on Crime Prevention and Control, *New Perspectives on Urban Crime.*

128. Discussion of this scapegoating forms the basis of several sobering essays, among them: James Vorenberg and James Q. Wilson, "Is the Supreme Court Handcuffing the Cops?" The *New York Times Magazine,* 1 May 1969; Yale Kamisar, "When the Cops Were Not 'Handcuffed'," The *New York Times Magazine,* 7 November 1965.

129. Richard Harris, *Decision* (New York: Ballantine Books, 1972), examines the case of court designee Harold Carswell.

130. Durkheim expounded this theory of anomie in several of his major works, including *On the Division of Labor in Society* (Glencoe, Ill.: The Free Press, 1949); *Suicide* (1951). The term was elaborated upon by Robert K. Merton in his famous article, "Social Structure and Anomie," *Amer. Soc. Review* 3 (Oct. 1938): 672-82.

131. The phrase was coined by J. Milton Yinger in "Contraculture and Subculture," *Amer. Soc. Review* 25 (October 1960): 625-635.

132. For a collection of essays assuming this position, see Theodore L. Becker and Vernon G. Murray, eds., *Government Lawlessness in America* (New York: Oxford U. Press, 1971).

133. Testifying before Congress in 1970, New York City Medical Examiner Dr. Milton Helpern stated that narcotics addiction was the greatest single cause of death among persons in the age group 15 to 35 in New York City. American Bar Association, *New Perspectives on Urban Crime.*

134. Such estimates vary enormously, however, and it is generally recognized that there are no precise statistics for either the number of addicts, or the proportion of street crime which can reliably be attributed to them. Law enforcement officials are virtually unanimous in their view, though, that addicts account for a major portion of urban street crime in the United States, and that New York Ciy has more heroin addicts, both proportionally and in number, than any other city in the world.

135. Some observers have argued that greater expenditures and additional manpower increments to police departments and other agencies might actually prove counterproductive in the effort to contain crime. See, for example, Alexander B. Smith and Harriet Pollack, "Less, Not More: Police, Courts, and Prisons," *Fed. Probation* 36 (September 1972): 12-18.

136. Similarly, in a large-scale study of U.S. federal probation and parole, there were found to be no significant differences in "success rates," between inmates who had randomly been assigned to "intensive," "ideal," or "normal" supervision. J. D. Lohman, A. Wahl, Robert M. Carter, *The San Francisco Project, Research Report No. 11: The Intensive Supervision Caseload* (Berkeley: U. of Calif., School of Criminology, 1967).

137. For a look at the nature of the police function see Albert J. Reiss, Jr., *The Police and the Public* (New Haven: Yale U. Press, 1970).

138. Marvin E. Wolfgang has noted that a 1950 reorganization of the New York City Police Department resulted in a recorded increase of 700 percent for larceny, 400 percent for robbery, and 200 percent for assault with a deadly weapon. *Crimes of Violence,* special report filed with the President's Commission on Law Enforcement and Administration of Justice (Washington, D.C.: U.S. Government Printing Office, 1967), p. 33. Another change in administration in 1966 resulted in a 37 percent increase for certain crimes, while in Chicago, a new police chief instituted new procedures resulting in an 83 percent increase in the official crime rate. Hood and Sparks, *Key Issues in Criminology.*

Chapter 2

Organization for Crime Control: Structure of the Criminal Justice System

SOURCES OF AUTHORITY OF THE CRIMINAL JUSTICE SYSTEM

The implementation of all crime control and preventive programs rests on government authority. The criminal justice system is a *legal* system. Its sources of authority come from each of the major branches of our government system: executive, legislative, judicial, and administrative. Crimes are defined by legislation. Appellate courts interpret these laws as they apply to specific situations, and, in a separate but critical function, such courts review legislation for constitutional conformity. The executive branch (the President, governor, or mayor) functions primarily to initiate legislation, appoint administrators, and propose budgets. Sometimes the executive exerts direct operational powers, such as pardoning prisoners or commuting sentences. The administrative agencies and offices—police, prosecutors, trial courts, probation agencies, prisons, and parole authorities—enforce the laws, collectively operate the overall criminal justice process, and assume various degrees of operational rule-making authority.

Traditionally the criminal justice system's authority structure has been seen as a hierarchy. On top is the legislative branch which is empowered to define crime, subject to judicial review on constitutional grounds. Appellate courts are immediately beneath, operating to interpret and apply statutes to specific criminal cases brought by the operating agencies. At the lowest level are the operating agencies with ministerial tasks (i.e., carrying out legislative mandates in conformity to court interpretation and decree). In this model the executive stands somewhere outside this hierarchy, feeding ideas, programs, and appointive personnel into it, but functioning indirectly as an influential source of power and authority.

While this hierarchical authority does exist, the criminal justice system normally operates in a more complex, less linear and less automatic way than this model suggests. It is true that the basic criminal code of any jurisdiction is a legislative creation and that statutes defining crimes enable courts and agencies to function. But the complete criminal law, or the activities and boundaries of criminal justice administration, cannot be found simply by reference to statute books. Each of the other components of the system, courts and agencies alike, has law-making as well as law-enforcement functions. To understand how any criminal justice system works, it is essential to know the role and functions of prosecutors, to observe the activities and trends of appellate court decisions, to comprehend police enforcement policies, and to be aware of the rule-making powers and implementation of practices of correctional agencies. A more realistic criminal justice model assumes the major sources of authority—the legislature, courts, and agencies—to be mutual and simultaneous partners (although not always equal) in crime definition, goal determination, and the implementation of crime control procedures.[1]

The greater accuracy and usefulness of this model stems from the need to apply legislative proscriptions to actual street crime situations. All statutes are necessarily broad and general, whether they refer to substantive criminal definitions or to such criminal procedures as search or trial.[2] It is virtually impossible to provide written formulas which cover all permutations and combinations of situations that arise, even within a single crime category such as burglary. It is equally impossible to specify all of the proper or improper actions of a police officer confronted with diverse and unpredictable street situations.

Legislative Authority

Legislatures exist on all levels of government, from the Federal Congress to city councils. For the most part, the crime-defining functions of legislatures are limited to Congress, which enacts and modifies federal criminal statutes, and to state legislatures, responsible for statewide criminal codes. Local, county, or city legislative bodies usually have limited authority to enact ordinances, but cannot define localized felonies. In criminal justice, the term *legislature* generally refers to Congress or to state legislatures having broad crime-defining powers. The primary legislative function is to define criminal conduct, along with such defenses as insanity or entrapment, as they specifically apply to common crime situations. Legislation typically provides basic definitions of crimes and also specifies elements that distinguish different degrees of criminal liability (i.e., a monetary standard to distinguish grand from petty larceny). However, even the most specific statute must be interpreted as it applies, or does not apply, to individual cases. Even apparently precise definitions (e.g., carrying concealed weapons) may prove to be inadequate in practical situations. What is a weapon? Is a starter-pistol a gun? The issue becomes much more complex with statutory definitions of the mental-state elements of crimes, such as "willful intent," "negligence," "reckless disregard for life."

Nevertheless our criminal laws must be specific, and their statutory terms need to be "strictly construed" by courts. Statutes which are not specific may, upon judicial review, be held unconstitutional on grounds of vagueness, for it is an important principle of our ideology that the boundaries of criminal conduct be legislatively fixed and definitive so that all may know the limits of the criminal law. Yet in many criminal codes there are offenses that are not precisely defined; these often include such public order misdemeanors as vagrancy, loitering, and unlawful assembly. Though rarely challenged because they typically involve the poor and homeless and because the penalties are less severe than jail-time awaiting trial, such offenses pose enforcement dilemmas, and many of them probably are unconstitutional on the grounds of vagueness. In recent years these and other victimless crimes have been the frequent targets for legislative reform.

Legislative attention to crime matters is erratic and fortuitous, except in rare periods of total penal code revision. In most jurisdictions, every year sees some new crimes added to the penal code, or old crimes modified in some way. There are numerous and diverse reasons for this: in some cases, the legislature attempts to resolve conflicting court interpretations of crimes or defenses, as in clarifying standards for the insanity defense which appellate courts have interpreted differently in recent years.[3] In others, a new or overlooked form of deviation may be brought to legislative attention, thus creating a new crime, as occurred in the case of glue sniffing in the mid-sixties. This was felt to be a serious matter by both police and health officials, but most states had no legal proscription against this behavior. In some cases, legislatures redefine crimes or procedures to make them constitutionally permissible after appellate courts have held earlier provisions to be unconstitutional. A number of states and the federal government are presently attempting to draft death penalty provisions which will meet constitutional requirements following the outlawing of capital punishment by the U.S. Supreme Court in *Furman* v. *Georgia*.[4] In still other instances, legislatures react to particularly heinous or notorious crimes, or perhaps to a "crime wave," by creating more inclusive statutes, by increasing penalties for particular offenses, or by both.[5]

63

It is important to note that the crime-defining function of the legislature includes drafting statutory provisions for sentences. In fact, many recent code revisions have been motivated by the need to more clearly codify the sentencing structure, reconciling what often were clearly disparate or disproportionate penalties. Though different jurisdictions have failed to adopt uniform sentencing provisions, the trend has been toward providing common sentencing limits for certain designated *classes* of crimes (i.e., class-A felonies or third-degree misdemeanors) in contrast to the earlier practice of attaching specific penalty limits to each criminal statute.

The law-making function of legislatures is not always the rational procedure it is widely assumed to be. Legislators are first and foremost politicians, who collectively represent a wide variety of constituencies. They are often pressured by various interest groups, lobbyists, mail campaigns, and sometimes by public demonstrations. While most legislative activity has little to do with crime and public interest in revision of a burglary statute may be minimal, the crime-defining or repealing function occasionally becomes a hot political issue. Recent abortion controversies in New York and elsewhere illustrate the intensity of public feeling and the political implications of each legislator's action in connection with this sensitive question.[6]

Many legislators feel duty-bound to express formal standards of public morality, though they realize that a number of laws which attempt to legislate such morality cannot be fully enforced.[7] Many criminal codes contain proscriptions against adultery, fornication and other consensual sexual misconduct, public intoxication, gambling, and other behavior deemed immoral. At best these can be enforced only loosely; in some cases, there may be no serious legislative intent that the laws be enforced in any manner. It may be comparatively easy for a determined legislator to introduce and perhaps push to passage a "crime" on the basis of high principle; it is very difficult to repeal such a law. A number of so-called blue laws—ancient legislation making it a crime to work on the Sabbath, to graze cattle on the public green, and so on—still exist in many states, often because they are ignored or because motions to repeal may be potentially damaging to the proponent.[8] Few legislators wish to be identified as supporters of adultery or consensual homosexual behavior. It is true that a number of victimless crimes, primarily sexual misconduct statutes, have disappeared from legislation in recent years. But usually this was achieved by simple omission during code revision, when the onus for repeal did not attach to any single legislator.

There are reasons other than fear of political retaliation for not repealing criminal laws, even ancient blue laws. The proliferation and accumulation of criminal statutes can be seen as advantageous to the state in providing technical means for "getting" certain dangerous or notorious deviants who cannot be apprehended in other violations. This has been called the "Al Capone theory of law making."[9] Several decades ago Thurman W. Arnold said:

Substantive criminal law for the most part consists not in a set of rules to be enforced, but in an arsenal of weapons to be used against such persons as the police or prosecutors may deem to be a menace to public safety.[10]

It is generally desirable for substantive criminal laws to be worded precisely, not only to avoid challenge on grounds of vagueness, but also to minimize uncertainty as to arrest, charging, and adjudication decisions. Occasionally, however, legislation is drafted in deliberately ambiguous terms. One reason for this is the inherent difficulty in specifying all possible varieties of conduct in certain crime categories. For example, few legislators doubt that sexual molestation of children is and must be a serious crime; the difficulty arises in wording statutes to fully cover the range of conduct to be outlawed. Making "carnal knowledge and abuse of a minor" a felony leaves the implementation of the statute to enforcement agencies and courts. Another reason for occasional ambiguity, but with somewhat differing expectations as to enforcement, is the prevention of loopholes by which serious or professional criminals can avoid liability. Gambling statutes in some jurisdictions are examples of this. Most often the legislative purpose in outlawing gambling is to curb professional gambling or the gambling activities of organized criminals, rather than to hinder neighborhood poker games or church bingo. To avoid the difficulties inherent in attempting to distinguish professional from amateur and friendly gambling, the statute may be written to forbid *all* gambling, with a tacit expectation that the law will be enforced *sensibly*—implying that enforcement officials will concentrate on bookies, numbers games, and other forms of professional gambling.[11]

1. LEGISLATIVE PROCEDURAL LAW. In addition to creating crimes, to defining some defenses to criminal liability, and to fixing penalties, legislatures also define some criminal justice procedures. Thus, in most jurisdictions, statutes establish conditions under which arrests can be made with or without warrants, standards which regulate the permissible amount of force to be used in making arrests, and the requirements for search warrants and similar documents. The legislative function has been much weaker and less precise in generating such procedural law than in drafting substantive criminal codes. The basic reason for this discrepancy is the nearly impossible task of spelling out in specific detail all the criteria and conditions necessary to cover the variety of enforcement situations confronted in daily operations. In most cases, there is no attempt to legislate *specific* conditions for arrest. Rather the effort is to state in general terms that the officer must have *probable cause* or a *reasonable belief* that a felony has been committed and that the person arrested is responsible for it; or if the offense is a misdemeanor, the law may require that arrest can take place only if the offense occurred "in view" of the arresting officer. Similarly, only such force as is "necessary" may be used to effect an arrest, and warrants can be issued only on probable cause. In most such statutory provisions, the determination of probable cause or reasonableness is determined first by the officer on the street, then by litigation at the trial court level, and finally, if necessary, by refinement of definition by appellate review.

Generally, such procedural law has been limited to police and trial court activities up to and including sentencing. Legislatures have done little about postsentencing procedures, preferring instead to create correctional agencies and to delegate complete authority to them, subject only to the statutory limits of sentence and constitutional prohibitions against cruel and unusual punishment.

There are some indications that legislatures now are taking a more active interest in all procedural matters, including procedures for processing inmates, probationers, and parolees. In some jurisdictions, as in New York, legislatures have passed "stop and frisk" laws which attempt codification of conditions under which police officers may pat-down suspects for weapons. Likewise, there are statutes prescribing criteria for eavesdropping warrants, for preventive detention, for procedures to be followed in parole revocation, and for other operational decisions. The *Model Penal Code,* which undoubtedly has had an effect on recent recodification of criminal laws in many jurisdictions, proposes a much broader, more inclusive role for the legislature in procedural matters. For example, this *Code* provides illustrative criteria that *could* be enacted in statutory form covering such matters as choice of sentence by the trial judge, criteria for probation and parole conditions, procedures for revocation, and so on.

2. MONETARY SUPPORT.   Providing budgetary support for crime control efforts is a critically important legislative function. Drafting statutes, creating agencies, and delegating authority while withholding adequate funds can be hollow and disappointing exercises. Although legislatures have become more liberal with funds as the crime problem has assumed greater political significance,[12] few agencies are adequately staffed and supported. One of the complex problems of budgeting is that some criminal justice agencies are locally autonomous, while other agencies have statewide jurisdiction, and still others are federal. Thus budgetary discrepancies may exist within the criminal justice system because different legislative bodies with different tax bases are responsible for monetary support. Some of these problems are being met by rather complex plans of revenue sharing and by federal grants to state and local crime control agencies. Nevertheless, the budgetary role of legislatures remains one of the most crucial and perhaps least understood functions in the entire criminal justice process. The hard fact is that the amount of monetary support that is or can be allocated for crime control purposes is limited. "Legislative intent" with respect to real desire for vigorous enforcement can perhaps be more accurately inferred from budget than from historical documents and position papers which are typically prepared prior to the enactment of new legislation or the recodification of old laws.

3. INVESTIGATORY POWERS. There are other legislative functions that occasionally play an important part in criminal justice administration. The investigatory power of legislative committees is a function that occasionally assumes major significance; certainly the activities of congressional investigations of organized crime from the Kefauver[13] to the McClellan[14] Commissions helped shape federal laws and stimulated public awareness of some dimensions of this crime problem. The Senate Watergate Hearings were standard television fare in 1973. Legislatures have impeachment power over certain criminal justice participants, including prosecuting attorneys, but impeachment is cumbersome and rarely used. Legislatures may also have authority to approve or disapprove executive appointments to courts or agencies. The rejection of two presidential nominations for the Supreme Court by the U.S. Senate in the first Nixon term illustrates the strength and importance of this function.[15]

The functions and powers of legislatures may vary from one jurisdiction to another, and in some instances rather unique powers exist. For example, in Vermont the legislature *elects* district court judges for the State. Legislatures thus play an important part in criminal justice; the system starts here, and the legislature sets the limits of intervention and provides the system with its monetary support.

Executive Authority

The chief executive of any jurisdiction, from the President of the United States to the mayor of a city, has a number of important functions in the criminal justice system. Some executives are directly active, while others act in more subtle and indirect fashion, though perhaps with equal effect. Though there are variations among jurisdictions, executive functions fall into four major categories: 1) the appointment of personnel, including judges, boards and commissions, and directors of major criminal justice agencies; 2) the introduction of legislation, requests for new programs, and submission of executive budgets;

3) direct intervention into the criminal justice process through powers of pardon or commutation, creation of investigatory commissions, appointment of special prosecutors, and removal of incompetent officeholders; and 4) use of the power and prestige of office to give direction or impetus to crime control efforts by proposals, by persuasion, and by skillful application of the pressure of political power.

The effectiveness of the executive in shaping criminal justice efforts depends in good part upon his individual style and the extent of his interest in crime control matters. Some executives have strong opinions about some aspects of crime control and may push vigorously to exert personal influence on the legislature, the bench, and the agencies. This type of executive may propose sweeping legislative reforms to fulfill campaign promises or out of personal conviction. Another executive may exhibit a quite different style, allowing for maximum legislative autonomy and waiting to react to legislation as it reaches his desk.

The function of the executive varies also by the opportunities and power available to him, particularly with respect to appointment of personnel. In some jurisdictions, the executive has no authority to appoint judges or prosecutors except on interim bases because these are elective offices; in others, the chief executive may be able to appoint judges at all court levels as vacancies occur; and in some states, prosecuting attorneys (and public defenders) serve at the pleasure of the governor. Similarly, the executive may be able to appoint parole board members, a police commissioner, a director of corrections, and perhaps even wardens and some lower echelon personnel to serve during his term in office. In some states, however, agency heads or parole board members have civil service tenure or overlapping term appointments that can be filled by the executive only when vacancies occur by retirement or resignation or when terms expire.

The governor may use his pardon and commutation powers frequently in some jurisdictions, particularly where long sentences are commonly imposed; in others, the use of pardon may be rare, limited to a few "Christmas commutations" and to exceptionally meritorious cases.[16]

One important function of executive power is the veto, an example of check-and-balance in our system of government. Even if rarely used, the veto tends to restrain legislative excesses. The executive may veto any legislation, whether it deals with substantive definitions of crimes or fund allocations. Though the veto ultimately may be overridden (usually by requiring a two-thirds vote of the legislative bodies) this is a difficult and cumbersome process, particularly

AMERICAN FEDERAL COURTS
SECTION 3.—AMERICAN FEDERAL COURTS

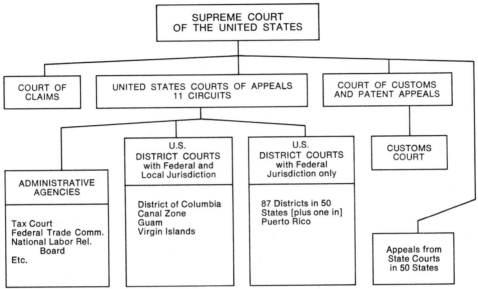

The United States Courts, by Joseph F. Spaniol, Jr. H.R.Doc. No. 180, 88th Cong., 1st Sess. 6 (1963).

if there is no overwhelming single-party domination of the legislature. Vetoes have been overridden by legislative coalition and near-consensus, but the executive veto potential remains a potent force for influencing legislative deliberation. Its power transcends that of an obstruction to easy passage of laws because the exercise of veto power usually attracts widespread publicity, crystallizing public support for or against the measure under consideration and thereby focusing political attention on individual legislators who may find themselves pitting their popularity against that of the President, governor, or mayor.

Appellate Court Authority

All jurisdictions have a hierarchy of courts, topped by the supreme court of each state.[17] At the apex of our judicial system is the U.S. Supreme Court. The courts of each jurisdiction form a dichotomy of *trial courts* and *appellate courts.* Trial courts have jurisdiction to conduct trials, to accept guilty pleas, and to act as fact finders and sentencers of the guilty in cases of persons accused of crimes. Appellate courts ordinarily do not conduct trials. They act only upon appeals from lower court decisions and function primarily to interpret and settle contro-

69

versies of law arising from litigation in the lower courts. The appellate process relies on the records of lower court processings, responding to briefs submitted by petitioners' and states' counsels. Higher courts normally do not deal directly with the defendant, nor (except in very unusual cases) review the actual factual evidence brought out at the trial. Instead, they decide points of law, determine the applicability of statutes to the case in question, examine the transcript for prejudicial errors, reexamine denial of motions to suppress evidence, and so on. Appellate courts have authority to reverse convictions or to remand cases back to the lower courts for retrial or other action. Not guilty findings may not be so remanded because of double jeopardy protection afforded all defendants.

In addition to the overall hierarchy of courts, trial and appellate courts are commonly organized from limited to increasingly broad jurisdiction. Some lower trial courts, presided over by a justice of the peace, have jurisdiction limited to traffic cases and other minor "violations" or petty misdemeanors. A step above these are courts with general misdemeanor jurisdiction, the judge having maximum sentencing authority of up to a year in jail for a convicted person. At the highest trial level are courts which try felonies and impose prison sentences, with their jurisdiction usually bounded by the county in which they are located.

Similarly, a jurisdiction may have intermediate appellate courts (these exist most commonly in large states and in the federal system) which hear appeals arising from trial courts within a particular region of the state, encompassing a number of counties; or, in the federal system, appeals from district courts in one of eleven federal circuits. The decisions of these intermediate courts can in turn be appealed to the supreme court of the jurisdiction, and in some state cases even beyond this, rising eventually to review by the U.S. Supreme Court.

The appellate process is complex and costly, particularly when a case initiated and appealed through state channels moves into the federal appellate process.[18] The right to appellate review of a lower court holding is by no means an automatic process; sufficient arguments must be made to convince the appellate court that the appeal is "meritorious," that it is not based on frivolous claims. The U.S. Supreme Court (and supreme courts of some states) has the power to select among petitions it receives to determine those it will act on, and its decision is transmitted either by a full-court written decision, or by a briefer *per curiam* holding. It may also decide not to consider the case at all. Once arrived at this level, a case is presented to the Court by a writ of *certiorari*—a request for review—and the Court may deny this without giving reasons. Denial of *certiorari* may not reflect a view that the case lacks merit, but rather that its implications are not broad enough to affect the law of land; or denial may indicate that the

Court does not wish to consider such matters at this time. There have been long periods of inactivity in Supreme Court review of criminal cases, but the Warren Court was vigorous in deciding many significant criminal law and procedural matters.[19]

The relationship between appellate courts and legislatures in law-making authority has been a long, stormy, and controversial one. An important form of check-and-balance in our system of government is the power, derived from the "supremacy clause"[20] of the U.S. Constitution, of judicial review to abrogate legislation found to be unconstitutional. The principle of judicial review is an important—indeed vital—appellate court function. Though all laws duly enacted are *presumed* to be constitutional, the law-making power of legislatures is by no means unfettered, and our history is replete with examples of Supreme Court nullification of statutes. This power of the courts illustrates the complexity of the basic authority structure of our criminal justice system—that the court function is not simply one of interpretation and application of statutes, and that in constitutional matters the Supreme Court is the apex of authority.

The controversy between legislatures and appellate courts is not limited to the matter of judicial review of the constitutionality of statutes. This is generally accepted as basic to our political ideology, although there have been strong disagreements in some legislatures with certain court interpretations—so much so that there have been occasional, usually abortive, attempts to get around judicial nullification by drafting new constitutional amendments. Following the Supreme Court's ruling on school integration, there was a great deal of activity of this kind. The issue of whether legislatures or courts should dominate in law reform and accompanying social change forms the basis of the controversy, and the intensity of the argument varies by jurisdiction. In some states, appellate courts tend to be passive and conservative, interpreting laws as cases arise, holding to the judicial principle of *stare decisis* (consistently following precedent from former cases), and unwilling to take the lead in shaping law or defining legal procedures. In other jurisdictions, the reverse is true, the U.S. Supreme Court during the Warren era being the best known illustration. Here the issue was not only most dramatically illustrated, but also had the most far-reaching implications for the law of the entire land. In discussing judicial activism, one author commented:

I wish merely to make the objective observation that the Court has become the most conspicuous source of legal change in the country . . . we had the earlier, long-standing image of the Supreme Court as essentially a resistant force, using constitutional doctrine and grudging statutory interpretation to slow the pace of legal change. This was followed, after the turnabout of the mid-thirties

71

by a permissive court, a court that exercised self-restraint in deference to the superior law making credentials of Congress and the state legislatures.

But in the Warren period we have seen a still further shift, the emergence of a court that is itself an architect of change. In one area of law after another, the Court has led and the country has followed . . .

There is not much need to document this view of the Court as a reforming institution, major areas in which it has accelerated the pace of legal change are familiar. The obvious and dramatic ones are segregation, reapportionment, and state criminal procedure.

. . . .

The fact that so much initiative in legal change has passed to the Supreme Court is in a sense paradoxical because it has occurred at a time when judicial lawmaking in general is very much in eclipse. It has been obvious for a long time that the creative era of the common law is a thing of the past and that legislation has become the dominant form of law. . . . The explanation of the paradox, of course, lies in the fact that the Federal Constitution is the principal remaining source of judicial power to make new law. We have had a Supreme Court that has exercised that power in a bold fashion.[21]

The paradox of recent judicial activism is quite accurate; the trend of past decades has been toward increasing legislative involvement in criminal law policy and practices. The immense effort expended in drafting the *Model Penal Code,* and the alignment of many prominent legal scholars with the general position that the legislative role should dominate in the definition of public policy regarding criminal behavior, in the setting of priorities, and even in the drafting of specific directives to courts and operational agencies has been an important development. Yet the controversy continues unabated, either because of legislative inadequacy in drafting laws, or as Judge Charles D. Breitel has charged, because management of the law is "incompatible with the political concerns and preoccupations of the legislature."[22] Nowhere, and certainly not at the level of the U.S. Supreme Court, is the appellate court function limited to refining and honing the words of statutes.

Executives have occasionally attempted to modify the inactivity or curb the activism of higher courts. A notable failure was President Franklin D. Roosevelt's attempt to "pack" (expand) a Supreme Court which was consistently ruling against the legality of his legislative proposals.[23] More recently, President Nixon expressed his intention to create a "strict constructionist" court to curb the trend of activism flowing from the Warren Court.[24] It remains to be seen whether executive or legislative attempts to curb or control the leadership role of appellate courts will succeed, but limited modification is the most likely result of such efforts. As a major source of authority for the criminal justice system, appellate courts will undoubtedly remain central and relatively independent from other branches of government.[25]

Agency Authority

Each of the on-line operational criminal justice agencies has rule-making power and a good deal of independence in decision making, whether by delegation, tradition, or functional necessity. The overall limits of police, prosecution, judicial, and correctional authority are set by legislation and modified by appellate court decisions; but within these boundaries the range of policy formulation and decision alternatives—the discretion left to the agencies—is great indeed. Such discretion may be more influential than either legislatures or appellate courts in the shaping and functioning of the criminal justice system in our society. To view on-line agencies as merely performing ministerial tasks, automatically carrying out legislative purposes or executive decrees, or following court dictates would be to oversimplify their role.

Sources of agency discretion vary, and the types and forms by which such discretion is exercised also differ. Legislative creation and funding of an agency is the most familiar source of discretionary authority.[26] This pattern is commonly found in the civil administrative law process, as illustrated by congressional creation of such federal agencies as the Securities and Exchange Commission, the Food and Drug Administration, and comparable agencies in which the development of operational policies and procedures is left to the agency. Such delegation is less commonly found in the criminal justice system, though it is approximated in most jurisdictions by the creation of correctional agencies and parole boards whose delegated authority is normally rather broad. Often there is little legislative direction other than specifying and funding a department of corrections for the "care and treatment" of prisoners, and perhaps providing for a parole board whose members are often appointed by the executive and who have power to "make rules and specify procedures for the release of inmates prior to expiration of their terms." However, the analogy of correctional and parole services and the more traditional administrative agencies of government is not exact. Though postconviction agencies have functioned like administrative agencies, until recently their actual legal status was—and to a large extent remains—anomalous. Legislation creating such agencies was typically so broad that their rule-making authority was assumed, rather than explicitly assigned, and eventual remedy by court appeal was foreclosed by the "hands off" doctrine which most appellate courts applied to all stages of the postsentencing treatment of offenders. In contrast, where legislatures have created agencies to regulate commerce, they have specifically delegated rule-making authority, and have

73

required the agencies to develop policies and practices conforming with principles of administrative due process and procedural regularity and have allowed dissatisfied petitioners the opportunity to appeal agency decisions to the courts. This has not been the case with corrections and parole. It is only within the past few years that the hands off doctrine has been modified by appellate courts so that today principles of administrative due process are required at some stages of postconviction treatment of offenders.[27]

1. THE TRIAL COURT FUNCTION. In operational terms, the trial court, presided over by a judge, is an on-line agency for the processing of cases of alleged offenders and the sentencing of those convicted. While the organizational structure of the court differs from those of the more traditional bureaucracies of police or corrections, the agency model is appropriate at the trial court level. In addition to his formal duties in adjudication and sentencing, the trial court judge finds himself chief of a retinue of court personnel, from clerks to probation staff. Not only is he given discretion by statute—particularly regarding sentencing alternatives and authority to set some conditions of sentences—but he may also have authority to delegate discretion to particular members of his staff.

The legislative delegation of sentencing discretion to trial judges is normally quite specific.[28] Except in comparatively rare cases where legislatures fix mandatory sentences for certain crimes (life imprisonment for first-degree murder, for example), judges are usually granted authority to choose among various sentencing alternatives with limits imposed only for upper and lower extremes. While there is wide variation in sentencing systems among the state and federal jurisdictions, in general judges are delegated some discretion to choose *types* of sentences (fines, probation, or imprisonment), to set some conditions of sentence—particularly rules of probation—and to fix minimum or maximum length of prison sentences within the outer limits set by statute. In some states, as in Wisconsin, judges can fix a maximum prison term at any point they wish below, but of course not above, the maximum sentence provided by statute. In other jurisdictions, for example, Michigan, judges have no discretion as to maximum terms for many crimes, but may at their discretion set a *minimum* period of years to be served before the prisoner is eligible for parole. Other states exhibit numerous and diverse variations on these patterns, but in all jurisdictions for *most* offenses, judges are delegated some sentencing discretion.

In adjudicatory matters, the discretion of the trial judge is less liberal and less often specifically delegated. In adjudication it is presumed that the judge will rely on impartial and expert analysis of evidence and that he will base his findings on his professional skills as a lawyer and jurist. Dismissals or acquittals on other than evidentiary grounds are not part of his delegated powers, although in practice such determinations occasionally occur. Conviction upon insufficient evidence is, of course, quite improper and subject to appellate review and reversal.

The discretion of trial juries is extremely broad, resting upon their creation by the Constitution.[29] Though they are subject to a directed verdict of acquittal by a trial judge (or may have a verdict of guilty set aside if, in the judge's opinion, the evidence presented at trial was insufficient) these are comparatively rare occurrences. Furthermore, trial juries are not required to give reasons for their findings, with respect to the crime charged or to a lesser offense. In seven states, trial juries have a sentencing function not unlike that of the judge, while in five other jurisdictions jury sentencing is limited to certain offenses, and in some others the jury may merely recommend a sentence to the judge.

2. THE PROSECUTORIAL FUNCTION.

The discretion of the prosecuting attorney is probably as broad as that of any office or agency in the criminal justice system.[30] It is of interest that this discretion is more often "recognized" than delegated. Some observers attribute the origin of the prosecutor's broad powers to common-law antecedents in both English and French legal history;[31] others argue that it is intrinsic to the task of screening the hundreds of cases brought to prosecutorial policy in his community. Whatever the origins and rationale of prosecutorial discretion, it is clearly broad in scope, ranging from the power of *nolle prosequi* (a decision not to initiate prosecution even with sufficient evidence to do so), to the selection of specific charges to be leveled against any defendant. Though in some jurisdictions there are specific statutes delegating charging discretion to the prosecutor in certain types of crimes, the more usual legislative role is to attempt to develop appropriate statutory checks on his authority. This may be done by requiring written reasons for *nol pros* decisions or, in some jurisdictions, requiring the prosecutor to continue once an information has been fixed or an indictment issued.[32] But in general, formal checks on the wide discretionary authority of the prosecutor have been ineffective. In some states, the attorney general may have some "supervisory" authority over local prosecutors, or may have concurrent jurisdiction to prosecute, but the power to intervene is rarely used.[33]

The prosecutorial process is really a series of decisions, ranging from deciding whether to initiate prosecution at all to the number and specific charges to be presented to a grand jury or to a judge at a preliminary hearing. Decisions *not* to initiate prosecution are virtually uncontrollable, short of evidence of corruption or other forms of malfeasance. Decisions to proceed to prosecution, however, are subject to the screening of the grand jury or to the magistrate at a preliminary hearing. In about half the states, the grand jury system can be used, although few use it as the *exclusive* way of charging serious crimes, while the other half use the preliminary hearing. Both procedures are designed to test whether there is probable cause to hold the defendant for trial on the crimes charged. Distinctions between these screening processes will be detailed in later chapters, but it should be noted here that they serve as a check on prosecutorial decisions to proceed and to select certain charges for trial.

There is little doubt that the prosecuting attorney in many jurisdictions establishes enforcement and prosecutorial *policies* in addition to his function as a decision maker in each case he confronts. The policy formulation powers of the prosecutor stem from his generally recognized "traditional" discretion and may be exercised in a number of ways.[34] The most indirect of these is his accumulated record of decisions in particular types of cases. For example, it may be observed by police and complainants that the prosecutor almost never charges assault growing out of family disputes. Or he may consistently *nol pros* bad check cases whenever restitution is made to the victim. In this manner, without directly saying so, he establishes policies regarding the processing of such offenses.[35] In other instances—particularly in large prosecutors' offices where the district attorney may have hundreds of assistants[36]—prosecutorial policy may be more explicitly stated, either as oral directives to chiefs of subdivisions, or by memoranda distributed to all assistants. Policies issued in these ways may relate to such diverse matters as suggested techniques and standards for determining evidence admissibility, the appropriate charge to be leveled in cases of attempted suicide or other crimes, or even procedures and guidelines for plea bargaining. In general, appellate courts have supported the prosecutor's policy role. A lower court in New York commented: "Just because a crime has been committed, it does not follow that there must necessarily be a prosecution for it lies with the District Attorney to determine whether acts which may fall within the literal letter of the law should *as a matter of public policy not be prosecuted.*"[37]

3. THE POLICE FUNCTION. Collectively, the police are the largest component of the criminal justice system.[38] In terms of both citizen and suspect contact, they are more directly involved than any other agency. Cases of traditional crime processed through the system may originate with a complaint or call for help. More commonly, police surveillance, other forms of detection, and the stopping and questioning of suspicious persons lead to police involvement. Yet with minor exceptions, the handling of juvenile delinquents, for example, police agencies have no formally delegated or traditional discretion with respect to enforcing criminal laws. In theory the police have a mandate to enforce equally and impartially every criminal law, to keep the peace, to search out crime and, when evidence warrants it, to take all violators into custody. But as every observer of police activity has pointed out, and as most citizens know, full enforcement is a myth. Selective enforcement is the rule: discretion is exercised by the police agency as a whole and by each individual officer in it. In recent years particularly, documentation of the extent of police discretion has accumulated rapidly.[39] Reasons for the existence of police discretion range from the impossibility of discovering all crimes and apprehending all violators, through community expectations of "sensible" enforcement, to police efforts to achieve desired objectives without utilizing the entire justice process, as, for example, in handling inebriates by helping them home, warning minor violators, and so on. The spectres of corruption and discrimination are present whenever discretion exists, but this potential misuse of authority is characteristic of the entire system of justice.[40] Why does the myth of full enforcement continue to exist if police, courts, prosecutors, researchers, legal scholars, and many laymen are aware of discretion? The primary reason is that legislatures and, with infrequent exceptions, courts have refused, primarily on ideological grounds, to sanction police discretion, which in turn puts police officials in a defensive position. As Herman Goldstein points out:

To acknowledge that law enforcement officials do exercise discretion requires an overt act—the articulation of a position—an action which is rare among those in the police field. . . . To acknowledge the exercise of discretion belies the very image which he strives so hard to achieve. This is the image of total objectivity—of impartiality—and of enforcement without fear or favor.[41]

Without express delegation of authority, the police official who admits to discretionary policies or practices puts himself in the untenable position of presuming to usurp legislative perogative. He also opens himself and his agency to the most complex and difficult task in all criminal justice administration: the challenge of defining, defending, and monitoring criteria for discretion.

Officially recognized or not, there is little doubt that the discretionary policies and practices of police are critical components of the basic structure of the criminal justice system. In recent years large departments have attempted to develop internal policy guidelines for the exercise of discretion. In some instances, methods of monitoring officer discretion have been tested, as, for example, requiring written reports of all citizen contacts whether or not these resulted in arrest. In general, however, without legislative delegation of authority and firm guidelines, the criteria for the actual exercise of police discretion remain obscure, resulting in what Professor Joseph Goldstein called a complex of "low visibility" decisions.[42] Lack of detailed policies and articulated criteria has resulted in a unique *structural* form of discretion, not commonly found in many other bureaucracies. James Q. Wilson comments:

In almost every other public organization discretion is exercised . . . but the police department has the special property (shared with a few other organizations) that within it discretion increases as one moves *down* the hierarchy . . . [T]he lowest-ranking police officer—the patrolman—has the greatest discretion and thus his behavior is of greatest concern to the police administrator. The patrolman is almost solely in charge of enforcing those laws that are the least precise, most ambiguous . . . or whose application is most sensitive to the availability of scarce resources and the policies of the administrator.[43]

Thus the complex underlying structure of the criminal justice system is what Sheldon Glueck some time ago called "a clumsy admixture of the oil of discretion and the water of rule."[44] In any operational sense—in the everyday world where suspects are arrested, jailed, charged, tried, convicted, sentenced, incarcerated, and paroled—the authority basis of the criminal justice system cannot be ordered, diagrammed, or even accurately described. It is evident that the basis for the criminal law, and for criminal justice processing, in the nation as a whole or in any jurisdiction within it, cannot be understood simply by reference to statutes, court decisions, the proclamations of chief executives, nor by observing rules or practices of on-line agencies. The criminal law as it operates is an amalgam of all these sources and the complexity of relationships, and tensions among sources of authority must be recognized before the system can be understood, altered, or reformed. Whether it will ever be possible to fully codify criminal justice processing, whether appellate courts will lead or follow legislation in shaping the law, whether executive influence will become more significant or of minor impact, and whether agency discretion can or should be eliminated, curbed, or controlled are all moot points of great current and future significance. Though it may be disheartening to those with suggestions for simple and quick changes or reforms, analysis of the system must begin with what is, and it must be recognized that the complexity of relationships between the basic authority sources of the system's structure is compounded by the equally complicated interrelationships of on-line criminal justice agencies.

THE AGENCIES AND OFFICES OF THE CRIMINAL JUSTICE SYSTEM

Scientists interested in studying bureaucracies and complex organizations, have argued that the criminal justice system is not a "system" at all because it has no core organizational pattern. Rather it is a series of *processes* by which persons are passed through a confederation of separate and distinct agencies and offices which, though functionally related, are structurally distinct and independent.[45] In a traditional sense, this is accurate. Apart from the separation of powers among the basic sources of authority, the on-line agencies of crime control and prevention are indeed separate and distinct one from another, without the line-staff relationships found in industrial, military, and many other large organizations. Yet the term "criminal justice system"[46] has come into common usage with full awareness that in a variety of ways it is different from more traditional bureaucratic "systems,"[47] "complex organizations,"[48] or even "administrative agencies."[49] The President's Commission commented:

The system of criminal justice America uses to deal with those crimes it cannot prevent and those criminals it cannot deter is not a monolithic, or even a consistent, system. It was not designed or built in one piece at one time. Its philosophic core is that a person may be punished by the Government if, and only if, it has been proved by an impartial and deliberate process that he has violated a specific law. Around that core layer upon layer of institutions and procedures, some carefully constructed and some improvised, some inspired by principle and some by expediency, have accumulated. Parts of the system— magistrate's courts, trial by jury, bail—are of great antiquity. Other parts— juvenile courts, probation and parole, professional policemen—are relatively new. The entire system represents an adaptation of the English common law to America's peculiar structure of government, which allows each local community to construct institutions that fill its special needs. Every village, town, county, city and State has its own criminal justice system and there is a Federal one as well. All of them operate somewhat alike. No two of them operate precisely alike.[50]

The organizational pattern of the on-line criminal justice agencies differs from more traditional, "monolithic" complex organizations in at least six major dimensions:

1. distinctness of agencies and offices one from another in terms of both non-interchangeable personnel and absence of formal continuum of authority,
2. separate, unrelated budgets,
3. differing jurisdictional boundaries,
4. separate manpower pools with personnel in each agency recruited in general from different professions or occupations,
5. differing patterns of personnel selection and tenure from one agency to another (and sometimes between the same agency in different jurisdictions), and
6. variations in the amount of direct and indirect citizen involvement in agency decision making or policy formulation.

The significance of these six dimensions is manifold, relating to both operational issues and ideological positions about the appropriateness of our form of criminal justice. Operationally, some of the dissonance in crime control efforts—involving both conflict between agencies and inefficiency—can be attributed to these unique variations in the way agencies are organized, funded, and staffed. Rooted in its structure are a number of problems that tend to obstruct easy changes or improvement of the system.

1. Distinct Agencies

The most unique structural characteristic of the on-line criminal justice system is the distinctness and relative independence of agencies that are contiguous and functionally interdependent. Generally, police are structurally, financially, professionally, and even socially *separate* from prosecutors; prosecutors are separate from trial judges, and judges from state correctional authorities. With minor exceptions there is no interchange of personnel: a policeman does not work up to a judgeship or by lateral transfer and promotion become a warden.[51] Some prosecutors may become judges, but this is because they share common antecedent characteristics—training in law and political aspirations—not because of any line-staff connection between the prosecutor's office and the trial bench.

In addition to the lack of a common, interchangeable manpower pool, there is no chain of command, no single line of authority, no central policy-making source, to order and systematize the criminal process. Unlike industrial and military complexes, there is no board of directors or chiefs of staff to oversee the interconnecting functions of the agencies. In short, there is no "boss" of the on-line criminal justice organization, so that decisions and policies emanate from separate sources and often are directed to specific agency goals which are not necessarily congruent.

Some trial judges may dispute the absence of leadership, claiming for the trial courts a central and dominating role. But in actual practice this is unrealistic. While significant, the influence of the trial court is not the conditioner of most major policies and practices of *any* agency. Trial judges neither hire nor fire police, prosecutors, wardens, or parole boards. The direct authority of the bench is limited to persons actively hired by the court or persons directly engaged in court functions. A judge may hold a policeman or perhaps even a prosecutor in contempt for defying a direct in-court order, but in daily operations the control of police, prosecutor, or correctional policies and practices is beyond the power of the trial court. Though the trial judge is often thought to occupy the pinnacle office of the process (in general, judges have the greatest prestige and often command the highest salaries of all criminal justice functionaries), and while

Estimated Expenditures by Function and Level of Government for Responding to Crime in New York State—1970

| FUNCTION | LEVEL OF GOVERNMENT | | |
	STATE	OTHER (LOCAL, FEDERAL)	TOTAL
1. Police	$ 65,340,000	$1,089,000,000	$1,154,340,000
2. Courts	36,125,000	142,504,000	178,629,000
3. Prosecution	0	23,066,000	23,066,000
4. Defense (public)	0	3,153,000	3,153,000
5. Correction—institutions	144,429,000	30,842,000	175,271,000
6. Correction—probation and parole	27,160,000	17,386,000	44,546,000
7. Other (planning, prevention, and so on)	3,993,000	0	3,993,000
8. Total	277,047,000	1,305,951,000	1,582,998,000

NOTE: Based on figures from New York State Office of Crime Control Planning.

the adjudicatory function of separating the guilty from the innocent is a natural demarcation line in the process of moving suspects to inmates, the actual operational significance of a trial judge probably is no more important that that of any decision maker in the process. Judges receive for their adjudicatory and sentencing functions only those persons initially screened by police and prosecutors; in the vast majority of the cases, adjudication involves merely the acceptance of a guilty plea, perhaps with sentencing prearranged by charge reduction. Following conviction the court loses jurisdiction over all offenders sentenced to state institutions.

2. Different Budgets

Each crime control agency draws from separate budgetary allocations, and these budgets in turn often depend upon different revenue sources. All agencies are tax supported, but some, like the police, rely on local taxes while others, like prisons, receive state revenue. In some places there may be various mixes of budgetary sources, such as partial state subsidy of local probation facilities. Though increasing infusion of federal monies into the states by distribution through statewide crime control planning agencies has brought some efforts to disburse funds in a rational manner according to the needs of each segment of the criminal justice organization, this is not the traditional way of allocating resources and is still in a developing stage. In general, the criminal justice system has not been viewed as an entity nor its resources allocated according to any superordinate plan for crime control or prevention. Instead each agency has traditionally scrambled and fought for its own support, competing with other agencies for a share of local or state revenue. Whether courts, corrections, or the police should receive more or less support in terms of overreaching system needs has rarely been considered, so that the budget for law enforcement is often unrelated in any way to that of prosecutors, courts, parole authorities, or the prison system. Such discrete budgets, achieved by political clout or simple historical drift, increase the fragmentation of the criminal justice system and remain a major challenge to any kind of rational crime control planning.

3. Different Jurisdictions

Apart from budgetary concerns, the differing jurisdictional limits of criminal justice agencies complicate the picture in other ways. Not only are some agencies locally autonomous while others are state directed, but even within the same agency jurisdictional boundaries are often confused, sometimes overlapping or unclear. In any given state, as well as in the federal system, there is not a single police agency, but many police agencies, with some functions and jurisdictional boundaries that occasionally differ and overlap. There are metropolitan police forces, state police, sheriffs, town police, and often various *special* police agencies, such as park police, transit authority police, campus police, and even private police. Likewise, in any given place there may be city courts, county courts, and district or circuit courts. There may also be local prosecutors and special state prosecutors, and metropolitan correctional systems may be as large as the state's own system. Thus police, prosecutors, courts, and correctional facilities exist as criminal justice agencies only in a generic sense; the details of their organizational patterns and the specifics of jurisdiction and authority vary markedly from place to place. Thus complexity of proliferation and overlap further complicates analysis of the total criminal justice system.

4. Different Manpower Sources

In general, criminal justice agencies and offices are staffed by persons who are recruited, trained, or educated in separate and distinct ways. With some exceptions—the FBI, for example—police are generally recruited from among high school graduates and receive on-the-job training within their own agency. Some

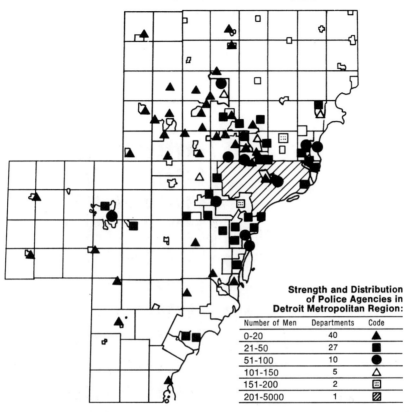

Strength and Distribution of Police Agencies in Detroit Metropolitan Region:		
Number of Men	Departments	Code
0-20	40	▲
21-50	27	■
51-100	10	●
101-150	5	△
151-200	2	▦
201-5000	1	▨

President's Commission on Law Enforcement and Administration of Justice, *Task Force Report: The Police* (Washington, D.C.: U.S. Government Printing Office, 1967), p. 69.

police agencies have training academies or send their recruits to the facilities of other agencies; but for *most* policemen, operational training is an in-house function.[52] Until very recently, police science was not a common component in college curricula, and it remains an uncommon requirement for police work. Furthermore, upward mobility in the police hierarchy has generally depended upon experience and years of service rather than upon increments in education or training.

In most places prosecutors and trial judges must be members of the bar, and, increasingly, this requires law school education rather than apprentice training as in Lincoln's time. However, the law degree or its equivalent is merely an entrance prerequisite to the office; normally there is no requirement and only

STATE ADULT INSTITUTIONS

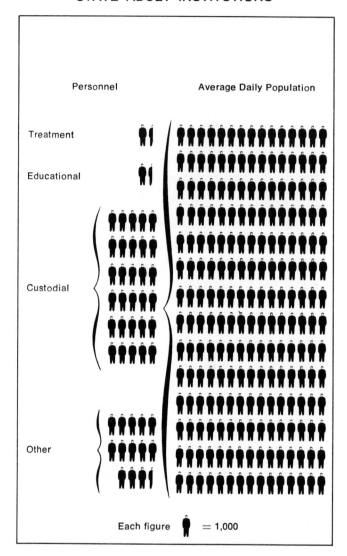

President's Commission on Law Enforcement and Administration of Justice, *Task Force Report: Corrections* (Washington, D.C.: U.S. Government Printing Office, 1967), p. 177.

very limited opportunities for specific training in prosecutorial or judicial functions.[53] It is assumed that general legal education will adequately equip incumbents for their roles in the criminal justice system, a questionable assumption because of some limitations in traditional legal education. For example, although recently there have been modifications in law school offerings with respect to criminal justice processing, judges who have responsibility for sentencing and adjudication usually learn little of this process in law school courses.[54]

Correctional manpower education and training issues are somewhat more complex than those of the police or the lawyers of the middle agencies of the process. This is so because corrections collectively is made up of a number of discrete subagencies (prisons, probation offices, parole boards, and parole field agents), and because of the distinction commonly made in prisons between professional and custodial staff. Corrections generally can be divided between institutional and community services. Institutional services comprise prisons, reformatories, training schools for delinquents, and jails. Institutions recruit manpower for two major purposes: custody and treatment. The first encompasses prison guards and jailers and the second social workers, psychologists, teachers, and other professionals. Custodial personnel are typically employed and trained much like policemen: they are mostly recruited from populations of high school graduates, trained on the job or in a correctional training academy, and rise within the custodial hierarchy according to their years of experience and successful performance on civil service examinations. Professional staff normally are college graduates, some with advanced training in their specialty. The ratio of custodial to professional personnel varies greatly from one correctional system to another and often even within different institutions in the same system, but necessity requires that custodial personnel outnumber professionals by substantial margins. However, beginning in the 1930s and with renewed impetus after World War II, corrections sought to become recognized as a "profession"—its major goal shifting from efficient restraint of convicted offenders to one of treatment and rehabilitation—and to achieve this, many correctional systems recruited college-educated personnel and vested more policy-making power in them.[55] The thrust toward professionalism was not uniform across all jurisdictions; it developed most clearly in community-based services like probation and parole, but was also evident in many prisons and other correctional institutions. Inevitably this development led to considerable friction between the numerically superior custodial forces in institutions and the fewer but administratively dominant treatment professionals. In some places the shift toward a rehabilitative goal and the corresponding increase in power of professionally trained personnel is alleged to have been an underlying factor in prison riots; in other areas these changes have resulted in strong unionization of guard forces and a hardening of the custody-treatment rift. In a few places, most often in institutions for juvenile or young offenders or where the correctional system built new medium- or minimum-security "open" institutions, the dominance of the correctional professional was amicably achieved. This occurred especially where the custodial staff were viewed as having treatment functions and were given opportunities for input into major policy decisions.

The greatest surge toward professionalism in corrections came in community-based services of probation and parole. At their start these services were staffed largely by volunteers, respectable citizens or private organizations who agreed to supervise and help offenders adjust to the community. For many reasons, including costs far below those of institutionalization, yet with high comparative effectiveness in preventing recidivism, these correctional services came to be viewed as very important. They soon became the dominant correctional agencies for handling the greatest numbers of offenders. This in turn caused some decline in the influence of the prison and other correctional institutions. The need for field staff soon outran available volunteers and these community programs became integral parts of county or state correctional systems. In some places probation and parole were joined into a single operating field agency; more commonly, however, probation remained court-attached and therefore a municipal or county service, while parole, involving primarily the supervision of inmates released from state institutions, became a statewide and state supported service. However, in terms of primary functions and the type of personnel most capable of providing such services, probation and parole were, and are, virtually identical. As the "rehabilitative ideal" came to dominate corrections, effective application of it seemed best assured by casework with individuals sentenced directly to the community without institutionalization (probation) or with those released from incarceration prior to expiration of the maximum sentence (parole). The professional skills most desired for performance of these tasks were perceived to be identical: graduate training in social work or in comparable clinically-oriented behavioral sciences. Thus the *ideal* qualification for field staff came to be specialized postgraduate social work education. This was nowhere fully achieved, but, with few exceptions, the minimum educational requirements for probation and parole officers came to be college graduation, usually with a degree in the social sciences.

The selection and staffing of parole boards is an exception to both the professionalism of field staff and to custodial recruitment patterns. These are commissions of varying size and permanence, which exist today in all correctional

SIZE OF STATE PAROLE AUTHORITIES, FELONY OFFENDERS
FEBRUARY 1966 AND JANUARY 1972

| | NUMBER OF BOARDS | |
BOARD SIZE	1966	1972
3	24	21
4	1	0
5	16	18
6	1	1
7	7	6
8	0	0
9 and over	1	4
Total number of board members	221	240

Vincent O'Leary and Joan Nuffield, "A National Survey of Parole Decision-Making," *Crime and Delinquency,* Vol. 19, No. 3 (July, 1973), p. 382.

systems, with the function of deciding when and under what conditions inmates are to be released on parole prior to expiration of maximum sentence. Parole boards are almost universally administratively independent of prison and reformatory systems as a deliberate check-and-balance within the correctional process. There are marked variations from one state to another in the way parole board members are selected, their tenure of office, the scope of their authority, and the procedures they follow in making parole determinations. Some parole board memberships are full-time jobs; some are part-time, really ancillary to the member's major profession or occupation. In most places parole board members are appointed by the chief executive to staggered terms and may or may not have professional correctional experience. In some areas the board is viewed as representing the "citizenry" in making such important decisions as those relating to release of inmates, and in these instances the governor commonly appoints prominent laymen to this agency; in others, the board may be a mixture of persons with no correctional experience and those with credentials of correctional "expertise." In only a few places are boards composed solely of career correctional administrators.

The variety of professions and occupations required to operate criminal justice agencies intensifies the problems inherent in the divergence and distinctness of the agencies themselves. There is no common manpower pool from which agency functionaries can be selected, and policemen are recruited, trained, and educated in isolation from the lawyers who staff prosecutors' offices and serve on the bench. In turn, correctional personnel, whether custodial or professional, are separately trained or recruited from educational fields that have virtually no contact with others—law or police science—from which other functionaries come. Not only are prior educational requirements and in-service training programs unique to each agency, but *continuing education* activities—conferences, seminars, workshops, and the like—are normally conducted within agency boundaries. Police meet with each other to discuss common problems, as do prosecutors with other prosecutors, and judges, probation staff, and other correctional personnel each with his own. Interagency conferences and training sessions are now coming into vogue, but only in limited and sporadic fashion. Isolation tends to be reinforced by the formation of discrete professional societies —the National Association of Chiefs of Police, the American Correctional Association, the National Association of Trial Court Judges, and others—which provide distinct professional reference groups and command intraoccupational loyalty. All of these factors combine to insulate agency concerns, to stress priorities within functions, and to diminish awareness and concern with total system operations.

5. Differential Selection

Incumbents of criminal justice agencies and offices are selected and advance within the agency hierarchy in a variety of ways, not only between agencies, but also within agencies, having the same function in different jurisdictions. There are three major methods of selection and promotion: competitive examination (after fulfilling educational or experience prerequisites), appointment, and election. In turn, these may vary in actual operational details. For example, in some places trial judges are elected after nonpartisan nomination; in others, major political parties support different judicial candidates. Though initial selection or promotion may be based primarily upon competitive examination, in many places the chief executive or head of an agency may be able to selectively appoint or promote individuals from among a list of top performers on the examination; placing first on the list does not insure appointment.

POLICE RECRUITMENT.   Most police are civil service career employees of municipal, county, state, or federal jurisdictions and compete by examination for original appointment and for promotions. However, police commissioners or chiefs are commonly appointed to the post by the chief executive of the jurisdiction, in some instances with the "advice and consent" of a city council, a state senate, or an advisory board such as a police and fire commission. Commonly the tenure of a police chief is at the pleasure of the appointing executive. In turn, the head of a police agency may be free to appoint, without competitive examination, some or perhaps all of his deputies and other top echelon personnel. Thus a typical police agency is a composite of lower-echelon career civil servants topped by an appointed administrative and policy-making staff, most of the latter, however, having advanced through the ranks from their initial entry as patrolmen.

The sheriff is an important exception to this selection pattern, since he is almost invariably an elected official. This is a significant variation for policing patterns in rural and many suburban areas, and it also has correctional implications, for in many places the sheriff operates local jails and workhouses. The office of sheriff thus exemplifies the most direct citizen involvement in police selection. Obviously the ballot influences the selection of all police commissioners, since the appointing executive is commonly an elected official and the police commissioner an important member of his cabinet, making police policies a correspondingly important plank in his political platform.

SELECTION OF PROSECUTORS. With few exceptions, the chief prosecutor (commonly called a district attorney) in most trial jurisdictions is a locally elected official as is the public defender in those jurisdictions where this office exists. Federal prosecutors are appointed by the President and serve at his pleasure, unlike judges who have life tenure when confirmed by the Senate. Only a few states provide for appointment of prosecutors, but political considerations play an important part in the selection process even in these states.[56] The pattern of selection of attorneys general is much like that of local prosecutors: in most places the attorney general is an elected official, but in some jurisdictions, including the federal, he is appointed by the chief executive, subject to legislative approval.

The tenure of office of the elected prosecutor is typically short, with most districts requiring election every two, three, or four years. A prerequisite for election or appointment is that the candidate be a lawyer. The organizational structure of his office will vary from one place to another; in small rural districts the district attorney may be a part-time officeholder with the bulk of his professional activity devoted to private law practice. In metropolitan counties, prosecutors are typically full-time and may have large staffs whose job security is protected by civil service entry and tenure provisions.

JUDICIAL SELECTION PATTERNS. Judges are selected for office in a variety of ways. In most states trial judges are nominated by a political party and elected on a partisan basis.[57] In several states judges stand for election as nonpartisans, getting their names on the ballot by circulating petitions to obtain a required number of voter signatures.[58] In nine states judges are appointed by the governor or by local executives, while in the federal system judges are appointed by the President with the consent of the Senate.[59] In five states judges are appointed (or, as in Vermont, elected) by the legislature.[60] In ten states judges are selected by the "Missouri Plan"[61] (first adopted in Missouri in 1940) which works as follows: a list of qualified candidates is prepared by a nonpartisan commission, and presented to the chief executive (governor, mayor, or other local authority). The executive then appoints judges selected from the list who are approved by voters at the next election. After a term of service the incumbent judge again runs for office unopposed, standing only on his own record. In effect, he asks the electorate for a vote of confidence. If the vote should be negative, the selection process begins again.

The term of office for a judge varies from jurisdiction to jurisdiction. The federal judiciary has life tenure, but in some states the terms may be as short as four years. More commonly terms range from six to ten years, with possible reelection for life or until reaching a mandatory retirement age defined by statute.

At the felony trial court level, all judges must have been admitted to the bar to qualify for office. This does not necessarily mean that each has received a legal education or has graduated from an accredited law school. Though by law and custom the apprenticeship system is disappearing, in some states persons can still become members of the bar by passing an examination upon fulfilling office practice training requirements. In lower courts (justice of the peace, coroners', and magistrates' courts) incumbents in some jurisdictions are not required to be members of the bar or trained lawyers.

THE JURY. Selection for jury duty involves a process that is quite different from the three major ways—examination, appointment, or election—that other criminal justice functionaries assume office. In general, jury members are selected by lot by a clerk of court or a jury commissioner from lists of eligible citizens. In half the states and in the federal system there are *grand* juries as well as trial juries, and the methods of selection of each jury type vary in some details. The two major functions of grand juries are to conduct investigations into certain types of crime or corruption, and to ratify or reject the request by the prosecutor for a formal charge—an indictment—to be levied against a specific defendant.[62] Sometimes a single grand jury performs both functions, but often the *investigatory* grand jury is separate from the *charging* grand jury and may be chosen from a separate panel. Where the law allows it, some executives can appoint a "blue ribbon" investigatory commission from among prominent citizens that has powers similar to those of a grand jury.

Charging grand juries are assembled much more frequently than their investigatory counterparts, and in general, grand jurymen are chosen by draws from panels obtained from city directories, voter registration lists, and similar sources. Though the same procedure is used to pick trial juries, in practice the basic panel lists may be different. Grand juries usually sit for a full term of court, unlike the trial jury, which meets to consider a particular case and exists only so long as the trial lasts. To minimize extended interference with employment and other activities, grand jury panels may be heavily composed of retired persons and others who have indicated their willingness to serve for an entire month, or as long as needed.

The grand jury is ready to function once chosen, if no members' requests for excuse from duty are honored. However, potential *trial* jurors, after being chosen, are subject to in-court examination and challenge by both the prosecutor and defense counsel. This is known as a *voir dire* (to speak the truth) examination and is an attempt to determine whether the juryman is sufficiently neutral in attitude, has neither a relationship with the defendant nor preconceived notions of guilt or innocence, and is otherwise competent to render a fair verdict. If bias, preconception, or some other element likely to prejudice a fair trial is discovered, the jury candidate will be excused by the judge and replaced by another person chosen from the panel.[63] In addition to jurymen candidates removed for a cause at *voir dire* by the judge, state and defense each have the option to make a specified number of peremptory challenges, that is, removal of persons from the jury without demonstrated cause.

SELECTION OF CORRECTIONAL PERSONNEL. Correctional personnel in institutional and community services are generally selected and promoted by competitive examination much like policemen. College education for probation and parole field staff and institutional professionals may be required in some jurisdictions. The heads of correctional agencies—corrections commissioners, chief probation officers, and parole board members—are most often appointed to their posts by the chief executive of the jurisdiction, or, as with some probation staff, by the appropriate judge. In some "integrated" correctional systems—in which all correctional personnel are employees of a single state superagency—there may be lateral or promotional movement of individuals, based on examination and accumulated experience, from probation to institutions, to parole field staff, and so on. Normally there is little or no lateral movement from one type of service to another where correctional services are discrete agencies.

91

6. Differential Citizen Involvement

An important trend in criminal justice administration, especially during the past two decades, has been the attempt of the major criminal justice agencies to become more "professional." For the most part, this has taken the form of raising educational and specialized training requirements of agency functionaries from policemen to parole officers. This movement reflects a desire by many participants to improve the efficiency and effectiveness of crime control efforts, supported by a belief that "higher standards" for personnel will bring this about.[64] Economic self-interest also is served by the achievement of recognized professional status. As in many occupations and professions, staff with education beyond high school or specialized training credentials can demand and receive higher salaries and other benefits not available to their less fortunate counterparts. In addition, criminal justice operations require every officeholder to exercise wide-ranging discretion, which is most easily justified by acknowledged expertise—skills more often associated with formal educational achievement than with simple street experience. Whatever the mix of motivations and pressures toward professionalism, the trend has virtually excluded laymen— untrained, unspecialized persons—from most significant decision roles in the criminal justice process. Generally, the town constable has been replaced by the professional policeman, the lay or apprentice-trained judge by the college-educated lawyer, and the correctional volunteer by the trained caseworker.

The point of most direct citizen involvement in criminal justice decision making is, of course, at the jury stages of the process. However, today only about half the states use the grand jury system in the charging decision, generally reserving it for felony cases. While performing a central function in contested cases, the trial jury is infrequently used in terms of the overall number of offenders adjudicated.[65] The majority of convicted offenders in every jurisdiction plead guilty, and a significant number of those who do not are adjudicated by means of a *bench trial,* that is, by trial before a judge sitting without a jury.[66]

As discussed earlier, citizens in some jurisdictions are indirectly involved in criminal justice processing by being able to elect prosecutors and judges or, more indirectly, by voting for executives who are given authority to appoint heads of agencies. In addition, limited citizen involvement may also be achieved by service on advisory boards or commissions, as perhaps a corrections commission, a board of prisons and welfare, a police and fire commission, which are generally composed of prominent laymen appointed by the mayor or governor and granted some degree of authority to establish policies, approve or disapprove

92

appointments or programs, or perhaps to review expenditures and to suggest budget.[67]

While the trend toward professionalism has increasingly insulated the criminal justice process from the influence of "laymen" in policy formulation and decision making, currently a backlash to many aspects of this trend seems to be developing. Stimulus for the backlash comes from many sources, but the dominant thrust originates in the increasing political awareness of the poor and of racial and ethnic minorities who find themselves frequent clients of criminal processing but only rarely among those in charge of processing. Thus there is increasing demand today for more direct public involvement in the criminal justice process, supported by numerous appellate court decisions which have expanded the rights of the poor and the rights of poor criminal defendants. This movement has also been bolstered by the dissatisfaction of some criminal justice administrators with the bureaucratic aloofness of many crime control agencies. Some communities have set up police *review* boards composed of citizens representing particular racial and ethnic groups whose task is investigating allegations of police misconduct. Other communities have police *advisory* panels, sometimes organized on a neighborhood basis, to react to police policy matters other than, or in addition to, misconduct. In a few communities—and in some correctional systems—*ombudsmen* who are civilians, that is, not employed by the agency, act as mediators in administrative disputes between those who administer an agency and those affected by it.[68] There is also a move toward establishment of *community-based* correctional institutions, a trend designed to decentralize the prison system by bringing correctional services into offenders' neighborhoods and giving neighborhood dwellers some say in correctional policies and practices. Volunteers are increasingly being recruited for use in all agencies from police to prisons and parole. Similarly, persons processed through the system are demanding and sometimes achieving, a greater voice in the determination of their own fate. A number of prisons today have elected inmate advisory councils and almost everywhere some ex-offenders are finding employment in criminal justice agencies, job opportunities formerly closed to persons with criminal records. *Paraprofessionals*—laymen, whether ex-offenders or not—are increasingly being used in all criminal justice agencies, even at the prosecution and court levels. *Paralegal* service, primarily involving investigation and referral duties, is a new criminal justice career opportunity. And various self-help organizations, many patterned after Alcoholics Anonymous, are being given new impetus and community monetary support to assist in reintegrating sex offenders, narcotics addicts, and other criminally deviant persons.

DEFENSE COUNSEL AND OTHER PARTICIPANTS IN THE CRIMINAL JUSTICE SYSTEM

In addition to the central participants in the on-line criminal justice agencies, there are a number of other actors in the criminal justice process who have no agency administrative responsibilities but who provide specialized services at one point or another. The most important of these is the defense attorney, a participant of major consequence.

Historically, the function of defense counsel was limited to representation of defendants at trial. But even in this capacity the extent of his role was determined by the ability of a defendant to pay for representation. Although the right to trial by jury was guaranteed by the Constitution, until recently the accused who could not afford a lawyer had no right to be represented at the trial or at any other stage of the process.[69] Affluent defendants could always retain private counsel if they wished, but without provisions in state statutes or state constitutions, poor defendants could properly be tried without legal assistance. Since most criminal defendants were (and are) poor, the presence or absence of lawyers for the defense varied from one jurisdiction to the next, depending upon statutory or constitutional vagaries. After an extended period of time during which the U.S. Supreme Court first held that even *poor* defendants had a right to counsel in state *capital* cases,[70] the Warren Court expanded the right to representation of indigent defendants at trial in all states on any charge which carries the possibility of a "substantial prison sentence."[71] This holding, at first interpreted as applying only to felony matters, subsequently has been expanded to include trials involving misdemeanor charges and to apply to defendants who plead guilty as well as those who go to trial.[72]

If the role of defense counsel were limited to trial or guilty plea functions, it would make the lawyer a major participant in only a small segment of the entire criminal justice process. But following the *Gideon* decision, the U.S. Supreme Court significantly expanded the right of representation to a number of "critical stages" of the process from in-custody interrogation by the police[73] through appeal[74] to various postconviction determinations.[75] The number and range of critical stages is still not finally settled, but at this writing it falls short of including every step in the process where decisions concerning defendants or offenders are made. In a recent case involving parole revocation, the Supreme Court, while requiring a hearing and other facets of due process, remained silent with regard to the right of parolees to have legal representation.[76] Nevertheless, the recent flow of cases from the Supreme Court has so greatly expanded the right to representation that the distribution of legal services has in some places become a serious problem.

Persons accused and convicted of crimes who desire to appeal or who otherwise seek release from custody can obtain legal counsel in a number of different ways. The major issue is payment for the lawyer's services, and this depends upon the type of legal services available in the particular jurisdiction. These tend to fall into four major categories: 1) private counsel, whereby the defendant or petitioner hires with his own funds a practicing lawyer who is willing to take his case; 2) court assignment, a procedure by which the judge appoints lawyers randomly from bar lists or from a panel of attorneys who have expressed willingness to serve, or if possible, attorneys chosen by petitioners (but in each case in which petitioners indigency is demonstrated, the attorney's fees are paid by the county or by other appropriate jurisdiction); 3) public defender, a system found in some jurisdictions in which a public defender's office is created and staffed much like the office of the prosecutor but with the mandate to defend indigents; and 4) legal aid services, involving a variety of programs, some subsidized by federal and state funds, others by local donations, whereby storefront law offices are set up and act very much like other Red Feather (i.e., "charitable") community resources for the poor, in this instance by providing both civil and criminal legal assistance.

From the defendant's, or petitioner's, point of view, the central issue is whether his attorney is chosen by him or assigned by the court. Studies of the comparative merits of different methods of providing legal services are generally inconclusive,[77] regardless of whether such analysis is based on cost or performance. One argument for a public defender system is that the lawyer in this office is a specialist in criminal defense and therefore more equal in skill to the prosecutor than a randomly assigned lawyer.[78] Not only is he knowledgeable in criminal law and procedure, but he also knows informal court practices, such as ways of obtaining reduced charges. Assigned lawyers may lack sufficient criminal law knowledge and defense skills and may not even be aware of hallway bargaining practices to obtain lesser charges. On the other hand, if an assignment system is used so that eventually all lawyers in a jurisdiction rotate through criminal cases, the result may be involvement of the "better" lawyers, usually concerned with more lucrative civil practice, in criminal matters. Such barwide involvement of attorneys may generate interest and concern about criminal justice issues among lawyers at large, and, because of their collective influence in politics and governmental administration, this could lead to improvements in the entire system.

With the exception of experienced public defenders and a handful of specializing criminal lawyers, few members of the bar are really familiar with criminal law and procedure, nor do they rely to any great extent on income derived from the defense of criminal cases. A major study of the *criminal lawyer* defined such

95

lawyers as those who specified that 10 percent or more of their practice was in criminal law.[79] There are a few courthouse regulars in larger communities whose practice is limited to criminal defense, but most attorneys who appear in criminal court receive the major share of their income from other types of law practice where their major professional interest lies.[80]

With the exception of public defender offices, the defense attorney function is not centered in a definable on-line agency of criminal justice. Defense attorneys are mainly entrepreneurs outside the organizational structure of the system and adversary to its processes. However, their presence throughout the process is now pervasive and their activities contribute directly and importantly to the shape and nature of criminal justice in our society.

In addition to lawyers, there are numerous other persons who represent various occupations and professions and who perform certain functions in criminal justice processing but who are, for the most part, peripheral to *major* decisions regarding policy or practices of the crime control agencies. At some point, depending upon need and the responsibility of particular agencies, physicians, dentists, psychiatrists, psychologists, experts in criminalistics[81] (fingerprinting, ballistics, and so on), and other professionals are called upon for some service. Thus prisons which provide medical and dental care for inmates often have appropriate medical personnel on permanent staff or part-time and on-call. Likewise, a court may have a "psychopathic clinic" attached for use in diagnosing defendants who appear from their actions or the nature of their crimes to be mentally disturbed or otherwise incompetent. Except in narrow areas of expertise, the persons performing such services normally have no overall responsibility for administering the agency which uses them. There are occasional exceptions, of course, as in the case of a psychiatrist who heads a hospital for the criminally insane, really a form of prison, or a psychologist who serves on a parole board. And a physician, as coroner or medical examiner, may play more than a passive, service role in the entire process. But in general, experts with particular skills who are utilized by the criminal justice agencies remain peripheral to core administrative tasks, though their activities may affect case processing from time to time.

IDEOLOGICAL VALUES IN CRIMINAL JUSTICE ORGANIZATION

There is little doubt that the hodge-podge structural array and diverse staffing patterns of the on-line criminal justice agencies compound inefficiency, create stresses and tensions in and between agencies, and present disturbing dilemmas for strategies of change and improvement in the processing of suspects, defendants, and offenders. From the standpoint of efficiency, it would be smoother and more businesslike to merge all the agencies and offices into a whole, perhaps even to "federalize" police, prosecutors, judges, and correctional services and to fix common personnel standards and prerequisites. Yet it must be remembered that efficiency and effectiveness of operation represent only one dimension, one desired value, of our criminal justice system. Just as our political philosophy supports separation of the powers of the legislative, judicial, and executive branches of governmental authority, so the mixture of agency structures and personnel selection patterns serve certain values which we espouse as well. At best, we give reluctant support to crime control efforts because we must. We want safety and domestic order, but we also fear the unfettered enforcement power of the state and wish to maintain a degree of community control over the way the law is administered. As attractive as a federally controlled criminal justice system may appear from an efficiency viewpoint—or, for that matter, as desirable as statewide control of presently local agencies may seem to be— any proposals in this direction tend to conflict with competing values which support home rule and local autonomy in the staffing and funding of agencies and to this extent in the control of enforcement policies and practices. Likewise, the professionalization of criminal justice roles and the removal of some jobs from patronage to the comparative political neutrality of civil service protection, while desirable from many perspectives, tend to prevent the involvement of ordinary citizens in criminal justice decisions. Thus differences in jurisdictions, budgets, methods of role selection, and degrees of lay involvement in on-line agencies serve multiple purposes, conforming to a number of basic principles that are not always congruent. The principle of home rule is maintained by local staffing patterns of most police, prosecutors, and judges, yet centralism exists as in prison systems, in which the problems are beyond local coping capacity. Most prosecutors, judges, and chief executives are chosen by ballot. But educational prerequisites and competitive examinations remove incumbents from direct political whim or threat in selection for many important roles. Juries continue to function and laymen volunteers are assuming new importance, but the trend toward professionalism goes on. The result is a mixture of lay and expert decision makers across the criminal justice process, or in some instances working side-by-side in a single agency.

It is clear that a careful analysis of the criminal justice system will show that its basic structure, cumbersome and inefficient though it may be, nevertheless serves values which are central to a democratic ideology. A more uniform system, less amorphous and better organized, might be achieved only by diminishing citizen control and forfeiting local autonomy. We are evidently unwilling to pay this price, in part because there is no assurance that a single, national criminal justice system would be more effective in crime prevention or control, nor would it necessarily be more honest and just. Corruption and unfairness also exist on national and state levels, but on a larger and more pervasive scale. However, we view centralized police power with deep suspicion—by which we mean the authority of *all* criminal justice agencies to compel conformity; and while we recognize the need for policemen, courts, and prisons, we have too many historical and contemporary examples of totalitarian police states to relinquish altogether the checks and balances on this power. The complex relationships among on-line agencies and the separation of sources of authority and power may not be ideal from any single perspective, but these arrangements serve many different ideals, each in its own way fitting notions of a proper form of justice for our society.

NOTES

1. See Frank J. Remington, Donald J. Newman, Edward L. Kimball, Marygold Melli, and Herman Goldstein, *Criminal Justice Administration: Materials and Cases* (Indianapolis: Bobbs-Merrill, 1969), esp. Introduction, for a leading example of this approach.

2. Henry M. Hart, "The Aims of the Criminal Law," *Law and Contemp. Prob.* 23, 401 (1958): esp. 412.

3. For a detailed examination of the insanity defense, see Abraham S. Goldstein, *The Insanity Defense* (New Haven: Yale U. Press, 1967).

4. 408 U.S. 238 (1972).

5. See Edwin M. Sutherland, "Diffusion of Sex Psychopath Laws," *J. Crim. Law, Criminology and Pol. Sci.* 40, 543 (January-February 1950).

6. Passed by the New York State Legislature by an extremely narrow margin in 1971, the state's liberal abortion law continued to stimulate fever-pitched debate for many months. In 1972 hospitals in the state reported performing more abortions than deliveries.

7. See Frank J. Remington and Victor G. Rosenblum, "The Criminal Law and the Legislative Process," *U. of Ill. Law Review* 481 (1960).

8. The Blue Laws, or Sabbath Laws, were created as a social control mechanism during Puritan times, and penalties for their violation included capital punishment. In 1961 the U.S. Supreme Court ruled that the matter would be left to the states. See McGowan v. Maryland, 366 U.S. 420 (1961).

9. The Capone theory is discussed in Monroe Freedman, "The Professional Responsibility of the Prosecuting Attorney," *Georgetown Law J.* 55, 1030 (1967). It should also be noted, however, that this approach is by no means limited to the prosecution of notorious gangsters. In 1972 for example, the IRS acknowledged that it had created special investigative units with the aim of building tax evasion cases against alleged political extremists and drug pushers.

10. Thurman W. Arnold, "Law Enforcement: An Attempt at Social Dissection," *Yale Law J.* 42, 1 (1932): esp. 17-18.

11. See Herbert A. Bloch, "The Gambling Business: An American Paradox," *Crime and Delin.* 8, 355 (1962). See also Herman Goldstein, "Police Discretion: The Ideal versus the Real," *Pub. Admin. Review,* 23, 140, 142 (1963); O. W. Wilson, *Police Administration* (New York: McGraw-Hill, 1963), pp. 301-04, 312, 313. There have been instances, however, where legislatures have sought to distinguish between social gamblers and professional gamblers. See, for example, Mich. Rev. Code, Final Draft, Comment to Sec. 6105-6106 (Sept. 1967).

12. For a penetrating political analysis of the federal budgetary process, see Aaron Wildavsky, *The Politics of the Budgetary Process* (Boston: Little, Brown, 1964). Perhaps the most striking example of this recent increase in crime control funding can be found in the formation of the federal Law Enforcement Assistance Administration. Created by Congress in 1968, under the Omnibus Crime Control and Safe Streets Act (P.L. 90-351), the LEAA undertook the first comprehensive assault on crime in the history of the United States. By 1971 it had expended 860 million dollars.

13. Convened in 1950, the Senate Crime Investigating Committee under Senator Kefauver held widely publicized public hearings into organized crime, calling more than 800 witnesses. See *Third Interim Report of the Special Committee to Investigate Organized Crime in Interstate Commerce* (Washington, D.C.: U.S. Government Printing Office, 1951).

14. Following the discovery of an apparent organized crime conference at Apalachin, N.Y., there emerged a great resurgence in interest in organized crime. See McClellan, Labor-Management Reports, *First Interim Report,* S. Rep. No. 1417, 85th Cong., 2d Sess. (1958), *Second Interim Report* (pts. 1 and 2), S. Rep. No. 621, 86th Cong., 1st Sess. (1959), *Final Report* (pts. 1-4), S. Rep. No. 1139, 86th Cong., 2d Sess. (1960).

15. The rejection of Clement Haynsworth and Harold Carswell are examined in detail in James F. Simon, *In His Own Image* (New York: David McKay Co., Inc., 1973).

16. For general discussions of executive clemency, see Winthrop Rockefeller, "Executive Clemency and the Death Penalty," *Catholic U. Law Review* 21, 94 (1971); Note, "Governor Reagan and Executive Clemency," *Calif. Law Review* 55, 407 (1967); Hugo Adam Bedau, "Death Sentences in New Jersey, 1907-1960," *Rutgers Law Review* 19, 1 (1964); Bedau, "Capital Punishment in Oregon, 1903-1964," *Ore. Law Review* 45, 1 (1965).

17. This does not necessarily mean, however, that such courts are called supreme courts. New York State, for instance, calls its highest court the Court of Appeals, while in New York a Supreme Court is a court of original jurisdiction impowered to try felony cases.

18. For a description of this intricate appellate process, with special emphasis on a landmark U.S. Supreme Court decision, see Anthony Lewis, *Gideon's Trumpet* (New York: Random House, 1964).

19. The record of the "activist" Warren Court is assessed in Archibald Cox, *The Warren Court: Constitutional Decisions as an Instrument of Reform* (Cambridge: Harvard U. Press, 1968); Fred P. Graham, *The Self-Inflicted Wound* (New York: Macmillan, 1970).

20. Article V, Section 2, *The Constitution of the United States.*

21. Phil C. Neal, "Judicial Activism, Nonjudicial Passivism, and Law Reform," *Chicago Bar J.* 49, 240 (1967): 241-44.

22. Charles D. Breitel, "The Court and Law Making," in Monrad Paulsen, ed., *Legal Institutions Today and Tomorrow,* 1959, p. 37.

23. On Feb. 5, 1937, in a speech to Congress, President Roosevelt proposed a far-reaching reorganization plan that would expand the Court from nine to fifteen members. Opposition quickly developed in Congress and elsewhere, and after a vigorous political tug-of-war, Roosevelt abandoned the plan. For a study of the interplay between public opinion and

legislative stance toward the plan, see Frank V. Cantwell, "Public Opinion and the Legislative Process," *Amer. Pol. Sci. Review* 55 (1946): 924-35.

24. Nixon's strategy is examined in Simon, *In His Own Image*. To some extent, Nixon may have succeeded in molding a Court that would rule consonant with his political philosophy, since in his first term alone, he had the good fortune of appointing four new justices, including Warren Burger as Chief Justice.

25. See William F. Swindler, *Court and Constitution in the Twentieth Century: The New Legality, 1932-1968* (Indianapolis: Bobbs-Merrill, 1970).

26. See, generally, Philippe Nonet, *Administrative Justice: Advocacy and Change in a Government Agency* (New York: Russell Sage Foundation, 1969); Kenneth Davis, *Administrative Law and Government* (St. Paul: West, 1960).

27. The nature and extent of this expanded due process are explored in Fred Cohen, "A Comment on Morrissey v. Brewer: Due Process and Parole Revocation," *Crim. Law Bull.* 7, 616 (September 1972); Comment, "Due Process: The Right to Counsel in Parole Release Hearings," *Iowa Law Review* 54, 497 (1968); Comment, "Rights v. Results: Quo Vadis Due Process for Parolees," *Pacific Law J.* 1, 321 (1970); Donald J. Newman, "Court Intervention in the Parole Process, *Albany Law Review* 36, 257 (1972).

28. Robert O. Dawson, *Sentencing: The Decision as to Type, Length, and Conditions of Sentence* (Boston: Little, Brown, 1969); President's Commission on Law Enforcement and Administration of Justice, *Task Force Report: The Courts* (Washington, D.C.: U.S. Government Printing Office, 1967), p. 14.

29. Article III, Section 2, *The Constitution of the United States*.

30. Kenneth Davis, *Discretionary Justice: A Preliminary Inquiry* (Baton Rouge: L.S.U. Press, 1969); Frank W. Miller, *Prosecution: The Decision to Charge a Suspect with a Crime* (Boston: Little, Brown, 1969); and Brian A. Grosman, *The Prosecutor: An Inquiry into the Exercise of Discretion* (Toronto: U. of Toronto Press, 1969).

31. Grosman, *The Prosecutor;* Newman F. Baker, "The Prosecutor—Initiation and Prosecution," *J. Crim. Law, Criminology and Pol. Sci.* 23, 770 (1933).

32. See generally, Miller, *Prosecution*.

33. President's Commission, *The Courts*, pp. 73-76.

34. See, Miller, *Prosecution*, pp. 151-72, 213-32, 293-345.

35. *Ibid*, p. 19.

36. President's Commission, *The Courts*, p. 73.

37. Hassan v. Magistrates Court, 20 Misc. 2d 509, 514, 191 N.Y.S. 2d 238, 248 (Sup. Ct. 1959), emphasis added. The courts have not been unanimous on this question, however. See, for example, Pugack v. Klein, 193 F. Supp. 630 (S.D.N.Y. 1961), and Miller, *Prosecution,* esp. Chap. 8.

38. See generally, President's Commission, *Task Force Report: The Police* (Washington, D.C.: U.S. Government Printing Office, 1967); Albert J. Reiss, Jr., *The Police and the Public* (New Haven: Yale U. Press, 1970).

39. See generally, Wayne R. LaFave, *Arrest: The Decision to Take a Suspect into Custody* (Boston: Little, Brown, 1965); President's Commission, *The Police;* Davis, *Discretionary Justice,* Jerome S. Skolnick, *Justice Without Trial* (New York: John Wiley and Sons, 1966); James Q. Wilson, *Varieties of Police Behavior: The Management of Law and Order in Eight Communities* (Cambridge: Harvard U. Press, 1968).

40. Recognizing this, some observers have called for the virtual elimination of all discretion. See, for example, American Friends Service Committee, *Struggle for Justice* (New York: Hill & Wang, 1971), esp. Chap. 8.

41. Herman Goldstein, "Police Discretion: The Ideal versus the Real," *Pub. Admin. Review* 23, 140 (1963).

42. Joseph Goldstein, "Police Discretion Not to Invoke the Criminal Process: Low Visibility Decisions in the Administration of Justice," *Yale Law J.* 69, 543 (1960).

43. From Wilson, *Varieties of Police Behavior,* pp. 7-8.

44. Sheldon Glueck, "Principles of a Rational Penal Code," *Harvard Law Review* 41, 453, 480 (1928).

45. See Remington, Newman, Kimball, Melli, and Goldstein, *Criminal Justice Administration,* esp. pp. 18-20. Herbert L. Packer, *The Limits of the Criminal Sanction* (Stanford: Stanford U. Press, 1968), esp. pp. 159-160, likens the criminal justice process as a conveyor belt process.

46. Remington, Newman, Kimball, Melli, and Goldstein, *Criminal Justice Administration,* pp. 6-12, provides an extensive examination of the geneology and implications of the term.

47. The term is too cumbersome and laden with political connotations, according to some observers. The term "bureaucracy," as well as several variations and application to criminal justice, are traced in Remington, Newman, Kimball, Melli, and Goldstein, pp. 6-7, note d.

48. *Ibid,* pp. 6-7, note d, in which the authors note that the terms "complex" and "organization" may conjure up exaggerated visions of formal organization, cohesiveness, or coordination.

49. *Ibid,* p. 7, note d, concludes that this description might suffer from several shortcomings. First, it might ignore the role of the courts and the rule of law. Second, it might place undo emphasis on internal administrative processes which can become extremely confusing, due to the multiplicity of agencies within the total criminal justice system.

50. President's Commission, *The Challenge of Crime in a Free Society* (Washington, D.C.: U.S. Government Printing Office, 1967), p. 7.

51. Moreover, there are commonly rigid career ladders within criminal justice agencies, so that all police recruits must first serve as beat patrolmen, and so on—despite individual strengths or weaknesses. This rigidity can sometimes reduce administrative effectiveness and frustrate personnel motivation.

52. A partial exception is found in New York State, where all police officers are required to undergo a minimum amount of certain types of training, some of it usually administered by the state's Municipal Police Training Council.

53. President's Commission, *The Courts,* pp. 74 (prosecutors) and 68-69 (trial judges).

54. *Ibid,* pp. 23-34. This lack of formal education, which has at least partially contributed to widespread sentence disparity, has recently resulted in the formation of numerous "sentencing councils," in which judges convene to study the sentencing process.

55. See President's Commission, *Corrections,* esp. Chap. 9; Charles S. Prigmore, ed., "Manpower and Training for Corrections" *Proceedings of an Arden House Conference,* June 24-26, 1964 (New York: Council on Social Work Education, 1964); Judith G. Benjamin, Marcia K. Freedman, and Edith F. Lynton, "Pros and Cons: New Roles for Non-professionals in Corrections" (New York: National Committee on Employment of Youth, 1965).

56. See Duane R. Nedrud, "The Career Prosecutor," *J. Crim. Law, Criminology and Pol. Sci.* 51, 461 (1961).

57. President's Commission, *The Courts,* p. 66.

58. *Ibid,* pp. 66-67.

59. *Ibid,* pp. 66-67.

60. *Ibid,* pp. 66-67.

61. *Ibid,* pp. 66-67.

62. The grand jury concept received considerable criticism during the Nixon administration. See Frank J. Donner and Eugene Cerruti, "The Grand Jury Network: How the

Nixon Administration Has Secretly Perverted a Traditional Safeguard on Individual Rights," *The Nation,* 3 January 1972, pp. 5-20.

63. In recent years, a growing number of lawyers acting as defense counsel for black extremists have sought to convince the courts that their clients should be judged by black juries. See for example, Charles R. Garry, "Minimizing Racism in Jury Trials," in Jonathan Black, ed., *Radical Lawyers: Their Role in the Movement and in the Courts* (New York: Avon, 1971), pp. 141-53. The point has also been made that a defendant's right to a trial by a jury composed of his "peers" might be interpreted as meaning juvenile jurors if the defendant was a juvenile. See *Matter of McCloud,* R. I. Family Court, 15 January 1971.

64. Although this plea for professionalization has been a major threat throughout most of the criminal justice literature of the last two decades, it has not been universally embraced. See Harold Wilensky, "The Professionalization of Everyone?" *Amer. J. Soc.* 70, 318 (Sept. 1964).

65. Donald J. Newman, *Conviction: The Determination of Guilt or Innocence Without Trial* (Boston: Little, Brown, 1966).

66. See Harry Kalven and Hans Ziesel, *The American Jury* (Boston: Little, Brown, 1966).

67. For a discussion of one of the earliest versions of this type of citizen participation, see Comment, "Philadelphia's Police Advisory Board—A New Concept in Community Relations," *Villanova Law Review* 7, 656 (Summer 1962).

68. The rationale and operation of ombudsmen is explored in Donald C. Rowat, *The Ombudsman: Citizens' Defender* (London: George Allen and Unwin, 1965); Walter Gellhorn, *Ombudsmen and Others: Citizen Protectors in Nine Countries* (Cambridge: Harvard U. Press, 1966).

69. This right was established in Gideon v. Wainwright, 372 U.S. 335 (1963).

70. Powell v. Alabama, 287 U.S. 45 (1932); Betts v. Brady, 316 U.S. 455 (1942).

71. Gideon v. Wainwright, 372 U.S. 335 (1963).

72. Argersinger v. Hamlin, 407 U.S. 25 (1972), extended the right to counsel to misdemeanor defendants.

73. Miranda v. Arizona, 384 U.S. 436 (1966).

74. Douglas v. California, 372 U.S. 353 (1963).

75. Mempa v. Rhay, 389 U.S. 128 (1967).

76. Morrissey v. Brewer, 92 S. Ct. 2576 (1972). For an incisive discussion of this case, see Cohen, "A Comment on Morrissey v. Brewer."

77. Lee Silverstein, *The Defense of the Poor in Criminal Cases in American State Courts* (Chicago: American Bar Foundation, 1965), p. 73.

78. Richard Harris, "Annals of Law: In Criminal Court—1," *The New Yorker,* 14 April 1965, esp. pp. 76-88, lists several advantages and disadvantages of the public defender system, especially in comparison to privately retained counsel.

79. Arthur L. Wood, *Criminal Lawyer* (New Haven, Conn.: College and University Press, 1967).

80. See Albert P. Blaustein, *The American Lawyer* (Chicago: U. of Chicago Press, 1954); Wood, *Criminal Lawyer.*

81. See C. E. O'Hara and J. W. Osterburg, *An Introduction to Criminalistics* (New York: Macmillan, 1949). Basically, the term refers to expertise in identification and comparison of criminal evidence.

Chapter **3**

The Criminal Justice Process

STAGES IN CRIMINAL JUSTICE PROCESSING

The structural complexity of the criminal justice system which involves the interplay of legislative mandates, appellate court decisions, and discretion and the profusion of professions and roles does not present a clear picture of a well-defined, conceptually manageable criminal justice system. The system appears even more amorphous when its structure is viewed along with its multiple objectives, such as rehabilitation, deterrence, incapacitation, and its ideological underpinnings—due process, equal protection, and other functions discussed earlier. Yet it becomes more clearly a system when its actual functions are detailed. For the glue which cements distant and often disparate agencies, offices, and courts is the criminal justice *process* which cycles individuals from the status of free citizen to that of suspect, then defendant, to convicted offender, probationer, inmate, parolee, and in most instances, to eventual discharge and return to society.

This processing of persons is the key to the system, for while its parts can be dissected for analysis, once it becomes functionally operative all components—the sources of authority, the objectives, the ideals, and the separate but contiguous agencies—coalesce at any single decision point and have relevance to all others. When a policeman decides to arrest a suspect, his decision, if properly made, rests on constitutional, legislative, and court authority and has implications not only for policing, but also for the prosecutor, the courts, and corrections.

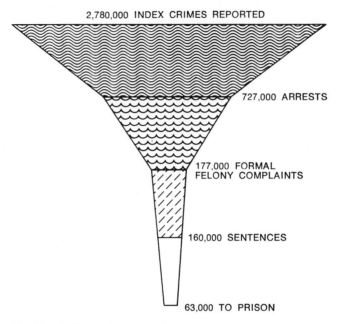

FUNNELING EFFECT FROM REPORTED CRIMES THROUGH PRISON SENTENCE

2,780,000 INDEX CRIMES REPORTED

727,000 ARRESTS

177,000 FORMAL FELONY COMPLAINTS

160,000 SENTENCES

63,000 TO PRISON

President's Commission on Law Enforcement and Administration of Justice, *Task Force Report: Science and Technology* (Washington, D.C.: U.S. Government Printing Office, 1967), p. 61.

Furthermore, the actions of the policeman in making an arrest, the available evidence, the amount of force used, and so on test, and are tested against, principles of propriety, due process, and other constitutional and legislative ideals basic to criminal justice in our society.

Because its processes tie the system together, analysis focused on the flow of operational decisions provides a means of understanding and evaluating criminal justice issues that goes beyond matters of authority structure and agency organizational patterns but that does not diminish their importance. As a system criminal justice can best be seen by what it does, or fails to do, rather than how it is put together. For this reason, the decision network of the system is the basis of analysis in later sections of this book. An overview of the major steps and stages in the process will be given here with relevant laws, policies, and practices fleshed out in subsequent chapters. But even in an overview it is important to note that no single description of the decision network precisely fits all crime categories or is equally applicable in all jurisdictions. For example, the number and forms of specific procedural steps vary depending upon whether a suspect is processed for a felony or a misdemeanor. Furthermore, there are some alternative procedures in different jurisdictions, as, for example, in the use of the grand jury or a preliminary hearing to ratify or reject the initial charging decision of the prosecutor. Also, it must be remembered that not all persons, even within a single jurisdiction and charged with comparable crimes, proceed in uniform fashion through each decision point. Some may be dropped out of processing for a variety of reasons at any step in the process; others may waive certain steps or proceedings. Many suspects "cooperate" in processing by confessing to crimes, waiving counsel and trial, pleading guilty, and accepting without contest or appeal any sentence imposed by the court. Their counterparts may fight processing the whole way by challenging arrest, demanding the state prove its case, and generally putting all decisions to adversary test.

Yet these differences are variations from a core series of procedural decision points that are roughly comparable in all jurisdictions, differing only in alternatives determined by local law or custom. For example, all convicted offenders are sentenced, but the actual sentencing process may vary in details (i.e., jury sentencing, sentencing committees of judges, or in alternatives such as fines, mandatory sentences, or indeterminate sentences) across jurisdictions. However, the core step in the process, sentencing, occurs everywhere as a critical stage in criminal justice processing.

The major steps and decision stages in the criminal justice process chiefly as it applies in felony cases are as follows.

Crime Investigation

In general, the criminal justice process begins when the police are led to believe that a crime has been committed. Police investigation may be initiated by a complaint of a victim, may begin when on routine patrol police observe a crime being committed or a person acting suspiciously, or may start when they decide to look for specific criminal activity which they believe is occurring or about to occur. In the latter instance, investigation may be triggered by a tip from an informer, but often results simply from accumulated police experience with crime conditions in the community. Typically the kinds of offenses involved in go-out-and-look investigations are gambling, prostitution, and other vice crimes. Techniques used by police in investigation include examination of physical evidence left at the scene of a crime, interrogation of suspicious persons, search of persons or premises, electronic eavesdropping including wiretapping, and undercover activities in which police infiltrate criminal conspiracies in order to obtain evidence.[1]

Arrest

Based on interrogation or other investigation, if a police officer accumulates sufficient evidence to cause him to reasonably believe that a crime has been committed by a particular person, he may make an arrest. Arrest involves taking the person into custody; that is, he is no longer free to leave. This usually means that he is transported to a police station where he is *booked* (where the arrest is registered).[2] In instances in which a complainant has identified a perpetrator not yet in custody, the police may obtain an arrest warrant from a judge and make arrest pursuant to the warrant. In practice, however, most arrests are made without warrants and are based on witnessing of offenses being committed, or on reasonable belief of the police officer following his observation and questioning of persons acting suspiciously. In a number of jurisdictions, statutes require that arrests for misdemeanors be made only if they are committed "in view" of the arresting officer, not as with felonies, on "reasonable belief." In some minor violations the police may be permitted to issue a *citation*, which is an order to appear before a judge at a later date, instead of taking the suspect into immediate physical custody. Generally, however, arrest involves taking physical custody; in making a felony arrest an officer may use such force as is necessary to detain and hold the suspect. At booking for felonies and some serious misdemeanors, the suspect is ordinarily fingerprinted, and his prints are sent to the FBI to determine if he is wanted elsewhere for an earlier crime. He may be placed in a police lineup for identification by the victim or witnesses and may be subject to further interrogation. Prior to in-custody interrogation, the police must notify a suspect of his right to remain silent and to have immediate assistance of counsel if he wishes.[3]

Initial Appearance Before a Magistrate

A short time after arrest—usually defined as a *reasonable* time—the suspect must be brought before a magistrate for consideration of bail. With the exception of certain crimes specified in statutes (usually very serious offenses like murder and kidnapping), suspects are eligible for release from custody on reasonable bail. In some jurisdictions, indigent offenders may be released on their own recognizance (their promise to appear at a later date) rather than on a monetary bond if they have a job, a home, and other ties to the community. The purpose of bail and recognizance investigation is to assure appearance at later proceedings.[4]

In certain minor offenses, such as traffic violations, the magistrate may be permitted to conduct a trial or accept a guilty plea at what for other offenders is a bail determination. But in felony cases the magistrate does not require the suspect to plead to charges, nor does he investigate the validity of the arrest. It is important to keep the bail-setting function of the initial appearance in mind, for this proceeding is often confused with a later step in the process, *arraignment,* at which a defendant is requested to plead to formal charges. The confusion is understandable because in a number of jurisdictions the initial appearance is variously called "arraignment on the warrant," "first arraignment," or sometimes simply "arraignment."

Initial Determination of the Charge

Although some suspects may be released by the police after having been taken into custody, in most serious cases the evidence held by the police is forwarded to the prosecuting attorney for the decision whether to charge the suspect with a crime at all, and if so, which statutory violations apply, and with how many counts. The prosecutor's initial task is to translate the fact situation which resulted in the arrest into formal statutory language and to determine whether the evidence held by the police or likely to be accumulated is sufficient to prove all required elements of the offense at trial. The evidentiary standard for a charge to be leveled is *probable cause to believe* that a crime was committed and that the individual committed it.[5] In routine cases the prosecutor does not see or question the suspect; he bases his initial determinations on evidence and records brought to him by the police.

Determination of Formal Charges

If the state's attorney decides to initiate prosecution, the next step is to seek formalization of charges. There are two major ways to do this, depending upon applicable provisions and customary practices in different jurisdictions. One way is to seek an *indictment* (a formal charging document) by presenting the case to a grand jury. Grand juries are available in about half the states and in the federal system, but are used as the exclusive way of bringing felony charges in only a few jurisdictions. A grand jury is composed of 23 members, with 16 required for a working quorum, and an indictment is issued on the affirmative vote of 12 members. Grand jury proceedings are secret with neither the defendant nor his counsel present. The prosecutor appears before the jury, presents his case, and asks for indictment. Members of the jury can ask any questions they wish and may vote to issue an indictment to the charge requested or to some other charge, or may decide not to indict at all. Grand juries honor prosecutors' requests in the great majority of cases.

The most common method of bringing formal charges today is by means of an *information,* a charging document similar to an indictment. Information procedures differ in a number of ways from the grand jury process. The information containing the formal charges he seeks is drafted by the prosecutor and is tested before a magistrate at a *preliminary hearing.* Unlike grand jury proceedings, the preliminary hearing is open to the public and attended by the defendant and his attorney. At this hearing the prosecutor presents some, but not necessarily all, of his evidence in open court. He need reveal only enough of his case to satisfy the judge there is probable cause that the defendant committed a crime and should be held for trial. The defendant may challenge state's evidence through cross-examination of witnesses. Unlike grand jury proceedings, the preliminary hearing may be waived by the defendant with the consent of the state.[6]

Arraignment on Indictment or Information

After indictment or when the defendant is bound over for trial on an information, he is brought before a court of competent jurisdiction, hears the charges read to him, and is asked to plead to them. Pleas available are 1) not guilty; 2) guilty as charged; and in some places, 3) *nolo contendere* (I will not contest it). This latter plea, which is available at the discretion of the judge in about half the states and in the federal jurisdiction, has the same criminal effect as a plea of guilty, but unlike the latter, may not be used in any subsequent civil action as proof that the defendant committed the act. If a defendant stands mute, a not guilty plea is entered for him.

A judge need not accept a guilty plea; before he does he is usually required to address the defendant personally, to officially notify him of his right to trial and to be represented by counsel, to make inquiry as to the "voluntary" nature of the plea, give warning of the possible sentencing consequences of his admission, and generally to determine that the defendant is competent and understands what he is doing. In many places today there is an additional requirement that the judge make some inquiry into the "factual basis" for the plea.[7] A defendant who enters a guilty plea may subsequently decide to withdraw his plea and go to trial by making a motion for withdrawal. Granting such motion is discretionary with the trial court; denial of the motion may be appealed.

In many jurisdictions today *plea bargaining* between prosecutor and the defense is a common practice. This may take place before or after arraignment up to and even during trial. In general, plea bargaining involves negotiation between the prosecutor and the defendant and his lawyer to enter a guilty plea in exchange for state reduction of charges to lesser offenses, or for a prosecutor's promise to "recommend" probation at the time of sentencing.[8] The U.S. Supreme Court recently approved such practices when properly conducted and controlled.[9]

Hearing on Pretrial Motions

In recent years a hearing to consider various pretrial motions has emerged as a distinct step in the process. At this proceeding defendants may enter motions to suppress evidence by alleging it was illegally obtained; may ask for a change of venue (relocation of trial); or may seek to "discover" some of the state's evidence, such as results of ballistic tests or names of witnesses. Trial court denial of such motions may become the basis of appeal.[10]

Trial

The next step in the process for defendants who enter not guilty pleas is trial on the charges contained in the indictment or information. In most places the defendant has an option of a jury trial or a bench trial (a trial before a judge sitting without a jury). The right to a jury trial in felony cases is absolute, but when an offense less than a felony is charged the situation is more variable. Many jurisdictions do not extend the right to jury trial to cases involving petty offenses generally encompassing such crimes as public intoxication, disorderly conduct, other public order crimes, and minor traffic offenses.

Usually, trial procedures are similar with or without a jury. In some places a judge at bench trial is required to file a memorandum in support of his finding of guilt, but juries are not required to give reasons for findings in either direction. Jury decisions to convict can be set aside by the judge if he does not think trial evidence was sufficient. In some cases he may not wait for a jury finding but may direct a verdict of acquittal. However, he cannot set aside a jury finding of not guilty, for this would violate the double jeopardy protections of the Constitution.

Procedures followed at trial are normally tightly circumscribed by constitutions, statutes, court rules, and appellate court decisions. Everywhere proof of a defendant's guilt must be beyond a reasonable doubt, the highest test of proof in the entire process. Conviction must be based only on properly obtained, presented, and interpreted evidence. At trial, evidence of culpability is presented by the prosecution, rebutted by the defense—which need do no more than raise a reasonable doubt of guilt—and appropriate statutory provisions and other instructions as to the meaning of the evidence is presented to the jury by the presiding judge. Following this the jury decides in a closed meeting the guilt or innocence of the defendant. It may find him not guilty or guilty of the crimes charged or of lesser offenses. At this writing most state constitutions require that trial jury verdicts be unanimous, but this provision is in a state of flux following a U.S. Supreme Court decision to the effect that states may allow other than unanimous verdicts.[11] A trial is a "critical stage" of the criminal process, and today defendants have a constitutional right to assistance of counsel. This was not always so, for until the Supreme Court held otherwise in *Gideon* v. *Wainwright*,[12] state jurisdictions were not required to provide counsel to indigent defendants on trial for noncapital charges. Following *Gideon* the right to counsel was expanded to apply to all criminal trials including those for minor offenses.[13] At the discretion of the court and with due warnings, a defendant may waive counsel and represent himself, but this rarely occurs in serious criminal matters.

Appeals and Postconviction Remedies

Convicted defendants may appeal to higher courts. In general, appeals must be instituted within a specified time after conviction and, with the exception of some provisions for automatic appeals, leave to appeal is discretionary with the appellate court. In addition to appeals of conviction, defendants may seek other remedies alleging, for example, inappropriate or improper sentences or treatment in confinement.[14]

The appellate process may ultimately involve the entire hierarchy of state and federal courts, eventually rising to the U.S. Supreme Court. However, before appeals move from state to federal review state remedies generally must be exhausted. Under certain restrictive conditions some states allow appeals to be taken by the prosecution. Usually the state cannot appeal a trial court finding of not guilty because the defendant is protected from retrial by prohibitions against double jeopardy. But in some places the prosecution may appeal controverted issues of law which may settle the legal controversy without consequences for the individual defendant.

Sentencing

After conviction by trial or guilty plea, the defendant is brought before the court for imposition of sentence. Most commonly, sentences are imposed by a trial judge, but there are some variations, depending upon statutory provisions in different jurisdictions. Twelve states provide for jury sentencing in noncapital cases, and in some jurisdictions sentencing councils of three or more judges may confer concerning sentence alternatives.[15]

Sentencing structures vary considerably among different jurisdictions. In some places legislatively fixed sentences for certain crimes allow the judge no discretion in sentencing. In others, certain offenses are designated as nonprobationable, and provisions for completely indeterminate sentences (from one day to life) for sex offenders are not uncommon.[16]

In *most* jurisdictions for *most* offenses, judges have some choice among alternative types and lengths of sentences. For some crimes fines may be imposed, but except for petty offenses these are rarely the sole penalty. For most offenses, misdemeanors and felonies alike, judges have the options of incarcerating offenders in a jail or prison or of placing them on probation. Probation is a sentence served without incarceration, in the community, under supervision of a probation officer, with the offender subject to rules and conditions imposed by the court. Where the decision is to incarcerate, the judge usually has discretion in fixing the minimum and maximum periods of time to be served in custody. In many jurisdictions a judge may impose a maximum prison term of any length under an absolute maximum fixed by statute. Also, he may be able to set a minimum term at no more than some fraction of the maximum, commonly one-third. The *maximum* period of incarceration fixes the time at which the offender must be released from confinement, but the *minimum* sentence merely determines the date at which he becomes eligible for parole. Parole is granted or denied at the discretion of a parole board.[17]

In most jurisdictions today there is an interval between conviction of a felony and the imposition of sentence during which a social worker attached to the court conducts a presentence investigation of the offender. The purpose of this investigation is to gather background material to help the judge select an appropriate sentencing alternative. The scope of the investigation and the contents of the report vary, but in general, the report contains records and reports about the offender (such as his "rap sheet" noting prior arrests and convictions, his employment history, school records, and so on) results of interviews with family and friends and may, if requested by the court, include the investigator's evaluation and analysis of the offender, perhaps with his recommendation as to sentence. Traditionally, such reports were considered confidential, to be read only by the judge and not shared with the defendant or his counsel. But in recent years there has been some relaxing of this rule so that at least partial disclosure of the report is more customary today. Disclosure gives the offender an opportunity to correct any errors, to rebut opinions, and to introduce material in his own behalf at the sentence hearing.[18]

There is considerable variation among jurisdictions in provisions for appellate review of sentences. Death sentences (when this was permissible) often were automatically reviewed, but in most other cases review must be initiated in a manner similar to appeal of convictions. A few states provide special courts or judicial panels to examine the propriety of sentences, but more commonly traditional appellate courts decide sentence controversies.

Conditions of Sentence

An offender sentenced to probation must agree to abide by rules and conditions imposed by the court and to submit to supervision by a probation agency. More or less standard rules found in many jurisdictions include a curfew, prohibition against drinking alcoholic beverages or using them immoderately, forbidding possession of firearms, prohibitions against leaving the community without permission of the probation service, and other restrictions on the probationer's freedom designed to prevent him from committing new offenses. Violation of these rules may result in revocation of probation and incarceration. The probation officer decides whether or not any infraction is serious enough to return the probationer to court and may thus *initiate* revocation at his discretion. However, since offenders on probation remain under control of the court, any formal decision to revoke is made by the judge.

In many places time served on probation *tolls,* that is, does not count toward completion of sentence. Thus an offender sentenced to five years imprisonment who has succeeded in obtaining instead a five-year probation term and who has served three years before revocation may still be incarcerated for the entire five-year period. However, successful completion of probation results in the offender being discharged from sentence.

Persons convicted of misdemeanors are usually confined in a city or county jail to serve sentences up to one year. Some jails have work release programs in which the individual continues his regular employment during the day but spends nights and weekends in lockup; however this is comparatively rare. Usually jail inmates are idle during their entire stay. Persons incarcerated for felonies are sent to state or federal prisons. In the past judges specified a particular prison, but today sentences are commonly directed to a department of correctional services, and the prisoner is sent to a reception center or a receiving institution to be classified and transferred to an appropriate correctional facility. Felony offenders generally begin their sentences in maximum-security prisons, walled facilities with gun turrets on the perimeter and prisoners housed in interior cell blocks. Control over the prisoner is virtually absolute. His time is divided between lockup in his cell and work in a prison industry that produces goods for state use. Today, in addition to maximum-security prisons, many correctional systems have medium- and minimum-security facilities to which low escape-risk prisoners may be transferred. Medium-security institutions are fenced rather than walled, and may have rooms instead of cells. Typically they have better education programs than do maximum-security prisons, and their industries may be more modern and oriented to outside employment opportunities. Minimum-security facilities are often prison farms or forestry camps, which are small and have no perimeter security. Young adult felons are often sent to reformatories which resemble prisons structurally but have more comprehensive educational and vocational training programs. Reformatory is sometimes taken to mean a place of confinement for juvenile delinquents, but this is technically incorrect. Delinquents are housed in training schools while reformatories hold young felons, generally those in the 18 to 21 year age group.[19]

Prison inmates are almost totally isolated from normal community contacts. Visits from approved family members are usually allowed but are severely circumscribed. Letters may be written and received, but traditionally outgoing and incoming mail is censored. Prisoners are subject to search without specific probable cause, cannot vote, and may be compelled to comply with a wide assortment of restrictions on personal freedom ranging from choice of clothing to physical movement within the institution. Maximum-security prisons maintain so-called segregation units for inmates who violate prison rules and regulations. Offenders are held in solitary confinement for various periods of time depending upon the seriousness of their infractions.

Release from Incarceration

Misdemeanant prisoners generally have *flat* sentences with no latitude between minimum and maximum time. Therefore, they remain in jail for the full time specified by the court. Incarcerated felons, however, usually have a minimum and a maximum sentence, and most inmates obtain release at a point between these dates. Release from incarceration may come in a number of ways: 1) upon completion of maximum sentence, 2) on parole, 3) at a mandatory release date, usually the maximum less time off for good behavior or 4) by pardon. Today most prisoners are released by parole.[20] Eligibility for parole depends upon completion of the minimum sentence, but release is discretionary with a parole board. Upon parole the inmate is released to community supervision and subject to rules and conditions similar to those provided for probationers. Length of supervision is determined by time remaining on the maximum sentence, and on successful completion of this period, parolees are discharged from sentence.

113

Revocation

Offenders on probation and inmates on parole or mandatory release are subject to supervision by field agents and must agree to abide by various rules and conditions of community supervision. Rule violation or the commission of a new crime makes him subject to revocation with subsequent incarceration. Revocation is a discretionary decision initiated by the supervising probation or parole agent and is not automatic. In the case of probationers who are still under court custody, the offender is returned to court for a revocation hearing. If the judge finds no infraction or if he feels the violation is a minor one, he may return the offender to probationer status. If violation is found and considered serious, the judge may impose a prison sentence or order execution of the earlier suspended sentence.

Parolees and inmates on mandatory release are under jurisdiction of a parole board rather than a local court. If an infraction is discovered by a parole officer and considered serious, he may order the parolee held in a local jail while he reports to his superiors and to the parole board. Parole revocation generally involves two steps: an initial fact-finding hearing at the site of the alleged violation which determines the weight of the evidence, and a later hearing before members of the parole board to decide whether, considering all circumstances, revocation is justified. A revoked parolee who is returned to prison begins to accumulate good time and will again become eligible for parole at a date fixed by the board at his revocation.

Most jurisdictions have statutory provisions for "time off for good behavior," which may be earned simply to serving time without getting in trouble. In some places a prisoner may accumulate a number of days of good time for every month served; others have sliding scales which allow prisoners with very long sentences to earn as much as six months good time for every year served after they have been in prison five or more years. Accumulated good time fixes a mandatory release date on which the prisoner is freed, but in many places he remains under supervision until expiration of his maximum term. Prisoners on such mandatory release may be revoked just like parolees.

The President of the United States and all governors have authority to pardon prisoners or to commute sentences, making prisoners eligible for parole at an earlier date. In general, pardon is not commonly used, although in a few jurisdictions, particularly where juries impose long sentences, pardons and commutations are somewhat more frequent.

114

Discharge from Sentence

The formal criminal justice process ends when an offender has successfully completed his sentence, whether in jail, on probation, in prison, or on parole or mandatory release. A number of jurisdictions have provisions for early discharge from sentence for offenders who have made exceptionally good adjustment under community supervision for a period of years.

Though the process ends when the offender is released from state control, the record of conviction and sentence remains, and collateral effects may continue throughout the life of the ex-offender. In most jurisdictions persons convicted of a felony lose a number of rights, ranging from eligibility to vote to ability to obtain licenses and to enter certain occupations and professions. Today some jurisdictions have procedures for restoration of rights, under which the ex-offender may apply to a court for restoration, commonly five years after discharge from sentence. In some places there are procedures for "expunging" records of youthful offenders who have successfully completed sentence and remain law-abiding for a period of time. Restoration or expungement procedures are variable and their success has been limited. Some negative aspects of conviction and sentence may be diminished, but the stigma of having been a prisoner tends to persist.

APPROACHES TO CRIMINAL JUSTICE ANALYSIS

The many facets of the criminal justice system pose such diverse issues that systematic analysis must proceed from rather well-defined reference points. The system might be described from any one or a combination of perspectives: analysis of its structure, the roles of participants, its decision stages, the common practices or policies of agencies, or the mandates and restraints of legislation and court decisions. The focus of any analysis will vary, depending upon what questions or issues are seen to be important, and any particular focus will largely predetermine the breadth of proposals for improvement or reform. If, for example, analysis centers on roles of actors in the process, matters such as the selection and training of judges or parole officers become paramount. But if analysis emphasizes procedural law at decision points, the evaluation will be dominated by issues such as state-federal relationships, trends in appellate court decisions, and the nature and extent of controls on decision processes.

Each analytic approach has its particular merit. However, it is important to note that the system must be viewed as a whole no matter what basis is chosen for analysis. Evaluation of only a single agency or decision point will provide

115

at best only fragmentary information about criminal justice; at worst, it may distort the overall aims and objectives of crime control. At the same time it is recognized that broad, total systems analysis cannot be completed quickly or easily, and that the number of variations in operations will receive only cursory attention.

Literature on various aspects of criminal justice ranges from compilations of procedural law to research studies of agency practices. An attempt to bring all such information together into a small collection would be nearly impossible because of its vast bulk and infinite detail. Here, we will merely identify some general approaches to analysis which will be utilized to explore the decision network of the process in subsequent chapters.

Criminal Procedure: Statutes and Case Law

One means of dealing with the criminal justice system is the study of procedural law relating to each decision point, from police investigation of crimes, to parole and discharge from sentence. This requires some familiarity with relevant legislation and appellate court decisions, not necessarily to "know" the law, for it constantly changes, but to gain understanding of legislative and jurisprudential approaches to criminal justice issues. There are, of course, discrete bodies of procedural law for each of the 50 states and for the federal jurisdiction. Up-to-date knowledge of all state and federal variations is really unnecessary for an overview of the system. It is more important to become familiar with legislative principles, with the way appellate courts decide issues, with the application of federal constitutional protections to state jurisdictions, with the limits of statutory law and case decisions, and with major current developments and trends in procedural law.

This is essentially the approach taken by legal scholars. There are a number of very good casebooks on criminal procedure, usually with annual supplements containing new legislative proposals and recent court decisions.[21] There are also collections of model laws and standards with commentaries that provide careful analysis of current issues in procedural law and offer suggestions for their resolution.[22] Such material is widely used in legal education, but also provides valuable reference for any student of criminal justice administration.

Analysis of the system based primarily on statutes and court decisions has the advantage of highlighting issues that are current and controversial, for the basis of appellate court intervention is litigation of actual disputes and challenges. However, too close study of unusual practices and policies that often become the basis for litigation may distort the view of more common practices and routines. Yet while it is commonly accepted that bad cases make bad law, the analysis of

116

laws and court decisions remains the only sure route to the ideological boundaries of the system. Even though thousands of persons are processed through the criminal justice system without challenge and dispute—without even a trial— it is fundamentally a *legal* system with the principles of procedural law forming its parameters.

No approach to criminal justice analysis can ignore statutes and court decisions if it is to prove of value. Detailed descriptions of daily police practices or prison procedures are important, but for full evaluation they must be referred to applicable laws and court holdings. Furthermore, major changes in criminal justice processing come more often from new laws and case holdings than from alterations in practices or changes in personnel requirements. Laws and appellate court interpretations of laws enable all criminal justice agencies to act, and restrain them as well. In short, no matter what other perspectives are applied in criminal justice analysis, some familiarity with procedural laws and principles is a fundamental prerequisite.

Agency Practices

Another significant analytic approach necessitates systematic study of day-by-day practices of police, prosecutors, judges, correctional personnel, defense counsel, and other participants in the criminal justice process. Most meaningful when combined with discussion of relevant procedural law, this approach is essentially descriptive of various ways agency functionaries exercise discretion in applying whatever their formal authority. It seeks to determine the criteria applied by police officers in investigating crimes and apprehending suspects, to analyze the charging practices of the prosecutor, including his role in negotiating for guilty pleas, to study the dismissal and sentencing practices of judges, and so on. While primary concern is the operation of the system in routine cases, attention is also given to deviations from normal practices.

Why a police officer stops and frisks a particular person and not another, or why a judge sentences one man to prison and puts another on probation—these and similar discretionary choices are no less criminal justice administration than are statutes and appellate court holdings authorizing such decisions.

Occasionally in combination, three major methods are used to analyze practices. One technique involves measuring discretionary alternatives. In its simplest form, tabulations are made at the major decision stages of the process. How many persons are stopped and questioned by the police? How many persons are arrested? For what crimes? How many suspects are indicted? Convicted? Sent to prison? As mentioned earlier, a more elaborate form of measurement is *cohort analysis,* which involves starting with a sample of persons at a specific point—

117

all citizens questioned by police in a given time period, for example—and tracking these individuals as they flow through the system or are dropped or diverted from it. Currently there is strong interest in this type of measurement because it permits computer technology and other techniques of systems analysis to be applied to the criminal justice process.[23] Such statistical assessment of the daily business of criminal justice administration is invaluable in forecasting and planning allocation of resources, in providing baseline measures for later evaluations of effectiveness, in highlighting such problems as court backlog and delay, and for the myriad other uses of accurate statistical data. Measurement of decision alternatives alone provides little understanding of the *reasons* for discretion, though statistics amply demonstrate its existence and pervasiveness across the entire process.

Another technique of analyzing practice is less concerned with counting discretionary choices than with describing their range and identifying reasons for variations. This approach was used in a comprehensive study conducted by the American Bar Foundation (the research wing of the American Bar Association) which was begun in the 1950s, but completed in 1970. Field teams of observers were placed in police departments, prosecutors' offices, courts, and correctional agencies in both urban and rural settings in three states—Kansas, Michigan and Wisconsin—to record practices and to determine by interviews as well as by observation the various purposes and objectives of the exercise of discretion. The results of this survey are reported in five books, one dealing with crime investigation by police,[24] another with arrest practices,[25] a third with prosecutorial discretion,[26] a fourth concentrating on the guilty plea process in adjudication,[27] and the last focusing on sentencing and parole.[28] These studies are essentially descriptive and analytical rather than statistical. They are not evaluative in the sense of assessing the effectiveness of variations in practice, but they do relate practice to both statutory and case law of the jurisdictions involved.

In addition to the American Bar Foundation study, there are numerous other studies of daily practice and discretion, many dealing with only one agency or decision point. For example, jury behavior has been studied,[29] and both police[30] and correctional decisions have been analyzed in numerous research projects.[31] A presidential crime commission surveyed criminal justice agencies and practices in the 1960s and reported its findings in a series of task force reports covering all of the major agencies and decision points of the process.[32] These reports are particularly valuable because they include assessments of manpower and other resources, while providing statistical descriptions of the crime control problem and highlighting the major decision network.

A third variation in this general approach of studying routine criminal justice processing is evaluative. Here the focus is on assessment of the effectiveness of decisions, whether of police, courts, or correctional agencies, and its literature consists of discrete studies of agencies or decision points. Because corrections in particular has often made effectiveness claims, many studies have evaluated correctional processing. In recent years the federal correctional system was thoroughly studied,[33] and there have been numerous evaluations of prisons.[34] Various techniques of parole prediction and evaluation of parole board decisions have been standard fare for decades.[35] In addition, various police practices[36] and sentencing decisions of judges[37] have also been subjected to evaluative research.

This analysis of day-by-day practices in criminal justice administration, whether statistical, descriptive, evaluative, or all of these, is an important approach to understanding the system. Together with information about relevant procedural law, such research studies provide a comprehensive picture of the way the criminal justice process works and changes. However, there are additional ways of looking at the system which have independent merit.

Models and Styles

In dealing with a mass of information about any phenomenon, the social scientist, like his physical scientist counterpart, attempts to order the material so that general statements about it may be made. The same is true for criminal justice. This approach has the advantage of providing overviews of the system without becoming lost in the myriad details of its parts.

One such technique applies various "models" of processing to the entire system, with the effect of highlighting different issues as models are changed. For example, Professor Herbert L. Packer suggests that two models, differing in operational significance, simultaneously apply to criminal justice processing: the *Crime Control Model* and the *Due Process Model*.[38] The former pictures the system as essentially geared to effective and efficient apprehension and processing of guilty persons.

Professor Packer comments:

The value system that underlies the Crime Control Model is based on the proposition that the repression of criminal conduct is by far the most important function to be performed by the criminal process. The failure of law enforcement to bring criminal conduct under tight control is viewed as leading to the breakdown of public order and thence to the disappearance of an important condition of human freedom. . . .

The model, in order to operate successfully must produce a high rate of apprehension and conviction, and must do so in a context where the magni-

119

tudes being dealt with are very large and the resources for dealing with them are very limited. There must be a premium on speed and finality. Speed, in turn, depends upon informality and on uniformity; finality depends on minimizing the occasions for challenge. . . . The image that comes to mind is an assembly-line conveyor belt down which moves an endless stream of cases, never stopping, carrying the cases to workers who stand at fixed stations and who perform on each case as it comes by the same small but essential operation that brings it one step closer to being . . . a closed file. The criminal process, in this model, is seen as a screening process in which each successive stage— prearrest investigation, arrest, post-arrest investigation, preparation for trial, trial or entry of plea, conviction, disposition—involves a series of routinized operations whose success is gauged primarily by their tendency to pass the case along to a successful conclusion.[39]

This model is indeed an accurate description of how criminal justice processing operates in the great bulk of cases where arrested persons proceed, without challenge or trial, from police intake to corrections. Packer correctly points out that this model rests on a presumption of guilt, not as a judicial norm, but as an operational prediction of outcome.[40]

Paradoxically, the system can be viewed from a due process perspective at the same time. Packer explains:

If the Crime Control Model resembles an assembly line, the Due Process Model looks very much like an obstacle course. Each of its successive stages is designed to present formidable impediments to carrying the accused any further along in the process. . . . (This model rests on) an insistence on formal, adjudicative, adversary factfinding processes in which the factual case against the accused is publicly heard by an impartial tribunal and is evaluated only after the accused has had a full opportunity to discredit the case against him.[41]

This perception of the criminal process is also correct, though less frequently experienced in practice. The models do not differ in their ultimate objective— the repression of crime—but in their methods of implementation and in the kinds of issues and short-range objectives that are seen as important. Are they simply alternative ways of processing cases? Packer believes the differences between them to be more fundamental, involving a basic conflict between a desire for efficiency and an ideology stressing the "primacy of the individual and the complementary concept of limitation on official power."[42]

John Griffiths suggests a third model of the process, a *Family Model*.[43] Viewing both of Packer's models as variations on one *Combat Model*, Griffiths minimizes punishment objectives of the process, dealing with the concept of criminal not as a special classification of persons different from the rest of us, but simply as persons who happen to be exposed to the criminal process.[44] He comments:

(W)e might expect more appreciation under a Family Model that one great advantage of the criminal law is the way it minimizes social intervention by limiting such intervention to situations in which an individual has failed to exercise the required self-control.[45]

A family analogy is used to explain:

Offenses, in a family, are normal, expected occurrences. Punishment is not something a child receives in isolation from the rest of his relationship to the family; nor is it something which presupposes or carries with it a change of status from "child" to "criminal child." When a parent punishes his child, both parent and child know that afterward they will go on living together as before.[46]

Essentially Griffiths' model building is less descriptive of what is than of what might be. He attempts to set the overall purposes of the criminal process within the cultural context of the family, relating them to the temporary interventions associated with child rearing.

(N)o list of the justifications for criminal prohibitions and punishments necessarily gives us the sum total of the substantive functions which should determine the shape of the criminal process. By contrast to the Battle Model, it is central to the Family Model that the function of the process involves far more than suppressing certain offenses.[47]

While the application of models to the criminal process has the advantages of broad conceptualization of the total system, there is a danger of overgeneralization. Packer warns:

There is a risk in an enterprise of this sort that is latent in any attempt to polarize. It is, simply, that values are too various to be pinned down to yes-or-no answers. The models are distortions of reality. And, since they are normative in character, there is a danger of seeing one or the other as Good or Bad . . . The attempt . . . is primarily to clarify the terms of discussion by isolating the assumptions that underlie competing policy claims and examining the conclusions that those claims, if fully accepted, would lead to.[48]

In addition to these techniques, a related approach involves analysis of criminal justice issues by isolating and contrasting *styles* of managerial behavior within criminal justice agencies. This is a form of typological assessment similar to the technique used by criminologists to differentiate types of offenders, such as the occasional property offender, the white-collar violator, the professional criminal, and others, with the focus instead on participants in the criminal process or on entire agencies. Based on observation and other research tech-

121

niques, the question is whether significant clusters of behavioral patterns can be separated and used to account for such differences as variations in enforcement practice among police departments, varieties of sentencing determinations among judges, differential parole board decisions, and so on. As with the application of models, style typology is an attempt at generalization; individual characteristics and actions are relevant only as they fall within some collective pattern.

There is a considerable body of research demonstrating the existence and importance of managerial styles as they relate to industry and commerce,[49] and many of the measurement techniques developed in industrial management are currently being applied in modified form to criminal justice administration.[50]

We will not attempt here to describe all typological research in criminal justice, but will confine ourselves to brief descriptions of a few studies to illustrate this general approach. On the basis of study of police behavior in eight New York communities, James Q. Wilson extracted three major police enforcement styles which accounted for significant differences in enforcement methods and patterns.[51] *Watchman* police agencies are primarily concerned with keeping order in the community, rather than with vigorous law enforcement; *legalistic* departments go by the book, issuing many traffic citations, detaining juveniles, and in general using arrest and detention powers vigorously, while *service* departments are omnipresent, intervening frequently to settle and otherwise assist in disputes, acting informally, off-the-record, and arresting only as a last resort.[52] Wilson related police styles to types of communities (i.e., service departments are often found in homogenous, middle-class communities) to department organizational patterns, leadership, and the political context of the communities.[53] For example, watchmen police exist in communities "led by politicians who appeal to a predominately working-class and lower-middle-class constituency on the basis of personal loyalty, ethnic identification, the exchange of favors, personal acquaintanceships, and the maintenance of a low tax rate."[54]

The way participants within an agency fulfill their roles is a variation on typing agency styles. For example, Lloyd Ohlin, Herman Piven, and Don Pappenfort identify three major types of probation and parole field agents: *punitive* officers who attempt to coerce their charges into conformity with middle-class moral standards; *protective* officers who vacillate between protecting the offender from situations which might lead to new crimes and threatening revocation to protect the community; and *welfare* officers, whose primary goal is the improved adjustment of offenders in their charge.[55] Daniel Glaser and his associates found similar classes among parole officers where different categories corresponded to the performance of parole supervision practices; that is, punitive officers place heavy emphasis on control and shun assisting offenders to adjust, while welfare officers do the opposite.[56]

In a similar fashion but involving the typing of entire organizations, Vincent O'Leary and David Duffee have identified four major models of correctional policies that determine the emphasis correctional agencies give to changing offenders, in contrast to changing opportunities for offender reintegration back into the community. *Reform* correctional organizations are oriented primarily to community protection with prison systems designed to instill "good habits" in inmates; *rehabilitative* organizations seek to change the personality characteristics of offenders by clinical interventions; *restraint* organizations simply hold offenders, stressing security from escape; while *reintegration* organizations seek to merge correctional agencies with community resources, stressing the necessity of on-the-street adjustment of offenders.[57]

There are many other techniques and approaches to typology and classification of criminal justice agencies and participants. John Hogarth, for example, attempts to account for sentencing differentials by measuring judicial attitudes and beliefs toward a wide variety of issues.[58] There have also been a number of studies of prison "communities" corresponding to criminological typology of offenders which produced typologies in terms of prisoner-keeper relationships.[59]

Recurrent Themes

Still another way of approaching criminal justice analysis is by identifying issues that are pervasive across the criminal justice process—issues that are commonly considered police, court, or correctional matters, but that actually arise at various decision points. For example, search is ordinarily thought to be a police technique and corresponding issues, such as the propriety of searches, evidentiary requirements, search warrants, or consent of persons searched, are assumed to be matters of police concern. Yet both search and its attendant issues arise elsewhere. Prisoners are subject to search, as are probationers and parolees. Though rarely addressed as a parole issue, questions of when, how, and under what conditions a parolee may be searched or have his premises searched by a parole officer is a concern at this postconviction stage of the process.

Recurring issues, or *themes* interwoven across the process, are not limited to techniques like search or interrogation, but may be phrased in more abstract terms. For example, *time* is a recurrent theme which assumes importance in a variety of ways. Requirement for initial appearance within a reasonable interval after arrest is a time issue. So is speedy trial, and, of course, sentences and parole or mandatory release dates are basically time concerns. The dimensions of issues alter as contexts change, but the isolation of pervasive themes does offer

123

an overall perspective of the criminal justice process that ties its various decision stages more closely together.

One current approach to criminal justice analysis utilizes five major analytical themes, each pervasive across the system:[60]

1. EVIDENCE SUFFICIENCY. The criminal justice process begins and proceeds on the basis of standards of evidence of wrongdoing. Police must have evidence to support *reasonable grounds* for arrest, charging rests on *probable cause,* and conviction at trial can be had only if the state proves its case *beyond a reasonable doubt.* The so-called evidentiary profile of the process does not end with conviction, but continues as a *criterion* for probation or incarceration, conditions of sentence, parole, and revocation. In short, evidence is an issue of recurring and pervasive concern at all criminal justice decision points. Without sufficient evidence, decisions become arbitrary or capricious and therefore improper in our system of justice.

2. CONSENT. The cooperation and consent of persons processed is another recurring theme of great operational significance. Consent takes a number of forms, including confessions to the police, waivers of preliminary hearings, guilty pleas, and agreements to abide by conditions of probation or parole. In effect, consent and waiver tend to nullify requirements for other, objective evidence, and become dominant themes in routine processing.

3. FAIRNESS AND PROPRIETY OF PROCEDURES. Another recurring issue has to do with the proper form of state intervention. As has been pointed out:

Our political ideology demands that justice be viewed from the standpoint of fair dealing with suspects, defendants and convicted criminals, and that methods of detection, apprehension, processing and treatment be fitting for our era and cultural heritage. There are, therefore, limits on the methods and techniques used to control crime. The end does not justify every means.[61]

4. THE EFFECTIVENESS AND EFFICIENCY OF CRIMINAL JUSTICE PRACTICES. Although not paramount factors in our democratic ideology, the cost, utilization of resources, and consequences of all criminal justice decisions are issues that continually arise. Within limits of propriety and with due attention to matters of evidence, we wish law enforcement, courts, and prisons to be as efficient as possible and to achieve what they set out to accomplish, whether solving crimes, deterring violators, or rehabilitating prisoners.

5. DISCRETION. The power and the need for participants in criminal justice processing to choose among alternative actions is, of course, a theme running from the earliest stages of police intervention to parole revocation. The exercise of discretion, and the effectiveness of controls on this discretion, is an analytical theme of primary importance.

Thematic analysis is a particularly valuable approach to understanding criminal justice processing, for it provides a bridge between the formal requirements of procedural law and the routine practices of agencies. The themes of evidence and propriety are most clearly reflected in case law and in statutes. Discretion and consent, though also eliciting court and legislative comment, are most clearly demonstrated by studies of operational policies and practices, while efficiency and effectiveness are illustrated in both places and also in behavioral and political science assessments.

ANALYSIS OF DOMINANT FUNCTIONS

Each of these various approaches is useful and can be of great help in any attempt to analyze and understand criminal justice administration. As the decision network of the process is tracked in subsequent chapters, questions from each of these approaches can be put not only to each major decision stage, but across them as well. The law of arrest, that is, cases and statutes, should be studied not as an end in itself, but rather in its relation to variations in actual arrest practices. Questions of evidence sufficiency at arrest should be compared and contrasted with evidentiary requirements elsewhere. In turn, the gathering of evidence, whether by police prior to arrest, or by a social worker conducting a presentence investigation, should be tested against standards of propriety. The details of each decision point should not dominate inquiry; common themes and models should be extracted and applied to give a sense of the overall functioning of the process. And it must be remembered that the study of criminal justice processing is not simply an intellectual exercise, and that the process is not an abstract problem, but is rather a set of decisions made by men which profoundly affect other men. It always operates within the context of community norms and expectations and its shape and form are determined significantly by the beliefs and styles of persons and the history of agencies.

In addition to the approaches already considered, another set of analytical perspectives relates to pervasive *functions* of the system. As pointed out earlier, the complexity of criminal justice processing is compounded by the fact that the system has multiple purposes. While its principal objective is to control crime and to maintain or restore public order, the system rests on a set of multiple and occasionally conflicting beliefs and expectations of how this is best achieved. Some of these expectations, such as control through punishment of violators, are ancient in origin, dating from the earliest conceptions of ordered society and

125

drawing philosophic justification from ideas about the nature of man, sin, and repentance. Others, such as the rehabilitation of offenders, are latter-day products of social science, stemming from more modern concepts of behavior, personality, and change. Still others, such as the accurate and fair separation of guilty from innocent, emanate from our democratic political ideology which stresses individual liberty, curbs on state power, and proper and humane treatment of even the worst among us.

Whether ancient or modern, whether rooted in beliefs about human behavior or in political principles, a variety of expectations about crime control permeates the structure and the process of the criminal justice system. These expectations ebb and flow in their relative importance as times and philosophies change, but all exist simultaneously, coloring all decisions from the drafting and enacting of statutes to parole revocation.

The fact that there are multiple expectations to crime control efforts has long been recognized. So too the paradoxical nature of some expectations, such as punishing offenders while desiring to rehabilitate them, has for many years generated comment and debate. But generally it is only at selected decision points that the historical and contemporary purposes of criminal processing have been seen as *operationally* significant. Punishment, for example, is commonly viewed as a relevant function (not necessarily a good one) at sentencing and as a condition of imprisonment. Decisions of the prosecutor or the judge at the trial are not commonly perceived in punitive terms. Likewise, the primary locus of rehabilitation is ordinarily assumed to be found in probation services and other correctional agencies. Yet is can be questioned whether preconviction stages serve a punitive as well as a fact-finding function and whether police determinations have rehabilitative significance. In brief, another way of analyzing the interlocking decisions of the criminal justice process is by perception of each decision point as it relates to and is colored by the different purposes assigned to crime control efforts. These various goals and purposes become functional imperatives in the daily operation of the system. Some major categories useful for functional analysis include the following.

The Punitive Function

There is little doubt that punishment of violators is an important purpose of the criminal justice process. The *punitive ideal*, though the most ancient approach to crime control, is still a force of major significance. In some degree punishment is an end in itself, for our moral sources support an eye-for-an-eye concept of justice. But the punitive aspects of our crime control system are also designed to compel conformity by conditioning violators to conforming behavior through imposition of sentence sanctions. And in a related though separate purpose, punishment is intended to deter potential violators by demonstrating that crime does not pay.

The application of punishment to law violators in proportion to the seriousness of their offenses is, of course, the cornerstone of criminal codes and sentencing structures. Beyond this, however, the punitive theme runs through all of the determinations of the criminal process, coloring the perceptions of all participants, including suspects and defendants as well as agency personnel, and even reflecting its influence in uniforms, accoutrements, and physical settings. At a minimum, the criminal justice process is designed to be stern and unpleasant; at its extreme, it is frankly punitive. Though punitiveness may be muted by competing objectives, there is no pretense, official or otherwise, that the system is designed to further the best interests of those processed. This contrasts sharply with the underlying philosophies of other systems where state power is employed to compel conformity, as in public schooling, hospital commitment of the mentally ill, or interventions with juvenile delinquents. From start to finish, the criminal process is "the state *versus* John Doe," not as in delinquency processing, "the state *in the interest* of Johnny Doe."

The punitive aura is pervasive throughout the process. It accounts in part for police behavior which is typically far from friendly, even when correct, once the process is invoked. It is reflected in the prosecutor's need for convictions to maintain community support. It is visible in emotionally cool, stern, and formal court proceedings. It is epitomized by prisons. The punitive function of the criminal justice system not only has a long tradition, but even today it is never far from the surface at any decision point or in any program. Attempts to change criminal processing inevitably confront punishment requirements. Early advocates of probation and parole achieved their objectives by demonstrating lower cost and greater effectiveness, but they also had to argue strongly that community sentences were indeed punishment. And modern correctional facilities, unwalled and without bars or cells, have been accepted slowly and grudgingly for fear they would diminish the punitive purposes of walled and turreted maximum-security prisons.

The Deterrent Function

A desire to use the criminal process in ways that deter others from committing crimes is closely tied to the punitive ideal. As might be expected, making examples of those caught and proved guilty is widely believed to be effective in achieving this purpose. This is a basic argument of those favoring severe sentences, including the death penalty.

127

However, deterrence has a broader base. The imminence of arrest and conviction may also deter; the *show* of force may accomplish conformity equally as well or better than the *use* of force. Consequently, many practices in all types of agencies are influenced in some degree by deterrent objectives. The omnipresence of police on patrol, the secrecy of grand juries and the public nature of trials, sentence pronouncement of judges, and the visibility of prisons and other correctional agencies not only display the punitive nature of the system, but demonstrate its readiness to act.

While some attempts are made in practice to *individualize* justice by fitting the consequences of intervention to the characteristics and circumstances of the individual being processed, more routinely what action is taken in a particular case is determined in part by its probable effect on others or, more abstractly, by how it may affect a general "respect for the law." In situations where he is unobserved, a police officer may release a suspect with a reprimand; in similar situations but faced with an observing crowd, he may feel compelled to make an arrest. Sentences meted in high publicity cases tend to be more severe than otherwise. Wherever and whenever decisions about a suspect, defendant, or offender are partly based on considerations of the likely effect of different alternatives on others, including the "public," the deterrent function is being served.

The Community Protection Function

There is a general expectation that the criminal justice process will protect the community from continued depravations of criminals and, for that matter, will offer protection from those suspected of being criminals. To accomplish this, authorities are permitted to take physical custody of suspects as well as offenders and restrain them, subject to legislative and court limitations and controls. The ultimate power of restraint is symbolized by maximum-security incarceration of convicted felons. In fact, a primary purpose of imprisonment is restraint and incapacitation of offenders to protect the community, an objective that most prisons achieve very well indeed. This is often overlooked when prisons are labelled as failures because they do not successfully rehabilitate many of their charges.

Custody and restraint for community protection is not limited to imprisonment and other postconviction processes. It is an important function from the very outset of the process. Police may arrest one suspect at gunpoint, handcuff him, and hold him in close detention until his bail hearing. Another suspect may be arrested without use of any force or hardware, experiencing little physical custody. Often high bail and always preventive detention reflect the community protection function. It may also be relevant to the charging decision; certainly community protection is a consideration in plea negotiation. Sentencing alternatives directly reflect this function, and it is a major factor in determining probation conditions, prison program and housing assignments, and selection for parole and revocation. The entire correctional process rests always on a balance between the needs and desires of the offender and concerns for community protection, even in systems giving high priority to remedial and rehabilitative programs.

The Corrective Function

It is generally expected that the criminal justice process will somehow reform or rehabilitate those caught up in it, or at least will not make them worse. It is recognized that virtually all persons who are processed, even those convicted and sentenced to life imprisonment, eventually return to community living. Thus it behooves participants and agencies to take actions designed to enable their charges to live law-abiding lives once they are discharged or diverted from the process. Some argue that this may be accomplished by conditioning individuals through punishment to avoid the unpleasant consequences of criminal activity much as animals can be conditioned to avoid painful stimuli. More commonly today, agencies attempt to provide positive programs designed to *rehabilitate* prison inmates by changing their attitudes and teaching them new vocational skills and work to *reintegrate* offenders by assisting them to adjust to normal community living.

Although the corrective mandate has traditionally been assigned specifically to postconviction agencies like prisons and probation and parole field services, there is increasing awareness that all stages of criminal justice intervention have relevance to the corrective function. In this respect the police are seen as an intake agency, making a wide range of decisions within their discretion that have long-range effect on the fate and conduct of persons with whom they have contact. For example, the way an arrest is made, the amount of force used, police behavior toward the suspect, and so on may influence his self-conception so as to harden criminal attitudes, or have the opposite and more desirable effect of creating respect for the police and, more generally, for the legal process. Police diversion of suspects to community treatment resources rather than arrest of them is seen as a significant corrective decision by many observers. While the police rarely think of themselves as social workers, the basic nature of their operations is increasingly seen—by the police as well as others—as critical to the overall objectives of rehabilitation and reintegration.

In the same manner, the discretion of the prosecutor to select among charges,

129

or to divert and not charge at all, may be exercised with corrective purposes in mind. A basic motivation in plea negotiation is to individualize the consequences of conviction, rather than simply to avoid trial. And a trial itself may have corrective relevance. An opportunity to be heard, a day in court, a fair hearing have purposes beyond fact finding, perhaps acting to dispel cynicism and the belief in "railroading" not uncommonly expressed by offenders hurried through a guilty plea at a brief arraignment. Sentencing discretion is often delegated to courts in the expectation that the judge's choice will not only satisfy the punitive ideal, but serve a corrective function as well.

Perhaps more than others the corrective function ties together the discrete stages of the criminal justice process. From the perspective of this function it can be seen that decisions made at one point have relevance elsewhere, and that any overall function is ultimately served by the degree of congruence of all decisions.

The Due Process Function

An objective of a different but equally important order is that the criminal justice process operate in a manner consistent with basic tenets of our political ideology. Among other requirements, there is a demand for accurate procedures for separating those guilty of crimes from those who are innocent. Standards for the amount of evidence necessary before the process can be invoked or continued are set in statutes and case law, and such evidence must be obtained in proper ways. There is concern for the balance of advantage between state and accused in adversary proceedings so that inequalities of wealth and social standing among persons processed are minimized. Thus this due process function is manifest in numerous ways, from express evidence standards and formal requirements for adversary proceedings, to provisions for defense counsel to assist both affluent and indigent defendants at critical stages of the process. Statutes and appellate court decisions define and control this function, curbing the discretion of all participants and operational agencies. In these ways, due process honors our ideals of fairness, procedural regularity, requirements of proof, and humane treatment. It acts to distinguish our system of justice from others and provides internal checks and balances on the other functions.

Other functions could be isolated and used in analysis, for notions about the purposes of criminal justice intervention have few limits or bounds. For example, a case could be made that providing general information about the crime problem and the way we meet it is yet another function. Hence we demand records and reports, public trials, media access to processes and decisions, and insist on an open, nonsecret process. And, of course, an efficiency function can be extracted, for the cost and effectiveness of crime control efforts is of concern to all. However long the list, it is important to recognize that all functions coexist and have simultaneous operational significance, each in its fashion influencing every decision stage. The fact that some functions seem to be incompatible with others accounts for many of the tensions and conflicts that characterize all crime control efforts, often presenting obstacles to implementation of programs of change or reform.

NOTES

1. See generally, Lawrence P. Tiffany, Donald M. McIntyre, Jr., and Daniel Rotenberg, *Detection of Crime* (Boston: Little, Brown, 1967).

2. See generally Wayne R. LaFave, *Arrest: The Decision to Take a Suspect into Custody* (Boston: Little, Brown, 1965).

3. Miranda v. Arizona, 384 U.S. 436 (1966).

4. See Livingston Hall, Yale Kamisar, Wayne R. LaFave, and Jerold Israel, *Modern Criminal Procedure,* 3rd ed. (St. Paul: West, 1969) *Supplement* (1973), Chap. 13.

5. See generally, Frank W. Miller, *Prosecution: The Decision to Charge a Suspect with a Crime* (Boston: Little, Brown, 1970).

6. See Hall, Kamisar, LaFave, and Israel, *Modern Criminal Procedure,* Chaps. 15 and 16.

7. Federal Rules of Criminal Procedures, Rule 11, *Pleas* (1968).

8. See Donald J. Newman, *Conviction: The Determination of Guilt or Innocence Without Trial* (Boston: Little, Brown, 1966).

9. Santobello v. New York, 404 U.S. 257 (1971).

10. See Frank J. Remington, *Cases and Materials on Criminal Law and Procedures* (Mundelein, Ill.: Callaghan & Co., 1969), pp. 970-999.

11. Williams v. Florida, 399 U.S. 78 (1970).

12. Gideon v. Wainwright, 372 U.S. 335 (1963).

13. Argersinger v. Hamlin, 407 U.S. 25 (1972).

14. See generally, American Bar Association, *Standards Relating to Criminal Appeals* (New York: Institute of Judicial Administration, 1970), and *Standards Relating to Post-Conviction Remedies* (New York: Institute of Judicial Administration, 1967).

15. See generally, President's Commission, *Task Force Report: The Courts* (Washington, D.C.: U.S. Government Printing Office, 1967).

16. See Note, "Statutory Structures for Sentencing Felons to Prison," *Columbia Law Review* 60, 1134 (1960).

17. See Robert O. Dawson, *Sentencing: The Decision as to Type, Length, and Conditions of Sentence* (Boston: Little, Brown, 1969).

18. For references to literature regarding the issue of disclosure of presentence reports, see American Bar Association, *Standards Relating to Sentencing Alternatives and Procedures* (New York: Institute of Judicial Administration, 1968), pp. 214-215.

19. See generally, President's Commission, *Task Force Report: Corrections* (Washington, D.C.: U.S. Government Printing Office, 1967).

20. See *National Prisoner Statistics* (Washington, D.C.: U.S. Department of Justice, Federal Bureau of Prisons).

21. See, for example, Hall, Kamisar, LaFave, and Israel, *Modern Criminal Procedure;* Monrad Paulsen and Sanford Kadish, *Criminal Law and its Processes,* 2nd ed. (Boston: Little, Brown, 1969).

22. See *Model Penal Code,* Proposed Official Draft (American Law Institute, 1967). American Bar Association, *Reports on Minimum Standards for Criminal Justice* (New York: Institute of Judicial Administration, 1967-1970). See also National Advisory Commission on Criminal Justice Standards and Goals, *A National Strategy to Reduce Crime* (Washington, D.C.: U.S. Department of Justice, 1973).

23. See President's Commission, *Task Force Report: Science and Technology* (Washington, D.C.: U.S. Government Printing Office, 1967); *Designing Statewide Criminal Justice Statistics Systems: An Examination of The Five-State Implementation,* Project SEARCH, Technical Report No. 5, 1972.

24. Tiffany, McIntyre, and Rotenberg, *Detection of Crime.*

25. LaFave, *Arrest.*

26. Miller, *Prosecution.*

27. Newman, *Conviction.*

28. Dawson, *Sentencing.*

29. Harry Kalven and Hans Zeisel, *The American Jury* (Boston: Little, Brown, 1966).

30. See, for example, Albert J. Reiss, Jr., *The Police and the Public* (New Haven: Yale U. Press, 1972).

31. See Robert M. Carter, Daniel Glaser, and Leslie T. Wilkins, *Correctional Institutions* (Philadelphia: J. B. Lippincott Company, 1972).

32. See President's Commission, *The Police; The Courts; Corrections.*

33. Daniel Glaser, *The Effectiveness of a Prison and Parole System* (Indianapolis: Bobbs-Merrill, 1964).

34. See, for example, Lawrence Hazelrigg, ed., *Prison Within Society* (Garden City, N.Y.: Doubleday, 1968).

35. See Lloyd Ohlin, *Selection for Parole* (New York: Russell Sage, 1951); Leslie T. Wilkins and P. MacNaughton-Smith, "New Prediction and Classification Methods in Criminology," *J. Res. in Crime and Delin.* 1 (January 1964): 19-32.

36. Jerome S. Skolnick, *Justice Without Trial* (New York: John Wiley and Sons, 1966).

37. Dawson, *Sentencing.*

38. See Herbert L. Packer, *The Limits of the Criminal Sanction* (Stanford, Calif: Stanford U. Press, 1968).

39. *Ibid,* pp. 158-160.

132

40. *Ibid,* pp. 161-162.

41. *Ibid,* pp. 163-164.

42. *Ibid,* pp. 164-165.

43. John Griffiths, "Ideology in Criminal Procedure or a Third 'Model' of The Criminal Process," *Yale Law J.* 79, 359 (1970).

44. *Ibid,* p. 374.

45. *Ibid,* p. 374.

46. *Ibid,* p. 376.

47. *Ibid,* p. 389.

48. Herbert L. Packer, *Limits of the Criminal Sanction,* pp. 153-154.

49. See, for example, Chris R. Argyris, *Integrating the Individual and the Organization* (1964); Robert R. Blake and Jane S. Mouton, *The Managerial Grid* (Houston, Tex.: Gulf Publ., 1964); Rensis Likert, *New Patterns of Management* (New York: McGraw-Hill, 1961).

50. See David Street, Robert Vinter, and Charles Perrow, *Organization for Treatment* (New York: The Free Press, 1966); Vincent O'Leary and David Duffee, "Correctional Policy: A Classification Designed for Change," *Crime and Delin.,* 1971.

51. James Q. Wilson, *Varieties of Police Behavior* (New York: Harvard Press, 1968).

52. *Ibid,* Chaps. 5, 6 and 7.

53. *Ibid,* passim.

54. *Ibid,* p. 236.

55. Lloyd Ohlin, Herman Piven, and Don Pappenfort, "Major Dilemmas of the Social Worker in Probation and Parole," *National Probation and Parole Association Journal* 2, 211 (1956).

56. See Daniel Glaser, *The Effectiveness of a Prison and Parole System,* pp. 431-442.

57. O'Leary and Duffee, "Correctional Policy: A Classification Designed for Change."

58. See John Hogarth, *Sentencing as a Human Process* (Toronto: Toronto U. Press, 1971).

59. See, for example, Donald Clemmer, *The Prison Community* (New York: Holt, Rinehart & Winston, 1940); Gresham Sykes, *Society of Captives* (1958); Donald R. Cressey, *The Prison* (1961); *Theoretical Studies in the Organization of the Prison,* Social Science Research Council, Pamphlet 15 (1960).

60. See Frank J. Remington, Donald J. Newman, Edward L. Kimball, Marygold Melli, and Herman Goldstein, *Criminal Justice Administration* (Indianapolis: Bobbs-Merrill, 1969), Chap. 1.

61. *Ibid,* pp. 33-34.

Part Two

The Decision Network

Preceding chapters have described the structure of the criminal justice system and its multiple purposes and ideological context. They have enumerated its decision stages and suggested various approaches for overall analysis. The chapters which follow will track the major decision points of the criminal process from intervention by the police through completion of sentence. Each chapter will be interspersed with excerpts from leading appellate court cases, statutes, "model" codes and standards, research studies, and other materials bearing on the particular decisions under consideration. It is important that the purposes served by nontextual material be understood, and that caution be exercised in generalizing from a court decision or a research study. There are, after all, 51 sets of criminal codes and procedures (counting all states and the federal jurisdiction), nearly 40,000 police agencies, thousands of prosecutors, and hundreds of trial courts and greatly varied correctional systems across our land. Laws, rules, and practices differ so widely that we can only provide *illustrative* material for particular issues. At the same time care will be exercised to introduce only material that is important and contemporary. Extracts will be given from significant *leading* court cases, often from the U.S. Supreme Court, from important and influential commission reports, from model standards, and from major research projects. Space limitations permit only excerpts from these materials, but ample citations will indicate where original and complete sources may be found.

A good deal of important criminal justice material is legal, not only in the form of case decisions, court rules, and statutes, but as comments and notes from law journals and treatises which are, perhaps, more familiar to lawyers than to other students of the process. This wealth of legal material is to be expected, for, as we have noted, the system *is* basically legal; it is justified and circumscribed by statutes and cases of substantive and procedural criminal law. But we must stress that our purpose here is *not* to survey and teach the criminal law. That would be too ambitious a goal and would not satisfy our needs, for the law constantly changes as new statutes are enacted and as old decisions are modified or overruled. Nonetheless, a thorough analysis of criminal justice requires some exposure to leading court decisions and demands some familiarity with contemporary developments and proposals in statutes and standards.

A few words of caution may be in order for those students who are dealing with legal materials for the first time. As we have mentioned, extracts from appellate court cases will be interspersed throughout subsequent chapters. Some of these will be from the U.S. Supreme Court, others from state supreme courts, or from such other appellate courts as federal circuit courts of appeal and occasionally federal district courts. By and large the *holding* in any case applies only to the jurisdiction of the deciding court, so that a decision of the Wisconsin Supreme Court, for example, applies only to Wisconsin and may not be the law in Illinois or in any other state. The scope of a decision of the U.S. Supreme Court is, however, sometimes confusing, for while this body may decide a constitutional matter which applies to all jurisdictions, it must be remembered that the Supreme Court is also the highest appellate body in the federal jurisdiction and some of its decisions apply only to federal criminal practices. This can be determined with accuracy only by reference to the complete, original decision.

The texts of appellate court decisions are collected in sequence by dates of the holdings in official reports of each state and of the federal system. For example, in 1963 in a leading case, the U.S. Supreme Court held that indigent defendants in all states have a constitutional right to be represented by counsel at trial for crimes carrying the possibility of a "substantial" sentence to incarceration. This case is cited as follows: *Gideon* v. *Wainwright,* 372 U.S. 355 (1963). Gideon is the *appellant,* at the time a prison inmate in Florida, while Wainwright represents the correctional system having custody of the appellant. The first number after the names indicates the volume number of *United States Reports* where the case will be found, the second number identifies the first page of the text of the holding in this volume, and the date is the year of the decision. A State Supreme Court decision may be cited as 52 Del. 550 (1960), the meaning of the numbers identical to those with the *Gideon* citation, but with the decision located in *Delaware Reports*. Decisions of intermediate federal courts are found in the *Federal Reporter* and may be cited as 365 F.2d 549 (4th Cir., 1966). This locates the decision in Volume 365, *Federal Reporter, Second Series,* at page 549 and indicates that the decision was handed down by the Fourth Circuit Court of Appeals in 1966. For federal purposes the nation is divided into districts and circuits, the boundaries of which can be found in maps that may be obtained from the U.S. Department of Justice.

The holding of any case is not only limited in its effect to the jurisdiction of the court, but all decisions are dated, and for their contemporary significance they must be examined along with any later decisions which may have modified, or even overruled, the holding. All decisions exist in a context of prior and con-current holdings which are sometimes directly opposite in outcome, so that any particular holding is much like a link in a chain, occasionally reinforcing many prior holdings and thus indicating a trend; or a decision may appear to be spurious and discordant and likely to be overruled, though even here events may prove it a harbinger of a new trend. The cases we have selected for inclusion are designed to highlight significant issues and must necessarily be presented without their antecedent decisions and contemporary refinements. For example, *Gideon* v. *Wainwright* is a leading case on right to counsel that should be familiar to all students of criminal justice. However, *Gideon* followed, in fact overturned, a chain of cases in the same area and has been subsequently expanded and refined, for the original holding left its full scope unclear. Therefore, when the decision stage of trial is reached, *Gideon* is essential, although it dates from 1963 and more recent cases have extended the right to counsel for trial even on minor offenses.

In addition to cases, selected statutes—such as the New York "Stop and Frisk" law—will be used to illustrate important issues at various decision points with no claim of universal, law-of-the-land applicability. Sections of model codes and standards, like the *Model Penal Code* and the American Bar Association's *Standards for Criminal Justice,* will be included along with commentaries, because they provide excellent summaries and suggested resolution of numerous contemporary issues. But it should be noted that models and standards are not viable law in any jurisdiction, though they are commonly phrased in statutory form. Instead, as their designation implies, they are suggestions for statutes or procedures advanced by eminent scholars and practitioners for possible use in law revision. In fact, the models from which we have taken extracts have influenced many recent changes in statutes and procedures.

Reference will also be made to various national commission reports, and occasionally extracts will be reproduced from hearings or from the summary volumes issued by these commissions. In recent years, a great many important problems in criminal justice have been investigated and analyzed by commissions appointed by the President. The reports of two of these commissions, The President's Commission on Law Enforcement and Administration of Justice, appointed by President Johnson, and the National Advisory Commission on Criminal Justice Standards and Goals, appointed by President Nixon, contain very important contributions to overall criminal justice analysis. Other commissions, such as the National Commission on Civil Disorders and the National Commission on the Causes and Prevention of Violence, have dealt with specific problems of central concern to criminal justice administration.

Some reference will be made to materials found in law reviews. Virtually all American law schools publish these journals which contain two major types of articles. Lead articles are prepared by mature scholars and are identified by title as well as authors' names. "Notes" and "Comments," generally unsigned, are produced by law students and often are surveys of law and practice as well as assessments of the significance of recent decisions and trends.

Selected extracts from research projects and the writings of criminal justice scholars will also appear where relevant. All research of legal or social science nature is limited in scope and applicability, but it is critically important to blend the everyday practices of criminal justice agencies with laws and rules extracted from court decisions and other legal sources.

Occasionally brief illustrations of real problems confronting agencies and the practices used in dealing with them will be presented. The purpose of these vignettes is to give some flavor of the kinds of issues confronted in routine operations, but they are necessarily selected examples which do not cover all possible contingencies, nor are they intended to demonstrate either good or bad policies or practices. The sources of these illustrations are varied, encompassing diverse examples from police response to complaints to materials contained in presentence reports. Some are extracted from reported studies and surveys, others from fact situations underlying appeals, still others from current research of the author and his colleagues.

Taken together, the text and materials in the chapters which follow demonstrate the multidisciplinary nature of criminal justice analysis. A student of criminal justice must be able to integrate materials from many fields and professions. He need not acquire professional expertise in law, economics, sociology, political science, and other relevant fields. But he should become familiar with the diverse sources of material in this field, sufficiently knowledgeable about court decisions and research findings to ask significant questions, and skilled enough to know where to find answers.

Chapter 4

Detection and Arrest

POLICE WORK

Collectively the police are the largest and most pervasive of all criminal justice agencies. Police activities are probably the most complex and certainly the most controversial of all in the criminal process. A dimension often overlooked in analysis is that the police, more than most other agencies, are involved only part-time in crime control and prevention. Much police activity has little to do with crime investigation, arrest, or interrogation of suspects. Most police work involves such things as directing traffic flow, providing emergency services for citizens who are injured or ill, maintaining an around-the-clock fire watch, locating missing persons, settling family and neighborhood disputes, handling chronic inebriates and mentally ill persons, and an endless list of other "service" functions. So much is expected and demanded of the police that the proper scope of policing has never been really defined. What a police agency does, should do, or should not do is literally unanswerable. Should the police provide an ambulance service? School crossing guards? Should they lead parades? Escort funerals? Dehydrate drunks? Settle family arguments? Rescue treed cats? Shoot mad dogs? Check parking meters? Guard dignitaries? The answer to all these questions, and more, is that many police agencies do these things, not always by desire, but often by default. The hard fact is that there are no other agencies, organizations, or institutions that have, or are willing or able to accept, responsibility for many of these diverse tasks. Police duties, in good part, fill a societal void; the police are not only the first summoned in emergencies and unusual situations, but often are the only resource available.

POLICE EMPLOYEE DATA

AVERAGE NUMBER OF POLICE DEPARTMENT EMPLOYEES, AND RANGE IN NUMBER OF EMPLOYEES, PER 1,000 INHABITANTS
BY POPULATION GROUPS, DECEMBER 31, 1971

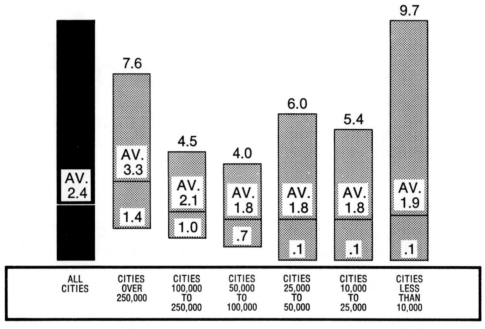

FBI *Uniform Crime Reports, 1971* (Washington, D.C.: U.S. Government Printing Office, 1972), p. 40.

The President's Commission points out:

It has been argued that many of the complex problems of the criminal process could be solved by more narrowly defining the police function. If drunkenness were dealt with by medically qualified people, for example, police would not have to contend with the habitual drunk. If family problems were handled by social work agencies, police would not have to deal with the many domestic and juvenile problems which now confront them. If the substantive law were revised, police would not be confronted with the difficult decisions resulting from broad prohibitions against narcotics, gambling, prostitution and homosexual activity. . . .

But little effective action has been taken to develop the kinds of resources required by the adoption of any of these alternatives.[1]

Moreover, police intervention in providing services, settling disputes, or giving emergency aid may be more closely related to their crime prevention function than first appears. A domestic disturbance or a barroom argument, left to boil, might erupt into serious assault or homicide. Public inebriates are prime targets for muggers; down-and-out drunks may freeze to death or be run over in the street. Street-walking prostitutes have been known to arrange robberies of their clients; assorted homeless, lost, and mentally disturbed persons are all potential crime victims.

The President's Commission concludes:

It might be desirable for agencies other than the police to provide community services that bear no relationship to crime or potential crime situations. But the failure of such agencies to develop and the relationship between the social problems in question and the incidence of crime suggest that the police are likely to remain, for some time, as the only 24-hour-a-day, 7 days-a-week agency that is spread over an entire city in a way that makes it possible for them to respond quickly to incidents of this kind.[2]

The actual percentage of police-citizen contacts in essentially noncriminal situations is not known with accuracy and, of course, varies by community, by time of day, and by specific assignment of each police officer. Police assigned to routine traffic control may have very few occasions to invoke the criminal process; on the other hand, officers in specialized crime intervention units may do little except participate in criminal investigations. An ordinary patrol officer in a metropolitan police agency probably devotes no more than 10 to 15 percent of his time to activities directly related to criminal law enforcement. And even here, "crime fighting" most often entails intervention in minor crime situations involving misdemeanant conduct and public order offenses. A patrolman may experience long intervals of on-duty assignment between felony arrests; and many officers serve years without necessity to use sidearms.

The varied activities of police involving actions other than crime investigation and arrest have received comparatively little attention in the form of authorization, guidance, or control. In contrast, their law-enforcement functions are heavily circumscribed by statutes, case law, internal policy guidelines and by extensive legal and sociological commentary. While there is widespread expectation that police will assist citizens, settle disputes, and perform many duties other than arresting suspects, formal recognition of this broader role is only now emerging. In 1973 the American Bar Association, in their *Standards Relating to the Urban Police Function,* addressed the broader police role:

Percentage Distribution of a Day's Telephone Communications to the Chicago Police Department, April 21, 1966 ($n = 6,172$)

TYPES OF COMMUNICATION (DEFINED BY CITIZENS)	PERCENTAGE OF COMMUNICATIONS
REQUEST ON CRIMINAL MATTERS:	
Dispute or breach of peace	26
Offense against property	16
Offense against persons	6
Auto violation	5
Suspicious person	3
Other	2
Subtotal	58
REQUEST FOR ASSISTANCE:	
Information	11
Personal/family	9
Medical	8
Traffic accident or hazard	6
Subtotal	34
COMPLAINT ABOUT POLICE SERVICE:	
Slow police service	2
Unsatisfactory police procedure	1
Subtotal	3
GIVE POLICE INFORMATION:	
Missing person	1
Other police matters	4
Subtotal	5
Total	100

NOTE: Tapes for April 21, 1966, supplied by the Chicago Police Department. Only calls made to PO5-1212 are included. Calls to administrative numbers and PAX (the Department's internal telephone system) are excluded.

Albert J. Reiss Jr., *The Police and the Public* (New Haven: Yale University Press, 1971), p. 71.

PART III. METHODS AND AUTHORITY AVAILABLE TO THE POLICE FOR FULFILLING THE TASKS GIVEN THEM.

3.1 ALTERNATIVE METHODS USED BY POLICE.

The process of investigation, arrest, and prosecution, commonly viewed as an end in itself, should be recognized as but one of the methods used by police in performing their overall function, even though it is the most important method of dealing with serious criminal activity. Among other methods police use are, for example, the process of informal resolution of conflict, referral, and warning. The alternative methods used by police should be recognized as important and warranting improvement in number and effectiveness; and the police should be given the necessary authority to use them under circumstances in which it is desirable to do so.

3.2 AVOIDING OVERRELIANCE UPON THE CRIMINAL LAW.

The assumption that the use of an arrest and the criminal process is the primary or even the exclusive method available to police should be recognized as causing unnecessary distortion of both the criminal law and the system of criminal justice.

3.3 NEED FOR CLARIFIED, PROPERLY LIMITED AUTHORITY TO USE METHODS OTHER THAN THE CRIMINAL JUSTICE SYSTEM.

There should be clarification of the authority of police to use methods other than arrest and prosecution to deal with the variety of behavioral and social problems which they confront. This should include careful consideration of the need for and problems created by providing police with recognized and properly-limited authority and protection while operating thereunder:

    i.   to deal with interferences with the democratic process. Although it is assumed that police have a duty to protect free speech and the right of dissent, their authority to do so is unclear, particularly because of the questionable constitutionality of many statutes, such as the disorderly conduct statutes, upon which police have relied in the past;

    ii. to deal with self-destructive conduct such as that engaged in by persons who are helpless by reason of mental illness or persons who are incapacitated by alcohol or drugs. Such authority as exists is too often dependent upon criminal laws which commonly afford an inadequate basis to deal effectively and humanely with self-destructive behavior;

    iii. to engage in the resolution of conflict such as that which occurs so frequently between husband and wife or neighbor and neighbor in the highly-populated sections of the large city, without reliance upon criminal assault or disorderly conduct statutes;

iv. to take appropriate action to prevent disorder such as by ordering crowds to disperse where there is adequate reason to believe that such action is required to prevent disorder and to deal properly and effectively with disorder when it occurs; and

v. to require potential victims of crime to take preventive action such as by a legal requirement that building owners follow a burglary prevention program similar to common fire prevention programs.[3]

Crime investigation and arrest are critical police activities even if less frequent than service functions and order maintenance. In fact, involvement in serious crime situations is often viewed as "real" police work by both the public and the police themselves. And the police *are* the front-line agency in crime control with a primary legal duty to function in this capacity. Entire police agencies, as well as individual officers within them, are often evaluated primarily in terms of crime control activity.

It has been said many times that a constable's lot is not a happy one, and indeed the police are continuously criticized for what they do and what they fail to do in all facets of their work. Castigation of police for brutality or corruption is, of course, justified. But criticism commonly leveled against the police is much broader, related in many ways to the intrinsic nature of policing and often resting on unreasonable expectations assigned to police agencies. The police, for example, are commonly criticized for failing to reduce or prevent crime. The President's Commission comments:

Americans are a people used to entrusting the solution of their social ills to specialists, and to expecting results from the institutions those specialists devise. They have entrusted the problems of crime to the police, forgetting that they still operate with many of the limitations of constables of years past, even though today's citizens are no longer villagers.[4]

The fact that our society has become urbanized is not alone the reason police cannot prevent or effectively control crime, although their functions are much more difficult in modern society. Primarily, however, criminal behavior is a product of a web of extremely complex societal and personality factors that can be neither corrected nor deterred by law enforcement alone. The President's Commission says:

The adjustment of conceptions of what can be expected of the police is particularly difficult for people who are themselves law-abiding and who live in a law-abiding community. For them the phenomenon of crime seems far

ORGANIZATION OF A POLICE DEPARTMENT
(1,000 Personnel, 500,000 City Population)

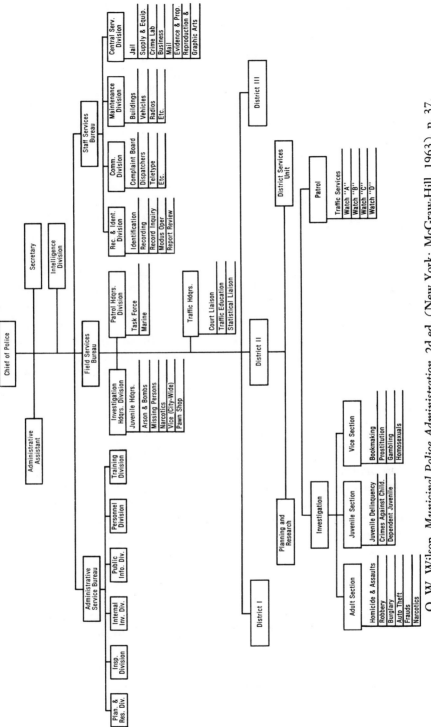

O. W. Wilson, *Municipal Police Administration*, 2d ed. (New York: McGraw-Hill, 1963), p. 37.

simpler than, in fact, it is. The voluntary controls of society work well for them and, since they have no desire to violate the criminal law, their supposition is that crime must be a choice between right and wrong for all men, and that more effective policing alone can determine this choice. Thus public concern about crime is typically translated into demands for more law enforcement, and often into making police the scapegoats for a crime problem they did not create and do not have the resources to solve.[5]

Though it may be unfair, even irrational, police agencies, especially chiefs and commissioners, are often held to blame if crime increases in a particular community or if it does not decrease following an increment in police budget. In addition to criticism for failing to correct the total crime problem, police are often criticized for failing to solve particular crimes. On its face, this seems much fairer, more closely related to efficiency claims of the police themselves and more clearly within the range of reasonable expectations about law enforcement. While the police may not be able to do much about environments which produce crime, they should be able to solve specific crimes by identifying and arresting suspects and recovering stolen property. Yet, detective stories to the contrary, this is not as simple as it sounds. Of course, police do solve crimes, arrest suspects, and recover property, but most crime investigations—particularly those involving forms of theft or fraud—are "cold," that is, the officer is summoned some time after the crime was committed, the perpetrator has left the scene, and often there are no witnesses and no telltale evidence. One observer has commented:

In truth, there is often little the police *can* do. Most crimes are crimes against property, and these are rarely solved because there are neither clues nor witnesses. Even when a suspect is identified, the police are often unable to make an arrest because, if the offense was a misdemeanor, they can only arrest when it is committed in their presence—or if a proper arrest is made, the man may be back on the street again within a day, in which case the public may blame the police when in fact the courts have released him on bail . . .[6]

Policemen are also sometimes criticized for standing at a fixed post, walking a beat, or driving around in a prowl car apparently "doing nothing." James Q. Wilson comments, "What he *is* doing, of course, is waiting to be called to cope with someone else's emergency and if he were not 'doing nothing' he would not be immediately available. The citizen, forgetting this, is likely to wonder why he isn't out 'looking for the man who stole my car' or whatever."[7]

146

Policing is a dangerous business, and police officers know only too well that they face the potential of violence in all confrontation situations, even when called to provide emergency services or to perform apparently uncomplicated peace-keeping functions. A speeding car is usually nothing more than a traffic violation, but now and then, it holds an armed felon fleeing the scene of a crime or wanted by police everywhere. All experienced police know, and continually repeat to colleagues, stories of officers hurt or killed in what appeared to be routine, nonthreatening calls, stops, or other investigations. This constant awareness of potential violence leads policemen to act with what often appears to citizens as undue suspicion and with unnecessary caution in situations in which there appears to be no reason for such protective action. Furthermore, over time a policeman becomes inured to crimes and other emergency situations, handling

LAW ENFORCEMENT OFFICERS KILLED—
BY TYPE OF ACTIVITY
1962-1971

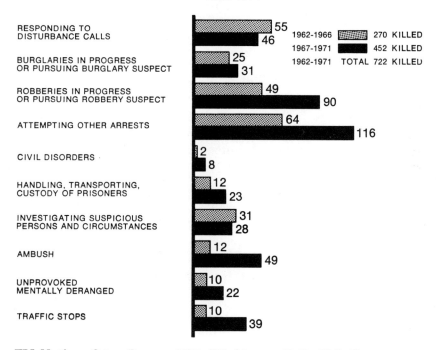

1962-1966	270 KILLED
1967-1971	452 KILLED
1962-1971 TOTAL	722 KILLED

RESPONDING TO DISTURBANCE CALLS — 55 / 46

BURGLARIES IN PROGRESS OR PURSUING BURGLARY SUSPECT — 25 / 31

ROBBERIES IN PROGRESS OR PURSUING ROBBERY SUSPECT — 49 / 90

ATTEMPTING OTHER ARRESTS — 64 / 116

CIVIL DISORDERS — 2 / 8

HANDLING, TRANSPORTING, CUSTODY OF PRISONERS — 12 / 23

INVESTIGATING SUSPICIOUS PERSONS AND CIRCUMSTANCES — 31 / 28

AMBUSH — 12 / 49

UNPROVOKED MENTALLY DERANGED — 10 / 22

TRAFFIC STOPS — 10 / 39

FBI *Uniform Crime Reports, 1971* (Washington, D.C.: U.S. Government Printing Office, 1972), p. 43.

these as routine matters, often to the dismay of victims and witnesses. Wilson comments: "When the police arrive to look for a prowler, examine a loss, or stop a fight, the victim and suspect are agitated, fearful, even impassioned. But the police have seen it all before and they have come to distrust victim accounts (to say nothing of suspect explanations) of what happened. Instead of offering sympathy and immediately taking the victim's side, the police may seem cool, suspicious, or disinterested. . . ."[8]

There is a good deal of solidarity among policemen with corresponding social isolation from others in the community.[9] Policing is often a thankless task; many police officers are disliked for doing their job effectively, for few people like to be questioned or to be given traffic citations even when such intervention is reasonable and warranted. Although most national polls show that most citizens have a high opinion of the work of police, members of racial, ethnic, and economic minorities who have the most contact with police tend to view them with a high degree of hostility and lack of confidence.[10]

Over the past few decades, particularly in the years since World War II, police have sought recognition as members of a "profession" rather than simply as job-holders. Success in this effort has been limited but noticeable. Many metropolitan and state police agencies have increased recruitment requirements and provided better training and education for all policemen, especially for command staff. While recognition of policing as a profession is developing slowly, the nature of their work supports the police claim for such recognition. Albert J. Reiss has said: "The police in America belong to one of the few occupations that includes all of the essential elements to qualify as a profession. They possess the power of coercive authority, and through their power to arrest and book for offenses, they control the fate of 'clients'. Furthermore, the code of ethics for law-enforcement officers is the same as for any profession. Law-enforcement officers are sworn to duty at all times and must discharge this duty with honor to themselves and others. . . . Policing is one of the few 'moral call' occupations. Police are duty bound to come when and where called, regardless of who calls them. Like clergymen, they serve others in matters of moral crisis and dilemma. But, as in the military, they must be prepared to follow orders and give their lives in the line of duty."[11]

The full range of police functions is beyond the scope of this book. Our analysis will focus on their decisions in the enforcement of criminal laws, recognizing that this activity exists in a much broader context of police work. Police activity in criminal law enforcement is a crucial function, not only in regard to those who are processed, but in terms of very basic values of our social order.

Investigating Crimes and Identifying Suspects

The criminal justice process usually begins when the police suspect that a crime has been committed, is being committed, or is about to be committed and when the situation is investigated to substantiate or dispel this suspicion. There are three major ways, with almost infinite variations, in which police suspicion is aroused. The first occurs when the police receive a complaint that a crime has taken place. Normally all complaints trigger an investigation which will vary in intensity depending upon the type of crime reported, the apparent credibility of the complainant, and the other specifics of the particular situation.

Illustration 1.   Police received a call from a homeowner who stated that his residence was burglarized while he was on vacation. The desk officer dispatched a patrol car to the scene. Officers observed signs of forcible entry, interviewed the complainant and neighbors, and filed a report with the Burglary Division. Detectives from Burglary followed up by dusting the scene for fingerprints, making an inventory of stolen property, and filing an MO report (method of operation of the burglar) with the Intelligence and Records Division.

Illustration 2.   At 1:30 A.M. a man appeared at a precinct station and reported that his wallet had been stolen while he was riding on a city bus. He was interviewed by a detective who became suspicious of the complaint, for the man appeared intoxicated and the officer knew that late at night there are few riders on the particular bus where the crime allegedly occurred. Further questioning elicited an admission that the complainant had lost all his money in a card game but was afraid to tell his wife. Consequently he invented the pickpocket story. He was reprimanded for filing a false report of a crime and sent home.

The second way in which police suspicion is aroused is by observation of street behavior on routine patrol. An officer working a beat, in a prowl car, or occasionally at a fixed post, may observe some occurrence—a person running from a warehouse in the early hours of the morning, a clean automobile with dirty license plates, and similar unusual situations—that in his experience may indicate the commission of a crime and justify further investigation. Or the officer on patrol may witness an actual crime or what appears to be a crime being committed. Many jurisdictions require that arrests for misdemeanors may be made only if the offense is committed "in view" of the police officer. Thus a driver cannot be arrested for speeding on the complaint of another driver; the infraction must be witnessed by the arresting officer.

1. FIELD INTERROGATION AND FRISK.   Persons acting in a suspicious manner may be stopped and questioned following a complaint, but most often this action is taken as a result of observation by officers on patrol. Normally at this point the police do not have sufficient evidence to make an arrest. Nonetheless, officers commonly approach persons who are found near the scene of a crime, or who otherwise arouse suspicion, and ask for identification. The field interrogation may confirm police suspicion so that arrest results or the person stopped may satisfactorily explain his actions and be allowed to move on.

The propriety of stopping and questioning is cloudy. In general, there has been little legislation or appellate court authorization of field interrogation practices, and such authority as exists is ambiguous.[12] Statutes in many jurisdictions permit police to stop automobiles to check registration, but often the law is silent concerning their authority to stop pedestrians in the absence of evidence sufficient to place them under arrest. For the most part, police rely on the consent of persons stopped to cooperate in a brief field interrogation, but a suspect may refuse to stop or to answer any questions. This presents the officer with a dilemma. Should he allow the person to proceed, or does his refusal to cooperate coupled with the original suspicious circumstances now constitute evidence sufficient to arrest?[13]

The right of police officers to frisk persons who are stopped for questioning is authorized by statute in some jurisdictions. *Frisk* involves a pat-down search of the suspect only to discover weapons, not to recover contraband. The scope of a frisk is much more circumscribed than a full-scale search and can occur only under specified conditions where the officer has reason to believe he is "in danger of life or limb."[14] An example of legislation authorizing frisk is:

STOP AND FRISK
NEW YORK CODE OF CRIMINAL PROCEDURE
Section 140.50 (1971)

1. In addition to the authority provided by this article for making an arrest without a warrant, a police officer may stop a person in a public place located within the geographical area of such officer's employment when he reasonably suspects that such person is committing, has committed, or is about to commit either a) a felony or b) a class A misdemeanor defined in the penal law, and may demand of him his name, address, and an explanation of his conduct.

2. When upon stopping a person under circumstances prescribed in subdivision one a police officer reasonably suspects that he is in danger of physical injury, he may search such person for a deadly weapon or any instrument, article, or substance readily capable of causing serious physical injury and of a sort not ordinarily carried in public places by law-abiding persons. If he finds such a weapon or instrument, or any other property possession of which he reasonably believes may constitute the

commission of a crime, he may take it and keep it until the completion of the questioning, at which time he shall either return it, if lawfully possessed, or arrest such person.

A police officer's decision to interrogate, and perhaps frisk, a suspect is often the result of his "street sense," his perception of suspicious and possibly dangerous situations based on years of experience on patrol. Like a trained hunter, an experienced officer may have suspicions aroused by circumstances that would not give pause to the ordinary citizen. Yet policemen, in contrast to such other participants as prosecuting attorneys and judges, are generally not recognized as "experts" in the sense that their actions can be justified on the basis of formal education, training, or experience. A significant exception was found by the U.S. Supreme Court:

TERRY V. OHIO
392 U.S. 1 (1968)

[Detective McFadden, a policeman for thirty-nine years was on afternoon patrol in a city when he observed two men standing at a corner. One would walk past a store, look in the window, go a short distance, and then return to the window for another look. The other man would then repeat the same pattern. After this took place a dozen times the men walked off together. Officer McFadden came to the conclusion that the men were "casing" the store for a possible robbery. He followed them, and when they stopped to confer with another man, he approached and asked them their names. When they mumbled in response, he turned one of the men around, patted him down and found a .38 caliber revolver in his overcoat pocket. Frisking the other two men, the officer found another gun. He took the men with the guns into custody and they were charged with carrying concealed weapons.]

MR. CHIEF JUSTICE WARREN delivered the opinion of the Court.

On the motion to suppress the guns the prosecution took the position that they had been seized following a search incident to a lawful arrest. The trial court rejected this theory, stating that it "would be stretching the facts beyond reasonable comprehension" to find that Officer McFadden had had probable cause to arrest the men before he patted them down for weapons. However, the court denied the defendant's motion on the ground that Officer McFadden, on the basis of his experience, "had reasonable cause to believe . . . that the defendants were conducting themselves suspiciously, and some interrogation should be made of their action." Purely for his own protection, the court held, the officer had the right to pat down the outer clothing of these men, whom he had reasonable cause to believe might be armed. The court distinguished between an investigatory "stop" and an arrest, and between a "frisk" of the outer clothing for weapons and a full-blown search for evidence of crime. The frisk, it held, was essential to the proper performance of the officer's investigatory duties, for without it "the answer to the police officer may be a bullet, and a loaded pistol discovered during the frisk is admissible."

After the court denied their motion to suppress, Chilton and Terry waived jury trial and pleaded not guilty. The court adjudged them guilty, and the Court of Appeals for the Eighth Judicial District, Cuyahoga County, affirmed. The Supreme Court of Ohio dismissed petitioner's appeal on the ground that no "substantial constitutional question" was involved. We granted *certiorari,* to determine whether the admission of the revolvers in evidence violated petitioner's right under the Fourth Amendment, made applicable to the States by the Fourteenth. We affirm the conviction. . . .

. . .

. . . [w]e consider first the nature and extent of the governmental interests involved. One general interest is of course that of effective crime prevention and detection; it is this interest which underlies the recognition that a police officer may in appropriate circumstances and in an appropriate manner approach a person for purposes of investigating possible criminal behavior even though there is no probable cause to make an arrest. It was this legitimate investigative function Officer McFadden was discharging when he decided to approach the petitioner and his companions. He had observed Terry, Chilton, and Katz go through a series of acts, each of them perhaps innocent in itself, but which taken together warranted further investigation. There is nothing unusual in two men standing together on a street corner, perhaps waiting for someone. Nor is there anything suspicious about people in such circumstances strolling up and down the street, singly or in pairs. Store windows, moreover, are made to be looked in. But the story is quite different where, as here, two men hover about a street corner for an extended period of time, at the end of which it becomes apparent that they are not waiting for anyone or anything; where these men pace alternately along an identical route, pausing to stare in the same store window roughly 24 times; where each completion of this route is followed immediately by a conference between the two men on the corner; where they are joined in one of these conferences by a third man who leaves swiftly; and where the two men finally follow the third and rejoin him a couple of blocks away. It would have been poor police work indeed for an officer of 30 years experience in the detection of thievery from stores in this same neighborhood to have failed to investigate this behavior further.

The crux of this case, however, is not the propriety of Officer McFadden's taking steps to investigate petitioner's suspicious behavior, but rather, whether there was justification for McFadden's invasion of Terry's personal security by searching him for weapons in the course of that investigation. We are now concerned with more than the governmental interest in investigating crime; in addition, there is the more immediate interest of the police officer in taking steps to assure himself that the person with whom he is dealing is not armed with a weapon that could unexpectedly and fatally be used against him. Certainly it would be unreasonable to require that police officers take unnecessary risks in the performance of their duties. American criminals have a long tradition of armed violence, and every year in this country many law enforcement officers are killed in the line of duty, and thousands more are wounded. Virtually all of these deaths and a substantial portion of the injuries are inflicted with guns and knives. . . .

. . .

Our evaluation of the proper balance that has to be struck in this type of case leads us to conclude that there must be a narrowly drawn authority to permit a reasonable search for weapons for the protection of the police officer, where he has reason to believe that he is dealing with an armed and dangerous individual, regardless of whether he has probable cause to arrest the individual for a crime. The officer need not be absolutely certain that the individual is armed; the issue is whether a reasonably prudent man in the circumstances would be warranted in the belief that his safety or that of others was in danger. And in determining whether the officer acted reasonably in such circumstances, due weight must be given, not to his inchoate and unparticularized suspicion or "hunch," but to the specific reasonable inferences which he is entitled to draw from the facts in light of his experience. . . . The sole justification of the search in the present situation is the protection of the police officer and others nearby, and it must therefore be confined in scope to an intrusion reasonably designed to discover guns, knives, clubs, or other hidden instruments for the assault of the police officer.

The scope of the search in this case presents no serious problem in light of these standards. Officer McFadden patted down the outer clothing of petitioner and his two companions. He did not place his hands in their pockets or under the outer surface of their garments until he had felt weapons, and then he merely reached for and removed the guns.

The policeman carefully restricted his search to what was appropriate to the discovery of the particular items which he sought. Each case of this sort will, of course, have to be decided on its own facts. We merely hold today that where a police officer observes unusual conduct which leads him reasonably to conclude in light of his experience that criminal activity may be afoot and that the persons with whom he is dealing may be armed and presently dangerous; where in the course of investigating this behavior he identifies himself as a policeman and makes reasonable inquiries; and where nothing in the initial stages of the encounter serves to dispel his reasonable fear for his own or others' safety, he is entitled for the protection of himself and others in the

153

area to conduct a carefully limited search of the outer clothing of such persons in an attempt to discover weapons which might be used to assault him. Such a search is a reasonable search under the Fourth Amendment, and any weapons seized may properly be introduced in evidence against the person from whom they were taken. Affirmed.

A third major way in which police investigation may be triggered differs significantly from response to complaints or reaction to observations on routine patrol, and involves instead a decision by police to go out and look for specific criminal activity. This originates primarily in the belief, sometimes supported by informer tips but more often based simply on accumulated knowledge of local conditions, that certain types of crimes, generally unreported, are occurring or will occur in the community. These investigations are usually directed toward so-called "victimless" crimes such as organized gambling, prostitution, sale of narcotics, and other vice offenses, but may also include various forms of criminal conspiracies ranging from robbery plots by professional criminals to meetings of groups of "political revolutionaries." Large police agencies often have specialized detective units such as vice squads, organized crime intelligence units and the like, specializing in the investigation of these offenses and in the observation and tracking of persons believed to be involved in vices, rackets, or conspiracies.

Illustration 3. Police received a call from a store owner who reported numerous customer complaints about homosexual solicitation in the store's restrooms. Vice squad officers went to the store and set up "peep hole" observation stations to attempt to gather evidence of criminal solicitation.

Illustration 4. Police received information from a number of informants that a "rumble" between rival motorcycle clubs was scheduled to take place in a local park. Members of the Tactical Unit were dispatched to the park with instructions to stake out the scene, remain hidden, but keep the area under surveillance.

The techniques used by police to seek out possible criminal activities are varied, depending upon the quality of their information, the extent of community pressures for enforcement, and the kinds of offenses toward which investigation is directed. Investigations may involve searches, electronic eavesdropping, and other kinds of surveillance in addition to undercover infiltration of ongoing criminal activities.

2. SEARCH.   Search is an investigatory technique that can be used at any time, before or after arrest of a suspect. Following a lawful arrest, a suspect may be searched without a warrant, but search prior to arrest normally requires a search warrant or the consent of the person searched.[15] Freedom from unreasonable searches is guaranteed by the Fourth Amendment to the Constitution, and the U.S. Supreme Court has held that evidence improperly seized cannot be admitted at trial. Prior to this decision, each state could make its own determination whether improperly seized evidence could be used; 22 states allowed it to be introduced at trial. Now, however, the "exclusionary rule" applies as a constitutional requirement in all states as well as in the federal jurisdiction. The court decision expanding the exclusionary rule is:

MAPP V. OHIO
367 U.S. 643 (1961)

[Three Cleveland police officers arrived at the home of Miss Mapp acting on information that a person was hiding there who was wanted for questioning in connection with a bombing and also believing that the home contained gambling paraphernalia. Miss Mapp, after conferring by phone with her attorney, refused to admit them. The officers placed the house under surveillance until joined some three hours later by four additional policemen. They approached the house and forcibly entered it. In the meantime Miss Mapp's attorney arrived, but the police would not allow him to enter the house or confer with Miss Mapp. When Miss Mapp demanded to see a search warrant, a paper claimed to be a warrant was held out and Miss Mapp seized it and placed it in her blouse. After a struggle the police recovered the paper, apparently not really a warrant, and handcuffed Miss Mapp because she resisted their recovery efforts. She was forcibly taken upstairs to her bedroom and restrained while police searched the entire house. In the basement they discovered and confiscated obscene materials, possession of which later became the basis of the charge for which Miss Mapp was convicted. At the time of all this Ohio did not require exclusion of evidence improperly seized. Under constitutional interpretation at the time, this was permissible for the U.S. Supreme Court held in *Wolf* v. *Colorado,* 338 U.S. 25 (1949) that "in a prosecution in a State court for a State crime the Fourteenth Amendment does not forbid the admission of evidence obtained by an unreasonable search and seizure." Now, however, this holding was reconsidered.]

MR. JUSTICE CLARK delivered the opinion of the Court.

. . .

. . . Today we once again examine Wolf's constitutional documentation of the right to privacy free from unreasonable state intrusion, and, after its dozen years on our books, are led by it to close the only courtroom door remaining open to evidence secured by official lawlessness in flagrant abuse of that basic right, reserved to all persons as a specific guarantee against that very same unlawful conduct. We hold that all evidence obtained by searches and seizures

155

in violation of the Constitution is, by that same authority, inadmissible in a state court. . . .

. . .

Moreover, our holding that the exclusionary rule is an essential part of both the Fourth and Fourteenth Amendments is not only the logical dictate of prior cases, but it also makes very good sense. There is no war between the Constitution and common sense. Presently, a federal prosecutor may make no use of evidence illegally seized, but a State's attorney across the street may, although he supposedly is operating under the enforceable prohibitions of the same Amendment. Thus the State, by admitting evidence unlawfully seized, serves to encourage disobedience to the Federal Constitution which it is bound to uphold. . . .

. . .

There are those who say, as did Justice (then Judge) Cardozo, that under our constitutional exclusionary doctrine "[t]he criminal is to go free because the constable has blundered." *People* v. *Defore,* 242 NY, at 21, 150 NE, at 587. In some cases this will undoubtedly be the result. But, as was said in *Elkins,* "there is another consideration—the imperative of judicial integrity." 364 US, at 222. The criminal goes free, if he must, but it is the law that sets him free. Nothing can destroy a government more quickly than its failure to observe its own laws, or worse, its disregard of the charter of its own existence. . . .

. . .

The judgment of the Supreme Court of Ohio is reversed and the cause remanded for further proceedings not inconsistent with this opinion.
Reversed and remanded.

Search of persons, premises, and vehicles is an extremely complex and controversial investigatory technique, yet one that is considered essential by most police agencies. In recent years, searches, with and without warrants, have been heavily litigated, resulting generally in new rules and proscriptions limiting police authority to search.[16]

3. SURVEILLANCE, ELECTRONIC EAVESDROPPING.

Surveillance encompasses a number of investigatory techniques, including police stakeout and sustained observation of suspicious premises, tailing of suspects, and various eavesdropping procedures such as wiretapping telephones and recording conversations with hidden microphones or "bugs." In general, surveillance is conducted by specialized units of detectives within police agencies rather than by officers on routine patrol. Its objective may be to gather evidence of a crime, or merely to accumulate "intelligence" information which may provide leads to the identity of vice rings or other criminal conspiracies.

Like search, surveillance techniques are also controversial, and as electronic eavesdropping techniques have become more sophisticated, they have been heavily litigated. Covert observation of suspects or premises is difficult to control but creates few problems if officers remain hidden. However, when a stakeout or tracking becomes obvious, it may border on harassment of the suspect, leading him to seek injunction against the practice.[17] Eavesdropping presents somewhat more complex problems and its scope and purposes have been increasingly circumscribed by the Supreme Court.[18] The Supreme Court dealt with this:

KATZ V. UNITED STATES
389 U.S. 347 (1967)

[Katz was convicted in a federal district court on charges that he had transmitted betting information by telephone from Los Angeles to Miami and Boston in violation of a federal statute. Evidence was obtained from an electronic listening and recording device attached to the outside of a public telephone booth from which he placed his calls. An intermediate court of appeals upheld his conviction based on this evidence finding that a public telephone booth is not a constitutionally protected area, like a person's home, and that in any event the device used did not actually penetrate and invade the area. Such physical "trespass" was commonly held to be necessary for violation of the Fourth Amendment. The Supreme Court granted *certiorari* to consider these matters.]

MR. JUSTICE STEWART delivered the opinion of the Court.

. . .

We decline to adopt this formulation of the issues. In the first place, the correct solution of Fourth Amendment problems is not necessarily promoted by incantation of the phrase "constitutionally protected area." Secondly, the Fourth Amendment cannot be translated into a general constitutional "right to privacy." That Amendment protects individual privacy against certain kinds of governmental intrusion, but its protections go further, and often have nothing to do with privacy at all. Other provisions of the Constitution protect personal privacy from other forms of governmental invasion. But the protection of a person's general right to privacy—his right to be let alone by other people—is, like the protection of his property and of his very life, left largely to the law of the individual states.

Because of the misleading way the issues have been formulated, the parties have attached great significance to the characterization of the telephone booth from which the petitioner placed his calls. The petitioner has strenuously argued that the booth was a "constitutionally protected area." The Government has maintained with equal vigor that it was not. But this effort to decide whether or not a given "area," viewed in the abstract, is "constitutionally protected" deflects attention from the problem presented by this case. For the

Fourth Amendment protects people, not places. What a person knowingly exposes to the public, even in his own home or office, is not a subject of Fourth Amendment protection. See *Lewis* v. *United States,* 385 U.S. 206, 210; *United States* v. *Lee,* 274 U.S. 563. But what he seeks to preserve as private, even in an area accessible to the public, may be constitutionally protected. See *Rios* v. *United States,* 364 U.S. 253; Ex parte *Jackson,* 96 U.S. 727, 733.
. . .

   We conclude that the underpinnings of *Olmstead* and *Goldman* have been so eroded by our subsequent decisions that the "trespass" doctrine there enunciated can no longer be regarded as controlling. The Government's activities in electronically listening to and recording the petitioner's words violated the privacy upon which he justifiably relied while using the telephone booth and thus constituted a "search and seizure" within the meaning of the Fourth Amendment. The fact that the electronic device employed to achieve that end did not happen to penetrate the wall of the booth can have no constitutional significance.
. . .

   The Government urges that, because its agents relied upon the decisions in *Olmstead* and *Goldman,* and because they did no more here than they might properly have done with prior judicial sanction, we should retroactively validate their conduct. That we cannot do. It is apparent that the agents in this case acted with restraint. Yet the inescapable fact is that this restraint was imposed by the agents themselves, not by a judicial officer. They were not required, before commencing the search, to present their estimate to probable cause for detached scrutiny by a neutral magistrate. They were not compelled, during the conduct of the search itself, to observe precise limits established in advance by a specific court order. Nor were they directed, after the search had been completed, to notify the authorizing magistrate in detail of all that had been seized. In the absence of such safeguards, this Court has never sustained a search upon the sole ground that officers reasonably expected to find evidence of a particular crime and voluntarily confined their activities to the least intrusive means consistent with that end. Searches conducted without warrants have been held unlawful "notwithstanding facts unquestionably showing probable cause," *Agnello* v. *United States,* 269 U.S. 20, 33, for the Constitution requires "that the deliberate, impartial judgment of a judicial officer . . . be interposed between the citizen and the police." *Wong Sun* v. *United States,* 371 U.S. 471, 481-482. "Over and over again this Court has emphasized that the mandate of the [Fourth] Amendment requires adherence to judicial processes," *United States* v. *Jeffers,* 342 U.S. 48, 51, and that searches conducted outside the judicial process, without prior approval by judge or magistrate, are per se unreasonable under the Fourth Amendment—subject only to a few specifically established and well-delineated exceptions.

158

It is difficult to imagine how any of those exceptions could ever apply to the sort of search and seizure involved in this case. Even electronic surveillance substantially contemporaneous with an individual's arrest could hardly be deemed an "incident" of that arrest. Nor could the use of electronic surveillance without prior authorization be justified on grounds of "hot pursuit." And, of course, the very nature of electronic surveillance precludes its use pursuant to the suspect's consent.

The Government does not question these basic principles. Rather, it urges the creation of a new exception to cover this case. It argues that surveillance of a telephone booth should be excepted from the usual requirement of advance authorization by a magistrate upon a showing of probable cause. We cannot agree. Omission of such authorization "bypasses the safeguards provided by an objective predetermination of probable cause, and substitiutes instead the far less reliable procedure of an after-the-event justification for the . . . search, too likely to be subtly influenced by the familiar shortcomings of hindsight judgment." *Beck* v. *State of Ohio*, 379 U.S. 89, 96. And bypassing a neutral predetermination of the scope of a search leaves individuals secure from Fourth Amendment violations "only in the discretion of the police."

These considerations do not vanish when the search in question is transferred from the setting of a home, an office, or a hotel room, to that of a telephone booth. Wherever a man may be, he is entitled to know that he will remain free from unreasonable searches and seizures. The government agents here ignored "the procedure of antecedent justification . . . that is central to the Fourth Amendment," a procedure that we hold to be a constitutional precondition of the kind of electronic surveillance involved in this case. Because the surveillance here failed to meet that condition, and because it led to the petitioner's conviction, the judgment must be reversed.

It is so ordered.

In 1968 Congress passed legislation providing stricter judicial control over eavesdropping and specified conditions and criteria limiting both the legitimate purposes and the scope of oral interceptions.[19] The American Bar Association has published model standards relating to electronic surveillance,[20] and there has also been much scholarly comment on this technique.[21]

4. UNDERCOVER OPERATIONS. Another police investigatory technique involves the infiltration of criminal conspiracies by policemen who conceal their identity with appropriate disguises. The extent to which a police officer must become personally involved, or participate, in illegal activity in order to maintain credibility while gathering evidence sufficient to arrest others is a major problem in undercover operations. Related to this is the question of the extent to which the undercover officer may "encourage" others to commit offenses in order to make arrests.[22] The nature of police encouragement has been described:

Some criminal offenses present the police with unique and difficult detection problems because they are committed privately or away from police officers or private citizens who might make a report to public officials and because they are committed with "victims" who are willing participants. As a consequence, these offenses are often not detectable by such means as search and seizure, routine or electronic surveillance, or the use of informants. Most but not all of these offenses are vice crimes, among them, solicitations by the prostitute and the homosexual, illegal sales of liquor, of narcotics, and of pornography, and gambling.

The suggestion that the state legislatures should stop trying to make discreet, consensual vice between adults criminal would not much simplify the police detection task, if adopted. Already, in the areas of homosexuality and prostitution, police agencies are primarily concerned with public solicitations, not with private activity. Controlling certain vice activities instead of prohibiting them only changes the police detection problem, as can be seen most clearly in the case of the liquor laws. Although the sale of liquor is now legal, the hours of this sale are subject to control and the liquor itself is subject to heavy taxation. As a result, enforcement of the liquor laws is still far from an easy task.

Greater police concern for the detection of one type of vice activity than for another can be explained by pressures from both within and without the police department. It is difficult to identify these pressures and to measure their significance in relation to current police practices. The police seldom explain why they concentrate their detection efforts in one direction rather than another. As a consequence, this aspect of current criminal justice administration is little understood. However, some of the pressures which motivate the police can be identified. Police are concerned about prostitutes apparently because a prostitute frequently robs her clients; may be part of an organized crime syndicate; spends her prostitution money on narcotics, thus supporting the narcotics trade; if a streetwalker, offends respectable citizens using the streets; and spreads venereal disease. Police are concerned about public solicitation by homosexuals because of pressure by private businesses and public agencies whose washroom facilities may be used as meeting places for homosexuals, and because public solicitation is offensive to the community. Police concern over liquor law violations undoubtedly reflects the fact that such violations are widely visible and the fact that the competitive situation is often such that all sellers must be made to conform to the law or none will. Sales of narcotics are of obvious concern to police and the general community.

When the police desire to enforce the criminal statutes applicable to a crime with willing victims, they know effective detection requires that a police officer gain firsthand knowledge of the crime. Other detection methods are ineffective because unless the victim has his money stolen or is assaulted, he will not complain to police. As a consequence, an officer must place himself in the position of a willing participant in the prescribed activity. The police issue is apparent: to what extent may police properly "encourage" suspects to engage in criminal conduct?

"Encouragement" is a word used to describe the activity of the police or police agent a) who acts as a victim; b) who intends, by his actions, to encourage a suspect to commit a crime; c) who actually communicates this encouragement to the suspect; and d) who has thereby some influence upon the commission of the crime. Encouragement does not usually consist of a single act but a series of acts, part of the normal interplay between victim and suspect.

Although encouragement is an important practice, used by national, state, and local enforcement agencies throughout the country, it has no generally accepted name. At times it is loosely or mistakenly referred to as "entrapment," a label properly reserved for illegal forms of encouragement. The term "encouragement," although imperfect and perhaps connoting impropriety to some, is intended only to be descriptive, a neutral word neither critical nor complimentary of the practice.

Encouragement is seldom discussed either by police or by persons outside a police agency. What discussion there is typically relates to entrapment. In part, no doubt, this reflects a general uneasiness as to whether it is ever proper for police to encourage the commission of crime. In part, it also no doubt reflects the fact that discussion has traditionally centered upon the limitations of police practice—what may not be done—rather than on proper police practice. More attention has been given to proper search practices, proper surveillance, and proper field interrogation than to proper encouragement. There are, for example, statutes authorizing searches and field interrogations, but there are no express legislative or judicial authorizations of encouragement. Little is known about the need for encouragement as a detection practice, the extent of its use, or the contribution it has made to effective law enforcement.[23]

In general, should an undercover officer happen to induce "otherwise innocent persons to commit crimes," they may have a defense of entrapment.[24] The *Model Penal Code* defines entrapment as follows:

Section 2.13. Entrapment.

1. A public law enforcement official or a person acting in cooperation with such an official perpetrates an entrapment if for the purpose of obtaining evidence of the commission of an offense, he induces or encourages another person to engage in conduct constituting such offense by either:

a.   making knowingly false representations designed to induce the belief that such conduct is not prohibited; or

b.   employing methods of persuasion or inducement which create a substantial risk that such an offense will be committed by persons other than those who are ready to commit it.

2.   Except as provided in Subsection (3) of this Section, a person prosecuted for an offense shall be acquitted if he proves by a preponderance of evidence that his conduct occurred in response to an entrapment. The issue of entrapment shall be tried by the Court in the absence of the jury.

3.   The defense afforded by this Section is unavailable when causing or threatening bodily injury is an element of the offense charged and the prosecution is based on conduct causing or threatening such injury to a person other than the person perpetrating the entrapment.[25]

Controversies over various police investigatory techniques center in the paradoxical way we view policing in our society. On one hand, we want lawbreakers apprehended or deterred efficiently and effectively; on the other, we fear police encroachment on the rights and privacy of innocent citizens. As a result, legislatures and courts have devoted a good deal of time and effort to setting curbs and limitations on various police investigation methods, while also trying to avoid crippling necessary procedures for the detection of crimes and the identification of suspects. The National Advisory Commission on Criminal Justice Standards and Goals suggests policies and procedures for limiting police authority:

LIMITS OF AUTHORITY

Every police chief executive immediately should establish and disseminate to the public and to every agency employee written policy acknowledging that police effectiveness depends upon public approval and acceptance of police authority. This policy at least:

1.   Should acknowledge that the limits of police authority are strictly prescribed by law and that there can be no situation which justifies extralegal police practices;

2.   Should acknowledge that there are times when force must be used in the performance of police tasks, but that there can be no situation which justifies the use of unreasonable force;

3.   Should acknowledge that in their exercise of authority the police must be accountable to the community by providing formal procedures for receiving both commendations and complaints from the public regarding individual officer performance. These procedures at least should stipulate that:

a.   There will be appropriate publicity to inform the public that complaints and commendations will be received and acted upon by the police agency;

b. Every person who commends the performance of an individual officer in writing will receive a personal letter of acknowledgment; and

c. Every allegation of misconduct will be investigated fully and impartially by the police agency and the results made known to the complainant or the alleged victim of police misconduct.

4. Should provide for immediate adoption of formal procedures to respond to complaints, suggestions, and requests regarding police services and formulation of policies. These procedures at least should stipulate that:

a. There will be appropriate notice to the public acknowledging that the police agency desires community involvement;

b. The public will be involved in the development of formal procedures as well as in the policies that result from their establishment; and

c. Periodic public surveys will be made to elicit evaluations of police service and to determine the law enforcement needs and expectations of the community.[26]

Arrest

In some instances, ordinarily where a suspect has been named by a complainant, police may obtain an arrest warrant as authority to apprehend the suspect. More commonly, felony arrests are made without warrants. Such arrests are proper if at the time the officer has reasonable grounds to believe that a felony has been committed and reasonable belief that the person arrested is the one who committed the crime.

Arrest involves taking the person into custody, meaning that he is no longer free to go his own way, and transporting him to a police station where he is "booked," that is, the arrest is registered.[27] There are some variations in this procedure and in the requirements for arrest. In some situations, primarily involving minor offenses, the suspect may be issued a *citation,* an order to appear at a later date rather than being taken into physical custody. And as already mentioned, statutory laws with some exceptions require the officer to actually witness a misdemeanor; simply "probable" or "reasonable" cause to believe the person committed the crime is insufficient ground for arrest. In making a felony arrest, a police officer may use such force as is necessary to take and maintain custody of the suspect.[28]

163

Illustration 5. Prowl car officers observed a man walking in a residential area in the early morning hours. This particular neighborhood had experienced a recent wave of burglaries. The officers stopped the man, but he could not satisfactorily explain his presence and gave as his home address a location in another part of the city. He was placed under arrest.

Illustration 6. Police responded to a call of a robbery at a liquor store. Upon arrival they were met by the owner who reported that two young men had taken money from him at gunpoint. The robbers had fled, but the owner said he thought he recognized one of them as a youth who lived nearby. The police went to the young man's home and placed him under arrest.

In the illustrations above, subsequent investigation revealed that both suspects were totally innocent of any crime. The question remains whether in each instance the police had "reasonable grounds" for arrest. If not, they might have been liable for damages in legal actions brought by the suspects.[29] If, however, a civil jury were to decide that the police acted reasonably, such arrests would have been proper, notwithstanding later evidence indicating innocence.

It is commonly assumed that when police arrest a suspect they will accumulate evidence and move the case along to the prosecutor for a charging decision. However, Wayne R. LaFave has identified a number of circumstances under which police take persons into custody with no intention of prosecution.[30] These include chronic inebriates who are taken into custody for their own protection, street-walking prostitutes detained to "control and contain" the problem, certain sex offenders who are public nuisances, and petty gamblers and liquor law violators where penalties are small and the inconvenience of arrest is considered sufficient punishment.[31] Where no prosecution is intended the police need not exercise special care to obtain evidence in ways that would make it admissible at trial.

In-Custody Investigation

A suspect taken into custody for an alleged felony or for certain misdemeanors is ordinarily fingerprinted and photographed during the booking procedure. He is often searched and, after appropriate notification of his right to remain silent and to have a lawyer present, interrogated regarding the offense for which he was arrested. The suspect has the right to refuse to answer questions; if he requests legal assistance, interrogation cannot proceed until he has conferred with counsel. This was not always the case before uniform requirements for notification of rights prior to in-custody interrogation were promulgated by the U.S. Supreme Court in 1966.

MIRANDA V. ARIZONA
384 U.S. 436 (1966)

[Ernesto Miranda was arrested in Phoenix, Arizona and charged with kidnapping and rape. He was taken to police headquarters where he was identified by the complainant. He was interrogated for two hours by detectives who admitted at trial that he was not advised of any right to have counsel present at the interrogation. Miranda signed a written confession, was subsequently convicted and appealed but his conviction was upheld by the Arizona Supreme Court. The *Miranda* case was joined with three others, *Vignera* v. *New York, Westover* v. *United States,* and *California* v. *Stewart,* all involving confessions following interrogation by police in the absence of defense counsel. The Supreme Court held such confessions to be improperly obtained not because of any specific "third-degree" tactics of the police but because the entire aura and atmosphere of police interrogation without notification of rights and an offer of assistance of counsel tends to "subjugate the individual to the will of his examiner."]

MR. CHIEF JUSTICE WARREN delivered the opinion of the Court.

The cases before us raise questions which go to the roots of our concepts of American criminal jurisprudence: the restraints society must observe consistent with the Federal Constitution in prosecuting individuals for crime. More specifically, we deal with the admissibility of statements obtained from an individual who is subjected to custodial police interrogation and the necessity for procedures which assure that the individual is accorded his privilege under the Fifth Amendment to the Constitution not to be compelled to incriminate himself.

. . .

Our holding will be spelled out with some specificity in the pages which follow but briefly stated it is this: the prosecution may not use statements, whether exculpatory or inculpatory, stemming from custodial interrogation of the defendant unless it demonstrates the use of procedural safeguards effective to secure the privilege against self-incrimination. By custodial interrogation, we mean questioning initiated by law enforcement officers after a person has been taken into custody or otherwise deprived of his freedom of action in any significant way. As for the procedural safeguards to be employed, unless other fully effective means are devised to inform accused persons of their right of silence and to assure a continuous opportunity to exercise it, the following measures are required. Prior to any questioning, the person must be warned that he has a right to remain silent, that any statement he does make may be used as evidence against him, and that he has a right to the presence of an attorney, either retained or appointed. The defendant may waive effectuation of these rights, provided the waiver is made voluntarily, knowingly and

Operational and Proposed ROR Programs and Summons-Citations in Lieu of Arrest

STATE	NUMBER PROGRAMS OPERATIONAL	NUMBER PROGRAMS PLANNED	NUMBER SUMMONS-CITATIONS OPERATIONAL
Alabama	—	1	—
Alaska	1	—	—
Arizona	1	—	—
Arkansas	—	—	—
California	13	2	5
Colorado	2	—	1
Connecticut	2*	—	2
Delaware	1*	—	—
D.C.	1*	—	1*
Florida	5	—	—
Georgia	1	—	—
Hawaii	1	—	—
Idaho	—	—	—
Illinois	1	—	—
Indiana	2	—	—
Iowa	1	—	—
Kansas	—	—	—
Kentucky	1	—	—
Louisiana	2	—	—
Maine	—	—	—
Maryland	2	—	—
Massachusetts	1	—	—
Michigan	4	1	—
Minnesota	1	—	—
Mississippi	—	—	—
Missouri	3	—	—
Montana	—	—	—
Nebraska	—	—	—
Nevada	—	—	—
New Hampshire	—	—	—
New Jersey	7	—	—
New Mexico	1	—	—
New York	9	—	1
North Carolina	1	—	—
North Dakota	—	—	—
Ohio	3	—	1
Oklahoma	1	—	—
Oregon	2	—	1
Pennsylvania	5	—	—
Rhode Island	—	—	—
South Carolina	—	—	—
South Dakota	—	—	—
Tennessee	1	1	—

Operational and Proposed ROR Programs and Summons-Citations in Lieu of Arrest (Continued)

STATE	NUMBER PROGRAMS OPERATIONAL	NUMBER PROGRAMS PLANNED	NUMBER SUMMONS-CITATIONS OPERATIONAL
Texas	5	1	—
Utah	1	—	—
Vermont	—	—	—
Virginia	—	—	—
Washington	4	—	—
West Virginia	2	—	—
Wisconsin	1	—	—
Wyoming	1	—	—

NOTE: Data from the Office of Economic Opportunity Pre-Trial Release Program.
* Statewide program.

National Advisory Commission on Criminal Justice Standards and Goals, *Corrections* (Washington, D.C.: U.S. Department of Justice, 1973), p. 108.

intelligently. If, however, he indicates in any manner and at any stage of the process that he wishes to consult with an attorney before speaking, there can be no questioning. Likewise, if the individual is alone and indicates in any manner that he does not wish to be interrogated, the police may not question him. The mere fact that he may have answered some questions or volunteered some statements on his own does not deprive him of the right to refrain from answering any further inquiries until he has consulted with an attorney and thereafter consents to be questioned. . . .

. . .

In announcing these principles, we are not unmindful of the burdens which law enforcement officials must bear, often under trying circumstances. We also fully recognize the obligation of all citizens to aid in enforcing the criminal laws. This Court, while protecting individual rights, has always given ample latitude to law enforcement agencies in the legitimate exercise of their duties. The limits we have placed on the interrogation process should not constitute an undue interference with a proper system of law enforcement. As we have noted, our decision does not in any way preclude police from carrying out their traditional investigatory functions. Although confessions may play an important role in some convictions, the cases before us present graphic examples of the overstatement of the "need" for confessions. In each case authorities conducted interrogations ranging up to five days in duration despite the presence, through standard investigating practices, of considerable evidence against each defendant.

A suspect held in custody may also be placed in a lineup which requires his appearance in company with other persons of roughly similar appearance for possible identification by the victim or witnesses. The Supreme Court has held this procedure to be a "critical stage" of the process, requiring assistance of counsel *if* the lineup takes place after the suspect is formally charged with a crime.[32] However, comparable protection is not required if the lineup occurs after arrest but before charging.[33]

Release from Police Custody: Initial Appearance Before a Magistrate

A short time after arrest, suspects must be taken before a magistrate for consideration of bail. How short the interval must be between arrest and initial appearance depends upon statutory law and relevant court decisions in each jurisdiction. Most jurisdictions require a bail hearing in a reasonable time after arrest: "promptly," or on the first occasion the court is open for business, but in some instances action must be "immediate." As with most criminal procedures, this time interval is a controversial matter, for the sooner bail is fixed (assuming the suspect can post a bond or is otherwise released by the magistrate) the shorter the opportunity for in-custody interrogation by the police. At the same time, prompt opportunity for bail acts as a restraint on arrests for "investigation" and on extended police interrogation, including such excesses as "third-degree" treatment—the improper use of coercion to get a confession.

In a federal case some years ago, the U.S. Supreme Court held that "immediate" appearance in all cases of federal felony arrests is required.[34] This necessitated the establishment of daily, 24-hour magistrate courts for federal cases and raised a storm of controversy.[35] Agencies charged court "handcuffing" of the police for interference with their mode of obtaining confessions to solve crimes. Most states have not followed the federal requirement and continue to allow a "reasonable" interval of time between custody and the bail hearing.

Except for those offenses which are specifically defined by statute as not bailable, suspects have a right to be released on reasonable bond. The determination of whether bail is reasonable is generally left to appellate court interpretation on a case-by-case basis in each jurisdiction.[36] In addition, some jurisdictions have established "release-on-own-recognizance" (ROR) programs, in which indigent suspects can be released without bond after signing an agreement to appear at later proceedings. These programs are patterned after the Manhattan Bail Project,[37] an experiment conducted in New York. This project demonstrated a high rate of return of suspects who were released after a brief investigation which established their residence in the community, local employment, and other community ties. ROR programs diminish the economic disparities of the bail system while offering as much assurance of later return as does monetary bail. The historic purpose for setting bail—return for pleading and trial—is thus fulfilled.

In recent years there has been increasing apprehension that some suspects may commit new crimes while on bail.[38] This concern has generated a number of proposals for *preventive detention* programs which would continue custody of suspects who *might* commit more crimes. While most of these proposals are of doubtful constitutional validity, some preventive detention programs have been instituted.[39]

SOME CONTEMPORARY LAW-ENFORCEMENT ISSUES

Policing modern society is an extremely complex task, always and everywhere controversial. Given the nature, extent, and variability of our crime problems, the old truism that the constable's lot is not a happy one is often vividly experienced by police officers who must balance their decisions between community demands for vigorous and effective crime control and various legal restraints on authority. Every action taken by a police officer, often based on a split-second street decision, is subject to criticism and challenge and may be physically dangerous to the officer as well. Even failure to act, or a decision not to investigate or to arrest, may result in criticism and reprimand. Officially, police have a mandate to fully enforce all laws; in practice, laws often are ambiguous, manpower and resources limited, and full, literal enforcement may in many situations be unnecessary and undesirable.

Currently, innumerable law-enforcement problems are of concern to both the police and the public. Many of these are not really new, but have existed throughout history and are perhaps intrinsic to the police function. Most of us reluctantly accept the need for policing but expect that its interference with our lives will be minimal and that the power will not be misused. We desire effective crime control tempered by restraint, fairness, and sensible patterns of enforcement. The extraordinary dimensions of the problems raised by these opposing pressures range from corruption to the proper dress for police officers. A complete listing is not possible here, but we will examine some problems of contemporary relevance.

Police Discretion: Decisions Not to Invoke the Criminal Process

Police have clear authority to investigate crimes and to arrest suspects when there is sufficient evidence to act. However, there is a question of whether they *must* act, must investigate or arrest, or whether they may properly decide, despite adequate evidence, not to follow through. The issue arises from the expectation of full enforcement conflicting with the desire for sensible use of the criminal process. Is intake into the criminal process a mechanical process, with the police mere automatons? Or is their expertise sufficient not merely to justify suspicions (as in *Terry* v. *Ohio*[40]), but also to decide when and under what conditions the criminal process should not be invoked? The drafters of the American Bar Association's *Standards Relating to the Urban Police Function* commented on the full enforcement myth, pointing out how police discretion has only recently received deserved attention:

There is a persistent myth that the responsibility of a police officer is narrowly prescribed by statute and that the police are, in effect, ministerial officers committed to "enforcing the law without fear or favor."

The statutes of a number of states, for example, leave no ambiguity on the question of whether, having learned of a criminal offense, a police officer is free to do anything other than initiate a criminal prosecution. . . .

At least one jurisdiction (the District of Columbia) goes so far as to make it a criminal offense for an officer to fail to make an arrest. . . .

. . .

Even among those police personnel who acknowledge the fact that the police exercise discretion, many think of it only in terms of the need to exercise common sense in those situations in which rigid application of the law or departmental policies would cause harm or bring embarrassment to the department. The situation calling for the exercise of discretion is considered an extraordinary occurrence—usually involving a rare combination of circumstances. This is particularly true in the "professional" police agencies that, in an effort to eliminate corrupt and politically-motivated practices, place a high value on rigidity as a means of achieving objective law enforcement.

While "full enforcement" has been the posture of many police agencies, there has always been a widespread awareness that many laws—especially those attempting to regulate public morals—have not been fully enforced.

. . .

It has only been since the early 1960s, however, that a number of studies have fully brought the exercise of discretion out into the open, documenting the fact that discretion is not limited to the enforcement of laws regulating public morals.

. . .

Increased concern with exercise of discretion by the police has gradually led to recognition of the fact that discretion is not limited to deciding whether or not to enforce the law; that police exercise broad discretion in deciding, for example, whether to ferret out criminal activity and whether to investigate a citizen's complaint that a crime has been committed. They exercise discretion, as well, in selecting from among available techniques for investigating crime and in determining how to process a person alleged to have committed a criminal offense. . . .

With this recognition of the numerous points in the criminal process at which police have the opportunity to exercise discretion, it began to become increasingly apparent that many of the problems within the criminal justice system stemmed from a failure to recognize the discretionary nature of the police role within the system.[41]

Statutes and court decisions authorizing police discretion not to invoke are rare. In many jurisdictions laws are equivocal or grant such discretion only in special circumstances. Studies of actual police practices, however, show that noninvocation is common, indicating an important dimension of the police function not revealed by arrest statistics. Based on his field observations, Wayne R. LaFave has described a number of circumstances in which the police do not use their full authority and has identified reasons for this exercise of discretion.[42] In some situations decisions rest on police beliefs that the legislature did not intend full enforcement, although the conduct is outlawed. This is shown by decisions not to arrest: a) when the law is ambiguous, as in complaints regarding obscene materials; b) when the statute is vague and appears to have been designed as a device to deal with nuisance behavior rather than to call for full criminal processing, as with vagrancy and loitering; c) when broad statutes are enacted to foreclose "loophole" opportunities for professional criminals, such as the case in which legislation prohibits all gambling but in which police come upon a friendly poker game; d) when the intent of the law is merely to express a moral standard without a real expectation of full enforcement, such as prohibition of "normal" adult consensual sexual misconduct; and e) when the legislation is out of date, as when "blue laws" remain on the books because of legislative oversight or traditional reluctance to repeal.[43]

In other circumstances the police may not act because to do so would strain limited resources. Included are situations: a) in which trivial offenses are confronted; b) in which the conduct is felt to be common, even normative, among a particular subgroup of the community although generally prohibited, as in cases of fistfights and family assaults in lower-class neighborhoods; c) in which the victim does not desire prosecution and refuses to sign a complaint or to testify at trial; and d) in which the victim is a party to the offense, as when the client of a prostitute complains of having been "rolled."[44]

LaFave identified still other circumstances, generally unrelated to interpretation of legislative intent or limited resources, in which police may decide not to arrest even though arrest would have been technically correct. These include situations: a) in which arrest would be inappropriate or ineffective, as in drunkeness arrests of skid-row inebriates; b) in which arrest would cause loss of public support, as in sudden crackdowns on public gambling or other technically illegal activities that have long been tolerated in a community; c) non-arrest of informants or persons who may become states' witnesses to assist long-range enforcement goals; and d) in which arrest would cause harm to the offender outweighing any risk from inaction, as when young first offenders or others with good reputations are involved in minor violations.[45]

Obviously, reasons for police noninvocation are not all alike or of the same magnitude. Some are self-serving, like rewarding informants; others rest on awareness that long-range objectives of crime control may be achieved in ways other than arrest and prosecution, like releasing a first offender with a reprimand rather than an arrest record. Some are matters of convenience, such as overlooking trivial offenses, while others rest on police attitudes toward differences in morality and life-styles among various social classes and minority groups in the community. Whether these patterns of police discretion are good or bad is open to controversy. The major issue is not whether police discretion exists, but how it can be controlled. There is a fine line between prudent selective enforcement and discriminatory enforcement that is clearly inimical to our social order.[46]

The National Advisory Commission on Criminal Justice Standards and Goals has proposed the following:

Standard 1.3. Police Discretion.

Every police agency should acknowledge the existence of the broad range of administrative and operational discretion that is exercised by all police agencies and individual officers. That acknowledgment should take the form of comprehensive policy statements that publicly establish the limits of discretion, that provide guidelines for its exercise within those limits, and that eliminate discriminatory enforcement of the law.

   1. Every police chief executive should have the authority to establish his agency's fundamental objectives and priorities and to implement them through discretionary allocation and control of agency resources. In the exercise of his authority, every chief executive:

   a. Should seek legislation that grants him the authority to exercise his discretion in allocating police resources and in establishing his agency's fundamental objectives and priorities;

   b. Should review all existing criminal statutes, determine the ability of the agency to enforce these statutes effectively, and advise the legislature of the statutes' practicality from an enforcement standpoint; and

    c.   Should advise the legislature of the practicality of each proposed criminal statute from an enforcement standpoint, and the impact of such proposed statutes on the ability of the agency to maintain the existing level of police services.

2.   Every police chief executive should establish policy that guides the exercise of discretion by police personnel in using arrest alternatives. This policy:

    a.   Should establish the limits of discretion by specifically identifying, insofar as possible, situations calling for the use of alternatives to continued physical custody;

    b.   Should establish criteria for the selection of appropriate enforcement alternatives;

    c.   Should require enforcement action to be taken in all situations where all elements of a crime are present and all policy criteria are satisfied;

    d.   Should be jurisdictionwide in both scope and application; and

    e.   Specifically should exclude offender lack of cooperation or disrespect toward police personnel, as a factor in arrest determination unless such conduct constitutes a separate crime.

3.   Every police chief executive should establish policy that limits the exercise of discretion by police personnel in conducting investigations and that provides guidelines for the exercise of discretion within those limits. This policy:

    a.   Should be based on codified laws, judicial decisions, public policy, and police experience in investigating criminal conduct;

    b.   Should identify situations where there can be no investigative discretion; and

    c.   Should establish guidelines for situations requiring the exercise of investigative discretion.

4.   Every police chief executive should establish policy that governs the exercise of discretion by police personnel in providing routine peacekeeping and other police services that, because of their frequent recurrence, lend themselves to the development of a uniform agency response.

5.   Every police chief executive should formalize procedures for developing and implementing the foregoing written agency policy.

6.   Every police chief executive immediately should adopt inspection and control procedures to insure that officers exercise their discretion in a manner consistent with agency policy.[47]

Aggressive Patrol: Arrests for Investigation

Police decisions not to act illustrate one aspect of police discretion. Another is demonstrated by the fairly common practice of "aggressive, preventive patrol."

Here a high crime area is saturated with officers who sweep down on pedestrians and drivers alike stopping, frisking, and searching almost at random. Harry W. More explains:

Preventive patrol often involves stopping persons using the streets in high-crime areas and making searches of both persons and vehicles. The purpose of this technique is not only to talk with individuals who may be suspected of having recently committed crimes but, more broadly, to find and confiscate dangerous weapons and to create an atmosphere of police omnipresence which will dissuade persons from attempting to commit crimes because of the likelihood of their being detected and apprehended.[48]

In many of these "aggressive patrol" instances the police do not have specific probable cause nor can the individuals stopped, questioned, and searched be "reasonably" individual suspects. Consequently, any admissions or evidence obtained cannot be used in prosecution. Why then do such practices persist?

Common street crimes—assaults, muggings, traffic in narcotics, rapes and even many homicides—do not occur in equal distribution throughout a community. In metropolitan areas particularly, police can easily identify high-crime neighborhoods with such accuracy that incidents of various types of offenses can be predicted for any week or month, or even daily. Respectable persons residing in these areas understandably demand protection and insist that the police do something to make the neighborhood safe. The police are also subject to outside pressures—from political figures, action groups, the press, and other sources, to clean up the city and to crack down on lawbreakers. In addition, it is often demanded that police prevent crime as well as solve it. In these circumstances the continued existence of high crime pockets in the city becomes frustrating. No matter that the root causes of such crime may be well beyond police capability to alleviate them. The urgency of the situation demands action, and aggressive patrol is the result. The police simply use techniques (i.e., field interrogation) that have been proved efficient in more orderly circumstances, but apply them intensively and at random.

Although not denying its extralegal nature, police justify aggressive patrol on the grounds that it is effective and that there is no alternative. Brief stops to identify persons abroad in the neighborhood fix them in time and place and become "intelligence" information that may be used later if a crime is reported. Frisks and searches "get the guns, knives and junk (narcotics) off the street," ostensibly preventing more serious crimes. Furthermore, the omnipresence of police acts to deter potential violators. Whether aggressive patrol accomplishes all these things is debatable. A recent experiment in Kansas City, involving different levels of patrol saturation in comparable crime-rate sectors, showed no significant differences in crime-rate reduction in heavily saturated sectors as compared to those with few police present.[49] One of the major difficulties with the practice of aggressive patrol is that it has negative effects on police-community relationships which may far outweigh any gains in seizing contraband weapons. The community costs of aggressive patrol are shown in the following excerpt from the report of the President's Commission:

Misuse of field interrogations, however, is causing serious friction with minority groups in many localities. This is becoming particularly true as more police departments adopt "aggressive patrol" in which officers are encouraged routinely to stop and question persons on the street who are unknown to them, who are suspicious, or whose purpose for being abroad is not readily evident. The Michigan State survey found that both minority group leaders and persons sympathetic to minority groups throughout the country were almost unanimous in labelling field interrogation as a principal problem in police-community relations:

> ***race has an undue influence on who is stopped.
> ***practice is o.k., but the way it was carried out was unfriendly, abusive, etc. Not against method, but how it is used.
> Personally, I found it offensive and was affronted on occasions of its use in New York.
> Spanish-Americans are picked up sooner.
> Many Negroes stopped in other neighborhoods and questioned. Happens more to Negroes than to others.

The Commission has found that field interrogations, used sometimes in conjunction with aggressive, preventive patrol, are often conducted on a broadscale basis by many police departments. First, field interrogations are often conducted with little or no basis for suspicion. In San Diego, written reports were made of over 200,000 stops in 1965 and there were probably about as many stops which were not recorded. The effect on attitudes which can result is revealed by the following comment of a lower income Negro:

"When they stop everybody, they say, well, they haven't seen you around, you know, they want to get to know your name, and all this. I can see them stopping you one time, but the same police stopping you every other day, and asking you the same old question."

A study of juvenile offenses in a western city with high police standards found that Negroes were stopped more frequently than other juveniles "often even in the absence of evidence that an offense had been committed."

. . .

In order to balance the need for field interrogations and the harmful effect on police-community relations which may result from their indiscriminate use, State legislatures should define the extent of police authority to stop and question persons, and police departments should adopt detailed policies governing this authority whether or not legislation exists. Such legislation and policies should have the following principles:

Field interrogations should be conducted only when an officer has reason to believe that a person is about to commit or has committed a crime, or that a crime has been committed and he has knowledge of material value to the investigation.

Field interrogations should not be used at all for minor crimes like vagrancy and loitering.

Adequate reason should be based on the actions of the person, his presence near the scene of a crime, and similar factors raising substantial suspicion, and not on race, poverty, or youth.

The stop should be limited in time. The sole purpose should be: (a) to obtain the citizen's identification; (b) to verify it by readily available information; (c) to request cooperation in the investigation of a crime; and (d) to verify by readily available information any account of his presence or any other information given by the person.

The citizen should be addressed politely and should receive a suitable explanation of the reason for the stop.

An officer should be allowed to conduct a search of the person only if he has reason to believe that his safety or the safety of others so requires.

Officers should be required to file a report each time a stop is made in order to record the circumstances and persons involved. Even greater care should be taken with these records than with arrest records, so that the police do not use them to establish the delinquency or bad character of the person stopped. Moreover, the records should not be available to persons outside of public law enforcement agencies.[50]

Aggressive patrol may also lead to arrests for investigation. These are not based on sufficient evidence at the time but used in order to obtain it later. Sometimes such arrests are simply harassment. The President's Commission comments on this practice:

Sixteen of fifty-five departments responding to a Commission survey in 1966 admitted the use of investigative arrests. In Baltimore, for example, 3,719 (6.6 percent) of the 56,160 nontraffic arrests during 1964 were recorded as arrests for investigation. Of those arrested on this basis, 98 percent were dismissed without going before a magistrate.

Occasionally, police departments engage in dragnet arrests on suspicion after serious crimes have been committed. In Detroit, in December 1960 and

January 1961, after a series of rapes and murders of women, persons were stopped on the street, searched, and in about 1,000 cases arrested. In 1964, after two brothers killed one policeman and seriously wounded another, Baltimore police officers searched more than 300 homes, most belonging to Negroes, looking for the gunman. The searches were often made in the middle of the night and were based almost entirely on anonymous tips. The U.S. Court of Appeals for the Fourth Circuit states:

> Lack of respect for the police is conceded to be one of the factors generating violent outbursts in Negro communities. The invasions so graphically depicted in this case "could" happen in prosperous suburban neighborhoods, but the innocent victims know only that wholesale raids do not happen elsewhere and did happen to them. Understandably they feel that such illegal treatment is reserved for those elements who the police believe cannot or will not challenge them. *Lankford* v. *Gelston,* 364 F 2d 197 (4th Cir. 1966)
>
> . . .

Arrests for investigation or on suspicion, whatever label is attached, should be abolished by all departments that now utilize them. This practice has long been a source of justified community hostility. They not only seriously inconvenience the citizen or even result in his incarceration, but they result in an arrest record which may greatly affect his present or future employment.[51]

The final costs of unfettered aggressive patrol and widespread arrests for investigation may be greater than simple feelings of community hostility toward police. Excesses in the patrol function may, in fact, precipitate riots and mass disorders. The National Advisory Commission on Civil Disorders pointed to both aggressive patrol practices and the increasing "motorization" of police as contributing to ghetto tensions and the outbreak of civil disorder. They commented:

Police administrators, pressed with concern about crime have instituted such patrol practices often without weighing their tension-creating effects and the resulting relationship to civil disorder.

Motorization of police is another aspect of patrol that has affected law enforcement in the ghetto. The patrolman comes to see the city through a windshield and hear about it over a police radio. To him, the area increasingly comes to consist only of lawbreakers. To the ghetto resident, the policeman comes increasingly to be only an enforcer.

Loss of contact between the police officer and the community he serves adversely affects law enforcement. If an officer has never met, does not know, and cannot understand the language and habits of the people in the area he patrols, he cannot do an effective police job. His ability to detect truly suspicious behavior is impaired. He deprives himself of important sources of information. He fails to know those persons with an "equity" in the community—homeowners, small businessmen, professional men, persons who are anxious to support proper law enforcement—and thus sacrifices the contributions they can make to maintaining community order.[52]

Police Response to Mass Disorders

The police function as commonly analyzed pictures one or two police officers questioning or arresting a single suspect, or at most a few suspects. However, police activities during mass disorders present quite a different picture and raise issues of contrasting and important dimensions.

In the past decade our society has experienced mass disorders with unprecedented frequency and simultaneously has witnessed fierce, sometimes lethal, state reactions. Fires, rioting, looting, and sniper fire have been met with gas, firepower, beatings, and mass arrests by police, national guardsmen, and prison officials. The distinctions between peaceful protest demonstrations and civil disobedience and crime and violence became blurred and, with few exceptions, police and other enforcement agencies lacked the kind of training and capabilities needed to maintain effective control. The results were tragic.

The frequency and intensity of mass disorders has waned recently, but it would be foolish to assume that the problem is solved. Though the riots and disorders of the 1960s were particularly widespread and intense, few decades in our history have been unmarked by riots. The first constitutional convention in 1787 saw mob violence, and massive draft riots occurred during the Civil War while great race riots plagued our country between and during the two world wars.[53] Whatever problems remain unsettled between citizens and government, we are compelled to recognize the fact that past disorders *did* accomplish change. This insures a high probability that there will be riots and demonstrations in the future.

The major street and campus disorders of the 1960s and the prison riots of the early 1970s were investigated by various official commissions, as were assassinations of political figures and the problem of violence in general.[54] A common finding of these investigatory bodies was that police actions often tended to escalate violence. The use of tear gas and massive forcible arrests were commonly the first reactions to demonstrations. Later, curfews were imposed, field booking procedures improvised, and stockades built to detain arrestees. Control of domestic disorders took on many of the aspects of guerrilla warfare. Metropolitan police, national guardsmen, state troopers, prison custodial forces—all of the "peace-keeping" forces of the state—faced enforcement dilemmas of major proportions, many of them unanticipated, for which there were neither plans nor experience upon which to draw. There were major problems of command. In a city street riot, does the police commissioner decide when, where, and how to use his force or is the mayor in charge? In the 1968 Chicago riots, the mayor at one point issued orders for the police to "shoot-to-kill" arsonists and "shoot-to-stop" looters, although he later softened this stand.[55] The issue of when, if ever, deadly force should be used by the police in mass disorders was, and is, a matter of great importance. The National Advisory Commission on Civil Disorders commented as follows on the use of deadly force by police agencies:

There are at least three serious problems involved in the use of deadly weapons in a civil disorder. The first is the risk of killing or wounding innocent persons—bystanders or passersby who may in fact be hundreds of feet away when a shot is fired.

The second is the justification for the use of deadly force against looting or vandalism. Are bullets the correct response to offenses of this sort? Major Gen. George Gelston told the Commission: "*** I am not going to order a man killed for stealing a six-pack of beer or a television set." Instead, he said, a nonlethal tear gas can stop any looting.

The third problem is that the use of excessive force—even the inappropriate display of weapons—may be inflammatory and lead to even worse disorder. As the FBI riot-control manual states:

> The basic rule, when applying force, is to use only the minimum force necessary to effectively control the situation. Unwarranted application of force will incite the mob to further violence, as well as kindle seeds of resentment for police that, in turn, could cause a riot to recur. Ill-advised or excessive application of force will not only result in charges of police brutality but also may prolong the disturbance.

Such counsel with respect to disorders accords with the clearly established legal and social principle of minimum use of force by police.

The major difficulty in dealing with all these problems, however, is the limited choice still presented to police in mass disorders: to use too much force or too little. The police who faced the New York riot of 1863 were equipped with two weapons—a wooden stick and a gun. For the most part, the police faced with urban disorders last summer had to rely on two weapons —a wooden stick and a gun.

Our police departments today require a middle range of physical force with which to restrain and control illegal behavior more humanely and more effectively.[56]

Former Attorney General Ramsey Clark traced how ill-prepared police agencies were for the massive demonstrations and disorders of the 1960s and how they only slowly evolved plans and principles to meet massive unrest:

Slowly the police departments in the major cities of the country trained and prepared for riot prevention and control. It was not easy. Understaffed, fragmented, untrained, unequipped and emotional, many police did not want riot control responsibility, viewing it as a military responsibility.

Intensive efforts by the International Association of Chiefs of Police with financing and support from the United States Department of Justice slowly led to the development of effective techniques of prevention and control. The best police leadership soon realized that riot prevention was possible and that police conduct itself was a major factor in prevention. In week-long conferences of police chiefs at Airlie House near Warrenton, Virginia, in January and February of 1968, followed by regional meetings in California, Oklahoma and West Virginia for key police personnel, 90 percent of the effort was devoted to analyzing and developing methods of riot prevention. Police-community relations were seen as the key. Only clear lines of communication with the ghetto could provide notice of and the opportunity to relieve tension. This rapport was considered indispensable.[57]

It became apparent that not only too quick and general use of force backfired by escalating violence, but that even the display of force sometimes acted to turn a peaceful demonstration into a riot. The National Advisory Commission on Civil Disorders warned against police use of sirens and flasher lights in crowd situations and pointed out that overt response to essentially minor incidents by summoning tactical units equipped with riot guns and helmets tended to aggravate tense situations.[58] "Restraint" became the keynote in planning and in police training.

Experiences with street disorders, courtroom disruptions, and prison riots have forced all criminal justice agencies to rethink their functions, to seek ways of preventing mass violence, and to establish riot plans if prevention fails. Many police agencies are now making serious attempts to establish better communication with residents of high-enforcement neighborhoods, to provide services rather than acting solely as outside "enforcers", to listen, learn, and act on feedback received from residents.[59] The American College of Trial Lawyers issued standards relative to courtroom disruptions[60] and correctional authorities are seeking to negotiate prisoner grievances to prevent riots in much the same manner as labor-management negotiations are designed to prevent strikes.[61] While some mass disorders may be prevented or kept nonviolent, the likelihood is that some agencies will confront full-blown riots in the future, and that today most police forces and other agencies have or are developing riot control plans.[62]

The issue of police response to mass disorders is more profound than simply the development of techniques and procedures to put down civil insurrection. Marches, protests, demonstrations, disruptions, and even violent outbursts and riots put to the test many values and ideals basic to our notion of proper policing in a free society. As a people we not only tolerate but encourage free assembly, free speech, and the right of our people to protest, demonstrate, and indeed engage in civil disobedience. We rightly fear encroachment of a police state and decry stormtrooper tactics. At the same time, we espouse ordered liberty and outlaw acts of violence, terror, and property destruction. The police stand as a fulcrum in this delicate but critical balance. If they intervene too soon and too harshly, our freedoms are destroyed; if they act too late or not at all, anarchy results. Most major disturbances and corollary state reactions of the past have been scrutinized after the fact by various grand juries and commissions. Likewise, riots and responses have elicited widespread scholarly assessments.[63] But the problem of the proper balance between the toleration of orderly dissent and prevention or control of violence remains. Ramsey Clark commented:

A fundamental purpose of government is to protect the lives and property of its citizens. This aim requires the maintenance of order under law. We cannot fail to make the effort essential to effective control. We know that riots can usually be prevented and can always be controlled. The question is whether we have the strength to act wisely, or will resort to the law of the pistol.

Even if our only purpose was order, and life meant little, still the most effective control technique would be balanced enforcement, not intimidation. All our experience tells us this.

. . .

Protesters are human beings like the rest of us, and however obnoxious they may seem to many, law enforcement must not deliberately injure them. When it does, it has violated the very principles that law relies on for the order which the rioters seem to threaten. When police exceed their authority, even while making arrests for serious crimes, ours is no longer a government of laws. If law enforcement yields to those who call for violence, only one response is possible among people who believe that what they are doing matters.[64]

CONCLUSION

For most citizens direct contact with the criminal justice system is through their local police. Few of us are actually arrested for crimes, put on trial, or serve sentences. Eventually, however, we all have some experiences with police, even if this is limited to our responses to routine traffic control. Many persons fear

181

police, and resent even slight intrusions into their privacy. Such fear, if not unreasonable, may be healthy in a democratic society where liberty and the right to be left alone are prized. Yet we need competent, efficient, and effective policing for without it there would be anarchy. To be effective, policing must occur in a context of citizen cooperation and support; lack of such support creates a dangerous division between police and the public. Because the need for proper policing is pervasive, and because the police more than any other agency directly touch our lives, it becomes critically important to understand and respond to the police function. Most observers of the criminal process agree that many of the most complex and most critical issues in criminal justice center around policing. This paradox of freedom yet control continues to be a central concern for all students of criminal justice.

NOTES

1. The President's Commission on Law Enforcement and Administration of Justice, *Task Force Report: The Police* (Washington, D.C.: U.S. Government Printing Office, 1967), p. 14. See also Raymond I. Parnas "The Police Response to the Domestic Disturbance," *Wis. Law Review* (1967): 914-960.

2. The President's Commission, *Police*, p. 14.

3. American Bar Association, *Standards Relating to the Urban Police Function*, Approved Draft (New York: Institute of Judicial Administration, 1973), Part III, Sec. 3.1, 3.2, 3.3.

4. The President's Commission, *Police*, p. 2.

5. *Ibid.*

6. James Q. Wilson, *Varieties of Police Behavior* (Cambridge, Mass.: Harvard U. Press, 1968), pp. 25-26.

7. *Ibid*, p. 26.

8. *Ibid*, p. 25.

9. See Jerome S. Skolnick, *Justice Without Trial: Law Enforcement in Democratic Society* (New York: John Wiley and Sons, 1966), especially chapter 3, pp. 42-70.

10. President's Commission, *Police*, pp. 145-146.

11. Albert J. Reiss, Jr., *The Police and the Public* (New Haven: Yale U. Press, 1971), p. 123.

12. See Lawrence P. Tiffany, Donald M. McIntyre, Jr., and Daniel Rotenberg, *Detection of Crime: Stopping and Questioning, Search and Seizure, Encouragement and Entrapment* (Boston: Little, Brown, 1967), Chapter 1.

13. *Ibid,* p. 10.

14. See Sibron v. New York, 392 U.S. 40 (1968).

15. See Tiffany, McIntyre, and Rotenberg, *Detection of Crime,* Part II, pp. 97-205.

16. See Chimel v. California, 395 U.S. 752 (1969).

17. See Giancana v. Johnson, 335 F. 2d 366 (7 Cir. 1964), but also see Scherer v. Brennan, 266 F. Supp. 758 (N.D. Ill. 1966). Affirmed, 379 F. 2d 609 (7th Cir. 1967).

18. In addition to the Katz case, see Alderman v. United States, 394 U.S. 165 (1969).

19. See Omnibus Crime Control and Safe Streets Act of 1968, Public Law 90-351.

20. American Bar Association, *Standards Relating to Electronic Surveillance* (New York: Institute of Judicial Administration, 1968).

21. See generally, Samuel Dash, Richard F. Schwartz, and Robert G. Knowlton, *The Eavesdroppers* (New York: DaCapo, 1959); Alan F. Westin, *Privacy and Freedom* (New York: Atheneum, 1967).

22. See Tiffany, McIntyre, and Rotenberg, *Detection of Crime,* Part III, "Encouragement and Entrapment," pp. 208-282.

23. From Tiffany, McIntyre, and Rotenberg, *Detection of Crime,* pp. 208-211.

24. See Sherman v. United States, 356 U.S. 369 (1958). See also Donnelly, "Judicial Control of Informants, Spies, Stool Pigeons and Agent Provocateurs," *Yale Law J.* 60, 1091 (1951).

25. American Law Institute, *Model Penal Code,* Proposed Official Draft, 1962. See 2.13.

26. National Advisory Commission on Criminal Justice Standards and Goals, *Police* (Washington, D.C.: U.S. Department of Justice, 1973), Standard 1.2, p. 17.

27. Wayne R. LaFave, *Arrest: The Decision to Take a Suspect into Custody* (Boston: Little, Brown, 1965).

28. See American Law Institute, *Model Penal Code,* Sec. 3.07, Comment 3 (Tentative Draft No. 8, 1958).

29. Citizens may sue police officers for damages if they are improperly arrested. In common parlance, the citizen's claim is called "false arrest," but technically suit is brought under the tort of "false imprisonment" meaning that the person's freedom of movement was wrongfully curtailed, even for a brief period of time. The police officer's defense to an allegation of false imprisonment is that the arrest was lawful. Whether in fact the officer had "probable cause" to arrest is determined by the civil jury. In general, civil actions by citizens against police are not an effective means of curbing abuses of police power. See Herman Goldstein, "Administrative Problems in Controlling the Exercise of Police Authority," *J. Crim. Law, Criminology and Pol. Sci.* 58, 160 (1967).

30. LaFave, *Arrest,* pp. 437-489.

31. *Ibid.*

32. United States v. Wade, 388 U.S. 218 (1967).

33. Kirby v. Illinois, 406 U.S. 682 (1972).

34. Mallory v. U.S., 354 U.S. 449 (1957).

35. The Omnibus Crime Control and Safe Arrests Acts of 1968 attempted to modify the Mallory Rule. See 18 U.S.C. See 3501 b. See also United States v. Keeble, 459 F. 2d. 757 (8th Cir. 1972).

36. See Stack v. Boyle, 342 U.S. 1 (1951).

37. See Herbert Sturz, "Experiments in the Criminal Justice System," *Legal Aid Briefcase* 25, 111 (1967).

38. See Herman Goldstein, "Setting High Bail to Prevent Pre-Trial Release," *Proceedings,* National Conference on Bail and Criminal Justice (1964).

39. See Nan C. Bases and William F. McDonald, *Preventive Detention in the District of Columbia: The First Ten Months* (Georgetown Institute of Criminal Law and Procedure and the Vera Institute of New York, 1972).

40. Terry v. Ohio, 392 U.S. 1 (1968).

41. American Bar Association, *Standards Relating to the Urban Police Function,* Sec. 4.1, Commentary, pp. 117-120.

42. LaFave, *Arrest,* pp. 61-226.

43. *Ibid,* Chapter 4, pp. 83-101.

44. *Ibid,* Chapter 5, pp. 102-124.

45. *Ibid,* Chapter 6, pp. 125-143.

46. See People v. Gray, 254 Cal. App. 2d 256 (1967).

47. National Advisory Commission, *Police,* pp. 21-22.

48. Harry W. More, Jr., *Critical Issues in Law Enforcement* (Cincinnati: The W. H. Anderson Co., 1972), p. 180.

49. See The *New York Times,* 11 November 1973.

50. President's Commission, *The Police,* pp. 184-185 (footnotes omitted).

51. *Ibid,* pp. 186-187.

52. *Report of the National Advisory Commission on Civil Disorders* (New York: Bantam, 1968), pp. 304-305.

53. Willard A. Heaps, *Riots U.S.A. 1765-1965* (New York: Seabury Press, 1966).

54. See for example, Final Report of the National Commission on the Causes and Prevention of Violence, *To Establish Justice, To Insure Domestic Tranquility* (1969); *Report of the New York Special Commission on Attica* (New York: Bantam, 1972); Daniel Walker, *Rights in Conflict: The Chicago Police Riot* (New York: Signet, 1968).

55. See Chicago *Sun-Times,* 16 April 1968, and Chicago *Daily News,* 18 April 1968.

56. *Report of the National Advisory Committee on Civil Disorders,* p. 176.

57. Ramsey Clark, *Crime in America* (New York: Simon & Schuster, 1970), pp. 167-168.

58. *Report of the National Advisory Commission on Civil Disorders,* pp. 267-272.

59. See generally, George Edwards, *The Police on the Urban Frontier* (New York: Institute of Human Relations, 1968), Gordon Misner, "The Response of Police Agencies," *The Annals* 376 (March 1968): 109-119; William P. Brown, *The Police and Community Conflict,* National Conference of Christians and Jews, Pamphlet 1962; Louis A. Radelet, *The Police and the Community* (Beverley Hills, Calif.: Glencoe Press, 1973); James Q. Wilson, "Police Morale, Reform and Citizen Respect: The Chicago Case," in David V. Bordua, ed., *The Police: Six Sociological Essays* (New York: John Wiley and Sons, 1967), pp. 137-162.

60. American College of Trial Lawyers, *Disruption of the Judiciary Process* (Chicago, American Bar Association, 1970).

61. See National Council on Crime and Delinquency, *Peaceful Resolution of Prison Conflict* (Hackensack, N.J.: NCCD 1973).

62. See for example, Joseph Coates, *Some New Approaches to Riot, Mob and Crowd Control* (Arlington, Va.: Institute for Defense Analysis, 1968); Robert H. Connery, *Urban Riots, Violence and Social Change* (New York: Vintage), 1969; Department of the Army, *Civil Disturbances and Disasters* (Washington, D.C.: U.S. Government Printing Office, 1968); Federal Bureau of Investigation, *Prevention and Control of Mobs and Riots* (Washington, D.C.: U.S. Department of Justice, 1967); R. Dean Smith and Richard W. Koblenz, *Guidelines for Civil Disorder and Mobilization Plannings* (Washington, D.C.: International Association of Chiefs of Police, 1968).

63. See for example, Louis H. Masotti and Don R. Bowen, eds., *Riots and Rebellion: Civil Violence in the Urban Community* (Beverly Hills, Calif.: Sage Publ., 1968); Jerome S. Skolnick, *The Politics of Protest* (New York: Simon & Schuster, 1969); Ralph W. Conant, "Rioting, Insurrection and Civil Disobedience," *The Amer. Scholar* 37 (September 1968): 420-433; Herman Goldstein, "Police Response to Urban Crisis," *Pub. Admin. Review* 28 (September-October 1968): 417-423; Elmer H. Johnson, "A Sociological Interpretation of Police Reaction and Responsibility to Civil Disobedience," *J. Crim. Law, Criminology and Pol. Sci.* 58 (1968): 405-409; Raymond M. Momboisse, "Demonstrations and Civil Disobedience," *Police* (November-December 1967): 76-82.

64. Clark, *Crime in America*, pp. 178-184.

Chapter 5

Prosecution and Adjudication

THE MIDDLE STAGES OF THE CRIMINAL PROCESS

After a felony suspect has been taken into police custody, and if he is not subsequently released or diverted to some community agency for "voluntary" treatment and control, his case is moved forward to the district attorney who determines whether prosecution will follow. At this point he may be free on bail or on his own recognizance, or failing to make bail, he may still be held in jail, for often by the time a prosecutor is aware of the arrest, the suspect has already been taken before a magistrate for bail consideration.

As pointed out in Chapter 4, police sometimes arrest suspects with no intention to proceed to prosecution. Generally, however, these are cases involving "nuisance" infractions—chronic inebriation, minor vice offenses, and other public order crimes. And today there are various, sanctioned diversion programs where young, first offenders are handled informally, short of prosecution and conviction, to avoid the long-range negative consequences of a criminal record. But the majority of arrested felony suspects move from police intake to the *middle stages* of the criminal process where formal charges are brought and guilt or innocence is determined. Here, for the most part, they experience the machinery of the law in a more formal, detached, and deliberate way than they do with police experience alone. Suspicion is increasingly focused on them, and their destiny within the system is increasingly subject to the scrutiny and determination of law-trained experts.

187

The middle stages of the process are lawyer dominated. After police intake, through charging and adjudication until the postsentencing stages of the process, the primary participants, other than the defendant, are the prosecuting attorney, the defendant's counsel, and the trial judge. In some cases grand or trial juries, or both, play a part, and by the time of sentencing, correctional personnel are beginning to make input into decision making. But the middle stages are primarily court-centered, with the first, and probably most important, actor being the prosecuting attorney.

For some important decisions in the middle stages the defendant is ordinarily not physically present; for others he is not only present, but he may be called on to plead or to testify. Some steps in the process may be waived by the defendant with concurrence of the state. The first decision, an initial determination of whether to prosecute and, if so, what charges to seek, is made by the prosecutor. In routine cases, the prosecutor acts upon the complaint forwarded by the police or the victim along with any evidence accumulated so far. In most instances, this initial decision rests on the basis of paper records and possibly a brief interview with arresting officers. Routinely, the defendant is elsewhere at this point.

If the prosecutor decides to seek a formal charge, the case is forwarded to a grand jury or scheduled for a preliminary hearing before a judge. The route followed depends upon law and custom in the particular jurisdiction. If an indictment is sought from a grand jury, this process ordinarily proceeds without the physical presence or participation of the defendant or his lawyer. But he and his attorney may attend a preliminary hearing and cross-examine any witnesses put on the stand by the state. Conversely, he can choose to waive this hearing, indicating a willingness to plead to charges as drafted by the prosecuting attorney.

Once the formal charge has been prepared—an *indictment* if it comes from a grand jury or an *information* if prepared by the prosecutor and tested at the preliminary hearing—the defendant is brought before a court of competent jurisdiction for pleading. The pleading process is known as *arraignment*. Here the formal charges are read, the defendant is once more notified of his rights, and a plea is requested. If he chooses to plead guilty and the court accepts the plea, a date is fixed for sentencing. If he pleads not guilty, he moves on to trial.

These are the formal steps from the point at which the police lose exclusive control until time for the imposition of sentence on those defendants convicted by plea or by trial. In some cases, other formal decision stages are necessary, such as hearings on pretrial motions to exclude evidence or to change venue, or psychiatric examinations if the defendant pleads insanity or appears incompetent. But in general, the middle stages involve interlocking charge determinations, pleading, and trial. For some defendants, progress through the middle stages is long, involved, and costly. When the state is put to full adversarial test, including a jury trial and appeals, the process may extend over months, sometimes years, before guilt or innocence is finally determined. Other defendants, who abandon rights, waive some steps, and plead guilty, may move very quickly from the police station to a sentencing hearing. At any point along the continuum, some defendants may have charges dropped or may be diverted out of the process, and some are released after being found not guilty at trial.

The formal steps in this decision network describe only its skeleton. In the office of the prosecutor, in the hallways of the courthouse, in the bull pens of the jail, a complicated process known as plea bargaining occurs in a high percentage of cases in most, if not all, jurisdictions around the country. In this process charges are reduced or sentencing promises made in exchange for the defendant's guilty plea. Although historically a nearly invisible, off-the-record procedure, plea bargaining has recently surfaced, is recognized today as a major characteristic of middle stage processing, and is currently an issue of controversy and concern to legislatures, appellate courts, commissions, and all informed observers of criminal justice administration.

Initial Determination of the Charge

In some cases, the invocation of the criminal process begins with a complaint made directly to the prosecutor's office. If the alleged perpetrator is identified by the complainant, the prosecutor may seek an arrest warrant from a judge and direct the appropriate police agency to take the suspect into custody. In other cases in which the suspect is identified by the complainant at the precinct level, the police may obtain an arrest warrant by showing probable cause to a judge for taking the suspect into custody.[1] In such cases the *initial* charge is determined by the warrant, but the final, formal charge may differ as evidence accumulates or dissipates. Arrests without warrants, however, are more common and in such instances the actual point of determination of the initial charge is less precise. Professor Frank Miller comments:

The decision to charge, unlike the decision to arrest, is not a unitary decision made at a readily identifiable time by a specified individual. It is, instead, a process consisting of a series of interrelated decisions, and the steps in the process do not always occur in the same sequence. Most often the decision is made after a suspect has already been taken into custody.[2]

189

In some jurisdictions, postcustody warrants are requested by the police and issued by courts after the suspect is already in custody.[3] More commonly, the complaint—whether of a victim or of the arresting police officer—is forwarded to the prosecutor's office together with any evidence to support it. The prosecutor then evaluates the situation and translates it into appropriate statutory charges.

The Prosecution Role

The prosecutor's discretion is very broad, and in practice is based on many considerations beyond his legal expertise in fitting charges to diverse fact situations. The prosecutor is a political figure as well as a lawyer, and like all politicians, he is responsive to community pressures and sensitive to community norms. The drafters of the American Bar Association's *Standards Relating to the Prosecution Function and the Defense Function* comment:

The political process has played a significant part in the shaping of the role of the American prosecutor. Experience as a prosecutor is a familiar stepping stone to higher political office. The "DA" has long been glamorized in fiction, films, radio, television, and other media. Many of our political leaders had their first exposure to public notice and political life in this office. A substantial number of executive and legislative officials as well as judges have served as prosecuting attorneys at some point in their careers. The political involvement of a prosecutor varies. In most jurisdictions he is required to run with a party designation. In some places prosecutors are elected on a nonpartisan basis. The powers of a prosecutor are formidable and he is an important personage in his community. If he is not truly independent and professional, his powers can be misused for political or other improper purposes. Perhaps even more than other American public officials, the prosecutor's activity is in large part open to public gaze—as it should be—and spotlighted by the press. The importance of his function is such that his least mistake is likely to be magnified, as are many of his successful exploits.[4]

At the same time, the prosecutor is a member of the bar, bound by its code of ethics, and the incumbent of an office with its own ethical traditions and standards. It is generally agreed that the basic duty of the prosecutor is to "seek justice, not merely to convict,"[5] but beyond this the ABA *Standards* posit a "duty to improve the law." These state: "It is an important function of the prosecutor to seek to reform and improve the administration of criminal justice. When inadequacies or injustices in the substantive or procedural law come to his attention, he should stimulate efforts for remedial action."[6] Sometimes the prosecutor is also referred to as the chief law-enforcement official of a district, and in this sense his role is seen as proactive (i.e., a duty to search out criminal activity) as well as reactive (i.e., responding in his charging function to cases brought by the police). The ABA *Standards* describe an investigatory responsibility:

A prosecutor, as the chief law-enforcement official of his jurisdiction, ordinarily relies on police and other investigative agencies for investigation of alleged criminal acts, but he has an affirmative responsibility to investigate suspected illegal activity when it is not adequately dealt with by other agencies.[7]

The scope of the prosecutor's duties—the community expectations commonly assigned to his role—coupled with his broad discretionary authority make this office one of the most powerful and most complex in the criminal justice system. Lawyer, politician, law-enforcement official, administrator, reform advocate, the "architect of fair trials," local "minister of justice" are all facets of his role. However approached or served, the office contains a basic duality of role that complicates analysis of the prosecutorial function. It has been observed:

The prosecutor has a dual role which reflects in a sense the ambivalence of public attitudes on law enforcement and is the source of some difficulties. On the one hand, the prosecutor is the leader of law enforcement in the community. He is expected to participate actively in marshaling society's resources against the threat of crime. When a crisis in the enforcement of criminal law arises in the community, the public press and others clamor for a "war against crime" and he may be drawn into the maelstrom of political controversy by the demand that he "stamp out the criminals." He is called upon to make public statements, to propose legislative reforms, or to direct the energies of the law-enforcement machinery of the community. On the other hand, the office demands, and on sober thought the public expects, that the prosecutor will respect the rights of persons accused of crime. Our nation began with resistance to oppressive official conduct and our traditions, embodied in the national and state constitutions, demand that the prosecutor accord basic fairness to all persons. Because of the power he wields, we impose on him a special duty to protect the innocent and to safeguard the rights guaranteed to all, including those who may be guilty. The conflicting demands on a prosecutor may exert pressures on him which his sense of fairness as a lawyer rejects. Both his public responsibilities as well as his obligations as a member of the bar require that he be something more than a partisan advocate intent on winning cases.[8]

Because the prosecutor's position is so central in the American criminal justice system, it is sometimes assumed that his broad discretionary authority and the dilemmas of his diverse duties are peculiar to our society and relatively absent

191

in other cultures. There is, however, increasing evidence that the situation is not that much different in other systems and that certain prosecutorial practices, such as plea bargaining, long thought to be an American phenomenon occur elsewhere.[9]

DISCRETION NOT TO CHARGE. Upon receiving a complaint and accompanying evidence from the police, the prosecutor, or one of his assistants, has several initial decisions to make. The first is whether to charge the suspect with a crime at all. As noted earlier, the prosecutor has the traditional power of *nolle prosequi*—discretion *not* to charge the suspect even though there is appropriate and sufficient evidence that he has committed a crime. As a lawyer, he may also decide that no law has been broken or that the evidence held by the police is insufficient, and likely to remain so, to support a formal charge. Or he may decide that the evidence would probably be held inadmissable at trial.

The prosecutor's right to decide *not* to prosecute, even with sufficient evidence, is one of the broadest, most powerful examples of discretionary authority in the entire criminal justice system. This traditional discretion, which traces its origins back to early common law, always has been controversial. Many years ago Thurman W. Arnold said: "The idea that a prosecuting attorney should be permitted to use his discretion concerning the laws he will enforce and those which he will disregard appears to the ordinary citizen to border on anarchy."[10] The common argument that the *nolle prosequi* power of the prosecutor is one-directional, that is, it is discretion not to act and therefore it is a form of leniency, has not gone unchallenged. For example, Professor Kenneth Culp Davis commented: "The discretionary power to be lenient is an impossibility without a concomitant discretionary power not to be lenient, and injustice from the discretionary power not to be lenient is especially frequent; the power to be lenient is the power to discriminate."[11]

Criticisms notwithstanding, the discretion of the prosecutor to *nol pros,* to engage in selective enforcement and to prosecute for less than the full extent possible, has been repeatedly upheld by appellate courts.[12] Recently the ABA issued the following standards for the exercise of charging discretion:

> a. In addressing himself to the decision whether to charge, the prosecutor should first determine whether there is evidence which would support a conviction. It is unprofessional conduct for a prosecutor to institute or cause to be instituted criminal charges when he knows that the charges are not supported by probable cause.
> b. The prosecutor is not obliged to present all charges which the evidence might support. The prosecutor may in some circumstances and for good cause consistent with the public interest decline to prosecute, not-

withstanding that evidence may exist which would support a conviction. Illustrative of the factors which the prosecutor may properly consider in exercising his discretion are:

    i.   the prosecutor's doubt that the accused is in fact guilty;

    ii.   the extent of the harm caused by the offense;

    iii.   the disproportion of the authorized punishment in 'relation to the particular offense or the offender;

    iv.   possible improper motives of a complainant;

    v.   reluctance of the victim to testify;

    vi.   cooperation of the accused in the apprehension or conviction of others;

    vii.   availability and likelihood of prosecution by another jurisdiction.

c.   In making the decision to prosecute, the prosecutor should give no weight to the personal or political advantages or disadvantages which might be involved or to a desire to enhance his record of convictions.

d.   In cases which involve a serious threat to the community, the prosecutor should not be deterred from prosecution by the fact that in his jurisdiction juries have tended to acquit persons accused of the particular kind of criminal act in question.

e.   The prosecutor should not bring or seek charges greater in number or degree than he can reasonably support with evidence at trial.[13]

In the tentative draft of this standard an additional criterion was included in the list of "illustrative factors" that might properly be considered by the prosecutor in exercising his discretion not to prosecute. This was stated as: "prolonged nonenforcement of a statute, with community acquiescence." It was deleted from the final draft "because the justification for exercise of discretion not to prosecute which it provides could be construed to go beyond the cases envisioned by the Advisory Committee, e.g., obsolete blue laws, to embrace matters which amount to a dereliction of duty, e.g., illegal gambling."[14]

THE PROBABLE CAUSE STANDARD. Technically, a formal, final charge may be levied against a defendant with evidence sufficient to show probable cause that the defendant is guilty of a crime, an evidence test that in many jurisdictions is phrased exactly like the evidentiary standard required for a lawful arrest. But in this respect probable cause is essentially backward-looking; the officer must have had sufficient evidence in hand to establish probable cause at the time he arrested the suspect. If he did not, he may be liable for damages in a civil suit for what is commonly called "false arrest," but which is, more precisely, an action in tort for false imprisonment. If the evidence is later refuted and the defendant released as innocent, the arrest may nevertheless stand as proper if at the time the officer acted reasonably on probable cause.

193

The prosecutor, however, is not interested in justifying past actions; he is looking ahead toward the trial at which the higher evidentiary standard of proof "beyond a reasonable doubt" is necessary for conviction. In this sense, his assessment of probable cause is forward looking and its application colored not only by the trial standard, but by such tactical considerations as the credibility of witnesses, the likelihood of a successful defense or of motions to exclude evidence, the probable effect on the jury of the reputation of the suspect or the victim, and similar factors.

CHARGING DECISIONS. If the district attorney or his assistant decides to proceed to prosecution, decisions must be made as to which specific charge or charges to levy and how many counts to seek in the formal charge. If more than one offense is contained in the complaint, or if more than one defendant is involved in the crime, the prosecutor must decide whether to join offenses and offenders in a single prosecution or whether to sever them for separate charges and trials.[15] If the record makes it possible to do so, the prosecutor must decide whether to levy additional charges, such as being an "habitual offender" against the suspect.

Illustration 1. Police arrested a suspect for homicide following a fatal knifing which occurred in a barroom. He was held without bail by the magistrate at initial appearance. The prosecutor reviewed police reports of interviews with witnesses, questioned the arresting officers, and finally decided to seek a charge of second-degree murder. He told the arresting officers that he did not think the evidence would support "premeditation" required in this jurisdiction for first-degree murder and that subsequent investigation might well reveal some mitigating circumstances that would preclude the higher charge.

Illustration 2. Police arrested a suspect they believed to be a "cat burglar" who had plagued the city in recent months. Following his arrest and pursuant to a search warrant, they recovered a good deal of stolen property hidden in an attic of a house owned by the suspect's uncle. The recovered property included loot from thirty-five reported burglaries. The prosecutor decided to charge three counts of burglary against the suspect but rejected police requests that his uncle be charged either as an accessory or for the crime of receiving stolen property.

In most routine cases the prosecutor's initial charging determination is made in the absence of the suspect, who at this point may be on bail or held in jail awaiting further processing. The prosecutor may interview the arresting officer and perhaps the complainant or available witnesses. And upon request, he may talk with the suspect's defense attorney if one has been hired or appointed by this time. In certain "hot" cases—generally those involving very serious crimes, famous or notorious suspects, or cases that otherwise have generated a good deal of publicity—the prosecutor may meet with and interrogate the suspect. In such cases he may become involved before or immediately after arrest and conduct all in-custody interrogation himself. But these are comparatively rare occurrences; usually the initial determination to charge or not to charge is made without contacting the suspect.

In practice, the actual decisions of the prosecutor in charging, like those of police in law enforcement, do not involve automatic application of the full force of statutes in all cases, but rather the fair use of his authority to make just and sensible distinctions among cases without abandoning his prerogatives or neglecting his duties. While he has authority to charge the highest crime supported by available evidence in each case he confronts, in practice he may charge a lesser crime or not charge at all, dismissing the case, "settling" it, or diverting the defendant to some other process. On the basis of his analysis of prosecutorial practices in three states, Professor Frank W. Miller comments as follows on the prosecutor's charging discretion:

Regardless of what position might be taken in law, there is general recognition everywhere that resources are simply not adequate to fully enforce every penal law. Recognition of the necessity for charging discretion, therefore, is most widespread in terms of limited resources. Enforcement practices designed to utilize resources most efficiently are adopted by prosecutors everywhere. A Detroit prosecutor reported, for example, that cases of nonsupport, conversion, fraud, and embezzlement are growing at such a rate that his office cannot prosecute all offenders; instead, private compromise settlements between the complainants and the offender are encouraged actively.

. . .

There is also wide recognition that factors other than limited resources may provide adequate bases for failure to enforce the law fully against the guilty. The wide variety of situations which may arise, including important differences in the characteristics of particular offenders, as well as inherent limitations in the use of language, force legislatures to proscribe conduct in broader terms than might be considered ideal. Indeed, there is evidence that full enforcement apart from resource limitations is not consistent with legislative expectations in some situations. On these assumptions, it follows that detailed distinctions must, in some measure, be drawn by front-line administrative officers, whether prosecutors, police or trial judges; that charging discretion is necessary to transform broad legislative proscriptions into pragmatically satisfactory social policy.[16]

Miller went on to analyze situations in which prosecutors commonly decide to settle cases without prosecution, to dismiss charges and to charge lesser crimes than possible with available evidence. These situations involve a wide variety of considerations and circumstances including: 1) decisions not to charge when there are more effective civil sanctions, such as license revocation; 2) decisions to drop charges because adequate alternatives exist, such as commitment to a mental hospital or revocation of parole on a prior sentence; 3) decisions to drop or reduce charges for informers or cooperating state's witnesses; 4) decisions to dismiss or reduce charges because full conviction would place an undue hardship on "deserving" defendants, that is, technical violations by otherwise law-abiding citizens or youthful first offenders; 5) dismissal or reduction because the victim either precipitated the offense by his own conduct or appears unwilling to cooperate fully in prosecution; 6) dismissal or reduction when the offender, otherwise not a serious or persistent violator, has made restitution or other amends and the victim is satisfied with the settlement; 7) charge reduction because maximum prosecution would be excessively costly and time-consuming and comparable sentencing results could be achieved by lesser charges; and, of course, 8) charge reductions as a part of overt plea bargaining to avoid trial.[17]

The Determination of Formal Charges

Assuming the initial decision is to prosecute, the next step in the charging process is to seek a formal, final charge which the suspect—now a defendant —must answer. As mentioned earlier, this may be done in two ways, depending upon provisions in particular jurisdictions. One involves seeking an *indictment* from a grand jury; the other requires the prosecutor to draft the formal charge as an *information* and to test for probable cause at a preliminary hearing before a judge.

THE GRAND JURY—INDICTMENT PROCESS.   Roughly half the states and the federal jurisdiction use grand juries as a major, occasionally exclusive, way of formalizing felony charges. In 22 states a felony may be prosecuted on an information *or* an indictment, though the former is more commonly used.[18]

A grand jury is composed of 23 members but may act with a quorum of 16 members present. An indictment will be issued upon vote of 12 members. Grand jury proceedings are secret, not only from the public and the press, but also from the defendant, except in rare instances and upon his own request. Defense counsel is likewise excluded from these hearings. With the permission of the trial judge, the minutes of grand jury deliberations *may* be shown in part or in whole to the defense immediately before or during the trial, but normally only if the defendant can show a "particularized need."[19]

When the grand jury is assembled, the prosecutor appears before it and requests an indictment. He need only show sufficient evidence to convince a majority that there is probable cause to hold the defendant for trial. He is not required at this stage to reveal all of the state's evidence or to bring forth all witnesses. Furthermore, evidence presented to the grand jury need not conform to trial standards of admissability. In one leading case the U.S. Supreme Court upheld the appropriateness of grand jury consideration of hearsay evidence, with Mr. Justice Black commenting: "[N]either the Fifth Amendment nor any other constitutional provision prescribes the kind of evidence upon which grand juries must act."[20] However, some states have more restrictive evidentiary rules. New York, for example, does not allow grand jurors to consider hearsay evidence.[21]

A major check on the use of inadmissable trial evidence before the grand jury is the prosecutor's professional awareness that unless other direct and appropriate evidence is available, he will be unable to convict the defendant at trial. Professor Miller comments:

The process may, therefore, be accurately conceived as one of self-limitation. Reasons are obvious why a prosecutor would find a situation intolerable in which a substantial number of persons were charged who later proved unconvictable. Not only would the ends of justice be disserved . . . but also the record of the prosecutor by which the public judges him—his success in obtaining convictions—would suffer.[22]

Because grand jurors hear only the state's evidence without opportunity for defense rebuttal or contradiction, it is to be expected that they will honor the prosecutor's request for an indictment in most cases. The rubber-stamp nature of this process came under fire following the various crime surveys of the early 1930s when both the American Law Institute and the Wickersham Commission (President Hoover's crime commission) recommended the initiation of all prosecutions by information rather than indictment. A study about this time demonstrated that the grand jury rejected prosecutor's requests only 5 percent of the time, leading the researcher, Wayne Morse, to call the grand jury "a fifth wheel in the administration of justice."[23] Though the grand jury system is cumbersome and expensive and in most cases does ratify the prosecutor's request for indictment, the "fifth wheel" condemnation did not gain uniform acceptance. For example, Professor George H. Dession argued that a low rate of disagreement is reasonable in light of the open-and-shut nature of most cases processed to this level. He pointed out that the real significance of the jury in acting as a citizen check on the prosecutor is demonstrated by the cases in which they do not indict—albeit a small fraction—when the prosecutor so requests.[24]

In most circumstances, if a grand jury fails to indict, the prosecutor can, if he wishes, take the case before another grand jury. Some states, however, require him to receive court approval before a second attempt.[25] If an indictment is issued by a first or subsequent grand jury, the defendant is not permitted a preliminary hearing, and the next step in the process is his plea to the charges.

More recent surveys have generally supported the finding of a low rate of grand jury rejection of prosecutor requests for indictment, with "no-bills" (i.e., no indictment) ranging from 1 to roughly 10 percent of cases presented to them.[26] Nevertheless the controversy over the relative merits of the indictment versus the information process continues.[27] Though the information-preliminary hearing process is more common today, the grand jury system is still alive and is used extensively in some of our larger and older state jurisdictions. As an important institution in our society, the grand jury has been called "A Sword and Shield" of justice: a sword because "it is the terror of criminals," and a shield because it protects the innocent against "unjust prosecution."[28] But it is a cumbersome and costly charging process and is falling into disuse even in those states where it has been the traditional means of charging felonies. In New York, for example, where the grand jury has been the exclusive method of felony charging, voters recently approved a proposed constitutional amendment to allow the preliminary hearing option. The role of grand juries is not limited to ratifying or rejecting charge requests of the prosecutor. Perhaps their most important function is investigation of possible crimes, corruption, and arrested wrongdoings of citizens, public officials, and agencies. Generally, investigatory grand juries are assembled for this purpose and are separate entities from charging grand juries, but this is not always the case. All grand juries can pursue almost unlimited investigations if they wish and may level charges on their own motions if they uncover crimes.[29] The investigatory grand jury has traditionally played a particularly important role in organized crime investigations, and official inquiries into such matters as police corruption and forceful state reactions to mass disorders, prison riots, and so on. In recent years, grand juries (and special prosecutors) played a central role in investigations arising from the Senate Watergate hearings. While the charging function of grand juries may be waning in use, their investigatory functions are likely to remain important and operational within the criminal justice system. Many jurisdictions which have abandoned the use of grand juries in charging retain them for investigatory purposes.

THE PRELIMINARY HEARING—INFORMATION PROCESS. The major way by which felony charges are formally levied against a defendant is by prosecutorial drafting of an information and, unless waived, a test of probable cause to support the charges at a preliminary hearing before a magistrate.

The preliminary hearing differs from grand jury proceedings in several significant ways. It is open to the public, and the testimony or evidence presented is available for dissemination in the press and other media. The defendant has a right to be present at the hearing and now has a constitutional right to assistance of counsel, even if he is indigent, for the U.S. Supreme Court has recently held the hearing to be a "critical stage" of the process. This represents another expansion of defendant protection by providing a right to counsel. The Supreme Court had already defined the trial, arraignment, sentencing, and even in-custody police interrogation as "critical stages," but the preliminary hearing was a point of some uncertainty, partly because it was, and is, an optional procedure in those jurisdictions which also can use the grand jury-indictment process. However, in the following case the Supreme Court resolved the critical stage issue:

COLEMAN V. ALABAMA
399 U.S. 1 (1970)
MR. JUSTICE BRENNAN announced the judgment of the Court and delivered the following opinion.

* * *

The preliminary hearing is not a required step in Alabama prosecution. The prosecutor may seek an indictment directly from the grand jury without a preliminary hearing. Ex parte *Campbell,* 278 Ala. 114, 176 So. 2d 242 (1965). The opinion of the Alabama Court of Appeals in this case instructs us that under Alabama law the sole purposes of a preliminary hearing are to determine whether there is sufficient evidence against the accused to warrant presenting his case to the grand jury and if so to fix bail if the offense is bailable.

. . .

This court is of course bound by this construction of the governing Alabama law . . . However from the fact that in cases where the accused has no lawyer at the hearing the Alabama courts prohibit the State's use at trial of anything that occurred at the hearing, it does not follow that the Alabama preliminary hearing is not a "critical stage" of the State's criminal process. The determination whether the hearing is a "critical stage" requiring the provision of counsel depends, as noted, upon an analysis "whether potential substantial prejudice

199

to defendant's rights inheres in the * * * confrontation and the ability of counsel to help avoid that prejudice." *United States* v. *Wade* supra, 388 U.S. at 227, 87 S. Ct. at 1932. Plainly the guiding hand of counsel at the preliminary hearing is essential to protect the indigent accused against an erroneous or improper prosecution. First, the lawyer's skilled examination and cross-examination of witnesses may expose fatal weaknesses in the State's case, that may lead the magistrate to refuse to bind the accused over. Second, in any event, the skilled interrogation of witnesses by an experienced lawyer can fashion a vital impeachment tool for use in cross-examination of the State's witnesses at the trial, or preserve testimony favorable to the accused of a witness who does not appear at the trial. Third, trained counsel can more effectively discover the case the State has against his client and make possible the preparation of a proper defense to meet that case at the trial. Fourth, counsel can also be influential at the preliminary hearing in making effective arguments for the accused on such matters as the necessity for an early psychiatric examination or bail.

The inability of the indigent accused on his own to realize these advantages of a lawyer's assistance compels the conclusion that the Alabama preliminary hearing is a "critical stage" of the State's criminal process at which the accused is "as much entitled to such aid [of counsel] * * * as at the trial itself." *Powell* v. *Alabama* supra, 287 U.S. at 57, 53 S. Ct. at 60.

. . .

Convictions vacated and case remanded with directions.

At the preliminary hearing the defendant is not asked to plead to any charge, and he need do nothing but listen to the evidence presented by the prosecutor. However, he may on his own, or through counsel, cross-examine state's witnesses and otherwise challenge evidence introduced by the prosecutor. In some jurisdictions the defendant is allowed to introduce an affirmative defense—for example, an alibi purporting to show that he was elsewhere and otherwise engaged when the crime was committed.[30]

Because the defendant has a right to cross-examine state's witnesses even though he may choose not to do so, direct testimony presented at the preliminary hearing may be used at the trial, if for any reason the witness is unavailable later. This is unlike the situation before a grand jury in which the defendant has no opportunity to confront and challenge his accusers.

Furthermore, unlike grand jury proceedings, the defendant may waive the preliminary hearing, in effect accepting the information as drafted by the prosecutor, and have his case go directly to pleading. But the state must agree to the waiver, for the prosecutor can insist on a preliminary hearing if he wishes. This is rare, however, occurring only when unusual tactics are considered desirable or necessary. The prosecutor may wish to record and certify the testimony of a witness whom he thinks may die, disappear, or perhaps become intimidated and change his story by the time of the trial. Occasionally he may wish to test his witnesses to see how they stand up under cross-examination. In general, however, the state gains little by insisting on a preliminary hearing.[31]

The defense may waive the preliminary for a variety of reasons ranging from an already firm decision to plead guilty to a desire to avoid the negative publicity which is likely to follow such a hearing. Typically, only the state's case is presented, while evidence in rebuttal is not revealed until the trial, perhaps months later. Even if the defendant is eventually acquitted, extensive damage to his reputation may flow from reported testimony of preliminary hearing witnesses. Thus waiver of the preliminary hearing has been the common practice, though this may change following the Supreme Court's definition of the hearing as a critical stage.[32]

A defendant may demand a preliminary hearing not only on the remote chance that the magistrate may find insufficient cause to hold him for trial, but also to get some inkling of the evidence against him. The latter reason is probably the chief defense motivation for desiring a preliminary hearing, but generally *discovery* is not sanctioned by appellate courts as a legitimate purpose. It is a common prosecutorial practice in those jurisdictions in which the grand jury may be used to schedule a grand jury hearing prior to any date set for a preliminary hearing in the hope of obtaining an indictment which would obviate the necessity for a preliminary and thus prevent any pretrial discovery by the defense. Occasionally, defendants confronted by this situation have demanded postindictment preliminary hearings, not on the basis that probable cause must be shown again, but on the grounds that a fundamental purpose of the preliminary is to provide defense discovery of at least some of the state's evidence. The Second Federal Circuit Court of Appeals confronted this issue:

SCIORTINO V. ZAMPANO
385 F. 2d. 132 (2nd CIR. 1967)
CERT. DENIED 390 U.S. 906 (1968)
Before FRIENDLY, HAYS, and ANDERSON, Circuit Judges.

HAYS, Circuit Judge. Petitioner seeks an order in the nature of a writ of mandamus directing the district court to order the U.S. Commissioner to conduct a preliminary examination of petitioner under Rule 5(c) of the Federal Rules of Criminal Procedure. We deny the writ.

Petitioner a Bridgeport, Connecticut physician, was arrested on June 22, 1967 upon a commissioner's warrant charging him with the unlawful sale of depressant and stimulant drugs. * * * He was brought before a commissioner,

201

advised of his rights, and admitted to bail. Petitioner's counsel asked the government to agree to a postponement of the preliminary examination until July 11 because his associate, who would be handling the case, was out of state. The government consented, but announced that it would present the case to a grand jury on July 10 and that, if an indictment was returned, it would contend that the commissioner no longer had power to hold a preliminary hearing.

On July 10 petitioner moved for an order enjoining the U.S. Attorney from presenting the case to the grand jury. The motion was denied, and later that day the grand jury returned an indictment.

. . .

Petitioner's principal contention is that the preliminary examination provided by Rule 5(c) of the Federal Rules of Criminal Procedure is intended to serve as a means of discovery for the accused as well as a forum for determining probable cause, so that the need for such an examination is not eliminated by the return of an indictment.

There is nothing in the language or the history of Rule 5 to suggest that the preliminary examination has any purpose other than to afford a person arrested upon complaint an opportunity to challenge the existence of probable cause for detaining him or requiring bail. The extensive review of the history of the drafting of Rule 5 contained in 1 Orfield Criminal Procedure under the Federal Rules, 203-224 (1966), contains not a word to suggest that in the drafting of the rule there was any purpose to provide the accused with a discovery procedure. See also 1 Orfield, Section 5:7, Functions of Preliminary Examination: "But the purpose is not to give discovery, before trial, of the governments case. The indictment plus a bill of particulars is all that the defendant is entitled to."

There is extensive authority in the cases for the proposition that the return of an indictment, which establishes probable cause, eliminates the need for a preliminary examination.

. . .

We cannot agree to elevating into a right to be enjoyed by an accused the pure fortuity that where a preliminary hearing is held there is necessarily some discovery of the government's evidence. It is quite clear from the logic as well as the history of the procedure that discovery is not one of its purposes. It defies logic, for example, to allow such discovery to defendants who happen to be arrested before indictment and to deny it to those who are arrested after indictment.

The subject of discovery in criminal cases received a great deal of attention at the hands of those responsible for the original preparation of the Federal Rules and their recent amendment. * * * It is most unlikely that having provided carefully for a limited discovery in Rules 7(f), 16, and 17.1 the draftsmen intended that the discovery adventitiously attached to the preliminary hearing should constitute a further right of the accused.

. . .

Petition denied.

Revelations made at the preliminary hearing may help the defendant prepare his defenses for trial, but in all probability the information will be most useful in helping him decide whether or not to plead guilty, and if so, to what charge.[33]

Though there are important differences between grand jury proceedings and the preliminary hearing, the purpose of each is identical: the demonstration of probable cause sufficient to hold the defendant for trial. Both processes are referred to as *pretrial screens* designed to act as curbs on police arrests for investigation and to reduce the possibilities for inappropriate or inaccurate charging by the prosecutor. In a statistical sense, both tend to rubber-stamp the initial charging decision of the prosecutor, for like the grand jury, the preliminary hearing most often results in a finding of probable cause.[34] If the magistrate finds probable cause, he will "bind over" the defendant for pleading and possible trial, just as he is bound over after indictment. The formal charging documents—the indictment and the information—have equal weight and significance when used as formal charging alternatives. The required quality of evidence used to establish probable cause varies by jurisdiction, as does that of evidence before the grand jury, though stringency is more common at preliminary hearings. While there is no uniform test of quality of evidence applicable in all jurisdictions, evidence such as hearsay, which is inadmissable at the trial, is also commonly inadmissable at the preliminary hearing.[35]

Ordinarily there is nothing to prevent a prosecutor taking a case dismissed at one preliminary hearing before another magistrate. Protection against double jeopardy does not apply until after the trial has commenced. However, such "magistrate shopping" by a prosecutor is likely to be frowned on by the bench, so that a dismissal at a preliminary hearing ends the case for all practical purposes unless significant new evidence is obtained by the state. Occasionally, when both procedures are available, a case dismissed at a preliminary hearing may be submitted to a grand jury and result in an indictment.

ARRAIGNMENT ON THE INDICTMENT OR INFORMATION. At some date after the filing of the indictment or information—ordinarily ranging from a few days to a few weeks, depending upon the court calendar—the defendant is brought before a court of competent jurisdiction where he is once more notified of his constitutional rights relating to trial, is presented with the formal charges against him, and is asked to plead to them.

Illustration 3.   COURT: You are charged in the information filed against you in this court with the crime of breaking and entering with intention to steal, two counts. Do you understand what this means?
DEFENDANT: Yes, sir.
COURT: What does it mean?
DEF.: Well, it means burglary, I guess. . . .
COURT: What actually did you do?
DEF.: Well, one time I took these tires from the gas station and the other time those TV sets from Shoppers' City. . . .
COURT: Did you use forcible entry to break into these places?
DEF.: Yes, sir.
COURT: And how do you plead to these charges?
DEF.: Guilty.
COURT: Do you realize that by pleading guilty you give up your right to trial?
DEF.: Yes.
COURT: Let the record show that the defendant is represented by counsel, Mr. Schuffstal, of this city. Have you consulted with your attorney? Does he agree that you should plead guilty?
DEF.: Yes, sir.
COURT: What say you, Mr. Schuffstal?
COUNSEL: I have advised my client to plead guilty as charged, your honor.
COURT: Do you realize that by pleading guilty you could be sent to prison for three years on each count in the charges?
DEF.: Yes, sir.
COURT: And you still wish to so plead?
DEF.: Yes, I do.
COURT: Has the prosecuting attorney, any officers of this court, or any other person threatened you or made any promises to induce you to plead guilty?
DEF.: No, sir.
COURT: You are pleading guilty freely and voluntarily?
DEF.: Yes.
COURT: Very well, I accept your plea of guilty and set the date for sentencing three weeks hence, that is, at 10:00 a.m. on August 15.

Pleas available to a defendant at arraignment are: 1) not guilty; 2) guilty; and in some places 3) not guilty because insane; and 4) *nolo contendere* (no contest). This latter plea, available at the discretion of the trial judge in about half the states and throughout the federal jurisdiction, has the same criminal effect as a plea of guilty, but unlike the guilty plea, may not be used in any subsequent civil action as proof that the defendant committed the act. It is commonly entered in white-collar cases in which a corporate defendant is likely to be sued for damages, and is used occasionally in cases involving traditional charges, such as assault in which the victim may be bringing civil suit.[36] This plea was accepted in the case involving former Vice President Spiro Agnew as part of his plea bargain with the federal government.[37]

If a defendant stands mute, or otherwise refuses to answer charges, a not guilty plea is entered for him. In a few jurisdictions, a defendant is required to indicate his intention to use an insanity defense by entering a plea of "not guilty because insane." More commonly, defense disclosure of the defenses of insanity or alibi are required five to ten days before trial as specified in statute, rather than at arraignment. However, in most places later entry of these defenses may be allowed with consent of the court, but this generally results in a delay of the trial to allow the state opportunity to investigate the alibi or submit the defendant to a psychiatric examination.

If the defendant pleads not guilty, the arraignment ends with the setting of a date for trial. Once again bail or recognizance release is considered with judicial options to continue bail or ROR, raise or lower the amount of bond, or deny release and remand the defendant to detention to await trial. When a plea of "not guilty because insane" is entered, the defendant is commonly held for psychiatric examination upon request of the prosecutor with trial time fixed for a date following the diagnostic interval.

GUILTY PLEA PROCEDURES. Even if a defendant pleads guilty or *nolo contendere,* the judge need not accept the plea. If, from the behavior, appearance, or words of the defendant during the brief arraignment process the judge is led to believe that he is mentally incompetent, that somehow he does not seem to understand what is happening, or that the plea may be involuntary or otherwise grossly inaccurate, he may delay arraignment for psychiatric diagnosis or to allow the defendant to confer with counsel, or he may simply reject the guilty plea and set a trial date as if the defendant had pleaded not guilty.

In deciding whether or not to accept a plea of guilty, both federal and state judges today are required to personally address the defendant and to make inquiry sufficient to establish: 1) that the defendant knows of his right to trial and that a guilty plea is a waiver of this right; 2) that the defendant is "voluntarily" pleading guilty; 3) that he understands the nature of the charges against him, and 4) that he is aware of the possible maximum sentence that can be imposed if he pleads guilty. The required scope of such judicial inquiry is still open to interpretation, but the Supreme Court has found a "silent record" of pleading procedures to be insufficient in state as well as federal courts.[38] Numerous state and federal appellate court decisions speak to dimensions of the judicial inquiry regarding voluntariness, understanding, and awareness of

UNITED STATES DISTRICT COURTS
METHOD OF DISPOSITION FOR CONVICTED DEFENDANTS
Fiscal Years 1964-1971

Number of
convicted
defendants

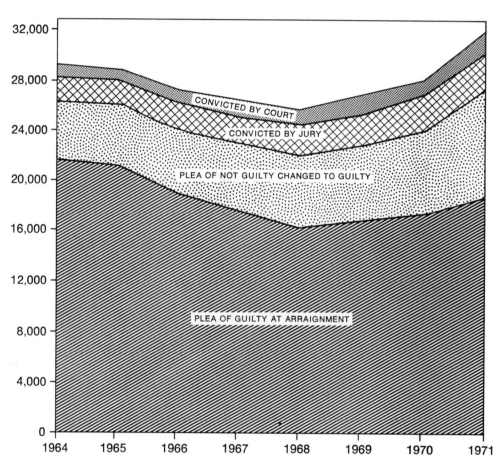

Note: Excludes District of Columbia and territories.

Administrative Office of U.S. Courts, *Federal Offenders in United States District Courts 1971* (Washington, D.C.: Administrative Office of U.S. Courts, 1972), p. 5.

consequences.[39] However, a more complex and unsettled matter is raised by a provision found in some state court rules or statutes and in the Federal Rules of Criminal Procedure which requires that the judge must inquire into the *factual basis* for the plea.[40] Other requirements deal with whether the defendant knows what he is doing and is willing to proceed, whereas the factual basis requirement relates more directly to the accuracy of the guilty plea, and to evidence supporting the charge. The extent of such inquiry, the amount and type of evidence sufficient to support a factual basis, is left to the discretion of the judge, requiring only that he be "satisfied that there is a factual basis for the plea" as stated in Federal Rule 11.[41] Presumably this could be less stringent than the beyond a reasonable doubt basis required for finding guilt at a trial. It is still unclear how extensive such judicial inquiries are in practice.

PLEA BARGAINING AND PLEA-AGREEMENT PROCEDURES. In all jurisdictions most defendants charged with both felonies and misdemeanors plead guilty to some crime, not uncommonly lesser offenses than originally charged. There is no doubt that the guilty plea, *not* the trial, is the chief form of criminal adjudication in our society.[42] A defendant who pleads guilty even to a very serious felony at a brief but properly conducted arraignment stands convicted just as surely as if he had been subjected to a three-month jury trial.

Guilty pleas are so pervasive across jurisdictions, occurring in proportions occasionally exceeding 90 percent of all charged offenders, that court calendars, staffing, and other resources are provided in anticipation of a high rate of pleas. Though it is sometimes assumed that high proportions of guilty pleas primarily occur in and are products of crowded, metropolitan courts, there is evidence to indicate that the proportion of guilty pleas is about the same in rural, less harried court systems.[43] For example, the percentage of guilty pleas in Vermont is about the same as that in Manhattan.[44]

In part, this record can be attributed to careful arrest practices and the effective use of pretrial screens to separate innocent or otherwise nonconvictable suspects and defendants. But the question remains: why would even guilty defendants waive trial, thus foregoing the evidentiary test of beyond a reasonable doubt which is met only at a trial? A guilty plea is, of course, a form of confession and in some cases may simply be the result of remorse or of some other motivation to confess. Operationally, however, ample evidence suggests that many defendants who plead guilty expect, and indeed receive, greater sentencing leniency than is shown to others convicted only after full trials.[45] In short, there is an *implicit bargain* with the state in each guilty plea, and though differential sentencing of those who plead in contrast to those who demand a trial is a controversial matter, this practice is generally considered proper today.[46]

Throwing oneself on the mercy of the court is one thing; arranging for charge or sentencing concessions *before* entering a guilty plea is an even more complex and controversial process. Nonetheless, negotiations between prosecution and defense to obtain guilty pleas is a common practice in most, perhaps all, jurisdictions.[47] Variously known as "plea bargaining," "plea negotiation," or "plea agreement," the actual point at which negotiations occur varies from any time after arrest, up to and during the trial. In some places it is customary for bargaining to occur prior to filing of an information; elsewhere agreements are commonly struck after preliminary hearing and before commencement of the trial. The kinds and types of bargains also differ among jurisdictions, just as sentencing structures vary from one place to another, for the primary motivation in bargaining by any defendant is to achieve a lenient sentence.

Illustration 4. Upon complaint of a woman and her young daughter, a suspect was arrested for child molestation (technically "carnal knowledge and abuse of a minor"), an offense carrying a prison sentence of 5 to 25 years. The defendant denied the allegation, and the only evidence against him was the testimony of the child, another young companion, and the hearsay complaint of the mother who did not witness the alleged crime. The defendant had been charged with a similar offense 5 years previously, but the charges had been dropped for unknown reasons. Defense counsel called on the prosecutor, first demanding that charges be dropped but later indicating that his client was willing to plead guilty to disorderly conduct or some other misdemeanor if he would be placed on probation. The prosecuting attorney, although "morally certain" that the defendant did indeed molest the child, came to the conclusion that the two children would be poor trial witnesses because there were some discrepancies in their stories. He offered to reduce the charge to "lewd and lascivious conduct," a misdemeanor, but would not recommend probation. The defendant accepted the offer of the lesser charge, pleaded guilty, and received a sentence of 90 days in jail.

Illustration 5. Two defendants, Roberts and Knapp, were arrested on a warrant charging them with armed robbery of a liquor store. The defendant Roberts, a man 47 years old, was apparently the ring leader and mastermind of the crime. He had an extensive rap sheet, with one prior conviction for armed robbery, two for assault, one for reckless use of a firearm, one for stolen auto, and numerous misdemeanor arrests and convictions. On the other hand, Knapp, 18 years old, had a clean prior record with the exception of one disorderly conduct arrest when he was 17 years old. In the present instance, Knapp had evidently fallen under the influence of the older man and played a relatively minor part in the robbery. Though he was carrying a loaded .22 caliber pistol, his active participation was as lookout, standing on the street in front of the store while Roberts entered, pointed a gun at the clerk, and took the money. Both defendants were charged with robbery in the first degree, a crime carrying a mandatory prison term of 15 to 25 years. The prosecuting attorney decided to press the armed robbery charge against Roberts, but reduced the charge against Knapp to "larceny from a commercial building" an offense carrying a 2-year maximum sentence and probationable at the discretion of the trial judge. In exchange for Knapp's willingness to plead guilty to the lesser charge, the prosecutor also promised to recommend probation at the time of his sentencing.

As the term implies, plea bargaining involves an active negotiation process by which the defendant offers to exchange a plea of guilty, thereby waiving his right to trial, for some concessions in charges or for a sentence recommendation from the prosecutor. Depending upon the crime or crimes charged and the sentencing structure of the jurisdiction, defendants seek one or more of the following concessions: 1) a charge reduction to some lesser offense with a correspondingly shorter maximum or minimum sentence; 2) prosecution on only one or two multiple charges with other counts dismissed; 3) alteration from a charge carrying a particularly damaging label which implies depravity on the part of the defendant to a charge with less negative connotations, for example, rape to assault; or 4) a promise from the prosecutor to recommend probation at the time of sentencing. There are other variations. For example, a defendant may express willingness to "consent" to revocation of probation or parole on an earlier sentence if current charges are dropped or reduced. There are combinations of these preconviction concessions, but in each case the result is the same: the defendant is allowed to plead guilty to charges less serious than warranted by his conduct and by state's evidence, or he receives a preadjudication sentence promise in exchange for his willingness to waive trial.

Only in recent years has plea negotiation surfaced to general public awareness as being a major characteristic of criminal justice processing in our society. Plea bargaining is not new; in all probability it has gone on as long as there have been criminal courts. But until recently various bargaining practices were discussed only by habitues of the courts—defendants, defense counsel, prosecutors, and trial judges. One reason for lack of public attention has been the private, virtually invisible nature of plea-agreement procedures. Out-of-court negotiations and arrangements have customarily taken place off-the-record, *sub rosa,* in the prosecutor's office or in the hallways of the courthouse. Another reason is that plea bargaining has rarely reached the appellate court level where, after all, controversial issues in criminal justice are aired and resolved. If plea bargaining is successful, that is, if the defendant wins concessions of charge or sentence and the state is assured of conviction, there is no injured party to bring an appeal. The victim of the crime, who may be dissatisfied with the deal, if in fact he is aware of it, has no independent standing to conduct private prosecution or to make an appeal.

Professional literature in law and social sciences made only scattered references to negotiation practices, and until recently it was of minimum interest to legal scholars and social scientists alike. In the 1950s the American Bar Association sponsored a research study of the criminal lawyer[48] from which came a few prominent journal articles that detailed some of the bargaining practices in selected jurisdictions.[49] These received scholarly attention but did little to modify or influence court decisions or practices. About ten years later the American Bar Foundation began a comprehensive survey of criminal justice administration in the United States. As part of this, one area of research (and one of the five volumes of results) was devoted to the guilty plea in general and to practices of plea negotiation in detail.[50] The advantages of plea bargaining, for the state and the accused, which underlie and serve to maintain this process as a major means of criminal adjudication were discussed in this book:

The advantages of the guilty plea over trial for the court, the prosecutor, the police, and in some instances for postconviction correctional authorities are many; some apparent, some more indirect. Not only does the guilty plea avoid the time, expense, and work of proving guilt at trial, but most, if not all, complex corollary issues such as the admissibility of evidence or the propriety of police investigation and arrest practices are largely avoided. In most cases, assuming a competent defendant, the plea assures conviction, whereas the result of a trial, no matter how carefully conducted, is an uncertainty, given the vagaries of jury decisions. Furthermore there is or may be a certain psychological satisfaction provided by an offender who admits his guilt. A defendant who continues to protest his innocence even though found guilty "beyond a reasonable doubt" after a full and fair trial may nevertheless leave some doubts about his guilt and the propriety of conviction. Furthermore from the viewpoint of correctional authorities, rehabilitation can only begin once the person has recognized his problem. The probationer or inmate who steadfastly denies the crime presents a very real dilemma to treatment personnel.

There are also other advantages of a guilty plea. The victim of a crime is often as reluctant to be exposed to the publicity and trauma of a trial as is the perpetrator. The guilty plea is quick and relatively anonymous. Not only are the details of the crime largely kept from public view, but there is ordinarily minimal interference with the daily routine of complainant and witnesses. The guilty plea, even if not preceded by charge reduction, offers the sentencing judge both a rationalization for showing leniency to deserving defendants and an opportunity to do so in a setting ordinarily free from the publicity which attends trial. Furthermore, law-enforcement agencies may benefit, directly and indirectly, from a guilty plea. They may escape the onerous duty of long court appearances and may avoid being challenged by the defense on their grounds for arrest or their apprehension procedures. Indirectly, a defendant pleading guilty may help them solve other crimes by admitting other offenses or may implicate other offenders in his crime. The police of course are under pressure to clear their books of unsolved crimes. A defendant who pleads guilty to one count of an offense is more likely to admit other counts and thereby "solve," to police satisfaction at any rate, a series of burglaries or whatever crime is involved.

These various advantages of conviction by plea of guilty in contrast to conviction by trial provide the incentive for the prosecution to participate in the negotiated plea process. But plea negotiation, like all bargaining, is a two-way street. While some guilty and remorseful defendants may plead guilty without any concessions being made to them, in the aggregate there must be clear advantages for most defendants who waive their right to trial. Apart from such matters as avoiding adverse publicity for themselves and their families and in addition to whatever self-satisfaction confession brings, the defendant who pleads guilty is typically most concerned with what will happen to him following conviction. In pleading guilty most defendants ordinarily expect a break, some leniency either in the seriousness of the offense of which they are convicted or in the sentence or, best of all, in both. Preconviction assurance of such leniency is the defendant's incentive in plea negotiation.

. . .

. . . More than one concession may be involved in any given case, but the most prominent and sought after is charge reduction. In general, this is the best all-round bargain from the defendant's point of view because it results in a less serious record than is warranted by the defendant's conduct, the avoidance of any mandatory sentencing provisions applicable to the original charge, and whatever intrinsic sentencing benefit is brought by the guilty plea. The sentence promise, assuming it is made and honored by appropriate officials, has the advantage of a lesser sentence but does not lessen the defendant's criminal record. The dropping of additional charges or the agreement not to invoke a habitual offender or sex deviate law are certainly important to the defendant, but he still stands convicted of the single, original charge.

Charge reduction as a form of plea bargaining also has a number of advantages from the point of view of both the prosecutor and the judge. In the first place, charge reduction can be rationalized if necessary on grounds of insufficient evidence, and evaluation of evidence is the area of particular competence of both prosecutor and judge. The overt sentence promise raises potentially more difficult questions for the judge who is supposed to accept a plea of guilty only if it is freely entered without threat or promise. Furthermore, responsibility for charge reduction is commonly divided between the prosecutor and court, and if there is any subsequent criticism of the bargain the diffuseness of the decision is a handy defense. The honored sentence promise, on the other hand, places accountability solely on the judge in his sentencing role. In only the comparatively rare cases of informants or helpful state's witnesses can he easily divert responsibility to recommendations of the prosecutor's office. Finally, to the extent that leniency is desired for defendants who, in the opinion of the court, do not deserve the severe treatment proscribed by legislation, a reduction in charge accompanied by a lesser sentence offers a maximum opportunity to achieve this objective. In this manner charge reduction offers the court an opportunity to individualize justice by distinguishing between technically similar cases in both sentence and conviction label, especially when sentencing discretion is denied by legislatively fixed terms.[51]

By the nature of his task, the prosecutor is in a position not simply to apply appropriate statutes to fact situations, but to apply the law, including inevitable sentencing consequences, to individuals whose criminal conduct occurs in varied contexts of mitigating and compounding circumstances. Statutes are by their nature broad and encompassing, but cases are specific and almost infinitely variable. Furthermore, sentencing provisions in many jurisdictions are very severe because those who write the law usually have in mind the worst offenders —the gangster, professional, hardened, or otherwise most vicious violator. In the routine of the typical prosecutor's office, however, this type of violator is comparatively rare. Most offenders, even those technically guilty of serious criminal conduct, are much less threatening and are not in any sense professional criminals. For example, severe mandatory prison sentences fixed to the sale of narcotics convictions are common today. The legislative purpose is clearly to deter large-scale trafficking in drugs and to incapacitate pushers by sentencing them to long years in prison. However, in the day-to-day operation of police and prosecutorial agencies, narcotics sellers who are apprehended are rarely professional heroin pushers, but are more likely to be young men and women who have sold marijuana or a few pills to acquaintances. Technically they are guilty of selling narcotics and face mandatory prison terms, commonly in the range of 20 years to life. Confronted with such cases, only a rare prosecutor or sentencing judge would wish to impose such long sentences. Yet the sentences are mandatory and the only way they can be avoided, assuming the state's unwillingness to dismiss the charges entirely, is to reduce a sales charge to some lesser offense—for example, "possession"—which normally has a lighter sentence, often with judicial discretion to impose probation.

Underlying plea bargaining there are a variety of equity concessions in which the state's motive is the arranging of a sentence appropriate to the actual harm done by the defendant. In addition to avoiding inappropriate maximum sentences, concessions are commonly made in cases in which there are codefendants of unequal culpability. As in the illustration given earlier in this chapter, an older, experienced robber may have as a lookout a youthful accomplice with a clean record. Technically both are equally guilty of the crime, but the prosecutor may feel it more fair and just to reduce the charges against the young accomplice, while making no concession to the experienced robber. Similarly, individuals may be charged with an offense whose label implies much more serious criminal behavior than actually took place. For example, a group of college students were arrested when a neighbor complained of a loud party. The tenant of the apartment was charged with "keeping a disorderly house," a misdemeanor. "Keeping a disorderly house," of course, implies more than arrest for a noisy party, and the court arranged for a plea of guilty to a noise ordinance infraction. Still another reason for charge reduction and similar concessions is that on-the-nose conviction might preclude some correctional alternative, like probation, that is likely to be more effective in the long run than imprisonment. Also a state motive of a somewhat different order is that charges be reduced in cases of informers or cooperative state's witnesses in order to assist the police in making "big" cases.

A basic question of particular concern to appellate courts and to various commissions in the past few years has been whether plea bargaining is a proper form of criminal justice in our society. For a variety of reasons resulting from research and from increasing appellate court attention to defendants who are unable to plea bargain or who are dissatisfied with the result, the issue has currently assumed great prominence and has evoked widespread comment in court decisions, model rules, and so on. Some observers of plea bargaining condemn it as intrinsically improper to our ideals of justice. In a case reaching the Fifth Circuit Court of Appeals in 1957, one judge stated: "Justice and liberty are not the subjects of bargaining and barter."[52] However, on a rehearing this Court found that "proper" bargaining (i.e., a settlement reached by a prosecutor with a fully-informed defendant and honored by the state) is not inappropriate and may be an administrative necessity.[53] Donald J. Newman and Edgar C. NeMoyer comment on this still active controversy:

. . . The propriety question about plea negotiation, as at many other points in the process, is whether an *inducement*-based system is any more proper than one which rests on *coercion,* which is clearly contrary to our system of government. Is a promise by a prosecutor to "recommend" probation really any different from a threat to "throw the book" at a defendant if he pleads not guilty? Is the dropping of a charge in an indictment to a lesser count, particularly to an "illogical" lesser offense, in exchange for a guilty plea a proper practice when the prosecutor, court, and defendant know that the defendant committed a more serious crime and that the evidence in fact supports conviction on the higher offense?

. . .

Debate over the propriety of plea negotiation rests upon multiple considerations, but the major conflict is between those who advocate recognition (and possible control) of plea negotiation on the grounds of expediency and those who see it as a distortion of our criminal justice ideology. In the latter viewpoint, plea negotiation is intrinsically improper and, furthermore, is dangerous and corrupting in its eventual consequences. The argument that plea bargaining is efficient, even "necessary," carries no weight against the fundamental impropriety of the state "dealing" with criminals by inducing pleas.

Those who take the opposite tack, namely that such dealing is not *necessarily* improper, rest their case in good part on the administrative realities of current adjudication practices. In fact, they argue that the "sociology" of our criminal justice world makes negotiation—expressed or implicit—normative. . . . Assuming this and accepting negotiated justice as not simply a minor variation of American justice but a major characteristic of it, the argument goes that independent considerations of propriety are not only irrelevant but are really ridiculous. The thing to do is get with it, to recognize plea bargaining, to legitimatize the norm, to make visible what is now an invisible process, and, in short, to bring into the open, with appropriate sanctions and controls, what are presently common and indeed inevitable practices no matter how much they deviate from the hypothetical postures of our criminal justice ideals.

. . .

Further, it can be argued that there is really nothing wrong in such an approach. Who is to say that full enforcement, maximum charging, and the full dress trial system are any better, fairer, more just, or more accurate than the system of plea negotiation as it operates in most district attorneys' offices and courtroom hallways? Indeed, perhaps it can be demonstrated that the negotiation system is in many ways more equitable and more just than its maximum implementation counterpart. Legislatures which define crimes and affix penalties to them are necessarily distant from individual defendants; and, by the nature of their tasks, they find it necessary to generalize, so that underlying the sentences in written law is the implicit assumption that all burglars are pretty much alike. Any distinctions between cases can be accommodated by whatever sentencing discretion is given the trial judge. Legislatures deal with offense and offender categories and not individual violators. They forbid forcible rape and assign a penalty to an anonymous collection of persons who may in fact be convictable of that crime. Prosecuting attorneys and judges, however, deal not in abstractions but with individual people and with single cases, all with a myriad of aggravating and mitigating circumstances. The flexibility created by charge reduction and sentencing leniency allows, or can allow, the system to operate more equitably.[54]

At present, there is a mixed response to the propriety of the plea-bargaining issue. Some appellate judges continue to castigate the practice and call for its elimination. In a Michigan case, Judge Levin commented:

The negotiated guilty plea is . . . fundamentally unsound. Besides the fact that it is inconsistent with established standards, those regarding the exercise of discretion by public officers and those surrounding the administration of justice generally, it is turning what used to be an accusatorial-adversary judicial system into an inquisitorial-administrative process. It encourages practices in which neither the profession nor the judiciary can take pride and establishes precedents which are bound to affect the administration of justice adversely in other areas . . .

. . .

The calendar problem is, of course, real. The administration of criminal justice has become so dependent upon plea bargaining that it could not be eliminated *instanter* by decree. To do so would be to inundate our presently overtaxed prosecutorial and judicial facilities. This, of course, is a matter for realistic concern—as is the fundamental soundness of a system of justice whose very ability to function is said to depend on the practices described.

The problem is not unlike that of segregated schools in that it is too ingrained to be eliminated forthwith. I suggest that we proceed to its eventual elimination.[55]

The National Advisory Commission on Criminal Justice Standards and Goals issued a report in 1973 calling for the abolition of all plea bargaining over a five-year period. The relevant standard is:

As soon as possible, but in no event later than 1978, negotiations between prosecutors and defendants—either personally or through their attorneys—concerning concessions to be made in return for guilty pleas should be prohibited. In the event that the prosecution makes a recommendation as to sentence, it should not be affected by the willingness of the defendant to plead guilty to some or all of the offenses with which he is charged. A plea of guilty should not be considered by the court in determining the sentence to be imposed.

215

Until plea negotiations are eliminated as recommended in this standard, such negotiations and the entry of pleas pursuant to the resulting agreements should be permitted only under a procedure embodying the safeguards contained in the remaining standards in this chapter.[56]

While the National Advisory Commission report includes a set of standards for the monitoring and control of plea negotiation during the five-year period necessary for elimination, the keynote is the total abolition of plea bargaining practices.[57] The timing of this standard was somewhat ironic, for shortly after the report of this Commission, which was appointed by the Nixon Administration, Vice President Agnew was convicted on the basis of a negotiated plea.[58]

While the propriety controversy is still very strong, courts and commissions which condemn plea negotiation are in a minority today. In recent years, the U.S. Supreme Court has considered a variety of cases involving forms of plea bargaining and has generally supported the practice.[59] Perhaps the most far-reaching decision is:

SANTOBELLO V. NEW YORK
404 U.S. 257 (1971)

[Defendant was convicted in Bronx County, New York upon a guilty plea to a lesser offense (reduced from the felony to Promoting Gambling in the First Degree) of Possession of Gambling Records in the Second Degree. The lesser charge was the result of negotiation between defense and an assistant prosecutor. The prosecutor also agreed "to make no recommendation" as to sentence. As the time of sentencing another prosecutor had replaced the one who had negotiated the plea. The new prosecutor recommended imposition of the maximum one-year sentence on the reduced charge, citing the defendant's prior record and alleged links with organized crime. Defense counsel immediately objected on the ground that the State had promised there would be no sentence recommendation by the prosecutor. The trial judge rejected this objection and sentenced the defendant to a year's incarceration. State appellate courts upheld the conviction and sentence and eventually the U.S. Supreme Court granted *certiorari*.]

MR. CHIEF JUSTICE BURGER delivered the opinion of the Court.

We granted *certiorari* in this case to determine whether the State's failure to keep a commitment concerning the sentence recommendation on a guilty plea required a new trial;

. . .

This record represents another example of an unfortunate lapse in orderly prosecutorial procedures, in part, no doubt, because of the enormous increase

216

in the workload of the often understaffed prosecutor's offices. The heavy work-load may well explain these episodes, but it does not excuse them. The disposition of criminal charges by agreement between the prosecutor and the accused, sometimes loosely called "plea bargaining," is an essential component of the administration of justice. Properly administered, it is to be encouraged. If every criminal charge were subjected to a full-scale trial, the States and the Federal Government would need to multiply by many times the number of judges and court facilities.

Disposition of charges after plea discussions is not only an essential part of the process but a highly desirable part for many reasons. It leads to prompt and largely final disposition of most criminal cases; it avoids much of the corrosive impact of enforced idleness during pretrial confinement for those who are denied release pending trial; it protects the public from those accused persons who are prone to continue criminal conduct even while on pretrial release; and by shortening the time between charge and disposition, it enhances whatever may be the rehabilitative prospects of the guilty when they are ultimately imprisoned.

. . .

This phase of the process of criminal justice and the adjudicative element inherent in accepting a plea of guilty, must be attended by safeguards to insure the defendant what is reasonably due in the circumstances. Those circumstances will vary, but a constant factor is that when a plea rests in any significant degree on a promise or agreement of the prosecutor, so that it can be said to be part of the inducement or consideration, such promise must be fulfilled.

On this record, the petitioner "bargained" and negotiated for a particular plea in order to secure dismissal of more serious charges, but also on condition that no sentence recommendation would be made by the prosecutor. It is now conceded that the promise to abstain from a recommendation was made, and at this stage the prosecution is not in a good position to argue that its inadvertent breach of agreement is immaterial. The staff lawyers in a prosecutor's office have the burden of "letting the left hand know what the right hand is doing" or has done. That the breach of agreement was inadvertent does not lessen its impact.

The judgment is vacated and the case is remanded for reconsideration not inconsistent with this opinion.

Commissions and standard setting groups other than the National Advisory Commission have generally supported plea negotiation practices as a proper form of justice if sufficiently controlled. The ABA, for example, adopts the following stance:

3.1 PROPRIETY OF PLEA DISCUSSIONS AND PLEA AGREEMENTS.

a. In cases in which it appears that the interest of the public in the effective administration of criminal justice (as stated in section 1.8) would thereby be served, the prosecuting attorney may engage in plea discussions for the purpose of reaching a plea agreement. He should engage in plea discussions or reach a plea agreement with the defendant only through defense counsel, except when the defendant is not eligible for or· does not desire appointment of counsel and has not retained counsel.

b. The prosecuting attorney, in reaching a plea agreement, may agree to one or more of the following, as dictated by the circumstances of the individual case:

i. to make or not to oppose favorable recommendations as to the sentence which should be imposed if the defendant enters a plea of guilty or *nolo contendere*;

ii. to seek or not to oppose dismissal of the offense charged if the defendant enters a plea of guilty or *nolo contendere* to another offense reasonably related to defendant's conduct; or

iii. to seek or not to oppose dismissal of other charges or potential charges against the defendant if the defendant enters a plea of guilty or *nolo contendere.*

c. Similarly situated defendants should be afforded equal plea-agreement opportunities.[60]

Likewise, the American Law Institute has adopted a set of plea-agreement procedures as part of their *Model Code of Pre-Arraignment Procedures*[61] and a 1974 revision of Rule 11 of the Federal Rules of Criminal Procedure contains detailed provisions for plea-agreement procedures.[62]

The recognition of overt plea negotiation as common, and under certain conditions as proper, has effected some changes in arraignment proceedings. For example, it was customary in the past for judges to inquire whether a tendered guilty plea was the result of "coercion" or "inducement" in order to assess its voluntariness. Today, the inducement question is rarely asked, or if it is, a positive response is not an absolute bar to accepting the plea. Instead, inquiry goes to the nature of any inducement. All current suggestions for monitoring and controlling bargaining practices require that an accurate record of any plea agreements be made and submitted to the court for approval, modification, or rejection. In a California case regarding making a record of plea agreements the appellate court stated:

Without limiting that [trial] court to those we set forth, we note four possible methods of incorporation: 1) the bargain could be stated orally and recorded by the court reporter, whose notes then must be preserved or transcribed;

2) the bargain could be set forth by the clerk in the minutes of the court;
3) the parties could file a written stipulation stating the terms of the bargain;
4) finally, counsel or the court itself may find it useful to prepare and utilize forms for the recordation of plea bargains.[63]

In general, both federal and state court arraignments where a guilty plea is entered require a more complex and detailed inquiry today than was necessary or common in the past. As part of this, plea bargaining is becoming an open process with an official record made of formal agreements. After prolonged neglect, the entire guilty plea process is being given the attention it deserves as the major way by which defendants are convicted of crimes in our society.

WITHDRAWAL OF A GUILTY PLEA. A defendant who has had a plea of guilty accepted by the court may subsequently decide to withdraw his plea and go to trial. This change of heart may occur at any time after arraignment, and may rest on a variety of factors, ranging from retention of a new attorney who advises a not guilty plea, to dissatisfaction with the sentence or a belief that the state has somehow reneged on a preplea promise. To withdraw his guilty plea the defendant must petition the court with a motion for withdrawal. In most jurisdictions, the judge has discretion as to whether such a motion should be granted. In the past, some jurisdictions allowed an absolute right to withdraw a plea up to the time of imposition of sentence, with postsentence withdrawal discretionary with the court. But generally, the trend has been to give the judge discretion in this matter both before and after sentencing.[64]

Often no specific criteria for withdrawal are contained in statute or court rule. A few states require the defendant to claim "total innocence" of the crime before considering withdrawal; a more common test, however, is that withdrawal should be granted to correct any "manifest injustice." This is the test in the federal system[65] and is the suggested test in the American Bar Association's *Standards Relating to Pleas of Guilty.* Here certain situations are listed which might meet the manifest injustice test, including failure of the defendant to "receive the charge or sentence concessions contemplated by [a] plea agreement."[66]

Denial of a motion for plea withdrawal is appealable, and such appeals occur fairly frequently. If denial by the trial court is upheld on appeal, the guilty plea stands; if withdrawal is allowed, the defendant is remanded for trial. An important issue then arises as to whether the fact that the defendant at one time pleaded guilty can be introduced at trial. There are differing opinions about this in various jurisdictions,[67] but the drafters of the ABA *Standards* suggest that a withdrawn plea "should not be received against the defendant in any criminal proceedings."[68]

Trial

In most jurisdictions, defendants who plead not guilty to felony charges have an option of a jury trial or a bench trial, with the judge acting alone as fact finder. In general, a jury trial is anticipated in felony cases and must be waived. In some places, the prosecutor must consent to such waiver.[69] In about one-third of state jurisdictions, the jury cannot be waived in any felony matter. In others waiver is permitted in all but capital cases, and the remainder allow waiver in all cases.[70]

The comparative tactical advantages and disadvantages of bench versus jury trial have elicited a good deal of discussion in legal literature. Waiver of the jury is often felt to be an advantage to the defendant in cases which have received a great deal of negative publicity, when a highly technical defense is going to be raised, or when it is believed laymen are otherwise unlikely to be sympathetic to the defense. On the other hand, studies of jury behavior in recent years have demonstrated that while judges and juries agree on the outcome of cases about 75 percent of the time, juries are significantly more lenient than judges in the remaining cases.[71]

The right to a jury trial in felony cases is absolute, but in cases where a lesser offense is charged, the situation is more variable. Constitutional provisions in many jurisdictions do not extend the right to jury trial to cases involving "petty offenses."[72] In general, these encompass the least severely punished misdemeanors and violations, such as public intoxication, disorderly conduct, other public order crimes, and minor traffic violations. However, their specific designation varies from one set of statutes to the next.[73]

The entire matter of when a state may refuse a defendant's request for a jury trial has been narrowed by a decision of the U.S. Supreme Court which held a right to a jury trial in a state case where the defendant was charged with a misdemeanor.[74] Taken in context with a recent decision expanding the right to counsel to defendants on trial for even "petty offenses,"[75] it may be that full-scale litigation will become more common at the lower register of criminal charges. Some state constitutions provide for a jury trial on appeal from a nonjury conviction for petty offenses, and the American Bar Association suggests such right of appeal as a desirable standard.[76] In some jurisdictions, the judge is required to file a memorandum in support of his factual finding of guilt after a bench trial. In contrast, juries do not give reasons for their findings of guilt or innocence. A jury decision to convict, however, may be set aside by the judge if he believes trial evidence failed to meet the reasonable doubt test. Occasionally he may direct a verdict of acquital without waiting for a jury finding.[77]

Procedures followed at a trial are tightly circumscribed by constitutions, statutes, court rules, and appellate court decisions. Everywhere, proof of a defendant's guilt must be "beyond a reasonable doubt" and based only on properly obtained, presented, and interpreted evidence.

At trial, evidence to prove guilt is presented by the prosecution, rebutted by the defense—which need do no more than raise a reasonable doubt of guilt —and instructions about the meaning of the evidence and the requirements of the law are presented to the jury by the presiding judge. The jury is then sequestered to decide the guilt or innocence of the defendant. It may find a defendant not guilty, guilty of the crimes charged, or guilty of lesser offenses.

Most jurisdictions require a jury of twelve members, but provisions in some states allow eight member juries for noncapital felony trials, while five or six member juries are often permitted in misdemeanor trials.[78] Most state constitutions now provide that trial jury verdicts be unanimous, but this provision, long debated,[79] is in a state of flux following U.S. Supreme Court holdings that states may properly have other than twelve member juries and that a unanimous verdict is not a federal constitutional requirement.[80]

Jury selection remains a controversial problem. In colonial times when we were a country of towns and villages, selecting a jury of peers in the common meaning of this term could sometimes be achieved, although even then major segments of the population (i.e., slaves and often women) were excluded from jury duty consideration. Today there is a question whether the peer ideal can even be approximated, not only in metropolitan courts, but also in smaller jurisdictions. Part of the problem is related to selection procedures, primarily certain exclusion practices, which by law or custom keep those without property or permanent residence (often members of ethnic and racial minorities) off jury panels. Because criminal defendants are often poor, transient, and members of minority groups, such exclusions are felt to weaken the spirit, if not the letter, of the law with respect to peer judgment. While the law does not require juries to mirror all of the economic, social, and personal characteristics of a defendant —in fact, a "peer" is simply any other citizen—systematic exclusion practices have tended to warp the ideology of the jury trial.[81]

Another part of the jury problem concerns grossly inadequate facilities and compensation for jurors (and also for witnesses) which in most jurisdictions make jury duty an unpleasant and unwelcome task for those selected. The President's Commission, in recommending improved treatment of both jurors and witnesses, commented:

Compensation is generally so low that service as a juror or witness is a serious financial burden . . . The economic impact bears most harshly on people whose

221

wages are usually paid on an hourly or daily basis. Such experiences can only aggravate the feeling of a major segment of the community that the law does them no good.[82]

RIGHT TO COUNSEL AT TRIAL.   From the very beginning of our system of justice, defendants who were financially able to do so could hire lawyers to represent them at trial. Indigent defendants, however, had to rely on whatever provisions existed in each jurisdiction with regard to state-assigned attorneys. In some places, provision was made to assign counsel to any defendant unable to afford a lawyer; in others, assistance of counsel was limited to very serious cases, usually those involving a capital offense. For many years, the U.S. Supreme Court took the position that there was no federal constitutional requirement that states provide counsel except in cases involving capital crimes. However, in a landmark decision in 1963, the Warren Court reversed this position, reasoning as follows:

GIDEON V. WAINWRIGHT
372 U.S. 335 (1963)

MR. JUSTICE BLACK delivered the opinion of the Court.

Petitioner was charged in a Florida state court with having broken and entered a poolroom with intent to commit a misdemeanor. This offense is a felony under Florida law. Appearing in court without funds and without a lawyer, petitioner asked the court to appoint counsel for him, whereupon the following colloquy took place:

> The Court: Mr. Gideon, I am sorry but I cannot appoint Counsel to represent you in this case. Under the laws of the State of Florida, the only time the Court can appoint counsel to represent a defendant is when that person is charged with a capital offense. I am sorry, but I will have to deny your request to appoint Counsel to defend you in this case.

> The Defendant: The United States Supreme Court says I am entitled to be represented by counsel.

Put to trial before a jury, Gideon conducted his defense about as well as could be expected from a layman. He made an opening statement to the jury, cross-examined the State's witnesses, presented witnesses in his own defense, declined to testify himself, and made a short argument "emphasizing his innocence to the charge contained in the Information filed in this case." The jury returned a verdict of guilty, and petitioner was sentenced to serve five years in the state prison. Later, petitioner filed in the Florida Supreme Court this *habeas corpus* petition attacking his conviction and sentence on the ground that the trial court's refusal to appoint counsel for him denied him rights "guaranteed by the Constitution and the Bill of Rights by the U.S. Government." Treating the petition for *habeas corpus* as properly before it, the State Supreme Court, "upon consideration thereof" but without an opinion, denied all relief. Since 1942, when *Betts* v. *Brady,* 316 U.S. 455, was decided by a divided Court, the problem of a defendant's federal constitutional right to counsel in a state court has been a continuing source of controversy and litigation in both state and federal courts. To give this problem another review here, we granted *certiorari.* 370 U.S. 908. Since Gideon was proceeding *in forma pauperis,* we appointed counsel to represent him and requested both sides to discuss in their briefs and oral arguments the following: "Should this Court's holding in *Betts* v. *Brady,* 316 U.S. 455, be reconsidered?"

. . .

The facts upon which Betts claimed that he had been unconstitutionally denied the right to have counsel appointed to assist him are strikingly like the facts upon which Gideon here bases his federal constitutional claim. Betts was indicted for robbery in a Maryland state court. On arraignment, he told the trial judge of his lack of funds to hire a lawyer and asked the court to appoint one for him. Betts was advised that it was not the practice in that county to appoint counsel for indigent defendants except in murder and rape cases. He then pleaded not guilty, had witnesses summoned, cross-examined the State's witnesses, examined his own, and chose not to testify himself. He was found guilty by the judge, sitting without a jury, and sentenced to eight years in prison. Like Gideon, Betts sought release by *habeas corpus,* alleging that he had been denied the right to assistance of counsel in violation of the Fourteenth Amendment. Betts was denied any relief, and on review this Court affirmed. It was held that a refusal to appoint counsel for an indigent defendant charged with a felony did not necessarily violate the Due Process Clause of the Fourteenth Amendment, which for reasons given the Court deemed to be the only applicable federal constitutional provision. The Court said:

> Asserted denial [of due process] is to be tested by an appraisal of the totality of facts in a given case. That which may, in one setting, constitute a denial of fundamental fairness, shocking to the universal sense of justice, may, in other circumstances, and in the light of other considerations, fall short of such denial. 316 U.S., at 462.

Treating due process as "a concept less rigid and more fluid than those envisaged in other specific and particular provisions of the Bill of Rights," the Court held that refusal to appoint counsel under the particular facts and circumstances in the *Betts* case was not so "offensive to the common and fundamental ideas of fairness" as to amount to a denial of due process. Since the facts and circumstances of the two cases are so nearly indistinguishable, we think the *Betts* v. *Brady* holding if left standing would require us to reject Gideon's claim that the Constitution guarantees him the assistance of counsel.

Upon full reconsideration we conclude that *Betts* v. *Brady* should be over-ruled. . . .

. . .

We accept *Betts* v. *Brady's* assumption, based as it was on our prior cases, that a provision of the Bill of Rights which is "fundamental and essential to a fair trial" is made obligatory upon the States by the Fourteenth Amendment. We think the Court in *Betts* was wrong, however, in concluding that the Sixth Amendment's guarantee of counsel is not one of these fundamental rights. Ten years before *Betts* v. *Brady,* this Court, after full consideration of all the historical data examined in Betts, had unequivocally declared that "the right to the aid of counsel is of this fundamental character." *Powell* v. *Alabama,* 287 U.S. 45, 68 (1932). While the Court at the close of its *Powell* opinion did by its language, as this Court frequently does, limit its holding to the particular facts and circumstances of that case, its conclusions about the fundamental nature of the right to counsel are unmistakable. . . .

. . .

. . . In returning to these old precedents, sounder we believe than the new, we but restore constitutional principles established to achieve a fair system of justice. Not only these precedents but also reason and reflection require us to recognize that in our adversary system of criminal justice, any person hailed into court, who is too poor to hire a lawyer, cannot be assured a fair trial unless counsel is provided for him. This seems to us to be an obvious truth. Governments, both state and federal, quite properly spend vast sums of money to establish machinery to try defendants accused of crime. Lawyers to prosecute are everywhere deemed essential to protect the public's interest in an orderly society. Similarly, there are few defendants charged with crime, few indeed, who fail to hire the best lawyers they can get to prepare and present their defenses. That government hires lawyers to prosecute and defendants who have the money hire lawyers to defend are the strongest indications of the widespread belief that lawyers in criminal courts are necessities, not luxuries. The right of one charged with crime to counsel may not be deemed fundamental and essential to fair trials in some countries, but it is in ours. From the very beginning, our state and national constitutions and laws have laid great emphasis on procedural and substantive safeguards designed to assure fair trials before impartial tribunals in which every defendant stands equal before the law. This noble ideal cannot be realized if the poor man charged with crime has to face his accusers without a lawyer to assist him. . . .

. . .

The Court in *Betts* v. *Brady* departed from the sound wisdom upon which the Court's holding in *Powell* v. *Alabama* rested. Florida, supported by two other States, has asked that *Betts* v. *Brady* be left intact. Twenty-two States, as friends of the Court, argue that *Betts* was "an anachronism when handed down" and that it should now be overruled. We agree.

The judgment is reversed and the cause is remanded to the Supreme Court of Florida for further action not inconsistent with this opinion.

Reversed.

The *Gideon* holding was first commonly interpreted to apply to all felony trials and to cases involving "serious" misdemeanors, usually those with a potential sentence of longer than six months. However, right to counsel has been subsequently expanded to apply at *all* criminal trials including those for petty offenses.[83]

There are a number of trial issues that remain controversial and often form the basis for appeal. These are extremely varied, ranging from such matters as the shackling of defendants—as one court commented, "the presumption of innocence requires the garb of innocence"[84]—to whether it is proper for jury members to make notes during the trial.[85] A matter of particular concern today has less to do with actual in-court proceedings than with the publicity aura that surrounds some trials. The American Bar Association and various other groups, including members of the press and other media, have struggled for some time with efforts to balance our desire for a free press with our need to have trials free from prejudicial publicity. The American Bar Association has issued a number of "Free Press-Fair Trial" standards and recommendations, including the following:

PART II. RECOMMENDATIONS RELATING TO THE CONDUCT OF LAW ENFORCE-MENT OFFICERS, JUDGES, AND JUDICIAL EMPLOYEES IN CRIMINAL CASES
2.1 DEPARTMENTAL RULES.

It is recommended that law enforcement agencies in each jurisdiction adopt the following internal regulations:

a. A regulation governing the release of information, relating to the commission of crimes and to their investigation, prior to the making of an arrest, issuance of an arrest warrant, or the filing of formal charges. This regulation should establish appropriate procedures for the release of information. It should further provide that, when a crime is believed to have been committed, pertinent facts relating to the crime itself and to investigative procedures may properly be made available but the identity of a suspect prior to arrest and the results of investigative procedures shall not be disclosed except to the extent necessary to aid in the investigation, to assist in the apprehension of the suspect, or to warn the public of any dangers.

b. A regulation prohibiting i) the deliberate posing of a person in custody for photographing or television by representatives of the news media and ii) the interviewing by representatives of the news media of a person in custody unless, in writing, he requests or consents to an interview after being adequately informed of his right to consult with counsel and of his right to refuse to grant an interview.

c. A regulation providing:

From the time of arrest, issuance of an arrest warrant, or the filing of any complaint, information, or indictment in any criminal matter, until the completion of trial or disposition without trial, no law enforcement officer within this agency shall release or authorize the release of any extra-judicial statement, for dissemination by any means of public communication, relating to that matter and concerning:

1. The prior criminal record (including arrests, indictments, or other charges of crime), or the character or reputation of the accused, except that the officer may make a factual statement of the accused's name, age, residence, occupation, and family status, and if the accused has not been apprehended, may release any information necessary to aid in his apprehension or to warn the public of any dangers he may present;

2. The existence or contents of any confession, admission, or statement given by the accused, or the refusal or failure of the accused to make any statement, except that the officer may announce without further comment that the accused denies the charges made against him;

3. The performance of any examinations or tests or the accused's refusal or failure to submit to an examination or test;

4. The identity, testimony, or credibility of prospective witnesses, except that the officer may announce the identity of the victim if the announcement is not otherwise prohibited by law;

5. The possibility of a plea of guilty to the offense charged or a lesser offense;

6. Any opinion as to the accused's guilt or innocence or as to the merits of the case or the evidence in the case.

It shall be appropriate during this period for a law enforcement officer:

1. to announce the fact and circumstances of arrest, including the time and place of arrest, resistance, pursuit, and the use of weapons;

2. to announce the identity of the investigating and arresting officer or agency and the length of the investigation;

3. to make an announcement, at the time of seizure of any physical evidence other than a confession, admission, or statement, which is limited to a description of the evidence seized;

4.   to disclose the nature, substance, or text of the charge, including a brief description of the offense charged;

5.   to quote from or refer without comment to public records of the court in the case;

6.   to announce the scheduling or result of any stage in the judicial process;

7.   to request assistance in obtaining evidence.

Nothing in this rule precludes any law enforcement officer from replying to charges of misconduct that are publicly made against him, precludes any law enforcement officer from participating in any legislative, administrative, or investigative hearing, or supersedes any more restrictive rule governing the release of information concerning juvenile or other offenders.

d.   A regulation providing for the enforcement of the foregoing by the imposition of appropriate disciplinary sanctions.

2.2 RULE OF COURT OR LEGISLATION RELATING TO LAW ENFORCEMENT AGENCIES.

It is recommended that if within a reasonable time a law enforcement agency in any jurisdiction fails to adopt and adhere to the substance of the regulation recommended in Section 2.1, c, as it related to both proper and improper disclosures, the regulation be made effective with respect to that agency by rule of court or by legislative action, with appropriate sanctions for violation.

2.3 RULE OF COURT RELATING TO DISCLOSURES BY JUDICIAL EMPLOYEES.

It is recommended that a rule of court be adopted in each jurisdiction prohibiting any judicial employee from disclosing, to any unauthorized person, information relating to a pending criminal case that is not part of the public records of the court and that may tend to interfere with the right of the people or of the defendant to a fair trial. Particular reference should be made in this rule to the nature and result of any argument or hearing held in chambers or otherwise outside the presence of the public and not yet available to the public under the standards of Section 3.1 and Section 3.5 d of these recommendations. Appropriate discipline, including proceedings for contempt, should be provided for infractions of this rule.

2.4 RECOMMENDATION RELATING TO JUDGES.

It is recommended that, with respect to pending criminal cases, judges should refrain from any conduct or the making of any statements that may tend to interfere with the right of the people or of the defendant to a fair trial.[86]

Other sections of these standards offer recommendations relating to the conduct of defense counsel and suggest controls ranging from revision of ethical codes to use of contempt power.[87] The publicity-fair trial issue has become especially critical in recent years because of great public interest in certain

227

crimes. The assassinations of President Kennedy and his brother, the killing of Dr. Martin Luther King, the shooting of Governor Wallace, the Senate inquiry into the Watergate break-in, as well as assorted hijacking and terrorist activities, all received extensive media coverage and comment. Under such conditions whether fair trials, free from prejudicial publicity, can be had is a most difficult question.

Appeals and Postconviction Remedies

With the exception of the military system of justice, which provides for automatic appeals, and a few jurisdictions where first appeal is a matter of right, the appeal of criminal convictions in U.S. jurisdictions is elective. Appeals by the defendant must ordinarily be instituted within a specified time after conviction, although for good cause appellate courts in some jurisdictions may extend this period.

In addition to appeal of conviction, there are a variety of writs and procedures used to seek other postconviction remedies normally relating to sentencing or sentence conditions. The use of any specific writ is dictated by the nature of remedy sought and the provisions available by law in each jurisdiction.

Generally there are two classes of appellate review sought by defendants. The first involves appeal of a final judgment of conviction, whether by trial or guilty plea (including appeal of denial of pretrial motions to supress certain evidence), and the second involves challenge of custody or the conditions of custody which follow conviction. Appeals of convictions proceed in varied ways, with a few jurisdictions first requiring approval of the trial court. But more commonly they proceed by a writ of error or other writ submitted to the appropriate appellate court and with its leave. Appeal of custody is commonly initiated by one of a variety of forms of the writ of *habeas corpus* (literally "you have the body," that is, the person in custody who must be presented to the court).[88]

The appellate process may ultimately involve the entire hierarchy of state and federal courts, eventually reaching the U.S. Supreme Court.[89] Before appeals move from state to federal review, state remedies must generally be exhausted. In recent years, however, many *habeas* actions involving state cases have originated directly in the federal appellate process under claims of violation of the Civil Rights Act. But recently the Supreme Court has substantially curbed this route, now requiring the state appellate process to be exhausted if the remedy is likely to result in shorter incarceration.[90]

Appeals and other postconviction remedies are usually decided on the basis of written petition and available records. Generally such documents are presented to and argued before the appellate court by counsel with the petitioner

228

not physically present. This is an expensive process beyond the means of most petitioners. However, a series of U.S. Supreme Court cases in recent years has substantially expanded the right of indigent petitioners to obtain transcripts and assistance of counsel at state expense, at least on first appeal.[91]

Under certain restricted conditions, appeals in some states may be taken by the prosecution. Normally the state cannot appeal a trial court finding of not guilty because the defendant is protected from retrial by constitutional prohibitions against double jeopardy. To avoid placing a defendant twice in jeopardy, a few states allow rather broad but "moot" prosecution appeals. These have the possible effect of settling the legal controversy, but have no consequences for the individual defendant.[92]

NOTES

1. Wayne R. LaFave and Frank J. Remington, "Controlling the Police: The Judge's Role in Making and Reviewing Law Enforcement Decisions," *Mich. Law Review* 63, 987 (1965).

2. Frank W. Miller, *Prosecution: The Decision to Charge a Suspect with a Crime* (Boston: Little Brown, 1970), p. 11.

3. *Ibid*, pp. 11-12.

4. American Bar Association, *Standards Relating to the Prosecution Function and the Defense Function* (New York: Institute of Judicial Administration, Approved Draft, 1971), pp. 18-19.

5. *Ibid*, p. 25.

6. *Ibid*, p. 47.

7. *Ibid*, p. 71.

8. *Ibid*, pp. 19-20.

9. See for example, Brian Grosman, *The Prosecutor: An Inquiry into the Exercise of Discretion* (Toronto: U. of Toronto Press, 1969); Robert Vouin, "The Role of the Prosecutor in French Criminal Trials," *Amer. J. Compar. Law* 18, 483 (1970); Shigemitsu Dando, "System of Discretionary Prosecution in Japan," *Amer. J. Compar. Law* 18, 518 (1970); Jonas Myhre, "Conviction Without Trial in the United States and Norway," *Houston Law Review* 5, 647 (1969); Anthony Davis, "Sentences for Sale: A New Look at Plea Bargaining in England and America," *Crim. Law Review* 150 (1971).

10. Thurman W. Arnold, "Law Enforcement—An Attempt at Social Dissection," *Yale Law J.* 42, 1, 7 (1932).

11. Kenneth Culp Davis, *Discretionary Justice* (Baton Rouge, La.: L.S.U. Press, 1969), p. 170.

12. See, for example, Oyler v. Boles, 368 U.S. 448 (1962); United States v. Cox, 342 F. 2d. 1967 (5th Cir. 1965); Moses v. Kennedy, 219 F. Supp. 762 (D.D.C. 1963); People v. Gray, 254 Cal. App. 2d (1967).

13. American Bar Association, *Standards Relating to the Prosecution Function and the Defense Function,* pp. 92-93.

14. *Ibid,* p. 4.

15. American Bar Association, *Standards Relating to Joinder and Severance* (New York: Institute of Judicial Administration, Approved Draft, 1968).

16. Miller, *Prosecution,* pp. 159, 161-162.

17. *Ibid,* Chapter 9-18, pp. 173-280.

18. See R. Spain, "The Grand Jury, Past and Present: A Survey," *Amer. Crim. Law Quar.* 2, 119 (1964).

19. See Pittsburgh Plate Glass Co. v. United States, 360 U.S. 395 (1959), and United States v. Procter and Gamble, 356 U.S. 677 (1958); but also see Dennis v. United States, 384 U.S. 855 (1966) and generally, Arthur Sherry, "Grand Jury Minutes: The Unreasonable Rule of Secrecy," *Va. Law Review* 48, 668 (1962).

20. Costello v. United States, 350 U.S. 359 (1956).

21. See New York Code of Criminal Procedure, Section 253 (1969). See also People v. Howell, 3 N.Y. 2d 672 (1958).

22. Miller, *Prosecution,* p. 15.

23. Wayne Morse, "A Survey of the Grand Jury Systems," *Ore. Law Review* 10, 101 (1931).

24. George H. Dession, "From Indictment to Information—Implications of the Shift," *Yale Law J.* 46, 163, 176 (1932).

25. See *New York Code of Criminal Procedure,* 1970, Sec. 190.75(3).

26. Note, *Columbia Law J.* 2, 88 (1966).

27. Frederick G. Watts, "Grand Jury, Sleeping Watchdog or Expensive Antique?" *N.C. Law Review* 37, 290 (1959). See also, Joseph Coates, "The Grand Jury, The Prosecutor's Puppet," *Pa. Bar Assoc. Quar.* 33, 311 (1962).

28. See United States v. Cox, 342 F. 2d. 167, 186 N.1. (5th Cir. 1965).

29. A charge issued by a grand jury on its own motion is called a "presentment" to distinguish it from an "indictment" which is a charge requested by the prosecutor. The documents, however, have identical weight at pleading and at trial. See, for example, Richard Kuh, "The Grand Jury 'Presentment': Foul Blow or Fair Play?" *Columbia Law Review* 55, 1103 (1955).

30. See Note, *Ga. Law J.* 56, 193 (1967).

31. See Harris Steinberg and Monrad Paulsen, "A Conversation With Defense Counsel on Problems of a Criminal Defense," *Prac. Lawyer* 7, 25, 30 (1961).

32. See Miller, *Prosecution,* Chapter 6 and Robert O. Dawson, "Non-use of the Preliminary Examination: A Survey of Current Practices," *Wis. Law Review* 252 (1964).

33. See, *Preliminary Hearing in the District of Columbia* (Washington, D.C.: Georgetown Law Center, 1967).

34. Miller, *Prosecution,* pp. 83-84.

35. See Livingston Hall, Yale Kamisar, Wayne R. LaFave, and Jerold Israel, *Modern Criminal Procedure,* 3rd ed. (St. Paul, Minn.: West, 1969), pp. 856-857. See also Miller, *Prosecution,* pp. 95-101.

36. See Comment, *Md. Law Review* 25, 227 (1965).

37. See Jack M. Kress, "The Agnew Case: Policy, Prosecution and Plea Bargaining," *Crim. Law Bull.* 10, 80 (January-February 1974), and Donald J. Newman, "The Agnew Plea Bargain," *Crim. Law Bull.* 10, 85 (January-February 1974).

38. See McCarthy v. United States, 394 U.S. 459 (1969), and Boykin v. Alabama, 395 U.S. 238 (1969).

39. See Donald J. Newman, *Conviction: The Determination of Guilt or Innocence Without Trial* (Boston: Little, Brown, 1966), Chapters 1, 2, 3.

40. See Federal Rules of Criminal Procedure for the United States District Courts, Rule 11, *Pleas.* Amended July 1, 1968.

41. *Ibid.*

42. Newman, *Conviction.*

43. See Frank Laurent, *The Business of a Trial Court: 100 Years of Cases* (Madison, Wis.: U. of Wis. Press, 1959).

44. See Donald J. Newman, "Reshape the Deal," *Trial* (May-June 1973), p. 11.

45. Judicial Conference of the United States, "Pilot Institute on Sentencing," *Federal Rules Decisions* 26, 231 (1969).

46. See American Bar Association, *Standards Relating to Pleas of Guilty* (New York: Institute of Judicial Administration), approved draft, 1968. Sec. 1.8. See also Comment, "The Influence of the Defendant's Plea on Judicial Determination of Sentence," *Yale Law J.* 66, 204 (1956).

47. See Newman, *Conviction;* President's Commission on Law Enforcement and Administration of Justice, *Task Force Report: The Courts* (Washington, D.C.: U.S. Government Printing Office, 1967), pp. 108-120; Note, "Guilty Plea Bargaining: Compromises by Prosecutors to Secure Guilty Pleas," *U. of P. Law Review* 112, 865 (1964).

48. See Arthur L. Wood, *Criminal Lawyer* (New Haven, Conn.: College and University Press, 1967).

49. See Donald J. Newman, "Pleading Guilty for Considerations: A Study of Bargain Justice," *J. Crim. Law, Criminology and Pol. Sci.* 46, 780 (1956).

50. See Newman, *Conviction.*

51. *Ibid,* pp. 95-98.

52. Shelton v. United States, 242 F. 2d. 101, 113 (5th Cir. 1957).

53. Shelton v. United States, 246 F. 2d 571 (5th Cir. 1957); rev'd on confession of error of Solicitor General, 356 U.S. 26 (1958).

54. Donald J. Newman and Edgar C. NeMoyer, "Issues of Propriety in Negotiated Justice," *Denver Law J.* 47, 367 (1970): 374-376.

55. People v. Byrd, 12 Mich. App. 186, 162 N.W. 2d. 777, 796-797 (1968).

56. National Advisory Commission on Criminal Justice Standards and Goals, *Courts* (1973), Sec. 3.1, p. 46.

57. *Ibid,* Standards 3.2, 3.3, 3.4, 3.5, 3.6, 3.7, 3.8, pp. 50-65.

58. See Newman, "The Agnew Plea Bargain."

59. See for example, Brady v. United States, 397 U.S. 742 (1970); Parker v. North Carolina, 397 U.S. 790 (1970); North Carolina v. Alford, 400 U.S. 25 (1970).

60. American Bar Association, *Standards Relating to Pleas of Guilty,* Sec. 3.1, p. 60.

61. American Law Institute, *Model Code of Pre-Arraignment Procedures,* Tentative Draft No. 5, 1972. Article 350.

62. Federal Rules of Criminal Procedure, Rule 11, *Pleas,* Sec. (e). (Amended July 1, 1974).

63. People v. West, 3 Cal. 3rd 385, 477 P. 2d. at 417, 418 (1970).

64. Hall, Kamisar, LaFave, and Israel, *Modern Criminal Procedure,* pp. 999-1000.

65. Federal Rules of Criminal Procedure, *Rule 32d* (1968).

66. American Bar Association, *Standards Relating to Guilty Pleas,* Part II, Sec. 2.1(4) 1968.

67. See, *Annotations,* 86 ALR 2d 326, 328-331 (1962).

68. American Bar Association, *Standards Relating to Guilty Pleas,* Sec. 2.2.

69. Article 3, Section 2 of the Constitution provides that "trial of all crimes . . . shall be by jury" but by and large court decisions have allowed waiver. See Patton v. United States, 281 U.S. 276 (1930). See also generally, Commentary, Sec. 1.2, American Bar Association, *Standards Relating to Trial by Jury* (1968).

70. See Note, *Cornell Law Quar.* 51, 339 (1966): 342-43.

71. Harry Kalven and Hans Zeisel, *The American Jury* (Boston: Little, Brown, 1966). p. 59.

72. See American Bar Association, *Standards Relating to Trial by Jury* (New York: Institute of Judicial Administration, Approved Draft, 1968). Commentary Sec. 1.1.

73. Title 18, Sec. 1 (3) of the U.S. criminal code defines a "petty offense" as "any misdemeanor, the penalty for which does not exceed imprisonment for a period of six months or a fine of not more than 500 dollars or both."

74. Duncan v. Louisiana, 391 U.S. 145 (1968).

75. Argersinger v. Hamlin, 407 U.S. 25 (1972).

76. American Bar Association, *Standards Relating to Trial by Jury,* Sec. 1.1(b).

77. See Federal Rules of Criminal Procedure, *Rule 29 (a)*; Winningham, "The Dilemma of the Directed Acquittal," *Vanderbilt Law Review* 15, 699 (1962) and American Bar Association, *Standards Relating to Trial by Jury,* Sec. 4.5(a).

78. American Bar Association, *Standards Relating to Trial by Jury,* Sec. 1.1(c).

79. See John V. Ryan, "Less Than Unanimous Verdicts in Criminal Trials," *J. Crim. Law, Criminology and Pol. Sci.* 58, 211 (1967); Kalven and Zeisel, *American Jury,* Chapters 36, 38.

80. Williams v. Florida, 399 U.S. 78 (1970); Apodaca v. Oregon, 406 U.S. 404 (1972).

81. Some discriminatory practices in jury selection have been addressed in Supreme Court decisions. See Swain v. Alabama, 380 U.S. 202 (1965); Glasser v. United States, 315 U.S. 60 (1942); Ballard v. United States, 329 U.S. 187 (1946).

82. President's Commission, *The Courts,* p. 90.

83. Argersinger v. Hamlin.

84. Eaddy v. People, 115 Colo. 488 (1946).

85. See generally, American Bar Association, *Standards Relating to Trial by Jury,* Sec. 4.1; Hall, Kamisar, LaFave, Israel, *Modern Criminal Procedure,* and *Supplement.*

86. American Bar Association, *Standards Relating to Fair Trial and Free Press* (New York: Institute of Judicial Administration, Approved Draft, 1968), pp. 4-7.

87. *Ibid,* Part I, pp. 1-4, Part IV, pp. 13-14.

88. See American Bar Association, *Standards Relating to Criminal Appeals* (New York: Institute of Judicial Administration, Approved Draft, 1970), and American Bar Association, *Standards Relating to Post-Conviction Remedies* (New York: Institute of Judicial Administration, Approved Draft, 1967).

89. For an example of this process, see Anthony Lewis, *Gideon's Trumpet* (New York: Random House, 1964), which follows the appellate process in the Gideon v. Wainwright case.

90. Preiser v. Rodriquez, 411 U.S. 475 (1973).

91. See Griffin v. Illinois, 351 U.S. 12 (1956) and Douglas v. California, 372 U.S. 353 (1963).

92. See American Bar Association, *Standards Relating to Criminal Appeals,* Sec. 1.4.

Chapter 6

Sentencing

THE LOCUS OF THE SENTENCE DECISION

After conviction by trial or guilty plea, the defendant is brought before a court for imposition of sentence. Today the hearing at which sentence is imposed is considered a "critical stage" of the process, and convicted offenders have a right to counsel at this time.[1]

Most commonly sentence is imposed by a judge, but there are variations depending upon statutory provisions in different jurisdictions. In California judges make a decision as to probation or incarceration, but if the offender is incarcerated, his actual sentence limits are set by a state agency called the Adult Authority. In the past a number of states provided for jury recommendations regarding imposition of the death penalty in capital cases, but this particular form of discretion formed part of the basis for the Supreme Court nullification of state death penalty provisions.[2] Today thirteen states provide for jury sentencing in noncapital cases. Eight of these give sentencing authority to juries in all serious crimes, four restrict the jury function to certain types of offenses, and one (Texas) allows the offender to request jury sentencing if he desires.[3] In a number of these states, jury sentencing has existed since colonial times. However, this practice has been questioned by a number of standard setting commissions. The National Advisory Commission on Criminal Justice Standards and Goals has recently called for abolition of jury sentencing because it is "nonprofessional and is more likely than judge sentencing to be arbitrary and based on emotions rather than the needs of the offender or society."[4]

Felony Sentencing in California

TYPE OF FELONY	TOTAL FELONS SENTENCED (PERCENT OF 40,477)	FELONS COMMITTED TO PRISON (PERCENT OF 5,492)
Homicide	1.8	7.5
Robbery	6.7	17.6
Assault	6.9	5.5
Burglary	19.5	18.4
Theft except auto	7.5	5.2
Auto theft	6.4	3.5
Forgery	11.2	12.0
Rape	1.9	2.3
Other sex offenses	2.5	2.6
Drug	25.2	10.2
All other	10.2	15.2
Total	100.0	100.0

Bureau of Criminal Statistics, *Crime and Delinquency in California* (Sacramento: State Printing Office, 1968), p. 97.

In some places, usually metropolitan areas where there are multijudge courts, there are sentencing councils of judges. However, this practice is still localized and experimental, although the National Advisory Commission recommends its use wherever feasible.[5] Sentencing by council commonly involves consultation between the judge who has ultimate sentencing responsibility, and two or more of his colleagues over the appropriateness of sentence alternatives. The purpose of such consultation is to reduce sentence disparities among judges of the same court.

Executions in the United States, 1930-1967

REGION AND STATE	ALL OFFENSES	MURDER	RAPE	ARMED ROBBERY	KIDNAP- PING	OTHER OFFENSES
UNITED STATES	3,859	3,334	455	25	20	25
FEDERAL	33	15	2	2	6	8
NORTHEAST	608	606	—	—	2	—
New Hampshire	1	1	—	—	—	—
Vermont	4	4	—	—	—	—
Massachusetts	27	27	—	—	—	—
Connecticut	21	21	—	—	—	—
New York	329	327	—	—	2	—
New Jersey	74	74	—	—	—	—
Pennsylvania	152	152	—	—	—	—

EXECUTIONS IN THE UNITED STATES, 1930-1967 (Continued)

REGION AND STATE	ALL OFFENSES	MURDER	RAPE	ARMED ROBBERY	KIDNAP-PING	OTHER OFFENSES
NORTH CENTRAL	403	393	10	—	—	—
Ohio	172	172	—	—	—	—
Indiana	41	41	—	—	—	—
Illinois	90	90	—	—	—	—
Iowa	18	18	—	—	—	—
Missouri	62	52	10	—	—	—
South Dakota	1	1	—	—	—	—
Nebraska	4	4	—	—	—	—
Kansas	15	15	—	—	—	—
SOUTH	2,306	1,824	443	23	5	11
Delaware	12	8	4	—	—	—
Maryland	68	44	24	—	—	—
District of Columbia	40	37	3	—	—	—
Virginia	92	71	21	—	—	—
West Virginia	40	36	1	—	3	—
North Carolina	263	207	47	—	—	9
South Carolina	162	120	42	—	—	—
Georgia	366	299	61	6	—	—
Florida	170	133	36	—	1	—
Kentucky	103	88	10	5	—	—
Tennessee	93	66	27	—	—	—
Alabama	135	106	22	5	—	2
Mississippi	154	130	21	3	—	—
Arkansas	118	99	19	—	—	—
Louisiana	133	116	17	—	—	—
Oklahoma	60	54	4	1	1	—
Texas	297	210	84	3	—	—
WEST	509	496	—	—	7	6
Montana	6	6	—	—	—	—
Idaho	3	3	—	—	—	—
Wyoming	7	7	—	—	—	—
Colorado	47	47	—	—	—	—
New Mexico	8	8	—	—	—	—
Arizona	38	38	—	—	—	—
Utah	13	13	—	—	—	—
Nevada	29	29	—	—	—	—
Washington	47	46	—	—	1	—
Oregon	19	19	—	—	—	—
California	292	280	—	—	6	6

Adapted from Bureau of Prisons, "Executions 1930-1967," *National Prisoner Statistics*, No. 42, Washington, D.C., 1968, pp. 10-11.

Richard Quinney, *The Social Reality of Crime* (Boston: Little, Brown, 1970), p. 187.

The question of who actually makes the sentencing determination, and when, is complicated by prevalent plea-bargaining practices discussed earlier. Overt recognition of the propriety of plea agreements between prosecution and defense means that, in effect, the sentence in a number of guilty plea cases is pre-determined by the prosecutor.[6] While the judge always has the option to reject such agreement, in practice this is uncommon.

A number of criminal codes stipulate mandatory sentences upon conviction of certain crimes. In some places certain offenses are defined as nonprobation-able, thus precluding the judge from using a suspended sentence. In others, the probation alternative may be left open, but if the judge imposes a sentence of incarceration, the minimum or maximum (or both) period of incarceration is fixed by statute, allowing the court no discretion to set sentence length. Although avoidance of mandatory sentences is often the objective of plea negotiation, convictions requiring mandatory sentences are not uncommon. In these cases the legislature in effect performs the sentencing function.

Although the completely indeterminate mandatory sentence—one day to life —is much less common in criminal codes today than it was some years ago, it still exists in some places, usually for sex crimes in which the offender is also diagnosed as a "sex deviate" or "sex psychopath." In such cases the actual determination of sentence is left to parolling authorities who decide when, if ever, the offender will be released from custody.

Sentencing Structures

Sentencing structures and sentencing practices vary considerably among juris-dictions.[7] A survey of sentencing provisions in the various states revealed five major types of structures for imposing prison sentences, with innumerable variations even within a single state for different types of offenses. The five general structures are as follows: 1) both maximum and minimum terms of imprisonment are set by the judge at any point within legislative outer limits; 2) maximum terms are fixed by statute, but the judge may set a minimum at any point up to the maximum; 3) maximum and minimum terms are set by the judge, but the minimum cannot exceed some fraction, usually one-third, of the maximum; 4) the maximum term is set by the judge, but the minimum is fixed by statute; and 5) both maximum and minimum terms are fixed by statutory law allowing the judge no discretion.[8]

This complex and somewhat confusing array of alternative structures illus-trates well the relationship and the conflicts between the major sources of authority in the criminal process. Mandatory sentences of any sort reserve sentencing power to the legislature, denying discretion to both the judiciary and to parole authorities. In systems where a judge may set a minimum term, his decision forecloses the possibility of parole until the minimum is served. On the other hand, systems which provide a large spread of time between minimum and maximum terms give a major share of the power to determine the time actually served to the parole board.

It is difficult to state with precision the most typical or prevalent sentencing structure, for there are often different provisions within jurisdictions from one offense to another. However, it can be said that in *most* jurisdictions for *most* crimes judges have some choice among alternative types and lengths of sentences. And today all jurisdictions have parole boards which have some degree of discretion as to release of *most* inmates.

In the past it was common for legislative draftsman to fix specific sentences to each statute defining a crime. Thus the range of available penalties for burglary could be found within the laws defining this offense, and the same was true for robbery, larceny, homicide, and all other crimes. The result was an extremely large, diffuse, complex, and often inconsistent list of penal sanctions scattered throughout each criminal code. Furthermore, statutes defining crimes and related penalties proliferated over time as new offenses or variations in old ones tended to be added by each legislative session with few prior statutes repealed. The result in most jurisdictions was not only a disarray of sentencing provisions, but a hodgepodge of criminal laws. In some places, for example, a separate statute outlawed horse stealing, another was required to cover cow theft, and neither applied to dog stealing. Consequently, many jurisdictions—at this writing one-third of the states—have recently revised their criminal codes. Commonly, penal code revision has two major purposes: a more rational and uniform categorization of offenses which eliminates the proliferation of single, separate laws for each variation of common crimes; and creation of standard sentencing provisions for various degrees of ordinary crimes and for extended sentences for dangerous offenders.

Code revision was both sparked and aided by various professional groups—the American Law Institute, The National Council on Crime and Delinquency, the American Bar Association, and various national commissions—who developed the model codes referred to earlier.[9] Some of these models suggested revision of the substantive law of crimes, and each proposed new sentencing structures. The models, though not the actual law of any jurisdiction, proved valuable to state code revisionists, because in addition to presenting summary proposals, each suggestion was fully researched and annotated with major alternatives extensively debated in accompanying commentaries. Revising law and creating a new sentencing structure is no easy task, for each provision is complex and controversial, with extensive case law and a variety of practices found on both sides of every issue. The models confronted major sentencing controversies and attempted to resolve them. Resulting proposals were not always identical or congruent, but each was well argued and documented, and gave state code revisors options in drafting their own proposals.

In confronting major sentencing issues, there were and remain points of consensus as well as residues of disagreement between the model builders and among the various legislative committees responsible for actual revision of state codes. In general, revisionists agreed that old maximum sentences for routine conventional crimes were too long.[10] They also agreed that legislatively mandated sentences should be eliminated or markedly reduced, with a corresponding increase in judicial sentencing discretion. Each modern proposal suggests a ranking of penalty ranges by degrees of seriousness of crimes. These penalty provisions are contained in a separate section of the penal code rather than attached to each criminal statute. In this scheme the legislature determines whether a particular crime is a "Class A" or "Class B" felony, or falls into similar categories which rank offenses from the most serious felonies through misdemeanors and violations. Upon conviction of a crime of a particular classification, the sentencing judge turns to the appropriate section to determine the permissable sentencing ranges. In addition to penalty ranges for "ordinary" crimes and offenders, model builders and revisionists also generally agreed that there should be "extended term" provisions for dangerous and persistent offenders, as well as for gangsters and racketeers. However, as will be seen, there are some differences in the proposed length of such extensions and in definitions of these special categories of violators.

Some issues were avoided by the model builders. For example, the drafters of both the *Model Penal Code* and the American Bar Association's *Standards Relating to Sentencing Alternatives and Procedures* take no position with respect to the death penalty. And in actual codes across the country, provisions regarding the death penalty remain variable, although for the present, the Supreme Court has forbidden use of capital punishment.

Although some issues were avoided and others were generally agreed upon, there were some points of controversy about sentencing alternatives. An important disagreement reflected in the model codes and found in practice concerns minimum sentences. The Advisory Committee of the National Council on Crime and Delinquency (NCCD) strongly urges that there be *no* minimum sentences for any crimes.[11] This would give full responsibility to parole authorities to determine on a case-by-case basis if and when offenders should be released to community supervision prior to expiration of maximum terms. In contrast, the drafters of the American Law Institute's *Model Penal Code* require the judge to set a minimum term of incarceration from one to ten years for first-degree felonies, one to three years for those of the second degree, and one to two years for third-degree offenses.[12] The American Bar Association supports the authorization of judicially set minima, but would not require it.[13]

The debates around this issue were long and vigorous and continue to this day. In general, proponents of judicial authorization to fix a minimum, which for this period would deny discretion to the parole board, argue that the sentencing judge is in the best position to evaluate the actual significance of the offense to the particular community in which it occurred. By setting a minimum, the judge is best able to reflect community sentiment, to provide extended community protection and to exercise the deterrent function of the law. Proponents of the minimum sentence argue that these are perfectly appropriate considerations in giving prison sentences. On the other hand, advocates of the no-minimum stance counter that the primary purpose of any sentence is to restrain and control the offender only as long as it takes to rehabilitate him. They assert that parole authorities, in consultation with correctional personnel, are better able to determine when it is best, and safest, to release any prisoner than the judge who imposes sentence at a particular moment in time, often when passions are still aroused by the crime and before any correctional interventions have been tried. Holding an offender beyond the point at which he is ready for release is counterproductive and often results in bitterness and "prisonization," a process by which the offender comes to strongly identify with and gain status in the inmate culture. Furthermore, no-minimum proponents stress the ability of parole authorities to correct inequities of maximum sentences imposed by scores of different judges when parole discretion is not curbed by differential minima. Prisoners who have similar criminal records and are otherwise comparable in risk to the community and readiness for parole can be released at roughly the same time regardless of different maxima if there are no minimum restrictions. These proponents see this "equalization" as a matter of fairness in uniform application of the law.

As we have noted, while there are marked variations in actual sentencing provisions among the states and federal jurisdictions, the ALI and NCCD models are prototypes of many modern codes. Singly and combined, their provisions have been liberally borrowed, modified, expanded, and paraphrased by many state draftsmen. The *Model Penal Code* is the most elaborate, for it encompasses not only substantive law revisions and sentencing recommendations, but suggests standards for correctional organization and staffing as well. While there is a single summary volume of its provisions entitled *The Proposed*

Official Draft, sections of the code with extensive commentary and citations were published over a period of 12 years in the form of tentative drafts of sections, council drafts, and proceedings of the American Law Institute. A collection of all this material would fill a six-foot shelf. In contrast, the NCCD *Model Sentencing Act* is a pamphlet of only 35 pages devoted exclusively to sentence structure proposals. Provisions from each model relating to prison sentences for ordinary offenders are reproduced below. Each model has additional sections dealing with sentences for youthful and for dangerous offenders, and elsewhere both stress the desirability of probation over incarceration as a sentence for most offenders.

AMERICAN LAW INSTITUTE
MODEL PENAL CODE
(Proposed Official Draft, 1962)

Section 6.06. Sentence of Imprisonment for Felony; Ordinary Terms.

A person who has been convicted of a felony may be sentenced to imprisonment, as follows:

1. in the case of a felony of the first degree, for a term the minimum of which shall be fixed by the Court at not less than one year nor more than ten years, and the maximum of which shall be life imprisonment;

2. in the case of a felony of the second degree, for a term the minimum of which shall be fixed by the Court at not less than one year nor more than three years, and the maximum of which shall be ten years;

3. in the case of a felony of the third degree, for a term the minimum of which shall be fixed by the Court at not less than one year nor more than two years, and the maximum of which shall be five years.

Alternate Section 6.06. Sentence of Imprisonment for Felony; Ordinary Terms.

A person who has been convicted of a felony may be sentenced to imprisonment, as follows:

1. in the case of a felony of the first degree, for a term the minimum of which shall be fixed by the Court at not less than one year nor more than ten years, and the maximum at not more than twenty years or at life imprisonment;

2. in the case of a felony of the second degree, for a term the minimum of which shall be fixed by the Court at not less than one year nor more than three years, and the maximum at not more than ten years;

3. in the case of a felony of the third degree, for a term the minimum of which shall be fixed by the Court at not less than one year nor more than two years, and the maximum at not more than five years.

No sentence shall be imposed under this Section of which the minimum is longer than one-half the maximum, or, when the maximum is life imprisonment, longer than ten years.

The well-known section of the *Model Sentencing Act* with its five-year maximum provision is reproduced below. Notice that this Section also provides for "consent probation," a procedure by which an offender, though convicted by a trial or his own plea, may be placed on voluntary probation and, if the probationary period is successfully completed, avoid a formal conviction record.

ADVISORY COUNCIL OF JUDGES
NATIONAL COUNCIL ON CRIME AND DELINQUENCY
MODEL SENTENCING ACT (1963)

Section 9. Sentencing for Felonies Generally.

Upon a verdict or plea of guilty but before an adjudication of guilt the court may, without entering a judgment of guilt and with the consent of the defendant, defer further proceedings and place the defendant on probation upon such terms and conditions as it may require. Upon fulfillment of the terms of probation the defendant shall be discharged without court adjudication of guilt. Upon violation of the terms, the court may enter an adjudication of guilt and proceed as otherwise provided.

If a defendant is convicted of a felony and is not committed under Section 5 or 7 [or 8] the court shall a) suspend the imposition or execution of sentence with or without probation, or b) place the defendant on probation, or c) impose a fine as provided by law for the offense, with or without probation or commitment, or d) commit the defendant to the custody of [director of correction] for a term of five years or a lesser term, or to a local correctional facility for a term of one year or a lesser term. Where a sentence of fine is not otherwise authorized by law, in lieu of or in addition to any of the dispositions authorized in this paragraph, the court may impose a fine of not more than $1000. In imposing a fine the court may authorize its payment in installments. In placing a defendant on probation the court shall direct that he be placed under the supervision of [the probation agency].

Section 10. Statement on the Sentence.

The sentencing judge shall, in addition to making the findings required by this Act, make a brief statement of the basic reasons for the sentence he imposes. If the sentence is a commitment, a copy of the statement shall be forwarded to the department or institution to which the defendant is committed.

The ABA *Standards Relating to Sentencing Alternatives,* citing the inappropriate length of common sentences in many jurisdictions, do not suggest specific maximum terms but state that: "Except for a very few particularly serious crimes (and except for special terms for dangerous offenders), the maximum authorized prison term ought to be five years and only rarely ten."[14] More recently, the National Advisory Commission proposed a sentencing scheme for the "nondangerous offender" very similar to the NCCD *Model Sentencing Act.* They recommend: "State penal code revisions should include a provision that the maximum sentence for any offender not specifically found to represent a substantial danger to others should not exceed five years for felonies other than murder. No minimum sentence should be authorized by the legislature."[15]

The five-year maximum commonly suggested in these models and reports, while considerably shorter than sentences possible under many state codes and, in fact, shorter than many sentences imposed by courts, is actually considerably longer than time really served by the vast majority of prison inmates in all jurisdictions.[16] The median length of time served for all offenses is somewhat less than two years, and in most states over half of all prison sentences imposed by courts are for five years or less.[17] This led the drafters of the *Model Sentencing Act* to point out that their proposed five-year maximum, if implemented by various states, would not really cause a very significant change in common practices.[18]

Straight, Partially Indeterminate, and Indeterminate Sentences

Both model codes and actual sentencing structures address the question of the distribution of sentencing discretion among legislatures, courts, and paroling authorities. With minor exceptions for certain serious crimes, all models and actual codes allow judges the power to choose between probation or incarceration. Today almost all felony sentences to incarceration are partially indeterminate, with a spread of years between a minimum (which may be zero), and maximum, whether set by statute, judge, or correctional agency. Thus within legislatively set limits, judges can impose sentences of different lengths, and, in turn, within judicial outer limits parole boards have discretion to release prisoners at different times. However, there is another alternative structure which is commonly found in misdemeanor sentences: "flat" or "straight" sentences for a specific period of time with no minimum or maximum spread. This is nowhere found as a general feature of felony sentencing structures and is not proposed as desirable in any of the model codes. Nonetheless, there are advocates of such a structure. The differential application of the criminal process generally, from police discretion through plea bargaining to sentencing structures, is under attack from many quarters, including groups of inmates and ex-offenders who have experienced criminal processing. The American

Friends Service Committee has issued a report calling for abolition of discretion across the criminal process, including elimination of indeterminancy in sentences.[19] This position rests chiefly on disillusionment with the rehabilitative ideal underlying correctional and parole discretion.[20]

In an address before the American Correctional Association, judge Lawrence Pierce proposed a sentencing scheme for nonviolent, nonrecidivist offenders which would start with a short period of incarceration (ranging from four to eight months), primarily to satisfy the retributive ends of the law and to provide a diagnostic interval. These sentences would be flat, and the incarceration period would not entail any rehabilitative efforts. Upon release, these offenders would be returned to the community, *not* on parole, but as free men, receiving such noncoercive support and help as could be provided by correctional and welfare resources. Should they commit new offenses, the more traditional sentencing and correctional system would be invoked. With respect to this proposal Judge Pierce commented: "As to these offenders, there would be no utilization of our limited parole resources for purposes of supervision, no commitment of valuable staff time to overseeing reporting, no tracking down of the offender to determine whether he's working, or living with a paramour, or has left the jurisdiction, or is associating with questionable companions. These valuable resources would be reserved for more intensive supervision of the violent offender and the inveterate recidivist."[21]

In general, proponents of straight sentences to reduce correctional and parole discretion argue that such sentences eliminate uncertainty of date of release, and that straight sentences are fixed by the seriousness of the crime. They also contend that release from servitude under discretionary schemes shifts from consideration of the offender's act to his perceived mental or moral condition. Furthermore, they claim that discretion as to time served, even if humanely intended, actually covers outrageous practices of racial discrimination and political intimidation.

In marked contrast to flat sentence proposals, another model endorses *completely* indeterminate sentences—from one day to life—for virtually all crimes. This was popularly espoused in the 1930s and 1940s when there was widespread belief that the expertise of medical and social scientists qualified them to "diagnose" and "treat" criminal behavior.[22] There is no serious support for such a scheme today for it has become too painfully obvious that such expertise is a myth. Furthermore, the operational consequences of the completely indeterminate sentence is to incarcerate for life "untreatable" and persistent minor violators, like alcoholic check forgers, who can neither be rehabilitated nor deterred. Residues of this type of sentencing structure are still found in sex deviate sentencing structures in some states.

The Sentencing Process: Presentence Investigations

After conviction, whether by plea or trial, the state's interest in the offender shifts from the question of whether he committed a crime to what to do with (or for) him. As we have indicated, most sentences are imposed by a judge who has a number of alternatives available to him, with the exception of those few cases where conviction carries legislatively mandated sanctions. In the vast majority of sentencing determinations, the judge knows little about the person he must sentence except for the formal conviction label. If a trial has been completed, the judge may have formed some opinion about the character and risk of the offender from testimony of witnesses or from the defendant himself if he took the stand. But in most cases, criminal defendants have pleaded guilty, and in this process the judge may actually see the offender for only a few minutes, exchanging only a few words with him.

To assist the court in imposing a fair and appropriate sentence, a presentence investigation is normally conducted to gather relevant information about the offender which will assist the judge in selecting among sentence alternatives. To accomplish this, there is usually a time interval—commonly from ten days to two weeks or a month—between conviction of a felony and sentencing, during which a social investigation of the offender is made by the probation staff attached to the court. In some jurisdictions such an investigation is mandated by statute or court rule; elsewhere it may be discretionary with the court. The American Bar Association recommends that such investigations be required (assuming no specific court order to the contrary in a particular case) in every instance where a sentence to incarceration for a year or longer is possible, where the offender is under 21 years of age or where he is a first offender.[23] Required presentence investigations are also recommended by the President's Commission and in the *Model Penal Code*.[24] The National Advisory Commission not only recommends presentence reports in cases involving felonies and with young offenders, but also "in every case where there is a potential sentencing disposition involving incarceration."[25] If this recommendation were followed, it would extend presentence investigation to cases involving at least the more serious misdemeanors, a practice that is comparatively rare at present.[26] In jurisdictions that use jury sentencing, such investigations may be superfluous, and in convictions for crimes where a mandatory sentence must follow, the judge may disdain presentence investigation, although in such instances the corrections service may conduct a similar "admissions investigation."

246

Presentence investigations vary in scope and focus, depending upon court resources and the desires of sentencing judges. Generally, a probation officer is given the task of conducting a background investigation of the person to be sentenced, bringing together facts and opinions about the offender that may inform and otherwise assist the judge in determining an appropriate sentence. Sometimes a clinical diagnosis of the offender is desired or mandated by law, and the offender may be sent to a clinic, hospital, or in some places to a prison for psychiatric and psychological assessment. In routine cases, however, the probation officer collects available records (the offender's police record, commonly called a "rap sheet," employment history, school reports, and so on), interviews persons knowing the offender (his family, friends, teachers, employers, sometimes the victim or witnesses, and so on), interviews the offender for his "own story" of the crime, and may, if desired by the court, offer his own "diagnosis" of the violator and make specific recommendations as to sentence.[27]

ILLUSTRATION 1

State of Madison
PRESENTENCE REPORT

CONFIDENTIAL   DATE: December 31, 1973
                                     P.O.: John R. Orkis

DISTRICT COURT OF MADISON
     UNIT 12, Jefferson County
          JUDGE: William P. Patterson
     DEFENDANT: Daniel Angus Defore
          AGE: 28 yrs. D.O.B.: 11/11/45
     RESIDENCE: 114 Adams, Jefferson, Madison
          P.O.B.: Rockway, Madison
     OFFENSE: Ct. 1 - Breaking and Entering
                    in the Nighttime
               Ct. 2 - Possession of Burglary Tools
     DATE CONVICTED: November 18, 1973, by Guilty Plea to
                      both counts.
     STATE'S ATTY.: Frank T. O'Neill, Jr.
     DEFENSE ATTY.: Mike B. Gage

ARREST SUMMARY OF THOMAS CAPRARI,
     JEFFERSON POLICE DEPARTMENT:

On February 27, 1973, at 12:30 a.m., Officer Caprari was on a routine patrol, and was returning to police headquarters, which is located next to the Acme Shopping Center in Jefferson, when he noticed a car coming out of that area. Officer Caprari then followed this car a short distance, marking down the registration and its description before turning on his Cruiser light and stopping the vehicle. When the car finally stopped, the operator got out and came back towards the Cruiser, acting very nervous. While Officer Caprari was approaching the stopped vehicle, he noticed that there were three other people in the car. Upon questioning the operator, it was determined that he was Robert Lee Morgan, Jr., of Concord, Madison. It was also determined that one of the passengers was his wife, Susan Ann Morgan. The other two individuals were Daniel A. Defore of Jefferson, and Peter Louis French of Jefferson. As Officer Caprari looked into the car he saw a tool box on the floor of the back seat. When he asked Morgan what the tools were for, Morgan told him that he had gotten them from his father. When Officer Caprari asked Morgan if he could look at them, he was given an OK. Officer Caprari then took the tools from the car and put them into the Cruiser. When Morgan was asked by the police officer where he was going, he stated that he and his friends had just come from Granville, and were headed back to Jefferson. Lt. Clarkson was then dispatched to come to the scene, and while waiting for the lieutenant to arrive, Officer Caprari made a list of the tools in question. Among them were:

    3 14-inch long black-handled screwdrivers, made in USA
    2 30-inch Drew #30 Pinch bar
    1 18-inch Flat bar, Stanley Handyman #H616
    1 16-inch Flat bar, C. Drew & Co.

All of these tools were new; then there was a 7-inch head wooden-handled sledgehammer which was old and rusty. Also present on the dash of the car was a 2-cell flashlight and one pair of brown cotton gloves.

After Lt. Clarkson arrived and the people were ordered to go to the police precinct, Officer Caprari noticed that Defore and French were wet up to the knee area. When they were asked how they got this way, they gave no answer.

The Jefferson police checked with the State Police, and it was learned that the men in question were known for breaking and entering into drugstores.

The officers then checked the drugstores in Jefferson and found them to be OK. After getting Morgan's permission to keep the tools, the men were allowed to proceed on their way. Just prior to their leaving, however, the boots of French and Defore were inspected by the police.

At 10:30 a.m., the following morning, Officer Caprari received a phone call from the Jefferson Country Properties, Inc., who advised him that their place had been broken into the night before. Upon investigation, Officer Caprari noticed that two sets of footprints led from the highway to the rear of the building, and that entry had been made through the rear door by someone using his shoulder to force the door open. The footprints were made by boots similar to those of the two men who were in the police station the night before. Two files had been broken into, but nothing had been taken.

Officer Caprari had also noted the night before that when he looked into the trunk of the car there were at least a dozen pairs of shoes, and also several changes of clothing. It was noted that Morgan did most of the talking.

STATEMENT OF ROBERT MORGAN TO SGT. RICHARD A. PEABODY, MADISON STATE POLICE:

On the night we were picked up in Jefferson, Danny Defore, Butch French, my wife, Susan, and myself, I had picked up Danny at his home, and he carried a gun box from his home that contained three big, black screwdrivers; a couple of pinch bars; and maybe a wedge bar. We had discussed going with him a few nights before this. He wanted my wife and I to go with him and his buddy, Butch. All we were to do was stay in the car while he and Butch went for a walk. We drove around and looked over a bowling alley. He wanted to hit the bowling alley, but I told him I didn't want to get involved in that. We went to the bowling alley and shot some pool. After we left the bowling alley we drove toward the edge of town, and when we went by a real estate office someone in the car mentioned it, so we drove by a couple of times. I dropped Danny and Butch off on the road above the real estate office, and my wife and I parked in a motel parking lot. When they left, they took some of the tools with them. They were gone about ten minutes and I saw light from cigarettes coming down the road, so I drove up and picked them up. When they got in the car I asked Defore if he got any money and he said, "screw the joint." We then went back down to the bowling alley and looked it over some more. I told them again that I didn't like the idea, as it was too near the police station. I then drove out and headed for home. We didn't go, for before we could we were stopped by a police officer. When he stopped us he noticed the box with the tools on the floor in the back seat. He asked what was in the box and I told him tools. He asked to see them so I took them back to the Cruiser, and he looked them over and called his lieutenant.

He then asked us to go to the station with him. They checked on our records and let us go. One of the officers asked me if I minded if they kept the tools to look them over for a while, and I told them they could.

STATEMENT OF PETER FRENCH, GIVEN TO P. O. ROBERT J. SOWALSKI:

The subject was interviewed at the jail in Jefferson and he readily admitted his guilt to the charges of Possession of Burglary Tools and Breaking and Entering in the Nighttime. French claims that on the day in question he had been drinking quite heavily. He was approached by the codefendants, Defore and Morgan. They wanted him to ride around with them to look around. Morgan had some burglary tools in the car, and French knew what they were up to. They looked over various stores. It was decided that they would break into the Jefferson Country Properties, Inc., and French and Defore got out of the car and went over to the building. French broke a window and crawled in. He then let Defore into the building. They looked around but could not find anything of value and eventually left the building and rejoined Mr. and Mrs. Morgan who were waiting a short way from the building.

STATEMENT OF DANIEL A. DEFORE TO P. O. ORKIS:

This man was interviewed at the jail on February 28, 1973. He stated that Morgan and his wife came over to pick up both him and Peter French, and they were just going riding around. When Defore got in the car, he noticed that there were tools on the back floor. While passing through the outskirts of Jefferson, Morgan stated that the Jefferson Country Properties place looked like a good place to break into, but Defore felt that Morgan wouldn't know what he was doing, so he and French decided they would go in. Because it was too early in the evening, the quartet went down to the bowling alley in the shopping center to play pool in order to kill time. They then returned to the property in question and Defore and French went into the building where they found a door open and just walked in. They then returned to the city to have some coffee in a diner, and were on the way home when the police stopped them.

Defore stated that it has been five years since he had last committed a felony, and he feels that he is now facing his roughest time because of his age, namely 28. He knows that he was a plain damn fool for doing this, especially since he didn't derive any benefit from the break. When asked whether he realizes

250

that his record indicates that he can certainly now be considered a habitual offender, and what it could mean, he stated yes, life imprisonment. However, this man stated that he is pretty sure he is going to get no more than two to ten years, and that if he doesn't he will certainly make an appeal.

Defore stated that he has certainly learned his lesson now, and knows that he could make it in the future. His wife has filed for a divorce but he doesn't care, because she was unfaithful to him, and as a result, he is finished with married life. However, he still intends to support his child, as he has done in the past.

Regarding a future job, Defore stated that he plans to return with the Green Tree Company. He has been working as a foreman, with take-home-pay of 96 dollars. That is the type of work he likes to do, and he has worked at it for the past year. This officer's impression of this man is that he is a real con artist who likes to twist things around to his advantage. He is also quite cocky. For instance, he stressed the fact that he didn't actually break into the building in question, but rather, walked in; for the door had been left unlocked. This officer advised him to do some research on the definition of breaking and entering.

PRIOR RECORD:

AGE

15 3/20/60 PD, Boston, Mass. Runaway-Larceny of Auto. Returned to Madison.

17 8/25/62 Spring Falls Municipal Court, Speeding Fine and Costs, $15.10.

18 4/6/63 Jefferson Municipal Court, Petty Larceny Fine and Costs, $46.95.

19 9/31/64 Sullivan County, Superior Court, Claremont, Madison, Breaking and Entering-Larceny, three years probation. Ordered to make restitution in amount of $300.00. Closed 9/1/67 due to incarceration in new offenses in Jefferson. (Goddy Realty and Bakery Co., Jefferson. Currency stolen to value of $60.00. Offense occurred 7/1/64 in nighttime). Ninety days in jail.

20 12/1/64 Jefferson Muncipal Court, Burglary in Nighttime --two counts, committed to Madison State Reformatory for not less nor more than one year on each

251

count, to be served concurrently. Released 9/6/65, served maximum less good time. (Smith's Store at Jefferson). (Tools, sawed-off shotgun and shells) also Crosse's Store (two bottles of wine).

22 6/18/67   Concord County Court, Grand Larceny, one to three years Madison State Prison. (The Woolen Mill at Ludlow, Madison). (Copper wire and aluminum type cable valued in excess of $100.00). Offense occurred about 2/16/67. Released on parole, 5/16/69.

22 9/28/69   Cheshire County Court, State of Lincoln, Breaking and Entering--Nighttime and Larceny, committed to State Prison one to three yrs. Transfer to Madison State Prison under Interstate Compact on 4/14/70. Paroled 8/24/70. Expired 9/28/72. (43 559A). (Offenses occurred about 5/16/69 in the nighttime at Dobbs and Sons, Inc. of Walpole. (Several handguns, one GE Stereo Record Player, one portable TV set, currency valued at $1,269.39.)

FAMILY:

FATHER:

Peter (NMI) Defore, age 62, was born at Dorset, Madison. He has been a machinist at Miller and Small Machine Shop in Jefferson for a total of 28 years. He has earned a poor reputation with law-enforcement officers in the area. With lay persons he presents an appearance of being a hard working, stable husband and father.

In 1943 he bought land at 19 Third Street in Traverse and attempted to settle his family into a shack. His wife rebelled and returned to Jefferson with Daniel. In 1947, the father joined his family and worked at Sure Moulding for some three years. In 1950 he returned to his employment at M & S Machine Shop.

The father claims that he has always bailed Daniel out of scrapes and that he has always maintained a close, supporting relationship with respondent. His lament is that no one can understand how Daniel could have become such a bad actor when he had so much. On the other hand, Daniel claims his father taught him to steal by sending him upstairs at Denby's Store to get shotgun shells while his father stood watch as "lookout." Daniel says that his father also used to use him to steal horse halters and equipment from the Saddlery Shop in Spring Falls. When Daniel was a little older he went back to Denby's to steal on his own, after he saw how easy it was.

Daniel also claimed that his father always made a pass at any woman, including his sister's girl friends, his teachers, and even Daniel's wife. The father reports that he was innocent and that he was falsely accused by these women, but this response was offered without being sought by me. Daniel said, "I have a lot of hate built into me because of him (father). He has led to much of my bad behavior."

Obviously there is deep conflict between father and son. The father appears to desire to gloss over this factor, while Daniel is now venting his problems. When I asked Daniel why he had not reported these problems earlier, he said it was to protect his mother who is now dead. Under these conditions, the father is not seen as being of any value toward reformation of respondent.

MOTHER:

Yolanda (Lyons) Defore was about 58 years of age when she died of cancer in July of 1967. She had worked as a store clerk during most of Daniel's formative years. Of her marriage, two children were born, respondent and his sister, Mary Finn, who was 12 years his senior. There was little brother/sister relationship during formative years due to difference in ages and Mary's early marriage. They are close now, and this relationship is seen as a resource for Daniel's future.

Daniel was very close to his mother and was very upset by her death. It appears the mother was a prudent homemaker and had accumulated several hidden hordes of money and savings bonds. Just before her death, she reportedly informed her daughter of this and told her of the location. The father learned of the money and converted it to his own estate although the children believed it was meant for their use. This has led to additional conflict between son and parent.

MARITAL:

Nancy Mae (Stewart) Defore was born October 13, 1946, and met Daniel after his release from prison in 1969. She was working at the A & W Drive In. After about a year, she stabbed herself with a butcher knife at his parent's home because Daniel was dating a girl from Spring Falls. She was hospitalized about one month and repeated threats to kill herself if respondent did not take her back. Daniel was on parole in 1970 and says he didn't want any trouble so renewed the relationship. She became pregnant and they were married in 1971 shortly after the birth of their child, Dominic, born 1/21/71.

Daniel reports they got along pretty well until "I came home in the Fall of 1971 and found she had run away with another man" (said to be Mr. Hicks of Westview in Springfield, and it is noted that respondent is currently reported to be a resident with a Mrs. Hicks at Westview). Daniel reports she was gone three days and when she came back told him she was pregnant and it was his. "I told her I didn't believe it. She eventually told me she was in love with the other man and didn't want to stay. We separated about one month. She came back and decided she didn't love the other fellow. I didn't take her back then and she tried to run me off the road near North Jefferson. All this started me on the 'pill road' and I was drinking a lot; the marriage plus my mother's death upset me and caused my present trouble with the Court. Nancy was willing to come to Court and say it was her fault, but I discouraged this. We are still friendly and communicate. I don't feel we could go back together because of her threats toward suicide and I don't want any more trouble. I visit the child and we get along all right." She has seen an attorney about a divorce.

PERSONAL HISTORY:

Daniel Angus Defore was born November 11, 1945, at Rockway, Madison Hospital. Daniel's earliest memory, dating from about four years of age, is that he and his mother lived at Oslo while the father worked in Jefferson and came home weekends. The mother had a baby-sitter who lived next door and who would take him to the store where his mother treated him to ice cream. Daniel started school at Oslo at six years of age and this led to friendship with Sandy Miller whose father was a TV repair man. After this he spent almost all his time with Sandy watching TV. Daniel believes he failed the second and fourth grades at Oslo and thus repeated the fourth grade when he entered Jefferson school system. Daniel has good memories of his mother and their early life at Oslo. In the village of about 300 people he had about six to eight close friends. He feels that it was the move to Jefferson that ruined his life.

Daniel had most of the usual childhood diseases without complications. He cut his foot with a homemade hatchet about seven to eight years of age but has no permanent disability. He was once involved in a head-on automobile collision and thrown through the windshield. Two years later, on the same road, he had a similar accident and was knocked unconscious. At present his health is good.

254

For a while Daniel worked as a bag boy at the First National Store with his mother. He used his earnings to purchase a car and automobile insurance plus pay for its running expenses. Because of this job, he dropped out of football but claims he was active in all sports during elementary schooling.

Respondent's work history is sporadic and seems to point toward a preference for work as a filling station attendant/mechanic. He is known to have had a previous interest in racing cars.

He was confined at Madison Reformatory on a felony conviction. He served his maximum sentence and was discharged. Later he served time in Madison Prison. He tried working at Miller and Small Machine Shop, but not for long. So far he has also had brief periods of experience working for an aluminum ladder company, and construction companies (Madison Foundry and Swanson Plastics) as a driver. His most consistent employment in recent years has been in service stations until he took up a recent job with Green Tree Service Co., where he claims he was advanced to foreman and is eligible for reemployment.

HOME ENVIRONMENT:

None. Daniel reports he is staying with friends in Jefferson. Informants told me he is staying with the wife of the man who broke up his marriage. Respondent offers to establish separate living quarters with a former, 70-year-old landlady from which he would seek reemployment as foreman for Green Tree Service Company.

FINANCIAL STATUS:

No savings, no checking account, no automobile. His assets consist of his personal wardrobe and hunting equipment. He earns an average weekly take home pay of $96.61 for a five-day week, nine hours daily. He is paying $25.00 a week to his wife on a temporary Court order and $20.00 a week to support his child. His only sizeable debt is $440.00 owed to Attorney Kent of Jefferson.

EDUCATION:

At Jefferson, Daniel entered North Street School in the fourth grade. He had good grades and relationships with his teachers until he entered the ninth grade, his first year of high school. At this point his grades slipped from a B-C average to D or incomplete. He completed the ninth grade but dropped out due to loss of interest during the third quarter of his tenth grade. An Iowa

Arithmetic Test when he was in the eighth grade shows that he was capable of only sixth-level work. A Gates Reading Test while still in the eighth, showed he was reading at fourth-grade level. Daniel admits it is a struggle to read and write at the present time, and as his former parole officer, I am well aware of his academic deficiency. This is an area that needs further exploration, as two separate IQ scores discovered were so low that they seem impossible to accept. Daniel says he received remedial courses in his last four years of elementary schooling and this may account for the higher achievement record in those years. The father told me that several teachers have said Danny was not up to his age.

INTERVIEWS:

Law-enforcement officers do not feel Defore can conform to society. They feel many unsolved crimes in the area were of his making and do not believe he is easily led, rather that he is, in fact, a leader in the deviant elements of the surrounding area.

Employers report that when he works he is a valued employee, but that he is impulsive and will walk off the job and go fishing.

His mother previously recorded that he was a bed wetter until eight years of age. He got along with his peer group and had many friends--was never sick; that he liked sports and also bowled, winning a trophy in high school. The mother reflected some hostility toward Daniel's later friends. She blamed Danny's choice of associates for his life of crime and said he was easily led.

Records of two state prisons show that Daniel makes a good adjustment to inmate life. Doctor Jagger reported--"this man's intelligence could not be tested properly as he missed both questions on orientation. It is possible he could be of dull intelligence . . . He does things and thinks afterward."

SUMMARY:

Daniel Angus Defore turned 28 in November of 1973. For the past twelve years he has been arrested numerous times for things ranging from a minor procuring malt beverages to breaking and entering in the nighttime, stealing guns. He has been incarcerated three times; twice in prison and once in a jail. This present offense makes his fourth conviction. Mr. Defore has entered the "habitual criminal" class.

256

True, this man is only 28 years old, but irregardless, he has the makeup to continue in a life of crime if he doesn't radically change his ways. As a result, he should therefore be considered the type of person who should be incarcerated for a long period of time, rather than one who would profit from any form of rehabilitation. Defore is smart enough to have taken advantage of a system that allows him and others to commit a series of similar crimes, only to be either charged with one, and/or actually serve time for one. In either case, this man couldn't care less as long as he is released on an early parole date. Certainly prior commitments haven't deterred him from a way of crime. As he mentioned to this officer, he is quite sure he will receive concurrent sentences and an early release on a long parole.

The only positive thing I can say about him is that he admits his crimes. He did plead guilty without any plea bargaining. On the other hand, the police had him cold.

In reviewing the statements given by the trio which was involved in the Jefferson break, their stories are not the same. It doesn't really matter, for there is no doubt as to their actions on the early morning of February 27, 1973. Actually, nothing was gained from this break; but it was quite obvious from all the burglary tools, and the changes of clothing in Morgan's car, that bigger things were in store for them.

Defore blames his life of crime on his "no-good father" and his unfaithful wife. Although his mother blames her son's downfall on his choice of poor associates, and his being led by them into doing these things, it is noted, however, that Morgan was 19 and French was 21, while Defore was 27 when they were caught in this act. It is also noted that neither of the codefendants had any felony charges against them until this one, so they certainly cannot be blamed for leading this respondent astray.

Because of this man's record and attitude, this officer feels that he shouldn't be given any consideration whatsoever.

RECOMMENDATION:

That this man not be considered probation material.

Respectfully submitted,

John R. Orkis
Probation and Parole Officer

Barry D. Martin, Supervisor

257

Except for changes of names and locations, this presentence report is a real one. It is not offered as a model of what a good report should be, nor is it necessarily typical, for the quality and contents of reports across the country vary so widely that no single illustration could claim to be representative. However, it is in no way unusual, and for this reason raises a series of questions about what materials and information are most helpful to a judge when making a sentencing determination. Some jurisdictions are experimenting with short-form reports, little more than a statement of the offender's prior criminal record, educational and work record, and present family status on the grounds that in practice judges can and do respond to only a few variables.

Some observers argue that much material in usual, long-form presentence reports is irrelevant to sentencing and essentially useless to the judge. For example, what is the significance of the statement by Daniel's mother in the Defore report that he was a bed wetter? Are his automobile accidents relevant in any way? Traditionally, the "diagnostic" parts of presentence investigations have heavily emphasized intrafamily relationships—parent-child conflicts, sibling rivalry, and so on—along with early developmental history—weaning, toilet training—in a modified psychoanalytic vein. In contrast, such variables as peer group relationships, neighborhood associational patterns, school gangs and other extrafamily influences have been omitted or downplayed, even though many criminologists feel that such factors are more relevant than family influences in the production of criminal behavior.

Aside from specific content, it can be demonstrated that differential phrasing of similar facts can color the reports, leading to diametrically opposite conclusions. For example, when confronted by an offender's erratic work record, one probation officer might interpret it as evidence of "instability" or "unreliability," while another could interpret it as evidence that the man is "searching for himself, seeking a way to make a meaningful contribution."

Whether such reports are sparse or detailed, whether they contain only easily verifiable facts, like employment history, or more nebulous and subjective elements, such as hearsay opinions of neighbors and diagnostic evaluations of the probation officer, they are generally considered necessary and valuable by the court. Because the judge typically has almost no information about the record and social history of the offender before him, he welcomes any additional information that may aid him in making the important, often painful, sentencing decision.

CONFIDENTIALITY OF THE PRESENTENCE REPORT. The history of the use of presentence investigations is a stormy one, for traditionally they were considered confidential documents to be seen only by the judge and not to be disclosed to the defendant or his counsel. But as the sentence hearing came to be defined as a critical stage, defense argued that a hearing based on a secret, unshared document of such importance was merely a hollow exercise. Probation staff countered with the claim that confidentiality must be promised to persons interviewed if worthwhile information is to be obtained.[28]

Proponents of nondisclosure of the presentence report long rested the propriety of their stance on a 1949 U.S. Supreme Court decision, *Williams* v. *New York*.[29] In this case Williams was convicted of murder, but the jury recommended leniency, that is, life imprisonment rather than execution. The judge, however, imposed a death sentence based on a presentence investigation which he did not fully disclose to the defense. Williams demanded to cross-examine witnesses who gave testimony in the presentence investigation. The trial court denied this request and the U.S. Supreme Court upheld the lower court denial. Actually this decision is really much narrower than disclosure of the report.[30] The Supreme Court merely concurred with the trial judge that Williams could not confront and cross-examine persons who provided information in the presentence investigation. Nevertheless, for many years the *Williams* case was widely interpreted as justification for not sharing the presentence report and not subjecting it to adversary testing at the sentence hearing.[31]

The situation is somewhat different today. In a few jurisdictions the entire contents of presentence reports, including even psychiatric diagnoses, are shared with both the defense and with the state's attorney. More commonly the disclosure controversy has resulted in a compromise. In a number of places today, a sentencing judge may, at his discretion, reveal *part* of the report, withholding identity of antagonistic respondents, for example, but "summarizing" their adverse statements. Some places distinguish the factual contents of the report (police records and so on) from opinions of respondents, allowing disclosure of the first part, but not revealing sources of information in the second part.[32] However, the National Advisory Commission, while cognizant of various partial disclosure provisions, rejects this compromise and calls instead for "requiring full disclosure, without exceptions as to confidentiality."[33] They reject as "unconvincing" the argument that sources of information will "dry up" if their identity and statements are related to the offender. They argue that "if the offender is to be convinced that his reintegration into society is desirable, he must be convinced that the society has treated him fairly" and if he is sentenced on the basis of "information he has not seen or had any chance to deal with and rebut, he cannot believe that he has been treated with impartiality and justice."[34]

However the confidentiality issue is resolved, the question of what is appropriate and relevant information for a presentence report is still open. Some dimensions of this issue have been discussed:

Can (or should) a presentence report include or make any references to or inferences about the criminality of the defendant—not on the basis of the present charge—but relying on evidence which may have been excluded at trial? As to this, the court in *U.S.* v. *Schipani* (315 F. Supp. 253, EDNY, 1970) held that a judge might properly consider evidence from wiretapping at sentencing although the same evidence was excluded from trial. This hardly is the final answer to the question, but it does illustrate the possible direction of litigious attack. Can a probation officer include in his presentence investigation report references to or allegation of other crimes of which the defendant was acquitted? As to this, the court in *U.S.* v. *Latimer* (415 F. 2d. 1288, 6th Cir. 1969) disapproved of a sentencing judge considering evidence of charges of which the defendant was acquitted.

The general issue, clearly just emerging at sentencing, is whether there are, should be, or will be, court imposed limitation on the *type* of information that may properly be included (and type of information that should be excluded) from presentence investigations. It is likely that this will rise either by the practice of disclosure or by judges giving reasons for sentencing in which they refer to information obtained from the report. Appellate courts will undoubtedly view this as a sentencing matter, thus only inferentially related to the presentence report, but nevertheless it seems likely that there will be *some* restrictions on the propriety of evidence used in the sentencing decision. It is doubtful that exclusion will reach the level of trial inadmissibility, but it would be excessively naive to assume that any or all information, no matter how inaccurate or irrelevant, can stand as a proper basis for sentence determination.[35]

Imposition of Sentence

Except when an offender is convicted of a crime with a sentence mandated or excluded by statute, the judge has discretion to select the type and to fix the length, and sometimes certain other conditions, of sentence. Depending upon the offense and statutory provisions, he may be able to choose among a fine, suspension of sentence without supervision, probation (which is suspension with community supervision), or incarceration in a jail or prison. The latter alternative, jail or prison, ordinarily depends upon whether the offense is a misdemeanor (jail) or felony (prison). Probation, and in some places nonconditional or nonsupervised suspension, can be given in either crime category. Fines are more commonly imposed in misdemeanor cases, alone or combined with probation or incarceration, but depending upon statutory law, they may also be imposed in some felony cases. Fines are commonly levied in white-collar violations like embezzlement, income tax evasion, and corporate fraud.

The *major* decision at sentencing involves a choice between probation (a sentence to community supervision without incarceration) or a sentence to jail or prison. A few jurisdictions, including the federal, provide for a "split sentence," even for felons, which involves a short term in jail (not prison) followed by a period of probation (not parole). Usually, however, the basic issue of particular concern to the offender at sentencing is whether he will remain in the community on probation or go to prison. If the decision is incarceration, questions of where and how long become paramount. If the decision is probation, determinations must be made of the length of sentence and the rules or conditions of supervision.

PROBATION. It is often thought that probation is a lenient sentence, and it is when compared with any kind of incarceration, but it *is* a sentence and not simply a dismissal of the case. The offender placed on probation generally must agree to a set of conditions—covering such things as curfew, regular employment, restricted travel, restitution to the victim, and so on—and to supervision by a probation officer. Should the probationer violate any condition or commit a new crime while on probation, he may, at the discretion of the probation staff, be returned to court for possible revocation and imprisonment. On successful completion of probation he is discharged from sentence.

A judge may sentence to probation in one of two ways: He may impose a prison sentence (three to ten years, perhaps), but suspend its *execution* and place the offender on probation; or he may suspend *imposition* of any prison sentence and place the offender directly on probation. In the first instance, if the offender is revoked the term of incarceration is already set, but in the second instance the term of incarceration is fixed after revocation. The latter is sometimes called "deferred sentencing."

Ordinarily the length of probation can be set within whatever limits are allowed by statute, though this may not necessarily be equal to the length of imprisonment provided by law for the crime. Thus if a crime carries a possible sentence of twenty years in prison, the term of probation may be only five years, or, conversely, if a one-year prison term is provided, a longer probationary period may be fixed by the court if probation statutes allow it. In many jurisdictions the conditions of probation can be modified from time to time by the court, and the length of the sentence can be reduced or extended.

Traditionally, at the point of sentencing, probation has been considered an alternative to imprisonment. That is, it has been assumed that a convicted felon should go to prison in the absence of substantial evidence that he is a good risk

PERCENTAGE DISTRIBUTION OF PROBATIONERS, BY SIZE OF
CASELOAD IN WHICH SUPERVISED, 1965

CASELOAD SIZE	JUVENILE PROBATION	FELONY PROBATION
Under 40	3.7	0.8
41–60	19.7	5.0
61–80	49.2	14.1
81–100	16.7	13.1
Over 100	10.7	67.0

National Survey of Corrections.

President's Commission on Law Enforcement and Administration of Justice, *Task Force Report: Corrections* (Washington, D.C.: U.S. Government Printing Office, 1967), p. 30.

and can be safely released and effectively supervised in the community. The drafters of the *Model Penal Code* sought to reverse this assumption by proposing legislation which would require the judge to place a convicted offender on probation unless he finds imprisonment is necessary for "protection of the public." They suggest three bases for rejecting probation, any of which is sufficient for imposition of a prison sentence:

   a. there is undue risk that during the period of a suspended sentence or probation the defendant will commit another crime; or
   b. the defendant is in need of correctional treatment that can be provided most effectively by his commitment to an institution; or
   c. a lesser sentence will depreciate the seriousness of the defendant's crime.[36]

The latter criterion is the most controversial, relating as it does to deterrence and a general respect for the law on the part of the public rather than to the characteristics or needs of the particular offender.

   In the same section of the *Model Panel Code,* there are suggested "grounds" for the court to consider in giving "weight in favor of withholding [a] sentence of imprisonment." These are not designed to be binding on the court nor to necessarily include all criteria that may be considered, but they do cover a broad range of factors important in the sentencing determination. The suggested grounds for probation are:

   a. the defendant's criminal conduct neither caused nor threatened serious harm;

b.   the defendant did not contemplate that his criminal conduct would cause or threaten serious harm;

c.   the defendant acted under a strong provocation;

d.   there were substantial grounds tending to excuse or justify the defendant's criminal conduct, though failing to establish a defense;

e.   the victim of the defendant's criminal conduct induced or facilitated its commission;

f.   the defendant has compensated or will compensate the victim of his criminal conduct for the damage or injury that he sustained;

g.   the defendant has no history of prior delinquency or criminal activity or has led a law-abiding life for a substantial period of time before the commission of the present crime;

h.   the defendant's criminal conduct was the result of circumstances unlikely to recur;

i.   the character and attitudes of the defendant indicate that he is unlikely to commit another crime;

j.   the defendant is particularly likely to respond affirmatively to probationary treatment;

k.   the imprisonment of the defendant would entail excessive hardship to himself or his dependents.[37]

The listing of such criteria in model legislation form represents a major contribution of the *Code*. While it is clear that these factors are offered merely as guidelines that "might" be considered by a court and although there is no claim that the list is exhaustive, this approach represents an attempt to articulate in legislation appropriate criteria for sentencing determinations, a situation rarely found in actual criminal codes. In general, legislatures have been silent with regard to factors judges may properly consider in deciding whether to send an offender to prison or to retain him under sentence in the community.

Actual sentencing practices in various courts were analyzed as part of the American Bar Foundation's survey of criminal justice during the 1960s. Along with other sentencing considerations, attention in this survey was focused on the use of probation by sentencing judges. Quite clearly the rehabilitative potential of probation was a major concern to judges and to probation staff. Professor Robert O. Dawson, however, comments on additional factors shown to be important in this decision:

. . . However, rehabilitation is not the only concern of persons who make probation decisions. Trial judges reflect their assessment of the seriousness of the offense in probation decisions. Offenses they view as very serious are likely to result in a prison sentence, despite the fact the defendant's potential for rehabilitation seems good; conversely, persons who commit offenses viewed as minor are likely to be placed on probation without regard to their prospects for rehabilitation. In part, this attitude doubtlessly reflects concern over the seriousness of the offense the defendant may commit if he is released on probation. But it also reflects a judgment that probation is leniency, and some offenses are so serious they require full community condemnation—a prison sentence.

In addition, the probation decision is used to accomplish some objectives that cannot be achieved by incarceration. The probation decision is sometimes used to relieve court congestion by encouraging the disposition of cases of guilty pleas. It may be used to support police efforts to detect crime and apprehend offenders through informants by rewarding their services with probation. The probation decision is often influenced by a desire to secure restitution to the victim of the offense or support for the offender's family—goals that cannot be achieved by a prison sentence.[38]

INCARCERATION.   Normally, misdemeanants are incarcerated in local jails, commonly the same institutions which hold defendants who are awaiting grand jury determinations, preliminary hearings, arraignments, or trials. Jail sentences are usually for specified times up to one year. Lesser sentences, up to a month, are commonly expressed in days, and longer sentences often in three month intervals—three months, six months, nine months, or a year. Some jails have work-release programs in which some inmates can go to work during the day and report to lockup at nights and on weekends. Though a few jurisdictions have a form of misdemeanor parole which allows a prisoner to be released under supervision prior to expiration of his full sentence, in most cases jail time is "flat," that is, there is no minimum and maximum spread. Instead the inmate serves precisely the term imposed by the court.

With felons, the sentencing options available to judges are extremely varied across the nation, not only from one jurisdiction to another, but often for different offense categories within a single state. The sentencing alternatives possible with a case involving burglary may be different from those provided by statute for cases of armed robbery. And minimum or maximum sentences provided by law for burglary in one state may not be the same as provisions in neighboring states. But in general, judges have some choice, not only as to probation, but in setting the length of incarceration if a prison term is decided upon.

In most jurisdictions for most offenses, legislation sets the outer limits of any sentence—the minimum and maximum period of incarceration—and though judges have some discretion to impose *lower* terms, they may not fix a time higher than that provided by statute. A *minimum* sentence is the time which an offender must spend in prison before becoming eligible for parole, although in some places this may be reduced somewhat for "good behavior" while in prison. Parole eligibility does not necessarily imply release; it merely fixes the date at which a prisoner may be considered for parole. The *maximum* sentence, however, sets the outer limit beyond which a prisoner cannot be held in custody. Unlike flat sentences for misdemeanors, most felony sentences today are partially indeterminate, with a spread of time between minimum parole eligibility and maximum servitude. Even life imprisonment sentences in most states today have a parole eligibility date fixed by law.

Statutes in some jurisdictions provide mandatory maximum sentences (in a few places for all felonies; more commonly only for specified crimes) which the court must impose, but they allow judicial discretion in setting a minimum up to the maximum or, more commonly, at some proportion of the maximum, usually one-third. Other states have low, legislatively fixed minimum sentences (for example, in Wisconsin the minimum is one year for all crimes but first- or second-degree murder) with judicial discretion to set a maximum term at any point from the minimum to an upper limit fixed by statute. Still other states, like New York, allow the judge to set a maximum within a legislative upper limit and a minimum within a fixed upper limit, *or* no minimum at all. Other jurisdictions have various combinations and permutations of these patterns.

Many judges consider sentencing, particularly determining length of incarceration, as their most difficult task. In recent years there have been numerous studies of criteria used by judges to make sentencing determinations, analyses of various correlates of judicial sentencing behavior, and attempts by judges themselves to articulate reasons for their choices, primarily to reduce sentence disparity.[39]

In most cases coming before a sentencing judge, there are myriad mitigating or aggravating circumstances which surround the crime itself or are revealed about the perpetrator in the presentence investigation. This gives any kind of statistical evidence of sentence disparity dubious validity. This is not to deny the reality of disparity nor minimize the possibility of arbitrary or capricious sentences. It merely suggests that sentence imposition in any particular case is rarely simple, so that uniformity and consistency are ideals that are difficult to accurately measure.

Like all men, judges often have idiosyncrasies which may affect their sentencing determinations. In any jurisdiction, certain judges may have deserved reputations for harsh or lenient sentencing decisions in certain types of cases. One judge may abhor narcotic violations and impose long sentences in these cases. Another may view narcotic violations as minor infractions, particularly if soft drugs are involved. There are "gun" judges who tend to impose long

265

sentences on any offender who had a gun during the commission of his crime, whether or not the gun was used. The same judge may be lenient with sex deviates, believing such persons to be sick rather than criminal. Defense lawyers who are aware of judicial foibles may spend considerable time judge-shopping to obtain sentence hearings for their clients in a sympathetic or at least non-hostile court.

Dawson found a wide variety of factors beyond the nature of the offense itself which influenced judicial setting of long or short periods of incarceration. Some of these he terms "administrative accommodations," including such things as showing more leniency to an offender who pleads guilty than to one who has had a full trial, or showing leniency to an offender who is a police informer or who has been a valuable state's witness. Conversely, judges sometimes impose very long sentences, not with the intention of burying the offender in prison for many years, but to provide an extended parole supervision period in the belief that intensive surveillance and assistance will be needed on his return to the community.[40] Furthermore, most conscientious judges wish to "individualize" sentences as much as possible, attempting to fit the actual consequences of sentences to the risk and reputation of the offender and also to consider the effect of the sentence on his family. But it should be noted that individualization is only one sentencing objective. Judges are lawyers, and in sentencing as in other matters, they often have strong allegiance to precedent. Over time it is not unusual for them to strive to impose comparable sentences for similar offenses and for similar offenders.

Sentencing Leniency for Guilty Plea Offenders

As we have pointed out, sentencing determinations are so intertwined with plea-negotiation practices that it is sometimes difficult to determine precisely where and by whom the sentence decision is actually made.[41] In general, overt plea bargaining principally affects selection for probation, avoids mandatory sentences, and, by reducing charges, acts to lower the outer limits of minimum or maximum sentences. Rarely does a bargain include a preconviction promise for a specific term of years in prison.

With minor exceptions, trial judges support the plea negotiation process by honoring bargains made between defense and the prosecutor. But apart from overt bargaining, there is a controversial sentencing issue regarding the common practice of judges showing greater leniency to defendants who have pleaded guilty than to those convicted only after trial. Sometimes called the "implicit bargain,"[42] defendants who plead guilty throw themselves on the mercy of the court and, in most instances, receive this mercy. Opponents of this practice—

often other judges—argue that such differential leniency penalizes defendants for exercising their constitutional right to trial. At a federal sentencing conference this issue was debated, and among those favoring more leniency to the guilty plea defendant one judge commented: "In a large metropolitan court it would be impossible to keep abreast of the large number of criminal cases if it were not generally known among the practicing bar that consideration is given to those who are willing to plead guilty."[43] Others supporting the practice felt that the pleading defendant has shown remorse and should be given a break, while the defendant who pleaded not guilty but was convicted anyway has added perjury to his original crime.

This leniency issue was aired in a federal case involving four codefendants charged with interstate transportation of stolen furs, where three pleaded guilty, but one demanded trial and was convicted. The judge sentenced the tried defendant to a longer prison term than his partners, although the record showed him to be the least criminal of the four. He had requested probation, but the judge said it was his "standard policy" not to grant probation to defendants who demanded trial, and added that his sentence would have been even longer if the defendant had demanded a jury trial instead of accepting a bench trial. The case was reversed on appeal and returned to the lower court for resentencing. The court of appeals said:

UNITED STATES V. WILEY
278 F. 2d. 500 (7th CIR. 1960)

The trial judge announced from the bench that it was the standard policy of his court that once a defendant stands trial, probation for such a defendant would not be considered. This policy or rule is self-imposed. It is contrary to the statute and the rule of criminal procedure authorizing probation. Such a rule should not be followed. A defendant in a criminal case should not be punished by a heavy sentence merely because he exercises his constitutional right to be tried before an impartial judge or jury.

In the case at bar, McGhee, the four-time convicted felon, and the ringleader; received a two-year term. The three defendants other than Wiley, all of whom had criminal records, received sentences of one year and a day. Yet Wiley, who had a good previous record except for one juvenile matter when he was thirteen years old, received a three-year term. A realistic appraisal of the situation compels the conclusion that Wiley's comparatively severe sentence was due to the fact that he stood trial. No other possible basis is suggested for the disparity. Consciously or not, the learned trial judge again applied the standard of his rule when he reimposed the three-year sentence. I agree this sentence should not be permitted to stand.

The matter does not rest here however. The American Bar Association in constructing its standards for pleading and sentencing took the following position:

Section 1.8. Consideration of Plea in Final Disposition.

a.　It is proper for the court to grant charge and sentence concessions to defendants who enter a plea of guilty or *nolo contendere* when the interest of the public in the effective administration of criminal justice would thereby be served. Among the considerations which are appropriate in determining this question are:

i.　that the defendant by his plea has aided in ensuring the prompt and certain application of correctional measures to him;

ii.　that the defendant has acknowledged his guilt and shown a willingness to assume responsibility for his conduct;

iii.　that the concessions will make possible alternative correctional measures which are better adapted to achieving rehabilitative, protective, deterrent, or other purposes of correctional treatment, or will prevent undue harm to the defendant from the form of conviction;

iv.　that the defendant has made public trial unncessary when there are good reasons for not having the case dealt with in a public trial;

v.　that the defendant has given or offered cooperation when such cooperation has resulted or may result in the successful prosecution of other offenders engaged in equally serious or more serious criminal conduct;

vi.　that the defendant by his plea has aided in avoiding delay (including delay due to crowded dockets) in the disposition of other cases and thereby has increased the probability of prompt and certain application of correctional measures to other offenders.

b.　The court should not impose upon a defendant any sentence in excess of that which would be justified by any of the rehabilitative, protective, deterrent, or other purposes of the criminal law because the defendant has chosen to require the prosecution to prove his guilt at trial rather than to enter a plea of guilty or *nolo contendere*.[44]

In contrast to this position, the National Advisory Commission states: "The fact that a defendant has entered a plea of guilty to the charge or to a lesser offense than that initially charged should not be considered in determining sentence."[45]

Extended Term Sentences

Each of the major model sentencing proposals and most newly revised state sentencing provisions provide separate sentencing provisions for youthful offenders and for dangerous or professional criminals. In general, sentences for young, first offenders are shorter, more indeterminate, and more clearly directed to treatment and rehabilitative programs in reformatories or other special diversion facilities than sentences for "ordinary" adult violators. Often there are provisions for expunging records if these young offenders show satisfactory correctional progress. It is generally believed that there is much more hope for successful rehabilitation and reintegration of the young, with corresponding attempts to reduce the stigma and the negative effects of labelling. In many jurisdictions the most modern facilities and a disproportionate number of professional staff are allocated to youth programs and facilities. For the most part, this approach is noncontroversial; a majority of all participants in criminal processing give high priority to early leniency and high quality correctional programs for youthful offenders.

Much more controversial, and exceptionally complex, are provisions for extended sentences for dangerous offenders and for gangsters and other persistent, professional criminals. Few would deny the existence of some very dangerous offenders—persons who have committed violent, atrocious crimes—who kill, maim, rape, and otherwise seriously jeopardize the safety of us all. The existence of career criminals, professionals who make crime their lifelong occupation, and gangsters and racketeers who traffic in heroin, and who extort, intimidate, and corrupt is an unpleasant reality. The problem of distinguishing these offenders with accuracy and by acceptable means from ordinary, limited-threat offenders is not easily solved. And the secondary problem, what to do with them once they have been convicted and identified, remains.

These problems generate very difficult legislative questions. Being a "dangerous person" is not in itself a crime. Nor is the appellation "gangster" constitutionally sufficient to lock someone up. Instead, model code draftsmen as well as state code revisionists have sought ways to distinguish both dangerous criminal activities and dangerous offenders. For example, the *Model Sentencing Act,* while limiting maximum terms for ordinary crimes to five years, distinguishes these from "atrocious crimes," providing longer sentences for persons convicted of the following acts:

Section 8. Atrocious Crimes.

If a defendant is convicted of one of the following felonies—murder, second degree; arson; forcible rape; robbery while armed with a deadly weapon; mayhem; bombing of an airplane, vehicle, vessel, building, or other structure— and is not committed under Section 5, [Dangerous Offenders] the court may commit him for a term of ten years or a lesser term or may sentence him under Section 9. [Ordinary Crimes. i.e., five years maximum][46]

269

This is an attempt to classify some crimes as worse than others, making long sentences appropriate because of the intrinsic "atrocious" nature of the criminal act. Another approach focuses on the criminal actor, rather than or in conjunction with the act, providing longer sentences if the person is found to be dangerous. Both the *Model Sentencing Act* and the *Model Penal Code* provide sections dealing with criteria for determining dangerous offenders, with correspondingly longer terms for each. The codes differ somewhat in their criteria and in methods of determiniing dangerousness. In addition to the maximum five-year term for ordinary offenders, ten years for atrocious crimes and life for first-degree murder, the *Model Sentencing Act* provides:

Section 5. Dangerous Offenders.

Except for the crime of murder in the first degree, the court may sentence a defendant convicted of a felony to a term of commitment of thirty years, or to a lesser term, if it finds that because of the dangerousness of the defendant, such period of confined correctional treatment or custody is required for the protection of the public, and if it further finds, as provided in Section 6, that one or more of the following grounds exist:

a. The defendant is being sentenced for a felony in which he inflicted or attempted to inflict serious bodily harm, and the court finds that he is suffering from a severe personality disorder indicating a propensity toward criminal activity.

b. The defendant is being sentenced for a crime which seriously endangered the life or safety of another, has been previously convicted of one or more felonies not related to the instant crime as a single criminal episode, and the court finds that he is suffering from a severe personality disorder indicating a propensity toward criminal activity.

c. The defendant is being sentenced for the crime of extortion, compulsory prostitution, selling or knowingly and unlawfully transporting narcotics, or other felony, committed as part of a continuing criminal activity in concert with one or more persons.

The findings required in this section shall be incorporated in the record.

Section 6. Procedure and Findings.

The defendant shall not be sentenced under subdivision a or b of Section 5 unless he is remanded by the judge before sentence to [diagnostic facility] for study and report as to whether he is suffering from a severe personality disorder indicating a propensity toward criminal activity; and the judge, after considering the presentence investigation, the report of the diagnostic facility, and the evidence in the case or on the hearing on the sentence, finds that the defendant comes within the purview of subdivision a or b of Section 5. The defendant shall be remanded to a diagnostic facility whenever, in the opinion of the court, there is reason to believe he falls within the category of sub-division a or b of Section 5. Such remand shall not exceed ninety days, subject to additional extensions not exceeding ninety days on order of the court.

The defendant shall not be sentenced under subdivision c of Section 5 unless the judge finds, on the basis of the presentence investigation or the evidence in the case or on the hearing on the sentence, that the defendant comes within the purview of the subdivision. In support of such findings, it may be shown that the defendant has had in his own name or under his control substantial income or resources not explained to the satisfaction of the court as derived from lawful activities or interests.[47]

In the past in many jurisdictions, the only provisions for extended periods of incarceration were for the "habitual criminal." In some places an offender became automatically eligible for a long habitual offender sentence upon his third or fourth conviction of specified crimes; in others, "being an habitual offender" was processed as a separate charge, with a trial, if any, devoted primarily to proof of his prior record. The operational consequences of habitual offender laws was that many essentially minor but persistent violators, not really dangerous or violent, were engulfed in the process and spent long stretches in prison. The drafters of the *Model Penal Code* attempted to address the issue of extended terms for the persistent violator as well as for the professional criminal and the dangerous offender:

Section 7.03. Criteria for Sentence of Extended Term of Imprisonment; Felonies.
The Court may sentence a person who has been convicted of a felony to an extended term of imprisonment if it finds one or more of the grounds specified in this Section. The finding of the Court shall be incorporated in the record.

1. The defendant is a persistent offender whose commitment for an extended term is necessary for protection of the public.

   The Court shall not make such a finding unless the defendant is over twenty-one years of age and has previously been convicted of two felonies or of one felony and two misdemeanors, committed at different times when he was over [insert Juvenile Court age] years of age.

2. The defendant is a professional criminal whose commitment for an extended term is necessary for protection of the public.

   The Court shall not make such a finding unless the defendant is over twenty-one years of age and:

   a. The circumstances of the crime show that the defendant has knowingly devoted himself to criminal activity as a major source of livelihood; or

271

    b.   The defendant has substantial income or resources not explained to be derived from a source other than criminal activity.

3.   The defendant is a dangerous, mentally abnormal person whose commitment for an extended term is necessary for protection of the public.

    The Court shall not make such a finding unless the defendant has been subjected to a psychiatric examination resulting in the conclusions that his mental condition is gravely abnormal; that his criminal conduct has been characterized by a pattern of repetitive or compulsive behavior or by persistent aggressive behavior with heedless indifference to consequences; and that such condition makes him a serious danger to others.

4.   The defendant is a multiple offender whose criminality was so extensive that a sentence of imprisonment for an extended term is warranted.

    The Court shall not make such a finding unless:

    a.   The defendant is being sentenced for two or more felonies, or is already under sentence of imprisonment for felony, and the sentences of imprisonment involved will run concurrently under Section 7.06; or

    b.   The defendant admits in open court the commission of one or more other felonies and asks that they be taken into account when he is sentenced; and

    c.   The longest sentences of imprisonment authorized for each of the defendant's crimes, including admitted crimes taken into account, if made to run consecutively would exceed in length the minimum and maximum of the extended term imposed.

Section 6.07. Sentence of Imprisonment for Felony; Extended Terms.

In the cases designated in Section 7.03, a person who has been convicted of a felony may be sentenced to an extended term of imprisonment, as follows:

1.   in the case of a felony of the first degree, for a term the minimum of which shall be fixed by the Court at not less than five years nor more than ten years, and the maximum of which shall be life imprisonment;

2.   in the case of a felony of the second degree, for a term the minimum of which shall be fixed by the Court at not less than one year nor more than five years, and the maximum of which shall be fixed by the Court at not less than ten nor more than twenty years;

3.   in the case of a felony of the third degree, for a term the minimum of which shall be fixed by the Court at not less than one year nor more than three years, and the maximum of which shall be fixed by the Court at not less than five nor more than ten years.[48]

    The federal jurisdiction, concerned as it is with interstate organized crime, has attempted to spell out criteria for including gangsters and racketeers under general provisions for extended sentences for dangerous criminals. The statutory framework of this approach is extremely complex and is much too long and detailed to be reproduced in full here. In general, the approach is to deal with "patterns" of crime, with "conspiracies," and with offender income acquired but not visibly earned. Some sampling of the statutory language includes the following:

. . . the defendant committed such felony as part of a pattern of conduct which was criminal under applicable laws of any jurisdiction, which constituted a substantial source of his income, and in which he manifested special skill or expertise; or

Such felony was, or the defendant committed such felony in furtherance of, a conspiracy with three or more other persons to engage in pattern of conduct criminal under applicable laws of any jurisdiction, and the defendant did, or agreed that he would, initiate, organize, plan, finance, direct, manage, or supervise all or part of such conspiracy or conduct, or give or receive a bribe or use force as all or part of such conduct.

. . . For purposes of . . . this subsection, special skills or expertise in criminal conduct includes unusual knowledge, judgment or ability, including manual dexterity, facilitating the initiation, organizing, planning, financing, direction, management, supervision, execution or concealment of criminal conduct, the enlistment of accomplices in such conduct, the escape from detection or apprehension for such conduct, or the disposition of the fruits or proceeds of such conduct. For purposes of paragraphs (2) and (3) of this subsection, criminal conduct forms a pattern if it embraces criminal acts that have the same or similar purposes, results, participants, victims, or methods of commission, or otherwise are interrelated by distinguishing characteristics and are not isolated events.

A defendant is dangerous for purposes of this section if a period of confinement longer than that provided for such felony is required for the protection of the public from further criminal conduct by the defendant.[49]

While most knowledgeable participants in the criminal process, and for that matter most citizens, fully agree that there are some very dangerous persons loose on our streets and in our prisons, the problem of actual diagnosis of *future* dangerousness is difficult, if indeed possible. If a person has killed once, will he kill again? Atrocious crimes and dangerous persons are of major concern across the entire criminal justice system, not just at sentencing. Techniques designed to prevent or deter violent crimes range from sidearms carried by police, to the walls and gun turrets of maximum-security prisons. Prediction of dangerousness is a critical operational concern from stop and frisk practices, to parole determinations. At preconviction stages of the process, however, except for such limited and controversial practices as preventive detention, most assessments of dangerousness apply to situations rather than to persons. Every passenger is subject to airport search, and except for those fitting the hijacker "profile," dangerousness is not individually predicted. Under certain conditions of even routine investigations, police officers always approach with drawn pistols without making individual assessments. But at sentencing, and in such post-sentencing determinations as the grant or denial of parole, predicting future dangerousness involves individual cases. While it is true that statistical analysis of past experiences with thousands of sentenced offenders or parolees can reveal correlates of dangerousness that will fairly accurately predict the probable frequency of its occurrence in large future samples, both judges and parole boards decide individual cases. The prediction of the frequency of future dangerous crimes in a large population is one thing; the prediction of such conduct in an individual case is quite another. In predicting dangerousness in the mass processing of hundreds of offenders through sentencing and parole, both judges and parole authorities face the dilemma of errors in two directions. Type I errors involve offenders who are not given extended terms or released on parole and who subsequently commit violent crimes. On the other hand, Type II errors are those where extended sentences are given to offenders or where parole is denied when the persons are not dangerous and would not commit future violence. The cost of the first type of error is repeated, serious criminal acts; the cost of the second is extended incarceration of offenders who could be safely returned to the community.

The difficulties with applying even the best predictive experience tables at the parole decision have been explained:

Even if a [parole] board were given all the psychiatrists, sociologists, statisticians, and other experts it desired to make a thorough investigation and analysis of each case, it is doubtful if it could achieve 80 percent accuracy in identifying the less than 5 percent of parolees who commit clearly violent offenses after release. Eighty percent accuracy is about the greatest precision that has been demonstrated by any man or any prediction system, applied to a cross-section of prisoners, for predicting parole violation in general, rather than the more difficult task of predicting violence on parole. Of course, a board might sharply reduce the number of violent offenses committed on parole if it stopped paroling, but this would merely mean releasing prisoners to commit violence as dischargees without the services of parole in facilitating a non-criminal life and restricting activities leading to crime.

If a board were 80 percent accurate in identifying the most violent parolees, they would still make more than 2 erroneous predictions in 10 as long as the violence they sought to predict occurred in less than 20 percent of the cases.

This is simply a matter of mathematics. For example, if violence were committed by 5 percent of prison releasees in every 1,000 releasees, a parole board would have to identify 50 men who would commit violence among 950 who would not. With 80 percent predictive accuracy, we could expect the board to predict violence for 20 percent of the 950, or 190 cases, and for 80 percent of the 50, or 40 cases. However, in this total of 230 designations as probably violent, one could not know in advance which actually would be the 40 who would be violent. They would make a total of 200 erroneous predictions, the 190 nonviolent designated as violent and the 10 violent not designated as violent, in identifying correctly the 230 cases in 1,000 which include 40 of the 50 violence cases. These errors are apart from others they might make in predicting more common types of parole infraction, such as nonviolent theft, burglary, or return to narcotics.

The foregoing theoretical analysis assumes 80 percent accuracy in predicting violent parole infractions, and that 5 percent of the men released will commit such infractions. If accuracy is lower, or the frequency of the behavior to be predicted is less than 5 percent, there will be more errors made in order to deny parole to a given proportion of those who could commit the predicted behavior. If we have 80 or even 90 percent accuracy in predicting an event occurring in only 1 percent of the cases, such as the commission of a violent sex offense by a paroled sex offender, our ratio of errors to predictions would be much greater than 200 to 40.[50]

The Treatment Mandate of Some Long Sentences

For the most part, extended sentences for dangerous or professional criminals are for the purposes of punishment and incapacitation, that is, simply holding them in prison for long periods of time to protect the community from their predatory activities. There is rarely any clear legislative intent that such sentences are for treatment and rehabilitation, and few correctional administrators have much faith in successfully rehabilitating persistently dangerous offenders, gangsters, or professional thieves.

However, a number of jurisdictions do provide long sentences for certain types of offenders, usually sex deviates, "defective delinquents," or others who are somehow "aberrant," with a specific mandate to the correctional service to provide "specialized treatment."[51] Whether we now have effective ways of treating and rehabilitating adult homosexual child molesters, mentally defective assaulters, or other offenders with bizarre mental or emotional quirks is doubtful. Nonetheless, the legislative mandate may be to treat as well as to hold. If a prisoner is found to be psychotic, he is commonly transferred to a hospital for the criminally insane, often a maximum-security institution much like the prison he left, for whatever psychiatric or psychological treatment modalities

275

exist there. But many inmates under long sentences with a treatment mandate are not insane by legal standards, nor psychotic by usual psychiatric diagnostic criteria. They remain in prison and are presumed to be receiving treatment for whatever condition led to or accompanied the criminal behavior for which they were convicted. In general, while appellate courts have recently shown increased willingness to intervene in cases where it is alleged that requirements for treatment in mental hospitals are not being carried out,[52] they have rarely addressed the question of whether correctional services have, or can, fulfill whatever "specialized treatment" has been demanded by legislation.

In addition to specific statutory language to the effect that the state must provide "treatment" for sex offenders or other specific categories of prisoners, some criminal codes differentiate correctional institutions according to rehabilitative or punishment purposes. For example, reformatories are sometimes specified as places for young prisoners who have "hopeful" futures and who should be given "rehabilitative opportunities." In contrast, prisons are for "hardened" or "dangerous" inmates and no rehabilitative expectations are specifically assigned in the law. This raises the issue of a young prisoner's right to serve his sentence in a reformatory which has rehabilitative programs. A federal district court in Iowa addressed this issue:

WHITE V. GILLMAN
360 F. SUPP. 64 (S.D. IOWA, 1973)
This action was instituted by Willie Heflin White for injunctive and declaratory relief regarding his transfer from the Iowa State Reformatory at Anamosa, Iowa to the Iowa State Penitentiary at Fort Madison, Iowa in June of 1972. The plaintiff alleges he was transferred without a hearing, notice, or reason given, and that as a result of this transfer he has lost rehabilitative opportunities available at the Reformatory and that the security at the Penitentiary is harsher than at the Reformatory, resulting in more severe punishment.

. . .

The Court first remarks that both the institutions involved in this lawsuit are prisons where the greatest deprivation of rights which inmates suffer is loss of their freedom. Beyond this, however, the Court does recognize on the basis of the affidavits submitted to the Court and laws regarding commitment to these institutions and the statutes governing transfer of these inmates, that there are important differences between the two institutions.

The statute governing the proper place of confinement in Iowa provides for the sentencing of younger criminals who are not convicted of one of a list of more serious crimes and who are first offenders to the Men's Reformatory at Anamosa. Older criminals over thirty years of age, recidivists, and those convicted of more serious crimes are to be confined in the Iowa Penitentiary at Fort Madison.

. . .

The legislature provided for transfer of the less hardened criminal and "promising" prisoners to the reformatory indicating a desire to maintain a certain type of prisoner in this institution. Again in Section 246.13 of the Code of Iowa the legislature indicated that more troublesome prisoners and those "not a hopeful subject for reformatory treatment" could be transferred to the penitentiary at Fort Madison.

The Iowa Legislature through these statutes has clearly recognized a substantial difference between these two institutions. This recognition of the difference between the institutions by Iowa law, coupled with plaintiff's numerous affidavits alleging loss of ability to participate in many rehabilitative programs and harsher discipline in the penitentiary supports the plaintiff's allegation that he has suffered a substantial loss by being transferred to and confined in an institution consisting of older inmates convicted of more serious crimes who are more likely to be habitual criminals.

The Court finds that although Willie White was notified of the transfer on or about June 29, 1972, and told the reasons for the transfer, he was not given a proper "due process" hearing prior to his transfer to Fort Madison.

In this case, as in the majority of appellate decisions dealing with extended or more harsh sentences, primary attention was given to such procedural matters as a right to a hearing, representation by counsel, and similar matters of due process.

The question of any right to treatment for sex deviates and others serving extended terms remains largely unresolved. In the decade after World War II an intense concern and fear about "sex criminals" dominated public opinion about our crime problem. Although the fears were disproportionate to the reality of the threat, the result was widespread adoption of sex psychopath legislation in many states.[53] These laws generally provided long indeterminate prison sentences for sex offenders with a mandate that prisons must attempt to treat and rehabilitate them. Prisons were often ill-equipped for this task, not only in terms of lack of clinical personnel and effective treatment techniques, but also because they found it difficult to house and care for such offenders separately from other prisoners as was often required by the new legislation. Correctional administrators confronted a small segment of their population who were not psychotic and therefore ineligible for treatment as criminally insane, but who required psychiatric intervention and could not simply be treated as routine inmates. The result was a series of internal prison accommodations in housing and programs that fall somewhere between a mental-hospital model and that of a regular

277

prison. Many adjustments were makeshift, tentative, and less than satisfactory to all concerned. In some instances certain cellhouses were designed as "treatment centers"; in others, "hospital" buildings for sex deviates appeared behind prison walls. Eventually appellate courts received prisoner complaints of lack of treatment, inadequate separation of classes of prisoners, and other allegations that the treatment mandate of the legislation was not being carried out. Usually, state appellate courts upheld the fulfillment of any treatment mandate if "some efforts" were being made to provide therapy, even though the setting and resources were less than ideal. The dilemmas presented by an in-prison treatment mandate and their resolution were addressed by the Massachusetts Supreme Court:

COMMONWEALTH V. HOGAN
170 N.E. 2d 327 (1960)

On March 4, 1959, the defendant was indicted for indecent assault and battery upon a child under the age of fourteen. He was arraigned on March 6 and pleaded not guilty. Subsequently, on March 18, he retracted his not guilty plea and pleaded guilty. At every stage of the proceedings herein discussed the defendant was represented by counsel. On the same day that the defendant pleaded guilty the district attorney moved, under G.L.C. 123A, Sec. 4, inserted by St. 1958, c 646, Sec. 1, that before sentence was imposed the defendant be committed to the treatment center mentioned in the statute for a period not exceeding sixty days for the purpose of examination and diagnosis. This motion was allowed and the defendant on March 18 was committed to the Correctional Institution at Concord for examination and diagnosis in accordance with Sec. 4. At Concord the defendant was examined by two psychiatrists, and on May 15 they filed their report stating that in their opinion the defendant was a sexually dangerous person.

On June 23, 1959 (doubtless as a result of our decision in *Commonwealth v. Page,* 339 Mass. 313, 159 N.E. 2d 82, rendered on June 2, 1959), the court heard evidence on whether a treatment center as prescribed in Sec. 2 for the care, treatment, and rehabilitation of sexually dangerous persons had been set up. At the conclusion of the evidence the judge made a general finding that such a treatment center had been established. To this finding the defendant excepted. On the following day (June 24) the judge, after notice and hearing, found that the defendant was a sexually dangerous person, and ordered him committed to the treatment center at the Massachusetts Correctional Institution at Bridgewater for the indeterminate period prescribed by Sec. 5, subject to the defendant's exception. The defendant was committed in accordance with this order.

On December 4, 1959, the defendant filed a motion for a "new hearing" on the question of whether a treatment center as prescribed by c. 123A had been established.

. . .

The evidence on this issue was as follows: On June 19, 1959 with the approval of the Commissioner of Correction, a treatment center was established at the Massachusetts Correctional Institution at Bridgewater. The center consisted of a four story wing of the State hospital to which the criminal insane are committed. Until recently the wing had been used to house the criminal insane. The center is separated from the rest of the hospital by double doors which were kept locked. There are seven individual rooms on each floor (twenty-eight all told) and a common room. The center is "staffed * * * by the general medical staff at the hospital, a purely diagnostic staff consisting of * * * [two doctors], and an administrative staff under a Mr. Krueger of the division of legal medicine consisting, for the time, of two psychiatric social workers." The center is under the control of the department of correction, and the "department of mental health is responsible for advising * * * [the department of correction] as to the type of mental staff and treatment." There are no full-time personnel assigned to the center but part-time personnel are available to meet the treatment needs of the center from day to day. The wing can accommodate twenty-eight persons, and more, if the common rooms are used as a ward. At the time of hearing there were probably twenty persons at the center. There are no dining or infirmary facilities available at the center separate from those used by the criminal insane.

The commissioner of correction testified when asked if the inmates mingled with the criminal insane, that the "plan is not to have them mix generally." He further testified that it was not intended that inmates of the center should go into the other parts of the institution; that if they did so it would be for some specific reason and they would be in custody of some correction officer or employee; that in matters pertaining to "recreating [in] the yard," eating in the dining room, and seeing "movies," the patients of the center may be in the same room with the criminal insane; but "the plan is to keep them separated."

In the *Page* case we expressly disclaimed any attempt to state the standards to be observed in a treatment center. We do not now undertake to state them. All that we decided there was that a confinement in a prison which is undifferentiated from the incarceration of convicted criminals was not confinement in a treatment center within the purview of the statute. The situation in the case at bar is not the same as that in the *Page* case. Here the defendant is segregated in a separate wing which has been established solely for those who have been committed as sexually dangerous persons. There is available to the center the general medical staff of the hospital, a diagnostic staff of two physicians, and two psychiatric social workers. To be sure, there is some mingling with the criminal insane at meal times and during periods of recreation. But that is not incarceration in a prison where there "was no separate staff for the treatment of sex offenders and the only treatment then available to persons committed to the center and not under diagnostic observation was the 'program of group and individual psychiatric therapy for the total prison population which might include sex offenders.' " *Commonwealth* v. *Page* supra, 339 Mass. at page 316, 159 N.E. 2d at page 85. It is to be noted that the center here was established on June 19 three weeks after the decision in the *Page* case and four days before the hearing in the court below. It can hardly be expected that within such a brief period a smoothly operating and adequately staffed treatment center could be established. It is apparent that the departments of correction and mental health were endeavoring to set up a center that would comply with the statutes. The center established (because of the mingling during meal times and recreation periods and the somewhat meager psychiatric treatment and therapy afforded) leaves much to be desired. The remedial purpose of the statute, namely the care, treatment and rehabilitation of the sexually dangerous person, must not be overlooked; indeed that is its primary objective and there must be more than mere incarceration if the statute is to "escape constitutional requirements of due process."

. . . We are of opinion in view of the brief period that the treatment Center had been in operation, that the finding that it satisfied the statute was not unwarranted. In reaching this conclusion we have assumed that, had there been no segregation of sexually dangerous persons at the center so that the defendant's incarceration would have been with the criminal insane the commitment would have been invalid.

. . .

Exceptions overruled.

Today, the situation regarding in-prison therapy for specific classes of offenders is not much changed. Some jurisdictions have opened special institutions designated as "Diagnostic and Treatment" centers or "Medical Facilities" for such inmates. However, courts are still coping with prisoner allegations that legislative treatment and rehàbilitative mandates are not being carried out in traditional prison settings.[54] Even when special treatment programs are available, the whole issue is further complicated today by inmate insistence upon a right to refuse coercive treatment or rehabilitative efforts if they wish. The National Advisory Commission, for example, suggests as a standard: "No offender should be required or coerced to participate in programs of rehabilitation or treatment nor should the failure or refusal to participate be used to penalize an inmate in any way."[55] The U.S. Supreme Court addressed the issue of whether an offender who refused to cooperate in a diagnostic determination of whether he was a "defective delinquent" could be held in custody beyond the sentence for his crime. The Court decided:

McNEIL V. DIRECTOR, PATUXENT INSTITUTION
407 U.S. 245 (1972)
Mr. Justice MARSHALL delivered the opinion of the Court.

Edward McNeil was convicted of two assaults in 1966, and sentenced to five years' imprisonment. Instead of committing him to prison, the sentencing court referred him to the Patuxent Institution for examination, to determine whether he should be committed to that institution for an indeterminate term under Maryland's Defective Delinquency Law. Md. Code Ann. Art 31B. No such determination has yet been made, his sentence has expired, and his confinement continues. The State contends that he has refused to cooperate with the examining psychiatrists, that they have been unable to make any valid assessment of his condition, and that consequently he may be confined indefinitely until he cooperates and the institution has succeeded in making its evaluation. He claims that when his sentence expired, the State lost its power to hold him, and that his continued detention violates his rights under the Fourteenth Amendment. We agree.

The Maryland Defective Delinquency Law provides that a person convicted of any felony, or certain misdemeanors, may be committed to the Patuxent Institution for an indeterminate period, if it is judicially determined that he is a "defective delinquent." A defective delinquent is defined as:

> an individual who by the demonstration of persistent aggravated antisocial or criminal behavior, evidences a propensity toward criminal activity, and who is found to have either such intellectual deficiency or emotional unbalance, or both, as to clearly demonstrate an actual danger to society so as to require such confinement and treatment, when appropriate, as may make it reasonably safe for society to terminate the confinement and treatment. Md. Code. Ann., Art. 31 B § 5.

Defective delinquency proceedings are ordinarily instituted immediately after conviction and sentencing; they may also be instituted after the defendant has served part of his prison term. §§ 6 (b), 6 (c). In either event, the process begins with a court order committing the prisoner to Patuxent for a psychiatric examination. §§ 6 (b), 6 (d). The institution is required to submit its report to the court within a fixed period of time. § 7 (a). If the report recommends commitment, then a hearing must be promptly held, with a jury trial if requested by the prisoner, to determine whether he should be committed as a defective delinquent. § 8. If he is so committed, then the commitment operates to suspend the prison sentence previously imposed. § 9 (b).

. . .

281

II

The State of Maryland asserts the power to confine petitioner indefinitely, without ever obtaining a judicial determination that such confinement is warranted. It advances several distinct arguments in support of that claim.

[1,2] A.   First, the State contends that petitioner has been committed merely for observation, and that a commitment for observation need not be surrounded by the procedural safeguards (such as an adversary hearing) that are appropriate for a final determination of defective delinquency. Were the commitment for observation limited in duration to a brief period the argument might have some force. But petitioner has been committed "for observation" for six years, and on the State's theory of his confinement there is no reason to believe it likely that he will ever be released. A confinement which is in fact indeterminate cannot rest on procedures designed to authorize a brief period of observation.
. . .

B.   A second argument advanced by the State relies on the claim that petitioner himself prevented the State from holding a hearing on his condition. The State contends that, by refusing to talk to psychiatrists, petitioner has prevented them from evaluating him, and made it impossible for the State to go forward with evidence at a hearing. Thus, it is argued, his continued confinement is analogous to civil contempt; he can terminate the confinement and bring about a hearing at any time by talking to the examining psychiatrist and the State has the power to induce his cooperation by confining him.

[5,6] Petitioner claims that he has a right under the Fifth Amendment to withhold cooperation, a claim we need not consider here. But putting that claim to one side, there is nevertheless a fatal flaw in the State's argument. For if confinement is to rest on a theory of civil contempt, then due process requires a hearing to determine whether petitioner has in fact behaved in a manner that amounts to contempt. At such a hearing it could be ascertained whether petitioner's conduct is willful or whether it is a manifestation of mental illness, for which he cannot fairly be held responsible. *Robinson* v. *California,* 370 U.S. 660, 82 S. Ct. 1417, 8 L.E.d 758 (1962). Civil contempt is coercive in nature, and consequently there is no justification for confining on a civil contempt theory a person who lacks the present ability to comply. *Maggio* v. *Zeitz,* 333 U.S. 56, 68 Ct. 401, 92 L.Ed 476 (1947). Moreover, a hearing would provide the appropriate forum for resolution of petitioner's Fifth Amendment claim. Finally, if the petitioner's confinement were explicitly premised on a finding of contempt, then it would be appropriate to consider what limitations the Due Process Clause places on the contempt power. The precise contours of that power need not be traced here. It is enough to note that petitioner has been confined, potentially for life, although he has never been determined to be in contempt by a procedure that comports with due process. The contempt analogy cannot justify the State's failure to provide a hearing of any kind.

[7] C. Finally, the State suggests that petitioner is probably a defective delinquent, because most noncooperators are. Hence, it is argued, his confinement rests not only on the purposes of observation, and of penalizing contempt, but also on the underlying purposes of the Defective Delinquency Law. But that argument proves too much. For if the Patuxent staff was prepared to conclude, on the basis of petitioner's silence and their observations of him over the years, that petitioner is a defective delinquent, then it is not true that he has prevented them from evaluating him. On that theory, they have long been ready to make their report to the Court, and the hearing on defective delinquency could have gone forward.

III

Petitioner is presently confined in Patuxent without any lawful authority to support that confinement. His sentence having expired, he is no longer within the class of persons eligible for commitment to the Institution as a defective delinquent. Accordingly, he is entitled to be released. The judgment below is reversed, and the mandate shall issue forthwith.

Reversed.

Sentence Review

Provisions for appellate review of sentence vary widely in different jurisdictions.[56] In the past, death sentences were often automatically reviewed, but in most other cases review had to be initiated much like an appeal. A few states provide special courts or judicial panels to examine the propriety of sentences; more commonly regular appellate courts decide sentence controversies.[57]

There is a general desire on the part of all criminal justice agencies for finality in criminal justice processing with corresponding reluctance to encourage seemingly endless appeals of all issues. In terms of sentencing, appellate courts have always been willing to correct sentences that are clearly improper; that is, those which exceed the limits set by statute. But traditionally courts have refused to review, or if reviewed to modify, sentences that fall within statutory limits, even though the sentence may seem excessive given the circumstances of the case.[58] However, sentence disparity (variations in sentences among like offenders convicted of the same crimes) has become a major concern to courts and correctional agencies and, of course, to differentially sentenced offenders. Today jurisdictions are increasingly providing review procedures, but even at the time of the American Bar Association assessment (1968) only 21 states allowed review of the merit of sentences.[59] The Bar Association recommends that sentence review be available in all cases where provision is made for review of conviction.[60]

The National Advisory Commission suggests that in the future sentencing courts should retain jurisdiction over all sentenced offenders to provide a continual monitoring of the conditions and lengths of sentences. They state:

Legislatures by 1975 should authorize sentencing courts to exercise continuing jurisdiction over sentenced offenders to insure that the correctional program is consistent with the purpose for which the sentence was imposed. Courts should retain jurisdiction also to determine whether an offender is subjected to conditions, requirements, or authority that are unconstitutional, undesirable, or not rationally related to the purpose of the sentence, when an offender raises these issues.

Sentencing courts should be authorized to reduce a sentence or modify its terms whenever the court finds, after appropriate proceedings in open court, that new factors discovered since the initial sentencing hearing dictate such modification or reduction or that the purpose of the original sentence is not being fulfilled.

Procedures should be established allowing the offender or the correctional agency to initiate proceedings to request the court to exercise the jurisdiction recommended in this standard.[61]

If adopted, this would be a radical departure from present practice. In all trial courts today, the sentencing jurisdiction of the judge is limited to offenders who are retained in the community under sentences to conditional discharge or probation. If an offender is sentenced to prison, the local court gives up its control, transferring jurisdiction to state correctional and parole authorities. If an offender feels aggrieved by prison conditions or parole decisions, remedies are available through the appellate process with the local sentencing court no longer involved. This standard would change this, allowing the trial court to retain jurisdiction and to modify its sentencing decision.

NOTES

1. See Mempa v. Rhay, 389 U.S. 128 (1967); Fred Cohen, "Sentencing, Probation and the Rehabilitative Ideal: The View from Mempa v. Rhay," *Tex. Law Review* 47, 1 (1968).

2. See Furman v. Georgia, 408 U.S. 238 (1972).

3. Texas Code Crim. Proc. Act. 37.07 (1966), see H. M. LaFont, "Assessment of Punishment—A Judge or Jury Function?" *Tex. Law Review* 38, 835 (1960); see also, Note, Jury Sentencing in Virginia," *Va. Law Review* 53, 968 (1967).

4. National Advisory Commission on Criminal Justice Standards and Goals, *Courts,* (1973), Standard 5.1 and Commentary, p. 110.

5. *Ibid,* Standard 5.13, pp. 182-183.

6. See Lloyd Ohlin and Frank Remington, "Sentencing Structure: Its Effect Upon Systems for the Administration of Criminal Justice," *Law and Contemp. Prob.* 23, 495 (1958).

7. See President's Commission on Law Enforcement and Administration of Justice, *Task Force Report: The Courts* (Washington, D.C.: U.S. Government Printing Office, 1967), pp. 24-25.

8. See Note, "Statutory Structures for Sentencing Felons to Prison," *Columbia Law Review* 60, 1134 (1960).

9. American Law Institute, *Model Penal Code* (Proposed Official Draft, 1962); National Council on Crime and Delinquency, *Model Sentencing Act* (1963); American Bar Association, *Standards Relating to Sentencing Alternatives and Procedures* (1968). National Advisory Commission on Criminal Justice Standards and Goals, *Corrections.*

10. See Alfred P. Murrah and Sol Rubin, "Penal Reform and the Model Sentencing Act," *Columbia Law Review* 65, 1167 (1965); Paul W. Tappan, "Sentencing Under the Model Penal Code," *Law and Contemp. Prob.* 23, 528 (1958); Randolph, "Are Long Sentences Necessary?" *Amer. J. Correc.* 21, 4 (1959).

11. National Council on Crime and Delinquency, *Model Sentencing Act,* Sec. 9.

12. American Law Institute, *Model Penal Code,* Sec. 6.06, Alternate 6.06.

13. American Bar Association, *Standards Relating to Sentencing Alternatives,* Sec. 3.2 and Commentary, pp. 142-160.

14. *Ibid,* Sec. 2.1, p. 48.

15. National Advisory Commission, *Corrections,* Standard 5.2, pp. 150-153.

16. See National Prisoner Statistics, *State Prisoners: Admissions and Releases 1970* (Washington, D.C.: Federal Bureau of Prisons, 1971).

17. *Ibid,* pp. 45, 47-81.

18. National Council on Crime and Delinquency, *Model Sentencing Act,* p. 26.

19. American Friends Service Committee, *Struggle For Justice* (New York: Hill & Wang, 1971).

20. John Irwin, *The Felon* (Englewood Cliffs, N.J.: Prentice-Hall, 1970).

21. Lawrence W. Pierce, "Rehabilitation in Corrections—A Reassessment," Keynote address, Annual Meeting of the American Correctional Association, Seattle, Washington, August 12, 1973.

22. See Louis E. Goodman, "Would a System Where Sentences Are Fixed By a Board of Experts Be Preferable?" *Fed. Rules Decisions* 30, 319 (1961).

23. American Bar Association, *Standards Relating to Sentencing Alternatives,* pp. 200-204.

24. National Advisory Commission, *Corrections,* p. 18 and American Law Institute, *Model Penal Code,* Sec. 7.07.

25. National Advisory Commission, *Corrections,* Standard 5.14, pp. 184-185.

26. See "Commentary," American Bar Association, pp. 201-204.

27. There is rather extensive literature about the appropriate contents of the presentence report as well as suggested standards in various model codes and commission reports. See

for example, "Standard 5.14 Requirements for Presentence Report and Content Specification" in National Advisory Commission, *Corrections*, pp. 184-185; *Model Penal Code*, Secs. 7.01, 7.07, pp. 106-107, 117-120; Paul W. Keve, *The Probation Officer Investigates* (St. Paul, Minn.: U. of Minnesota Press, 1960), Victor H. Evjen, "Some Guidelines in Preparing Presentence Reports," *Fed. Rules Decision* 37, 177 (1964).

28. For a collection of references to literature in which both sides of presentence disclosure are debated, see American Bar Association, *Standards Relating to Sentencing Alternatives and Procedures*, pp. 214-215.

29. Williams v. New York, 337 U.S. 241 (1949).

30. For a discussion of the significance of Williams, see Sol Rubin, Henry Weihofen, George Edwards, and Simon Rosenzweig, *The Law of Criminal Correction* (St. Paul, Minn.: West, 1963).

31. Williams was not executed. His sentence was commuted to life imprisonment by the governor. Fourteen years later he obtained his release from prison by a *habeas corpus* action on the grounds that his confession, the principle evidence at his trial, was coerced. See U.S. ex rel. Williams v. Fry, 323 F. 2d 65 (2d Cir. 1963).

32. See, Federal Rules of Criminal Procedures, Rule 32 (c), *Presentence Investigation* (1968). See also provisions in the American Law Institute, *Model Penal Code*, Sec. 7.07, Proposed Official Draft (1962) and National Council on Crime and Delinquency, *Model Sentencing Act*, Art. II, Sec. 4 (1962).

33. National Advisory Commission, *Corrections*, p. 189.

34. *Ibid.*

35. Donald J. Newman, "Perspectives of Probation: Legal Issues and Professional Trends," from *The Challenge of Change in the Correctional Process* (Hackensack, N.J.: National Council on Crime and Delinquency, 1972), pp. 7-8.

36. American Law Institute, *Model Penal Code*, Sec. 7.01.

37. *Ibid.*

38. Robert O. Dawson, *Sentencing: The Decision as to Type, Length and Conditions of Sentence* (Boston: Little, Brown, 1969), pp. 79-80.

39. See for example, John Hogarth, *Sentencing As a Human Process* (Toronto: U. of Toronto Press, 1971); Edward Green, *Judicial Attitudes in Sentencing* (London: Macmillan, 1961). Frank Remington and Donald J. Newman, "The Highland Park Institute on Sentence Disparity," *Fed. Probation* 26 (March 1962): 3-9.

40. See Dawson, *Sentencing*, pp. 173-202.

41. See Ohlin and Remington, "Sentencing Structure."

42. See Donald J. Newman, *Conviction: The Determination of Guilt or Innocence Without Trial* (Boston: Little, Brown, 1966), pp. 60-66.

43. Pilot Institute on Sentencing, *Fed. Rules Decision* 26, 233 (1959): 288.

44. American Bar Association, *Standards Relating to Pleas of Guilty* (Approved Draft, 1968), Sec. 1.8, pp. 36-37.

45. National Advisory Commission, *Corrections*, Standard 3.8, p. 64.

46. See National Council on Crime and Delinquency, *Model Sentencing Act*, Sec. 8.

47. *Ibid*, Secs. 5 and 6.

48. American Law Institute, *Model Penal Code*, Secs. 7.03, 6.07.

49. *Organized Crime Control Act of 1970,* Sec. 1001 (a), Chapter 227, Title 18, United States Code, Sec. 3575 (e).

50. Daniel Glaser, Donald Kenefick, and Vincent O'Leary, *The Violent Offender* (Washington, D.C.: U.S. Department of Health, Education, and Welfare, 1966).

51. See for example, Seymour Halleck and Asher Pacht, "The Current Status of the Wisconsin State Sex Crimes Law," *Wis. Bar Bull.* 33, 17, No. 6 (1960).

52. See Welsh v. Likins, U.S.D.C., Minn. 1974, 42 L.W. 2476, March 19, 1974. See also Grant Morris, ed. *The Mentally Ill and the Right to Treatment* (Springfield, Ill.: Charles C Thomas, 1970).

53. See Edwin H. Sutherland, "The Diffusion of Sexual Psychopath Laws," *Amer. J. Soc.* 56 (September 1950): 142-148.

54. See for example, People v. DeLong, 64 Misc. 999, 316 N.Y.S. 2d 81 (1970).

55. National Advisory Commission, *Corrections, Standard* 2.9 (6).

56. For a collection of state sentence review statutes see American Bar Association, *Standards Relating to Appellate Review of Sentences* (Approved Draft, 1968), Appendix A.

57. *Ibid,* Commentary, Sec. 2.1.

58. See Dawson, *Sentencing,* pp. 386-387. See also G. O. W. Mueller, "Penology on Appeal: Appellate Review of Legal but Excessive Sentences," *Vanderbilt Law Review* 15, 671 (1962).

59. American Bar Association, *Standards Relating to Appellate Review of Sentences,* Commentary, Sec. 1.1 (a).

60. *Ibid.*

61. National Advisory Commission, *Corrections,* Standard 5.9, p. 173.

Chapter **7**

Conditions of Sentence

THE NATURE AND IDEOLOGY OF CORRECTIONS

The term "corrections" encompasses almost all postconviction and postsentencing interventions with offenders. In its broadest sense, corrections involves the use of such techniques as fines, jail sentences, imprisonment, probation, parole, and various combinations of incarceration and community supervision. Correctional systems are complex organizations, comprising much more than probation and parole field services and a few prisons. Modern correctional systems employ a wide variety of programs, facilities, and techniques for the classification, processing, treatment, control, and care of their charges. Within the ambit of correctional services are hospitals for the criminally insane, group counselling programs, work-release projects, halfway houses, farms, forestry camps, diagnostic centers, schools, factories which produce goods for state use, special programs for narcotic addicts, sex deviates, and physically ill prisoners, and even geriatric programs for those who become old and senile while under sentence. Maximum-security prisons are administratively linked with medium- and minimum-security facilities, with reformatories for young felons, and with training schools for juvenile delinquents. There are separate facilities and programs for female offenders, and the vast network of centralized prisons and other facilities is often incorporated with a wide variety of community-based institutions and programs.

There is, of course, much variety in the types and use of different correctional settings and programs among the states and the federal jurisdiction. Some correctional systems have very large offender populations and very diverse programs and facilities. Others are smaller, with only traditional prisons and perhaps with limited use of parole and other forms of noninstitutional correctional services. Some systems are old, entrenched, set in their ways, and not readily amenable to change or experimentation. Others welcome diversity and continuously evaluate past efforts in a search for new and more effective programs.

Whatever the structural varieties of correctional systems, all reflect a basic ideology, full of paradoxes and dilemmas about the nature of man, of crime, and of crime control and prevention. The problem of what to do with Cain once it is proved that he murdered his brother has not changed essentially over the centuries. A sophisticated answer may be "nothing," but this has not been the historical response since we left the era of private vengeance and family feuds. We impose and execute sentences, moving offenders into correctional settings not merely in righteous wrath, but to accomplish some purposes beyond simple punishment of the offender.

While all sorts of intentions and goals have been expressed for different types and conditions of correctional interventions, these purposes have traditionally clustered around several main themes related to our beliefs about the best way to reduce crime and about proper ways to treat even the worst violators. These beliefs directly influence conditions imposed on sentenced individuals, ranging from the secure and austere architecture and rigid controls of prisons, to rules for offenders serving sentences on probation or parole. There seems to have been an historical shift in the major emphasis of corrections that is reflected today in the kinds of institutions and programs and conditions most commonly found in correctional services or that may be desired as *future* correctional interventions. These shifting emphases have been identified as the four "R's": restraint, reform, rehabilitation, and reintegration.[1]

While each in turn became dominant at different times in the past, none disappeared entirely. All these infuse corrections today, so that in any sentence, whether to prison or probation, the drama of multiple objectives is played out on all levels. But discrepancies between the objectives exist and probably will persist. Strong emphasis on restraint may prevent or cripple serious reintegrative efforts. Yet restraint, the "incapacitation" of offenders as a legitimate purpose for sentence, will undoubtedly continue to be operative in the future. Strong reform motives, including use of punitive techniques to condition offenders into "good work habits" and other patterns of conforming behavior, may exist simultaneously with rehabilitative goals in sentences to probation as well as to prison. In short, though the place where sentence is served may range from the

MODELS OF CORRECTIONAL POLICIES

EMPHASIS ON THE COMMUNITY

		LOW	HIGH
EMPHASIS ON THE OFFENDER	HIGH	Rehabilitation (Identification Focus)	Reintegration (Internalization Focus)
	LOW	Restraint (Organizational Focus)	Reform (Compliance Focus)

Reform Model: high emphasis on the community; low emphasis on the offender.
Rehabilitation Model: low emphasis on the community; high emphasis on the offender.
Restraint Model: low emphasis on the community; low emphasis on the offender.
Reintegration Model: high emphasis on the community; high emphasis on the offender.

Vincent O'Leary and David Duffee, "Correctional Policy: A Classification of Goals Designed for Change," *Crime and Delinquency* 17, 4 (October, 1971): 379.

community to a maximum-security prison, the purposes of the sentence—punishment, control, rehabilitation, reintegration—apply simultaneously, though with some differences in emphasis and priority. Not all of the rules and regulations of a prison are designed solely to punish, nor are all the conditions and restrictions of probation directed to rehabilitation and reintegration. Conditions of all sentences reflect a mixture of purposes, often conflicting and not easily reconciled.

COMMUNITY SUPERVISION

Most convicted offenders serve all or part of their sentences in the community under the supervision of parole or probation staff. At present more than half of all sentenced offenders are placed on probation by courts,[2] and nationally about 70 percent of prison inmates are released on parole.[3] Projections prepared for the President's Commission in the mid-1960s indicate that community sentences will be used even more frequently in the future. For example, it is estimated that populations of adults on probation will grow at a rate 2½ times greater than offender populations in prisons.[4] The National Advisory Commission, which strongly supports both preadjudication diversion and community sentences, recommends that each state develop "a systematic plan with timetable and scheme for implementing a range of alternatives to institutionalization" by 1978.[5]

The origin of probation in the United States is usually traced to the activities of a Boston bootmaker who volunteered to be responsible for a number of

291

Sentenced Prisoners Received from Court in State and Federal Institutions, for the United States, 1940-1970

YEAR	NUMBER			RATE PER 100,000 OF THE ESTIMATED CIVILIAN POPULATION OF THE U.S.		
	ALL INSTITUTIONS	FEDERAL INSTITUTIONS	STATE INSTITUTIONS	ALL INSTITUTIONS	FEDERAL INSTITUTIONS	STATE INSTITUTIONS
1970	79,351	12,047	67,304	39.1	5.9	33.1
1969	75,277	11,589	63,688	37.6	5.8	31.8
1968	72,058	11,120	60,938	36.3	5.6	30.7
1967	77,850	11,447	66,403	39.6	5.8	33.8
1966	77,857	11,508	66,349	40.0	5.9	34.1
1965	87,505	12,781	74,724	45.4	6.6	38.8
1964	87,578	12,482	75,096	46.0	6.6	39.4
1963	87,826	12,882	74,944	46.8	6.9	39.9
1962	89,082	13,514	75,568	48.1	7.3	40.8
1961	93,513	13,517	79,996	51.3	7.4	43.9
1960	88,575	13,723	74,852	49.3	7.6	41.7
1959	87,192	13,872	73,320	49.5	7.9	41.6
1958	88,633	13,803	74,830	51.2	8.0	43.3
1957	80,482	13,305	67,177	47.4	7.8	39.5
1956	77,924	13,454	64,470	46.7	8.1	38.6
1955	78,414	15,286	63,128	47.9	9.3	38.5
1954	80,900	16,685	64,215	50.3	10.4	40.0

Year						
1953	74,240	16,376	57,864	47.1	10.4	36.7
1952	70,892	15,305	55,587	45.8	9.9	35.9
1951	67,165	14,120	53,045	44.1	9.3	34.9
1950	69,473	14,237	55,236	46.1	9.5	36.7
1949	68,925	13,130	55,795	46.3	8.8	37.5
1948	63,777	12,430	51,347	43.6	8.5	35.1
1947	64,804	12,948	51,856	45.0	9.0	36.0
1946	61,338	14,950	46,388	43.7	10.6	33.0
1945	53,212	14,171	39,041	40.0	10.7	29.4
1944	50,162	14,047	36,115	39.5	11.0	28.4
1943	50,082	12,203	37,879	39.4	9.6	29.8
1942	58,858	13,725	45,133	45.5	10.6	34.9
1941	68,700	15,350	53,350	52.3	11.7	40.6
1940	73,104	15,109	57,995	55.5	11.5	44.1

NOTE: State figures exclude Hawaii prior to 1960; Alaska for all years; Arkansas and Rhode Island for years 1968, 1969, and 1970. As rates were computed individually, sum of State and Federal rates may not exactly equal "All Institutions" rate.

National Prisoner Statistics 1970 (Washington, D.C.: U.S. Department of Justice, April 1972), p. 3.

offenders convicted of minor crimes.[6] It received great impetus as a correctional technique with the spread of the juvenile court movement after the turn of the century. Parole was first used with young adult offenders released from the prototype reformatory at Elmira, New York, in the 1870s.[7]

The history of community sentences for adult felons is a stormy one, for both probation and parole were, and to some extent still are, controversial measures. In general, however, they have proved effective and are now widely used in most jurisdictions. Opposition to these measures is motivated by a variety of beliefs, such as fear that unrestrained criminals will commit further crimes or the feeling that probation or early release is too lenient, and not sufficiently punitive to satisfy this purpose of the law. While selective cases of crimes committed by probationers and parolees can be marshalled along with illustrations of apparently unwarranted leniency, today most experienced observers of the criminal justice system support such sentence settings as viable and effective alternatives to incarceration. Obviously, community supervision is much cheaper than incarceration, for the capital and operating costs of a prison are astronomical. Also, records of probationers and parolees universally demonstrate a high "success" rate, showing that the majority of probationers and parolees complete their sentences without committing further crimes.[8]

Offenders on probation or parole are under the supervision of a "field agent," sometimes a fully-trained social worker, but more commonly a career professional selected for his job on the basis of competitive examination, often with a prerequisite that he be a college graduate, perhaps, but not necessarily, with some training in behavioral science and some clinical skills.[9] In general, probation and parole supervision involves some surveillance—the probation officer must somehow keep track of his charges—although in routine cases this may involve only regular office visits. In addition, the supervising field agent is generally charged with helping the offender adjust, become "reintegrated," to all aspects of a law-abiding life, including relationships with his family, his work, and his use of leisure time. The probation or parole officer may provide counselling when needed, or may refer his charges to appropriate clinical or welfare resources in the community. Field staff may also offer direct assistance by helping offenders find jobs or enroll in educational programs, and otherwise guide and assist those who have adjustment problems of any sort. The task of supervising offenders involves both authority and helpfulness, a mixture which is not always easily reconciled. Probation and parole officers have a duty to "protect the community" as well as to assist their charges. In fulfilling this responsibility, they have wide discretion to *initiate* revocation proceedings if offenders under their supervision violate rules or conditions, or otherwise fail to adjust satisfactorily to community living. This dual loyalty—to the interests of the general community and to offenders in their caseload—results in different "styles" of supervision. Some field agents frequently use threats of revocation to obtain conformity; others give high priority to casework and counselling as a major supervisory style.[10] There are disagreements among probation and parole officers as to the relative importance of their law-enforcement and social work functions. And these disagreements over field staff roles may lead to conflict with other criminal justice participants, primarily the police.[11]

The effectiveness of field supervision has been continuously hampered by a shortage of budget and manpower which often results in excessively large caseloads assigned to each officer. It is commonly agreed that a single field agent should not have more than 35 or 40 felony offenders in his caseload for effective surveillance and supervision. However, the President's Commission revealed that 67 percent of the probation officers in a national sample had more than 100 persons under their supervision. Only 4 percent of those sampled were carrying caseloads of 40 or less.[12]

While it is common for offenders to be assigned at random to any particular probation or parole officer, some communities are experimenting with different size caseloads of specially selected offenders. Many probationers and parolees present little risk of revocation and have few adjustment needs, so that supervision need not be rigorous. In other instances, because of higher risk of revocation or because of complex adjustment needs, intensive supervision is called for. In the latter cases, specially-trained agents may have reduced caseloads to permit intensive surveillance and counselling. A few places also are experimenting with team supervision. Here every offender is supervised by a three or four member panel of field agents, each with different skills. Some of these teams have an ex-offender as a member, in this way seeking to develop better rapport and greater credibility with their charges.[13]

The traditional distinction between sentences served in the community and those served in correctional institutions is disappearing today. Many modern probation and parole services use a variety of "halfway houses" and "residential treatment centers" which provide a mixture of partial institutionalization with community supervision. Offenders in halfway houses (halfway into prison if on probation, halfway out of prison if on parole) are housed in special facilities similar to dormitories or motels rather than in their own homes like offenders in traditional probation and parole caseloads. Typically, they are confined to these quarters nights and weekends, but are allowed to leave during the day to go to (or look for) work, or go to school or to counselling sessions, and so on. This type of program retains some of the security measures demanded of

295

prisons while at the same time allowing selected offenders to retain some community ties, to support their families, and to gradually adjust to community living.[14]

Probation and Parole Conditions

In addition to general supervision, the probationer is subject to rules and conditions fixed by the court, while the parolee must abide by similar rules fixed by the parolling authority. Commonly these are standard rules which are applied to all probationers and parolees, but occasionally special rules or prohibitions are imposed if, in the opinion of the board or court, these are necessary to help the offender adjust and to prevent him from committing new crimes. Thus a sex offender may be required to participate in psychiatric counselling as a special condition of his community sentence.

The standard regulations of probation are virtually identical to those required of persons on parole. For the most part, they are designed to exert control over a wide variety of activities, particularly those that might lead the offender to commit new offenses. For example, it is common to require probationers and parolees to refrain from associating with known criminals, to abstain from liquor or to use it only in moderation, not to possess firearms, to remain in the community, not to change jobs, and not to marry or move without permission of the field agent. In general, they must keep their activities and whereabouts known and not change status in any way without prior notification and consent of the probation or parole service. In addition, they may be required to maintain a "cooperative" posture with supervising officers. These rules and conditions, as well as any special conditions, are normally given to probationers and parolees in written or printed form with a requirement that they sign agreement to them if they wish community sentences.

Whatever the specific set of rules and conditions imposed in any jurisdiction, a person on probation or parole is held to a higher standard of morality and is more restricted in his movements than citizens not under sentence. Violation of any rule or condition is grounds for revocation with subsequent incarceration. A probationer is under control of both his probation officer and the sentencing judge, and like the Sword of Damocles, imprisonment constantly hangs over his head.[15] Parolees also face possible return to prison for any infraction of rules or conditions. Standard conditions of community supervision under probation and parole are similar; for example, there are no significant differences which seem to rest on any policy consideration, between the *Model Penal Code's* suggested standard conditions for probation and its suggested conditions for parole.[16] While there are some common rules and conditions for both parolees and probationers in *most* jurisdictions, a survey of regulations in all states showed that no rule is common to all jurisdictions.[17] Twenty-nine different *categories* of rules were tabulated in this survey (with a potential of some 50 violations), and it was pointed out that while a few states have recently reduced their rules in number, most jurisdictions have added to their regulations.[18]

Both probationers and parolees are convicted felons—some courts view a parolee as merely an inmate outside the walls—and as such have lost many of the rights of free citizens and are subject to restraints and controls not applicable to law-abiding persons. This poses the question whether *any* rules and conditions may be imposed on offenders serving community sentences or whether there are limits, constitutional or otherwise, on such restraints. Some argue that any rule is permissable, excluding those which might violate Eighth Amendment prohibitions against cruel and unusual punishment, since both probationers and parolees are free to refuse community sentence and to opt for prison if they object to the conditions. At best, this argument seems impractical and coercive. Initially, most probationers and parolees are willing to agree to almost any condition to escape confinement, preferring instead to challenge the appropriateness of conditions while they are on the street.

Although there are exceptions, challenge of such conditions is not normally concerned with the common requirements that the offender remain law-abiding, sober, and keep his whereabouts known. More often litigated are special conditions which are attached to a particular offender or class of offenders. Likewise, interpretation of essentially vague conditions, such as a requirement to "cooperate with your probation officer," become the basis of litigation when unique or peculiar interpretations are given as the basis for revocation.

Illustration 1. An offender convicted of assault on a police officer was placed on probation for two years by the court. In addition to imposing standard rules of supervision, the sentencing judge ordered the offender to pay medical costs incurred by the victim and to write an essay entitled "Why the Police Should be Entitled to the Respect of the Citizenry" to be submitted to the Court for approval.

Illustration 2. A youthful offender convicted of robbery (purse-snatching) was placed on probation for three years with a special condition that he "regularly attend a church of his choice" and present evidence to the court that he has complied with this condition.

It would appear that special, unusual, and possibly legally improper conditions are more often imposed in cases involving probationers than in those involving parolees. At any rate, the frequency of litigation is greater in probation than in parole cases with fairly extensive plaintiff success. The relative prevalence

297

of unusual conditions in probation, some of them clearly in violation of constitutional rights, is perhaps explained by the fact that in most jurisdictions any sentencing judge can set whatever rules and conditions he deems fit, without review by a centralized probation authority, and without mandatory adherence to any fundamental policy considerations underlying the use of probation. While it is true that judges are trained in the law and normally are sensitive to constitutional rights and restrictions, there are literally hundreds of independent court enclaves through the nation; consequently, probation conditions are set by many different individuals, even within a single state, resulting in much variation in their content and purposes. In contrast, parole rules are usually standardized within a particular state by a central paroling authority and offer limited opportunity for individual parole agent rule making. Although there are provisions in some jurisdictions for setting special parole conditions for particular types of offenders (e.g., sex deviates, narcotic addicts), and in many places a parole agent has discretion to require some forms of unique performance under the general condition that the parolee "cooperate" with his parole officer, litigated conditions, some of them quite excessive, have occurred mostly in probation cases.

Challenge of conditions is sometimes raised by a petitioner asking relief from a rule which is excessively "onerous," unrelated to his offense, and unnecessary as part of his supervision. Other times, he may claim that a particular condition should be voided because it is "impossible" to comply with; still other challenges seek relief from conditions which deny or chill his remaining constitutional rights. The effective challenge of conditions is often clouded by the contractual nature of the probation or parole agreement which the offender signed to gain freedom or permission to remain in the community. Furthermore, while the offender usually seeks relief from only a single rule or condition, he faces the possibility that even a sympathetic appellate court may void all of the conditions, in effect nullifying the sentence, with the result that all the offender wins is incarceration or return to incarceration. This dilemma has been noted by observers of the "prisoners' rights" movement:

Efforts to challenge the conditions present awkward situations for lawyer and client. If the client agrees to the condition and later is revoked, the contractual theory may prove an embarrassment. If the client refuses probation or parole and tests the condition by *habeas corpus,* he faces the substantial chance the condition will be upheld. If he appeals the question of the condition's propriety and wins, the result may be invalidation of the whole probation or parole order rather than merely the particular condition and the client may be faced with the unwillingness to admit him to probation or parole on the remaining conditions.[19]

298

The types of special conditions of community sentence that have been litigated vary from the severity of involuntary sterilization to compulsory church attendance. A number of appeals have originated in California, which requires that conditions of community supervision be "reasonable."[20] Legislation in most states is silent with regard to conditions, making any challenge that much more difficult. In one case, the California Court of Appeals of the Second District reversed a revocation of probation involving a woman convicted of robbery who was placed on probation on condition that she not become pregnant until she married.[21] The court applied the following test:

A condition of probation which 1) has no relationship to the crime of which the offender was convicted, 2) relates to conduct which is not in itself criminal, and 3) requires or forbids conduct which is not reasonably related to future criminality does not serve the statutory ends of probation and is invalid.[22]

The court concluded that "Appellant's future pregnancy was unrelated to robbery. Becoming pregnant while unmarried is a misfortune, not a crime."[23]

In earlier cases, the California reasonable provision was given some dubious interpretations. In 1936 a California appellate court upheld a decision requiring the sterilization of a syphillitic offender convicted of statutory rape on the ground that it would prevent transmission of the venereal disease to his children.[24] And in 1965 the U.S. Supreme Court declined to review a California decision ordering sterilzation as a condition of probation for an offender convicted of nonsupport.[25] But recently a California superior court held void an order of sterilization imposed as a probation condition on a young woman convicted of possession of narcotics, who was unmarried but living with a man and receiving welfare payments for an illegitimate child. The woman refused to accept the condition and was sentenced to three months in jail. In voiding the sterilization order the court deemed the other conditions of probation to be accepted, and released the offender to probationary status.[26]

Not all cases of litigated conditions come from California. For example, in the past, it was a fairly common practice in some other states to use "banishment" as a condition of probation. In these instances the offender would be placed on probation and instructed to leave the state or the community until his sentence expired. Called in some places "Sundown Parole," appellate courts usually voided banishment orders when they were appealed. In the 1930s the Michigan Court, for example, held improper an order requiring a probationer to remove himself from the state for five years[27] and in another case voided an order requiring a defendant convicted of disturbing the peace to move from his neighborhood.[28] More recently, however, an Oklahoma Court upheld banishment of a 9-year-old child from her family until the age of 18 on the grounds that it was in her best interest and was not designed to punish her.[29] A short time ago a California court reached a strange decision involving separation of a husband and wife. In this case a young woman who had pleaded guilty to possession of marijuana married a college student while awaiting sentence for her conviction. Her husband was under investigation for drug use, although she claimed to have no knowledge of this. At sentencing she was placed on probation on condition that she live with her parents and refrain from associating with "known or reputed" drug users. She petitioned the court for elimination of these conditions, and instead was sentenced to 60 days in jail to be followed by a probationary period with exactly the same conditions. In effect, the court required her to live apart from her husband. The order was appealed, but the appellate court upheld the conditions, pointing out that they did not "permanently sever" the marriage.[30]

Other special conditions found to be improper are varied. With respect to the two illustrative probation conditions given earlier in this chapter, a District of Columbia Court found it improper to require an offender to write an essay on "Why the Police Should be Entitled to the Respect of the Citizenry"[31] and conditions requiring compulsory church attendance generally have been held unconstitutional.[32]

A question of a parolee's First Amendment right to free speech was decided by a federal district court in California. In this case, the parolee was required, as a special condition, to obtain permission from his parole officer before giving any public speech. On two occasions permission was denied, and the parolee sought appellate relief from this rule. The federal court held for the parolee, enjoining the State of California from prohibiting addresses to lawful public assemblies because of the "expected content" of such speeches. The Court said:

That the condition here imposed on plaintiff's parole is a prior restraint of his First Amendment rights seems clear.
. . .
But it is not only the apparent abridgement of First Amendment rights which concerns the Court. California as well as federal law imposed the due process rule of reasonableness upon the State's discretion in granting or withholding "privileges" from prisoners, parolees, and probationers. . . . The defendants herein have made no showing that the condition imposed on plaintiff's parole is in any way related to the valid ends of California's rehabilitation system.[33]

The imposition of unusual, even weird, special conditions on probationers or parolees can be fairly easily remedied by appellate courts, if the offender is sufficiently outraged, resolute, and otherwise able to bring an appeal. However, a somewhat more complicated problem arises when standard and widely applied conditions work some special hardship on an individual offender. For example, a rule against drinking alcoholic beverages—or in some places, a rule against "immoderate" drinking—is routine and generally accepted as a reasonable restriction on offenders under community supervision. On its face, it violates no constitutional protections as applied to convicted offenders. Yet for probationers who may be alcoholic as well as criminal, compliance with this condition can be virtually impossible. In a federal case involving a Dyer Act violation (interstate transportation of a stolen motor vehicle), an offender was placed on probation for five years with a condition that he refrain from drinking. He was revoked for being drunk, and he subsequently appealed, alleging that he should have had a psychiatric examination prior to imposition of sentence, and that such examination would have shown that he was, and is, a chronic alcoholic. The appellate court ordered the case remanded for such an examination, and in its remand order said:

It appears from the record that when probation was granted, the district court knew petitioner's history of chronic alcoholism and had indications of its pathological nature. We think, consequently, the probation condition under the facts of this case, would be unreasonable, as impossible if psychiatric or other expert testimony was to establish that petitioner's alcoholism has destroyed his power of volition and prevented his compliance with the condition.[34]

This court went on to cite the applicability of *Robinson* v. *California*[35] in which the U.S. Supreme Court struck down a California statute which made being a narcotic addict a criminal offense. In the *Robinson* case the court commented, ". . . in the light of contemporary human knowledge, a law which made a criminal offense of such a disease would doubtless be universally thought to be an infliction of cruel and unusual punishment in violation of the Eighth and Fourteenth Amendments."[36] The Supreme Court of Idaho also found improper a condition with which a petitioner found it impossible to comply.[37]

There is an additional and even more complex issue that occasionally arises when a probationer or parolee is alleged to have violated some standard of behavior "implicit" in his community sentence, but not specifically enumerated in the list of rules and conditions which he signed prior to community release. Sometimes the list of requirements ends with a broad, catchall condition like "I agree to lead a clean, temperate, and honest life" which gives very wide discretion to probation or parole agents. Even beyond this, however, situations sometimes arise in which an offender has neither violated any specific rule nor committed a new crime, but in which revocation is nevertheless sought. In a

301

federal case, a defendant pleaded guilty to the sale of narcotics, and was placed on probation agreeing, as required, to abide by a set of standard rules and conditions. Some time later he was called before a federal grand jury and asked to disclose the source from which he obtained the narcotics that he had earlier confessed to selling. He refused to respond to the grand jury and his probation was revoked on the general grounds that his refusal was inconsistent with the good citizenship required of all probationers. He appealed, pointing out that he had violated none of the conditions he had agreed to when placed on probation. The court of appeals, however, upheld the revocation order, commenting:

The appellant's argument that he violated none of the specific terms of his probation and that the terms were never modified would not, even if true, be persuasive. The determinative question is whether the conduct of the probationer was inconsistent with his duties as such. One on probation is not at liberty; he is in law and in fact in the custody and under the control of the court granting probation.

. . .

We also think there can be no doubt but what, aside from the written conditions of probation, there is an implied condition that the probationer will follow the reasonable directions and orders of both the probation officer and the District Judge. In the instant case, the appellant's refusal to follow the court's direction that he disclose to the grand jury the source of his heroin was a sufficient ground for the revocation of probation and we think the trial court did not abuse its discretion in so doing.[38]

Searching Probationers and Parolees

An offender sentenced to prison is under virtually total control of the state. While inmates do retain many constitutional rights and protections afforded to all citizens, they are not entitled to citizen restrictions on search and seizure under the Fourth Amendment. Prison inmates can have their persons and cells searched at any time, randomly or at the whim of prison officials, without warrant and with no need to show probable cause. Whether the same broad authority exists to search persons under sentence in the community is not an easy question to answer because of different interpretations existing across jurisdictions and between the different statuses of probationer and parolee. A number of courts take the position that a parolee is really an inmate who is serving part of his sentence on the street by the grace of the parole board. From this view, it would follow that parolees as "inmates outside the walls" can be searched under exactly the same conditions as prisoners still in confinement. But probationers, not having been inmates, present a somewhat different problem. For this reason, some courts distinguish authority to search on the inmate model, allowing parolees to be searched readily without probable cause but restricting probationer search to the Fourth Amendment requirements applying to all citizens. This is by no means universally agreed upon. For example, a New York court found such distinction insufficient to distinguish grounds for search in the following case:

PEOPLE V. CHINNICI
273 N.Y.S. 2d 538 (1968)

[Defendant moved to suppress a revolver found in the trunk of his car. He was on probation and his probation officer had caused his arrest for a traffic violation after receiving confidential information that Chinnici was in possession of a revolver.]

DOUGLAS F. YOUNG, Judge. There is little in the reported opinions to provide authority upon the question of the rights of a probationer. There are some cases concerning the rights of a parolee. Whether a probationer has greater or lesser protection from an invasion of his constitutional privileges than a parolee appears to be an open question.

However, in my opinion there is sufficient similarity between the status of the two to permit the cases concerning a parolee to be used as guidance in the cases of a probationer.

The probation officer had received a telephone call that defendant had a revolver. True, we do not know what information the probation officer had as to the reliability of the informer. However, there existed a serious potential danger, involving a convicted person, under the supervision of the court, allegedly in possession of a dangerous weapon. The probation officer had the responsibility of dealing with this possible danger to protect members of the community.

I believe that where there is some reason based either on the necessities of supervision or danger to the public the probationer and his dwelling and his automobile must be held to be subject to summary search. Any alternative involving the interposition of constitutional barriers to the strict supervision and control of probationers would render the program less useful and perhaps entirely unworkable. The ultimate result would be that courts would find it necessary to incarcerate many defendants who otherwise would obtain the benefits of probation. For example, if it had happened that the officer had received the telephoned warning and a prompt search had not been made, and if this probationer had used his gun to injure or kill a person, the probation officer might well feel that he had failed in his obligation of supervision, and the judge who had placed the defendant on probation would be reluctant to extend the privilege of probation to convicted defendants thereafter. A

303

probation officer is under the control of the court and would be restrained by the court from unbridled and unreasonable harassment of a probationer.

In the circumstances of this case I find that no constitutional rights of the defendant were violated by the search and, therefore, that the search was legal. It is ordered that the motion is denied.

Occasionally the authority of parole officers to search their charges rests—or is claimed to rest—on a condition found in a few places under which the released inmate is required to give his permission in advance for parole authorities to search his person or premises.[39] Under this form of agreement, it is assumed that the parolee has consented to any search, making a warrant or a valid arrest unnecessary prerequisites. In other places, parolees may only be searched pursuant to an administrative warrant or parole board order issued on the belief that the parolee has violated some condition of his supervision. About one-half of the states require issuance of a warrant or "hold order" from the parole board, while others allow the field agent—sometimes with police assistance—discretion to apprehend, detain, and search parolees without any warrant or other document.[40] Evidence of the violation of rules or the commission of a new crime found by searching parolees may, of course, be used to revoke their paroles.

A more difficult question is whether evidence seized during an administrative or warrantless search of a parolee can be used to convict him of a new crime. In general, appellate courts have upheld the introduction of evidence discovered during the search of a parolee at prosecution for a new crime. In a California case parole agents searched a parolee's apartment while he was absent and discovered marijuana. In addition to having his parole revoked, the offender was charged and convicted of a new crime—possessing narcotic drugs. He moved to have the marijuana found by the parole officer excluded from trial on the grounds that the search was unreasonable and unlawful. However, the California Court of Appeals upheld the conviction, commenting:

The situation in the instant matter differs significantly from that involved in the Cahan case, and all others decided since the adoption of the exclusionary rule, since the problem confronting the court in those cases was either the propriety of the arrest of a private person with which the complained of search and seizure was conjoined, or whether the search incidental to the arrest of the private individual was reasonable, or whether in the particular case the suspected person had apparently given his voluntary assent to the search. The vital distinction here is that on the occasion of the search defendant was not an ordinary individual merely suspected of a crime but a convict on parole. A prisoner released on parole is not a free man.

. . .

The parole system, as an enlightened penological technique, enables him to pay his debt to society in a prison without bars. But he continues at all times to remain in penal custody, the same as the prisoner allowed the privilege of working on the prison's "honor farm." Parole has simply pushed back the prison walls for him, allowing him wider mobility and greater personal opportunity while serving his sentence.[41]

In general, other appellate courts have reached the same conclusion.[42] The National Advisory Commission, however, recommends that "except where periodic searches (in the case of former addicts, for example) are specifically authorized by the court or parolling authority as a condition of release, the correctional authority must comply with the requirements of the fourth amendment regarding searches."[43]

Electronic Control over Probationers and Parolees

An emerging issue in community supervision is the possible applicability of behavioral modification techniques to probationers and parolees. Various conditioning devices—rewarding good behavior, punishing bad—are currently used (and are currently very controversial) in correctional institutions. Sometimes conditioning interventions, ranging from a "token economy" in which inmates earn certain amounts of paper currency for conforming behavior and use this money to buy "privileges," to "aversion-suppression therapy" involving punishment of bad conduct, are used in combination with prescription drugs, such as tranquilizers and antidepressants. In general, while these techniques have been used primarily in institutional settings, they may also be applicable to community sentences. Postrelease chemotherapy has revolutionized the field of mental health, and it may be that the use of certain behavior modification drugs, as a condition of field supervision, will play a more important part in the future. More complex and controversial than drugs, however, is the possibility that the use of electronic monitoring and intervention systems (which have been used in prototype form with probationers) may prove to be more feasible for widespread use with parolees. The applicability of such electronic monitoring devices (designed originally for "hazard prevention" by allowing persons with certain diseases or in high-risk occupations to rapidly summon assistance) to probation and parole supervision has been noted:

Another use of tracking would involve those released on parole or probation or sentenced to treatment not involving full separation from society.

Requiring the wearing of a tracking device as a condition of parole or probation would permit parole officers to know whether their charges were obeying

305

conditions of release. It would deter the tracked person's former criminal associates from reenlisting him in their activities. If he obeyed the law, it would protect him from the tendency of the police to fasten on ex-convicts as suspects. Most important of all, tracking would make it possible to extend the relatively free and therapeutic experience of parole to convicts who would otherwise have to be imprisoned until their terms expired.

On the other hand, tracking—entirely apart from its possible offensiveness to human dignity—might in practice impede parole therapy. The parolee or probationer might experience anxiety or fail to develop self-confidence as a result of excessive surveillance. He might curtail proper as well as improper activities. If third persons become aware that their conversations with him were being recorded by parole officers, he might find it impossible to get a job and might undergo social isolation. Despite these drawbacks, however, tracking may be more effective than imprisonment.[44]

The propriety, constitutional or otherwise, of such surveillance and intervention techniques has not been determined. There is much current concern about this whole matter by both legal scholars and those who have developed and experimented with such devices.[45]

Model Conditions of Community Sentence

Because conditions commonly imposed on probationers vary so greatly from place to place, it is not possible to present a representative list. However, the drafters of the *Model Penal Code* prepared a set of "reasonable" conditions which courts might follow if they chose. They propose:

Section 301.1. Conditions of Suspension or Probation.

1.   When the Court suspends the imposition of sentence on a person who has been convicted of a crime or sentences him to be placed on probation, it shall attach such reasonable conditions, authorized by this Section, as it deems necessary to insure that he will lead a law-abiding life or likely to assist him to do so.

2.   The Court, as a condition of its order, may require the defendant:

    a.   to meet his family responsibilities;

    b.   to devote himself to a specific employment or occupation;

    c.   to undergo available medical or psychiatric treatment and to enter and remain in a specified institution, when required for that purpose;

    d.   to pursue a prescribed secular course of study or vocational training;

    e.   to attend or reside in a facility established for the instruction, recreation or residence of persons on probation;

f. to refrain from frequenting unlawful or disreputable places or consorting with disreputable persons;

g. to have in his possession no firearm or other dangerous weapon unless granted written permission;

h. to make restitution of the fruits of his crime or to make reparation, in an amount he can afford to pay, for the loss or damage caused thereby;

i. to remain within the jurisdiction of the Court and to notify the Court or the probation officer of any change in his address or his employment;

j. to report as directed to the Court or the probation officer and to permit the officer to visit his home;

k. to post a bond, with or without surety, conditioned on the performance of any of the foregoing obligations;

l. to satisfy any other conditions reasonably related to the rehabilitation of the defendant and not unduly restrictive of his liberty or incompatible with his freedom of conscience.[46]

Most of these conditions are not unusual, although they are by no means uniformly imposed by courts across the nation. The most unique and most controversial condition is the final one requiring any special condition to be related to rehabilitation, not unduly restrictive and not "incompatible" with the probationer's "freedom of conscience." In another section, the *Code* provides a similarly phrased restriction on conditions set for parolees.[47]

The drafters of the American Bar Association's *Standards Relating to Probation* similarly suggest that no condition be imposed that is incompatible with the probationer's "freedom of religion." The basic position taken in these *Standards* is stated more succinctly than in the *Model Penal Code,* as follows:

Section 3.2.

a. It should be a condition of every sentence to probation that the probationer lead a law-abiding life during the period of his probation. No other conditions should be required by statute; but the sentencing court should be authorized to prescribe additional conditions to fit the circumstances of each case. Development of standard conditions as a guide to sentencing courts is appropriate so long as such conditions are not routinely imposed.

b. Conditions imposed by the court should be designed to assist the probationer in leading a law-abiding life. They should be reasonably related to his rehabilitation and not unduly restrictive of his liberty or incompatible with his freedom of religion. They should not be so vague or ambiguous as to give no real guidance.[48]

307

These *Standards* go on, however, to suggest matters that are appropriate for the court to address in setting conditions beyond the law-abiding-life requirement. Among others, these matters include "cooperating with a program of supervision" and "making restitution of the fruits of the crime or reparation for loss or damage caused thereby."[49]

The National Advisory Commission would require only those conditions "necessary to provide a benefit to the offender and protection to the public safety."[50] They go on to recommend: "The conditions imposed in an individual case should be tailored to meet the needs of the defendant and society, and mechanical imposition of uniform conditions on all defendants should be avoided."[51]

CONDITIONS OF IMPRISONMENT

Persons convicted of misdemeanors may be incarcerated in a city or county jail to serve sentences up to a year. Occasionally jail sentences may be longer, particularly if they are imposed consecutively for multiple violations. In some places, for example, New York, overflow jail populations may be held in state prisons. Normally, however, misdemeanants serve sentences of a year or less in local jails.

Conditions in most jails in the United States range from bad to appalling. The Corrections Task Force of the President's Commission concluded:

The national survey of corrections estimated that there were about 3,500 local institutions for misdemeanants in the Nation in 1965. Three-quarters of the institutions in the 250 county sample were jails and the remainder were designated as workhouses, camps, farms, or institutions having some of the characteristics of all three. Not only are the great majority of these facilities old, but many do not meet the minimum standards in sanitation, living space, and segregation of different ages and types of offenders that have obtained generally in the rest of corrections for several decades.[52]

Most jails have neither rehabilitative programs nor meaningful work opportunities. In the absence of furlough or work-release projects, jail inmates are idle and in most places dismally cared for throughout their sentences.

Felons are incarcerated in prisons or reformatories. In common usage, "reformatory" is often understood to indicate a place of incarceration for juvenile delinquents, but technically this is incorrect. Juveniles are housed in training schools, while reformatories hold young felons, generally those in the 18- to 21-year age group.

308

POPULATION OF STATE CORRECTIONAL FACILITIES FOR ADULTS,
BY SECURITY CLASSIFICATION OF INMATES

CLASSIFICATION	INMATES	PERCENT OF TOTAL POPULATION
Maximum	109,920	56
Medium	57,505	30
Minimum	28,485	15
Total	195,910	100

American Correctional Association, *1971 Directory of Correctional Institutions and Agencies of America, Canada, and Great Britain* (College Park, Md.: ACA, 1971) and poll taken by the American Foundation's Institute of Corrections, which contacted the head of every state department of corrections.

Formerly it was common for the sentencing judge to specify the prison or reformatory where sentence would be served. Today judges ordinarily do not select a particular prison but instead transfer custody of the offender to a department of correctional services. The offender is then transported to a reception center or a receiving prison where he is classified and assigned to an available correctional facility to complete his sentence. Although different jurisdictions will vary, today the federal and most state correctional systems have diversified facilities for felons, so that some choice of correctional setting is available at the time of intake.

Prisons and reformatories are generally classified by their degree of security, which relates not only to stringent perimeter control and internal gates and bars, but also to types of industrial and treatment programs within the institution. Maximum-security institutions are typically completely surrounded by high walls with gun towers placed at strategic intervals. Inmates are housed in individual cells that rise in tiers (called galleries) in cellblocks which do not touch the cellhouse wall. Prisons commonly operate industries, or shops, which produce goods used by state agencies. There may also be schools and other treatment programs designed for inmate rehabilitation and, of course, services for feeding and clothing and for the health needs of the inmates. Sections of maximum-security prisons are separated by gates, interior fences and walls, and prison staff are much concerned with prevention of escape, riots, and inmate possession of contraband.

Medium-security institutions typically are enclosed by chain-link fences, may provide inmates with rooms instead of cells, and generally are much less regi-

Date of Opening, State Maximum Security Prisons Still in Operation

DATE OF OPENING	NUMBER OF PRISONS
Prior to 1830	6
1831 to 1870	17
1871 to 1900	33
1901 to 1930	21
1931 to 1960	15
1961 to date	21
Total	113

American Correctional Association, *1971 Directory of Correctional Institutions and Agencies of America, Canada and Great Britain* (College Park, Md.: ACA, 1971).

mented and security-oriented than walled institutions. In some places inmates are permitted to wear civilian clothing, unlike their counterparts in maximum-security facilities. Industries tend to be more modern—computer programming or television repair—in contrast to the launderies and auto-tag shops found in maximum-security prisons. Generally, medium-security institutions receive only prisoners who have been carefully screened for risk of escape or assault. These prisoners do not come directly from courts, but are transferred from maximum-security prisons or reception and diagnostic centers.

Prison farms and forestry camps are often designated as minimum-security facilities. These tend to be small and to house carefully selected prisoners who are unlikely to escape. However, these facilities offer little in way of rehabilitative or remedial services.

Maximum-security prisons and reformatories and indeed the concept of imprisonment as the principal way of dealing with criminals began and developed in the United States. While there were dungeons, "gaols," workhouses, and similar facilities for incarceration of criminals in medieval Europe and in Asia, in general these were short term lockup arrangements designed to hold perpetrators only until they could be executed, pilloried, branded, or transported to overseas penal colonies.

Among other reasons for the development and spread of imprisonment as a major method of dealing with felons was the lack of suitable new locations for penal colonies. The early American colonies and Australia had served as penal colonies, receiving prisoners banished and transported from European countries. With only a few exceptions, such as Siberia for Russian criminals or Devil's

Island for French prisoners, transportation as such ended in the early 1800s. Boatloads of offenders from other societies became increasingly unwelcome on most foreign shores. Prisons were thus developed as alternative *internal* penal colonies, receiving and holding "outlaws" banished from local communities and transported to the closed, walled communities called penitentiaries. In addition, denial of freedom as punishment for crime had a particular attraction in the early years of our Republic, for we had just emerged from a revolutionary struggle over freedom. What could be more punitive than taking freedom away from deviant citizens?

But expediency and punishment did not alone support the idea of incarceration. In the years between 1820 and 1840 when the first prisons were built, there was a good deal of intellectual interest in utopia's which, combined with strong religious fervor, came to justify and rationalize imprisonment on philosophical and moral grounds. Though it may seem strange to us today, early prisons were designed to be utopian societies, models not only for control and treatment of criminals, but examples of a social order that could be more generally applied. David Rothman, an historian who has done extensive research into the origin of prisons, asylums for the insane and other "welfare" institutions, all of which developed about the same time, comments:

Americans' understanding of the causes of deviant behavior led directly to the invention of the penitentiary as a solution. It was an ambitious program. Its design—external appearance, internal arrangement, and daily routine—attempted to eliminate the specific influences that were breeding crime in the community, and to demonstrate the fundamentals of proper social organization. Rather than stand as places of last resort, hidden and ignored, these institutions became the pride of the nation. A structure designed to join practicality to humanitarianism, reform the criminal, stabilize American society, and demonstrate how to improve the condition of mankind, deserved full publicity and close study.

. . .

Europeans came to evaluate the experiment and the major powers appointed official investigators. France in 1831 dispatched the most famous pair, Alexis de Tocqueville and Gustave Auguste de Beaumont; in 1832 England sent William Crawford, and in 1834, Prussia dispatched Nicholas Julius. Tourists with no special interest in penology made sure to visit the institutions. Harriet Martineau, Frederick Marryat, and Basil Hall would no more have omitted this stop from their itinerary than they would have a Southern plantation, a Lowell textile mill, or a frontier town. By the 1830's, the American penitentiary had become world famous.[53]

311

Two types of prisons were developed in the United States, and for a number of years advocates of one kind argued with advocates of the other over their relative merits. One type of prison was developed in Pennsylvania and reflected a strong Quaker influence. Its major characteristic was solitary confinement of prisoners; it is sometimes called the "segregate" prison system. Inmates, placed in solitary confinement, were allowed no contact with the outside world or with each other and were expected to remain in their cells, read the Bible, reflect on their crimes and "repent." Hence the term "penitentiary." A different kind of prison was built at Auburn in New York, where prison inmates were held in cells at night but were released in the daytime to work together at various forms of hard labor. This "congregate" system rested on the belief that the way to repentance and reform, and indeed the way to salvation, is by hard work. Both systems imposed total silence on prisoners, and in New York an elaborate form of marching—a shuffle called the "lock step"—was imposed to move prisoners, in silence, from their cells to their places of work.

As Rothman points out, both types of prisons became world famous, were visited, evaluated, and their merits debated by scholars, politicians, and reformers. In this battle over the "best" system, the Auburn plan generally prevailed. The extended solitary confinement of the Pennsylvania system tended to drive prisoners insane and was very costly, whereas the congregate, work prison could help support itself by the labor of inmates.

Auburn prison, built between 1819 and 1823, was quickly followed by similar prisons at Ossining (Sing-Sing) and Dannemora (Clinton Prison), and eventually the Auburn plan spread nationwide and become an international prototype for maximum-security confinement. In the 1870s a reformatory for young adult felons was established at Elmira, New York. Structurally it was maximum-security, built very much like Auburn prison, but its program included education and vocational training opportunities as well as work. As Auburn became the prototype prison, so Elmira became the prototype reformatory, copied throughout the nation and the world.

Although the Pennsylvania segregation system did not become the basic pattern for prisons generally, its techniques and ideology are still very much in evidence. All maximum-security prisons contain within them other prisons, more severe forms of incarceration, for inmates who are troublemakers or who otherwise violate prison rules. Such prisoners are commonly placed in solitary confinement, segregated from the general prison population for periods of time under conditions similar to those found in the early Pennsylvania institutions.

The conditions experienced by prison inmates was at minimum drab and unpleasant, at worst degrading and brutal. In theory, however, prisons were not designed to be places *for* punishment but rather places *of* punishment; that is, the mere fact of being in prison was punitive; additional punishment was added only for internal control, not as an end of the law. In this punitive setting, prisoner life-style was controlled by the principle of "least eligibility" applied in our society to all forms of "welfare" programs. This principle limits the kind of food, housing, and care and treatment afforded prisoners to levels common to the poorest, "least eligible," free citizen. In short, prison conditions were not permitted to exceed bare minimum necessities. Both structurally and in their internal programs, prisons were austere, stark, and uniform, providing minimum caloric diets, minimum standards of heat, light, education, training, and recreation.

How much have conditions of imprisonment changed since the early days of Auburn? Many of the prototype prisons built in the early 1800s still exist; Auburn, Sing-Sing, and Clinton at Dannemora are still operating in New York, modernized, of course, and now called "correctional facilities." The lock step and the silent system are gone and the ready use of whip and lash to force conformity is no longer allowed. Yet incarceration in maximum-security prisons is still a harsh existence, unpleasant and degrading at best, brutal and brutalizing at worst. Modern medium- and minimum-security prisons have softened the architecture and reduced the drabness of steel bars and grey paint. Educational and training programs in many of these "pastel prisons" are better, more closely related to outside work opportunities than the original forms of hard labor. But these modern prisons hold only a few selected prisoners. In the main, the walls, cellhouses, treeless yards, and regimented existence of early prisons remain the pattern in maximum-security institutions today. Measured against progress in society generally, changes in conditions of imprisonment are minimal. In the early days of Auburn even horses were a luxury in our society, and since then our technology has placed men on the moon. We have educated our population, increased life expectancy, become a leading world power; confronted Freud, Marx, and Darwin; changed in size and perhaps in morality. Yet prisons remain very much what they have always been. Such changes as have been made were made slowly and reluctantly. The life of an inmate today, while certainly better in many ways than that of his early Auburn counterpart, is still one of strict regimentation, of rigid rules and conditions, as illustrated below.

PRISONER RULES AND REGULATIONS
[Issued to all newly received inmates in _____ Prison, 1973]
Read, remember, and abide by the following rules. Bear in mind that those men who are given such privileges as working outside the walls, who are allowed to

313

leave on short furloughs or have been granted parole are men who have made an effort to cooperate. It goes without saying that your time spent here can be much more pleasant if you abide by the rules.

You will have the opportunity to work while here and if you indicate enough interest and show good application to your work, you may have the opportunity to learn at least the fundamentals of the crafts employed in our industries.

Your name will be placed on a waiting list for the job for which you are considered best fitted and when your turn is reached and the job available, you may be placed on that job if your conduct and work merit such a change.

You will have the opportunity to fulfill your religious obligations. Catholic, Protestant, Jewish, and Muslim services are held weekly. Other services are held from time to time. We urge you to attend the services of your faith regularly.

GENERAL RULES OF CONDUCT

In the interest of your protection and the protection of others, it is necessary that we have discipline and order in an institution of this size. You will get along well here by taking the attitude that you will respect the rights of others, cooperate with them, and govern your dealings with them by the principles of good sportsmanship.

If you refuse to cooperate with members of our staff, they will have no choice but to file a disciplinary report describing your misconduct. The report will be referred to the Disciplinary Court for action and the results of the hearing, as well as the disciplinary report, will become a part of your record. Your attitude and frankness before the Disciplinary Court will have much to do with the final outcome of the Court action.

Upon entering the prison, you will be placed in First Grade and entitled to all First Grade privileges.

For wilful violation of any of the following rules, in addition to punishment by solitary confinement with loss of good time, or by records—a mark with loss of good time, or deprivation of privileges, the warden may, at his discretion, reduce the offender to Second or Third Grade.

CELL HOUSE RULES

Keep your cell neat and clean. To draw, paint or paste pictures on the walls of your cell, or in any way to make or mar the walls, floors, furniture, fixtures, or bed clothes, would not be good sportsmanship because when you leave that cell, someone else must move in. You will, of course, be expected to keep your wash basin and toilet clean.

So that men can study and rest, refrain from singing and whistling or making unnecessary noise. To talk or call to men in other cells would not be conducive to quiet and study.

When entering your cell, close the door quietly, it will be locked automatically. When leaving the cell, leave the door open. Whenever a count is being made, stand at the door with your hands on the bars.

Sleep with your feet toward the door.

Arise at the first gong signal in the morning—not before—and wash, dress, make your bed, sweep out your cell, and be ready to march out.

Your keeper will instruct you as to when laundry, books, etc., are to be put out for exchange.

When you return to the cell hall, go at once to your cell. Never enter any cell but your own. You are not to pass any articles from one cell to another.

If you are sick, notify any officer who passes your cell. You should not remain in bed without permission after the signal to arise.

At the 10:00 p.m. signal, go to bed at once. Place your shoes at the door and the rest of your clothing on the chair next to the door. Sleep with your head uncovered or the officer will be forced to awaken you.

No smoking between 10:00 p.m. and 6:00 a.m. Smoking is permitted between the hours of 6:00 a.m. and 10:00 p.m. when you are in your cell.

Your door is not to be opened until the signal for your range is sounded after the cells have been automatically unlocked.

Your clothing or shoes are not to be altered in any way. If your clothing or shoes do not fit or need repair, report the matter to your officer at your place of work.

Always be fully dressed when you leave your cell.

You must not have money, jewelry, or other valuables in your cell.

MARCHING RULES

At the signal to fall in for marching, take your place in line promptly, forming a column of two's. Stand erect in line, arms folded, until the order to march is given.

There will be no talking in line or while marching.

LETTER WRITING AND VISITORS

All letters and papers will be examined under the direction of the warden before being mailed or delivered.

Letters must refer to family or personal matters only, or to proper matters of business. No references may be made to criminal matters generally. Do not refer to prison employees by name, or fellow inmates by name.

Obscene or vulgar language, of course, is out of order. Such language would of itself render you liable for prosecution under both Federal and State Laws if the letter were mailed. Letters containing threats of any kind would also render you liable for prosecution.

Those in First Grade may write one letter every Sunday at state expense, and those in Second and Third Grade may write one letter on the first and third

Sundays of every month at the state expense. First Graders may write two or more letters during the week but must use their own stationery and stamps, which may be purchased at the canteen.

Letters must be left unsealed and placed on the cross bar of the cell door for collection.

Persons with whom you correspond must be listed on your writing list. To add a person to your writing list, secure a request blank from your cell-hall keeper.

You are allowed visits from relatives and are credited with one (1) hour visiting time for the current month upon entrance and each calendar month thereafter. Visiting time is cumulative up to 12 hours. Saturday visits will be limited to one hour. Visits will not be allowed on Sundays or the following legal holidays: New Year's Day, Decoration Day, Fourth of July, Labor Day, Thanksgiving Day, Christmas Day, or on the afternoons of Good Friday, December 24th and December 31st.

Visits cannot be started before 8:00 a.m. and the last visiting hour must be started by 3:30 p.m., as positively no visiting is permitted after 4:30 p.m. You are allowed interviews with your attorneys on regular visiting hours and days when legal business should be cared for. Officers are not available for legal visits on Saturdays except by prior arrangement with the warden.

It is often asserted that prison rules are imposed with malevolent intent, as part of a "degradation ceremony" required to satisfy the punitive ideal in our treatment of felons. And there is little doubt that many present-day prison rules and regulations can be traced directly to the prototype prisons at Auburn and in Pennsylvania, reflecting the beliefs then held about the nature and cure of criminal behavior. But a number of regulations, though abrasive in their impact, are simply the artifacts of bureaucracy, the occasionally mindless result of the logistics of processing thousands of men not unlike the often irrational assignment practices of the military.

Early decisions were made about the *size* of prisons as well as their other features. Generally, maximum-security prisons were designed to hold one thousand to five thousand inmates, with the average holding between one and two thousand men, depending upon state size and need. While prisons are often smaller than mental hospitals and similar institutions, their traditional size today is criticized as too large and cumbersome to accomplish what is expected of a correctional facility. Prisons are "total institutions"[54] with reluctant populations requiring intensive security measures as well as provisions for feeding, housing, work, recreation, and all other aspects of life in a single-sex community. Given the size and nature of prisoner populations and the requirements to maintain security as well as to treat and rehabilitate, prison rules and regulations tend to proliferate simply to efficiently meet requirements of mass care, feeding, and custody.

There is considerable variation in prison regulations and in general prison conditions from one place to another and among different types of facilities. Usually there are fewer rules and a more relaxed, less regimented life-style in medium- and minimum-security institutions. Nonetheless prisoners are almost totally isolated from normal community contacts. Visits from approved family members are allowed but severely circumscribed. A few jurisdictions today permit some inmates to have conjugal visits with lawful wives. And increasingly prison systems are allowing selected prisoners to go home on short furloughs during their sentences. Prisoners may write and receive mail, though traditionally both outgoing and incoming mail is censored. Conferences with attorneys are not limited, and some prisons permit phone calls to families at specified intervals.

In a very real sense prison inmates are "outlaws." Their status places them outside many of the legal protections afforded ordinary citizens. They are subject to search without specific probable cause, they cannot vote and they can be forced to comply to a wide assortment of restrictions on personal freedom ranging from choice of clothing to physical movement around the institution. Inmates in maximum-security prisons spend a good deal of time locked in their cells when they are not working in one of the prison industries. The locked cell is not only punishment, but also is protection, for it keeps other inmates out. Perhaps the worst and most dangerous aspect of imprisonment is forced association with other felons, for prisons hold some offenders who are aggressive and dangerous within the prison as well as on the street.

Sociologists, in particular, have conducted considerable research on the "prison community."[55] Prisons, after all, are small self-contained societies with rules, norms of behavior, ethical codes, formal and informal sanctions, and a whole range of complex relationships between keepers and inmates and inmates and their fellow prisoners. The accommodations between guards and prisoners necessary to allow the "total institution" to function have been noted.[56] Inmate types—the "right guy," the "gorilla," the "merchant," the "punk," and the "rat" —have been identified and the whole "inmate code" has been described.[57] The code represents a survival response, not only to the rigors of prison life, but to the label of "criminal" and to the damage to self-conception brought by the fact of incarceration. Sykes and Messinger explain:

. . . [T]he dominant theme of the inmate code is group cohesion, with a "war of all against all"—in which each man seeks his own gain without considering

317

the rights or claims of others—as the theoretical antipode. But if a war of all against all is likely to make life "solitary, poor, nasty, brutish, and short" for men with freedom, as Hobbes suggested, it is doubly so for men in custody. Even those who are most successful in exploiting their fellow prisoners will find it a dangerous and nerve-wracking game, for they cannot escape the company of their victims. No man can assure the safety of either his person or his possessions, and eventually the winner is certain to lose to a more powerful or more skillful exploiter.

. . .

As a population of prisoners moves toward a state of mutual antagonism, then, the many problems of prison life become more acute. On the other hand, as a population of prisoners moves in the direction of solidarity, as demanded by the inmate code, the pains of imprisonment become less severe. They cannot be eliminated, it is true, but their consequences at least can be partially neutralized.

. . .

Finally, a cohesive inmate social system institutionalizes the value of "dignity" and the ability to "take it" in a number of norms and reinforces these norms with informal social controls. In effect, the prisoner is called on to endure manfully what he cannot avoid.

. . .

Dignity, composure, courage, the ability to "take it" and "hand it out" when necessary—these are the traits affirmed by the inmate code. They are also traits that are commonly defined as masculine by the inmate population. As a consequence, the prisoner finds himself in a situation where he can recapture his male role, not in terms of its sexual aspects, but in terms of behavior that is accepted as a good indicator of virility.[58]

Prisoners' Rights and Prison Reform

In years past the outlaw status of prisoners was almost complete. There was no viable way to protest conditions of imprisonment, for communication with the outside world was extremely curtailed and appellate courts, even if reached, would rarely respond to inmate petitions.[59] Today this situation is somewhat different, though prisoner status is still very much restricted. Appellate courts have mostly abandoned their hands-off policy and are increasingly willing to consider prisoner appeals, particularly where a constitutional infringement is alleged.[60] While still recognizing the necessity for administrative discretion in maintaining custody of inmates, recent appellate decisions have tended to more sharply distinguish between rights retained by inmates and those lost by conviction and incarceration. The scope of appellate intervention has gone beyond curbing cruel and unusual punishment, reaching to such matters as censorship of mail, freedom of speech and religion, access to courts and to counsel, the further deprivation of liberty resulting from placing unruly inmates in segregation, and a variety of other internal control decisions.[61]

While the full dimensions of the trend toward more comprehensive prisoners' rights have yet to be played out, it is clear that inmates today are afforded a greater measure of administrative due process in challenging decisions made about them while in prison. Hearings on such matters as segregation (solitary confinement), loss of "good time" (i.e., time off for good behavior), and similar matters are now permitted in many jurisdictions. A federal district court addressed the issue of in-prison discipline:

LANDMAN V. ROYSTER
333 F. SUPP. 621 (E.D. VA. 1971)

[This decision was the result of a class action by Virginia prison inmates against correctional officials. Among other things, the prisoners alleged, and the court heard corroborative testimony, of the extensive use of solitary confinement and of other punishments for prison rule infractions including bread and water diets, placing inmates in chains, keeping prisoners nude in solitary confinement in unheated cells and denial of medical treatment.]

MERHIGE, District Judge. In these adjudicatory proceedings the Court concludes that certain due process rights are both necessary and will not unduly impede legitimate prison functions.

First, the decision to punish must be made by an impartial tribunal. This bars any official who reported a violation from ruling.

Second, there shall be a hearing. Disposition of charges on the basis of written reports is insufficient.

Necessarily a hearing encompasses the right to present evidence in defense, including the testimony of voluntary witnesses.

A hearing must be preceded by notice in writing of the substance of the factual charge of misconduct. Only with written notice can a prisoner prepare to meet claims and insist that the hearing be kept within bounds. A reasonable interval to prepare a defense must be allowed as well, but the Court declines to fix any definite period. Rather whether a trial has been too speedy must be determined on a case-by-case basis.

Cross-examination of adverse witnesses likewise is necessary. The Court appreciates the concern of prison officials that interrogation by prisoners of the guard force may be at variance with their ordinary respective positions in the penal hierarchy. Because most disciplinary cases will turn on issues of fact, however, the right to confront and cross-examine witnesses is essential.

Fundamental to due process is that the ultimate decision be based upon evidence presented at the hearing, which the prisoner has the opportunity to refute.

"To demonstrate compliance with this elementary requirement, the decision maker should state the reasons for his determination and indicate the evidence he relied on," *Goldberg* v. *Kelly,* 397 U.S. 271.

The Court will not require an appellate procedure. However, if higher authorities than the disciplinary committee feel duty bound to reexamine decisions, their review must be restricted to the charge made and the evidence presented.

In addition, for the reason that the evidence shows that some inmates are unfortunately intellectually unable to represent themselves in discipline hearings, the tribunal should permit a prisoner to select a lay advisor to present his case. This may be either a member of the noncustodial staff or another inmate, serving on a voluntary basis. Notice of charges shall include the information that such assistance is available .

These minimum due process standards are necessary when solitary confinement, transfer to maximum-security confinement, or loss of good time are imposed, or a prisoner is held in padlock confinement more than ten days.

. . .

Few of the opinions to date on prison discipline treat in depth the real problem of vagueness in institutional regulations. The evidence, however, shows that the purposes of the constitutional requirement of reasonable specificity—fair warning so that one may conform to the rules, and exactness so that arbitrary penalties or penalties for protected conduct will not be imposed—have been ill-served by the rules enforced against Virginia prisoners.

Virginia prisoners have been penalized for such ill-defined offenses as "misbehavior" and "agitation." Recent amendments to discipline procedure have not sharpened the outlines of these offenses. On the other hand, existing regulations governing maximum-security facilities, which are in the record, demonstrate that the prison authorities are capable of phrasing their requirements with reasonable specificity.

The Court concludes, therefore, that the existence of some reasonably definite rule is a prerequisite to prison discipline of any substantial sort. Regulations must in addition be distributed, posted, or otherwise made available in writing to inmates.

"Misbehavior" or "misconduct," for which, for example, Jefferson and Scott were penalized, offers no reasonable guidance to an inmate.

"Agitation" appears to encompass discussing litigation with other prisoners, assisting them in litigation, or advising them as to the law. It also includes, as is apparent from Thompson's case, complaining to the authorities, and according to *Cunningham,* it may include the giving of incorrect legal advice. Prison authorities may legitimately fear the incitement of rule violations and the interruption of orderly activities, and may punish men who engage in such conduct. However, the ban on "agitation" at once gives no fair warning that certain conduct is punishable and, in practice, includes the rendition of legal advice and the preparation of legal pleadings, protected activities.

On the other hand, the Court is not persuaded that the offenses of "insolence," "harassment," and "insubordination," directed against custodial or administrative personnel, are unduly vague.

In a followup case with the same title in 1973, *Landman* v. *Royster*,[62] the court awarded 15,000 dollars damages to Landman for extended solitary confinement in disregard of his constitutional rights. The court also imposed a 25,000 dollar fine for contempt on correctional officials. The fine was suspended, however, on prompt compliance with the injunction issued after the 1971 case.

The U.S. Supreme Court recently decided a prisoners' rights case originating in the State of Nebraska. The decision is sweeping and inclusive, dealing with such matters as due process requirements in loss-of-good-time proceedings and in disciplinary procedures generally, including questions of an inmate's right to call and examine witnesses and his right to assistance of counsel. Other issues dealt with include mail-censorship, the retroactivity of appellate court holdings in prisoners' rights cases, and other prison administration matters. As with other case excerpts, only part of the decision can be reproduced here. However, this is an important, landmark decision tending to round out the pattern of Supreme Court intervention into postconviction determinations which started with *Mempa* v. *Rhay* and was carried through *Morrissey* v. *Brewer* and *Gagnon* v. *Scarpelli* (see Chapter 8). The original and complete decision, including dissenting opinions omitted here, should be familiar to all students of criminal justice and in particular to those interested in prisoners' rights.

WOLFF V. McDONNELL

_____ U.S. _____ 1974

15 CRIMINAL LAW REPORTER 3304

(JUNE 26, 1974)

MR. JUSTICE WHITE delivered the opinion of the Court.

We granted the petition for writ of *certiorari* in this case, —— U.S. ——, because it raises important questions concerning the administration of a state prison.

Respondent, on behalf of himself and other inmates of the Nebraska Penal and Correctional Complex, Lincoln, Nebraska, filed a complaint under 42 U.S.C. § 1983 challenging several of the practices, rules, and regulations of the Complex. For present purposes, the pertinent allegations were that disciplinary proceedings did not comply with the Due Process Clause of the Federal Constitution; that the inmate legal assistance program did not meet constitutional standards and that the regulations governing the inspection of mail to and from attorneys for inmates were unconstitutionally restrictive. Respondents requested damages and injunctive relief.

. . .

The State of Nebraska asserts that the procedure for disciplining prison inmates for serious misconduct is a matter of policy raising no constitutional issue. If the position implies that prisoners in state institutions are wholly without the protections of the Constitution and the Due Process Clause, it is plainly untenable. Lawful imprisonment necessarily makes unavailable many rights and privileges of the ordinary citizen, a "retraction justified by the considerations underlying our penal system." *Price* v. *Johnston,* 334 U.S. 266, 285 (1948). But though his rights may be diminished by the needs and exigencies of the institutional environment, a prisoner is not wholly stripped of constitutional protections when he is imprisoned for crime. There is no iron curtain drawn between the Constitution and the prisons of this country. Prisoners have been held to enjoy substantial religious freedom under the First and Fourteenth Amendments.

. . .

We also reject the assertion of the State that whatever may be true of the Due Process Clause in general or of other rights protected by that clause against state infringement, the interest of prisoners in disciplinary procedures is not included in that "liberty" protected by the Fourteenth Amendment. It is true that the Constitution itself does not guarantee good-time credit for satisfactory behavior while in prison. But here the State itself has not only provided a statutory right to good-time but also specifies that it is to be forfeited only for serious misbehavior. Nebraska may have the authority to create, or not, a right to a shortened prison sentence through the accumulation of credits for good behavior, and it is true that the Due Process Clause does not require a hearing "in every conceivable case of government impairment of private interest." *Cafeteria Workers* v. *McElroy,* 367 U.S. 886, 894 (1961). But the State having created the right to good time and itself recognizing that its deprivation is a sanction authorized for major misconduct, the prisoner's interest has real substance and is sufficiently embraced within Fourteenth Amendment "liberty" to entitle him to those minimum procedures appropriate under the circumstances and required by the Due Process Clause to insure that the state-created right is not arbitrarily abrogated.

. . .

We think a person's liberty is equally protected, even when the liberty itself is a statutory creation of the State. The touchstone of due process is protection of the individual against arbitrary action of government, *Dent* v. *West Virginia,* 129 U.S. 114, 123 (1889). Since prisoners in Nebraska can only lose good-time credits if they are guilty of serious misconduct, the determination of whether such behavior has occurred becomes critical, and the minimum requirements of procedural due process appropriate for the circumstances must be observed.

. . .

In striking the balance that the Due Process Clause demands, however, we think the major consideration militating against adopting the full range of procedures suggested by *Morrissey* for alleged parole violators is the very different stake the State has in the structure and content of the prison disciplinary hearing. That the revocation of parole be justified and based on an accurate assessment of the facts is a critical matter to the State as well as the parolee; but the procedures by which it is determined whether the conditions of parole have been breached do not themselves threaten other important state interests, parole officers, the police or witnesses, at least no more so than in the case of the ordinary criminal trial. Prison disciplinary proceedings, on the other hand, take place in a closed, tightly controlled environment peopled by those who have chosen to violate the criminal law and who have been lawfully incarcerated for doing so. Some are first offenders, but many are recidivists who have repeatedly employed illegal and often very violent means to attain their ends. They may have little regard for the safety of others or their property or for the rules designed to provide an orderly and reasonably safe prison life. Although there are very many varieties of prisons with different degrees of security, we must realize that in many of them the inmates are closely supervised and their activities controlled around the clock. Guards and inmates co-exist in direct and intimate contact. Tension between them is unremitting. Frustration, resentment, and despair are commonplace. Relationships among the inmates are varied and complex and perhaps subject to the unwritten code that exhorts inmates not to inform on a fellow prisoner.

It is against this background that disciplinary proceedings must be structured by prison authorities; and it is against this background that we must make our constitutional judgments, realizing that we are dealing with the maximum-security institution as well as those where security considerations are not so paramount. The reality is that disciplinary hearings and the imposition of disagreeable sanctions necessarily involve confrontations between inmates and authority and between inmates who are being disciplined and those who would charge or furnish evidence against them. Retaliation is much more than a theoretical possibility; and the basic and unavoidable task of providing reasonable personal safety for guards and inmates may be at stake, to say nothing of the impact of disciplinary confrontations and the resulting escalation of personal antagonisms on the important aims of the correctional process.

. . .

Two of the procedures that the Court held should be extended to parolees facing revocation proceedings are not, but must be, provided to prisoners in the Nebraska Complex if the minimum requirements of procedural due process are to be satisfied. These are advance written notice of the claimed violation and a written statement of the fact findings as to the evidence relied upon and the reasons for the disciplinary action taken. As described by the Warden in his oral testimony, on the basis of which the District Court made its findings, the inmate is now given oral notice of the charges against him at least as soon as the conference with the chief correction officer and charging party. A written record is there compiled and the report read to the inmate at the hearing before the Adjustment Committee where the charges are discussed and pursued. There is no indication that the inmate is ever given a written statement by the Committee as to the evidence or informed in writing or otherwise as to the reasons for the disciplinary action taken.

Part of the function of notice is to give the charged party a chance to marshal the facts in his defense and to clarify what the charges are, in fact. See In re Gault, 387 U.S. 1, 33-34 & n. 54 (1967). Neither of these functions was performed by the notice described by the Warden. Although the charges are discussed orally with the inmate somewhat in advance of the hearing, the inmate is sometimes brought before the Adjustment Committee shortly after he is orally informed of the charges. Other times, after this initial discussion, further investigation takes place which may reshape the nature of the charges or the evidence relied upon. In those instances, under procedures in effect at the time of trial, it would appear that the inmate first receives notice of the actual charges at the time of the hearing before the Adjustment Commitee. We hold that written notice of the charges must be given to the disciplinary action defendant in order to inform him of the charges and to enable him to marshal the facts and prepare a defense. At least a brief period of time after the notice, no less than 24 hours, should be allowed to the inmate to prepare for the appearance before the Adjustment Committee.

We also hold that there must be a "written statement by the factfinders as to the evidence relied on and reasons for the disciplinary action." Morrissey, 408 U.S., at 489. Although Nebraska does not seem to provide administrative review of the action taken by the Adjustment Committee, the actions taken at such proceedings may involve review by other bodies. They might furnish the basis of a decision by the Director of Corrections to transfer an inmate to another institution because he is considered "to be incorrigible by reason of frequent intentional breaches of discipline," Neb. Rev. Stat. § 83-185 ([4] Supp. 1972), and are certainly likely to be considered by the state parole authorities in making parole decisions. Written records of proceedings will thus protect the inmate against collateral consequences based on a misunderstanding of the nature of the original proceeding. Further, as to the disciplinary action itself, the provision for a written record helps to insure that administrators, faced with possible scrutiny by state officials and the public, and perhaps even the courts, where fundamental constitutional rights may have been abridged, will act fairly. Without written records, the inmate will be at a severe disadvantage in propounding his own cause to or defending himself from others. It may be that there will be occasions when personal or institutional safety are so implicated, that the statement may properly exclude certain items of evidence, but in that event the statement should indicate the fact of the omission. Otherwise, we perceive no conceivable rehabilitative objective or prospect of prison disruption that can flow from the requirement of these statements.

We are also of the opinion that the inmate facing disciplinary proceedings should be allowed to call witnesses and present documentary evidence in his defense when permitting him to do so will not be unduly hazardous to institutional safety or correctional goals. Ordinarily, the right to present evidence is basic to a fair hearing; but the unrestricted right to call witnesses from the prison population carries obvious potential for disruption and for interference with the swift punishment that in individual cases may be essential to carrying out the correctional program of the institution. We should not be too ready to exercise oversight and put aside the judgment of prison administrators. It may be that an individual threatened with serious sanctions would normally be entitled to present witnesses and relevant documentary evidence; but here we must balance the inmate's interest in avoiding loss of good time against the needs of the prison, and some amount of flexibility and accommodation is required. Prison officials must have the necessary discretion to keep the hearing within reasonable limits and to refuse to call witnesses that may create a risk of reprisal or undermine authority, as well as to limit access to other inmates to collect statements or to compile other documentary evidence. Although we do not prescribe it, it would be useful for the Committee to state its reason for refusing to call a witness, whether it be for irrelevance, lack of necessity or the hazards presented in individual cases. Any less flexible rule appears untenable as a constitutional matter, at least on the record made in this case. The operation of a correctional institution is at best an extraordinarily difficult undertaking. Many prison officials, on the spot and with the responsibility for the safety of inmates and staff, are reluctant to extend the unqualified right to call witnesses; and in our view, they must have the necessary discretion without being subject to unduly crippling constitutional impediments. There is this much play in the joints of the Due Process Clause, and we stop short of imposing a more demanding rule with respect to witnesses and documents.

Confrontation and cross-examination present greater hazards to institutional interests. If confrontation and cross-examination of those furnishing evidence against the inmate were to be allowed as a matter of course, as in criminal trials, there would be considerable potential for havoc inside the prison walls. Proceedings would inevitably be longer and tend to unmanageability. These procedures are essential in criminal trials where the accused, if found guilty, may be subjected to the most serious deprivations, *Pointer* v. *Texas,* 380 U.S. 400 (1965), or where a person may lose his job in the society, *Greene* v. *McElroy,* 360 U.S. 474, 496-497 (1959). But they are not rights universally applicable to all hearings. See *Arnett* v. *Kennedy, supra.* Rules of procedure may be shaped by consideration of the risks of error. *In re Winship, supra,* 397 U.S. 358, 368 (1970) (HARLAN, J., concurring); *Arnett* v. *Kennedy, supra* (WHITE, J., concurring), and should also be shaped by the consequences which will follow their adoption. Although some States do seem to allow cross-examination in disciplinary hearings, we are not apprised of the conditions under which the procedure may be curtailed; and it does not appear that confrontation and cross-examination are generally required in this context. We think that the Constitution should not be read to impose the procedure at the present time and that adequate bases for decision in prison disciplinary cases can be arrived a without cross-examination.

Perhaps as the problems of penal institutions change and correctional goals are reshaped, the balance of interests involved will require otherwise. But in the current environment, where prison disruption remains a serious concern to administrators, we cannot ignore the desire and effort of many States, including Nebraska and the Federal Government, to avoid situations that may trigger deep emotions and that may scuttle the disciplinary process as a reha-bilitation vehicle. To some extent, the American adversary trial presumes contestants who are able to cope with the pressures and aftermath of the battle, and such may not generally be the case of those in the prisons of this country. At least, the Constitution, as we interpret it today, does not require the contrary assumption. Within the limits set forth in this opinion we are content for now to leave the continuing development of measures to review adverse actions affecting inmates to the sound discretion of corrections officials administering the scope of such inquiries.

We recognize that the problems of potential disruption may differ depending on whom the inmate proposes to cross-examine. If he proposes to examine an unknown fellow inmate, the danger may be the greatest, since the disclosure of the identity of the accuser, and the cross-examination which will follow, may pose a high risk of reprisal within the institution. Conversely, the inmate accuser, who might freely tell his story privately to prison officials, may refuse to testify or admit any knowledge of the situation in question. Although the dangers posed by cross-examination of known inmate accusers, or guards, may be less, the resentment which may persist after confrontation may still be substantial. Also, even where the accuser or adverse witness is known, the disclosure of third parties may pose a problem. There may be a class of cases where the facts are closely disputed, and the character of the parties mini-mizes the dangers involved. However, any constitutional rule tailored to meet these situations would undoubtedly produce great litigation and attendant costs in a much wider range of cases. Further, in the last analysis, even within the narrow range of cases where interest balancing may well dictate cross-examination, courts will be faced with the assessment of prison officials as to the dangers involved, and there would be a limited basis for upsetting such judgments. The better course at this time, in a period where prison practices are diverse and somewhat experimental, is to leave these matters to the sound discretion of the officials of state prisons.

. . .

The insertion of counsel into the disciplinary process would inevitably give the proceedings a more adversary cast and tend to reduce their utility as a means to further correctional goals. There would also be delay and very practical problems in providing counsel in sufficient numbers at the time and place where hearings are to be held. At this stage of the development of these procedures we are not prepared to hold that inmates have a right to either retained or appointed counsel in disciplinary proceedings.

Where an illiterate inmate is involved, however, or where the complexity of the issue makes it unlikely that the inmate will be able to collect and present the evidence necessary for an adequate comprehension of the case, he should be free to seek the aid of a fellow inmate, or if that is forbidden, to have adequate substitute aid in the form of help from the staff or from a sufficiently competent inmate designated by the staff. We need not pursue the matter further here, however, for there is no claim that the named plaintiff McDonnell is within the class of inmates entitled to advice or help from others in the course of a prison disciplinary hearing.

Finally, we decline to rule that the Adjustment Committee which conducts the required hearings at the Nebraska Prison Complex and determines whether to revoke good time is not sufficiently impartial to satisfy the Due Process Clause. The Committee is made up of the Associate Warden for Custody as chairman, the Correctional Industries Superintendent and the Reception Director. The Chief Corrections Officer refers cases to the Committee after investigation and an initial interview with the inmate involved. The Committee is not left at large with unlimited discretion. It is directed to meet daily and to operate within the principles stated in the controlling regulations, among which is the command that "full consideration must be given to the causes for the adverse behavior, the setting and circumstances in which it occurred, the man's accountability, and the correctional treatment goals," as well as the direction that "disciplinary measures will be taken only at such times and to such degrees as are necessary to regulate and control a man's behavior within acceptable limits and will never be rendered capriciously or in the nature of retaliation or revenge." We find no warrant in the record presented here for

327

concluding that the Adjustment Committee presents such a hazard of arbitrary decisionmaking that it should be held violative of due process of law.

Our conclusion that some, but not all, of the procedures specified in *Morrissey* and *Scarpelli* must accompany the deprivation of good-time by state prison authorities is not graven in stone. As the nature of the prison disciplinary process changes in future years, circumstances may then exist which will require further consideration and reflection of this Court. It is our view, however, that the procedures we have now required in prison disciplinary proceedings represent a reasonable accommodation between the interests of the inmates and the needs of the institution.

The question of retroactivity of new procedural rules affecting inquiries into infractions of prison discipline is effectively foreclosed by this Court's ruling in *Morrissey* that the due process requirements there announced were to be "applicable to *future* revocations of parole," 408 U.S., at 490 (emphasis supplied). Despite the fact that procedures are related to the integrity of the fact-finding process, in the context of disciplinary proceedings, where less is generally at stake for an individual than at a criminal trial, great weight should be given to the significant impact a retroactivity ruling would have on the administration of all prisons in the country, and the reliance prison officials placed, in good faith, on prior law not requiring such procedures. During 1973, the Federal Government alone conducted 19,000 misconduct hearings, as compared with 1,173 parole revocation hearings, and 2,023 probation revocation hearings. If *Morrissey-Scarpelli* rules are not retroactive out of consideration for burden on federal and state officials, this case is *a fortiori.* We also note that a contrary holding would be very troublesome for the parole system since performance in prison is often a relevant criterion for parole. On the whole, we do not think that error was so pervasive in the system under the old procedures to warrant this cost or result.

The field of administrative law dealing with prisoners' rights has mushroomed in recent years, and as with many trends, the causes of the change are varied but closely related. The increasing willingness of appellate courts to intervene at postsentence stages of the process is occurring in a cultural context of expanded legal services for the poor, coupled with increased concern for the civil rights of racial and ethnic minorities who are disproportionately represented in prison populations, and at a time of widespread cynicism about governmental claims of benevolence or effectiveness. In recent years prison riots have focused public and professional attention on prisons. And the riots are both cause and effect of increasing political awareness among prisoners. One result of this has been the creation of various commissions empowered not only to investigate prison riots, but to look at the whole problem of prisons and make suggestions for remediation and reform.[63] Another result of the riots has been the creation of study groups charged with developing model rules and regulations concerning prisons and prisoners' rights. The areas covered in these model rules are too varied and extensive to be reproduced in full here. In general, these model rules call for greater attention to standards of evidence, procedural due process, and other requirements similar to those required for police or court interventions with suspects outside the walls. Two illustrations from a compendium of model rules are reproduced below to give some notion of the kinds of issues addressed:

RULE ID-3. PERSONAL SEARCHES.
a.   Weapons frisk.

1.   A correctional officer may perform a limited search for weapons upon suspicion that a particular inmate is carrying a weapon.

2.   Such suspicion is not to be wholly groundless but is to be based on facts observed, tips received, reasoned opinion as "known" character and temperament of the inmate, even rumors indicating that the inmate will be carrying weapons.

3.   The search is to be limited to a "pat-down" or "frisk" of the outer clothing calculated to reveal concealed weapons.

4.   A weapons frisk is not to be used as a cover for a full personal search. If illicit matter other than weapons is revealed in a frisk and used against the inmate in disciplinary proceedings, the presumption arises that the officer was conducting a personal search and accordingly must meet the standards set for a personal search. This violation shall be handled as described in subsection ID-3b.

b.   Personal search.

1.   A correctional officer may perform a personal search whenever he reasonably concludes that an inmate is likely to be carrying contraband of any description.

2.   Such conclusion is to be based on

a.   The observation of facts, which may be interpreted in light of the correctional officer's experience and his knowledge of the character of the inmate, or

b.   Incriminating information from a third party where there is not reason to believe the third party is motivated by the desire to harass the inmate.

3.   Authorization to conduct a personal search must be obtained from the shift supervisor. Authorization shall be given except where it is clear from the officer's description of the facts that there is no cause to search.

4. The supervisor shall grant authorization in writing and the supervisor shall immediately record, for evidentiary purposes, the

    a.   Time, date and name of the searching officer.

    b.   The observations or information on which the searching officer has based his conclusion that an inmate is likely to be carrying contraband.

    c.   The nature of the matter the officer expects to find.

    d.   The inmate to be searched.

    e.   Name and signature of the supervisor.

    f.   Time and date.

5. Copies of this record shall be made available upon request to any concerned party.

6. Failure to produce this record raises the presumption that the searching officer failed to obtain the requisite authorization.

7. The personal search may constitute reaching into the clothing, but an inmate will not be required to undress beyond the removal of shoes (or cap).

c.   Emergency personal search.

1. A correctional officer may perform a personal search whenever he reasonably concludes that

    a.   An inmate is likely to be carrying contraband, and

    b.   There is reason to believe that it is highly probable the inmate will dispose of the contraband in the interval required to obtain authorization for personal search.

2. The correctional officer's reasonable conclusion is to be judged by the standards provided in subsection ID-2b(2).

3. An after-action report of the emergency search, whether or not contraband is discovered, shall be filed.

d.   Strip search.

In order for a strip search to be considered reasonable, each of the factors in subsection ID-3b (1-3) must be met.

e.   Standing cause for personal searches.

1. If visiting hours permit close physical contact with minimal supervision, the manner and extent of the search to which the inmate is subjected following the visit is at the inspecting officer's discretion.

2. In any situation where the inmate has ready access to dangerous or valuable items (e.g., kitchen or shop tools), the inmate, prior to departure from the area, may be subjected to a search designed in scope and manner to discover the items to which the inmate had access. The superintendent shall make a written finding as to which areas of the institution will be protected by this provision. Such finding, along with a description of the procedure to be followed and

reasons why, shall be posted for the information of the inmates and correctional personnel.

3. After-action reports shall be filed whenever contraband is discovered.[64]

Today a number of prisons have elected inmate councils to funnel complaints to administrative officials and in some correctional systems there are *ombudsmen,* persons neutral to the correctional system who hear and attempt to negotiate inmate complaints or demands.

Despite such developments, incarceration in prisons and reformatories remains the most extreme and most socially degrading example of the full power of the state to punish and to force compliance. It is the vortex, not the apex, of our criminal justice system, a method of control that is controversial and presently in a state of change but currently used to punish, restrain, and perhaps rehabilitate 200,000 offenders.

NOTES

1. See Vincent O'Leary and David Duffee, "Correctional Policy: A Classification of Goals Designed for Change," *Crime and Delin.* 373 (1971); and by the same authors, "Managerial Behavior and Correctional Policy," *Pub. Admin. Review* 31 (November-December 1971): 603.

2. President's Commission on Law Enforcement and Administration of Justice, *Task Force Report: Corrections* (Washington, D.C.: U.S. Government Printing Office, 1967), pp. 27-37.

3. Federal Bureau of Prisons, *National Prisoner Statistics* (Washington, D.C.: U.S. Department of Justice, 1970).

4. President's Commission, *Corrections.*

5. National Advisory Commission on Criminal Justice Standards and Goals, *Corrections* (Washington, D.C.: U.S. Department of Justice, 1973), Standard 7.1, p. 237.

6. See Paul Tappan, *Crime, Justice and Correction* (New York: McGraw-Hill, 1960), pp. 546-549.

7. See Zebulon R. Brockway, *Fifty Years of Prison Service* (New York: Charities Publication, 1912).

8. See George F. Davis, "A Study of Adult Probation Violation Rates by Means of the Cohort Approach," *J. of Crim. Law, Criminology and Pol. Sci.* 55, 70 (March 1964); *The Saginaw Probation Demonstration Project* (New York: National Council on Crime and Delinquency, 1963); Daniel Glaser, *The Effectiveness of a Prison and Parole System*

(Indianapolis: Bobbs-Merrill, 1964); Don M. Gottfredson, M. G. Neithercutt, Joan Nuffield, and Vincent O'Leary, *Four Thousand Lifetimes: A Study of Time Served and Parole Outcomes* (Davis, California: National Council on Crime and Delinquency Research Center, 1973).

9. See Herman Piven and Abraham Alcabes, *The Crisis of Qualified Manpower for Criminal Justice: An Analytic Assessment with Guidelines For New Policy,* Vol. I *Probation and Parole* (Washington, D.C.: U.S. Department of Health, Education, and Welfare, nd.).

10. See Lloyd Ohlin, Herman Piven, and Donald Pappenfort, "Major Dilemmas of the Social Worker in Probation and Parole," *Nat. Prob. and Parole Assoc. J.* 2, 211 (1956).

11. See Vincent O'Leary and Donald J. Newman, "Conflict Resolution in Criminal Justice," *J. Res. in Crime and Delin.* 7, 99 (1970).

12. President's Commission, *Corrections.* See also, Stuart Adams, "Some Findings From Correctional Caseload Research," in Robert M. Carter and Leslie T. Wilkins, eds., *Probation and Parole* (New York: John Wiley and Sons, 1970), pp. 364-378.

13. See President's Commission, *Corrections,* pp. 38-44.

14. See Marguerite Q. Warren, *Correctional Treatment in Community Settings: A Report of Current Research* (Rockville, Md.: National Institute of Mental Health, 1971); Oliver J. Keller, Jr. and Benedict S. Alper, *Halfway Houses: Community-Centered and Treatment* (Lexington, Mass.: Lexington Books, 1970); Bertram S. Griggs and Gary R. McCune, "Community-Based Correctional Programs: A Survey and Analysis" *Fed. Probation* 36, 7 (June 1972); Robert M. Carter, Daniel Glaser, and Leslie T. Wilkins, eds., *Correctional Institutions* (Philadelphia: J. B. Lippincott Company, 1972).

15. See generally, Donald J. Newman, "Perspectives of Probation: Legal Issues and Professional Trends," *The Challenge of Change in the Correctional Process* (New York: National Council on Crime and Delinquency, 1972).

16. Compare Sec. 301.1, "Conditions of Suspension of Probation" and Sec. 305.13, "Conditions of Parole," in American Law Institute, *Model Penal Code* (Proposed Official Draft, 1962). See commentaries to these Sections, in *Tentative Draft No. 2,* p. 141 (Probation) and *Tentative Draft No. 5,* p. 103 (Parole).

17. Nat R. Arluke, "A Summary of Parole Rules—Thirteen Years Later," *Crime and Delin.* 15, 267 (1969).

18. *Ibid,* at 268.

19. Frank J. Remington, Donald J. Newman, Edward L. Kimball, Marygold Melli, and Herman Goldstein, *Criminal Justice Administration: Materials and Cases* (Indianapolis: Bobbs-Merrill, 1969), p. 805.

20. California Penal Code, Sec. 203.1 (Supp. 1966).

21. People v. Dominquez, 256 Cal. App. 623, 64 Cal. Rptr. 290 (Ct. of App. 1967).

22. *Ibid,* p. 293.

23. *Ibid.*

24. People v. Blankenship, 16 Cal. App. 2d 606, 61 P. 2d 352 (1936).

25. In re. Andrada, 380 U.S. 953 (1965).

26. Matter of Hernandez, No. 76757 at 12 (Cal. Super. Ct., Santa Barbara County, June 8, 1966).

27. People v. Baum, 251 Mich. 187, 231 N.W. 95 (1930).

28. People v. Smith, 252 Mich. 4, 232 N.W. 397 (1930). See also Note, "Banishment: A Medieval Tactic in Modern Criminal Law," *Utah Law Review* 5, 365 (1957).

29. Ex Parte Walters, 221 P. 2d 659 (Okla. Ct. of App. 1950).

30. In re. Peeler, 266 Cal. App. 2d 483, 72 Cal. Rptr. 254, 261 (Ct. of App. 1968).

31. Butler v. District of Columbia, 346 F. 2d 789 (D.C. Cir. 1965).

32. Jones v. Commonwealth, 185 Va. 335, 38 S.E. 2d 444 (1946).

33. Hyland v. Procunier, 311 F. Supp. 749, 750 (N.D. Cal. 1970).

34. Sweeney v. United States, 353 F. 2d 10 (7th Cir. 1965).

35. Robinson v. California, 370 U.S. 660 (1962).

36. *Ibid,* p. 666.

37. State v. Oyler, 92 Idaho 43 (1968).

38. Kaplan v. United States, 234 F. 2d 345, 348-49 (9th Cir. 1956).

39. See Arluke, "A Summary of Parole Rules," p. 274.

40. For a list of such jurisdictions see *Model Penal Code* (Tentative Draft No. 5, 1956) p. 180 or Sol Rubin, Henry Weihofen, George Edwards, and Simon Rosenzweig, *The Law of Criminal Correction* (St. Paul, Minn.: West, 1963), Chapter 15, Section 10.

41. People v. Denne, 141 Cal. App. 499 (Cal. Dist. Ct. of App. 1956).

42. See People v. Randazzo, 15 N.Y. 2d 526 (1964): DiMarco v. Greene, 385 F. 2d 556 (6th Cir. 1967).

43. National Advisory Commission, *Corrections,* Standard 2.7, Commentary, p. 39.

44. Note, "Anthropotelemetry: Dr. Schwitzgebel's Machine," *Harvard Law Review* 80, 403, 406-407 (1966).

45. Further details on tracking devices and their social and legal implications can be found in Schwitzgebel, Schwitzgebel, Pahnke and Hurd, "A Program of Research in Behavioral Electronics," *Behavioral Sci.* 9, 233 (1964); Ralph Schwitzgebel, *Streetcorner Research: An Experimental Approach to the Juvenile Delinquent* (Cambridge, Mass.: Harvard U. Press, 1964); and Ralph Schwitzgebel, "Electronic Innovations in the Behavioral Sciences: A Call to Responsibility," *Amer. Psychol.* 22, 364 (1967); Ralph Schwitzgebel, "Electronically Monitored Parole," *Prison J.* 48, 34 (1968). See also Jose Delgado, *Physical Control of the Mind* (New York: Harper and Row, 1969).

46. *Model Penal Code,* pp. 242-243.

47. *Ibid,* Sec. 305.13.

48. American Bar Association, *Standards Relating to Probation* (New York: Institute of Judicial Administration, Approved Draft, 1970), Sec. 3.2, pp. 44-45.

49. *Ibid,* Sec. 3.2(c), p. 45.

50. National Advisory Commission, *Corrections,* Standard 5.4, p. 158.

51. *Ibid.*

52. President's Commission, *Corrections,* p. 75.

53. David J. Rothman, *The Discovery of the Asylum* (Boston: Little, Brown, 1971), pp. 79, 81.

54. See Erving Goffman, *Asylums* (Garden City, N.Y.: Doubleday, 1961).

55. See especially, Donald Clemmer, *The Prison Community,* rev. ed. (New York: Holt, Rinehart & Winston, 1958); Gresham Sykes, *The Society of Captives* (Princeton, N.J.: Princeton U. Press, 1958), Donald R. Cressey, ed., *The Prison: Studies in Institutional Organization and Change* (New York: Holt, Rinehart & Winston, 1961).

56. Goffman, *Asylums.*

57. Sykes, *Society of Captives.*

58. Gresham Sykes and Sheldon L. Messinger, "Inmate Social System," in *Theoretical Studies in the Social Organization of the Prison* (New York: Social Science Research Council Pamphlet 15, 1960), pp. 14-15.

59. See generally, Note, "Beyond the Ken of the Courts: A Critique of Judicial Refusal to Review the Complaints of Convicts," *Yale Law J.* 72, 506 (1963), and Note, "Constitutional Rights of Prisoners: The Developing Law," *U. of P. Law Review* 110, 985 (1962).

60. See Note, "Judicial Intervention in Corrections: The California Experience—An Empirical Study," *UCLA Law Review* 20, 452 (1973). See also Fred Cohen, *Legal Norms in Corrections,* Consultant Paper, President's Task Force on Corrections, (1967) and Edward L. Kimball and Donald J. Newman, "Judicial Intervention in Correctional Decisions": Threat and Response," *J. Res. Crime and Delin.* 14, 1 (1968).

61. See South Carolina Department of Corrections, *The Emerging Rights of the Confined* (1972). See also, R. Singer, *Prisoners' Legal Rights: A Bibliography of Cases and Articles* (Columbia, S.C., 1972).

62. Landman v. Royster, 354 F. Supp. 1302 (E.D. Va. 1973).

63. See for example, New York State Special Commission on Attica, *Attica* (Official Report, Bantam 1972); *Report of the Select Committee on Correctional Institutions and Programs* (Mimeo; New York, N.Y., 1972).

64. Sheldon Krantz, Robert Bell, Jonathan Brant, and Michael Magruder, *Model Rules and Regulations on Prisoners' Rights and Responsibilities,* Center for Criminal Justice, Boston University (St. Paul, Minn.: West, 1973), pp. 63-64.

Chapter 8

Release and Revocation

RELEASE FROM INCARCERATION

Most offenders who are sent to jails or prisons, even those with life sentences, are eventually released. Of course, some inmates die of natural causes, kill themselves, or are murdered in prison, and a few very dangerous lifers are held in custody all of their natural lives. Inmates who die while serving sentences are few, not more than 1 or 2 percent of all prisoners. However, some offenders are repeatedly sent to prison, released and returned on new convictions, in effect serving life on an installment plan. While this sometimes occurs with criminals who persistently commit very serious crimes—successive homicides, rapes, armed robberies, and so on—very often installment-plan lifers are essentially minor violators—check forgers, petty thieves—whose basic problem is alcoholism, addiction, or some aberrant mental or emotional condition which may be uncurable, and who are not deterred by incarceration. Thus it is that most prison populations are composed of a mixture of "heavy" and perhaps dangerous offenders and a somewhat larger proportion of essentially minor but persistent violators.

Incarcerated misdemeanants generally serve their full sentences in jail; misdemeanant parole is found only in a few jurisdictions. There is no data available for the nation as a whole with respect to the average length of all jail sentences. A sample study in two California counties showed two-thirds of jail sentences to be three months or less.[1] In many places a misdemeanant is incarcerated

Sentence and Actual Time Served by First Releases* from State Correctional Institutions in 1970

	1†	2	3	4	5	6
	1–5 YEARS		5–10 YEARS		10+ YEARS	
	(PERCENT)		(PERCENT)		(PERCENT)	
STATE	SENTENCED	SERVED	SENTENCED	SERVED	SENTENCED	SERVED
Arizona	34.56	88.54	42.44	9.22	23.00	2.44
California	15.21	81.32	66.51	16.13	9.49	2.55
Colorado	21.30	95.70	32.45	3.42	46.25	.88
Connecticut	51.59	97.86	42.39	1.58	6.02	.56
Delaware	87.00	98.65	10.31	.90	2.24	.45
Georgia	56.68	88.80	27.84	9.48	15.47	1.72
Hawaii	4.26	80.85	17.02	13.83	78.72	5.32
Idaho	47.26	94.56	32.88	3.40	19.86	2.04
Illinois	48.47	89.00	30.16	8.00	21.37	3.00
Kansas	8.50	91.51	39.44	6.73	52.05	1.76
Kentucky	72.55	94.14	12.20	5.28	15.25	.58
Louisiana	56.98	88.84	26.97	9.84	16.04	1.32
Maine	76.95	95.20	13.26	3.00	9.80	1.80
Maryland	78.97	97.17	15.12	2.14	5.91	.69
Massachusetts	14.66	92.30	65.43	6.47	19.91	1.23
Minnesota	21.94	5.81	39.35	31.61	38.71	62.58
Mississippi	63.38	87.36	19.89	6.69	16.73	5.95
Missouri	74.81	96.05	19.39	2.74	5.80	1.21
Montana	54.70	95.30	25.17	4.03	20.13	.67
Nevada	38.53	93.51	29.87	6.49	31.60	0.00
New Hampshire	54.44	97.78	34.44	2.22	11.11	0.00
New Mexico	8.54	86.65	47.49	10.83	43.97	2.52
New York	57.40	89.79	28.26	7.61	15.86	2.59
North Dakota	68.47	96.40	19.82	2.70	11.71	.90
Ohio	5.43	84.77	19.95	10.74	74.62	4.49
Oklahoma	73.80	95.57	17.82	3.61	8.37	.82
Oregon	65.90	95.62	25.09	4.26	9.01	.12
South Carolina	64.41	92.62	20.46	5.16	15.12	2.22
South Dakota	86.19	95.24	38.10	4.29	4.29	.48
Tennessee	61.69	90.20	19.46	8.33	18.84	1.47
Utah	10.55	90.45	21.11	9.55	68.34	0.00
Vermont	70.37	100.00	25.93	0.00	3.70	0.00
Washington	3.06	95.78	2.75	3.06	94.19	1.16
West Virginia	0.00	87.15	10.10	10.76	89.90	2.08
Wyoming	73.72	94.89	16.06	3.65	10.22	1.46

* A first release is a prisoner released for the first time on his current sentence.

† Explanation of Table:
    Column 1: Percent of first releases sentenced to 1 to 5 years.
    Column 2: Percent of first releases who actually served less than 6 months to 5 years.
    Column 3: Percent of first releases sentenced to 5 to 10 years.
    Column 4: Percent of first releases who actually served 5 to 10 years.
    Column 5: Percent of first releases sentenced to 10 or more years.
    Column 6: Percent of first releases who actually served 10 or more years.

National Prisoner Statistics: State Prisoners, Admissions and Releases, 1970 (Washington: Federal Bureau of Prisons, 1971), pp. 45, 47-81.

when he is unable to pay a fine, in effect making jail a sort of "debtor's prison" reminiscent of 19th-century England. This practice has long been condemned.[2] The drafters of the American Bar Association *Standards Relating to Sentencing Alternatives and Procedures* commented:

A system which routinely provides for imprisonment following default in the payment of a fine carries with it numerous disadvantages. Many have commented on the unfairness—and perhaps the unconstitutionality—of permitting the severity of the sanction to turn on the means of the defendant.

. . .

. . . Not so frequently recognized, however, is the fact that there can be little constructive effect of such a short-term commitment, particularly in an often substandard local institution. Frequently, for example, there is little or no attempt to segregate types of offenders, resulting in associations which may promote future crime rather than deter it. The most ironic aspect of the practice, however, is the fact that it often involves undergoing the expense of maintaining an offender in an institution and at the same time preventing him from earning the very sum for the lack of which he is being detained. The economic absurdity of this is compounded by the effect on those who are dependent on the defendant. And all of this is brought about, it should be kept in mind, after there has been an initial determination that jail—or at least the time which is due to nonpayment—is unnecessary in terms of the protection of the public, the gravity of the offense, and other factors which normally determine the need for the incarceration.[3]

In 1970 and 1971 the U.S. Supreme Court considered the matter of imprisonment in lieu of fine in two separate cases.[4] While the court cast doubt on this practice when applied to those who cannot pay, in contrast to those who refuse to do so, it did not forbid the practice in all circumstances.

Maximum prison sentences imposed by statute or by a judge on convicted felons in the United States are probably the longest in the world.[5] Awareness of this, and awareness of considerable variations among different jurisdictions across the nation, had much to do with the creation of model sentencing proposals in the 1960s and 1970s, all calling for a shortening of sentences for all but dangerous or professional criminals. The length of imposed maximum sentences is deceptive, however, if taken to mean the actual time spent in prison. While there is considerable variation from one jurisdiction to the next according to a somewhat dated national survey, felony inmates received in state and federal prisons serve, on the average, less than two years (21.2 months) before *first* release.[6] This statistic needs several qualifications. The average time given is the *median,* meaning that 50 percent of the prisoners served this amount of time or less while the remainder served more time. It is important to note that the time refers to first release; prisoners who were paroled, revoked, and perhaps reparoled or held to maximum discharge date are not included. Neither are prisoners who are never released included. The date of release from incarceration does not necessarily, nor even usually, mean that the prisoner has completed his sentence. Most prisoners must still serve time under community supervision by a parole officer until their maximum sentence expires.

At sentencing itself, only one out of three maximum terms are for ten years or more. Though the median time of first release is somewhat less than two years, it varies among jurisdictions from about three-and-one-half years to a low of about twelve months. The drafters of the *Model Sentencing Act* who proposed a five-year maximum for all felons except those who are convicted of murder, other atrocious crimes or who were diagnosed as dangerous, argued that their five-year maximum would not effect any operational difference in prison sentences, since the majority of inmates in *all* jurisdictions are released in less than five years anyway.[7]

Across the nation inmates are released from prison in a number of ways: 1) upon completion of maximum sentence, 2) on parole, 3) at a mandatory release date which generally is the maximum sentence less time off for good behavior, and 4) by pardon. All methods are used in each jurisdiction, but their frequency of use varies considerably. Part of this variation stems from differences in statutory provisions from one state to the next, part to the type and structure of correctional systems, including differences in the availability and quality of parole services and other resources, part simply to local customs and historical drift, and part to the characteristics of populations held in prisons. In jurisdictions with strong and frequently used probation services, prison populations may be heavily composed of "residue" violators—those who are dangerous or so persistent in criminality that community supervision on probation has proved unsafe and ineffective. In this type of situation, parole authorities may be seeing quite different types of offenders than those parole boards in states where probation is less often used and where prisons are used to hold less serious but recidivistic violators along with the "heavies" and the dangerous.

While there are some gross differences in prison populations depending upon the availability and use of other alternatives, all prison populations are composed of a complex mixture of differences in personalities, offense categories, age groupings, and persons from divergent outside life-styles. These combine to make matters and methods of release more than a simple exercise of application of easily determined criteria. The President's Task Force on Corrections had this to say about correctional populations:

The American correctional system is an extremely diverse amalgam of facilities, theories, techniques, and programs. It handles nearly 1.3 million offenders on an average day; it has 2.5 million admissions in the course of a year; and its annual operating budget is over a billion dollars. Correctional operations are administered by Federal, State, county and municipal governments. Some jurisdictions have developed strong programs for the control and rehabilitation of offenders. But most lack capacity to cope with the problems of preventing recidivism—the commission of further offenses. Some fail even to meet standards of humane treatment recognized for decades.

. . .

Individual offenders differ strikingly. Some seem irrevocably committed to criminal careers; others subscribe to quite conventional values or are aimless and uncommitted to goals of any kind. Many are disturbed and frustrated boys and young men. Still others are alcoholics, narcotic addicts, victims of senility, or sex deviants. This diversity poses immense problems to correctional officials, for in most institutions or community treatment caseloads a wide range of offender types must be handled together.

. . .

But beneath such diversities, certain characteristics predominate. About 95 percent of all offenders are male. Most of them are young, in the age range between 15 and 30.

. . .

Many come from urban slums. Members of minority groups that suffer economic and social discrimination are present in disproportionate numbers. In fact, the life histories of most offenders are case studies in the ways in which social and economic factors contribute to crime and delinquency. Education, for example, is as good a barometer as any of the likelihood of success in modern America. Census data show that over half of adult felony inmates in 1960 had no high school education.

Offenders also tend to lack vocational skills. Census data show a higher proportion of unskilled laborers among prisoners than in the civilian labor force.

Many too have had failures in relationships with family and friends. This pattern of cumulative failure has prevented many offenders from developing a sense of self-respect, thus creating another obstacle to rehabilitation.[8]

Maximum Discharge

Normally a prisoner cannot be held in custody beyond the expiration of his maximum sentence. It is possible, however, for an offender to spend a combination of time incarcerated and time under community supervision in excess of

339

AVERAGE DAILY POPULATION IN CORRECTIONS

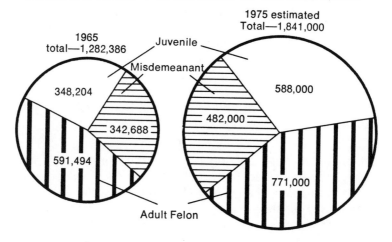

* 1965 data from National Survey of Corrections and tabulations provided by the Federal Bureau of Prisons and the Administrative Office
of the U.S. Courts. Projections by R. Christensen, of the Commission's task force on science and technology. Adopted from the President's Commission on Law Enforcement and the Administration of
Justice, *Task Force Report: Corrections* (Washington, D.C.: U.S.
Government Printing Office, 1967), p. 7.

the years specified in a maximum sentence. For example, in a number of jurisdictions time on probation or mandatory release "tolls," that is, it does not count
toward sentence expiration unless the period of community supervision is
successfully completed. Thus an offender sentenced to prison for five years who
has his sentence suspended and is placed on probation, but who is revoked after
four years on probation may still owe the state the full five-year prison sentence.
In this instance, though incarceration is limited to five years, if the full time
is served, the offender will actually have been under sentence for nine years.

Servitude to maximum discharge date is rare today except for offenders who
are sentenced to very short maximum terms—a year or a year and a day, for
example—and to offenders who commit crimes in sequence while on probation,
parole, or mandatory release. Persons incarcerated for the first time are almost
invariably released prior to completion of maximum sentence. Release, whether
on parole or at a "good time" date, is usually under supervision of a parole
officer. The primary reason for this is the awareness that return to the community from prison is a traumatic and difficult task better accomplished with

supervisory help than simply with "gate money" (usually a few dollars plus any funds earned in prison industry) and a bus ticket home.

Parole

Most inmates—about 70 percent nationally with a range from 9 to 99 percent among various jurisdictions—are released on parole at the discretion of a parole board after expiration of minimum sentences, but prior to dates of mandatory discharge.[9] All states and the federal jurisdiction now have parole statutes and prescribe some procedures for discretionary release of most inmates. The prisoner who is granted parole is generally required to agree to abide by rules and conditions not unlike those imposed by courts on probationers and to cooperate in supervision by parole officers.[10] In some jurisdictions, a single agency supervises both probationers and parolees; more commonly parolees are under supervision of a statewide parole authority, but the conditions of both forms of community supervision are much the same.

In general, parolees remain under supervision from the time of release until expiration of their maximum sentence. Though there are variations, time on parole usually counts toward expiration of sentence and does not "toll" as is often the case with probation. This presents a dilemma in that good risk inmates released early in their sentences have longer time under supervision but may need it less than poorer risk offenders released near the end of their terms. To meet this the drafters of the *Model Penal Code* suggest separate parole terms, not to exceed five years, which would divorce time on parole from sentence remainder.[11] While this provision has not been widely adopted, many jurisdictions do provide early discharge for those offenders who have made successful adjustment and for whom supervision to the maximum appears unnecessary.

THE DEVELOPMENT OF PAROLE.   The actual structure of the paroling process, including the composition and selection of the parole board, the caseloads, training, and authority of field staff, and procedures used for grant and for revocation, varies markedly from one jurisdiction to another,[12] as does the comparative use of parole. These variations in the structure and use of the parole process, as well as differences in sentencing provisions from one jurisdiction to another, account in good part for lack of agreement about the legal status of parole across the nation. Where parole is the common method of release from prison, it comes more often to be viewed as a right—indeed it is the norm—than where it is granted reluctantly and rarely. And in jurisdictions with long statutory sentences, infrequent use of pardon, and with no other alternative to sentence mitigation, parole becomes crucially important to inmates and an obvious focus of litigation. Whether the parole system of a particular jurisdiction is elaborate or simple, and whether discretionary release is frequently or rarely used, there is little doubt that today parole systems everywhere are experiencing an increase in appellate litigation which challenges both their formal procedures and common practices.[13]

The history of parole in this country is a stormy one. The idea of releasing convicts before expiration of their duly imposed sentences was vigorously opposed by many individuals and groups, including law-enforcement officials and a number of prominent newpaper editors.[14] Very early in its development the constitutionality of the concept of parole was challenged on a number of grounds, among them that it was an infringement on judicial sentencing authority, that it usurped the pardoning powers of the chief executive, and even that it was an unlawful delegation of the legislative function. Generally these arguments were rejected and the basic foundation of the parole function today is legally accepted.[15]

Despite this opposition, the idea of parole caught on and spread to every jurisdiction. The reasons for its growth and greater acceptance today are mixed. In part, parole is simply more humanitarian than long prison sentences. It also offers mitigation of statutory prison terms to certain offenders who while guilty of serious crimes in the past, are no longer likely to violate. Partly also parole was seen as a way to control inmate behavior by offering the possibility of early release for those willing to participate in prison programs and to cooperate with officials. Parole was also advocated for economic reasons, since street supervision is much less costly than incarceration. Finally, parole itself was seen as rehabilitative, for supervised reentry into the community is almost always safer and more effective than simply opening the gates. In general, years of experience with parole have proved its effectiveness on all these levels.[16]

In its origins, however, the grant of parole was defined as an act of grace, of mercy, on the part of the state; a privilege afforded to a few but the right of none. Eligibility for parole was, and remains, fixed by a statutory minimum sentence, or, where permitted by law, a minimum set by the court at sentencing. In some places, a fixed minimum may be reduced a few months, occasionally years, by "good time" credits earned by a prisoner for good behavior while incarcerated. In a number of other jurisdictions, some sentences carry no minimum which allows the paroling authority to fix a date for "first appearance." In some places, prior to first eligibility date, inmates must "apply" for parole consideration; in others, consideration for parole is automatic as the eligibility date approaches. In general, the grant, deferral, or denial of parole at the first appearance and subsequently is discretionary with a parole board, commonly a panel of officials appointed by the chief executive who are administratively independent from both the correctional services and the sentencing courts.[17]

Illustration 1. Parole Hearing

COMMISSIONER: Take a seat please . . . your name is Charles Edward Robinson?

INMATE: Yes, sir.

COMM.: You were received here on December 21, 1969, is that right?

INMATE: Yes, sir.

COMM.: You received a sentence of from three to seven-and-one-half years for burglary while armed, to which you pleaded guilty. Is that correct?

INMATE: Yes, sir.

COMM.: The original charge was robbery, wasn't it?—Did you cop a plea?

INMATE: Well, I guess you could call it robbery—I took this money off this guy. I guess it was robbery or burglary.

COMM.: Now the record shows that you have a drinking problem, Charles, although you don't seem to have been in any serious trouble before.

INMATE: Yes sir. I was drunk alright.

COMM.: What have you been doing about this problem? Are you in the AA group here?

INMATE: Yes, sir. I joined AA and have gone to every meeting since I been here.

COMM.: Where are you working?

INMATE: Now I'm in the shoe factory. Before that I was in the laundry.

COMM.: Have you been involved in any other programs while here?

INMATE: Yes, sir. I'm in Mr. Crawford's counselling group. I've taken an auto mechanics course in the school and I volunteered in the Blood Drive—

COMM.: What good has the group counselling done you?

INMATE: Well, I learned more about myself—my problems, I guess you'd call it. I learned to control myelf.

COMM.: It says here that you intend to live with your sister if you make parole. Is this right?

INMATE: Yes, sir.

COMM.: And you have a job lined up as a mechanics helper in this garage?

INMATE: Yes, sir. They said they'd hire me right away—

COMM.: Alright, Charles. That will be all. Thank you for coming. You will receive our decision in a day or two.

This brief dialogue is not designed to illustrate an ideal parole hearing, nor is it offered as being representative of hearings everywhere. Nonetheless, it is not atypical in brevity or focus; most hearings, especially in large states, are only too short and cursory. The actual procedures followed in deciding whether

343

AVERAGE NUMBER OF CASES HEARD PER DAY DURING PAROLE CONSIDERATION HEARINGS: 51 JURISDICTIONS,* FELONY OFFENDERS

AVERAGE NUMBER OF CASES HEARD PER DAY	NUMBER OF PAROLE BOARDS
1–19	11
20–29	15
30–39	14
40 and over	11

* Excludes Georgia, Hawaii, and Texas, where no parole hearings are conducted.

Vincent O'Leary and Joan Nuffield, *The Organization of Parole Systems in the United States,* 2nd ed. (Hackensack, N.J.: National Council on Crime and Delinquency, 1972), p. xxx.

or not to parole an inmate vary in a number of significant ways among the 51 jurisdictions in the United States.[18] In most jurisdictions, members of a parole board personally interview an inmate at, or shortly before, the time he becomes eligible for parole. This is not a universal practice, however. A comprehensive survey of parole decision making revealed that in three states interviews are not held with inmates; instead the board depends entirely on a review of case file materials, while in three additional states personal hearings are conducted only in selected cases.[19] In the federal jurisdiction and in California, parole authorities employ a staff of "hearing representatives" to conduct interviews in routine cases and report their findings to the board. The National Advisory Commission, which like all recent national commissions strongly supports the wide use of parole, suggests that all larger state jurisdictions employ full-time hearing examiners to conduct initial parole hearings. In this scheme, the parole board itself would act as a policy-making body, would monitor hearing officer interviews, and would serve as an appellate body in cases where inmates are dissatisfied with hearing examiner decisions.[20] The advantage of such a structure is that it makes individual hearings possible and more careful and deliberate than where inmate populations are large or, as in the federal system, where there are great distances between institutions. At present, many parole boards are comparatively small and in large states must travel constantly, often making the parole hearing a hurried and harried experience.

The size of parole boards varies from two or three to twelve or more members, and, as discussed earlier, some boards are composed of full-time members, others of part-time representatives whose major careers are elsewhere. In some jurisdictions, each parole applicant is heard by the full board; in others, particularly in large jurisdictions having many correctional facilities, boards may be split into panels with the hearing actually conducted by one or two parole commissioners. In the latter instance, certain cases—in which the single member is in doubt, in which there is a split opinion, or in which the case is otherwise particularly complex—the panel may refer the matter to the entire board.

The course of the hearing itself is variable, ranging from a few cursory questions to, more rarely, a full-scale hearing with witnesses, lawyers, and evidence for or against release subject to adversary examination. Some boards may hear only a few inmate cases each day; others may handle forty or more applications daily.[21] The National Advisory Commission, strongly supporting careful and deliberate parole hearings, had this to say about the behavioral significance of the hearing:

Development of guidelines for desirable parole hearings should attend to several concerns simultaneously. First, such hearings should provide parole authorities with as much relevant and reliable information about each case as possible. Second, the hearing process itself should carry the hallmark of fairness. Not only should it be a fair determination in substance, but to the extent possible it also should be perceived by the inmate as fair. Third, as far as practicable the hearing should enhance the prospects for an inmate's successful completion of his parole.

To these ends the hearing can make a number of contributions. The manner in which the inmate is interviewed and notified of decisions affecting him can support or undermine respect for the system of justice. Any opportunity for the offender's active participation in decisions can greatly affect his commitment to the plans made. In the final analysis, his commitment is the crucial factor in whether or not these plans will be carried out.[22]

In deciding whether to grant or deny parole, the board does not rely solely on information from the interview, but typically has before it the complete correctional and police file on the prisoner (often including his original presentence investigation) and some form of "parole plan" which has been prepared by the prisoner with the assistance of correctional staff. A typical parole plan contains information as to where he will be employed (or where he reasonably expects to obtain employment) and his other intentions regarding his life-style if returned to the community.

The traditional assumption has been that the prisoner must make some affirmative claims as to why he should be paroled; otherwise parole would be denied.

The drafters of the *Model Penal Code* proposed a reversal of this assumption and suggested criteria to be used by the board:

MODEL PENAL CODE
(Proposed Official Draft, 1962)
Section 305.9. Criteria for Determining Date of First Release on Parole.

1. Whenever the Board of Parole considers the first release of a prisoner who is eligible for release on parole, it shall be the policy of the Board to order his release, unless the Board is of the opinion that his release should be deferred because:

 a. there is substantial risk that he will not conform to the conditions of parole; or

 b. his release at that time would depreciate the seriousness of his crime or promote disrespect for law; or

 c. his release would have a substantially adverse effect on institutional discipline; or

 d. his continued correctional treatment, medical care or vocational or other training in the institution will substantially enhance his capacity to lead a law-abiding life when released at a later date.

2. In making its determination regarding a prisoner's release on parole, it shall be the policy of the Board of Parole to take into account each of the following factors:

 a. the prisoner's personality, including his maturity, stability, sense of responsibility and any apparent development in his personality which may promote or hinder his conformity to law;

 b. the adequacy of the prisoner's parole plan;

 c. the prisoner's ability and readiness to assume obligations and undertake responsibilities;

 d. the prisoner's intelligence and training;

 e. the prisoner's family status and whether he has relatives who display an interest in him, or whether he has other close and constructive associations in the community;

 f. the prisoner's employment history, his occupational skills, and the stability of his past employment;

 g. the type of residence, neighborhood or community in which the prisoner plans to live;

 h. the prisoner's past use of narcotics, or past habitual and excessive use of alcohol;

 i. the prisoner's mental or physical makeup, including any disability or handicap which may affect his conformity to law;

 j. the prisoner's prior criminal record, including the nature and circumstances, recency and frequency of previous offenses;

SELECTED PAROLE HEARING PRACTICES OF
51* STATE AND FEDERAL PAROLE BOARDS: FELONY OFFENDERS
JANUARY 1972

	NUMBER OF BOARDS	
SELECTED PRACTICE	YES	NO
Counsel permitted at hearing	21	30
Inmate permitted to present witnesses	17	34
Reasons for decision recorded	11	40
Verbatim record of proceedings made	20	31

* Georgia, Hawaii, and Texas not included since no hearings
  are conducted in these jurisdictions.

Vincent O'Leary and Joan Nuffield, *The Organization of Parole
Systems in the United States*, 2nd ed. (Hackensack, N.J.:
National Council on Crime and Delinquency, 1972), p. xxxiv.

k. the prisoner's attitude toward law and authority;
l. the prisoner's conduct in the institution, including particularly
whether he has taken advantage of the opportunities for self-
improvement afforded by the institutional program, whether he has
been punished for misconduct within six months prior to his hearing
or reconsideration for parole release, whether he has forfeited any
reductions of term during his period of imprisonment, and whether
such reductions have been restored at the time of hearing or reconsideration;
m. the prisoner's conduct and attitude during any previous experience of probation or parole and the recency of such experience.

DUE PROCESS AT THE PAROLE HEARING. The traditional discretionary power of parole authorities to grant or deny release has come under vigorous
attack in recent years, primarily on the ground that boards act arbitrarily and
capriciously and do not follow proper forms of due process and procedural
regularity in their hearings. For these reasons some critics have called for
abolition of parole.[23] More commonly, prisoners have sought by the appellate
process to alter the nature of parole hearings, and to curb the discretion of parole
boards. Challenges to denial of parole have raised a number of issues and
demands: 1) parole boards must consider only proper and relevant information
in making their decisions, and this information should be available to the
inmate; 2) reasons for denial of parole must be given and be appealable;

347

Parole Outcome for 60,202 Offenders Convicted of Five Property Crimes, According to Time Served Before Release and Prior Prison Record: Age Adjusted, One Year Follow-up

OFFENSE CATEGORIES	NUMBER	PERCENT FAVORABLE OUTCOME BY TIME SERVED PENTILES				
		FIRST	SECOND	THIRD	FOURTH	FIFTH
NO PRIOR NONPRISON SENTENCES						
Auto theft	1,454	76.1	73.6	73.8	68.4	64.1
(months served)		(0–7)	(8–10)	(11–14)	(15–21)	(22–394)
Check offense	2,482	73.4	71.8	75.3	73.5	65.1
(months served)		(0–7)	(8–10)	(11–14)	(15–21)	(22–230)
Burglary	8,487	81.5	79.7	79.1	75.2	75.9
(months served)		(0–7)	(8–11)	(12–16)	(17–25)	(26–374)
Larceny	2,755	81.7	81.1	81.1	79.7	76.2
(months served)		(0–6)	(7–9)	(10–12)	(13–20)	(21–267)
Fraud	335	88.6	84.7	85.6	86.6	76.8
(months served)		(0–6)	(7–9)	(10–12)	(13–19)	(20–108)
Overall*	15,513	79.8	78.4	78.4	75.4	73.0
PRIOR NONPRISON SENTENCES						
Auto theft	4,285	64.5	65.7	62.5	58.9	63.3
(months served)		(0–7)	(8–11)	(12–16)	(17–24)	(25–231)
Check offense	8,493	66.3	66.1	66.3	62.8	60.4
(months served)		(0–8)	(9–12)	(13–17)	(18–25)	(26–281)
Burglary	23,790	70.7	69.3	68.3	69.3	69.0
(months served)		(0–9)	(10–13)	(14–19)	(20–30)	(31–494)
Larceny	7,448	76.4	72.6	74.3	69.7	66.0
(months served)		(0–7)	(8–11)	(12–15)	(16–23)	(24–362)
Fraud	673	71.1	74.3	77.0	79.6	71.6
(months served)		(0–7)	(8–10)	(11–14)	(15–22)	(23–241)
Overall*	44,689	70.2	68.9	68.5	67.3	66.3

* The results reported in the rows labeled "Overall" were obtained by combining subjects from each offense category based on the time served pentile assignments for their respective offenses.

Don M. Gottfredson, M. G. Neithercutt, Joan Nuffield, and Vincent O'Leary, *Four Thousand Lifetimes: A Study of Time Served and Parole Outcomes* (Davis, Calif.: National Council on Crime and Delinquency, June 1973), p. 21.

3) prisoners should have a right to representation by counsel at parole hearing; and 4) prisoners should be allowed to present witnesses in their own behalf and to cross-examine hostile witnesses.

The traditional response of appellate courts to such demands was to hold them inappropriate under their usual "hands-off" policy with respect to correctional determinations. For example, in the early 1960s a prisoner in Wisconsin who was denied parole claimed unequal protection of the law and brought action against paroling authorities, requesting that they be ordered to "show cause" why his case was different from other lifers convicted of similar offenses who were paroled. In denying his request, the Wisconsin Supreme Court stated:

The gist of petitioner's claim illustrates the virtual impossibility of a meaningful judicial review of refusal of parole. . . . He alleges that he "has been arbitrarily and capriciously" denied equal parole consideration given other 'lifers' who have served less time and whose rehabilitative efforts do not surpass petitioners own; that numerous 'lifers' have been paroled whose rehabilitative efforts are questionable and whose criminal records far exceed the petitioner's own. He claims that he has been denied equal protection under the law. No sound determination could be made concerning those allegations without a detailed knowledge of many cases and the factors which had motivated the parole board and director of the department to exercise their power in the manner they did in each.

The foregoing considerations lead us to the conclusion that a prisoner's interest in parole is not a legal right or privilege and that the department's refusal to parole is not a decision reviewable under Sec. 227.15 ff., Stats.[24]

Over the next decade, the access of prisoners to appellate courts expanded rapidly and the "hands-off" doctrine as a general court stance was abandoned.[25] As we shall see, appellate courts, including the U.S. Supreme Court, have recently intervened in the parole process where *revocation* of parole is involved,[26] but the situation remains much the same today as it did in the early 1960s with respect to requirement of due process at parole *grant* hearings. Not long ago a Federal Court of Appeals considered the following petitioner demands: 1) notice of charges, including a substantial summary of the evidence and reports before the Board; 2) a fair hearing, including the right to counsel, to cross-examination and confrontation, and to present favorable evidence and compel the attendance of favorable witnesses; and 3) a specification of the grounds and underlying facts upon which the determination is based. In affirming the decision of the district court which denied the prisoner's petition, the Court of Appeals commented as follows on various procedural aspects of the entire parole release process:

349

PAROLE OUTCOME FOR 30,908 OFFENDERS CONVICTED OF FIVE CRIMES AGAINST PERSONS, ACCORDING TO TIME SERVED BEFORE FIRST RELEASE AND PRIOR PRISON RECORD: AGE ADJUSTED, ONE YEAR FOLLOW-UP

OFFENSE CATEGORIES	NUMBER	PERCENT FAVORABLE OUTCOME BY TIME SERVED PENTILES				
		FIRST	SECOND	THIRD	FOURTH	FIFTH
NO PRIOR NONPRISON SENTENCES						
Armed robbery	3,450	81.8	84.0	85.6	83.9	83.2
(months served)		(0–14)	(15–23)	(24–35)	(36–58)	(59–449)
Aggravated assault	1,812	86.8	87.5	87.0	84.3	85.7
(months served)		(0–6)	(7–11)	(12–18)	(19–31)	(32–312)
Forcible rape	886	90.3	87.2	87.3	90.5	86.0
(months served)		(0–15)	(16–32)	(33–59)	(60–108)	(109–496)
Manslaughter	863	96.9	94.0	92.6	94.9	90.6
(months served)		(0–9)	(10–15)	(16–23)	(24–39)	(40–278)
Homicide	3,311	94.7	93.0	93.9	95.4	90.0
(months served)		(0–21)	(22–44)	(45–79)	(80–124)	(125–637)
Overall*	10,322	88.8	88.6	89.2	89.1	86.7
PRIOR NONPRISON SENTENCES						
Armed robbery	8,851	73.2	71.8	73.6	75.0	75.1
(months served)		(0–17)	(18–27)	(28–41)	(42–63)	(64–537)
Aggravated assault	4,487	77.6	78.0	79.9	77.5	74.8
(months served)		(0–6)	(7–12)	(13–19)	(20–30)	(31–396)
Forcible rape	1,480	83.6	79.4	76.6	81.4	83.0
(months served)		(0–23)	(24–40)	(41–62)	(63–105)	(106–455)
Manslaughter	1,030	86.5	84.6	86.7	84.2	80.9
(months served)		(0–10)	(11–16)	(17–26)	(27–45)	(46–275)
Homicide	4,738	88.3	87.9	87.3	89.6	86.5
(months served)		(0–23)	(24–42)	(43–71)	(72–120)	(121–720)
Overall*	20,586	79.5	78.2	79.0	79.7	78.2

* The results reported in the rows labeled "Overall" were obtained by combining subjects from each offense category based on the time served pentile assignments for their respective offenses.

Don M. Gottfredson, M. G. Neithercutt, Joan Nuffield, and Vincent O'Leary. *Four Thousand Lifetimes: A Study of Time Served and Parole Outcomes* (Davis, Calif.: National Council on Crime and Delinquency, June 1973), p. 23.

. . .

On the erroneous assumption that the Board's determination of whether the prisoner should be paroled is an adversary proceeding, the complaint alleges that the Board fails to give appellant "notice of charges" against him and demands that such notice be furnished.

There are no "charges" or accusations against appellant. Nor is the Board necessarily called upon, in deciding whether he should be released on parole, to resolve disputed issues of fact, which might be the occasion for use of skills associated with lawyers, judges and the judicial process.

The Board's function is a different one. It must make the broad determination of whether rehabilitation of the prisoner and the interests of society generally would best be served by permitting him to serve his sentence beyond the confines of prison walls rather than by being continued in physical confinement. In making that determination the Board is not restricted by rules of evidence or procedures developed for the purpose of determining legal or factual issues. It must consider many factors of a nonlegal nature, such as psychiatric reports with respect to the prisoner, his mental and moral attitudes, his vocational education and training, the manner in which he has used his recreation time, his physical and emotional health, his intrapersonal relations with prison staff and other inmates, his habits, and the nature and extent of community resources that will be available to him upon his release, including the environment to which he plans to return.

Without suggesting that legal counsel or a social worker could not render any assistance at all with respect to the numerous facets of the picture before the Board, the problem to be resolved is not one which usually demands the traditional skills, training and expertise of legal counsel. Far more important is an understanding of the numerous other factors we have mentioned, which have to do with medicine, psychiatry, criminology, penology, psychology, and human relations.[27]

While the legal requirements concerning hearing procedures have not changed significantly, there have been some modifications in practices of many boards. According to the survey of parole decision making referred to above, about 40 percent of all parole boards now allow inmates to be represented by counsel at parole hearings, and about one-third permit inmates to present witnesses in their behalf. Forty percent now inform the inmate directly of their decisions as to release or denial (a major change from past practice, which was to inform the prisoner of the results of the hearing in writing at a later date), but only some 20 percent of the boards record reasons for their decisions.[28]

351

Mandatory Release

Most jurisdictions today allow prison inmates to earn a reduction in sentence for good behavior. "Good time" statutes generally express a formula by which a sentence is reduced by a specified number of days or weeks for each month served. Some states have sliding scales which increase the amount of reduction each year so that prisoners with very long sentences may earn as much as six months good time for every year served after the first five.

The primary purpose of good time allowance is institutional control, for it gives hope of earlier release to inmates who conform with prison regulations. However, another purpose is to provide supervised reentry into the community of offenders who, for whatever reasons, were not paroled, for mandatory release usually requires the prisoner to agree to street supervision until his maximum sentence expires. Historically, good time was given by prison officials only to inmates who demonstrated good behavior, but for the most part good time now is automatically calculated for all prisoners, though it can be taken away, in whole or part, for misbehavior.

Depending upon statutes in each jurisdiction, good time reduces the minimum sentence, the maximum sentence, or both. When taken off the minimum it simply makes the prisoner eligible for parole at an earlier date. But good time taken from the maximum fixes a mandatory release date at which time the prisoner must be released, subject, however, to supervision and the rules of parole until expiration of his court-imposed or statutory maximum. Mandatory release has been called "parole-of-right" to distinguish it from parole granted at the discretion of a parole board. Like a parolee, an offender on mandatory release can be revoked and returned to prison to complete his full sentence.

Persons sentenced to life imprisonment are not eligible for mandatory release, but good time provisions may affect them too. In most jurisdictions a life sentence is translated into a minimum term of years, generally from twenty to thirty, and lifers may earn good time from this minimum, thereby becoming eligible for parole at some earlier date. For example, in Wisconsin a life sentence is interpreted to be twenty years, and a statute provides a formula for calculation of good time for sentences over five years. The formula is: one-half the sentence, plus one year and three months. This means that Wisconsin lifers become eligible for parole (but not mandatory release) in eleven years, three months.

Executive Clemency: Commutation and Pardon

The governor of any state, and, of course, the President of the United States, has power to pardon any prisoner in his jurisdiction or to reduce his sentence, making him eligible for parole. Sometimes pardon or commutation of sentence is made on the executive's own motion, but more commonly a prisoner files a formal petition with the governor who, if it seems warranted, may order the parole board or correctional authorities to investigate the case and make recommendations.

For the nation as a whole, pardon is not a major method of prisoner release. In most states only a handful of inmates may be granted executive clemency in any year.[29] However, in some places, as in Texas, executive intervention is much more common, possibly because of relatively long jury-imposed sentences.

REVOCATION

As we have seen, inmates released on parole or mandatory release as well as offenders placed on probation by the court are subject to supervision by field agents and must agree to abide by various rules and conditions. Violation of these or commission of a new crime makes the offender subject to revocation with subsequent incarceration or reincarceration. There is nothing automatic about revocation, which is a discretionary decision initiated in the first instance by the supervising probation or parole field agent. In some places the revocation process begins with the field agent seeking an administrative warrant charging the offender with a violation. Other jurisdictions use a written report of alleged violations, with the offender often jailed on a "hold order" until final determination can be made.

Revocation of probation is a judicial function, since probationers are still under court jurisdiction. When an infraction is alleged the probationer is returned to the court for a hearing and for the imposition or execution of sentence.

In general, revocation of probation, parole, or mandatory release requires a more elaborate procedure than is necessary for initial selection for community sentence. This is consistent with a general tradition in administrative law surrounding the removal of a privilege once granted, and in which the holder has a vested interest, with more procedural safeguards than are required for denial of the privilege in the first instance.[30] In an analogous manner, a university may deny a student admission in a much more cursory fashion than it may use later to expel him.

This was by no means always the case. In the past, appellate courts often adopted the familiar "hands-off" stance with regard to revocation, just as they did with all matters of correctional discretion. In many jurisdictions, probationers and prisoners were held to have no right to challenge most postconviction determinations including revocation of probation or parole.[31] This situation has changed markedly since the mid-1960s.

In 1966 the Supreme Court of the State of Washington considered a petition from a probationer whose probation was revoked without what he alleged to be a proper hearing conforming to principles of procedural due process, including the right to be represented by counsel. The state court rejected his petition, saying:

No appeal, or a petition for a writ of *habeas corpus,* will be successful in this court where the question is whether the probationer was accorded his constitutional due process rights at the hearing. He simply has none.[32]

The case was appealed, and the U.S. Supreme Court granted *certiorari:*

MEMPA V. RHAY
389 U.S. 128 (1967)
MR. JUSTICE MARSHALL delivered the opinion of the Court.

These consolidated cases raise the question of the extent of the right to counsel at the time of sentencing where the sentencing has been deferred subject to probation.

Petitioner Jerry Douglas Mempa was convicted in the Spokane County Superior Court on June 17, 1959, of the offense of "joy-riding," Wash. Rev. Code, Sec. 9.54.020. This conviction was based on his plea of guilty entered with the advice of court-appointed counsel. He was then placed on probation for two years on the condition, inter alia, that he first spend 30 days in the county jail, and the imposition of sentence was deferred pursuant to Wash. Rev. Code, Sec. 9.95.200, Sec. 9.95.210.

About four months later the Spokane County prosecuting attorney moved to have petitioner's probation revoked on the ground that he had been involved in a burglary on September 15, 1959. A hearing was held in the Spokane County Superior Court on October 23, 1959. Petitioner Mempa, who was 17 years old at the time, was accompanied to the hearing by his stepfather. He was not represented by counsel and was not asked whether he wished to have counsel appointed for him. Nor was any inquiry made concerning the appointed counsel who had previously represented him.

At the hearing Mempa was asked if it was true that he had been involved in the alleged burglary and he answered in the affirmative. A probation officer testified without cross-examination that according to his information petitioner had been involved in the burglary and had previously denied participation in it. Without asking petitioner if he had anything to say or any evidence to supply, the court immediately entered an order revoking petitioner's probation and then sentenced him to 10 years in the penitentiary, but stated that it would recommend to the parole board that Mempa be required to serve only a year.
. . .

The State, however, argues that the petitioners were sentenced at the time they were originally placed on probation and that the imposition of sentence following probation revocation is, in effect, a mere formality constituting part of the probation revocation proceeding. It is true that sentencing in Washington offers fewer opportunities for the exercise of judicial discretion than in many other jurisdictions. The applicable statute requires the trial judge in all cases to sentence the convicted person to the maximum term provided by law for the offense of which he was convicted. Wash. Rev. Code, Sec. 9.95.010. The actual determination of the length of time to be served is to be made by the Board of Prison Terms and Paroles within six months after the convicted person is admitted to prison. Wash. Rev. Code Sec. 9.95.040.

On the other hand, the sentencing judge is required by statute, together with the prosecutor, to furnish the Board with a recommendation as to the length of time that the person should serve, in addition to supplying it with various information about the circumstances of the crime and the character of the individual. Wash. Rev. Code Sec. 9.95.030. We were informed during oral argument that the Board places considerable weight on these recommendations, although it is in no way bound by them. Obviously to the extent such recommendations are influential in determining the resulting sentence, the necessity for the aid of counsel in marshaling the facts, introducing evidence of mitigating circumstances and in general aiding and assisting the defendant to present his case as to sentence is apparent.

. . .

Without undertaking to catalog the various situations in which a lawyer could be of substantial assistance to a defendant in such a case, it can be reiterated that a plea of guilty might well be improperly obtained by the promise to have a defendant placed on the very probation the revocation of which furnishes the occasion for desiring to withdraw the plea. An uncounseled defendant might very likely be unaware of this opportunity.

The two foregoing factors assume increased significance when it is considered that the eventual imposition of sentence on the prior plea of guilty is based on the alleged commission of offenses for which the accused is never tried.

In sum, we do not question the authority of the State of Washington to provide for a deferred sentencing procedure coupled with its probation provisions. Indeed, it appears to be an enlightened step forward. All we decide here is that a lawyer must be afforded at this proceeding whether it be labeled a revocation of probation or a deferred sentencing. We assume that counsel appointed for the purpose of the trial or guilty plea would not be unduly burdened by being requested to follow through at the deferred sentencing stage of the proceeding. Reversed and remanded.

The *Mempa* decision affirmed the right to representation at sentencing—in this case "deferred sentencing"—and to probation revocation generally. Subsequent appellate court decisions generally applied the *Mempa* requirement of hearing and counsel to all forms of probation revocation, in addition to the somewhat unique procedures found in the State of Washington. However, the question of whether this decision was, or would be, generalized to *parole* revocation remained open. Shortly after the *Mempa* decision, Professor Fred Cohen put the question: "The most fundamental question . . . is whether *Mempa* is to be regarded as simply a rearguard mopping-up operation or whether it is an important step designed to bring lawyers and the rule of law to the correctional process."[33] In general, the answer is the *Mempa* was more than a rearguard decision. Though the process is by no means complete, both probationers and parolees have been extended much fuller rights to due process by later court decisions.

Until recently, procedures used in revocation of parolees varied considerably from jurisdiction to jurisdiction.[34] Probationers still under court authority, were generally returned to the judge for a revocation determination even before the *Mempa* ruling, which merely fleshed out the requirements for this hearing. However, parolees, and persons on mandatory release, are no longer under court jurisdiction, and revocation orders were, and continue to be, issued by parole authorities, not by a judge.

The parole revocation process begins when a parole officer discovers, or has reason to believe, a parolee has violated a rule or condition, or when the parolee is arrested for a new crime. The field agent makes an initial determination as to whether the infraction or arrest is serious enough to call for revocation. If he makes a positive finding, his decision is usually referred to a supervising parole officer for ratification. Then, depending upon requirements in the particular jurisdiction, an administrative warrant sufficient to detain the parolee may be sought from a parole board member or, if this is not required, the supervising field agent may issue a hold order to detain the parolee until a revocation hearing can be held.

Although there have been marked variations both in statutory requirements and common practices with regard to parole revocation hearings, in general most jurisdictions provided at least a nominal revocation hearing before a parole commissioner or before the entire parole board. There have been some exceptions; a number of appellate courts in the past held that no hearing is required if the parolee admitted the violation or if he was convicted of a new crime.[35]

Until 1972 the logistics of parole revocation differed markedly from probation revocation. The common practice in many jurisdictions was for a parolee to be taken into custody when a revocation order was issued, returned from the community to a prison where, at some later date—days, weeks, or even months later—a hearing into the appropriateness of his revocation was held. This worked an obvious hardship on any parolee where it turned out that revocation was inappropriate, inaccurate, or otherwise wrongful. In many ways it was comparable to denial of bail to a person arrested for a crime, or lack of prehearing release to an alleged probation violator. But in the case of return to prison, the logistics of the situation were often more extreme. Removal from the community to the prison, even for short duration, not only meant interruption of the parolee's family life and employment, but, since prisons are often distant from the scene of violation, serious problems were created should witnesses, complainants, or others, including local counsel, be required or desirable at the hearing. All this was changed by the Supreme Court in 1972:

MORRISSEY V. BREWER
408 U.S. 471 (1972)

MR. CHIEF JUSTICE BURGER. Petitioner asserts he received no hearing prior to revocation of his parole.

The parole officer's report on which the Board of Parole acted shows that petitioner's parole was revoked on the basis of information that he had violated the conditions of parole by buying a car under an assumed name and operating it without permission, giving false statements to police concerning his address and insurance company after a minor accident, and obtaining credit under an assumed name and failing to report his place of residence to his parole officer. The report states that the officer interviewed Morrissey, and that he could not explain why he did not contact his parole officer despite his effort to excuse this on the ground that he had been sick. Further, the report asserts that Morrissey admitted buying the car and obtaining credit under an assumed name and also admitted being involved in the accident. The parole officer recommended that his parole be revoked because of "his continual violating of his parole rules."

In practice not every violation of parole conditions automatically leads to revocation. Typically a parolee will be counseled to abide by the conditions of parole, and the parole officer ordinarily does not take steps to have parole revoked unless he thinks that the violations are serious and continuing so as to indicate that the parolee is not adjusting properly and cannot be counted on to avoid antisocial activity. The broad discretion accorded the parole officer is also inherent in some of the quite vague conditions, such as the typical requirement that the parolee avoid "undesirable" associations or correspondence. Cf. *Arciniega* v. *Freeman*, 404 U.S. 4 (1970). Yet revocation of parole is not an unusual phenomenon, affecting only a few parolees. It has been

357

estimated that 35-45 percent of all parolees are subjected to revocation and return to prison. Sometimes revocation occurs when the parolee is accused of another crime; it is often preferred to a new prosecution because of the procedural ease of recommitting the individual on the basis of a lesser showing by the State.

Implicit in the system's concern with parole violations is the notion that the parolee is entitled to retain his liberty as long as he substantially abides by the conditions of his parole.

If a parolee is returned to prison, he often receives no credit for the time "served" on parole. Thus the returnee may face a potential of substantial imprisonment.

Release of the parolee before the end of his prison sentence is made with the recognition that with many prisoners there is a risk that they will not be able to live in society without committing additional antisocial acts. Given the previous conviction and the proper imposition of conditions, the State has an overwhelming interest in being able to return the individual to imprisonment without the burden of a new adversary criminal trial if in fact he has failed to abide by the conditions of his parole. Yet the State has no interest in revoking parole without some informal procedural guarantees.

In analyzing what is due, we see two important stages in the typical process of parole revocation.

a. *Arrest of Parolee and Preliminary Hearing.* The first stage occurs when the parolee is arrested and detained, usually at the direction of his parole officer. The second occurs when parole is formally revoked.

In our view due process requires that after the arrest, the determination that reasonable grounds exist for revocation of parole should be made by someone not directly involved in the case. The officer directly involved in making recommendations cannot always have complete objectivity in evaluating them. This independent officer need not be a judicial officer.

It will be sufficient, therefore, in the parole revocation context, if an evaluation of whether reasonable cause exists to believe that conditions of parole have been violated is made by someone such as a parole officer other than the one who has made the report of parole violations or has recommended revocation.

With respect to the preliminary hearing before this officer, the parolee should be given notice that the hearing will take place and that its purpose is to determine whether there is probable cause to believe he has committed a parole violation. The notice should state what parole violations have been alleged. At the hearings the parolee may appear and speak in his own behalf; he may bring letters, documents, or individuals who can give relevant information to the hearing officer. On request of the parolee, persons who have given adverse information on which parole revocation is to be based are to be made available for questioning in his presence. However, if the hearing officer determines that the informant would be subjected to risk of harm if his identity were disclosed, he need not be subjected to confrontation and cross-examination.

The hearing officer shall have the duty of making a summary, or digest, of what transpires at the hearing in terms of the responses of the parolee and the substance of the documents or evidence given in support of parole revocation and of the parolee's position. Based on the information before him, the officer should determine whether there is probable cause to hold the parolee for the final decision of the parole board on revocation. Such a determination would be sufficient to warrant the parolee's continued detention and return to the state correctional institution pending the final decision. No interest would be served by formalism in this process: informality will not lessen the utility of this inquiry in reducing the risk of error.

b. *The Revocation Hearing.* There must also be an opportunity for a hearing if it is desired by the parolee, prior to the final decision on revocation by the parole authority. This hearing must be the basis for more than determining probable cause; it must lead to a final evaluation of any contested relevant facts and consideration of whether the facts as determined warrant revocation. The parolee must have an opportunity to be heard and to show, if he can, that he did not violate the conditions, or, if he did, that circumstances in mitigation suggest the violation does not warrant revocation. The revocation hearing must be tendered within a reasonable time after the parolee is taken into custody. A lapse of two months, as the State suggests occurs in some cases, would not appear to be unreasonable.

We cannot write a code of procedure; that is the responsibility of each state. Most states have done so by legislation, others by judicial decision usually on due process grounds. Our task is limited to deciding the minimum requirements of due process. They include a) written notice of the claimed violations of parole; b) disclosure to the parolee of evidence against him; c) opportunity to be heard in person and to present witnesses and documentary evidence; d) the right to confront and cross-examine adverse witnesses (unless the hearing officer specifically finds good cause for not allowing confrontation); e) a "neutral and detached" hearing body such as a traditional parole board, members of which need not be judicial officers or lawyers; and f) a written statement by the factfinders as to the evidence relied on and reasons for revoking parole. We emphasize there is no thought to equate this second stage of parole revocation to a criminal prosecution in any sense; it is a narrow inquiry; the process should be flexible enough to consider evidence including letters, affidavits, and other material that would not be admissible in an adversary criminal trial.

We do not reach or decide the question whether the parolee is entitled to the assistance of retained counsel or to appointed counsel if he is indigent.

We reverse and remand to the Court of Appeals for further proceedings consistent with this opinion.

The full operational significance of the mandates of the *Morrissey* decision, particularly the requirement for a two-stage procedure involving an on-site factual determination prior to a formal revocation hearing, remain to be assessed. There is limited evidence from some states which employed on-site hearings prior to *Morrissey* that the parolee is less likely to be revoked if a parole board member meets in the community with both the parolee and the parole officer before the decision is made to return him to prison. As pointed out by Vincent O'Leary and Joan Nuffield, "Once removed from the community and returned to an institution, even for the purpose of a hearing, the result is more likely to be to sustain a revocation of parole than to overturn it."[36]

As is clear from the *Morrissey* decision, the court pointedly avoided the issue of whether parolees have a right to counsel at revocation proceedings, thus leaving a possible distinction between parole and probation revocation requirements as mandated by *Mempa*. Distinctions were lessened, however, by a 1973 decision of the U.S. Supreme Court in a case involving probation revocation. Here the probationer was not afforded a hearing, presumably because a prison sentence had been imposed with execution suspended rather than, as in *Mempa*, served under "deferred" sentencing. Although this case involved probation revocation, the Court found no "difference relevant to the guarantee of due process" between this and parole revocation. The decision is:

GAGNON V. SCARPELLI
411 U.S. 778 (1973)
MR. JUSTICE POWELL delivered the opinion of the Court.

Respondent, Gerald Scarpelli, pleaded guilty in July, 1965, to a charge of armed robbery in Wisconsin. The trial judge sentenced him to 15 years' imprisonment, but suspended the sentence and placed him on probation for seven years in the custody of the Wisconsin Department of Public Welfare ("the Department").

On August 6, respondent was apprehended by Illinois police, who had surprised him and one Fred Kleckner, Jr., in the course of the burglary of a house. After being apprised of his constitutional rights, respondent admitted that he and Kleckner had broken into the house for the purpose of stealing merchandise or money, although he now asserts that his statement was made under duress and is false. Probation was revoked by the Wisconsin Department on September 1, without a hearing.

The stated grounds for revocation were that:
1. [Scarpelli] has associated with known criminals, in direct violation of his probation regulations and his supervising agent's instructions;
2. [Scarpelli] while associating with a known criminal, namely Fred Kleckner, Jr., was involved in, and arrested for, a burglary . . . in Dearfield, Illinois. App., p. 20.

On September 4, 1965, he was incarcerated in the Wisconsin State Reformatory at Green Bay to begin serving the 15 years to which he had been sentenced by the trial judge. At no time was he afforded a hearing.

Some three years later, on December 16, 1968, respondent applied for a writ of habeas corpus. On the merits, the District Court held that revocation without a hearing and counsel was a denial of due process. 317 F. Supp. 72 (ED Wis. 1970). The Court of Appeals affirmed *sub nom. Gunsolus* v. *Gagnon,* 454 F. 2d. 416 (CA7 1971), and we granted certiorari. 408 U.S. 921 (1972).

[I]n *Morrissey* v. *Brewer* we held the revocation of parole is not a part of a criminal prosecution.

Even though the revocation of parole is not a part of the criminal prosecution, we held that the loss of liberty entailed is a serious deprivation requiring that the parolee be accorded due process. Specifically, we held that a parolee is entitled to two hearings, one a preliminary hearing at the time of his arrest and detention to determine whether there is probable cause to believe that he has committed a violation of his parole and the other a somewhat more comprehensive hearing prior to the making of the final revocation decision.

Petitioner does not contend that there is any difference relevant to the guarantee of due process between the revocation of parole and the revocation of probation, nor do we perceive one.

Accordingly, we hold that a probationer, like a parolee, is entitled to a preliminary and a final revocation hearing, under the conditions specified in *Morrissey* v. *Brewer.*

The second, and more difficult, question posed by this case is whether an indigent probationer or parolee has a due process right to be represented by appointed counsel at these hearings.

In *Morrissey,* we recognized that the revocation decision has two analytically distinct components:

"The first step in a revocation decision, thus involves a wholly retrospective factual question: whether the parolee has in fact acted in violation of one or more conditions of his parole. Only if it is determined that the parolee did violate the conditions does the second question arise: should the parolee be recommitted to prison or should other steps be taken to protect society and improve chances of rehabilitation?"

When the officer's view of the probationer's or parolee's conduct differs in

361

this fundamental way from the latter's own view, due process requires that the difference be resolved before revocation becomes final. Both the probationer or parolee and the State have interests in the accurate finding of fact and the informed use of discretion, the probationer or parolee to insure that his liberty is not unjustifiably taken away and the State to make certain that it is neither unnecessarily interrupting a successful effort at rehabilitation nor imprudently prejudicing the safety of the community.

It was to serve all of these interests that *Morrissey* mandated preliminary and final revocation hearings.

[T]he effectiveness of the rights guaranteed by *Morrissey* may in some circumstances depend on the use of skills which the probationer or parolee is unlikely to possess. Despite the informal nature of the proceedings and the absence of technical rules of procedure or evidence, the unskilled or uneducated probationer or parolee may well have difficulty in presenting his version of a disputed set of facts where the presentation requires the examining or cross-examining of witnesses or the offering or dissecting of complex documentary evidence.

By the same token, we think that the Court of Appeals erred in accepting respondent's contention that the State is under a constitutional duty to provide counsel for indigents in all probation or parole revocation cases.

The role of the hearing body itself, aptly described in *Morrissey* as being "predictive and discretionary" as well as fact finding, may become more akin to that of a judge at a trial, and less attuned to the rehabilitative needs of the individual probationer or parolee. In the greater self-consciousness of its quasi-judicial role, the hearing body may be less tolerant of marginal deviant behavior and feel more pressure to re-incarcerate rather than continue non-punitive rehabilitation. Certainly, the decision-making process will be prolonged, and the financial cost to the State—for appointed counsel, counsel for the State, a longer record, and the possibility of judicial review—will not be insubstantial.

[T]here are critical differences between criminal trials and probation or parole revocation hearings, and both society and the probationer or parolee have stakes in preserving these differences.

In a criminal trial, the State is represented by a prosecutor; formal rules of evidence are in force; a defendant enjoys a number of procedural rights which may be lost if not timely raised; and, in a jury trial, a defendant must make a presentation understandable to untrained jurors. In short, a criminal trial under our system is an adversary proceeding with its own unique characteristics. In a revocation hearing, on the other hand, the State is represented not by a prosecutor but by a parole officer with the orientation   described above; formal procedures and rules of evidence are not employed; and the members of the hearing body are familiar with the problems and practice of probation or parole. The need for counsel at revocation hearings derives not from the invariable attributes of those hearings but rather from the peculiarities of particular cases.

We thus find no justification for a new inflexible constitutional rule with respect to the requirement of counsel. Although the presence and participation of counsel will probably be both undesirable and constitutionally unnecessary in most revocation hearings, there will remain certain cases in which fundamental fairness—the touchstone of due process—will require that the State provide at its expense counsel for indigent probationers or parolees.

It is neither possible nor prudent to attempt to formulate a precise and detailed set of guidelines. Presumptively, it may be said that counsel should be provided in cases where, after being informed of his right to request counsel, the probationer or parolee makes such a request, based on a timely and colorable claim i) that he has not committed the alleged violation of the conditions upon which he is at liberty; or ii) that, even if the violation is a matter of public record or is uncontested, there are substantial reasons which justified or mitigated the violation and make revocation inappropriate and that the reasons are complex or otherwise difficult to develop or present. In passing on a request for the appointment of counsel, the responsible agency also should consider, especially in doubtful cases, whether the probationer appears to be capable of speaking effectively for himself. In every case in which a request for counsel at a preliminary or final hearing is refused, the grounds for refusal should be stated succinctly in the record.

We return to the facts of the present case. As to whether the State must provide counsel, respondent's admission to having committed another serious crime creates the very sort of situation in which counsel need not ordinarily be provided. But because of respondent's subsequent assertions regarding that admission, see *ante,* we conclude that the failure of the Department to provide respondent with the assistance of counsel should be re-examined in light of this opinion. The general guidelines outlined above should be applied in the first instance by those charged with conducting the revocation hearing.

One problem with parole revocation practices that has been rarely addressed is the availability of sanctions short of revocation for infractions of rules. In general, revocation has been handled as an either/or proposition; either the field staff who discover rule infractions do nothing, or they commence full-scale revocation proceedings. The drafters of the *Model Penal Code* suggest some other alternatives:

MODEL PENAL CODE
(Proposed Official Draft, 1962)
Section 305.16. Sanctions Short of Revocation for Violation of Condition of Parole.

1. If the Parole Administrator has reasonable cause to believe that a parolee has violated a condition of parole, he shall notify the Board of Parole, and shall cause the appropriate district parole supervisor to submit the parolee's record to the Board. After consideration of the records submitted, and after such further investigation as it may deem appropriate, the Board may order:

    a. that the parolee receive a reprimand and warning from the Board;

    b. that parole supervision and reporting be intensified;

    c. that reductions for good behavior be forfeited or withheld;

    d. that the parolee be remanded, without revocation of parole, to a residence facility specified in Section 305.14 for such a period and under such supervision or treatment as the Board may deem appropriate;

    e. that the parolee be required to conform to one or more additional conditions of parole which may be imposed in accordance with Section 305.13;

    f. that the parolee be arrested and returned to prison, there to await a hearing to determine whether his parole should be revoked.

The *Model Penal Code* elsewhere suggests that parolees be able to earn "good time" off the remainder of their supervision, much as prisoners earn good time from their maximum sentences.[37] The *Code* further suggests that parolees who no longer require supervision and guidance be granted early discharge from parole if it is not "incompatible with the protection of the public."[38]

Discharge from Sentence

The formal criminal process ends when an offender has successfully completed his sentence, whether in jail, on probation, in prison, or on parole or mandatory release. Normally the "ex-offender's" conviction record remains on file, as does all of the other material and information gathered about him by the court and correctional authorities. Many of the corollary effects of felony conviction, including loss of voting rights, inability to obtain certain licenses or franchises or to enter certain occupations or professions, may persist throughout his lifetime, affecting him for many years after he has served his sentence. And the status of "ex-con" may haunt him forever.

Today some jurisdictions have procedures for restoration of rights lost by conviction.[39] In general, the ex-offender must apply to a court for restoration some time after sentence completion, commonly five years, and cooperate in whatever investigation is ordered by the court. The National Advisory Commission has called for the repeal of some and the modification of other "collateral consequences" of conviction. They propose the following:

Each State should enact by 1975 legislation repealing all mandatory provisions depriving persons convicted of criminal offenses of civil rights or other attributes of citizenship. Such legislation should include:

1. Repeal of all existing provisions by which a person convicted of any criminal offense suffers civil death, corruption of blood, loss of civil rights, or forfeiture of estate or property.

2. Repeal of all restrictions on the ability of a person convicted of a criminal offense to hold and transfer property, enter into contracts, sue and be sued, and hold offices of private trust.

3. Repeal of all mandatory provisions denying persons convicted of a criminal offense the right to engage in any occupation or obtain any license issued by government.

4. Repeal of all statutory provisions prohibiting the employment of ex-offenders by State and local governmental agencies.

Statutory provisions may be retained or enacted that:

1. Restrict or prohibit the right to hold public office during actual confinement.

2. Forfeit public office upon confinement.

3. Restrict the right to serve on juries during actual confinement.

4. Authorize a procedure for the denial of a license or governmental privilege to selected criminal offenders when there is a direct relationship between the offense committed or the characteristics of the offender and the license or privilege sought.

The legislation also should:

1. Authorize a procedure for an ex-offender to have his conviction expunged from the record.

2. Require the restoration of civil rights upon the expiration of sentence.[40]

There is an effort today to do more than simply restore certain specified lost rights to persons who have successfully served their sentences, on the general grounds that the continuing negative effects of convictions work excessive hardship on many persons who are now fully law-abiding. To this end, there are provisions in some places for the "expunging" of all records of those who have successfully adjusted to society. The National Council on Crime and Delinquency proposed a model act in this regard:

MODEL ACT TO AUTHORIZE COURTS TO
ANNUL A RECORD OF CONVICTIONS

The Court in which a conviction of crime has been had may, at the time of discharge of a convicted person from its control, or upon his discharge from imprisonment or parole, or at any time thereafter, enter an order annulling, canceling, and rescinding the record of conviction and disposition, when in the opinion of the Court it would assist in rehabilitation and be consistent with the public welfare. Upon the entry of such order the person against whom the conviction had been entered shall be restored to all civil rights lost or suspended by virtue of the arrest, conviction, or sentence, unless otherwise provided in the order, and shall be treated in all respects as not having been convicted, except that upon conviction of any subsequent crime the prior conviction may be considered by the court in determining the sentence to be imposed.

In any application for employment, license, or other civil right or privilege, or any appearance as a witness, a person may be questioned about previous criminal record only in language such as the following: "Have you ever been arrested for or convicted of a crime which has not been annulled by a court?"

Upon entry of the order of annulment of conviction, the court shall issue to the person in whose favor the order has been entered a certificate stating that his behavior after conviction has warranted the issuance of the order, and that its effect is to annul, cancel, and rescind the record of conviction and disposition.

Nothing in this act shall affect any right of the offender to appeal from his conviction or to rely on it in bar of any subsequent proceedings for the same offense.

In actual practice, procedures for restoration or expungement vary widely across the nation and are of limited success. Some damaging effects of conviction and sentence may be diminished, but the negative status of having been convicted or having been a convict tends to persist throughout the lifetime of the ex-offender.

NOTES

1. President's Commission on Law Enforcement and Administration of Justice, *Task Force Report: Corrections* (Washington, D.C.: U.S. Government Printing Office, 1967), p. 77.

2. See Note, "Equal Protection and the Use of Fines as Penalties for Criminal Offenses," *U. of Ill. Law Forum* 460 (1966); Note, "The Equal Protection Clause and Imprisonment of the Indigent for Non-Payment of Fines," *Mich. Law Review* 64, 938 (1966); Note, "Fines and Fining—An Evaluation," *U. of P. Law Review* 101, 1013 (1953).

3. American Bar Association, *Standards Relating to Sentencing Alternatives and Procedures* (Approved Draft, 1968), Sec. 2.7(b), pp. 120-122.

4. Williams v. Illinois, 399 U.S. 235 (1970) and Tate v. Short, 401 U.S. 395 (1971).

5. Marvin Frankel, *Criminal Sentences* (New York: Hill & Wang, 1972), B. J. George, "An Unsolved Problem: Comparative Sentencing Techniques," *ABA J.* 45, 250 (1959); William P. Rogers, "The Geneva Conference on Crime: Its Significance for American Penology,"—*Fed. Probation* 40 (1955), H. Mannheim, "Comparative Sentencing Practice," *Law and Contem. Prob.* 23, 577 (1958).

6. Federal Bureau of Prisons, *National Prisoner Statistics* (Washington, D.C.: U.S. Department of Justice, 1964). There have been subsequent reports from the Federal Bureau of Prisons, the most recent summaries issued in 1970, but these suffer from lack of total state reporting. For example, in the 1970 report, the Bureau notes that only 33 of the 50 states reported on time or in sufficient detail to have their data included. The Report states: "Since 17 of the 50 state's data are missing, no nationwide or region-wide totals were accumulated." Federal Bureau of Prisons, *National Prisoner Statistics* (1970), p. 2.

7. Advisory Council of Judges of the National Council on Crime and Delinquency, *Model Sentencing Act* (1963), p. 26.

8. President's Commission, *Corrections*, pp. 1-2.

9. See Federal Bureau of Prisons, *National Prisoner Statistics* (1970) and President's Commission, *Corrections*.

10. For an update of a survey on parole rules and conditions see Nat R. Arluke, "A Summary of Parole Rules—Thirteen Years Later," *Crime and Delin.* 15, 267 (1969).

11. American Law Institute, *Model Penal Code,* Proposed Official Draft (1962), Sec. 6.10 (2). The "separate parole term" is opposed, however, by the National Advisory Commission. See National Advisory Commission on Criminal Justice Standards and Goals, *Corrections* (1973), pp. 589-590.

12. President's Commission, *Corrections*, pp. 60-61.

13. See generally, Donald J. Newman, "Court Intervention in the Parole Process," *Albany Law Review* 36, 257 (1972). See also, Fred Cohen, *Legal Norms in Corrections* (Consultant Paper, President's Task Force on Corrections, 1967); Chapter 8, "The Legal Status of Convicted Persons," in President's Commission, *Corrections*, pp. 82-92; Edward L. Kimball and Donald J. Newman, "Judicial Intervention in Correctional Decisions: Threat and Response," *J. Crime and Delin.* 14, 1 (1968).

14. For historical developments of parole see Harry Elmer Barnes and Negley Teeters, *New Horizons in Criminology*, 2nd ed. (New York: Prentice-Hall, 1951); Frederick Moran, "The Origins of Parole." *NPPA* Yearbook (1954), pp. 71-98; Charles Newman, *Sourcebook on Probation, Parole and Pardons,* 2nd ed. (Springfield, Ill.: Charles C Thomas, 1964); Sol Rubin, Henry Weihofen, George Edwards, and Simon Rosenzweig, *The Law of Criminal Corrections* (St. Paul, Minn.: West, 1963), Chapter 11.

15. See cases collected at Annot., *American Law Review* 143, 1473 (1942).

16. See Don M. Gottfredson, M. G. Neithercutt, Joan Nuffield, and Vincent O'Leary, *Four Thousand Lifetimes: A Study of Time Served and Parole Outcomes* (Davis, Calif.: National Council on Crime and Delinquency Research Center, Report, June 1973); See also Daniel Glaser, *The Effectiveness of a Prison and Parole System* (Indianapolis: Bobbs-Merrill, 1964).

17. See generally, Vincent O'Leary and Joan Nuffield, *The Organization of Parole Systems in the United States* (Hackensack, N.J.: National Council on Crime and Delinquency, 1972); See also Vincent O'Leary, "Issues and Trends in Parole Administration in the United States," *Amer. Crim. Law Review* 11, 97 (1972).

18. Although there are 51 jurisdictions, counting the federal system and all states, there are more parole boards. Some states have special boards to make parole decisions about women, others have special boards for sex deviates, narcotics violators, and youthful offenders in addition to "regular" parole boards.

19. Vincent O'Leary and Joan Nuffield, "Parole Decision Making Characteristics: Report of a National Survey," *Crim. Law Bull.* 8, 651, 659 (1972).

20. National Advisory Commission on Criminal Justice Standards and Goals, *Corrections,* 1973, Standard 12.1, pp. 417-419.

21. O'Leary and Nuffield, "Parole Decision Making Characteristics," p. 658.

22. National Advisory Commission, *Corrections,* p. 401.

23. See American Friends Service Committee, *Struggle For Justice* (New York: Hill & Wang, 1971) and *Summary Report on New York Parole* (New York: Citizen's Inquiry on Parole and Criminal Justice, Inc., Mimeo, 1974).

24. Tyler v. State Department of Public Welfare, 19 Wis. 2d 166, 168 (1963).

25. See generally, Goldberg v. Kelly, 397 U.S. 254 (1970); Dixon v. Alabama State Board of Education, 294 F. 2d 150 (5th Cir., 1961), and In re Ruffalo, 390 U.S. 544 (1968). See also, Comment: "Due Process and the Right to a Prior Hearing in Welfare Cases," *Ford. Law Review* 604 (1965) and Witham VanAlstyne, "The Demise of the Right-Privilege Distinction in Constitutional Law," *Harvard Law Review* 81, 1439 (1968).

26. See Morrissey v. Brewer, 408 U.S. 471 (1972). See also, Comment: "Rights v. Results: Quo Vadis Due Process for Hearings in California and the Federal System," *Cal. West. Law Review* 4, 18 (1968).

27. Menechino v. Oswald, 430 F. 2d 403, 407-408 (2nd Cir. 1970).

28. O'Leary and Nuffield, "Parole Decision Making Characteristics," p. 658.

29. See Reed Cozart, "The Benefits of Executive Clemency," *Fed. Probation* 32, 33 (1968).

30. See generally, Charles Reich, "The New Property," *Yale Law J.* 73, 733 (1964); Charles Reich, "Individual Rights and Social Welfare: The Emerging Legal Issues," *Yale Law J.* 74, 1245 (1965) and Goldberg v. Kelly, 397 U.S. 254 (1970).

31. See generally, Note, "Beyond the Ken of the Courts: A Critique of Judicial Refusal to Review the Complaints of Convicts," *Yale Law J.* 72, 506 (1963); Note, "Constitutional Rights of Prisoners. The Developing Law," *U. of P. Law Review* 110, 985 (1962). See also Comment, "Rights v. Results: Quo Vadis Due Process for Parolees?" *Pac. Law J.* 1, 321 (1970).

32. Mempa v. Rhay, 68 Wash. 2d 882, 892 (1966).

33. Fred Cohen, "Sentencing, Probation and the Rehabilitative Ideal: The View from Mempa v. Rhay," *Tex. Law Review* 47, 1 (1968).

34. See Ron Sklar, "Law and Practice in Probation and Parole Revocation Hearings," *J. Crim. Law, Criminology, and Pol. Sci.* 55, 175 (1964).

35. See Savage v. U.S. Parole Board, 422 F. 2d. 1248 (6th Cir. 1970); Boswell v. United States Board of Parole, 388 F. 2d. 467 (D.C. Cir. 1967): United States ex rel Heacock v. Meyers, 251 F. Supp. 773 (E.D. Pa.), Aff'd 367 F. 2d. 583 (3rd Cir. 1966) (per curiam cert. denied Heacock v. Rundle, 386 U.S. 925 (1967). Avrutine v. United States, 313 F. Supp. 19 (D. Conn. 1970); Hughey v. Speaker, 320 F. Supp. 191 (E.D. Pa. 1970).

36. O'Leary and Nuffield, "Parole Decision Making Characteristics," p. 675.

37. American Law Institute, *Model Penal Code,* Proposed Official Draft (1962), Sec. 306.6. See also, President's Commission, *Corrections* (1967), Chapter 8, "The Legal Status of Convicted Persons," pp. 88-92.

38. *Model Penal Code,* Sec. 305.12.

39. See *Model Penal Code,* Sec. 306.6. See also, President's Commission, *Corrections* (1967), Chapter 8, "The Legal Status of Convicted Persons," pp. 88-92.

40. National Advisory Commission, *Corrections,* Standard 16.17, p. 592.

Part Three

Contemporary Issues and Trends in Criminal Justice Administration

In preceding sections, discussion and analysis focused on the structure of the criminal justice system and on the major stages in the decision network that form its process. If nothing more, the material presented should amply demonstrate the complexity of the system. Anyone attempting serious analysis of criminal justice must confront separation of powers of the legislative, executive, judicial, and administrative branches of government, but still be aware of their combined impact. He must also deal with the amorphous but interdependent relationships of many agencies and offices of crime control, with the multiplicity of occasionally conflicting purposes of criminal justice efforts, and with variability in the sequential stages of the process from crime detection to parole revocation. The awesome complexity of the system precludes quick and simplistic solutions for changes or reform, or even for amelioration of what may appear to be dysfunctional practices. There is no common procedure by which courts can be ordered to be more efficient, police more just, or corrections more effective. No single source of authority dominates others; the agencies and offices of the system, contiguous to each other and functionally interdependent, are nevertheless administratively distinct, often jealously guarding their own identities, budgets, and functions. There are no universal personnel requirements, nor is there a common manpower pool. The desire for uniformity in the application of the law and for common procedures is countered by an equally strong desire to individualize justice, to have and to use diverse procedures and techniques. The purposes of the whole process are mixed and often antagonistic.

While participants may offer allegiance to the superordinate but vague objectives of *crime control* and *crime prevention,* strong disagreements exist, and are reflected in statutes, court decisions, and agency practices, as how these ends may best be achieved.

As if this were not enough, the entire system is constantly changing. Every legislative session passes new laws, and though less frequently, some old laws are repealed or significantly modified. Litigation is endless. Every day appellate courts decide new cases, and in recent years each term of the U.S. Supreme Court has brought new decisions affecting criminal justice. Agency policies and practices are continuously renewed, modified, discarded, and replaced. Older personnel retire to be replaced by newcomers in a never-ending stream. Agencies and offices expand, and despite Parkinson's law occasionally contract, with the ebbing and flowing of concern—and budget—among police, prosecutors, courts, and the correctional agencies.

Although crime waves may indeed be largely inventions of the media rather than real epidemics, new crimes or new varieties of old ones present the system with constant crises. We are bombarded with reports of terror bombings, kidnapings, airplane hijacking, heroin addiction, street and prison riots, political assassinations, corruption in government, upsurges in muggings, newly discovered mass murders, bank robberies, and reported increments in most other crimes. Careful statistical analysis may show the crime problem to be less threatening than it sometimes appears, but bombings, riots, assassinations, hijacking, and other crimes do occur and are widely reported. The result is that today public concern and fear about crime make it a domestic issue of major importance. As the public is bombarded with reports of crime, so the components of the criminal justice system are bombarded with demands that "something" be done. New programs, procedures, and techniques are constantly being tried, and old, ineffective ones discarded in perennial crisis response.

Because of its intrinsic complexity and dynamism, attempts to analyze the criminal justice system often raise more issues than they resolve. And these issues are rarely one dimensional, nor are resolutions final. Since so few generalizations can be made about practices or processes, analysis is always encumbered by cautions that "it all depends" and notations that laws, procedures, and policies "vary considerably." Furthermore, the ends and means of crime control often become intermingled and confused so that any issue, such as the propriety of certain enforcement practices, takes on different coloration in different contexts. Wiretapping to trap marijuana sellers may be viewed as improper by legislatures, courts, or any observer, but it is often unclear whether the decision about its impropriety is based on the means—wiretapping—or whether it really rests on a belief that use and sale of marijuana should not be criminal. Would the same observer abhor wiretapping to catch a kidnaper?

A number of approaches to analysis and evaluation were suggested earlier as means to cope with the multiple facets of the total crime control system without becoming enmeshed in all its myriad details. Any single agency—the police, the courts, or corrections—and any decision stage in the process—arrest, charging, adjudication, sentencing, or postconviction intervention—is worthy of intensive examination, analysis, and evaluation in its own right. Our focus, however, has been on the total criminal justice system, beginning with a description of its authority structure and the organizational patterns of its agencies. This was followed by more detailed descriptions of laws, policies, and practices at major decision points across the entire process from crime detection to parole revocation. Our purpose has been to give an overview, to present materials relevant to the entire system, not simply as information, but also to create awareness of common issues and perspectives that tie together what often appear to be discrete agencies and unique functions. Even a cursory overview will reveal that no single agency embodies or represents the entire criminal process and that decisions made at any point by any participant have effects elsewhere. Police activities (or inactivity) affect the prosecutor, the courts, and are the first step in correctional intake. In turn, parole board decisions have implications for policing and so on. Likewise, it becomes evident that the responsibility for policies and practices of crime control is shared by the legislative, executive, judicial, and administrative branches of the government, thus complicating the development and implementation of proposals for change or reform.

All these factors, all this complexity, must be faced directly. Awareness of the interdependence of participants and the interrelationship of functions is a prerequisite for the kind of total systems analysis that is necessary today for research, evaluation, and planning in criminal justice administration. It is necessary to conceptualize the whole system, to be attuned to the linkage among decisions, to be aware that change at any point radiates to all others. The various analytical approaches suggested earlier—applying models to the entire system, factoring out themes and using perspectives that occur over and over again, assessing functions common to all agencies and incorporated in all decisions, and the others—are merely tools for use in seeing the whole system. These are suggested techniques for evaluating similarities and differences in the activities of a policeman, a prosecutor, a probation officer, and of all other participants in the process.

Criminal justice analysis is rarely undertaken as simply an intellectual exercise. While it might proceed from a desire to assess and evaluate current or past crime control efforts, there is usually an expectation, sometimes quite explicit, that analysis will lead to suggestions for improvement in our methods of crime control or prevention. To this extent, analysis is prospective, focused in the present but always with implications for the future. In this respect, the student of criminal justice must be attuned to the changing nature of the crime problem and to emerging forces and trends in crime control efforts. Forecasting is one of the most difficult and least certain of all analytic efforts, yet change is certain. The criminal justice system, like all institutions in the social order, responds to myriad forces from population growth to economic cycles, and many of these forces are unplanned, unforeseen, and perhaps unforeseeable. Patterns, policies, and programs of crime control are perhaps more unstable than those of other institutions, for the system is engaged in constant crisis response. A brutal killing by a parolee may cause the whole parole process to totter, a serious courtroom disruption may lead to new trial procedures. Some changes may be a matter of historical drift: an agency created at one time simply grows and becomes entrenched, or a practice developed for one need continues long after the need is gone. Other changes are reflective, their impetus coming from forces outside the criminal justice system but felt within it. The civil rights movement began in the communities and in the public schools, but today is a basic issue in all phases of crime control and prevention.

In general, change in criminal justice administration can be characterized as either unintended—the result of crisis, or as a reflection of broader societal trends—or planned. It is the latter, planned change, that is most distinctly within the ambit of the criminal justice analyst.

No one, no matter how skilled, can be expected to develop a blueprint for all aspects of criminal justice administration. Nevertheless, careful analysis and evaluation of criminal justice issues should, if warranted, lead to suggestions for improvement of many aspects of crime control. However, implementation of change may be beyond the power of the analyst and no matter how well prepared, may never be achieved, for as we have seen, the criminal justice system is not fully amenable to rational modification. Many of our procedures and practices have symbolic, ceremonial importance that cannot be undermined by demonstrating their ineffectiveness. However, when and wherever our system of justice needs modification and improvement, we have the choice of change by default, by drift, or by change through careful planning. It is in such planning that the analyst can make a major contribution.

The imperative of change and the opportunity to contribute in a meaningful fashion to change requires the student of criminal justice to be aware of current developments and trends in crime control and prevention. While some forecasting can be done by population projections, by predictions of crime rates, and by other statistical "futures" techniques, many developments are not amenable to mathematical prediction. Changes in ideas, philosophies, and beliefs are even more important than population growth. In this respect, it is important to try to isolate major trends in criminal justice proposals and changes in ideology and to assess, if possible, the likely impact of these developments on future practices and policies. This is no easy task. No trend is linear; there is always a backlash, always some evidence of countertrend. Nor are ideas about any facet of crime control universally accepted. Arguments in favor of abolishing prisons are countered by those calling for wider use of incarceration. All criminal justice planners face a basic paradox: as a people we want more of less; that is, we want a more effective and efficient system for crime control but we want less interference with our basic freedoms. This paradox colors all forecasting and affects every proposal for change. Nevertheless, our criminal justice system will change, and analysis must proceed within the context of paradox and conflict.

Chapter 9

Trends and Unresolved Issues in Criminal Justice Administration

Most of the problems confronted by our criminal justice system are as old as mankind. Moreover, the same basic problems faced by our forebears are likely to be confronted by our children. Obviously, we have not effectively prevented, controlled, or significantly diminished crime and related deviant behavior. We have made no breakthroughs in crime control or prevention at all comparable to those in medicine or to those in science and technology which have become so common as to be almost routine in our society. Such analogies may be unfair, however, for crime is not a disease, nor is crime control a science in the same sense as physics or biochemistry. Given the values and value conflicts about the causes of crime, the mixed tenets of our political philosophy, and the fact that crime encompasses a wide range of conduct and is subject to shifts in cultural definitions, perhaps it is not surprising that breakthroughs have not occurred. Nonetheless, we continue to spend an enormous amount of time, energy, and money in a continuous effort to control and prevent crime. But by almost any measure, our efforts have generally failed.

Some observers, including many criminal justice scholars, feel that we have failed because our basic approach has been wrong from the start. They see as the ultimate goal a form of prevention requiring a basic modification of many societal values and a fundamental realignment of the society's reward and opportunity structures. In this view, crime is a symptom of underlying tensions and conflicts in the structure of our massive industrial society and is inevitable as long as we stay the way we are, as long as we stress values of competition and capitalism while we create social barriers to equal opportunities by entrenching differential social classes, by practicing racial discrimination, and so on. In short, such observers see our elaborate efforts in ferreting out crime and apprehending and processing violators as essentially endless and futile, so long as we fail to overhaul our entire culture in the direction of a more equitable and utopian social order.[1]

Other observers and commentators regard our failure to be primarily the result of ineffectiveness and inefficiency of present law-enforcement techniques. They believe that crime control objectives can be achieved by increasing the certainty of crime detection and more effectively processing those who are caught and convicted.[2] Failure of past efforts is a common predicate to both positions; there are few, if any, serious observers of the system who think we are doing a fine job the way things are.

Although the two positions are ideologically very different, both have merit, for crime control and prevention pose both long-range and immediate problems. It may well be that the "banishment," or even the significant reduction of crime, will require basic modifications in our social structure and a reversal or shift in many present-day values. However, it seems clear that such changes will not come about overnight, and indeed may never come about, not only because of reluctance and resistance to change, but also because no one is really sure which modifications will lead to crime reduction. Nor do we know the other costs of change, even if certain modifications could be agreed upon.

Some critics of our present system feel that waiting for desirable social changes to evolve is too slow and uncertain. They advocate sudden revolutionary change, designed to overthrow all or most of our institutions and to replace them with a new social order which is fairer and more just.[3] Our own society was formed as a result of revolution, and we have numerous examples of revolutionary and radical change in other societies around the world. While crime reduction has never been a primary revolutionary motive,[4] in theory it is possible that the overturning of entrenched power, the revision of social and economic institutions, and similar sudden changes might lead to the formation of more representative and equitable societies in which conventional crime need not occur. However, we have no evidence for this. Crime rates of suddenly changed countries are sometimes difficult to obtain and often of questionable validity, and about the only thing that is certain is that there is no crime-free society of any size and complexity anywhere in the world. This is not to denigrate long-range crime control efforts, nor to suggest that certain social reforms are unwarranted. But it does suggest that, at present, we simply do not know enough to be certain that specific sudden changes will bring about crime reduction.

The problem of crime is immediate and constant. Even if we accept the necessity for long-range cultural change and recognize the limits of our traditional approaches to crime control, the hard fact is that we must take continual action to at least curb and contain criminal behavior, for unless we do, we face very real threats to the safety and security of all. We are saddled with the present crime situation, and, though we may have doubts about its ultimate effectiveness, we do have an ongoing criminal justice system that most persons want to be more effective and more just. It is unnecessary to fully accept the proposition that the improvement of present approaches to crime control will ultimately lead to a crime-free society in order to demand greater effectiveness and closer adherence to standards of propriety.

Pessimism about our crime control efforts is easily reinforced. One merely has to read current newspapers. At the same time, we have both the need and the obligation to keep trying, and though we have not achieved our ultimate objectives, our whole approach to the crime problem is better in many ways today than our efforts of the past. Few will deny that we have progressed from the days of Salem witchcraft trials, or that we have introduced higher standards of propriety in processing suspects and defendants, or that we have become more humane in the treatment of most offenders. Progress has admittedly been snail-slow, and neither linear nor uniform. Nowhere have we fully achieved our ideals of equal protection under the law, due process, and effective and humane treatment of violators. But progress has been made and is ongoing. The basic issue of proper and effective crime control which faces us today, while fundamentally the same as confronted by earlier generations, exists in a different cultural context.

It is unnecessary to list here all the basic, unresolved issues in our criminal justice efforts; they are too painfully obvious. Instead, attention will be given to some immediate problems and trends in crime control which are likely to be important in the foreseeable future. This chapter will deal with these problems in three categories: trends which appear to be recent and ongoing; divergent trends or "paradoxes," which are trends moving in two directions simultaneously; and some basic unresolved issues that are likely to persist in importance.

TRENDS IN CRIMINAL JUSTICE ADMINISTRATION

In criminal justice, as in any dynamic field, it is often hard to say whether any development is a trend that will persist and flower or whether it is a "sport," an anomalous development, that will wither and die and is in no way predictive of future happenings. A few years ago, for example, an informed observer might have seen as a trend the full application of a "medical model" to criminal justice processing, particularly at postconviction stages.[5] Criminological literature espoused various theories of personality disorders as the root of criminal behavior with a corresponding need to "diagnose" offenders and prescribe "treatment," primarily psychological and psychiatric counselling.[6] Rehabilitation was the measure of effectiveness, new prisons took on many of the characteristics of hospitals or clinics, while probation and parole were analogized to "out-patient" care. A widespread belief in the expertise of social scientists led a number of states to adopt completely indeterminate sentencing sanctions—one day to life for many crimes—on the assumption that offenders could be treated as needed and only released when expert panels determined they were "cured."

Today, while there are some residues of the medical model, in general there is no universal support for dominance of this approach.[7] Completely indeterminate sentences, so popular at the time, have been virtually abandoned.[8] Intensive clinical psychiatry is reserved for a few emotionally disturbed violators, while expertise for determining sentence length has been returned to the legislature and sentencing judges with parole authorities able to act only within prescribed limits.

Trend forecasting is an uncertain business at best. The most that can be done is to marshal whatever evidence and arguments exist which indicate a *pattern* in legal decisions, in agency practices, and in past and current ideas about various aspects of crime control. One event is never a trend, nor can it be foretold whether a single court decision or a new statute is a bellwether. Trends can only be observed over an extended period of time so that a determination can be made about the consistency and direction of movement. Even then, there is room for error. Developments must be evaluated in context with the various forces that gave impetus to change in the first place. Trends in criminal justice, like all cultural change, are always related to the *zeitgeist*—"the spirit of the times"—meaning the various developments, pressures, and beliefs in the society as a whole—indeed in the world—that affect behavior patterns generally and criminal behavior specifically. The criminal justice system is not entirely a self-generating or self-determining entity, but rather is part of the warp-and-woof of the entire social fabric. Developments in criminal justice rarely lead in cultural change; more often the system reflects and responds to modifications in broader forces, in changing ideas, new views of morality, surges and recessions of economic cycles, and shifts in political fortunes and power.

In spite of the difficulties and the risks in identifying trends, there appear to be some developments in criminal justice that seem sufficiently stable in direction to be designated as trends. Given the complex nature of criminal justice and all the value conflicts surrounding each aspect of crime control, it is not surprising that there are more paradoxes—apparent trends in one direction but with strong countertrends—than there are linear, single-direction, high-consensus developments. Nevertheless, over the past few decades certain patterned changes have occurred and give every indication of continuing into at least the immediate future. Some of these are agency-specific, relating primarily to the police, courts, or corrections, but others are systemwide, affecting all agencies and processes. Included among what appear to be current and stable trends are:

1. Increasing Emphasis on Due Process

This is a systemwide trend spreading outward from the court stages of the process to increasingly distant decisions made about suspects and defendants before adjudication and in the postconviction decision stages. Our crime control efforts have always been tested against two general standards: the *effectiveness* of intervention procedures and their *propriety* in terms of our political and legal ideology. In the past, effectiveness often appeared to be given highest priority. Historically, we have been concerned with such issues as whether the death penalty deters potential criminals, whether police techniques for discovering crime and apprehending violators are efficient, with the question of whether prisons can effectively restrain and rehabilitate offenders, whether parole is safe, and similar matters. Past research was heavily committed to evaluating programs and procedures in terms of their enforcement objectives, that is, increase in arrests, decrease in recidivism, and so on. However, beginning in the 1960s and continuing through the present, increasing priority has been given to the propriety of *methods* of decision making and control rather than to their results. In a sense we retreated from the medical model—can it be cured?—and the business model—how much does it cost?—to an earlier, constitutional position which stresses adherence to the civil rights of those processed, and which places priority on means, not ends.

The due process trend was led by the Supreme Court in the Warren era, but it had roots in various contemporary social movements which dramatized the demands of the poor, of blacks and other racial and ethnic minorities for fair treatment and equal opportunities. The war on crime became intertwined with the war on poverty, with the civil rights movement, with youth protesting the Vietnam War, with women's liberation, and with similar developments which challenged both the objectives and the procedures of governmental control and largesse.

In this general shift in emphasis toward what Reich has called "The New Property,"[9] citizens became increasingly concerned with their *right* to obtain

381

welfare payments, social security, equal education, fair employment, and their *right* to be free from arbitrary and capricious interference with their lives. The result has been a blurring of a former legal distinction between "rights" and "privileges," with corresponding court controls on unfettered discretion and on the concept of expertise by which former distinctions and distributions were made.[10] There was, and is, not only a demand that privileges become rights, but that governmental giving or taking away of material goods, opportunities, or changes in status, including freedom, be done only by appropriate and circumscribed procedures of due process. In criminal justice terms, many major decisions about suspects, defendants, offenders, and inmates formerly made without opportunity for challenge or review are now subject to adversary testing and open to appellate review.

In general, courts, legislatures, and criminal justice agencies have responded positively to due process demands, though slowly and reluctantly in many cases, with the result that many of the administrative procedures which were followed for years in the regulation of commerce and industry are now applied to an increasing array of decision points in criminal justice administration. While most enforcement and postconviction decisions are not yet required to fully meet trial standards of evidence or procedure, it is clear that our criminal process today is heavily "judicialized" with requirements for hearings, with opportunities for adversary testing, and with the necessity for procedural regularity at *most* of the major stages and decision points in the process.

Part of the due process trend has involved increasing the "balance of advantage" between state and accused.[11] Its primary manifestation has been provision of counsel for indigent defendants, not only at trial, but outward in both directions to early pretrial stages, at sentencing, on appeal, and at other postconviction determinations. In addition to provisions for counsel, there have been other changes designed to equalize material resources (e.g., indigent access to transcripts for appeal, prisoners' access to law books) and to provide more open and shared information to lessen the "battle model"[12] formerly characteristic of criminal processing. In contrast to only a few years ago, greater pretrial discovery is allowed today, settlement of cases by plea negotiation is out in the open, and at least partial disclosure of the presentence report is common. The trend toward balance of advantage, as with the entire move toward increasing due process, is far from complete. It does, however, appear to be viable; lawyers for defendants and petitioners are presently active at an increasing number of points in the criminal justice process and appear to be in the system to stay.

The due process trend was, and is, an embattled one. While the movement was led by the Supreme Court and sometimes supported by legislatures, at other times statutes were sought to nullify court decisions. At the start, operating agencies, from police to parole boards, universally fought the trend. The *Mapp v. Ohio*[13] decision allegedly "handcuffed" the police.[14] Trial courts were reputedly "overwhelmed" by *Gideon* v. *Wainwright*[15] and subsequent decisions.[16] *Mempa v. Rhay*[17] and *Morrissey* v. *Brewer*[18] were seen as threats to the expertise of probation and parole authorities and destructive of correctional ideology.[19] Some politicians railed against court decisions which hampered the "peace forces" of the nation,[20] and President Nixon pledged to appoint "strict constructionists" to the Supreme Court to curb this trend.[21] Nonetheless, increasing due process prevailed, and though there may be a slowdown in future developments, at present the trend seems likely to continue.

Most objective observers of criminal justice agree that the expansion of due process requirements was long overdue. However, as is often the case, there is a danger that too much will be expected from these changes. It must be remembered that the trend is procedural, not substantive, and does not directly address important effectiveness objectives and goals of criminal processing. It merely provides increased attention to the *methods* by which persons are arrested, interrogated, searched, convicted, and sentenced, but does not really touch the whys and wherefores of processing itself. Suspects are still arrested and offenders still serve long sentences in prison, but now only after they have been afforded a fuller measure of due process. A dilemma created by some broader expectations assigned to this trend has been commented on:

Defendants' rights generally, procedural regularity, fundamental fairness, access to lawyers and courts have preoccupied our system of justice, including corrections, over the past decade. Though there have been and continue to be administrative costs and inconveniences connected with this trend as it applies to corrections, most fair observers probably would agree that it was long overdue and perhaps is necessary to curb unfettered discretion, to hold correctional processing within proper bounds, to prevent cruel and unusual punishment, and so forth. The interesting thing about the trend was the implicit promise it held out to those persons incarcerated in prisons. Early "victories" in prisoner's rights cases, particularly in those providing access to counsel and the courts, were widely hailed as a major force for change and reform in the correctional system. This has not worked out in the way it was initially hoped for some very interesting reasons. When prisoners demand right to counsel, or similar rights, they are really asking for a right to be released or to have their sentences mitigated in some way. After all, capital punishment following a full and fair trial is no more welcomed by the person executed than if he were railroaded. The fact is access to counsel proved to be a hollow victory for a number of prisoners. What has been gained by the prisoner who in demanding and receiving the right to a hearing on parole revocation for example, finds himself revoked anyway and not only still incarcerated, but incarcerated with all options for rights expended? An interesting thing about the impact of prisoners' rights on correctional populations is, of course, the fact that those persons who have been successful in using new rights to the point where they are released from the criminal justice system are not those who make up present prison populations. Prison populations today are composed of increasing numbers of persons who have had a fuller measure of due process and have lost. Perhaps it is of little wonder that the "system's" way to effect change by using legal process has less credibility.[22]

2. Establishment of Standards and Articulation of Criteria for Decision Making

In the past, many important decisions about persons processed through the criminal justice system were made by officials without well-developed written standards or decision-making guidelines. Very broad discretion was delegated to most criminal justice functionaries by legislation or by tradition, or in some cases (e.g., the police) it was simply assumed as functionally necessary in the absence of expressly delegated authority. This situation is rapidly changing; the system is not only becoming more "judicialized," but also more "legislated."

Due process challenges to decision making rested basically on allegations of abuse of discretion. As appellate courts listened to demands for rights, examined dimensions of fundamental fairness, decided matters of equal protection, and as they provided defense lawyers to challenge the bases for decisions, *reasons* for alternative choices and *criteria* for decisions became central concerns. Agencies were forced to respond to appellate insistence on notice, precedent, reasonableness, and propriety by stating policies, procedures, and criteria for their various critical decisions. Appellate litigation was always intended to be more than case-specific; appellate decisions demanded fundamental changes in continuing practices, changes which were necessarily implemented by agency issuance of policy manuals and practice guidelines.

Courts alone did not provide sole impetus for the articulation of decision standards. Legislation, both actual and in model form, has had a profound influence on the shape of the criminal justice network and continues to be a major force for change. The principles of the *Model Penal Code,* the *Standards* of the American Bar Association and the National Council on Crime and Delinquency, the recommendations of various governmental commissions, including the two presidential crime commissions, have all expressed standards and model criteria for most of the major decision points in criminal justice processing. This same thrust is reflected in the many new state codes adopted in the past decade.

The result today is a system of criminal processing with various decision points more clearly defined, with standards and criteria openly expressed from very early police stages through parole revocation. Discretion has not been totally circumscribed, nor are there fully agreed upon, precisely articulated standards and criteria for every decision made by a policeman, prosecutor, judge, or correctional authority. But, today, in contrast to even five years ago, the bases for most decisions are more clearly expressed in statutes or formal policies, making them more visible and more easily challenged on the basis of reasonableness, fairness, and congruence with the aims of the criminal process. It may be impossible, indeed undesirable, to completely eliminate discretion. But the continuing trend is to make it more visible and to articulate its rationale in order to curb its excesses.

3. Mitigation of Harshness

It may be somewhat risky to define this as a trend, for backlash movements in criminal justice have been frequent. Nevertheless, for a number of years there have been, and there continue to be, serious attempts to mitigate the punitiveness and the harshness of our criminal justice system at all stages. We have abolished corporal punishment, and we make continuous attempts to eradicate overt brutality which is and always has been improper. The use of the death penalty fell into steady decline and was not used (though it was imposed) for a number of years before the Supreme Court declared a moratorium on it in 1972.[23] There have been attempts to better train police in order to sensitize them to differential community life-styles and to diminish as much as possible police use of force. While this has not been universally accomplished, police training today places heavy stress on restraint and on noninvocation of the process, rather than, as in the past, concentrating almost exclusively on the use of firearms and other techniques for forcibly apprehending and detaining suspects.

Sentences are getting shorter. Probation and parole are more frequently used than in the past.[24] Diversion from the system, from the early stages of intake to sentencing, is the *desideratum* today. There are even attempts to soften forced confinement in maximum-security prisons. Furloughs are used more often and some jurisdictions now permit limited conjugal visits. The American Correctional Association has called for a moratorium on construction of maximum-security prisons, and, in fact, most new correctional facilities are of medium and minimum classification.[25] This implies not only a reduction in perimeter control, including absence of fire power on the walls, but programs and life-styles of inmates in new institutions are markedly different from traditional prisons. At a minimum new correctional facilities are less harsh and brutal; hopefully they are more "rehabilitative" in terms of meeting needs of prisoners to return to community living.

For anyone currently caught up in the criminal justice network, all this may sound pollyannaish. There still are, of course, large and harsh prisons. There is police brutality, there are only too frequent examples of excessive use of force, and jails and lockups for the most part remain substandard by almost any test. Being processed through the criminal justice system, being housed in even the most modern, pastel-colored correctional institution is hardly a pleasant experience. Arrest, prosecution, trial, sentencing, and postconviction intervention are not, and never will be, pleasant experiences. Nevertheless, there appears to be a trend toward mitigation of harshness, a desire on the part of most informed observers to make our criminal justice system not only more proper in terms of procedure and processing, but also less punitive and degrading than it has been in the past. There are plenty of exceptions, oversights, retrogressive pressures, and change is painfully slow. Nonetheless, the weight of evidence would seem to indicate that we can, and will, consistently strive to reduce severity, lessen the punitive ideal, and build a system that is both less excessive and less self-defeating than has been our historical experience.

4. Focus on the Total System

This trend is of a somewhat different order from the ones above, but it has many of the same implications. Today, most participants in criminal justice and many other observers and scholars (hopefully including readers of this book) are viewing the crime control process as a system, as a whole entity, with increased awareness of the interrelationships of its many parts. This was not always the case. As noted previously, the various crime control agencies and offices grew in a hodge-podge fashion, each—the police, prosecutors, courts, and corrections—concerned with its own problems and seeking to determine its own destiny. Agencies were not only physically discrete—recruiting their own man-power, establishing their own policies, competing for separate budgets, evaluating their own effectiveness on their own terms—they were psychologically distinct as well. While there was always superficial awareness that the activities of the police were related to those of the prosecutor, and those of the prosecutor to the courts and so on, and while there was some vaguely expressed allegiance to the superordinate goals of crime control and prevention, there was no real sense of systemic functions, no shared awareness of the operational significance of the interlocking decision network. This has begun to change. Awareness of total system relevance was brought about largely by criminal justice scholars who demonstrated the now obvious relationships between divergent agencies and discrete decisions. Scholarship in turn influenced federal agencies and national commissions, particularly the two presidential crime commissions, to look at total system issues.

With the creation of the Law Enforcement Assistance Administration (LEAA), which became federal headquarters in the war on crime, system awareness became a necessity in the competition of federal funds. In general, educational and training grants were conditioned on the recipient's ability to offer some sort of "total system" curriculum; sole focus on police issues or correctional administration would not suffice. The requirements were the same for a good deal of federally funded research.

While there has been some token accommodation (by police administration programs adding a course on prisons and some corrections programs offering only one course on the law of arrest), in general, both colleges and training academies have responded by establishing criminal justice curricula based on a serious attempt to cover major issues running across the entire criminal justice process. The result has been the emergence of criminal justice as a viable and distinct academic field, with corresponding credentialing consequences for agency employment and promotion.

Given built-in economic rewards for total system education and training and the increasing accumulation of total-system scholarly literature, there appear to be lasting effects on the way criminal justice issues are and will be perceived. It seems likely that the police will never return to exclusive focus on law-enforcement practices without being aware of their impact on and relationships with the other agencies and decision points of the process. So too with other agencies and participants. Furthermore, criminal justice education is producing an increasing number of graduates who carry with them this new awareness and perception of the total system, and these alumni are taking places in the on-line crime control agencies as well as in planning and research positions. There is every indication that criminal justice is stabilizing as an academic discipline and that its perceptions, values, and contributions will continue to be significant in the future.

DIVERGENT TRENDS

As demonstrated throughout preceding chapters, probably the two most characteristic attributes of criminal justice administration are rapid change and jurisdictional variation in laws, policies, and practices. Every day appellate courts decide new issues or redecide old ones; every year some new criminal laws are passed or repealed; agencies periodically merge or separate and adopt new procedures or refine older ones. Criminal behavior is continuous, but types of crimes vary in frequency, while characteristics of offenders change with shifting population trends and with the ebb and flow of economic conditions and changing social forces generally.[26] In this context, and given constant pressures for improvement from within the criminal justice system itself, it is little wonder that at any one time changing patterns emerge which often appear contradictory, even paradoxical, making it difficult to assess the direction of any long-term change. For lack of a better term, these can be called *divergent trends,* for while some change appears likely, the most prominent direction is still obscure.

While the different tracks of divergent trends often appear to be mutually exclusive, indeed conceptually antagonistic, operationally they may coexist for extended periods of time. That is, there is no necessary implication that one direction of change must prevail over the other. A strong movement toward law-and-order, get-tough law enforcement may coexist with an equally strong movement toward due process along with softer, more humanitarian processing of suspects and offenders. There will be clashes and compromises to be sure. But programs embodying both basic stances may simultaneously develop. Our society is so large and complex, our criminal justice jurisdictions so variable, that different and opposing trends can exist simultaneously in different places. One state can be building new correctional facilities while a neighboring jurisdiction is phasing out its prisons. Within jurisdictions, even within single agencies, divergent programs can receive equal support. It is not uncommon for large police agencies to equip some officers with riot gear while others are issued blazers and are trained in community relations. The point is that given tremendous in-system variations in practices and even greater variation in crime control philosophies and theories there are many more divergent and conflicting developments in criminal justice than there are agreed upon, single-direction trends. Furthermore, divergent trends are not necessarily zero-sum, win-lose developments but may indeed represent equally strong and persistent simultaneous changes, however antithetical in philosophy and approach.

Much of the uncertainty reflected by divergent trends rests on a deeper uncertainty about the aims and objectives of crime control and about means of achieving even those objectives that might be agreed upon. We have not settled in any definitive way the basic question of the kind of criminal justice system, if any, that we want, nor do we know the full costs of alternative approaches. Beyond the desire for a crime-free society—or more realistically, for a significant reduction in our crime problem—there is very little agreement on any issue in criminal justice administration. Proponents can be found for virtually any stance. Critics of every program or policy are easy to find and often have counterproposals, many of which have equally strong supportive evidence. Given this, it is fairly easy to expect change but extremely difficult to determine direction.

Divergent trends could be discussed in their broadest, most abstract forms. The significance of differential focus on crime control versus crime prevention is a case in point, as are values (and corresponding operational developments) which stress deterrence versus rehabilitation, full enforcement versus discretion, cultural change versus individual treatment, and so on. The list could be endless. The most that can be done here is to highlight some current divergent trends *in* criminal justice administration rather than *about* criminal justice that will probably be significant in shaping the future of our crime control system. In most cases, one can only speculate about long-range effects of alternative paths on the goals of crime reduction and prevention.

As used here, divergent trends are not simply conflicting or contradictory philosophies, opinions, or viewpoints. In each case, there is some evidence of more than simply alternative desires. To be considered a divergent trend there must be some overt programs or measurable developments that have lasted for at least a few years and indicate that parallel directions of change will likely continue into the future. Unlike the full-scale trends discussed earlier, these differ by lack of agreement about major directions and results. This makes them no less important than other trends—in fact, it may increase their importance, for many of them represent polar positions in extremely important criminal justice controversies, some of which have always existed, others of which may be moving toward resolution.

1. Diversion versus Formal Processing

In recent years it has become popular to advocate diversion from the formal criminal justice system to other processes of intervention and control on the general grounds that diversionary alternatives are both more effective and more humane.[27] Diversion takes two forms. The first involves keeping otherwise eligible persons totally out of criminal processing by "adjusting" or "settling" whatever issues are involved without arrest or charging or by moving the offender into another treatment process such as the mental health system. The second is exemplified by practices and techniques designed to ameliorate the crime problem or treat the offender without invoking the *full* process. If criminal processing cannot be completely avoided, steps are taken as early as possible to keep the person from moving *deeper* into the criminal justice system. This is done by postarrest, middle-stages diversion, or, at the very end, by seeking alternatives to incarceration.

Diversionary alternatives have mushroomed at all agency levels from the police to corrections. These new "community-based" programs and facilities range from alcoholic rehabilitation centers and police-run youth counselling services to halfway houses and community sponsored offender treatment programs. Sometimes diversionary programs represent little more than articulation and justification of existing discretionary practices. Police, for example, have traditionally settled many family disputes by reprimand, counselling, and referral. The establishment of Family Crisis Intervention Units within police agencies simply formalizes, makes visible, and provides some control over long-standing practices. Other diversionary programs emanate from legislative changes, especially those which redefine certain criminal behaviors as forms of mental illness. For example, a number of states have developed procedures and accompanying facilities for civil commitment of narcotic offenders similar to the procedures used for the civil commitment of mentally ill persons. Here, as an alternative to conviction and sentence in the formal criminal justice system, the addict-pusher "voluntarily" submits to incarceration in a nonpenal facility and to participation in accompanying treatment programs. In return, he escapes the onus of a conviction record and avoids going to a traditional prison or other correctional facility. However, his term of commitment is related to his "condition" rather than his offense, and sometimes incarceration is shorter but more often longer than the period of confinement provided in the penal law.

Diversion rests on a number of assumptions which determine its objectives and provide its rationale. It is often assumed, and sometimes demonstrated, that full-scale criminal processing has the long-range effect of producing persons who are more dangerous or certainly more psychologically damaged than they were upon entry.[28] In part, this is a result of the degrading and physically harsh nature of the criminal process. In another part, damage is presumably the result of the labelling process by which individuals internalize the negative connotations of arrest, conviction, and incarceration and come to think of themselves as deeply criminal and are thereby likely to continue in an outlaw role.[29] Furthermore, it is assumed, though intrinsically difficult to demonstrate with accuracy, that full-scale criminal processing of one person does not really deter others from criminal conduct. Thus full invocation of the process is seen as counterproductive to its own objectives of rehabilitation and deterrence.

It is also assumed that diversion is less expensive than criminal processing ("It costs more to send a man to prison than to put him through college") and above all, apart from effectiveness and cost, it is more humane, more fitting to modern ideology than the punitive ideal which underlies every step in criminal procedure.[30]

Although diversionary tactics are currently popular and most informed observers admit the credibility of many claims of diversion proponents, there is some evidence of a countertrend. One of the major problems with diversion is that it bypasses many of the formal criminal law safeguards. "Voluntarily" agreeing to rehabilitative treatment or "consenting" to be on probation prior to conviction raises fundamental issues of due process that have long been established as necessary prior to formal state intervention with those suspected of crimes. The formal criminal process operates only with statutory authority; it rests on matters of evidence and proof, has built-in procedural safeguards, and in general, has an elaborate set of checks and balances designed to minimize errors, to accurately separate the guilty from the innocent, and to exercise controls over the treatment of even the most guilty and dangerous. Diversionary techniques often bypass these procedures and controls—indeed some diversion practices are deliberately utilized to avoid challenge and to bypass proof—and the question remains of whether the gains are worth the costs.

Apart from avoidance of admittedly cumbersome due process requirements, diversion tends to diffuse control and accountability. Individuals "disappear" from the criminal process so that there is no easy way to keep track of them, to monitor their treatment, or to assess the effectiveness of diversionary alternatives.

As a result of these informal, dispersal characteristics, diversion no longer enjoys uncritical acceptance as the wave of the future. Some opponents argue that diversionary tactics usurp legislative prerogative, are intended to deliberately bypass courts and the rule of law, and act to conceal unfettered and possibly improper discretion. From this perspective, the diffusion of diversionary programs is likely to result in more arbitrary and capricious decision making, without controls, than is possible in formal processing. Other critics claim that diversion results in excessive and inappropriate leniency without corresponding effectiveness in crime reduction.

The result is a renaissance in a modified "full enforcement," reduced-discretion perspective of criminal processing. This exists side-by-side with the currently strong emphasis on informality, negotiation, out-of-system treatment of persons caught in the enforcement net. Both approaches will probably exist side-by-side even within single jurisdictions, with differences highlighted between different criminal categories. In other words, at a minimum most jurisdictions will probably develop (if they haven't already) diversionary programs for first offenders, minor property violators like check forgers, family dispute violators, and the like. Heavy offenders—murderers, robbers, narcotics pushers—and chronic violators will probably be processed more fully and formally. This is not unlike the situation that has long existed, but there are at least two major differences. First, as the idea receives official support, diversion will be more openly expressed as a desirable and proper approach, with more clearly defined alternative programs. In short, it will involve more than the simple, sub-rosa exercise of discretion, resting instead on articulated criteria and having specified procedures for selection at all stages from the police, through plea bargaining to community corrections. Second, the number and types of offenders diverted will probably increase. Diversion limited to easy cases would make little impact on the criminal justice system. Battles will be fought over the use of diversion for more serious and higher risk cases, and here diversionary programs will find their real test as viable alternatives to formal processing.

2. Uniformity versus Individualization

A long-standing tenet of our criminal justice system is that the law be applied equally and uniformly to all. Many challenges to criminal justice processing rest on claims of denial of equal protection as guaranteed by the Constitution. Individuals differentially treated at all stages of the process from police intake to sentencing and beyond often claim they were improperly selected for intervention in discriminatory or arbitrary and capricious fashion, while others equally guilty were let go or were treated much more leniently. Indeed arbitrary and capricious intervention, discriminatory enforcement, and sentence disparity are considered inappropriate in our system of justice. The equal protection test no doubt will be a major challenge to simple discretion as it will to diversionary programs and practices.

At the same time, however, there continues to be a propensity to "individualize" justice, to employ discretion in a manner that distinguishes between superficially similar cases, that takes into account mitigating and aggravating circumstances often not discernible from formal labels. There is a desire to achieve justice by fitting the consequences of criminal intervention to the actual harm done by the person and to his individual and unique circumstances.

The apparent paradox between these two positions may rest on operational definitions of "uniformity" or its opposite "disparity." For example, is uniformity of the law achieved if all persons observed to be publically intoxicated are arrested? Suppose police see two persons who are drunk. One is a skid-row derelict, a chronic inebriate who has been arrested dozens of times in the past. The other is a theology student who is drunk for the first, and perhaps the only, time in his life. Is it more just to arrest both or to consider the consequences of the arrest record on the reputation and career of the two individuals confronted by the police? Likewise, if one codefendant is offered a reduced charge by a prosecutor in exchange for becoming a state's witness, does his partner have a valid equal protection demand that he should also be offered a reduced charge?

In its broader sense, the conflict is between demands for full enforcement (automatic implementation of the laws) versus selective enforcement (the exercise of discretion in proper fashion to achieve sensible and just distinctions in law enforcement). It is doubtful that full enforcement can ever be realistically achieved, even if desired. But even if it could be more closely approximated, the question remains of whether it would result in either a more just or more effective criminal justice system. Historically, uniformity in processing was a basic political ideal, but individualization became popular with the growth of social science with its stress on individual differences and on variations in life-styles and with its focus on the behavioral consequences of official intervention.[31]

As with the use of diversion, there is a backlash today against discretion at all stages of the criminal justice process.[32] This is illustrated by demands for abolition of plea bargaining, and for increased controls on police discretion. Critics of discretion argue that it makes our system of justice subject to the whims and caprices of men rather than to the rule of law. It is argued that to the extent we delegate or otherwise permit great power to accrue to persons who operate the criminal justice agencies, we perpetuate racial and economic discrimination under the guise of expertise. Furthermore, even if not discriminatory, discretion, whether exercised by police or parole boards, makes our system unpredictable, uneven, and basically unfair.[33] A lawbreaker may or may not be arrested, an offender serving an indeterminate sentence has no way of knowing when he will be released or upon what criteria. It would be fairer and intrinsically more proper for there to be certain and sure enforcement and sentences, not variable at the whim of police and parole authorities. In essence, advocates of nondiscretionary processing put their faith in the legislative process for precise formulas of criminal conduct and appropriate punishments. The agents and functionaries of the process would simply apply the correct formula to each instance in which sufficient evidence of illegal conduct exists.

The consequences of the discretion versus uniformity conflict are manifold, having implications beyond the nature of the criminal process itself. Each position effects the way criminal justice personnel are viewed and the way they view themselves. One recent development in virtually all agencies has been increased professionalization of personnel. Prosecutors and judges of all but the most minor justice courts have achieved this; corrections has approximated it, particularly in community supervision agencies, and the police have taken significant steps in this direction. In general, the move toward professionalism resulted from and relies on a highly discretionary criminal process. To the extent police are seen as merely automaton gatekeepers of the system, this perception is antithetical to professionalism. So, of course, is the abolishment of parole, adoption of legislatively fixed mandatory sentences, the curtailing of plea negotiation, and other similar proposals which reflect the uniform treatment, nondiscretionary approach. The basic conflict is whether we will rely on a system of expertise or will demand automatic implementation of all procedures. The operational significance of this divergent theme will undoubtedly continue as a major criminal justice issue in the foreseeable future.

3. Central Control, Federalism versus Local Autonomy

As a matter of increased efficiency and effectiveness there is a trend toward the merging of discrete criminal justice agencies into statewide, centrally administered superagencies.[34] These large bureaucracies, often the respositories of significant state and federal crime control budgets, have become powerful in determining the shape and priorities of both statewide and local crime control efforts. With significant input of federal funds, there is also a move toward federal direction and economic control of many state and local criminal justice policies and practices. Here, however, the bureaucratic influence is more indirect than physical merger of agencies. Federalism is occurring primarily by persuasion, by suggested "model" programs, and above all by discretionary distribution of federal funds.

Our system of criminal justice, with admittedly great variations in organizational arrangements from one jurisdiction to another, has been characterized by a mixture of locally autonomous and locally funded agencies with those of statewide jurisdiction which are state-funded. Certain problems—for example, the incarceration of felons—have been traditionally considered to be beyond local coping capacity and therefore properly a state function. On the other hand, the activities of police, prosecutors, and trial courts have been viewed as local issues, and generally these agencies have remained locally controlled. While there are some state police forces, state attorneys general, and statewide appellate courts, most police, prosecutory, and trial court functions have community reference bases with only some rather remote statewide and federal controls.

The tendency to merge agencies and to increase state and federal controls has its roots in many social and political forces. First, a number of modern crime problems are well beyond local efforts, indeed are cross-jurisdictional, national, even international, in scope. Then, to the extent that desire for uniformity in criminal processing is a viable objective, existing local variations in policing, court processing, and sentencing make central control of personnel and standards attractive. Not only is uniformity offered in support of merger, but paradoxically so is expertise. Professionalism rarely flowers on a local level. Both a wider funding base and greater employment choices are necessary prerequisites for serious attempts at professionalism by police and other criminal justice functionaries.

Efficiency is probably the major driving force in merger. The endless proliferation and duplication of functions and services by city boundaries, town lines, counties, or other delimiting factors is not only cumbersome, but expensive. In short, it is good business to streamline operations, merge functions, and monitor "production" with the ubiquitous computer.

Evidence of merger is most dramatic at the postconviction stages of the process. Here what were formerly distinct agencies, many of them local in orientation and funding, like probation services, have been pulled together into large, state-operated departments of corrections. Where established, these central agencies encompass prisons, reformatories, training schools, parole boards and parole field agents, probation, halfway houses, and all other correctional programs under one bureaucratic umbrella. One advantage offered by proponents of such merger is increased personnel flexibility. Under central management, an adult probation officer can be assigned to work with juvenile parolees if needed, while some prison employees can be moved into field supervision or parole officers can be used in prisons as demands shift. Moreover, over time with the experience of interchangeable positions, a "complete" correctional administrator will be produced. A single, trained professional may accumulate experience as a probation officer, a deputy warden, a parole board member, have experience in central office planning, and be as familiar with youth programs as with adult corrections. All of this is not possible where probation is local and distinct from parole and where both are separate from the prison system.

Merger and central control are not limited to corrections. Virtually all criminal justice agencies are experiencing some movement toward centralization. Most states today are in the process of establishing central offices for court administration. There are an increasing number of statewide "special prosecutors" for dealing with such problems as organized crime and official corruption. There are even state public defenders to monitor and assist indigents in the appellate process. While many police agencies have jealously guarded their local roots, there is not only an increase in the powers and functions of many state police, but new statewide police agencies (some of temporary duration commonly known as "strike forces") are mushrooming. "Lateral entry" into the officer ranks of some large police forces is now possible, whereas formerly every police officer had to be a local resident and work up to higher rank from beat patrolman.

Every state now has a crime control and planning agency, separate from the on-line agencies and acting as the link between federal and local efforts in crime control planning. These agencies are concerned with more than the in-house merger of correctional services or the streamlining of police functions. They attend to the relationships among police, courts, and correctional functions. More than the others, these agencies stress the continuity and congruency of the total, overall criminal process. By power to disperse federal monies to regions and localities, to underwrite educational endeavors of participants, and to support demonstration and research projects that meet federal standards, these agencies represent the spearhead of federalism in modern criminal justice developments.[35]

There is, of course, backlash to centralization, to the merger of agencies, and to federal influence. Part of it emanates from local entrenchment and resentment of outside interference with traditional ways of doing things. Merger, efficiency, and professionalism are all seen by some as threats to job security, as likely to destroy local power enclaves, for it is only too obvious that many participants in the criminal justice process have a vested interest in the status quo. Indeed sudden change emanating outside local control would work economic hardships; imagine the effect on some of the small rural prison communities if these major industries were to be suddenly moved or closed.

Partly, too, resistance comes from a traditional widespread fear of federal control, of "too much government," and from distrust and dislike of large, impersonal bureaucracies. This is more than simply a state's rights stance designed to perpetuate practices of racial discrimination—although this indeed may be involved—but has deep roots in our ideology. As a people we have maintained a long-standing fear of a police state. Efficiency alone has never been a hallmark of our criminal justice system; if it were, we would have replaced the jury with a computer long ago. We prize freedom from official intervention and espouse restraint on official power even more than we admire efficiency. This means that while most people concede the necessity for central direction in *some* aspects of our crime control effort, there is strong resistance to uncritical acceptance to total, centralized control and merger.

The countertrend involves more than simply an ideological reluctance to accept centralization. There are a variety of programs and projects designed to enhance local antonomy, to highlight and capitalize on regional differences, and to vary standards and procedures to better serve divergent life-styles. Efficiency and uniformity are viewed as deadening and ineffective in both enforcement and in reintegration of offenders. Furthermore, crime control is viewed as too important an issue to be left to "experts," no matter what their professional qualifications. Many locally autonomous programs are linked with the diversion efforts discussed earlier, but many go beyond this for diversion can also be centrally administered and controlled. "Community-based" corrections, for example, which is designed, staffed, and administered by a state superagency is quite distinct from "community-run" corrections where projects are locally tailored, personnel is indigenous, and policies are determined by citizen input.

The countermovement toward local control and life-style variation is not limited to correctional stages, though here programs of this sort are most advanced. There is increasing demand for local citizen input into policing, prosecutory policies, and sentencing. The major thrust of all these efforts is not efficiency or uniformity, but variation and "relevance." Whether unique and locally-responsive variations will spread and come to characterize our criminal justice system, or whether the pressures toward merger, central control, and professionalism will prevail is a drama that will continue to be played out across the nation in future years.

4. Secrecy versus Openness

Our basic approach to crime control has been to declare "war" on crime and to literally wage it.[36] We arm our "peace forces" for battle, robe our judges, sequester our juries, turn the prosecutor's office into a command post, and build and staff stockades to detain and incapacitate "enemy" prisoners. The war model not only characterizes the actual apprehension and processing of those caught by our crime fighters, but also colors preparations for battle. It has been common for crime control strategies and tactics to be developed secretly, less perpetrators get wind of the plans and escape. Like all armies, our criminal justice agencies seek and accumulate "intelligence" about the enemy. With sophisticated electronic devices, large data banks, and the ever-ready computer, intelligence gathering has become a major enterprise in criminal justice.

The war on crime, however, is a domestic war. Thus the question arises as to the appropriateness of pervasive secrecy in this effort. The enemies of our peace forces are our own people, albeit deviant or allegedly so, yet the criminal justice net is thrown very wide, particularly in the intelligence gathering function. There are, of course, very significant issues and controversies about the nature and propriety of choices at each decision point in the criminal justice system. These were discussed previously as the flow of the process was traced from early police investigatory activity through parole and revocation. An overriding issue all these points in the process is the question of secrecy. To what extent is it proper, necessary, and desirable for the criminal justice effort to proceed in secrecy, to keep information about policies and activities from the public, from persons suspected but untouched, from those processed, and, internally, to keep each agency's activities secret from the others?

The traditional stance across the system has been toward secrecy, toward keeping records and plans confidential within limits of mandated accountability. Total secrecy has never existed, for police, courts, and corrections, as public agencies, normally have been required to issue annual reports of their activities. But as pointed out earlier, these have been largely gate-keeping, summary statements about workload, not unlike the "body-counts" required of our military forces in Vietnam. The basic issue in secrecy is not workload, but the extent to which operational details and raw records are shared with the public and with persons processed. In general, police, court, and correctional files have been closed to public scrutiny, although periodically and selectively the press and other media have gained some access. The aura of secrecy has been so pervasive, however, that even in-system sharing of records and information has been far from common. Not only is there some resistance to share information cross-agencies (police access to probation records, police awareness of prosecution policies, etc.), but sharing even between agencies with common functions has not been the practice. In short, the system has been relatively closed both internally and with outsiders including suspects, defendants, offenders, and the public.

The rationales for secrecy are many, ranging from necessity to prevent the escape of lawbreakers, to a desire to protect innocent persons from reputational damage of premature disclosure of strictly "intelligence" information. Today, as provided in the Omnibus Crime Control Act,[37] (and as the basis of one scenario in the Watergate tapes) secrecy may rest on considerations of "national security."

There is currently a backlash to secrecy in criminal justice, a countertrend that is partly rooted in the consumer movement. Here there are numerous challenges to commercial secrecy, particularly the closed nature of credit information. At the same time, there has been increased public awareness that the very size of many crime data banks means that they must include information about a much larger proportion of the population than is actually criminal. Fingerprint files and the establishment of data banks based on social security and Internal Revenue information mean that probably most adult Americans have some sort of official "record," even though these are by no means criminal records. According to a recent survey there are more than 850 separate personal data banks in some 50 federal agencies.[38] For the most part they are readily available to most criminal justice agencies. The desire of many to discover what

398

information is gathered about them, by whom, and for what uses has surfaced the issue of individual access to relevant files across our entire government and even private enterprise systems. The existence of political "enemies lists," and their possible operational consequences, has intensified this concern.

Secrecy is being challenged within and about the criminal justice system at many levels and in many forms. As discussed previously, agencies are being pressured to articulate policies and to state decision criteria. Some of this pressure emanates from appellate court intervention into operational decision making; some from the desire of participants to be recognized as professional, and for this they need to express and justify the bases of their discretion. Greater openness is also demanded by legislatures and courts as they become aware of some possibly improper consequences of closed operations. The misuse of police files, hidden opportunities for graft and corruption, and inarticulated residues of racial discrimination are all covered by the blanket of secrecy. The poor and the criminally processed have new supporters on the bench and in public opinion so that their demands for equal protection, and allegations of its denial, require a more open view to know how the process actually works.

As most credit-card holders know, computers make (or perpetuate) errors. To the extent that our system of justice prides itself on accuracy in separating the guilty from the innocent, there is a corresponding necessity to check and recheck records for factual accuracy. As the system becomes judicialized and increasingly adversary, sharing the information basis for decisions comes to be viewed as necessary, a matter of fairness as well as of increased accuracy. New provisions for both wider pretrial discovery and more complete disclosure of the presentence report illustrate this trend.[39]

The right of the general public to know both the details of crimes and the steps taken to control them is the basis of long-standing controversy. Secrecy, official or otherwise, is anathema to a free press and contrary to the widely held view that in a democracy the public has a "right to know" the nature of social threats and the details of steps taken to cope with them.[40] However, some serious problems are intrinsic to full and complete public airing of both crimes and crime control programs. The crime problem is such that extensive publicity about any phase of it can sometimes serve to increase rather than diminish it. This dilemma was dramatically highlighted during the street and campus rioting of the 1960s. Extensive media coverage of riots, especially television reporting, seemed to intensify the problem and cause it to spread.[41] Recently the director of the FBI pointed to the possible mimicry basis of political kidnappings, laying part of the blame for its increment on extensive and intensive press coverage. However, he did not call for a media moratorium and confessed his inability to suggest an acceptable solution to this type of dilemma. At the court stages of the process, representatives of the media and of the bar and bench have been working on standards to maximize freedom of reporting without jeopardizing fair trials by release of prejudicial, pretrial publicity.[42]

The secrecy-openness dilemma will not be easily solved. As with many of the countertrend issues, there are advantages and costs to be weighed in each alternative at each stage of the process. In general, it is likely that our system will become increasingly open in routine matters at most decision points. At the same time, there will probably remain compelling reasons for at least some secrecy varying with the perceived nature of the crime threat and the possibly damaging ancillary effects of disclosure on innocent persons. There may also be greater reportorial discretion to withhold or delay detailed reports in instances where premature disclosure might compound the problem. And with better electronic techniques for instantaneous and complete coverage of events everywhere, it may well be that new controls on *when* the public has a right to know will occupy our legislatures and courts in the future.

UNRESOLVED ISSUES IN CRIMINAL JUSTICE

A cynic might well ask for a list of *resolved* criminal justice issues, and it would be a tough question indeed. Virtually everything relating to crime control and prevention is unresolved, existing in a state of flux and uncertainty and surrounded by controversy. The most abstruse generalizations about criminal behavior are subject to challenge. Even the truisms of yesterday—"criminal behavior is learned," "crime is a matter of cultural definition," and the like—evoke challenge today by some biological and social scientists.[43] A number of dedicated crime preventers have become disillusioned with utopian experimentation, coming to doubt the possibility of a stable, crime-free culture. Needless to say, every crime control effort from law enforcement to reintegration receives less than full consensus of *any* group, whether participants in the process, those affected by it, or informed observers on the outside. It is even possible at present to resurrect "resolved" issues of the past and find modern supporters for their return. For example, today there are proponents of corporal punishment—long thought abandoned as barbarous—as an alternative sanction for what is perceived to be the more brutalizing use of long periods of incarceration. And in many cities there are officially recognized and supported vigilante law-enforcement groups, a phenomenon commonly thought *passe* with the closing of the Western frontier.[44] What American would bet against the possibility of penal colonies on distant planets if we eventually conquer space travel? The death penalty, fallen into disuse and condemned by the Supreme Court, is again finding strong legislative support in many of our states. In short, nothing is finally settled in crime control, a fact that should have become apparent from the first page of this book. At this point, the most that can be done is to highlight a few general present concerns about the future direction, shape, and objectives of our criminal justice system. These are offered with full recognition that literally all other matters, large and small, are really unresolved issues and are likely to remain unsettled in any definite sense for a long time to come.

1. A Double System of Crime Control

Although sustained efforts to systemically analyze the total, overall criminal justice system are relatively new, it appears that before this process has even begun, our whole crime control effort is already changing toward bifurcation, a split into two major crime control efforts. It has been recognized for some time, of course, that the criminal justice system is not a single operational entity.[45] It is a system in a conceptual sense, but there are clearly different origins and pathways for processing different offense categories, even within the general heading of conventional crime. The standard processing of chronic inebriates is quite different from that invoked when armed robbery is involved. Routine enforcement against many victimless crimes, public order offenses, and misdemeanors is generally simpler, ordinarily less adversarial, and often more truncated than full-scale processing of serious felonies. However, types of abbreviated processing, as with the revolving door treatment of inebriates, and the merger of arrest, charging, adjudication, and sentencing at initial appearance with minor misdemeanors, have been treated as simply variations from the full formal processing found with many felonies but still part of the main criminal justice system. Processes with less distinct steps have been referred to as "subsystems," just as the consent-based, guilty-plea, nonadversarial flow of the process has been called the "routinized" system to distinguish it from the trial process in which most decision points are subject to challenge, adversarial testing, and possible appeal.[46]

The double system referred to here involves a more fundamental change than simple variations on a common process. There appears to be a desire, with corresponding serious attempts, to develop a separate set of policies and procedures for dealing with "dangerous" criminal behavior in contrast to "ordinary," nonviolent crimes. Various ways of delineating dangerous crimes and offenders were discussed in earlier chapters. In general, dangerousness encompasses a number of subdefinitions with two primary trunks. There are intrinsically dangerous *crimes* (e.g., homicide or assault) which result in death, serious

401

physical injury, or threats of great bodily harm to the victim. The other trunk encompasses dangerous *criminals* whose definition rests less on the criminal act than on the psychiatric characteristics of the perpetrator. Measurement of an offender's dangerousness is sometimes inferred from the repeated nature of his criminality (the persistent, chronic, or habitual offender), but more often from clinical diagnosis. Generally, the test is not simply one of likely recidivism, but, as with intrinsically dangerous conduct, whether he will likely become violent in the future. In short, the clinical question with a young, two-time car thief is not solely whether he will steal another car, but whether he is likely to injure or kill someone someday. "Dangerousness" also commonly serves as a categoric repository for the organized criminal—the gangster and the racketeer.

Today the dangerous-ordinary dichotomy is more than merely an expression of concern and more than a clinical exercise. There is evidence of sustained efforts to make this distinction operational from the earliest police stages of the process through sentencing and postconviction treatment.[47] Great impetus was given to this distinction by the model sentencing codes discussed earlier, each of which attempted to make dangerousness distinctions at the sentencing stage. Most newly adopted state codes have followed these leads. In addition, a number of programs and procedures based on concepts of dangerousness were developed by agencies themselves. Some of these were pushed through the legislative process. Stop-and-frisk laws, for example, rest on experiences of police officers killed or injured in routine street questioning. These laws relate dangerousness to the surroundings in which police often find themselves, allowing for weapon-retrieval pat-down searches of suspects not yet arrested. Preventive detention provisions reflect concern for potentially dangerous conduct by some suspects who otherwise would be released on bail.[48] Some accommodations to potential danger, like massive, encompassing airport searches are outgrowths from the anger, frustration, and fear aroused by repeated airplane hijackings, as are such techniques as the intensive, pervasive police sweep-questioning practiced at the height of the Zebra killings in San Francisco.

Serious attempts to develop a set of separate processes for the control of dangerous criminal behavior confront two very critical stumbling blocks. The first is the feasibility of predicting dangerousness, particularly future dangerous conduct by an individual. The second is the Constitution.

Various statistical devices, similar to those used in insurance actuarial tables, can be used to make probability statements about the frequency of future dangerous conduct in large, well-defined populations. Of course, these are never 100 percent accurate, but even more crucial, there is no present way of isolating which *individuals* in the population will engage in this conduct. The most that can be done is to predict, within margins of error, the probable frequency of homicide, assault, or other violent crimes within populations of persons sharing certain common traits. This is a far cry from saying with assurance that John Doe will rob or kill, or rob or kill again. Yet, as with the sale or denial of insurance, John Doe can be selected for special treatment (like preventive detention, a long sentence, even the death penalty) based on his closeness to the population characteristics which correlate with future dangerousness. There are very serious problems with this. Because the characteristics are never perfectly predictive, some individuals will be selected for harsh treatment who would not violate in the future, and some who will violate will escape selection. To increase assurance of future safety, more and more persons who would not violate must be subject to severe restraints in order to include more of those who will. At its most grotesque, it is comparable to preventing parole violations by holding all prisoners for life.

Prediction of individual dangerousness is primarily a detention, sentencing, and release concern. But some dangerous provisions are not primarily based on individual diagnosis; they are really collective responses. In the early days of hijacking, all passengers were searched at airports because the problem was considered serious enough to warrant massive intervention, and such selective devices as the hijacker "profile" were not considered sufficiently accurate to pick out likely suspects. Stop-and-frisk laws are encompassing, relating to time of day or night and street environment based on past police experience under similar conditions. Even in postconviction treatment some severe control methods are applied collectively. The walls and gun turrets of prisons are admittedly necessary for only a small proportion of possibly dangerous inmates, but form the boundaries for all prisoners.

Reaction to amorphous dangerousness is not limited to criminal justice agencies. Television cameras in elevators or on street corners photograph all riders and passersby. Secure buildings and neighborhoods, "defensible space,"[49] are increasingly common in metropolitan areas. In fact, the dangerous-ordinary dichotomy is very real in contemporary public opinion. The safe streets emphasis is strong; at the same time there appears to be greater public compassion for minor property violators and perpetrators of victimless crimes and other nonviolent offenses.

The second major obstacle to a separate process for "dangerous" persons involves constitutional interpretations. In general, constitutional protections do not vary according to the nature of the threat. That is, such issues as fundamental fairness, equal protection, freedom from cruel and unusual punishment, prohibitions against self-incrimination, and the like apply across-the-board. The exclusionary rule generally has been applied whether the illegal search involved recovery of lottery tickets or evidence of more serious crimes. There are, of course, constitutionally permissible variations in processing based on the application of appropriate criteria within delegated legislative limits. That is, for conviction of comparable crimes, one offender can be sent to prison with a counterpart placed on probation. This does not violate equal protection provisions, assuming both choices are permissible within existing and proper legislation and that appropriate procedures and criteria for selection are carefully followed.

The double-system issue, however, goes beyond the proper exercise of discretion. In full flower, a system based on dangerousness would allow some police intervention techniques not permissible under present laws, would deny bail and permit pretrial detention of potentially dangerous suspects, would have implications at the middle stages (prohibitions against plea bargaining with dangerous categories of crimes, for example), and would be reflected, as proposed by the model codes, in extended prison terms. Not all of these steps, or other comparable ones, involve the same legal issues. A number of dangerousness distinctions, particularly those in postconviction processing like mandatory sentences, special diagnosis, and extended incarceration of addicts and sex deviates, have been generally upheld as constitutionally proper if appropriate administrative procedures are adhered to in the selection process. Others, in particular preconviction interventions like preventive detention, while operational in some places exist under the uneasy cloud of possible constitutional defects. Some practices are bootlegged into operation (e.g., airport searches under a "consent" doctrine) but are now in litigation. Still others, while questionable, enjoy at least tenuous support. A number of differential police practices rely for justification on the type of distinction made by Mr. Justice Robert Jackson in 1949 in *Brinegar* v. *United States*:

If we assume, for example, that a child is kidnapped and the officers throw a roadblock about the neighborhood and search every outgoing car, it would be a drastic and undiscriminating use of the search. The officers might be unable to show probable cause for searching any particular car. However, I should candidly strive hard to sustain such an action, executed fairly and in good faith, because it might be reasonable to subject travelers to that indignity if it was the only way to save a threatened life and detect a vicious crime. But I should not strain to sustain such a roadblock and universal search to salvage a few bottles of bourbon and catch a bootlegger.[50]

There is additional evidence that the seriousness of an offense involved in appellate litigation does influence judicial rulings.[51]

Whether a double set of procedures will evolve and survive constitutional tests is uncertain. If not, our system will remain very much as it is now. If so, we may have to deal with two parallel sets of policies, procedures, statutes, and case law. In effect, a double criminal justice process will exist. These will not be two totally distinct systems, of course, for many of the present crime control agencies will be common but have double authority. That is, it is unlikely that there will be two prosecutors, one for dangerous crimes, one for ordinary offenses, or two police forces, although separate courts and separate correctional agencies are not that unfeasible.

2. The Prevention of Crime

Crime prevention is a major challenge to our society. The goal of prevention is clearly expressed by the term itself and is generally agreed to be a desirable one. The major problem is with the *means,* for here there are some fundamental controversies of philosophy, of political ideology, of semantics, and some very serious questions about the costs and effectiveness of different approaches. It is generally agreed, even by those with a vested interest in crime control, that it would be idyllic if necessity for criminal behavior could be removed, if somehow we could inoculate our citizens or alter our social environment so that crimes would diminish or disappear much as certain diseases are prevented by vaccination or by environmental hygiene. But the crime problem is neither this straightforward nor simple. Collectively, criminal behavior is no more an entity than disease, nor does it lend itself to medical analogies. The roots of crime are neither in germs nor genes, but rather are bound intricately into the values, relationships, and all other elements of our social fabric. The search for universal biological or psychological "causes" of criminal tendencies has largely proved fruitless. The apprehension, diagnosis, and clinical treatment of offenders has not significantly reduced the incidence of crime in our society. If the causes of crime are so elusive of definition and so intricately interwoven with societal traits, how can prevention proceed? This is the challenge, and, as evidenced by our continually high crime rate, the response has been less than effective.

Operationally, crime prevention is one of the most encompassing, vague, and misused concepts in criminological endeavors. Practically any activity, or lack of activity, has been hailed as crime prevention at one time or another. Some preventive measures are outrageous; others are ludicrous. Sterilization and psychosurgery have been used to prevent crimes. So has comic-book censorship, new patterns of toilet training, improved bank locks, community psychiatry, the electric chair, the boy scouts and police athletic associations, and preventive detention. Virtually every public endeavor has at one time or another rested on

405

crime prevention claims, so that any complete list of past and present preventive measures would be eclectic and limitless.

Today, crime prevention activities fall into a number of major categories that differ markedly in approach and in underlying theories of human behavior, deviation, and control. These include:

A. DETERRENCE.

General deterrence rests on a pleasure-pain principle, namely that potential offenders will be prevented from seeking the pleasures of crime if there is sufficient assurance that swift and certain punishment will follow any violation.[52] Operationally, many crime deterrence devices resemble those we employ in seeking to deter an international nuclear holocaust by maintaining strong military capabilities. As with the international arms race, crime deterrence requires the constant development and omnipresent display of the law-enforcement and punitive capabilities of the state. Theoretically it is less important that we actually achieve efficient law enforcement than it is that we maintain a convincing posture in this regard. The physical presence of prisons not only serves to incapacitate and rehabilitate prisoners, it also exemplifies the cost of crime. Since crimes occur anyway, whether because of weakness in the certainty of apprehension or forgetfulness on the part of perpetrators, periodic examples of strict and harsh treatment are necessary to revitalize the deterrence concept. To the deterrence proponent, one execution is worth a thousand words.

The idea of deterrence is evidently attractive, for it has existed as a form of social control from the very earliest times.[53] It persists as operationally viable, even in the face of evident failure. It rests on a strange mixture of conceptions about the nature of man and of human behavior, in part viewing man as rational, able to calculate gains and losses, and in part treating him as an animal, able to be conditioned to obey. As its rational basis, the pleasure-pain principle adopts the legal fiction of the reasonable and prudent man. What prudent human is motivated more by pain than pleasure? Deterrence is also seen as a conditioning process resting on the same principle involved in Pavlov's experiments with dogs, not only imprinting avoidance on those subject to painful stimuli, but also conditioning all others who know about and identify with the punished. It is a sort of conditioning-once-removed approach.

Some persons can be deterred or conditioned from at least some deviant acts under ideal laboratory conditions. However, even under controlled conditions the most serious crimes, the ones most desired to be deterred (e.g., murder, assault, and sex crimes) are probably the least amenable to deterrence. In addition, the real world is not a laboratory, and there are significant gaps in the speed and certainty of deterrent responses. Most crimes are not solved, and it is generally known that most perpetrators get away at least for a long time.

A policeman cannot be put into every household, in every warehouse, or on every street corner. Yet despite its conceptual weakness and its operational difficulties, deterrence persists as a major response to the challenge of crime prevention.

As discussed previously, deterrence is a pervasive theme running through all criminal justice decision points. It accounts, in part, for every policy, every procedure, even every ritual and gesture in the criminal process. It is probably the most popular of all crime prevention approaches because it is the cheapest and most simplistic. Witness the resurgence of death penalty provisions which almost always rest on deterrence claims. Given the horrors of kidnapping and murder, and the usually vague, infinitely complex, and controversial proposals of other long-range prevention proposals, it is easy to see the political attractiveness of reestablishing the electric chair. No matter that it is likely to fail in its objective. It represents precise and immediate action in the face of pressures to do something about these crimes. In brief, there is little doubt that deterrence in one form or another will remain a major approach to crime prevention in the future.

B. VIGOROUS ENFORCEMENT. This approach relies on the military maxim that the best defense is a strong offense. The underlying assumption is that crime can be abolished, or significantly reduced, by our present methods of crime control, if only these can be made more efficient and effective. This viewpoint is generally consistent with deterrence, but it also encompasses punitive and rehabilitative efforts with active offenders.

Unlike preventive approaches which call for sweeping societal changes, vigorous enforcement demands no fundamental realignment of values or cultural behavior patterns. It accepts the status quo and merges the objectives of control with prevention. More efficient police, quicker and surer court processing, and more effective correctional interventions not only solve crimes, but if completely successful, eradicate the problem. If all lawbreakers were arrested, convicted, and rehabilitated, the crime problem would begin to diminish. Ideally, there would be no recidivism so that *chronic* criminality would no longer exist. However, the criminal justice process—police, courts, and corrections—would always be necessary for new offenders, but these would be quickly processed to law-abiding status.

In its most idealized form, this approach appears to many as unrealistic, for it has been the major way we have responded to crime in the past without achieving these desirable ends. Yet it is probably the most prevalent, most widely accepted crime prevention theory in our society today. Control and prevention have long been seen as inseparable, for it is difficult to admit that vast efforts and major expenditures in the war on crime have not really reduced the problem. As with many activities where great commitment has been made, there is a tendency to call for more vigorous efforts, to blame failures on shortages, on inefficiency, on personnel failures or corruption, and to demand a beefing-up of the original thrust. The police can be blamed for failure to stop crime, or, more indirectly, those who fund and support the police can be blamed. In like manner delay in the courts and failure of prisons to rehabilitate are at fault. It is generally believed that with more or better police, prosecutors, and judges control can be achieved, while prisons with better staff and new programs can accomplish the rehabilitative ideal.[54] In this view, hindrances to efficient and effective processing, such as appellate court controls on agency functions, should be removed. New attention should be given to the rights of victims rather than as in the past to the rights of criminals.

Stress on greater efficiency and effectiveness of control efforts will undoubtedly occupy our society in the future. Few persons oppose this if done in balance with procedural fairness and sufficient attention to constitutional protections. Furthermore, an effective system of criminal processing can be demanded without confusing control with prevention. Many accept the necessity for police and prisons reluctantly, necessary as crisis response, but having little impact on long-range prevention. Some, however, see crime control as an end in itself, with increased enforcement effectiveness the real solution to crime prevention.

C. DEFENSIVE MEASURES. Another popular approach involves developing measures to prevent the *possibility* of crimes.[55] While this is essentially defensive, it is not incompatible with a vigorous enforcement offensive attack. However, unlike the offender focus of enforcement proposals, this approach deals with crimes, not criminals. It is age-old in its simplest form, represented by the first locks on household doors and by walled villages designed to bar roving brigands and outlaws.

Defensive measures today are varied, with different techniques used for different purposes. Some, like locks, bank vaults, burglar alarms, automobile keys, windowless buildings, and similar security measures are intended to keep thieves from property by making it impossible or very difficult to obtain. Of course, there never has been a thief-proof lock, at least not for long, but we have an extensive history of experimentation with antitheft devices. All forms of property security, including safety devices in modern architecture are currently big busines. So is personal security. Added to the guns, mace, whistles, and karate expertise possessed by many of our citizens—no one knows how many, but estimates are large—are personal bodyguards, a phenomenon becoming increasingly common following a rash of recent kidnappings.

A variation on methods designed to keep thieves from property or to afford personal protection are devices intended to identify or catch criminals who break through protective barriers while simultaneously deterring other potential offenders from crime attempts. Television cameras in banks, elevators, on street corners, and in schoolyards, watchmen and doormen, dogs in warehouses and after hours in department stores, private and industrial police, blockwatchers and citizen patrols are all prevalent in our society today. A private police force equipped with guard dogs patrolling walled or fenced neighborhoods is becoming increasingly common. Some defensible space architecture—walled and windowless—with accompanying perimeter manpower gives the impression of a prison in reverse—citizens on the inside with potential criminals held without.[56]

A third defensive variation involves removing the *object* of crimes, thus fundamentally frustrating crime attempts. If money is the object of theft, replace it with credit cards. If credit cards are stolen, move to a checkbook economy. If personal checks are forged, use checkwriters or interlocking computers to record transactions. This general approach is limited, of course—there still must be some cash—but such techniques are becoming common. Exact change fares on buses reduce the chances of bus-driver stickups. Gas stations which accept only credit cards are another illustration. Some techniques are informal, like "buddy-system" shopping and daily, neighborhood phonechecks designed to discover or deter crimes by lessening victim risk. Others are more elaborate and scientific, with some intended to prevent serious crimes and others to curb minor offenses like vandalism. A few years ago, car radio antennas were objects of vandals, whether to build zip guns or merely to hear the snap of broken metal. As a result, many newer autos have no extended antennas; appropriate wiring is invisibly imbedded in windshield glass. Today there are experiments with "erasable" masonry and writeproof paint designed to reduce the incidence, or at least the permanence, of graffiti that color our buildings, statues, buses, and trains.

Defensive reactions are generally born of desperation rather than desired as a life-style. They have obvious limits of applicability unless we are willing and able to return to a walled-village type of society. Essentially they are mechanistic, seeking to avoid the manifestation of trouble rather than to deal with either the motivation for or the follow-up results of criminal behavior. They stand in relation to crime prevention like a bulletproof vest relates to homicide prevention.

D. MODIFICATION OF SOCIAL FORCES. Many informed observers of criminal justice believe that the root causes of most criminal behavior are inextricably bound into the fabric of our political, economic, and social system.[57] From this perspective, crime prevention can come about only to the extent that we are willing and able to alter those cultural values, behavior patterns, and social structures which produce a reality in which crime is inevitable. There are disagreements, differences in emphasis, and some deep theoretical conflicts about *which* values, patterns, and structures must change, and in which direction and how far. Nonetheless, the basic stance is that crime prevention cannot be achieved by enforcement alone, by deterrence or protective entrenchment, or by patchwork improvements on the fringes of our social and economic system. Instead we must make some basic alterations in our present life-styles in order to eliminate the need for theft and violence.

Specific alterations felt necessary by these prevention proponents vary, but range from modification of family structure and child-rearing practices to reduction of social class differentials, realignment of our societal reward system, and elimination of all forms of social, racial, and economic discrimination. None of these are minor or simple; all relate the crime problem to broader, more basic cultural issues.

This fundamental-change approach to prevention sometimes is labelled "radical" or "socialist," just as vigorous enforcement is sometimes denigrated as "hardhat" or "fascist." Like most appellations, these are not accurate and serve only to stereotype and depreciate sincere beliefs in contrary approaches to the same problem. This does not mean that full-fledged advocates of socialism on the one hand or fascism on the other would be found equally distributed between both approaches. It means that most proponents of basic crime prevention measures are by no means socialists any more than those who desire more effective crime control are fascists. In fact, virtually all American research criminologists, of widely diverse political orientations, espouse the necessity for societal modifications if long-range crime prevention is to occur.[58] Simultaneously, most accept crime control measures as necessary and wish them to be more efficient and effective. Proponents other than criminologists include senators, judges, policemen, and clergymen, along with other observers and participants in criminal justice from all walks of life and of every political hue. Of course, some change proponents, disillusioned by past efforts to evolve into a crime-free society, call for politically radical, even revolutionary, measures to dramatically modify the structures of our institutions.[59] Others believe needed alterations can come about by procedures consistent with the democratic process, requiring only awareness of the problem and willingness to change. This too is a radical stance, but radical in a surgical rather than political sense. In any event, proposals to equalize life chances and to otherwise achieve a less crime-motivating social environment will undoubtedly continue to occupy criminal justice planning along with the more mechanistic deterrence, protective, and vigorous enforcement efforts.

3. The Search for Justice

Quite naturally most persons would like to live in a crime-free society or if this is not immediately possible, to enjoy an efficient and effective crime control system. Prevention and efficiency, although important concerns, are not the sole determinants of appropriate criminal justice efforts. Whatever preventive or control measures are taken must stand the test of propriety, must be consistent with our sense of justice. And this term—justice—is as elusive of definition, as difficult to measure or evaluate, as any concept in our language.

The search for justice is an age-old quest. Undoubtedly it will remain unresolved as long as mankind lives in ordered society. At times in the past we thought it solved, or at least better defined. An-eye-for-an-eye, the wisdom of Solomon, the Declaration of Independence, the teachings of Freud, and the early claims of social science all promised new insights and new solutions to the crime problem. Yet for every variation in definition, for each new solution, significant questions and challenges were raised, and justice still somehow fails to be caught in a word formula and to be simply achieved. From our origins as a colonial people to the present day, our entire history can be fairly characterized as a search for justice. We have slowly and often painfully constructed a government, a constitution, and a highly intricate set of administrative machinery intended to maximize liberty, to afford wide opportunities for the pursuit of happiness, to give and protect the civil liberties of all our citizens. Needless to say we have never fully achieved this goal. We have at times collectively supported repressive institutions, like slavery, that in hindsight seem unbelievable and that took a civil war to change. Rejecting aristocracy, we still developed a class-entrenched society. Our treatment of all minorities, racial, political, sexual, and economic has been less than consistent with our ideals. In short, our history is littered with examples of injustice and with only too frequent cases of corruption of our own institutions. Yet the search continues.

Criminal justice has two parts, as the words themselves clearly express. It is not enough to emphasize the "criminal" part and to mute "justice," for they are related and inseparable. If anywhere, the parameters of justice will be defined and tested by the criminal justice system. Here is where our basic notions of the nature of deviant behavior are most clearly expressed and here is where we put to the test our principles regarding the treatment of even the "worst" among us. The criminal justice system of our society, as of all societies, is more than just a reluctant necessity; it is the final, most significant expression of our basic ideology. This is why study, analysis, and change in this field are so important.

411

NOTES

1. See, for example, Edwin Schur, *Our Criminal Society: The Social and Legal Sources of Crime in America* (Englewood Cliffs, N.J.: Prentice-Hall, 1969).

2. Most criticism probably falls in this category. See, for example, Whitney North Seymour, Jr., *Why Justice Fails* (New York: William Morrow & Co., 1973).

3. A leading proponent of this view has been Richard Quinney. See Quinney, *Critique of Legal Order* (Boston: Little, Brown, 1973).

4. *Ibid.* See also Ian Taylor, Paul Walton, and Jock Young, *The New Criminology: For a Social Theory of Deviance* (New York: Harper & Row, 1973).

5. See, for example, Barbara Wooton, *Social Science and Social Pathology* (London: Macmillan, 1959); Karl Menninger, *The Crime of Punishment* (New York: The Viking Press, 1966).

6. Marguerite Q. Grant, *Interaction Between Kinds of Treatment and Kinds of Delinquents* (Sacramento, California: Printing Division, July 1961), Marguerite Warren, "Classification of Offenders as an Aid to Efficient Management and Effective Treatment," *J. Crim. Law, Criminology and Pol. Sci.* 62 (1971): 239-258.

7. Recent criticisms of the medical model are found in Leslie T. Wilkins, *Evaluation of Penal Measures* (New York: Random House, 1969); Nicholas N. Kittrie, *The Right to Be Different* (Baltimore: Johns Hopkins Press, 1971).

8. Ramsey Clark, the former U.S. Attorney General, for example, strongly supported the indeterminate sentence shortly after leaving the Justice Department. See Clark, *Crime in America* (New York: Simon & Schuster, 1970). However by 1973, he had abandoned it in equally strong terms.

9. Charles Reich, "The New Property," *Yale Law Journal* 73, 5 (April 1964): 733-787. See also Reich, "Individual Rights and Social Welfare: The Emerging Legal Issues," *Yale Law Journal* 74, 7 (June 1965): 1245-1258.

10. See William Van Alstyne, "The Demise of the Rights-Privilege Distinction in Constitutional Law," *Harvard Law Review* 81, 7 (May 1968): 1439-1464; Goldberg v. Kelly, 397 U.S. 254 (1970).

11. See Abraham S. Goldstein, "The State and the Accused: Balance of Advantage in Criminal Procedure," *Yale Law Journal* 69, 7 (1960): 1149-1199.

12. The term "battle model" is described in John Griffiths, "Ideology in Criminal Procedure, or a Third 'Model' of the Criminal Process," *Yale Law Journal* 79 (1970): 359-417.

13. Mapp v. Ohio, 367 U.S. 643 (1961).

14. See James Vorenburg and James Q. Wilson, "Is the Court Handcuffing the Cops?" The *New York Times Magazine*, 11 May 1969, in Donald R. Cressey, ed. *Crime and Criminal Justice* (New York: Quadrangle, 1971), pp. 82-88.

15. Gideon v. Wainwright, 372 U.S. 335 (1963).

16. Although Gideon was limited to felony cases, one Federal Court of Appeals interpreted the ruling to extend to an indigent defendant charged with a misdemeanor punishable by a maximum sentence of 90 days in jail and a 500 dollar fine. Harvey v. Mississippi, 340 F. 2d. 263 (5th Cir. 1965). More recently the U.S. Supreme Court held that counsel was required for an indigent defendant charged with an offense punishable by imprisonment up to six months and a 1,000 dollar fine. See Argersinger v. Hamlin, 407 U.S. 25 (1972). The Court also ruled that no person could be imprisoned as the result of a criminal prosecution in which he was not accorded the right to public representation.

17. Mempa v. Rhay, 389 U.S. 128 (1967).

18. Morrissey v. Brewer, 408 U.S. 471 (1972).

19. See Fred Cohen, "A Comment on Morrissey v. Brewer: Due Process and Parole Revocation," *Crim. Law Bull.* 8, 7 (September 1972): 616-622; Cohen, "Sentencing, Probation, and the Rehabilitative Ideal: The View from Mempa v. Rhay," *Texas Law Review* 47, 1 (1968): 1-59.

20. For an excellent account of this phenomenon, see Richard Harris, *Justice: The Crisis of Law, Order, and Freedom in America* (New York: Dutton, 1970).

21. Nixon's strategy is examined in James F. Simon, *In His Own Image: The Supreme Court in Richard Nixon's America* (New York: David McKay Co., Inc., 1973).

22. Donald J. Newman, "Corrections of the Future: Some Paradoxes in Development," in Doris Baker, ed., *Corrections in Context: The Criminal Justice System and the Corrective Function* (Madison, Wis.: University Extension Division, 1972), pp. 9-10.

23. When the U.S. Supreme Court declared its moratorium in 1972, there had not been a legal execution since 1967. See Furman v. Georgia, 408 U.S. 238 (1972).

24. In 1970, 72 percent of the felons released from state and federal institutions were released by parole, as compared to 61 percent in 1966. National Advisory Commission on Criminal Justice Standards and Goals, *Corrections* (Washington, D.C.: U.S. Department of Justice, 1973), p. 389. The National Advisory Commission on Criminal Justice Standards and Goals urged in its 1973 report on corrections that probation be made the standard sentence in criminal cases (p. 159), contending that broad use of probation does not increase risk to the community. Results of probation, it concluded, are as good, if not better, than those of institutionalization (p. 311).

25. The National Advisory Commission on Criminal Justice Standards and Goals also endorsed a moratorium on construction, adding that "every effort must be made to phase out existing mega-institutions at the earliest possible time." Failure to stop new construction," it concluded, "could repeat a two-century-old error and fail to benefit from the lessons of history." (*Ibid*, p. 597).

26. See, for example, Emile Durkheim, *Suicide*, John A. Spaulding and George Simpson, trans. (Glencoe, Ill.: The Free Press, 1951); Andrew F. Henry and James F. Short Jr., *Suicide and Homicide: Some Economic, Sociological, and Psychological Aspects of Aggression* (New York: The Free Press, 1954).

27. By 1973 advocates of diversion included the Law Enforcement Assistance Administration, the Youth Development and Delinquency Prevention Administration, the American Correctional Association, the National Advisory Commission on Criminal Justice Standards and Goals, and many more criminal justice agencies and organizations.

28. National Advisory Commission on Criminal Justice Standards and Goals, *Corrections,* esp. pp. 74-76.

29. The acceptance or internalization of such deviant labels by the labelled has been termed "secondary deviance." "When a person begins to employ his deviant behavior or a role based on it as a means of defense, attack, or adjustment and the overt and covert problems created by the consequent societal reaction to him, his deviance is secondary." Edwin M. Lemert, *Social Pathology* (New York: McGraw-Hill, 1951), p. 71.

30. For example, the Project Crossroads diversion program in the District of Columbia operated on a per capita program cost of 6 dollars per day, compared to the 17 dollars spent in the district's institutionalized corrections facilities; recidivism for the diversion population was 22 percent, compared to the 46 percent among a control group that did not receive its services. American Correctional Association, *Juvenile Diversion: A Perspective* (College Park, Md.: ACA, 1972), pp. 1-2.

31. See, for example, R. Saleilles, *The Individualization of Punishment* (Boston: Little, Brown, 1911).

32. See, for example, American Friends Service Committee, *Struggle for Justice* (New York: Hill & Wang, 1971).

33. Judge Marvin E. Frankel put it this way: "The basic evil in sentencing is its lawlessness. There's too little law and too much discretion." Lesley Oelsner, "Wide Disparities Mark Sentences Here," *The New York Times*, 26 September 1972, p. 1.

34. Most states, for instance, have established a centralized court administration. See National Advisory Commission on Criminal Justice Standards and Goals, *Courts* (Washington, D.C.: U.S. Department of Justice, 1973), pp. 177-178. In New York State, the Division of Criminal Justice Services was established in 1972 to consolidate and coordinate the activities of several state agencies.

35. National Advisory Commission on Criminal Justice Standards and Goals, *Criminal Justice System* (Washington, D.C.: U.S. Department of Justice, 1973), esp. pp. 5-31. For an example of such a planning agency, see Division of Criminal Justice Services, *State of New York 1973 Comprehensive Crime Control Plan* (Albany, New York: DCJS, 1973).

36. For an examination of the war on crime, see Robert M. Cipes, *The Crime War* (New York: New American Library, 1968); Scott Christianson, "The War Model in Criminal Justice: No Substitute for Victory," *Crim. Justice and Behavior* 1, 3 (September 1974).

37. The Omnibus Crime Control and Safe Streets Act of 1968, Public Law 90-351, 90th Cong., June 1968, 18 U.S.C., Sec: 2518(7).

38. See *U.S. News and World Report*, 1 July 1974, p. 41.

39. See National Advisory Commission on Criminal Justice Standards and Goals, *Corrections*, esp. pp. 188-189; The *Model Sentencing Act* recommends that disclosure of the contents of the presentence report be mandatory wherever the sentence is for more than five years for a "dangerous offender." National Council on Crime and Delinquency, *Model Sentencing Act* (New York: NCCD, 1963). The *Model Penal Code* recommends that the court advise the defendant or his counsel of the factual contents and the conclusion of any presentence investigation. American Law Institute, *Model Penal Code: Proposed Official Draft* (Philadelphia: ALI, 1962). The American Bar Association Project on Standards for Criminal Justice urges that the report should be available for inspection by the defendant or his attorney, but provides for exclusion of some parts "which are not relevant to a proper sentence . . . diagnostic opinion which might seriously disrupt a program of rehabilitation, or sources of information which has been obtained on a promise of confidentiality." American Bar Association Project on Standards for Criminal Justice, *Standards Relating to Sentencing Alternatives and Procedures* (New York: Institute of Judicial Administration, 1968), Sec. 4.4.

40. See David Wise, *The Politics of Lying: Government Deception, Secrecy, and Power* (New York: Random House, 1973).

41. National Commission on the Causes and Prevention of Violence, *Violence and the Media* (Washington, D.C.: U.S. Government Printing Office, 1969).

42. See, for example, American Bar Association Project on Criminal Justice Standards and Goals, *Standards Relating to Fair Trial and Free Press* (New York: Institute of Judicial Administration, 1968).

43. See, for example, Hans Eysenck, *Crime and Personality*, rev. ed. (London: Paladin, 1970); T. Sarbin and J. Miller, "Demonism Revisited: the XYY Chromosomal Anomaly," *Issues in Criminology* 5 (Summer 1970): 195-207.

414

44. See "Sheriff's Reserves Given $1.00 for Year's Services," *Crime Control Digest* (March 31, 1972); "Reserve Deputies Handle Tough Assignments on Job," *California Council on Criminal Justice* 5 (February 11, 1972); National Advisory Commission on Criminal Justice Standards and Goals, *Police* (Washington, D.C.: U.S. Department of Justice, 1973), pp. 255-257.

45. Frank J. Remington, Donald J. Newman, Edward L. Kimball, Marygold Melli, and Herman Goldstein, *Criminal Justice Administration: Materials and Cases* (Indianapolis: Bobbs-Merrill, 1969), pp. 18-20.

46. *Ibid.*

47. Stanley Brodsky has concluded there are several problems in defining dangerousness: "(a) There seems to be no such behavioral entity as dangerousness, that mental health professionals (or others) can define, apart from social contexts or attitudes . . . (b) There is limited knowledge about base rates of certain types of 'Dangerousness,' such as battery, in the general population . . . (c) The statistical prediction of any rare event, such as an aggressive threat to safety, is a difficult burden for any professional to assume. (d) In making these kinds of judgments, an estimate has to be made of the acceptable fail rate." Stanley L. Brodsky, *Psychologists in the Criminal Justice System* (Chicago: U. of Ill. Press, 1972), pp. 142-143.

48. See Comment, "Preventive Detention: An Empirical Analysis," *Harvard Civil Rights-Civil Liberties Law Review* 6, 2 (March 1971): 289-396; Comment, "Preventive Detention Before Trial," *Harvard Law Review* 79, 7 (May 1966): 1489-1510.

49. See Oscar Newman, *Defensible Space* (New York: Macmillan, 1972).

50. Brinegar v. United States, 338 U.S. 160, 183 (1949).

51. See United States v. Soyka, 394 F. 2d. 443 (2d. Cir. 1968).

52. See, generally, Johannes Andenaes, "Does Punishment Deter Crime?", *Crim. Law Quarterly* II (1968): 76-93; Andenaes, "General Prevention—Illusion or Reality?", *J. Crim. Law, Criminology and Pol. Sci.* 43 (1952): 176-198; Franklin Zimring and Gordon Hawkins, *Deterrence* (Chicago: U. of Chi. Press, 1973).

53. Many Biblical references illustrate this—for example, hell as a deterrent.

54. This position is assailed by an increasing number of writers, however. See Alexander Smith and Harriet Pollack, "Less, Not More: Police, Courts, Prisons," *Fed. Probation* 36, 3 (September 1972): 12-19.

55. Law Enforcement Assistance Administration, National Institute on Law Enforcement and Administration of Justice, *Residential Security* (Washington, D.C.: U.S. Government Printing Office, 1973).

56. Newman, *Defensible Space.*

57. See, for example, Edwin M. Schur, *Our Criminal Society* (Englewood Cliffs, N.J.: Prentice-Hall, 1967); Leon Radzinowicz, *Ideology and Crime* (New York: Columbia U. Press, 1966).

58. See, generally, Richard A. Cloward and Lloyd E. Ohlin, *Delinquency and Opportunity: A Theory of Delinquent Groups* (New York: The Free Press, 1960); Walter C. Reckless and Simon Dinitz, *The Prevention of Juvenile Delinquency* (Columbus, Ohio: Ohio State U. Press, 1972).

59. See, for example, Richard Quinney, *Critique of Legal Order: Crime Control in Capitalist Society* (Boston: Little, Brown, 1974).

SELECTED BIBLIOGRAPHY

Arranged According to the Following General Topics

1. The Criminal Justice System
2. Theory in Law and Punishment
3. Criminology, The Nature of Crime and Delinquency
4. The Police
5. Prosecution and the Courts
6. Corrections

The Criminal Justice System

Allen, Francis A. *The Borderland of Criminal Justice.* Chicago: University of Chicago Press, 1964.

American Bar Association, Special Committee on Crime Prevention and Control. *New Perspectives on Urban Crime.* Washington, D.C.: American Bar Association, 1972.

American Friends Service Committee. *Struggle for Justice.* New York: Hill & Wang, 1971.

Argyris, Chris R. *Integrating the Individual and the Organization.* New York: John Wiley and Sons, 1964.

Beattie, Ronald H. "Sources of Statistics on Crime and Correction." *Journal of American Statistical Association* 54 (September 1959): 582-592.

Blake, Robert R. and Mouton, Jane S. *The Managerial Grid.* Houston, Tex.: Gulf Publ., 1964.

Blau, Peter M. *Bureaucracy in Modern Society.* New York: Random House, 1956.

Brakel, Samuel J. "Diversion from the Criminal Process: Informal Discretion, Motivation and Formalization." *Denver Law Journal* 48, 2 (1971): 211-238.

Casper, Jonathan D. *American Criminal Justice: The Defendant's Perspective.* Englewood Cliffs, N.J.: Prentice-Hall, 1972.

Christianson, Scott. "The War Model in Criminal Justice: No Substitute for Victory." *Criminal Justice and Behavior* 1 (September 1974).

Churchman, C. West. *The Systems Approach.* New York: Dell, 1968.

Cicourel, Aaron V. *The Social Organization of Juvenile Justice.* New York: John Wiley and Sons, 1968.

Cipes, Robert M. *The Crime War.* New York: New American Library, 1968.

417

Cohen, Bernard and Chaihen, Jan M. *Police Background Characteristics and Performance: Summary*. New York: Rand Institute, May 1972.

Dash, Samuel. "Cracks in the Foundation of Criminal Justice." *Illinois Law Review* 46, 3 (July-August 1951): 385-406.

Etzioni, Amitai. *A Comparative Analysis of Complex Organizations*. New York: The Free Press, 1964.

Gardiner, John A. *The Politics of Corruption*. New York: Russell Sage Foundation, 1970.

Gellhorn, Walter. *Ombudsmen and Others: Citizen Protectors in Nine Countries*. Cambridge, Mass.: Harvard University Press, 1966.

Goldfarb, Ronald. *Ransom: A Critique of the American Bail System*. New York: Harper & Row, 1965.

Handler, Joel F. "The Juvenile Court and the Adversary System: Problems of Function and Form." *Wisconsin Law Review* 1965 (Winter 1965): 7-51.

Harris, Richard. *Justice: The Crisis of Law, Order, and Freedom in America*. New York: Dutton, 1970.

Hills, Stuart L. *Crime, Power, and Morality: The Criminal Law Process in the United States*. Scranton, Pa.: Chandler Publ. Co., 1971.

Kadish, Mortimer R. and Kadish, Sanford H. "On Justified Rule Departures by Officials." *California Law Review* 59, 4 (June 1971): 905-961.

Kadish, Sanford H. and Paulsen, Monrad G. *Criminal Law and Its Processes*, 2d ed. Boston: Little, Brown, 1969.

Kamisar, Yale; Inbau, Fred E.; Arnold, Thurman. *Criminal Justice in Our Time*. Charlottesville, Va.: University of Virginia Press, 1965.

Kerper, Hazel B. *Introduction to the Criminal Justice System*. St. Paul, Minn.: West, 1972.

Kolodney, S. E. *Offender Tracking—Information for Criminal Justice System Planning, Analysis and Evaluation*. Sunnyvale, Calif.: Public Systems, Inc., 1970.

Law Enforcement Assistance Association. *3rd Annual Report of the Law Enforcement Assistance Administration*. Washington, D.C.: U.S. Government Printing Office, 1972.

Leonard, V. A. *The Police, the Judiciary and the Criminal*. Springfield, Ill.: Charles C Thomas, 1969.

Likert, Rensis. *New Patterns of Management*. New York: McGraw-Hill, 1961.

Nagel, Stuart S. "Disparities in Criminal Procedure." *UCLA Law Review* 14 (1967): 1272-1305.

National Advisory Commission on Criminal Justice Standards and Goals. *Criminal Justice System*. Washington, D.C.: U.S. Department of Justice, 1973.

———. *A National Strategy to Reduce Crime*. Washington, D.C.: U.S. Department of Justice, 1973.

Navansky, Victor S. *Kennedy Justice*. New York: Atheneum, 1971.

Newman, Donald J. "The Effect of Accommodations in Justice Administration on Criminal Statistics." *Sociology and Social Research* 46 (January 1962): 144-155.

———. "Perspectives of Probation: Legal Issues and Professional Trends" from the *Challenge of Change in the Correctional Process.* Hackensack, N.J.: National Council on Crime and Delinquency 1972.

Nonet, Philippe. *Administrative Justice: Advocacy and Change in a Government Agency.* New York: Russell Sage Foundation, 1969.

Note. "Juvenile Delinquents, the Police, State Courts, and Individualized Justice." *Harvard Law Review* 79, 4 (February 1966): 775-810.

Oaks, Dallin H. and Lehman, Warren. *A Criminal Justice System and the Indigent.* Chicago: University of Chicago Press, 1968.

Pound, Roscoe. *Criminal Justice in America.* New York: Holt & Co., 1930.

President's Commission on Law Enforcement and Administration of Justice. *Task Force Report: Science and Technology.* Washington, D.C.: U.S. Government Printing Office, 1967.

Remington, Frank J.; Newman, Donald J.; Kimball, Edward L.; Melli, Marygold; and Goldstein, Herman. *Criminal Justice Administration: Materials and Cases.* Indianapolis: Bobbs-Merrill, 1969.

Remington, Frank J. and Rosenblum, Victor G. "The Criminal Law and the Legislative Process." *University of Illinois Law Forum* 1960 (Winter 1960): 481-499.

Rosett, Arthur. "Discretion, Severity and Legality in Criminal Justice." *Southern California Law Review* 46, 1 (December 1972): 12-50.

Rowat, Donald C. *The Ombudsman: Citizen's Defender.* London: George Allen and Unwin, 1965.

Silver, Isidore. "Crime and Punishment." *Commentary* (March 1968): 68-73.

Smith, Alexander and Pollack, Harriet. "Less, Not More: Police, Courts, Prisons." *Federal Probation* 36, 3 (September 1972): 12-19.

Tappan, Paul. *Crime, Justice and Correction.* New York: McGraw-Hill, 1960.

Tolchin, Martin and Tolchin, Susan. *To the Victor . . . Political Patronage From the Clubhouse to the White House.* New York: Random House, 1971.

Wildavsky, Aaron. *The Politics of the Budgetary Process.* Boston: Little, Brown, 1964.

Wilensky, Harold. "The Professionalization of Everyone?" *American Journal of Sociology* 70 (September 1964): 138-140.

Wilkins, Leslie T. "New Thinking in Criminal Statistics." *Journal of Criminal Law, Criminology and Police Science* 56 (1965): 277-284.

Wolfgang, Marvin E. "Uniform Crime Reports: A Critical Appraisal." *University of Pennsylvania Law Review* 111 (April 1963): 709-738.

Ziegler, Harmon. *Interest Groups in American Society.* Englewood Cliffs, N.J.: Prentice-Hall, 1964.

Theory in Law and Punishment

Akers, Ronald L. "Toward a Comparative Definition of Law," *Journal of Criminal Law, Criminology and Police Science* 56 (September 1965): 301-306.

Allen, Francis A. *The Borderland of Criminal Justice.* Chicago: University of Chicago Press, 1964.

Andenaes, Johannes. "The General Preventive Effects of Punishment." *University of Pennsylvania Law Review* 114, 7 (May 1966): 949-983.

Aptheker, Bettina and Davis, Angela, eds. *If They Come in the Morning.* New York: New American Library, 1971.

Arnold, Thurman W. "Law Enforcement: An Attempt at Social Dissection." *Yale Law Journal* 42, 1 (November 1932): 1-24.

Barnes, Harry Elmer. *The Story of Punishment: A Record of Man's Inhumanity to Men.* Montclair, N.J.: Patterson-Smith Publishing Co., 1972.

Beccaria, Cesare B. *On Crimes and Punishments.* Translated by Henry Paolucci, 1963. Indianapolis: Bobbs-Merrill, 1968.

Bentham, Jeremy. *An Introduction to the Principles of Morals and Legislation,* corrected ed. Oxford: Clarendon Press, 1823.

Brant, Irving. *The Bill of Rights.* New York: New American Library, 1967.

Chwast, Jacob. "Value Conflicts in Law Enforcement." *Crime and Delinquency* 11, 2 (1965): 151-162.

Cohen, Morris R. "Moral Aspects of the Criminal Law." *Yale Law Journal* 49, (April 1940): 987-1026.

Davis, Kenneth C. *Administrative Law and Government.* St. Paul, Minn.: West, 1960.

———. *Discretionary Justice: A Preliminary Inquiry.* Baton Rouge, La.: Louisiana State University Press, 1969.

Devlin, Patrick. *The Enforcement of Morals.* London: Oxford University Press, 1959.

Duster, Troy. *The Legislation of Morality.* New York: The Free Press, 1970.

Ezorsky, Gertrude, ed. *Philosophical Perspectives on Punishment.* Albany, N.Y.: State University of New York Press, 1973.

Falk, Richard A.; Kolko, Gabriel; and Lifton, Robert Jay. *Crimes of War.* New York: Vintage, 1971.

Friedmann, Wolfgang. *Law in a Changing Society.* Harmondsworth, Eng.: Penguin Books, 1964.

Fuller, Lon L. *The Morality of Law.* New Haven, Conn.: Yale University Press, 1964.

Fuller, Richard C. "Morals and the Criminal Law." *Journal of Criminal Law, Criminology and Police Science* 32 (March-April 1942): 624-630.

Glueck, Sheldon. "Principles of a Rational Penal Code." *Harvard Law Review* 41 (1928): 453-482.

Hall, Jerome. "Objectives of Federal Criminal Procedural Revision." *Yale Law Journal* 51 (1942): 723-747.

Hart, Henry M., Jr. "The Aims of the Criminal Law." *Law and Contemporary Problems* 23 (Summer 1958): 401-441.

Hart, H. L. A. *The Concept of Law.* London: Oxford University Press, 1961.

———. *Law, Liberty, and Morality.* Stanford, Calif.: Stanford University Press, 1963.

Hills, Stuart L. *Crime, Power, and Morality.* Scranton, Pa.: Chandler Publ. Co., 1971.

Hindelang, Michael J. "Equal Justice Under Law." *Journal of Criminal Law, Criminology and Police Science* 60 (1969): 306-313.

Holmes, Oliver Wendell. *The Common Law*. Edited by Mark DeWolfe Howe. Cambridge, Mass.: Belknap Press of Harvard University Press, 1963.

Kadish, Sanford H. "The Crisis of Overcriminalization." *Annals of the American Academy of Political and Social Science* 374 (November 1967): 157-170.

———. "Legal Norm and Discretion in the Police and Sentencing Process." *Harvard Law Review* 75, 5 (March 1962): 904-931.

Kirchheimer, Otto. *Political Justice: The Use of Legal Procedure for Political Ends*. Princeton, N.J.: Princeton University Press, 1961.

Kittrie, Nicholas N. *The Right to Be Different: Deviance and Enforced Therapy*. Baltimore, Md.: Johns Hopkins Press, 1971.

Knowles, Louis and Prewitt, Kenneth, eds. *Institutional Racism in America*. New York: Spectrum Books, 1969.

Korn, Richard. "Of Crime, Criminal Justice and Corrections." *San Francisco Law Review* 27, (October 1971): 27-75.

Lewis, C. S. "The Humanitarian Theory of Punishment." *Res Judicatae* 6 (1954): 224-229.

Mead, George Herbert. "The Psychology of Punitive Justice." *American Journal of Sociology* 23 (March 1918): 577-602.

Milgram, Stanley. *Obedience to Authority*. New York: Harper & Row, 1974.

More, Harry W., Jr. *Critical Issues in Law Enforcement*. Cincinnati, Ohio: The W. H. Anderson Co., 1972.

Morris, Norval and Hawkins, Gordon. *The Honest Politicians Guide to Crime Control*. Chicago: University of Chicago Press, 1970.

Packer, Herbert L. *The Limits of the Criminal Sanction*. Stanford, Calif.: Stanford University Press, 1968.

Pfeffer, Leo. *The Liberties of an American*. Boston: Beacon Press, 1956.

Pritchett, C. Herman. *The American Constitution*, 2d ed. New York: McGraw-Hill, 1968.

Quinney, Richard. "Crime Control and Capitalist Society: A Critical Philosophy of Legal Order." *Issues in Criminology* 8 (Spring 1973): 75-100.

———. "The Ideology of Law: Notes for a Radical Alternative to Legal Oppression." *Issues in Criminology* 7, 1 (Winter 1972): 1-36.

Radzinowicz, Leon. *Ideology and Crime*. New York: Columbia University Press, 1966.

Rawls, John. *A Theory of Justice*. Cambridge, Mass.: Harvard University Press, 1971.

Reasons, Charles E. and Kuykendall, Jack L. *Race, Crime and Justice*. Pacific Palisades, Calif.: Goodyear Publishing, 1972.

Reich, Charles. "Individual Rights and Social Welfare: The Emerging Legal Issues." *Yale Law Journal* 74, 7 (June 1965): 1245-1258.

———. "The New Property." *Yale Law Journal* 73, 5 (April 1964): 733-787.

Ryan, William. *Blaming the Victim*. New York: Vintage, 1971.

Saleilles, R. *The Individualization of Punishment*. Boston: Little, Brown, 1911.

Schafer, Stephen. "The Concept of the Political Criminal." *Journal of Criminal Law, Criminology and Police Science* 62, 3 (1971): 380-387.

Schur, Edwin M. *Crimes Without Victims,* Englewood Cliffs, N.J.: Prentice-Hall, 1965.

Skolnick, Jerome. "Coercion to Virtue." *Southern California Law Review* 41 (1968): 588-641.

Sykes, Gresham M. "The Corruption of Authority and Rehabilitation." *Social Forces* 34 (March 1956): 257-262.

Tappan, Paul W. "Who Is the Criminal?" *American Sociological Review* 12 (February 1947): 96-102.

Turk, Austin. *Criminality and Legal Order.* Chicago: Rand McNally, 1969.

Van Alstyne, William W. "The Demise of the Rights-Privilege Distinction in Constitutional Law." *Harvard Law Review* 81, 7 (May 1968): 1439-1464.

Walker, Nigel. "Aims of Punishment." In Leon Radzinowicz and Marvin E. Wolfgang, eds., *The Criminal In the Arms of the Law.* New York: Basic Books, 1971, 48-65.

Warren, Samuel D. and Brandeis, Louis D. "The Right to Privacy." *Harvard Law Review* 4, 5 (December 1890): 193-220.

Westin, Alan F. *Privacy and Freedom.* New York: Atheneum, 1967.

Wooten, Barbara. *Social Science and Social Pathology.* London: George Allen and Unwin, 1959.

Zimring, Franklin. "Is Gun Control Likely to Reduce Violent Killing?" *University of Chicago Law Review* 35 (1968): 720-737.

————. *Perspectives on Deterrence.* Washington, D.C.: National Institute of Mental Health, 1971.

———— and Hawkins, Gordon. *Deterrence.* Chicago: University of Chicago Press, 1973.

Criminology, The Nature of Crime and Delinquency

Abrahamsen, David. *Who Are the Guilty?* New York: Holt, Rinehart & Winston, 1952.

Anderson, Robert T. "From Mafia to Cosa Nostra." *American Journal of Sociology* 16 (November 1965): 302-310.

Aschaffenburg, Gustave. *Crime and Its Repression.* Translated by Adalbert Albrecht. Boston: Little, Brown, 1913.

Barnes, Harry E. and Teeters, Negley K. *New Horizons in Criminology,* 2nd ed. New York: Prentice-Hall, 1951.

Becker, Howard S. *Outsiders: Studies in the Sociology of Deviance.* New York: The Free Press, 1963.

————, ed. *The Other Side.* Glencoe, Ill.: The Free Press, 1964.

Becker, Theodore L. and Murray, Vernon G., eds. *Government Lawlessness in America.* New York: Oxford University Press, 1971.

Bell, Daniel. "Crime as an American Way of Life." *Antioch Review* 13 (June 1953): 131-154.

Biderman, Albert D. and Reiss, Albert J. Jr. "On Exploring the 'Dark Figure' of Crime."

Annals of the American Academy of Political and Social Science, 374 (November 1967): 1-15.

————; Johnson, Louis A.; McIntyre, Jennie; and Weir, Adrianne W. "Report on a Pilot Study in the District of Columbia on Victimization and Attitudes Toward Law Enforcement." *Field Survey I,* President's Commission on Law Enforcement and Administration of Justice. Washington, D.C.: U.S. Government Printing Office, 1967.

Biggs, John Jr. *The Guilty Mind: Psychiatry and the Law of Homicide.* Baltimore, Md.: Johns Hopkins Press, 1955.

Bloch, Herbert A. "The Gambling Business: An American Paradox." *Crime and Delinquency* 8 (October 1962): 355-364.

———— and Geis, Gilbert. *Man, Crime, and Society.* New York: Random House, 1962.

Boggs, Sarah L. "Urban Crime Patterns." *American Sociological Review* 30 (December 1965): 899-908.

Bonger, Willem. *Criminality and Economic Conditions.* Bloomington, Ind.: Indiana University Press, 1969.

————. *Introduction to Criminology.* Translated by Emil Van Loo. London: Methuen, 1918.

Bordua, D. J. "Delinquent Subcultures: Sociological Interpretations of Gang Delinquency." *The Annals of the American Academy of Political and Social Science* 338 (November 1961): 119-136.

Brace, Charles Loring. *The Dangerous Classes of New York,* 3d ed. Montclair, N.J.: Smith Patterson, 1880.

Brown, Claude. *Manchild in the Promised Land.* New York: Macmillan, 1965.

Burgess, Ernest W. "The Study of the Delinquent as a Person." *American Journal of Sociology* 28 (May 1923): 657-680.

Cameron, Mary Owen. *The Booster and the Snitch.* Glencoe, Ill.: The Free Press, 1964.

Cavan, Ruth Shonle. *Criminology,* 3d ed. New York: Thomas Y. Crowell, 1962.

Chambliss, William. *Crime and the Legal Process.* New York: McGraw-Hill, 1969.

———— and Seidman, Robert B. *Law, Order and Power.* Reading, Mass.: Addison-Wesley Publishing Co., 1971.

————. "Types of Deviance and the Effectiveness of Legal Sanctions." *Wisconsin Law Review* (Summer 1967): 703-719.

————. "A Sociological Analysis of the Law of Vagrancy." *Social Problems* 12 (Summer 1964): 66-77.

Clark, Alexander L. and Gibbs, Jack P. "Social Control: A Reformulation." *Social Problems* 12 (Spring 1965): 402-406.

Clark, John P. and Tifft, Larry L. "Polygraph and Interview Validation of Self-Reported Deviant Behavior." *American Sociological Review* 31 (August 1966): 516-523.

Clark, Kenneth B. *Dark Ghetto.* New York: Harper & Row, 1965.

Clark, Ramsey. *Crime in America: Observations on Its Nature, Causes, Prevention and Control*. New York: Simon & Schuster, 1970.

Cleaver, Eldridge. *Soul on Ice*. New York: Delta, 1968.

Clinard, Marshall B., ed. *Anomie and Deviant Behavior*. New York: The Free Press, 1964.

————. "Sociologists and American Criminology." *Journal of Criminal Law, Criminology and Police Science* 41 (January 1951): 549-577.

————. *Sociology of Deviant Behavior*. New York: Holt, Rinehart & Winston, 1968.

———— and Quinney, Richard. *Criminal Behavior Systems: A Typology*. New York: Holt, Rinehart & Winston, 1967.

Cloward, Richard A. and Ohlin, Lloyd E. *Delinquency and Opportunity*. New York: The Free Press, 1960.

Cohen, Albert K. *Delinquent Boys*. New York: The Free Press, 1955.

————; Lindesmith, Alfred; and Schuessler, Karl F., eds. *The Sutherland Papers*. Bloomington, Ind.: Indiana University Press, 1956.

Conklin, John E. *Robbery and the Criminal Justice System*. New York: J. B. Lippincott Company, 1972.

Conot, Robert. *Rivers of Blood, Years of Blackness*. New York: Bantam, 1967.

Coser, Lewis. *The Functions of Social Conflict*. New York: The Free Press, 1956.

————. "Some Functions of Deviant Behavior and Normative Flexibility." *American Journal of Sociology* 68 (September 1962): 172-181.

Cressey, Donald R. *Other People's Money*. New York: The Free Press, 1953.

————. *Theft of a Nation: The Structures and Operations of Organized Crime in America*. New York: Harper & Row, 1969.

Davis, F. J. "Crime News in Colorado Newspapers." *American Journal of Sociology* 57 (January 1952): 325-330.

Deutsch, Albert. *The Mentally Ill in America*, 2d ed., revised. New York: Columbia University Press, 1949.

Durkheim, Emile. *The Rules of the Sociological Method*. New York: The Free Press, 1956.

————. *Suicide*. Glencoe, Ill.: The Free Press, 1951.

Duster, Troy. *The Legislation of Morality*. New York: The Free Press, 1970.

Elmhorn, K. "Study on Self-Reported Delinquency Among School Children in Stockholm." In K. O. Christianson, ed., *Scandinavian Studies in Criminology*. London: Tavistock, 1965, pp. 117-146.

Empey, L. T. and Erickson, M. L. "Hidden Delinquency and Social Status." *Social Forces* 44 (1966): 546-554.

Ennis, Philip, H." Criminal Victimization in the United States: A Report of a National Survey." Field Surveys II, President's Commission on Law Enforcement and Administration of Justice. Washington, D.C.: U.S. Government Printing Office, 1967.

Erickson, Kai T. *Wayward Puritans*. New York: John Wiley and Sons, 1966.

424

Erickson, M. L. and Empey, L. M. "Court Records, Undetected Delinquency and Decision-Making." *Journal of Criminal Law, Criminology and Police Science* 54 (1963): 456-469.

Eysenck, H. J. *Crime and Personality*. London: Granada Publishing Ltd., 1964.

Ferri, Enrico. *Criminal Sociology*. Translated by J. I. Kelly and John Lisle. Boston: Little, Brown, 1917.

Fink, Arthur E. *Causes of Crime: Biological Theories in the United States, 1800-1915*. Philadelphia: University of Pennsylvania Press, 1938.

Foucault, Michel. *Madness and Civilization: A History of Insanity in the Age of Reason*. New York: New American Library, 1967.

Freud, Sigmund. *A General Introduction to Psychoanalysis*. New York: Liveright Publishers, 1948.

Friendly, Alfred and Goldfarb, Ronald L. *Crime and Publicity: The Impact of News on the Administration of Justice*. New York: Vintage, 1968.

Garofalo, Raffaele. *Criminology*. Translated by Robert Wyness. Boston: Little, Brown, 1914.

Geis, Gilbert. "White Collar Crime: The Heavy Electrical Equipment Antitrust Cases of 1961." In M. B. Clinard and R. Quinney, eds., *Criminal Behavior Systems: A Typology*. New York: Holt, Rinehart & Winston, 1967, pp. 139-151.

―――. *White Collar Criminal: The Offender in Business and The Professions*. New York: Atherton Press, 1968.

Genet, Jean. *The Thief's Journal*. New York: Bantam, 1965.

Gold, Martin. "Undetected Delinquent Behavior." *Journal of Research in Crime and Delinquency* 3 (1966): 27-46.

Gibbs, Jack P. "Conceptions of Deviant Behavior: The Old and the New." *The Pacific Sociological Review* 9 (Spring 1966): 9-14.

Glueck, Sheldon and Glueck, Eleanor. *Five Hundred Criminal Careers*. New York: Alfred A. Knopf, Inc., 1930.

Hall, Jerome. *Theft, Law, and Society*, 2d ed. Indianapolis: Bobbs-Merrill, 1952.

Hardt, Robert H. and Bodine, George E. *Development of Self-Report Instruments in Delinquency Research: A Conference Report*. Syracuse: Syracuse University Youth Development Center, 1965.

Harris, Richard. *The Fear of Crime*. New York: Praeger, 1969.

Hartogs, Renatus and Artzt, Eric, eds. *Violence: Causes and Solutions*. New York: Delhi, 1970.

Hood, Roger and Sparks, Richard. *Key Issues in Criminology*. New York: World University Library, 1970.

Hooten, Ernest A. *Crime and the Man*. Cambridge, Mass.: Harvard University Press, 1939.

Hunt, Morton. *The Mugging*. New York: Atheneum, 1972.

Kiester, Edwin. *Crimes With No Victims*. New York: Alliance for a Safer New York, 1972.

Kitsuse, John I. "Social Reaction to Deviant Behavior: Problems of Theory and Method." *Social Problems* 9 (Winter 1962): 247-256.

Korn, Richard R. and McCorkle, Lloyd W. *Criminology and Penology.* New York: Holt, Rinehart & Winston, 1959.

Lemert, Edwin M. "The Behavior of the Systematic Check Forger." *Social Problems* 6 (Fall 1958): 141-149.

————. *Human Deviance, Social Problems, and Social Control.* Englewood Cliffs, N.J.: Prentice-Hall, 1967.

Lindesmith, Alfred R. *The Addict and the Law.* Bloomington, Ind.: Indiana University Press, 1965.

————. *Addiction and Opiates.* Chicago: Aldine, 1968.

Lofland, John and Lofland, Lyn H. "Some Benefits of Crime and Other Nonconformity." *Forum, The University of Houston* 6 (Spring 1968): 41-45.

Malinowski, Bronislav. *Crime and Custom in Savage Society.* New York: Humanities Press, 1926.

Matza, David. *Delinquency and Drift.* New York: John Wiley and Sons, 1964.

Maurer, David W. *The Big Con.* New York: Signet, 1962.

————. *Whiz Mob.* New Haven, Conn.: College and University Press, 1955.

McClintock, F. H. *Crimes of Violence.* London: MacMillan, 1963.

Merton, Robert K. "Social Structure and Anomie." *American Sociological Review* 3 (October 1938): 672-682.

————. *Social Theory and Social Structure.* Glencoe, Ill.: The Free Press, 1949.

Morris, Terrence. *The Criminal Area.* London: Routledge & Kegan Paul, 1957.

———— and Gibson, E. *Robbery in London.* London: MacMillan, 1961.

Myren, Richard A. and Swanson, Lynn D. *Police Work with Children.* Washington, D.C.: U.S. Department of Health, Education, and Welfare, 1962.

National Commission on the Causes and Prevention of Violence. *To Establish Justice, To Insure Domestic Tranquility.* New York: Bantam, 1970.

Newman, Donald J. "Public Attitudes Toward a Form of White Collar Crime." *Social Problems* 4 (January 1957): 228-232.

————. "White Collar Crime." *Law and Contemporary Problems* 23, 4 (Autumn 1958): 735-753.

Newman, Graeme, R. "Normality and Crime Revisited: A View from the Sociology of Deviance." *British Journal of Criminology* (January 1970): 64-73.

Piven, Frances Fox and Cloward, Richard A. *Regulating the Poor.* New York: Random House, 1971.

Platt, Anthony. *The Child-Savers: The Invention of Delinquency.* Chicago: University of Chicago Press, 1969.

Polsky, Ned. *Hustlers, Beats, and Others.* Chicago: Aldine, 1967.

Powell, Edwin H. "Crime as a Function of Anomie." *Journal of Criminal Law, Criminology and Police Science* 57 (June 1966): 161-171.

President's Commission on Law Enforcement and Administration of Justice. *The Challenge of Crime in a Free Society*. Washington, D.C.: U.S. Government Printing Office, 1967.

———. *Task Force Report: Crime and Its Impact—An Assessment*. Washington, D.C.: U.S. Government Printing Office, 1967.

———. *Task Force Report: Drunkenness*. Washington, D.C.: U.S. Government Printing Office, 1967.

———. *Task Force Report: Juvenile Delinquency and Youth Crime*. Washington, D.C.: U.S. Government Printing Office, 1967.

———. *Task Force Report: Organized Crime*. Washington, D.C.: U.S. Government Printing Office, 1967.

Quinney, Richard. *Critique of Legal Order: Crime Control in Capitalist Society*. Boston: Little, Brown, 1974.

———. *The Social Reality of Crime*. Boston: Little, Brown, 1970.

Reckless, Walter. *The Crime Problem*. New York: Appleton-Century-Crofts Inc., 1961.

Redl, Fritz and Wineman, David. *Children Who Hate*. New York: The Free Press, 1956.

Report of the National Advisory Commission on Civil Disorders. New York: Bantam, 1968.

Rights in Conflict, A Report Submitted by Daniel Walker to the National Commission on the Causes and Prevention of Violence. New York: Bantam, 1968.

Roche, Philip Q. *The Criminal Mind: A Study of Communications Between the Criminal Law and Psychiatry*. New York: Grove Press, 1958.

Roebuck, Julian B. *Criminal Typology: The Legalistic, Physical-Constitutional-Heredity, Psychological-Psychiatric and Sociological Approaches*. Springfield, Ill.: Charles C Thomas, 1967.

———. "The Negro Drug Addict as an Offender Type." *Journal of Criminal Law, Criminology and Police Science* 53 (March 1962): 36-43.

——— and Cadwallader, Marvyn. "The Negro Armed Robber as a Criminal Type: The Construction and Application of a Typology." *Pacific Sociological Review* 4 (Spring 1961): 2-26.

Salisbury, Harrison. *The Shook-up Generation*. New York: Harper & Brothers, 1958.

Schafer, Stephen. *The Victim and His Criminal: A Study in Functional Responsibility*. New York: Random House, 1968.

Schuessler, Karl F. and Cressey, Donald R. "Personality Characteristics of Criminals." *American Journal of Sociology* 55 (March 1950): 476-484.

Schur, Edwin M. *Crimes Without Victims*. Englewood Cliffs: Prentice-Hall, 1965.

———. *Labelling Deviant Behavior*. New York: Harper & Row, 1971.

Sellin, Thorsten. *Culture Conflict and Crime*. New York: Social Science Research Council, 1938.

——— and Wolfgang, Marvin E. *The Measurement of Delinquency*. New York: John Wiley and Sons, 1964.

427

Shaw, Clifford; Zorbaugh, Frederick M.; McKay, Henry D.; and Cottrell, Leonard S. *Delinquency Areas.* Chicago: University of Chicago Press, 1929.

Shaw, Clifford. *The Jack-roller: A Delinquent Boy's Own Story.* Chicago: University of Chicago Press, 1930.

———, and McKay, Henry D. *Juvenile Delinquency and Urban Areas.* Chicago: University of Chicago Press, 1942.

——— and Moore, Maurice E. *The Natural History of a Delinquent Career.* Chicago: University of Chicago Press, 1931.

Skolnick, Jerome H. *The Politics of Protest.* New York: Ballantine, 1969.

Smigel, Edwin O. and Ross, H. Lawrence. *Crimes Against Bureaucracy.* New York: Van Nostrand Reinhold Co., 1970.

Spradley, James P. *You Owe Yourself a Drunk: An Ethnography of Urban Nomads.* Boston: Little, Brown, 1970.

Sutherland, Edwin H., ed. *The Professional Thief.* Chicago: University of Chicago Press, 1937.

———. *White Collar Crime.* New York: Dryden Press, 1949.

——— and Cressey, Donald R. *Criminology,* 9th ed. Philadelphia: J. B. Lippincott Company, 1974.

Sykes, Gresham M. and Matza, David. "Techniques of Neutralization: A Theory of Delinquency." *American Sociological Review* 22 (December 1957): 664-670.

Szasz, Thomas S. *Law, Liberty and Psychiatry.* New York: Macmillan, 1963.

———. *The Manufacture of Madness.* New York: Harper & Row, 1970.

———. *The Myth of Mental Illness.* New York: Hoeber-Harper Books, 1961.

———. *Psychiatric Justice.* New York: Macmillan, 1965.

Tannenbaum, Frank. *Crime and the Community.* New York: Columbia University Press, 1938.

Taylor, Ian; Walton, Paul; and Young, Jack. *The New Criminology: For a Social Theory of Deviance.* New York: Harper & Row, 1973.

Thrasher, Frederick. *The Gang,* 2d ed. Chicago: University of Chicago Press, 1936.

Toch, Hans. *Violent Men: An Inquiry into the Psychology of Violence.* Chicago: Aldine, 1969.

Tyler, Gus. *Organized Crime in America.* Ann Arbor, Mich.: University of Michigan Press, 1962.

Vold, G. B. *Theoretical Criminology.* New York: Oxford University Press, 1958.

von Hentig, Hans. *The Criminal and His Victim.* New Haven, Conn.: Yale University Press, 1948.

Wallerstein, James S. and Wyle; Clement J. "Our Law Abiding Law-Breakers." *National Probation* 25 (March-April 1947): 107-112.

Westley, William A. "The Escalation of Violence through Legitimation." *Annals of the American Academy of Political and Social Science* 364 (March 1966): 120-126.

Whyte, William F. *Street Corner Society,* 2d ed. Chicago: University of Chicago Press, 1955.

428

Wilkins, Leslie T. "The Concept of Cause in Criminology." *Issues in Criminology* 3, 2 (1968): 147-165.

———. "Crime in the World of 1990." *Futures* (1970): 202-214.

———. "New Thinking in Criminal Statistics." *Journal of Criminal Law, Criminology and Police Science* 56, 3 (September 1965): 277-284.

———. *Social Deviance: Social Action, Policy, and Research.* London Tavistock, 1964.

Winick, Charles and Kinsie, Paul M. *The Lively Commerce: Prostitution.* New York: Signet, 1971.

Wolfgang, Marvin E. *Patterns in Criminal Homicide.* Philadelphia: University of Pennsylvania Press, 1958.

——— and Cohen, Bernard. *Crime and Race.* New York: Institute of Human Relations, 1970.

——— and Ferracuti, Franco. *The Subculture of Violence: Towards an Integrated Theory of Criminology.* London: Tavistock, 1967.

———; Figlio, Robert M.; and Sellin, Thorsten. *Delinquency in a Birth Cohort.* Chicago: University of Chicago Press, 1972.

———; Savitz, Leonard; and Johnston, Norman, eds. *The Sociology of Crime and Delinquency.* New York: John Wiley and Sons, 1962.

X, Malcolm. *The Autobiography of Malcolm X.* New York: Grove Press, 1966.

Yablonsky, Lewis. *The Violent Gang.* New York: Macmillan, 1962.

Yinger, J. Milton. "Contraculture and Subculture." *American Sociological Review* 25 (October 1960): 625-635.

The Police

American Bar Association. Project on Standards for Criminal Justice. *Standards Relating to Electronic Surveillance.* New York: Institute of Judicial Administration, 1971.

———. *Standards Relating to the Urban Police Function.* New York: Institute of Judicial Administration, 1973.

Aubry, Arthur S. *The Officer in the Small Department.* Springfield, Ill.: Charles C Thomas, 1961.

Banton, Michael. *The Policeman in the Community.* London: Tavistock, 1964.

Bard, Morton. "Family Intervention Police Teams as a Community Mental Health Resource." *Journal of Criminal Law, Criminology and Police Science* 60 (1969): 247-250.

———. *Training Police as Specialists in Family Crisis Intervention.* Washington, D.C.: U.S. Government Printing Office, 1970.

Bass, Nan C. and McDonald, William F. *Preventive Detention in the District of Columbia: The First Ten Months.* New York: Vera Institute of Justice and Georgetown Institute of Criminal Law and Procedure, 1972.

Bayley, David H. and Mendelsohn, Harold. *Minorities and the Police.* New York: Macmillan, 1968.

429

Bercal, Thomas E. "Calls for Police Assistance: Consumer Demands for Government Service." *American Behavioral Scientist* 13 (May-August 1970): 681-691.

Berger, Mark. "Police Field Citations in New Haven." *Wisconsin Law Review* 1972, 2 (1972): 382-417.

Bittner, Egon. *The Functions of the Police in Modern Society.* Rockville, Md.: National Institute of Mental Health, 1970.

———. "Police Discretion in Emergency Apprehension of Mentally Ill Persons." *Social Problems* 14 (1967): 287-292.

———. "The Police on Skid Row: A Study of Peace Keeping." *American Sociological Review* 32 (October 1967): 669-715.

Black, Algernon D. *The People and the Police.* New York: McGraw-Hill, 1968.

Blum, Richard H., ed. *Police Selection.* Springfield, Ill.: Charles C Thomas, 1964.

——— and Osterloh, William. "The Polygraph Examination as a Means for Detecting Truth and Falsehood in Stories Presented by Police Informants." *Journal of Criminal Law, Criminology and Police Science* 59 (1968): 133-137.

Bordua, David J., ed. *The Police: Six Sociological Essays.* New York: John Wiley and Sons, 1967.

——— and Reiss, Albert J., Jr. "Command, Control and Charisma: Reflections on Police Bureaucracy." *American Journal of Sociology* 72 (1966): 68-76.

Bristow, Allen P. and Gabard, E. C. *Decision Making in Police Administration.* Springfield, Ill.: Charles C Thomas, 1961.

Bristow, Allen P. *Effective Police Manpower Utilization.* Springfield, Ill.: Charles C Thomas, 1969.

Brown, William P. "Narcotics Squad: The Golden Arm of the Law." *The Nation* (October 25, 1971): 392-397.

———. *A Police Administration Approach to the Corruption Problem.* Washington, D.C.: U.S. Government Printing Office, 1973.

Buchsbaum, Peter. "Police Infiltration of Political Groups." *Harvard Civil Rights - Civil Liberties Review* 4, 2 (Spring 1969): 331-344.

Carter, Robert M. "The Evaluation of Police Programs." *The Police Chief* 38 (November 1971): 57-60.

Chapman, Samuel G. *The Police Heritage in England and America.* East Lansing, Mich.: Michigan State University Press, 1962.

Chevigny, Paul. *Cops and Rebels.* New York: Pantheon Books, 1972.

———. *Police Power: Police Abuses in New York City.* New York: Vintage, 1969.

Christianson, Scott. "The Cops Can't Find the Pusher." *The Nation* (November 29, 1971): 462-464.

Coates, Joseph. *Some New Approaches to Riot, Mob and Crowd Control.* Arlington, Va.: Institute of Defense Analysis, 1968.

Cohen, Bernard and Chaiken, Jan M. *Police Background Characteristics and Performance: Summary.* New York: Rand Institute, 1972.

Cohen, Bernard. *The Police Internal Administration of Justice in New York City.* New York: Rand Institute, 1970.

Cohen, Fred. "Police Perjury: An Interview with Martin Garbus." *Criminal Law Bulletin* 8, 5 (June 1972): 363-375.

Comment. "At the Border of Reasonableness: Searches by Customs Officials." *Cornell Law Review* 53, 5 (May 1968): 871-885.

———. "Border Searches and the Fourth Amendment." *Yale Law Journal* 77, 5 (April 1968): 1007-1018.

———. "Interrogations in New Haven: The Impact of Miranda." *Yale Law Journal* 76, 8 (July 1967): 1519-1648.

———. "Judicial Control of Secret Agents." *Yale Law Journal* 67, 5 (April 1967): 994-1019.

———. "Kill or Be Killed?" Use of Deadly Force in the Riot Situation." *California Law Review* 56, 3 (May 1968): 829-877.

———. "Philadelphia's Police Advisory Board—A New Concept in Community Relations." *Villanova Law Review* 7, 4 (Summer 1962): 656-673.

———. "Police Perjury in Narcotics 'Dropsey' Cases: A New Credibility Gap." *Georgetown Law Journal* 60, 2 (1971): 507-523.

———. "The Role of 'Booking' in the Administration of Criminal Justice." *University of Illinois Law Forum* 1963, 4 (Winter 1963): 685-692.

Commission to Investigate Allegations of Police Corruption. *Final Report.* New York: City of New York, 1972.

Conant, Ralph W. "Rioting, Insurrection and Civil Disobedience." *The American Scholar* 37 (September 1968): 420-433.

Connery, Robert H. *Urban Riots, Violence and Social Change.* New York: Vintage, 1969.

Cook, Fred J. *The FBI Nobody Knows.* New York: Pyramid, 1964.

Cray, Ed. *The Big Blue Line: Police Power versus Human Rights.* New York: Coward McCann, 1967.

Cumming, Elaine; Cumming, Ian; and Edell, Laurel. "Policeman as Philosopher, Guide and Friend." *Social Problems* 12 (1965): 276-286.

Daley, Robert. "The Deadly Score of the Stakeout Squad." *New York Magazine* (April 24, 1972): 30.

Dash, Samuel; Schwartz, Richard F.; and Knowlton, Robert E. *The Eavesdroppers.* New York: Da Capo Press, 1959.

Deutsch, Albert. *The Trouble With Cops.* New York: Crown Publishers, 1954.

Donnelly, Richard C. "Judicial Control of Informants, Spies, Stool Pigeons, and Agent Provocateurs." *Yale Law Journal* 60, 6 (June 1951): 1091-1131.

Driver, Edwin. "Confessions and the Social Psychology of Coercion." In Marion Summers and Thomas Barth, eds., *Law and Order in a Democratic Society.* Indianapolis: Bobbs-Merrill, 1970, pp. 71-90.

431

Editorial Note. "Police Undercover Agents: New Threat to First Amendment Freedoms." *George Washington Law Review* 37, 3 (March 1969): 634-668.

Edwards, George. "Order and Civil Liberties: A Complex Role for the Police." *Michigan Law Review* 64, 1 (November 1965): 47-62.

———. *The Police on the Urban Frontier.* New York: Institute of Human Relations Press, 1968.

Federal Bureau of Investigation. *Prevention and Control of Mobs and Riots.* Washington, D.C.: U.S. Department of Justice, 1967.

Gamsen, William A. and McEnvoy, James. "Police Violence and Its Public Support." *The Annals* 391 (September 1970): 98-110.

Germann, A. C.; Day, Frank D.; and Gallati, Robert R. J. *Introduction to Law Enforcement.* Springfield, Ill.: Charles C Thomas, 1966.

Goldstein, Herman. "Administrative Problems in Controlling the Exercise of Police Authority." *Journal of Criminal Law, Criminology and Police Science* 58, 2 (1967): 160-172.

———. "Police Discretion: The Ideal versus the Real." *Public Administration Review* 23, 1 (September 1963): 140-148.

———. "Police Response to Urban Crisis." *Public Administration Review* 28 (September-October 1968): 417-423.

Goldstein, Joseph. "Police Discretion Not to Invoke the Criminal Process: Low Visibility Decisions in the Administration of Justice." *Yale Law Journal* 69 (March 1960): 543-594.

Greenwood, Peter W. *An Analysis of the Apprehension Activities of the New York City Police Department.* New York: Rand Institute, 1970.

Heaps, Willard A. *Riots U.S.A. 1765-1965.* New York: Seabury Press, 1966.

Hersey, John. *The Algiers Motel Incident.* New York: Bantam, 1968.

Hunt, Issac C., Jr. and Cohen, Bernard. *Minority Recruiting in the New York City Police Department.* New York: Rand Institute, 1971.

Inbau, Fred E. "Democratic Restraints Upon the Police." *Journal of Criminal Law, Criminology and Police Science* 57, 3 (1966): 265-270.

Ingersoll, John E. "The Police Scandal Syndrome: Conditions Leading to an Apparent Breakdown in Police Service." *Crime and Delinquency* 10, 3 (July 1964): 269-275.

Johnson, Elmer H. "A Sociological Interpretation of Police Reaction and Responsibility to Civil Disobedience." *Journal of Criminal Law, Criminology and Police Science* 58 (1968): 405-409.

Klein, Herbert T. *The Police: Damned If They Do—Damned If They Don't.* New York: Crown Publishers, 1968.

LaFave, Wayne R. *Arrest: The Decision to Take a Suspect into Custody.* Boston: Little, Brown, 1965.

——— and Remington, Frank. "Controlling the Police: The Judge's Role in Making and Reviewing Law Enforcement Decisions." *Michigan Law Review* 63, 6 (April 1965): 987-1013.

Larson, Richard C. *Urban Police Patrol Analysis.* Cambridge, Mass.: Massachusetts Institute of Technology Press, 1972.

Lipset, Seymour M. "Why Cops Hate Liberals—and Vice Versa." *The Atlantic* (March 1969): 76-83.

Masotti, Louis H. and Bowen, Ron R., eds. *Riots and Rebellion: Civil Violence in the Urban Community.* Beverly Hills, Calif.: Sage Publications, 1968.

McIntyre, Donald M. and Chabraja, Nicholas D. "The Intensive Search of a Suspect's Body and Clothing." *Journal of Criminal Law, Criminology and Police Science* 58, 1 (1967): 18-26.

Mendalie, Richard J.; Zeitz, Leonard; and Alexander, Paul. "Custodial Police Interrogation in Our Nation's Capital. The Attempt to Implement Miranda." *Michigan Law Review* 66, 7 (May 1968): 1347-1422.

Michener, James A. *Kent State: What Happened and Why.* New York: Random House, 1971.

Milton, Catherine. *Women in Policing.* Washington, D.C.: Police Foundation, 1972.

Misner, Gordon. "The Response of Police Agencies." *The Annals* (March 1969): 109-119.

National Advisory Commission on Criminal Justice Standards and Goals. *Police.* Washington, D.C.: U.S. Department of Justice, 1973.

Nelson, Jack and Bass, Jack. *The Orangeburg Massacre.* New York: Ballantine, 1970.

Niederhofer, Arthur. *Behind the Shield: The Police in Urban Society.* Garden City, N.Y.: Doubleday, 1967.

Nimmer, Raymond T. "The Public Drunk: Formalizing the Police Role as a Social Help Agency." *Georgetown Law Journal* 58, 6 (June 1970): 1089-1116.

———. "St. Louis Diagnostic and Detoxification Center: An Experiment in Non-Criminal Processing of Public Intoxicants." *Washington University Law Quarterly* 1079 (Winter 1970): 1-28.

Note. "The Administration of Complaints by Civilians Against the Police." *Harvard Law Review* 77 (January 1964): 499-519.

———. "Anderson v. Sills: The Constitutionality of Police Intelligence Gathering." *Northwestern University Law Review* 65, 3 (1970): 461-485.

———. "Philadelphia Police Practice and the Law of Arrest." *University of Pennsylvania Law Review* 100 (1952): 1182-1216.

———. "Program Budgeting for Police Departments." *Yale Law Journal* 76, 4 (March 1967): 822-838.

Packer, Herbert L. "Policing the Police." *The New Republic* (September 4, 1965): 17-21.

Parnas, Raymond I. "The Police Response to Domestic Disturbance." *Wisconsin Law Review* 1967 (Fall 1967): 914-960.

Pepinsky, Harold E. "A Theory of Police Reaction to Miranda v. Arizona." *Crime and Delinquency* 16 (October 1970): 379-392.

President's Commission on Law Enforcement and Administration of Justice. *Task Force Report: The Police*. Washington, D.C.: U.S. Government Printing Office, 1967.

Radelet, Louis A. *The Police and the Community*. Beverly Hills, Calif.: Glencoe Press, 1973.

Reiss, Albert J., Jr. *The Police and the Public*. New Haven, Conn. Yale University Press, 1971.

Remington, Frank J. "The Role of the Police in a Democratic Society." *Journal of Criminal Law, Criminology and Police Science* 56 3 (1965): 361-365.

Rotenberg, Daniel L. "The Police Detection Practices of Encouragement." *Virginia Law Review* 49, 5 (June 1963): 871-903.

Rubinstein, Jonathan. *City Police,* New York: Farrar, Straus & Giroux, 1973.

Savitz, Leonard. "The Dimensions of Police Loyalty." *American Behavioral Scientist* 13 (May-August 1970): 693-704.

Schaefer, Walter V. *The Suspect and Society*. Evanston, Ill.: Northwestern University Press, 1967.

Schwartz, Louis B. "Excluding Evidence Illegally Obtained: American Idiosyncrasy and Rational Response to Social Conditions." *Modern Law Review* 29 (1966): 635-638.

Smith, Bruce. *Police Systems in the United States,* 2d rev. ed. New York: Harper & Row, 1960.

Smith, R. Dean and Koblenz, Richard W. *Guidelines for Civil Disorder and Mobilization Plannings*. Washington, D.C.: International Association of Chiefs of Police, 1968.

Stinchcombe, Arthur. "Institutions of Privacy in the Determination of Police Administrative Practice." *American Journal of Sociology* 69 (September 1963): 150-160.

Tiffany, Lawrence P.; McIntyre, Donald M.; Rotenberg, Daniel. *Detection of Crime: Stopping and Questioning, Search and Seizure, Encouragement and Entrapment*. Boston: Little, Brown, 1967.

Toch, Hans. "Cops and Blacks: Warring Minorities." *The Nation* (April 21, 1969): 491-493.

Turner, William. *The Police Establishment*. New York: G. P. Putnam's Sons, 1968.

Westley, William A. *Violence and the Police*. Cambridge, Mass.: Massachusetts Institute of Technology Press, 1970.

Weston, Paul B. and Wells, Kenneth M. *Criminal Investigation: Basic Perspectives*. Englewood Cliffs, N.J.: Prentice-Hall, 1970.

Wilson, James Q. "The Police and Their Problems: A Theory." *Public Policy* 12 (1963): 189-216.

———. *Varieties of Police Behavior*. Cambridge, Mass.: Atheneum, 1968.

Wilson, O. W. *Police Administration,* 2d ed. New York: McGraw-Hill, 1963.

Wisenand, Paul M. and Tamara, Tug T. *Automated Police Information Systems*. New York: John Wiley and Sons, 1970.

Prosecution and the Courts

Abrams, Norman. "Internal Policy: Guiding the Exercise of Prosecutorial Discretion." *UCLA Law Review* 19, 1 (October 1971): 1-58.

Agovina, Pier and Parisi, Alfred J. "Post-Conviction Relief from Pleas of Guilty: A Diminishing Right." *Brooklyn Law Review* 38 (Summer 1971): 182-210.

Alschuler, Albert W. "The Prosecutor's Role in Plea Bargaining." *University of Chicago Law Review* 36 (1968): 50-112.

American Bar Association. Advisory Committee on Sentencing and Review. *Sentencing Alternatives and Procedures.* New York: Institute of Judicial Administration, 1967.

————. Project on Standards for Criminal Justice. *Standards Relating to Criminal Appeals.* New York: Institute of Judicial Administration, 1970.

————. *Standards Relating to Fair Trial and Free Press.* New York: Institute of Judicial Administration, 1968.

————. *Standards Relating to Joinder and Severance,* approved draft. New York: Institute of Judicial Administration, 1968.

————. *Standards Relating to Pleas of Guilty,* approved draft. New York: Institute of Judicial Administration, 1968.

————. *Standards Relating to Post-Conviction Remedies,* approved draft. New York: Institute of Judicial Administration, 1967.

————. *Standards Relating to Probation.* New York: Institute of Judicial Administration, 1970.

————. *Standards Relating to the Prosecution Function and the Defense Function,* approved draft. New York: Institute of Judicial Administration, 1971.

————. *Standards Relating to Sentencing Alternatives and Procedures.* New York: Office of the Criminal Justice Project, 1968.

————. *Standards Relating to Trial by Jury,* approved draft. New York: Institute of Judicial Administration, 1968.

American College of Trial Lawyers. *Disruption of the Judiciary Process.* Chicago: American Bar Association, 1970.

American Law Institute. *Model Penal Code: Proposed Official Draft.* Philadelphia: American Law Institute, 1962.

Ares, Charles E.; Rankin, Anne; and Sturz, Herbert. "The Manhattan Bail Project: An Interim Report on the Use of Pre-Trial Parole." *New York University Law Review* 38 (January 1963): 67-95.

Ariano, Frank V. and Countryman, John W. "The Role of Plea Negotiations in Modern Criminal Law." *Chicago-Kent Law Review* 46 (Spring 1969): 116-122.

Baker, Newman F. "The Prosecutor—Initiation of Prosecution." *Journal of Criminal Law and Criminology* 23 (1933): 770-796.

Barkin, Eugene N. "The Emergence of Correctional Law and the Awareness of the Rights of the Convicted." *Nebraska Law Review* 45, 4 (1966): 669-689.

435

Bedau, Hugo Adam, ed. *The Death Penalty in America.* New York: Anchor, 1967.

Bennett, David E. "Competency to Stand Trial: A Call for Reform." *Journal of Criminal Law, Criminology and Police Science* 59, 4 (1968): 569-582.

Bickel, Alexander M. *Politics and the Warren Court.* New York: Harper & Row, 1965.

Black, Jonathan, ed. *Radical Lawyers: Their Role in the Movement and in the Courts.* New York: Avon Books, 1971.

Black's Law Dictionary, 4th ed. St. Paul, Minn.: West, 1968.

Blaine, Gerald S. "Computer-Based Information Systems Can Help Solve Urban Court Problems." *Judicature* 54, 4 (November 1970): 149-153.

Blaustein, Albert P. *The American Lawyer.* Chicago: University of Chicago Press, 1954.

Blumberg, Abraham S. *Criminal Justice.* Chicago: Quadrangle Books, 1967.

————, ed. *The Scales of Justice.* New Brunswick, N.J.: Transaction Books, 1973.

Borkin, Joseph. *The Corrupt Judge.* New York: Meridian Books, 1962.

Bress, David G. "Professional Ethics in Criminal Trials: A View of Defense Counsel's Responsibility." *Michigan Law Review* 64 (June 1966): 1493-1498.

Cardozo, Benjamin N. *The Nature of the Judicial Process.* New Haven, Conn.: Yale University Press, 1921.

Carter, Robert M. "The Presentence Report and the Decision-Making Process." *Journal of Research in Crime and Delinquency* 4 (July 1967): 203-211.

Cicourel, Aaron V. *The Social Organization of Juvenile Justice.* New York: John Wiley and Sons, 1968.

Clinton, John and Hester, Samuel. "A Survey of Student Prosecutor Programs in the United States." *Prosecutor* 7 (January-February 1971): 28-38.

Cohen, Fred. "The Function of the Attorney and the Commitment of the Mentally Ill." *Texas Law Review* 44, 3 (February 1966): 424-459.

————. "Sentencing, Probation, and the Rehabilitative Ideal: The View from Mempa v. Rhay." *Texas Law Review* 47, 1 (December 1968): 1-59.

Cole, George. "The Decision to Prosecute." *Law and Society Review* 4 (1970): 331-343.

Comment. "Constitutional Limitations on the Conditions of Pretrial Detention." *Yale Law Journal* 79, 5 (April 1970): 941-960.

————. "The Influence of Defendants Plea on Judicial Determination of Sentence." *Yale Law Journal* 66, 2 (December 1956): 204-222.

————. "Official Inducements to Plead Guilty: Suggested Morals for a Market Place." *University of Chicago Law Review* 32, 1 (Autumn 1964): 167-187.

————. "Preventive Detention." *George Washington Law Review* 36, 1 (October 1967): 178-189.

————. "Preventive Detention: An Empirical Analysis." *Harvard Civil Rights - Civil Liberties Law Review* 6, 2 (March 1971): 289-396.

————. "Preventive Detention Before Trial." *Harvard Law Review* 79, 7 (May 1966): 1489-1510.

Conrad, Richard P. "Profile of a Guilty Plea: A Proposed Trial Court Procedure for Accepting Guilty Pleas." *Wayne Law Review* 17, 4 (September-October 1971): 1195-1239.

Cox, Archibald. *The Warren Court: Constitutional Decisions as an Instrument of Reform.* Cambridge, Mass.: Harvard University Press, 1968.

Cozart, Reed. "The Benefits of Executive Clemency." *Federal Probation* 32 (June 1968): 33-35.

Dawson, Robert O. *Sentencing: The Decision as to Type, Length, and Conditions of Sentence.* Boston: Little, Brown, 1969.

Donner, Frank J. and Cerruti, Eugene. "The Grand Jury Network: How the Nixon Administration Has Secretly Perverted a Traditional Safeguard of Individual Rights." *The Nation* (January 3, 1972): 5-20.

Douglas, William O. *We the Judges.* Garden City, N.Y.: Doubleday, 1956.

Downie, Leonard. *Justice Denied: The Case for Reform of the Courts.* New York: Praeger, 1971.

Enker, Arnold. "Perspectives on Plea Bargaining." In President's Commission on Law Enforcement and Administration of Justice. *Task Force Report: The Courts.* Washington, D.C.: U.S. Government Printing Office, 1967, pp. 109-119.

Foote, Caleb. "The Bail System and Equal Justice." *Federal Probation* 23 (September 1959): 43-48.

———. "The Coming Constitutional Crisis in Bail." *University of Pennsylvania Law Review* 113, 8 (June 1965): 1125-1185.

———, ed. *Studies on Bail.* Philadelphia: University of Pennsylvania Press, 1967.

Friedmann, Wolfgang. *Law in a Changing Society.* London: Stevens and Sons, 1959.

Frank, Jerome. *Courts on Trial.* Princeton, N.J.: Princeton University Press, 1949.

Frankel, Marvin. *Criminal Sentences.* New York: Hill & Wang, 1972.

Freed, Daniel J. and Wald, Patricia M. *Bail in the United States: 1964.* Washington, D.C.: U.S. Department of Justice and Vera Foundation, 1964.

Freed, Roy N. "Computers in Judicial Administration." *Judicature* 52, 10 (May 1969): 419-421.

Friendly, Henry J. "Is Innocence Irrelevant? Collateral Attack on Criminal Judgements." *University of Chicago Law Review* 38, 1 (Fall 1970): 142-172.

Ginsberg, Morris. *On Justice in Society.* Baltimore, Md.: Penguin Books, 1965.

Glaser, Daniel; Kenefick, Donald; and O'Leary, Vincent. *The Violent Offender.* Washington, D.C.: U.S. Department of Health, Education and Welfare, 1966.

Goldfarb, Ronald. *Ransom: A Critique of the American Bail System.* New York: Harper & Row, 1965.

Goldstein, Abraham S. *The Insanity Defense.* New Haven, Conn.: Yale University Press, 1967.

———. "The State and the Accused: Balance of Advantage in Criminal Procedure." *Yale Law Journal* 69, 7 (June 1960): 1149-1199.

Goldstein, Herman. "Trial Judges and the Police—Their Relationships in the Administration of Criminal Justice." *Crime and Delinquency* 14, 1 (January 1968): 14-25.

Graham, Fred P. *The Self-Inflicted Wound.* New York: Macmillan, 1970.

Green, Edward. *Judicial Attitudes in Sentencing.* London: Macmillan, 1961.

Griffiths, John and Ayres, Richard E. "A Postscript to the Miranda Project: Interrogation of Draft Protestors." *Yale Law Journal* 77, 2 (December 1967): 300-319.

Grosman, Brian A. *The Prosecutor: An Inquiry into the Exercise of Discretion.* Toronto: University of Toronto Press, 1969.

Hall, Livingston; Kamisar, Yale; LaFave, Wayne R. and Israel, Jerold H. *Modern Criminal Procedure,* 3d ed. St. Paul, Minn.: West, 1969.

Hogarth, John. *Sentencing as a Human Process.* Toronto: University of Toronto Press, 1971.

Hughes, Graham. "Criminal Omissions." *Yale Law Journal* 67, 4 (February 1958): 590-637.

Kalven, Harry Jr. and Ziesel, Hans. *The American Jury.* Boston: Little, Brown, 1966.

Kaplan, John. "The Prosecutorial Discretion—A Comment." *Northwestern University Law Review* 60 (1965-66): 174-193.

Katz, Lewis R. *Justice is the Crime: Pretrial Delay in Felony Cases.* Cleveland, Ohio: Press of Case Western Reserve University, 1972.

Kempton, Murray. *The Briar Patch: The People of the State of New York v. Lumumba Shakur, et al.* New York: Dutton, 1973.

Klein, Daniel. "Judicial Participation in Guilty Pleas: A Search for Standards." *University of Pittsburgh Law Review* 33, 1 (Fall 1971): 151-160.

Klonoski, James; Mitchell, Charles; and Gallagher, Edward. "Plea Bargaining in Oregon: An Exploratory Study." *Oregon Law Review* 50, 2 (Winter 1971): 114-137.

Knowlton, Robert E. "Problems of Jury Discretion in Capital Cases." *University of Pennsylvania Law Review* 101, 8 (June 1953): 1099-1136.

Kress, Jack M. "The Agnew Case: Policy, Prosecution and Plea Bargaining." *Criminal Law Bulletin* 10, 1 (January-February 1974): 80-84.

Kuh, Richard H. "The Grand Jury 'Presentment': Foul Blow or Fair Play?" *Columbia Law Review* 55, 8 (December 1955): 1103-1136.

LaFave, Wayne R. "Alternatives to the Present Bail System." *University of Illinois Law Forum* 1965 (Spring 1965): 8-19.

———— and Remington, Frank J. "Controlling the Police: The Judge's Role in Making and Reviewing Law Enforcement Decisions." *Michigan Law Review* 63, 6 (April 1965): 987-1013.

Laurent, Francis W. *The Business of a Trial Court: 100 Years of Cases.* Madison, Wis.: University of Wisconsin Press, 1959.

Lemert, Edwin M. *Social Action and Legal Change: Revolution Within the Juvenile Court.* Chicago: Aldine, 1970.

Levine, Mark L.; McNamee, George C.; and Greenburg, Daniel. *The Tales of Hoffman.* New York: Bantam, 1970.

Lewis, Anthony. *Gideon's Trumpet.* New York: Vintage, 1964.

Lineberry, W. P., ed. *Justice in America.* New York: H. W. Wiss & Co., 1972.

Mayer, Martin. *The Lawyers.* New York: Dell, 1968.

Mayers, Lewis. *The American Legal System,* rev. ed. New York: Harper & Row, 1964.

McCafferty, James A. "The Need for Criminal Court Statistics." *Judicature* 55, 4 (November 1971): 149-154.

Meyer, Hermine H. "Constitutionality of Pretrial Detention." *The Law Journal* 60, 5 (May 1972): 1139-1194.

Miller, Frank W. *Prosecution: The Decision to Charge a Suspect With a Crime.* Boston: Little, Brown, 1969.

——— and Dawson, Robert O. "Non-Use of the Preliminary Examination: A Survey of Current Practices." *Wisconsin Law Review* 1964 (March 1964): 252-277.

——— and Tiffany, Lawrence P. "Prosecutor Dominance of the Warrant Decision: A Study of Current Practices." *Washington University Law Quarterly* 1 (February 1964): 1-23.

Mitford, Jessica. *The Trial of Dr. Spock.* New York: Alfred A. Knopf, Inc., 1969.

Mueller, G. O. W. "Penology on Appeal: Appellate Review of Legal But Excessive Sentences." *Vanderbilt Law Review* 15, 3 (June 1962): 671-697.

Murrah, Alfred P. and Rubin, Sol. "Penal Reform and the Model Sentencing Act." *Columbia Law Review* 65 (1965): 1167-1183.

Myhre, Jonas A. "Conviction Without Trial in the United States and Norway." *Houston Law Review* 5 (March 1968): 647-663.

National Advisory Commission on Crime Justice Standards and Goals. *Courts.* Washington, D.C.: U.S. Department of Justice, 1973.

National Council on Crime and Delinquency. *Model Sentencing Act.* New York: National Council on Crime and Delinquency, 1963.

Nedrud, Duane R. "The Career Prosecutor—Prosecutors of Forty-Eight States." *Journal of Criminal Law, Criminology and Police Science* 51, 3 (September-October 1960): 343-355.

Newman, Donald J. "The Agnew Plea Bargain." *Criminal Law Bulletin* 10, 1 (January-February 1974): 85-90.

———. *Conviction: The Determination of Guilt or Innocence Without Trial.* Boston: Little, Brown, 1966.

———. "Pleading Guilty for Considerations: A Study of Bargain Justice." *Journal of Criminal Law, Criminology and Police Science* 46 (March-April 1956): 780-790.

——— and NeMoyer, Edgar C. "Issues of Propriety in Negotiated Justice." *Denver Law Journal* 47, 3 (1970): 367-407.

Noonan, John T., Jr. "The Purposes of Advocacy and the Limits of Confidentiality." *Michigan Law Review* 64, 8 (June 1966): 1485-1492.

439

Note. "Beyond the Ken of the Courts: A Critique of Judicial Refusal to Review the Complaints of Convicts." *Yale Law Journal* 72, 3 (January 1963): 506-558.

————. "Constitutional Limitations on the Conditions of Pre-Trial Confinement." *Yale Law Journal* 79, 5 (April 1970): 941-960.

————. "The Costs of Preventive Detention." *Yale Law Journal* 79, 5 (April 1970): 926-940.

————. "Criminal Law—Pleas of Guilty—Plea Bargaining—The American Bar Associations Standards on Criminal Justice and Wisconsin's Statutory Section 971.08." *Wisconsin Law Review* 1971, 2 (1971): 583-594.

————. "The Equal Protection Clause and Imprisonment of the Indigent for Non-Payment of Fines." *Michigan Law Review* 64, 5 (March 1966): 938-947.

————. "Equal Protection and the Use of Fines as Penalties for Criminal Offenses." *University of Illinois Law Forum* 460 (1966).

————. "Fines and Fining—An Evaluation." *University of Pennsylvania Law Review* 101 (1953): 1013-1030.

————. "Guilty Plea Valid Even When Accompanied by Profession of Innocence." *Fordham Law Review* 39, 4 (May 1971): 773-781.

————. "Jury Sentencing in Virginia." *Virginia Law Review* 53, 4 (May 1967): 968-1001.

————. "Statutory Structures for Sentencing Felons to Prison." *Columbia Law Review* 60, 8 (December 1960): 1134-1172.

————. "The Unconstitutionality of Plea Bargaining." *Harvard Law Review* 83, b (April 1970): 1387-1411.

Oaks, Dallin and Lehman, Warren. *A Criminal Justice System and the Indigent.* Chicago: University of Chicago Press, 1967.

Ohlin, Lloyd E. and Remington, Frank J. "Sentencing Structure: Its Effect upon Systems for the Administration of Criminal Justice." *Law and Contemporary Problems* 23 (1958): 495-507.

Owens, Richard C. "People v. West, Recorded Plea Bargains." *Willamette Law Journal* 7 (June 1971): 347-354.

Pitler, Robert M. "The Fruit of the Poisonous Tree Revisited and Shepardized." *California Law Review* 56, 3 (May 1968): 579-651.

Portman, Sheldon. "The Defense Lawyer's New Role in the Sentencing Process." *Federal Probation* 34, 1 (March 1970): 3-8.

President's Commission on Law Enforcement and Administration of Justice. *Task Force Report: The Courts.* Washington, D.C.: U.S. Government Printing Office, 1967.

Radzinowicz, Leon and Wolfgang, Marvin E., eds. *Crime and Justice, Volume 2: The Criminal in the Arms of the Law.* New York: Basic Books, 1971.

Rankin, Anne. "The Effect of Pretrial Detention." *New York University Law Review* 39 (1964): 641-655.

Remington, Frank and Newman, Donald J. "The Highland Park Institute on Sentence Disparity." *Federal Probation* 26, 1 (March 1962): 3-9.

Rubin, Sol. "Allocation of Authority in the Sentencing - Correction Decision." *Texas Law Review* 45, 3 (February 1967): 455-469.

———; Weihofen, Henry; Edwards, George; and Rosenzweig, Simon. *The Law of Criminal Correction*. St. Paul, Minn.: West, 1963.

Ryan, John V. "Less Than Unanimous Verdicts in Criminal Trials." *Journal of Criminal Law, Criminology and Police Science* 58, 2 (1967): 211-217.

Schafer, Stephen. *Restitution to Victims of Crime*. London: Stevens and Sons, 1960.

Sellin, Thorsten, ed. *The Death Penalty*. New York: Harper & Row, 1967.

Silverstein, Lee. *The Defense of the Poor in Criminal Cases in American State Courts*. Chicago: American Bar Foundation, 1965.

Simon, James F. *In His Own Image: The Supreme Court in Richard Nixon's America*. New York: David McKay Co., Inc., 1973.

Simon, Rita James. *The Jury and the Defense of Insanity*. Boston: Little, Brown, 1967.

Stephens, Otis H. "The Burger Court: New Dimensions in Criminal Justice." *Georgetown Law Journal* 60, 2 (November 1971): 249-278.

Suffet, Frederic. "Bail Setting: A Study of Courtroom Interaction." *Crime and Delinquency* 12 (October, 1966): 318-331.

Swindler, William F. *Court and Constitution in the Twentieth Century: The New Legality, 1932-1968*. Indianapolis: Bobbs-Merrill, 1970.

Tappan, Paul W. "Sentencing Under the Model Penal Code." *Law and Contemporary Problems* 23, 3 (1958): 528-543.

Vera Institute of Justice. *Bail and Parole Jumping in Manhattan in 1967*. New York: Vera Institute of Justice, August 1970.

Vetri, Dominick R. "Guilty Plea Bargaining: Compromises by Prosecutors to Secure Guilty Pleas." *University of Pennsylvania Law Review* 112 (1964): 865-908.

Wald, Michael; Ayres, Richard; Hess, David; Schantz, Mark; and Whitebread, Charles II. "Interrogations in New Haven: The Impact of *Miranda*." *Yale Law Journal* 76 (1967): 1519-1648.

Watts, Lewis P. "Grand Jury: Sleeping Watchdog or Expensive Antique?" *North Carolina Law Review* 37 (1959): 290-315.

Wechsler, Herbert. "The Challenge of a Model Penal Code." *Harvard Law Review* 65, 7 (May 1952): 1097-1133.

———. "Codification of Criminal Law in the United States: The Model Penal Code." *Columbia Law Review* 1425, 68 (1968).

Wellman, Francis L. *The Art of Cross-Examination*. New York: Collier, 1962.

White, Welsh S. "A Proposal for Reform of the Plea Bargaining Process." *University of Pennsylvania Law Review* 119, 3 (January 1971): 439-465.

Wood, Arthur L. *The Criminal Lawyer*. New Haven, Conn.: College and University Press, 1967.

Work, Charles R. "A Prosecutor's Guide to Automation." *The Prosecutor* 7 (November-December 1971): 479-480.

Wright, Charles Allan. "Must the Criminal Go Free if the Constable Blunders?" *Texas Law Review* 50, 4 (April 1972): 736-746.

Wyzanski, Charles E., Jr. "A Trial Judge's Freedom and Responsibility." *Harvard Law Review* 65, 8 (June 1952): 1281-1304.

Zastrow, William G. "Disclosure of the Presentence Investigation Report." *Federal Probation* 35, 4 (December 1971): 20-23.

Corrections

American Bar Association. Project on Minimum Standards for Criminal Justice. *Standards Relating to Probation.* New York: Institute of Judicial Administration, 1970.

American Correctional Association. *Causes, Preventive Measures and Methods of Controlling Riots and Disturbances in Correctional Institutions.* Washington, D.C.: American Correctional Association, 1970.

———. *Manual of Correctional Standards,* 3d ed. Washington, D.C.: American Correctional Association, 1966.

Arluke, Norman. "A Summary of Parole Rules." *National Probation and Parole Association Journal* 2 (January 1956): 6-13.

Arluke, Nat R. "A Summary of Parole Rules—Thirteen Years Later." *Crime and Delinquency* 15 (April 1969): 267-274.

Bennett, James V. *I Chose Prison.* New York: Alfred A. Knopf, Inc., 1970.

Berk, Bernard B. "Organizational Goals and Inmate Organization." *American Journal of Sociology* 71 (March 1966): 522-534.

Brockway, Zebulon R. *Fifty Years of Prison Service.* New York: Charities Publication, 1912.

Bruce, Andrew A.; Burgess, Ernest W.; Harno, Albert J.; and Landesco, John L. "A Study of the Indeterminate Sentence and Parole in the State of Illinois." *Journal of the American Institute of Criminal Law and Criminology* Vol. IX, No. 1, Part 2 (1928), pp. 5-306.

Carter, Robert M. and Wilkins, Leslie T., eds. *Probation and Parole: Selected Readings.* New York: John Wiley and Sons, 1970.

Carter, Robert M.; Glaser, Daniel; and Wilkins, Leslie T., eds. *Correctional Institutions.* Philadelphia: J. B. Lippincott Company, 1972.

Clark, Robert E. "Size of Parole Community as Related to Parole Outcome." *American Journal of Sociology* 57 (July 1951): 43-47.

Clegg, Reed K. *Probation and Parole: Principles and Practices.* Springfield, Ill.: Charles C Thomas, 1964.

Cohen, Fred. "A Comment on Morrissey v. Brewer: Due Process and Parole Revocation." *Criminal Law Bulletin* 8, 7 (September 1972): 616-622.

———. *The Legal Challenge to Corrections: Implications for Manpower and Training.* Washington, D.C.: American Correctional Association, 1969.

Cohen, William M. "Due Process, Equal Protection and State Parole Revocation Proceedings." *University of Colorado Law Review* 42, 3 (November 1970): 197-230.

Comment. "Due Process: The Right to Counsel in Parole Release Hearings." 54, 3 *Iowa Law Review* (1968): 497-533.

———. "The Parole System." *University of Pennsylvania Law Review* 120 (December 1971): 284-377.

———. "Rights v. Results: Quo Vadis Due Process for Parolees." *Pacific Law Journal* 1, 1 (January 1970): 321-349.

Conrad, John P. *Crime and Its Correction: An International Survey of Attitudes and Practices.* Berkeley, Calif.: University of California, 1967.

Cressey, Donald R., ed. *The Prison: Studies in Institutional Organization and Change.* New York: Holt, Rinehart & Winston, 1961.

———. "The State of Criminal Statistics." *National Probation and Parole Association Journal* 3 (July 1957): 240-241.

Davis, George F. "A Study of Adult Probation Violation Rates by Means of the Cohort Approach." *Journal of Criminal Law, Criminology and Police Science* 55, 1 (March 1964): 70-85.

Dawson, Robert O. "The Decision to Grant or Deny Parole: A Study of Parole Criteria in Law and Practice." *Washington University Law Quarterly* 1966, 3 (June 1966): 243-303.

Dean, Charles W. and Duggan, Thomas J. "Problems in Parole Prediction: A Historical Analysis." *Social Problems* 15 (Spring 1968): 450-459.

Dean, Charles W. "Treatment Concepts and Penology." *South Carolina Law Review* 21 (1970): 40-52.

de Beaumont, Gustave and de Tocqueville, Alexis. *On the Penitentiary System in the United States and Its Application in France.* Carbondale, Ill.: Southern Illinois University Press, 1964.

Delgado, Jose. *Physical Control of the Mind.* New York: Harper & Row, 1969.

Dressler, David. *Practice and Theory of Probation and Parole,* 2d ed. New York: Columbia University Press, 1969.

Edwards, George and Rosenzweig, Simon. *The Law of Criminal Correction.* St. Paul, Minn.: West, 1963.

Fox, Vernon. *Violence Behind Bars: An Explosive Report on Prison Riots in the United States.* New York: Vantage Press, 1956.

Gallington, Daniel. "Prison Disciplinary Decisions." *Journal of Criminal Law, Criminology and Police Science* 60, 2 (1969): 152-164.

Gaylin, Willard. *In the Service of Their Country: War Resisters in Prison.* New York: Grosset's University Library, 1970.

Gibbons, Don C. *Changing the Lawbreaker.* Englewood Cliffs, N.J.: Prentice-Hall, 1965.

Glaser, Daniel. *The Effectiveness of a Prison and Parole System.* Indianapolis: Bobbs-Merrill, 1964.

————; Kenefick, Donald; and O'Leary, Vincent. *The Violent Offender*. Washington, D.C.: Department of Health, Education and Welfare, 1966.

———— and O'Leary, Vincent. *Personal Characteristics and Parole Outcome*. Washington, D.C.: U.S. Government Printing Office, Department of Health, Education and Welfare, 1966.

Goffman, Erving. *Asylums: Essays on the Social Situation of Mental Patients and Other Inmates*. Chicago: Aldine, 1961.

Goldfarb, Ronald and Singer, Linda. "Redressing Prisoners' Grievances." *George Washington Law Review* 39, 2 (December 1970): 175-320.

Goring, Charles. *The English Convict*. London: His Majesty's Stationery Office, 1913.

Gottfredson, Don M.; Neithercutt, M. G.; Nuffield, Joan; O'Leary, Vincent. *"Four Thousand Lifetimes: A Study of Time Served and Parole Outcomes."* Davis, Calif.: National Council on Crime and Delinquency Research Center, 1973.

Griswold, H. Jack; Misenheimer, Mike; Powers, Art; and Tromanhauser, Ed. *An Eye for an Eye*. New York: Pocket Books, 1970.

Gross, Seymour Z. "Biographical Characteristics of Juvenile Probation Officers." *Crime and Delinquency* 12 (April 1966): 109-116.

Grunhut, Max. *Penal Reform*. New York: The Clarendon Press, 1948.

Hartinger, Walter; Eldefonso, Edward; and Coffey, Alan. *Corrections: A Component of the Justice System*. Pacific Palisades, Calif.: Goodyear Publishing, 1973.

Hayner, Norman S. "Correctional Systems and National Values." *British Journal of Criminology* 3 (October 1962): 163-175.

Hindelang, Michael J. "A Learning Theory Analysis of the Correctional Process." *Issues in Criminology* 4 (1969): 43-58.

Hirschkop, Philip J. and Millemann, Michael A. "The Unconstitutionality of Prison Life." *Virginia Law Review* 55, s (June 1969): 795-839.

Hollen, Charles R. "Emerging Prisoners' Rights." *Ohio State Law Journal* 33, 1 (Winter 1972): 1-79.

Holtzoff, Alexander. "The Power of Probation and Parole Officers to Search and Seize." *Federal Probation* 31 (December 1967): 3-7.

Hopper, Columbus B. *Sex in Prison: The Mississippi Experiment with Conjugal Visiting*. Baton Rouge, La.: Louisiana State University Press, 1969.

Irwin, John. *The Felon*. Englewood Cliffs, N.J.: Prentice-Hall, 1970.

Jackson, George. *Soledad Brother: The Prison Letters of George Jackson*. New York: Bantam, 1970.

Jacob, Bruce R. "Prison Discipline and Inmates' Rights." *Harvard Civil Liberties Law Review* 5, 2 (April 1970): 227-277.

Kassenbaum, G.; Ward, D.; and Wilner, D. *Prison Treatment and Its Outcome*. New York: John Wiley and Sons, 1971.

Keller, Oliver J. Jr. and Alper, Benedict S. *Half-Way Houses: Community-Centered and Treatment*. Lexington, Mass.: Lexington Books, 1970.

Keve, Paul W. *The Probation Officer Investigates*. St. Paul, Minn.: University of Minnesota Press, 1960.

Key, Barbara A. and Vedder, Clyde B., eds. *Probation and Parole*. Springfield, Ill.: Charles C Thomas, 1963.

Kimball, Edward L. and Newman, Donald J. "Judicial Intervention in Correctional Decisions: Threat and Response." *Crime and Delinquency* 14, 1 (January 1968): 1-13.

Krantz, Sheldon; Bell, Robert; Brant, Jonathan; and Magruder, Michael. *Model Rules and Regulations on Prisoners' Rights and Responsibilities*. St. Paul, Minn.: West, 1973.

Lewis, W. David. *From Newgate to Dannemora: The Rise of the Penitentiary in New York 1796-1848*. Ithaca, N.Y.: Cornell University Press, 1965.

Lohman, J. D.; Wahl, A.; and Carter, R. M. "The San Francisco Project, Research Report No. 11; the Intensive Supervision Caseload." Berkeley, Calif.: School of Criminology, University of California Press, 1967.

Lunden, Walter A. *The Prison Warden and the Custodial Staff*. Springfield, Ill.: Charles C Thomas, 1965.

Mandell, Wallace. "Making Correction a Community Agency." *Crime and Delinquency* 17 (1971): 281-288.

Mannheim, Hermann and Wilkins, Leslie T. *Prediction Method in Relation to Borstal Training*. London: Her Majesty's Stationery Office, 1955.

Martin, John Bartlow. *Break Down the Walls*. New York: Ballantine, 1954.

————. *Offenders as Employees*. London: Macmillan, 1962.

Menninger, Karl. *The Crime of Punishment*. New York: The Viking Press, 1966.

Miller, Herbert S. *The Closed Door: The Effect of a Criminal Record on Employment With State and Local Public Agencies*. Washington, D.C.: Manpower Administration, U.S. Department of Labor, 1972.

Milligan, William D. "Parole Revocation Hearings in California and the Federal System." *California Western Law Review* 4, 1 (Spring 1968): 18-34.

Minton, Robert J. Jr., ed. *Inside: Prison American Style*. New York: Random House, 1971.

Nagel, William G. *The New Red Barn: A Critical Look at the Modern American Prison*. New York: Walker and Co., 1973.

National Advisory Commission on Criminal Justice Standards and Goals. *Corrections*. Washington, D.C.: U.S. Department of Justice, 1973.

National Council on Crime and Delinquency. *A Model Act for the Protection of Rights of Prisoners*. New York: National Council on Crime and Delinquency, 1972.

————. *Peaceful Resolution of Prison Conflict*. Hackensack, N.J.: National Council on Crime and Delinquency, 1973.

Newman, Charles L., ed. *Sourcebook on Probation, Parole and Pardons*, 2d ed. Springfield, Ill.: Charles C Thomas, 1964.

445

Newman, Donald J. "Court Intervention in the Parole Process." *Albany Law Review* 36, 2 (1972): 257-304.

———. "In Defense of Prisons," *Psychiatric Annals* 4, 3 (March 1974): 6-17.

New York State Special Commission on Attica. *Attica.* New York: Bantam, 1972.

Norman, Sherwood. *The Youth Service Bureau.* Paramus, N.J.: National Council on Crime and Delinquency, 1972.

Note. "Addict Diversion: An Alternative Approach for the Criminal Justice System." *Georgetown Law Journal* 60, 3 (February 1972): 667-710.

———. "Anthropotelemetry: Dr. Schwitzgebel's Machine." *Harvard Law Review* 80, 2 (December 1966): 403-421.

———. "Civil Restraint, Mental Illness, and the Right to Treatment." *Yale Law Journal* 77, 1 (November 1967): 87-116.

———. "Constitutional Rights of Prisoners: The Developing Law." *University of Pennsylvania Law Review* 110 (1962): 985-1008.

———. "Judicial Review of Probation Conditions." *Columbia Law Review* 67, 1 (January 1967): 181-207.

———. "Legal Services for Prison Inmates." *Wisconsin Law Review* 1967, 514 (Spring 1967): 514-531.

———. "Parole: A Critique of Its Legal Foundations and Conditions." *New York University Law Review* 38 (June 1963): 702-739.

———. "Prison Mail Censorship and the First Amendment." *Yale Law Journal* 81, 1 (November 1971): 87-111.

———. "Symposium on Prisoners' Rights." *Journal of Criminal Law, Criminology and Police Science* 63, 2 (June 1972): 154-256.

Ohlin, Lloyd E. *Selection for Parole: A Manual for Parole Prediction.* New York: Russell Sage Foundation, 1951.

———; Piven, Herman; and Pappenfort, Donnell M. "Major Dilemmas of the Social Worker in Probation and Parole." *National Probation and Parole Association Journal* 2, 3 (July 1956): 211-225.

O'Leary, Vincent. "Issues and Trends in Parole Administration in the United States." *The American Criminal Law Review* 11 (Fall 1972): 97-140.

——— and Duffee, David. "Correctional Policy: A Classification of Goals Designed for Change." *Crime and Delinquency* 373 (1971).

——— and Nuffield, Joan. *The Organization of Parole Systems in the United States.* Hackensack, N.J.: National Council on Crime and Delinquency, 1972.

———. "Parole Decision-Making Characteristics: Report of a National Survey." *Criminal Law Bulletin* 8, 8 (October 1972): 651-680.

Oswald, Russell G. *Attica: My Story.* Garden City, N.Y.: Doubleday, 1972.

President's Commission on Law Enforcement and Administration of Justice. *Task Force Report: Corrections.* Washington, D.C.: U.S. Government Printing Office, 1967.

"Professional Standards Endorsed by the Federal Probation Officers Association." *Federal Probation* 21 (March 1957): 48-50.

Pugh, George W. and Carver, M. Hampton. "Due Process and Sentencing: From Mapp to Mempa to McGautha." *Texas Law Review* 49, 1 (December 1970): 25-49.

Reed, John P. and King, Charles E. "Factors in the Decision-Making of North Carolina Probation Officers." *Journal of Research in Crime and Delinquency* 3 (July 1966): 120-128.

Rogers, William P. "The Geneva Conference on Crime: Its Significance for American Penology." *Federal Probation* 29, 4 (December 1955): 39-42.

Rothman, David J. *The Discovery of the Asylum: Social Order and Disorder in the New Republic.* Boston: Little, Brown, 1971.

Rubin, Sol. "Due Process Is Required in Parole Revocation Proceedings." *Federal Probation* 27 (June 1963): 42-46.

———; Weihofen, Henry; Edwards, George; and Rosenzweig, Simon. *The Law of Criminal Correction.* St. Paul, Minn.: West, 1963.

Rudovsky, David. *The Rights of Prisoners: The Basic American Civil Liberties Union Guide to a Prisoner's Rights.* New York: Avon Books, 1973.

Schwitzgebel, Ralph K. "Electronically Monitored Parole." *Prison Journal* 34, 48 (1968).

———. "Limitation on the Coercive Treatment of Offenders," *Criminal Law Bulletin* 8, 4 (May 1972): 267-320.

Sklar, Ron B. "Law and Practice in Probational Parole Revocation Hearings." *Journal of Criminal Law, Criminology and Police Science* 55, 2 (June 1964): 175-198.

South Carolina Department of Corrections. *The Emerging Rights of the Confined.* Columbia, S.C.: South Carolina Department of Corrections, 1972.

Special Project. "Collateral Consequences of a Criminal Conviction." *Vanderbilt Law Review* 23, 5 (October 1970): 929-1241.

Stollery, Peter L. "Families Come to the Institution: A Five Day Experience in Rehabilitation." *Federal Probation* 36, 3 (September 1970): 46-53.

Street, David; Vinter, Robert; and Perrow, Charles. *Organization for Treatment.* New York: The Free Press, 1966.

Studt, Elliot. *The Reentry of the Offender into the Community.* Washington, D.C.: U.S. Department of Health, Education and Welfare, 1967.

Sykes, Gresham. "The Corruption of Authority and Rehabilitation." *Social Forces* 34 (March 1956): 257-262.

———. *The Society of Captives: The Study of a Maximum Security Prison.* Princeton, N.J.: Princeton University Press, 1958.

Turner, William B. "Establishing the Rule of Law in Prisons: A Manual for Prisoner's Rights Litigation." *Stanford Law Review* 23, 3 (February 1971): 473-518.

Urbaniak, Eugene T. "Due Process Should Not Be a Requirement at a Parole Revocation Hearing." *Federal Probation* 27 (June 1963): 46-50.

447

Wallace, Robert. "Ecological Implications of a Custody Institution." *Issues in Criminology* 2, 1 (Spring 1966): 47-60.

Warren, Marguerite Q. *Correctional Treatment in Community Settings: A Report of Current Research.* Rockville, Md.: National Institute of Mental Health, 1971.

———. *Interpersonal Maturity Level Classification (Juvenile): Diagnosis and Treatment of Low, Middle, and High Maturity Delinquents.* Community Treatment Project Report. Sacramento, Calif.: California Youth Authority, 1966.

———. "Other Things Being Equal." *Criminal Law Bulletin* 9 (July-August 1973): 473-490.

Wilkins, Leslie T. *Evaluation of Penal Measures.* New York: Random House, 1969.

Wolfgang, Marvin E. "Corrections and the Violent Offender." *Annals of the American Academy of Political and Social Science* 381 (January 1969): 119-124.

Yablonsky, Lewis. *Synanon: The Tunnel Back.* Baltimore, Md.: Penguin Books, 1967.

APPENDIX

Constitution of the United States
(Adopted in Convention, September 17, 1787)
(Effective March 4, 1789)

PREAMBLE

WE THE PEOPLE OF THE UNITED STATES, *in order to form a more perfect union, establish justice, insure domestic tranquillity, provide for the common defense, promote the general welfare, and secure the blessings of liberty to ourselves and our posterity, do ordain and establish this Constitution for the United States of America.*

ARTICLE I. LEGISLATIVE DEPARTMENT[1]

Section 1. Congress[1]

Powers Are Vested in Senate and House[1]

1.[1] All legislative powers herein granted shall be vested in a Congress of the United States, which shall consist of a Senate and House of Representatives.

Section 2. House of Representatives

Election of Representatives

1. The House of Representatives shall be composed of members chosen every second year by the people of the several States, and the electors in each State shall have the qualifications requisite for electors of the most numerous branch of the State Legislature.

Qualifications of Representatives

2. No person shall be a Representative who shall not have attained to the age of twenty-five years, and been seven years a citizen of the United States, and who shall not, when elected, be an inhabitant of that State in which he shall be chosen.

Apportionment of Representatives

3. Representatives and direct taxes shall be apportioned among the several States which may be included within this Union, according to their respective numbers, which shall be determined by adding to the whole number of free persons, including those bound to service for a term of years, and excluding Indians not taxed, three-fifths of all other persons. The actual enumeration shall be made within three years after the first meeting of the Congress of the United States, and within every subsequent term of ten years, in such manner as they shall by law direct. The number of Representatives shall not exceed one for every thirty thousand, but each State shall have at least one Representative; and until such enumeration shall be made, the State of New Hampshire shall be entitled to choose three, Massachusetts eight, Rhode Island and Providence Plantations one, Connecticut five, New York six, New Jersey four, Pennsylvania eight, Delaware one, Maryland six, Virginia ten, North Carolina five, South Carolina five, and Georgia three.

(This clause has been superseded, so far as it relates to representation, by section 2 of Amendment XIV to the Constitution.)

Vacancies

4. When vacancies happen in the representation from any State, the executive authority thereof shall issue writs of election to fill such vacancies.

Officers of the House—Impeachment

5. The House of Representatives shall choose their Speaker and other officers; and shall have the sole power of impeachment.

Section 3. The Senate

Number of Senators

1. The Senate of the United States shall be composed of two Senators from each State, chosen by the Legislature thereof, for six years; and each Senator shall have one vote.

(Superseded by Amendment XVII.)

Classification of Senators

2. Immediately after they shall be assembled in consequence of the first election, they shall be divided as equally as may be into three classes. The seats of the Senators

of the first class shall be vacated at the expiration of the second year, the second class at the expiration of the fourth year, and of the third class at the expiration of the sixth year, so that one third may be chosen every second year; and if vacancies happen by resignation, or otherwise, during the recess of the Legislature of any State, the executive thereof may make temporary appointments until the next meeting of the Legislature, which shall then fill such vacancies.

(Modified by Amendment XVII.)

Qualifications of Senators

3. No person shall be a Senator who shall not have attained to the age of thirty years, and been nine years a citizen of the United States, and who shall not, when elected, be an inhabitant of that State for which he shall be chosen.

President of Senate

4. The Vice President of the United States shall be President of the Senate, but shall have no vote, unless they be equally divided.

Officers of Senate

5. The Senate shall choose their other officers, and also a President pro tempore, in the absence of the Vice President, or when he shall exercise the office of the President of the United States.

Trial of Impeachment

6. The Senate shall have the sole power to try all impeachments. When sitting for that purpose, they shall be on oath or affirmation. When the President of the United States is tried the Chief Justice shall preside: And no person shall be convicted without the concurrence of two-thirds of the members present.

Judgment on Conviction of Impeachment

7. Judgment in cases of impeachment shall not extend further than to removal from office, and disqualification to hold and enjoy any office of honor, trust or profit under the United States: but the party convicted shall nevertheless be liable and subject to indictment, trial, judgment and punishment, according to law.

Section 4. Election of Senators and Representatives—Meetings of Congress

Election of Members of Congress

1. The times, places and manner of holding elections for Senators and Representatives, shall be prescribed in each State by the Legislature thereof; but the Congress may at any time by law make or alter such regulations, except as to the places of choosing Senators.

(See Amendment XX.)

Congress to Meet Annually

2. The Congress shall assemble at least once in every year, and such meeting shall be on the first Monday in December, unless they shall by law appoint a different day. (Changed to January 3 by Amendment XX.)

Section 5. Powers and Duties of Each House of Congress

Sole Judge of Qualifications of Members

1. Each House shall be the judge of the elections, returns and qualifications of its own members, and a majority of each shall constitute a quorum to do business; but a smaller number may adjourn from day to day, and may be authorized to compel the attendance of absent members, in such manner, and under such penalties as each House may provide.

Rules of Proceedings—Punishment of Members

2. Each House may determine the rules of its proceedings, punish its members for disorderly behavior, and, with the concurrence of two-thirds, expel a member.

Journals

3. Each House shall keep a Journal of its proceedings, and from time to time publish the same, excepting such parts as may in their judgment require secrecy; and the yeas and nays of the members of either House on any question shall, at the desire of one-fifth of those present, be entered on the Journal.

Adjournment

4. Neither House, during the session of Congress, shall, without the consent of the other, adjourn for more than three days, nor to any other place than that in which the two Houses shall be sitting.

Section 6. Compensation, Privileges and Disabilities, of Senators and Representatives

Compensation—Privileges

1. The Senators and Representatives shall receive a compensation for their services, to be ascertained by law, and paid out of the Treasury of the United States. They shall in all cases, except treason, felony and breach of the peace, be privileged from arrest during their attendance at the session of their respective Houses, and in going to and returning from the same; and for any speech or debate in either House, they shall not be questioned in any other place.

Disability to Hold Other Offices

2. No Senator or Representative shall, during the time for which he was elected, be appointed to any civil office under the authority of the United States, which shall have been created, or the emoluments whereof shall have been increased during such time; and no person holding any office under the United States, shall be a member of either House during his continuance in office.

(See also section 3 of Amendment XIV.)

Section 7. Mode of Passing Laws

Special Provision as to Revenue Laws

1. All bills for raising revenue shall originate in the House of Representatives; but the Senate may propose or concur with amendments as on other bills.

Laws, How Enacted

2. Every bill which shall have passed the House of Representatives and the Senate, shall, before it becomes a law, be presented to the President of the United States; if he approve he shall sign it, but if not he shall return it, with his objections to that House in which it shall have originated who shall enter the objections at large on their Journal, and proceed to reconsider it. If after such reconsideration two-thirds of that House shall agree to pass the bill, it shall be sent, together with the objections, to the other House, by which it shall likewise be reconsidered, and if approved by two-thirds of that House, it shall become a law. But in all cases the votes of both Houses shall be determined by yeas and nays, and the names of the persons voting for and against the bill shall be entered on the Journal of each House respectively. If any bill shall not be returned by the President within ten days (Sundays excepted) after it shall have been presented to him, the same shall be a law, in like manner as if he had signed it, unless the Congress by their adjournment prevent its return, in which case it shall not be a law.

Resolutions, Etc.

3. Every order, resolution, or vote to which the concurrence of the Senate and House of Representatives may be necessary (except on a question of adjournment) shall be presented to the President of the United States; and before the same shall take effect, shall be approved by him, or being disapproved by him, shall be repassed by two-thirds of the Senate and House of Representatives, according to the rules and limitations prescribed in the case of a bill.

Section 8. Powers Granted to Congress

Taxation

1. The Congress shall have power to lay and collect taxes, duties, imposts and excises,

to pay the debts and provide for the common defense and general welfare of the United States; but all duties, imposts and excises shall be uniform throughout the United States;

Loans

2. To borrow money on the credit of the United States;

Commerce

3. To regulate commerce with foreign nations, and among the several States, and with the Indian tribes;

Naturalization and Bankruptcies

4. To establish an uniform rule of naturalization, and uniform laws on the subject of bankruptcies throughout the United States;

Coin

5. To coin money, regulate the value thereof, and of foreign coin, and fix the standard of weights and measures;

Counterfeiting

6. To provide for the punishment of counterfeiting the securities and current coin of the United States;

Post Office

7. To establish post offices and post roads;

Patents and Copyrights

8. To promote the progress of science and useful arts, by securing for limited times to authors and inventors the exclusive right to their respective writings and discoveries;

Courts

9. To constitute tribunals inferior to the Supreme Court;

Piracies

10. To define and punish piracies and felonies committed on the high seas, and offenses against the law of nations;

War

11. To declare war, grant letters of marque and reprisal, and make rules concerning captures on land and water;

Army

12. To raise and support armies, but no appropriation of money to that use shall be for a longer term than two years;

Navy

13. To provide and maintain a navy;

Military and Naval Rules

14. To make rules for the government and regulation of the land and naval forces;

Militia, Calling Forth

15. To provide for calling forth the militia to execute the laws of the Union, suppress insurrections and repel invasions;

Militia, Organizing and Arming

16. To provide for organizing, arming, and disciplining, the militia, and for governing such part of them as may be employed in the service of the United States, reserving to the States respectively, the appointment of the officers, and the authority of training the militia according to the discipline prescribed by Congress;

Federal District and Other Places

17. To exercise exclusive legislation in all cases whatsoever, over such district (not exceeding ten miles square) as may, by cession of particular States, and the acceptance of Congress, become the seat of the government of the United States, and to exercise like authority over all places purchased by the consent of the Legislature of the State in which the same shall be, for the erection of forts, magazines, arsenals, dockyards, and other needful buildings;—And

Make Laws to Carry Out Foregoing Powers

18. To make all laws which shall be necessary and proper for carrying into execution the foregoing powers, and all other powers vested by this Constitution in the Government of the United States, or in any department or officer thereof.

(For other powers, see Article II, section 1; Article III, sections 2 and 3; Article IV, sections 1-3; Article V; and Amendments XIII-XVI and XIX-XXI.)

Section 9. Limitation on Powers Granted to the United States

Slave Trade

1. The migration or importation of such persons as any of the States now existing shall think proper to admit, shall not be prohibited by the Congress prior to the year one thousand eight hundred and eight, but a tax or duty may be imposed on such importation, not exceeding ten dollars for each person.

Habeas Corpus

2. The privilege of the writ of habeas corpus shall not be suspended, unless when in cases of rebellion or invasion the public safety may require it.

Ex Post Facto Law

3. No bills of attainder or ex post facto law shall be passed.

Direct Taxes

4. No capitation, or other direct tax shall be laid, unless in proportion to the census or enumeration hereinbefore directed to be taken.
(Modified by Amendment XVI.)

Duties on Exports

5. No tax or duty shall be laid on articles exported from any State.

No Commercial Discrimination to Be Made Between States

6. No preference shall be given by any regulation of commerce or revenue to the ports of one State over those of another; nor shall vessels bound to, or from, one State, be obliged to enter, clear or pay duties in another.

Money, How Drawn from Treasury

7. No money shall be drawn from the Treasury, but in consequence of appropriations made by law; and a regular statement and account of the receipts and expenditures of all public money shall be published from time to time.

Titles of Nobility

8. No title of nobility shall be granted by the United States: And no person holding any office or profit or trust under them, shall, without the consent of the Congress, accept of any present, emolument, office, or title, of any kind whatever, from any King, Prince, or foreign State.
(For other limitations see Amendments I-X.)

Section 10. Powers Prohibited to the States

Powers Prohibited, Absolutely

1. No State shall enter into any treaty, alliance, or confederation; grant letters of marque and reprisal; coin money; emit bills of credit; make anything but gold and silver coin a tender in payment of debts; pass any bill of attainder, ex post facto law, or law impairing the obligation of contracts, or grant any title of nobility.

Powers Concerning Duties on Imports or Exports

2. No State shall, without the consent of the Congress, lay any imposts or duties on imports or exports, except what may be absolutely necessary for executing its inspection laws: and the net produce of all duties and imposts, laid by any State on imports or exports, shall be for the use of the Treasury of the United States; and all such laws shall be subject to the revision and control of the Congress.

Powers Permitted with Consent of Congress

3. No State shall, without the consent of Congress, lay any duty of tonnage, keep troops, or ships of war in time of peace, enter into any agreement or compact with another State, or with a foreign power, or engage in war, unless actually invaded, or in such imminent danger as will not admit of delay.

ARTICLE II. EXECUTIVE DEPARTMENT

Section 1. The President

Executive Power Vested in President—Term of Office

1. The executive power shall be vested in a President of the United States of America. He shall hold his office during the term of four years, and, together with the Vice President, chosen for the same term, be elected, as follows:

Appointment and Number of Presidential Electors

2. Each State shall appoint, in such manner as the Legislature thereof may direct, a number of electors, equal to the whole number of Senators and Representatives to which the State may be entitled in the Congress: but no Senator or Representative, or person holding an office of trust or profit under the United States, shall be appointed an elector.

Mode of Electing President and Vice President

3. The electors shall meet in their respective States, and vote by ballot for two persons, of whom one at least shall not be an inhabitant of the same State with themselves. And they shall make a list of all the persons voted for, and of the number of votes for each; which list they shall sign and certify, and transmit sealed to the seat of the Government of the United States, directed to the President of the Senate. The President of the Senate shall, in the presence of the Senate and House of Representatives, open all the certificates, and the votes shall then be counted. The person having the greatest number of votes shall be the President, if such number be a majority of the whole number of electors appointed; and if there be more than one who have such majority, and have an equal number of votes, then the House of Representatives shall immediately choose by a ballot one of them for President; and if no person have a majority, then from the five highest on the list the said House shall in like manner choose the President. But in choosing the President, the votes shall be taken by States, the representation from each State having one vote; a quorum for this purpose shall consist of a member or members from two-thirds of the States, and a majority of all the States shall be necessary to a choice. In every case, after the choice of the President, the person having the greatest number of votes of the electors shall be the Vice President.

457

But if there should remain two or more who have equal votes, the Senate shall choose from them by ballot the Vice President.

(This paragraph has been superseded by Amendment XII to the Constitution. See Amendment XX.)

Time of Choosing Electors and Casting Electoral Vote

4. The Congress may determine the time of choosing the electors, and the day on which they shall give their votes; which day shall be the same throughout the United States.

Qualifications of President

5. No person except a natural-born citizen, or a citizen of the United States, at the time of the adoption of this Constitution, shall be eligible to the office of President; neither shall any person be eligible to that office who shall not have attained to the age of thirty-five years, and been fourteen years a resident within the United States.

(See also Article II, section 1 and Amendment XIV.)

Presidential Succession

6. In the case of the removal of the President from office, or of his death, resignation, or inability to discharge the powers and duties of the said office, the same shall devolve on the Vice President, and the Congress may by law provide for the case of removal, death, resignation or inability, both of the President and Vice President declaring what officer shall then act as President, and such officer shall act accordingly, until the disability be removed, or a President shall be elected.

Salary of President

7. The President shall, at stated times, receive for his services, a compensation, which shall neither be increased nor diminished during the period for which he shall have been elected, and he shall not receive within that period any other emolument from the United States, or any of them.

Oath and Office of President

8. Before he enter on the execution of his office, he shall take the following oath or affirmation:—"I do solemnly swear (or affirm) that I will faithfully execute the office of President of the United States, and will to the best of my ability, preserve, protect and defend the Constitution of the United States."

Section 2. Powers of the President

Commander in Chief

1. The President shall be Commander in Chief of the Army and Navy of the United States, and of the militia of the several States, when called into the actual service of

the United States: he may require the opinion, in writing, of the principal officer in each of the executive departments, upon any subject relating to the duties of their respective offices, and he shall have power to grant reprieves and pardons for offenses against the United States, except in cases of impeachment.

Treaties and Appointments

2. He shall have power, by and with the advice and consent of the Senate, to make treaties, provided two-thirds of the Senators present concur; and he shall nominate, and by and with the advice and consent of the Senate, shall appoint ambassadors, other public ministers and consuls, Judges of the Supreme Court, and all other officers of the United States, whose appointments are not herein otherwise provided for, and which shall be established by law: but the Congress may by law vest the appointment of such inferior officers, as they think proper, in the President alone, in the courts of law, or in the heads of departments.

Filling Vacancies

3. The President shall have power to fill up all vacancies that may happen during the recess of the Senate, by granting commissions which shall expire at the end of their next session.

Section 3. Duties of the President

Message to Congress—Adjourn and Call Special Session

He shall from time to time give the Congress information of the state of the Union, and recommend to their consideration such measures as he shall judge necessary and expedient; he may, on extraordinary occasions, convene both Houses, or either of them, and in case of disagreement between them, with respect to the time of adjournment, he may adjourn them to such time as he shall think proper; he shall receive ambassadors and other public ministers; he shall take care that the laws be faithfully executed, and shall commission all the officers of the United States.

(See also Article I, section 5.)

Section 4. Removal of Executive and Civil Officers

Impeachment of President and Other Officers

The President, Vice President and all civil officers of the United States, shall be removed from office on impeachment for, and conviction of, treason, bribery, or other high crimes and misdemeanors.

(See also Article I, sections 2 and 3.)

ARTICLE III. JUDICIAL DEPARTMENT

Section 1. Judicial Powers Vested in Federal Courts

Courts—Terms of Office and Salary of Judges

The judicial power of the United States, shall be vested in one Supreme Court, and in such inferior courts as the Congress may from time to time ordain and establish. The judges, both of the Supreme and inferior courts, shall hold their offices during good behavior, and shall, at stated times, receive for their services, a compensation, which shall not be diminished during their continuance in office.

Section 2. Jurisdiction of United States Courts

1. The judicial power shall extend to all cases, in law and equity, arising under this Constitution, the laws of the United States, and treaties made, or which shall be made, under their authority;—to all cases affecting ambassadors, other public ministers and consuls;—to all cases of admiralty and maritime jurisdiction;—to controversies to which the United States shall be a party;—to controversies between two or more states;—between a State and citizens of another State;—between citizens of different States; —between citizens of the same state claiming lands under grants of different States, and between a State, or the citizens thereof, and foreign States, citizens or subjects.
(See also Amendment XI.)

Jurisdiction of Supreme and Appellate Courts

2. In all cases affecting ambassadors, other public ministers and consuls, and those in which a State shall be party, the Supreme Court shall have original jurisdiction. In all the other cases before mentioned, the Supreme Court shall have appellate jurisdiction, both as to law and fact, with such exceptions, and under such regulations as the Congress shall make.

Trial of Crimes

3. The trial of all crimes, except in cases of impeachment, shall be by jury; and such trial shall be held in the State where the said crimes shall have been committed; but when not committed within any State, the trial shall be at such place or places as the Congress may by law have directed.
(See also Amendments V-VIII.)

Section 3. Treason

Treason Defined

1. Treason against the United States, shall consist only in levying war against them, or in adhering to their enemies, giving them aid and comfort.

460

Conviction

2. No person shall be convicted of treason unless on the testimony of two witnesses to the same overt act, or on confession in open court.

Punishment

3. The Congress shall have power to declare the punishment of treason, but no attainder of treason shall work corruption of blood, or forfeiture except during the life of the person attained.

ARTICLE IV. THE STATES AND THE FEDERAL GOVERNMENT

Section 1. Official Acts of the States

Full Faith and Credit

Full faith and credit shall be given in each State to the public acts, records, and judicial proceedings of every other State. And the Congress may by general laws prescribe the manner in which such acts, records and proceedings shall be proved, and the effect thereof.

(See also Amendment XIV.)

Section 2. Citizens of the States

Interstate Privileges of Citizens

1. The citizens of each State shall be entitled to all privileges and immunities of citizens in the several States.

Fugitives from Justice

2. A person charged in any State with treason, felony, or other crime, who shall flee from justice, and be found in another State, shall on demand of the executive authority of the State from which he fled, be delivered up, to be removed to the State having jurisdiction of the crime.

Fugitives from Service

3. No person held to service or labor in one State, under the laws thereof, escaping into another, shall, in consequence of any law or regulation therein, be discharged from such service or labor, but shall be delivered up on claim of the party to whom such service or labor may be due.

(*Person* here includes slave. This was the basis of the Fugitive Slave Laws of 1793 and 1850. It is now superseded by Amendment XIII, by which slavery is prohibited.)

461

Section 3. New States

Admission or Division of States

1. New States may be admitted by the Congress into this Union; but no new State shall be formed or erected within the jurisdiction of any other State; nor any State be formed by the junction of two or more States, or parts of States, without the consent of the Legislatures of the States concerned as well as of the Congress.

Control of the Property and Territory of the Union

2. The Congress shall have power to dispose of and make all needful rules and regulations respecting the territory or other property belonging to the United States; and nothing in this Constitution shall be so construed as to prejudice any claims of the United States, or of any particular State.

Section 4. Protection of States Guaranteed

Republican Form of Government

The United States shall guarantee to every State in this Union a republican form of government, and shall protect each of them against invasion; and on application of the Legislature, or of the executive (when the Legislature cannot be convened) against domestic violence.

ARTICLE V. AMENDMENTS

Amendments, How Proposed and Adopted

The Congress, whenever two-thirds of both Houses shall deem it necessary, shall propose amendments to this Constitution, or, on the application of the Legislatures of two-thirds of the several States, shall call a convention for proposing amendments, which, in either case, shall be valid to all intents and purposes, as part of this Constitution, when ratified by the Legislatures of three-fourths of the several States, or by conventions in three-fourths thereof, as the one or the other mode of ratification may be proposed by the Congress; provided that no amendment which may be made prior to the year one thousand eight hundred and eight shall in any manner affect the first and fourth clauses in the ninth section of the first article; and that no State, without its consent, shall be deprived of its equal suffrage in the Senate.

ARTICLE VI. GENERAL PROVISIONS

The Public Debt

1. All debts contracted and engagements entered into, before the adoption of this

Constitution, shall be as valid against the United States under this Constitution, as under the Confederation.

(See also Amendment XIV, section 4.)

Supreme Law of the Land

2. This Constitution, and the laws of the United States which shall be made in pursuance thereof; and all treaties made, or which shall be made, under the authority of the United States, shall be the supreme law of the land; and the judges in every State shall be bound thereby, anything in the Constitution or laws of any State to the contrary notwithstanding.

Oath of Office—No Religious Test Required

3. The Senators and Representatives before mentioned, and the members of the several State Legislatures, and all executive and judicial officers, both of the United States and of the several States, shall be bound by oath or affirmation, to support this Constitution; but no religious test shall ever be required as a qualification to any office or public trust under the United States.

ARTICLE VII. RATIFICATION OF THE CONSTITUTION

Ratification of Nine States Required

The ratification of the conventions of nine States, shall be sufficient for the establishment of this Constitution between the States so ratifying the same.

Done in convention by the unanimous consent of the States present the seventeeth day of September in the year of our Lord one thousand seven hundred and eighty-seven and of the Independence of the United States of America the twelfth. In witness whereof we have hereunto subscribed our names,

> G° Washington
> Presidt and deputy
> from Virginia

New Hampshire { John Langdon
{ Nicholas Gilman

Massachusetts { Nathaniel Gorham
{ Rufus King

Connecticut	{	Wm Saml Johnson Roger Sherman
New York		Alexander Hamilton
New Jersey	{	Wil: Livingston David Brearley. Wm Paterson. Jona: Dayton
Pennsylvania	{	B Franklin Thomas Mifflin Robt. Morris Geo. Clymer Thos FitzSimons Jared Ingersoll James Wilson Gouv Morris
Delaware	{	Geo: Read Gunning Bedford jun John Dickinson Richard Bassett Jaco: Broom
Maryland	{	James McHenry Dan of St Thos Jenifer Danl Carroll
Virginia	{	John Blair— James Madison Jr.
North Carolina	{	Wm Blount Richd Dobbs Spaight. Hu Williamson
South Carolina	{	J. Rutledge Charles Cotesworth Pinckney Charles Pinckney Pierce Butler
Georgia	{	William Few Abr Baldwin

AMENDMENTS

AMENDMENT I

Restrictions on Powers of Congress

(SECTION 1.) Congress shall make no law respecting an establishment of religion, or prohibiting the free exercise thereof; or abridging the freedom of speech, or of the press; or the right of the people peaceably to assemble, and to petition the Government for a redress of grievances.

(Proposed September 25, 1789; ratified December 15, 1791.)

AMENDMENT II

Right to Bear Arms

(SECTION 1.) A well-regulated militia, being necessary to the security of a free State, the right of the people to keep and bear arms, shall not be infringed.

(Proposed September 25, 1789; ratified December 15, 1791.)

AMENDMENT III

Billeting of Soldiers

(SECTION 1.) No soldier shall, in time of peace be quartered in any house, without the consent of the owner, nor in time of war, but in a manner to be prescribed by law.

(Proposed September 25, 1789; ratified December 15, 1791.)

AMENDMENT IV

Seizures, Searches and Warrants

(SECTION 1.) The right of the people to be secure in their persons, houses, papers, and effects, against unreasonable searches and seizures, shall not be violated, and no warrants shall issue, but upon probable cause, supported by oath or affirmation, and particularly describing the place to be searched, and the persons or things to be seized.

(Proposed September 25, 1789; ratified December 15, 1791.)

AMENDMENT V

Criminal Proceedings and Condemnation of Property

(SECTION 1). No person shall be held to answer for a capital, or otherwise infamous crime, unless on a presentment or indictment of a grand jury, except in cases arising in the land or naval forces, or in the militia, when in actual service in time of war or public danger; nor shall any person be subject for the same offense to be twice put in jeopardy of life or limb; nor shall be compelled in any criminal case to be a witness against himself, nor be deprived of life, liberty, or property, without due process of law; nor shall private property be taken for public use, without just compensation.

(Proposed September 25, 1789; ratified December 15, 1791.)

AMENDMENT VI

Mode of Trial in Criminal Proceedings

(SECTION 1.) In all criminal prosecutions, the accused shall enjoy the right to a speedy and public trial, by an impartial jury of the State and district wherein the crime shall have been committed, which district shall have been previously ascertained by law, and to be informed of the nature and cause of the accusation; to be confronted with the witnesses against him; to have compulsory process for obtaining witnesses in his favor, and to have the assistance of counsel for his defense.

(Proposed September 25, 1789; ratified December 15, 1791.)

AMENDMENT VII

Trial by Jury

(SECTION 1.) In suits at common law, where the value in controversy shall exceed twenty dollars, the right of trial by jury shall be preserved, and no fact tried by a jury, shall be otherwise re-examined in any court of the United States, than according to the rules of the common law.

(Proposed September 25, 1789; ratified December 15, 1791.)

AMENDMENT VIII

Bails—Fines—Punishments

(SECTION 1.) Excessive bail shall not be required, nor excessive fines imposed, nor cruel and unusual punishments inflicted.

(Proposed September 25, 1789; ratified December 15, 1791.)

AMENDMENT IX

Certain Rights Not Denied to the People

(SECTION 1.) The enumeration in the Constitution, of certain rights, shall not be construed to deny or disparage others retained by the people.

(Proposed September 25, 1789; ratified December 15, 1791.)

AMENDMENT X

State Rights

(SECTION 1.) The powers not delegated to the United States by the Constitution, nor prohibited by it to the States, are reserved to the States respectively, or to the people.

(Proposed September 25, 1789; ratified December 15, 1791.)

AMENDMENT XI

Judicial Powers

(SECTION 1.) The judicial power of the United States shall not be construed to extend to any suit in law or equity, commenced or prosecuted against one of the United States by citizens of another State, or by citizens or subjects of any foreign State.

(Proposed March 4, 1794; ratified February 7, 1795; declared ratified January 8, 1798.)

AMENDMENT XII

Election of President and Vice President

(SECTION 1.) The electors shall meet in their respective States and vote by ballot for President and Vice President, one of whom, at least, shall not be an inhabitant of the same State with themselves; they shall name in their ballots the person voted for as President, and in distinct ballots the person voted for as Vice President, and they shall make distinct lists of all persons voted for as President, and of all persons voted for as Vice President, and of the number of votes for each, which lists they shall sign and certify, and transmit sealed to the seat of the government of the United States, directed to the President of the Senate;—The President of the Senate shall, in the presence of the Senate and House of Representatives, open all the certificates and the votes shall then be counted;—the person having the greatest number of votes for President, shall be the President, if such number be a majority of the whole number of electors appointed; and if no person have such majority, then from the persons having the highest numbers not exceeding three on the list of those voted for as President, the House of Representatives shall choose immediately, by ballot, the President. But in choosing the President, the votes shall be taken by States, the representation from each State having one vote; a quorum for this purpose shall consist of a member or members from two-thirds of the States, and a majority of all the States shall be necessary to a choice. And if the House of Representatives shall not choose a President whenever the right of choice shall devolve upon them, before the fourth day of March next following, then the Vice President shall act as President, as in the case of the death or other constitutional disability of the President—The person having the greatest number of votes, as Vice President, shall be the Vice President, if such a number be a majority of the whole number of electors appointed, and if no person have a majority, then from the two highest numbers on the list, the Senate shall choose the Vice President; a quorum for the purpose shall consist of two-thirds of the whole number of Senators, and a majority of the whole number shall be necessary to a choice. But no person constitutionally ineligible to the office of President shall be eligible to that of Vice President of the United States.

(Proposed December 12, 1803; declared ratified September 25, 1804.)

AMENDMENT XIII

Slavery

(SECTION 1.) Neither slavery nor involuntary servitude, except as a punishment for crime whereof the party shall have been duly convicted, shall exist within the United States, or any place subject to their jurisdiction.

(SECTION 2.) Congress shall have power to enforce this article by appropriate legislation.

(Proposed January 31, 1865; ratified December 6, 1865; certified December 18, 1865.)

AMENDMENT XIV

Citizenship, Representation and Payment of Public Debt

Citizenship

(SECTION 1.) All persons born or naturalized in the United States and subject to the jurisdiction thereof, are citizens of the United States and of the State wherein they reside. No State shall make or enforce any law which shall abridge the privileges or immunities of citizens of the United States; nor shall any State deprive any person of life, liberty, or property, without due process of law; nor deny to any person within its jurisdiction the equal protection of the laws.

Apportionment of Representatives

(SECTION 2.) Representatives shall be apportioned among the several States according to their respective numbers, counting the whole number of persons in each State, excluding Indians not taxed. But when the right to vote at any election for the choice of electors for President and Vice President of the United States, Representatives in Congress, the executive and judicial officers of a State, or the members of the Legislature thereof, is denied to any of the male inhabitants of such State, being twenty-one years of age, and citizens of the United States, or in any way abridged, except for participation in rebellion, or other crime, the basis of representation therein shall be reduced in the proportion which the number of such male citizens shall bear to the whole number of male citizens twenty-one years of age in such State.

Disqualification for Public Office

(SECTION 3.) No person shall be a Senator or Representative in Congress, or elector of President and Vice President, or hold any office, civil or military, under the United States, or under any State, who, having previously taken an oath, as a member of Congress, or as an officer of the United States, or as a member of any State Legislature, or as an executive or judicial officer of any State, to support the Constitution of the United States, shall have engaged in insurrection or rebellion against the same, or given aid or comfort to the enemies thereof. But Congress may by a vote of two-thirds of each House, remove such disability.

Public Debt, Guarantee of

(SECTION 4.) The validity of the public debt of the United States, authorized by law, including debts incurred for payment of pensions and bounties for services in suppressing insurrection or rebellion, shall not be questioned. But neither the United States nor any State shall assume or pay any debt or obligation incurred in aid of insurrection or rebellion against the United States, or any claim for the loss or emancipation of any slave; but all such debts, obligations and claims shall be held illegal and void.

Power of Congress

(SECTION 5.) The Congress shall have power to enforce, by appropriate legislation, the provisions of this article.

(Proposed June 13, 1866; ratified July 9, 1868; certified July 28, 1868.)

AMENDMENT XV

Elective Franchise

Right of Citizens to Vote

(SECTION 1.) The right of citizens of the United States to vote shall not be denied or abridged by the United States or by any State on account of race, color, or previous condition of servitude.

Power of Congress

(Section 2.) The Congress shall have power to enforce this article by appropriate legislation.

(Proposed February 26, 1869; ratified February 3, 1870; certified March 30, 1870.)

AMENDMENT XVI

Income Tax—Congress Given Power to Lay and Collect

(Section 1.) The Congress shall have power to lay and collect taxes on incomes, from whatever source derived, without apportionment among the several States, and without regard to any census or enumeration.

(Proposed July 12, 1909; ratified February 3, 1913; certified February 25, 1913.)

AMENDMENT XVII

Popular Election of Senators

(Section 1.) The Senate of the United States shall be composed of two Senators from each State, elected by the people thereof, for six years; and each Senator shall have one vote. The electors in each State shall have the qualifications requisite for electors of the most numerous branch of the State Legislatures.

(Section 2.) When vacancies happen in the representation of any State in the Senate, the executive authority of such State shall issue writs of election to fill such vacancies: *Provided,* That the Legislature of any State may empower the executive thereof to make temporary appointments until the people fill the vacancies by election as the Legislature may direct.

(Section 3.) This amendment shall not be so construed as to affect the election or term of any Senator chosen before it becomes valid as part of the Constitution.

(Proposed May 13, 1912; ratified April 8, 1913; certified May 31, 1913.)

Note—Amendment XVII was proposed as a direct amendment of Article I, Section 3 of the Constitution.

AMENDMENT XVIII

Prohibition—States Given Concurrent Power to Enforce

(Section 1.) After one year from the ratification of this article the manufacture, sale, or transportation of intoxicating liquors within, the importation thereof into, or the exportation thereof from the United States and all territory subject to the jurisdiction thereof for beverage purposes is hereby prohibited.

(SECTION 2.) The Congress and the several States shall have concurrent power to enforce this article by appropriate legislation.

(SECTION 3.) This article shall be inoperative unless it shall have been ratified as an amendment to the Constitution by the Legislatures of the several States, as provided in the Constitution, within seven years from the date of the submission hereof to the States by the Congress.

(Proposed December 18, 1917; ratified January 16, 1919; certified January 29, 1919; effective January 29, 1920. For repeal see Amendment XXI.)

AMENDMENT XIX

Equal Suffrage

(SECTION 1.) The right of citizens of the United States to vote shall not be denied or abridged by the United States or by any State on account of sex.

(SECTION 2.) Congress shall have power to enforce this article by appropriate legislation.

(Proposed June 4, 1919; ratified August 18, 1920; certified August 26, 1920.)

AMENDMENT XX

Commencement of Congressional and Presidential Terms

End of Terms

(SECTION 1.) The terms of the President and Vice President shall end at noon on the 20th day of January, and the terms of Senators and Representatives at noon on the 3d day of January, of the years in which such terms would have ended if this article had not been ratified; and the terms of their successors shall then begin.

Assembling of Congress

(SECTION 2.) The Congress shall assemble at least once in every year, and such meeting shall begin at noon on the 3d day of January, unless they shall by law appoint a different day.

Congress Provides for Acting President

(SECTION 3.) If, at the time fixed for the beginning of the term of the President, the President-elect shall have died, the Vice-President-elect shall become President. If a President shall not have been chosen before the time fixed for the beginning of his term, or if the President-elect shall have failed to qualify, then the Vice-President-elect shall act as President until a President shall have qualified; and the Congress may by law provide for the case wherein neither a President-elect nor a Vice-President-elect

471

shall have qualified, declaring who shall then act as President, or the manner in which one who is to act shall be selected, and such person shall act accordingly until a President or Vice President shall have qualified.

Congress Has Power over Unusual Elections

(SECTION 4.) The Congress may by law provide for the case of the death of any of the persons from whom the House of Representatives may choose a President whenever the right of choice shall have devolved upon them, and for the case of the death of any of the persons from whom the Senate may choose a Vice President whenever the right of choice shall have devolved upon them.

Date in Effect

(SECTION 5.) Sections 1 and 2 shall take effect on the 15th day of October following the ratification of this article.

Conditions of Ratification

(SECTION 6.) This article shall be inoperative unless it shall have been ratified as an amendment to the Constitution by the Legislatures of three-fourths of the several States within seven years from the date of its submission.

(Proposed March 2, 1932; ratified January 23, 1933; certified February 6, 1933.)

AMENDMENT XXI

Repeal of Prohibition

Repeal of 18th Amendment

(SECTION 1.) The eighteenth article of amendment to the Constitution of the United States is hereby repealed.

Control of Interstate Liquor Transportation

(SECTION 2.) The transportation or importation into any State, Territory, or possession of the United States for delivery or use therein of intoxicating liquors, in violation of the laws thereof, is hereby prohibited.

Condition of Ratification

(SECTION 3.) This article shall be inoperative unless it shall have been ratified as an amendment to the Constitution by conventions in the several States, as provided in the Constitution, within seven years from the date of the submission hereof to the States by the Congress.

(Proposed February 20, 1933; ratified December 5, 1933; certified December 5, 1933.)

AMENDMENT XXII

Terms of Office of the President

Limitation on Number of Terms

(SECTION 1.) No person shall be elected to the office of the President more than twice, and no person who has held the office of President, or acted as President, for more than two years of a term to which some other person was elected President shall be elected to the office of the President more than once. But this article shall not apply to any person holding the office of President when this article was proposed by the Congress, and shall not prevent any person who may be holding the office of President, or acting as President, during the term within which this article becomes operative from holding the office of President or acting as President during the remainder of such term.

Condition of Ratification

(SECTION 2.) This article shall be inoperative unless it shall have been ratified as an amendment to the Constitution by the Legislatures of three-fourths of the several States within seven years from the date of its submission to the States by the Congress.

(Proposed March 24, 1947; ratified February 27, 1951; certified March 1, 1951.)

AMENDMENT XXIII

Voting Rights in the District of Columbia

(SECTION 1.) The district constituting the seat of government of the United States shall appoint in such manner as the Congress may direct:

A number of electors of president and Vice President equal to the whole number of Senators and Representatives in Congress to which the District would be entitled if it were a State, but in no event more than the least populous state; they shall be in addition to those appointed by the states, but they shall be considered, for the purposes of the election of President and Vice President, to be electors appointed by a State; and they shall meet in the District and perform such duties as provided by the twelfth article of amendment.

(Certified March 29, 1961.)

AMENDMENT XXIV

Prohibition of Poll Tax

(SECTION 1.) The right of citizens of the United States to vote in any primary or other election for President or Vice President, for electors for President or Vice President, or the Senator or Representative in Congress, shall not be denied or abridged by the United States or any State by reason of failure to pay any poll tax or other tax.

(SECTION 2.) The Congress shall have power to enforce this article by appropriate legislation.

(Certified January 23, 1964.)

AMENDMENT XXV

Presidential Succession

(SECTION 1.) In case of the removal of the President from office or of his death or resignation, the Vice President shall become President.

(SECTION 2.) Whenever there is a vacancy in the office of the Vice President, the President shall nominate a Vice President who shall take office upon confirmation by a majority vote of both Houses of Congress.

(SECTION 3.) Whenever the President transmits to the President pro tempore of the Senate and the Speaker of the House of Representatives his written declaration that he is unable to discharge the powers and duties of his office, and until he transmits to them a written declaration to the contrary, such powers and duties shall be discharged by the Vice President as Acting President.

(SECTION 4.) Whenever the Vice President and a majority of either the principal officers of the executive departments or of such other body as Congress may by law provide, transmit to the President pro tempore of the Senate and the Speaker of the House of Representatives their written declaration that the President is unable to discharge the powers and duties of his office, the Vice President shall immediately assume the powers and duties of the office as Acting President.

Thereafter, when the President transmits to the President pro tempore of the Senate and the Speaker of the House of Representatives his written declaration that no inability exists, he shall resume the powers and duties of his office unless the Vice President and a majority of either the principal officers of the executive department or of such other body as Congress may by law provide, transmit within four days to the President pro tempore of the Senate and the Speaker of the House of Representatives their written declaration that the President is unable to discharge the powers and duties of his office. Thereupon Congress shall decide the issue, assembling within forty-eight hours for that purpose if not in session. If the Congress, within twenty-one days after receipt of the latter written declaration, or, if Congress is not in session, within twenty-one days after Congress is required to assemble, determines by two-thirds vote of both Houses that the President is unable to discharge the powers and duties of his office, the Vice President shall continue to discharge the same as Acting President; otherwise, the President shall resume the powers and duties of his office.

(Certified February 10, 1967.)

AMENDMENT XXVI

Lowering Voting Age to 18 Years

(SECTION 1.) The right of citizens of the United States, who are 18 years of age or older, to vote shall not be denied or abridged by the United States or any State on account of age.

(SECTION 2.) The Congress shall have the power to enforce this article by appropriate legislation.

(Proposed March 23, 1971; ratified June 30, 1971.)

AMENDMENT XXVII

Equal Rights

(SECTION 1.) Equality of rights under the law shall not be denied or abridged by the United States or by any State on account of sex.

(SECTION 2.) The Congress shall have the power to enforce, by appropriate legislation, the provisions of this article.

(SECTION 3.) This amendment shall take effect two years after the date of ratification.

(Proposed March 22, 1972; ratification completed by 20 states; needs 18 more for final adoption.)

NOTE

1. Headings and paragraph numbers have been inserted to assist the reader and are not part of the Constitution. The original Constitution contains only article and section numbers. These headings and paragraph numbers were prepared under the direction of the chief clerk of the California Assembly.

GLOSSARY

ADJUDICATION. The determination of guilt or innocence by a trial court.

AGGRAVATED ASSAULT. An unlawful attack by one person upon another for the purpose of inflicting severe bodily injury, usually accompanied by the use of a weapon or other means likely to produce death or serious bodily harm.

AGGRESSIVE PATROL. A controversial police practice usually involving the saturation of a high-crime area with policemen who stop, question, frisk, and search pedestrians and motorists, almost at random, in an effort to prevent crimes and confiscate weapons.

AMERICAN BAR ASSOCIATION (ABA). A national professional organization of lawyers.

AMERICAN BAR FOUNDATION (ABF). A research wing of the ABA.

AMERICAN LAW INSTITUTE (ALI). A national association of prominent lawyers and legal scholars who voluntarily draft model laws, such as the *Model Penal Code.*

ANARCHY. The absence of law or supreme authority. Anarchism regards any form of politically organized government as unnecessary and undesirable.

ANOMIE. A state of normlessness, of uncertainty of goals, purposes, identities, roles, procedures, and norms necessary for a properly ordered society to function.

APPELLANT. One who appeals a legal decision to a higher court.

ARRAIGNMENT. The pleading process; legal proceeding at which formal charges are read, the defendant is notified of his rights, and a plea to the charges is requested.

ARREST. The physical taking into custody of a person believed to have committed a crime.

BAIL. A method of pretrial release of an accused person by means of having him post financial security to insure his appearance at later proceedings, such as trial.

BARGAIN, IMPLICIT. A sentencing practice by which the defendant pleads guilty and throws himself on the mercy of the court, with the implied understanding that he will receive a lighter sentence than if he pleaded not guilty and demanded trial.

BOOKING. The official registering of an arrest by the police, occurring at the police stationhouse and requiring the physical presence of the person arrested (for fingerprinting, and so on).

BURGLARY. Some states define burglary as "breaking and entering," while others merely require "unlawful entry with intent to commit a crime."

BUST. To arrest.

CHARGING. The process of formal criminal accusation usually involving the prosecutor and sometimes a grand jury. The term is also used to mean the judge's instruction of a jury on matters of law.

CITATION. An order, issued by the police, to appear before a magistrate or judge at a later date. Usually used for minor violations; avoids the taking of a suspect into immediate physical custody.

COERCION. Compulsion by force or by threat; constraint.

COHORT ANALYSIS (See TRACKING). The study over a period of time of a number of persons possessing some common characteristic.

COMMUNITY-BASED CORRECTIONS. The location and operation of correctional services in offenders' neighborhoods or other places outside the prison or jail, usually accompanied by the input of community opinion and decision making.

COP OUT. To plead guilty, often in return for a lesser charge.

COURTS, APPELLATE. Courts of appeal which interpret and apply statutes to specific criminal cases, but ordinarily do not conduct trials, accept guilty pleas, or impose sentences. Their primary purpose is to settle legal controversies arising from litigation in the lower courts.

COURTS, TRIAL. Federal, state, or local courts with jurisdiction to conduct trials, accept guilty pleas, and act as fact finders and sentencers of persons convicted of crimes.

CRIMINAL INTELLIGENCE. Information concerning alleged criminals which is not necessarily substantiated by a determination of guilt or the result of public proceedings.

CRIMINALISTICS. The science of crime detection, based upon the application of chemistry, physics, physiology, psychology, and other sciences. Criminalistics is a highly specialized and complicated field involving extensive laboratory work in ballistics, handwriting analysis, drug analysis, and other scientific methods. It is ordinarily used by the police in identification and case preparation.

CRIMINAL JUSTICE. A system for the enforcement of traditional penal laws, analysis of which involves describing the structural interrelationships of legislatures, appellate courts, and enforcement and administrative agencies as well as their corresponding processes of decision making from arrest of suspects through charging, adjudication, sentencing, imprisonment, and release on parole. Criminal justice is mostly concerned with the decisions of the various crime control agencies.

CRIMINOLOGY. The scientific study of crime and criminal behavior; the body of knowledge regarding crime as a social phenomenon, largely concerned with finding "causes" of criminal behavior.

CRITICAL STAGE. A stage of the criminal justice process which the courts have determined to be a crucial point capable of effecting the outcome of a criminal case. The number and range of critical stages remains unsettled and still in evolution; it does not yet include every stage in the process where decisions concerning criminal offenders or defendants are made.

CRUEL AND UNUSUAL PUNISHMENT. The Eighth Amendment guarantees freedom from cruel and unusual punishment; however the term's definition has rested with the courts. In recent years, the U.S. Supreme Court has revised various sentences as unconstitutional and set certain standards for their lengths and conditions.

DANGEROUSNESS. The term designating the ranking of offenders and offenses along some sort of "seriousness" or violent-proneness continuum. Generally denotes physical threat or harm rather than theft or property damage.

DETERRENCE, GENERAL. The threat of punishment which is directed to all members of society, and which seeks to restrain them from engaging in future criminal conduct.

DETERRENCE, SPECIFIC. The preventive effect of actual punishment on the offender, so that he does not repeat his crime.

DISCRETION. The authority to choose among alternative actions or of not acting at all.

DIVERSION. A decision or program designed to divert offenders from official processing to less formal, less adversary and noninstitutionalized community-based settings.

DOUBLE JEOPARDY. The common-law and constitutional prohibition against trial of a defendant more than once for the same crime.

DUE PROCESS. The fundamental yet ambiguous constitutional principle stating that no person shall be deprived of his life, liberty, or property without due process of law. This broad principle has undergone constant refinement and reinterpretation in appellate court decisions. Essentially it means that the state cannot intervene arbitrarily or capriciously into the lives of citizens, even those properly convicted and sentenced for crimes.

479

EFFECTIVENESS. The extent to which the criminal justice process (or any agency or individual functionary therein) achieves its objectives in a manner consistent with its long-range responsibilities. Effectiveness requires clear objectives and the capacity to achieve them.

EFFICIENCY. A variable in the measurement of effectiveness, involving evaluation of effectiveness within existing constraints of budget, manpower, and other resources over time.

ENTRAPMENT. A defense to criminal responsibility that arises from improper acts committed against the accused by another, usually a police undercover agent. When police encouragement plays upon the weaknesses of an innocent person and beguiles him to commit crimes he normally would not attempt, it can be deemed improper as entrapment and the evidence excluded under the exclusionary rule.

EQUAL PROTECTION. The constitutional principle asserting that the law must be applied equally and impartially to all, regardless of race, economic class, sex, and so on.

EXCLUSIONARY RULES. Legal rules, established by the U.S. Supreme Court and State Courts, which hold that the Fourth Amendment prohibition against unreasonable searches and seizures requires that illegally obtained evidence is impermissible and must be excluded as evidence at trial. Exclusionary rules apply as a constitutional requirement in all states as well as in the federal jurisdiction.

Ex parte. On one side only; done for, or in behalf of, one party only.

EXPUNGE. The act of physically destroying information—including criminal records—in files, computers, or other depositories.

FELONY. A serious criminal offense punishable by at least one year in prison.

FENCE. The selling of stolen goods; a receiver of stolen property.

FRISK. A pat-down search of a suspect by police, designed to discover weapons not to recover contraband. The scope of a frisk has been limited by the courts to be less than a full-scale search; it can occur only under specified conditions where the officer has reason to believe he is "in danger of life or limb."

FUNDAMENTAL FAIRNESS. This basic principle, which is essential under a democratic system, rests on the belief that crime control efforts must be fair even if it means an impairment of enforcement efficiency (e.g., the accused is entitled to a fair trial, confessions cannot be obtained unfairly by coercion, and so on).

GATE KEEPING. A process of simple tabulation or headcounting, such as the gate keeping conducted by prison authorities who count the number of prisoners who enter and leave an institution.

GOOD TIME. Credit allowed on the sentence which is given for satisfactory conduct in prison. Introduced as an incentive for inmates, it has become practically automatically awarded. It may reduce the minimum or maximum sentence or both.

GRAND JURY, CHARGING. The grand jury attached to a court whose purpose is to ratify or reject the prosecutor's request for a formal charge to be levied against a specific defendant.

GRAND JURY, INVESTIGATORY. The grand jury attached to a court empowered to conduct investigations into possible crimes or corruption.

HABITUAL OFFENDER. A legal category effective in some states by which severe penalties up to life imprisonment can be imposed on criminals convicted of any crime the third or fourth time.

HOMICIDE. This offense includes all willful killings without due process (e.g., murder and nonnegligent manslaughter).

INCAPACITATION. An objective of sentencing, the aim of which is to restrain a potential offender from committing new and/or different crimes, usually by holding him in a maximum-security prison.

INCARCERATION. Imprisonment in a state, federal, or local institution.

INDEX OFFENSES. The term designating the seven classes of offenses reported annually by the FBI in its *Uniform Crime Reports*. They include: willful homicide, forcible rape, robbery, burglary, aggravated assault, larceny over 50 dollars, and motor vehicle theft.

INDICTMENT. A written accusation presented by a grand jury to the court in which it is impaneled, charging that a person or persons named has done some specified criminal act. An indictment is a formal charging instrument.

INFORMATION. A formal charging document similar to an indictment; this is the most common method of bringing formal charges. An information is drafted by a prosecutor and tested before a magistrate at a preliminary hearing, not before a grand jury. The evidentiary standard for the information, like that of the indictment, is probable cause that the defendant committed a crime and should be "bound over" for trial.

INSANE. A legal classification meaning not guilty (technically not responsible) because of court determination that the defendant lacked control over his actions, could not tell right from wrong, and so on, at the time he committed the offense.

JURY, GRAND. A jury of inquiry impaneled for the term of the court, and whose functions include investigation of alleged crime and corruption and the

481

ratification or rejection of the prosecutor's request for a formal charge (indictment). Grand juries are usually comprised of 23 members, and serve for a fixed term as opposed to the smaller trial jury which functions only as long as the trial. A working quorum for a grand jury is commonly 16, and an indictment is issued on the affirmative vote of 12 members.

JUVENILE DELINQUENT. An individual youth who has not yet reached a specific age (e.g., 18) who has been adjudicated by a juvenile court to have committed a crime or to be incorrigible or in need of supervision by the state.

LARCENY-THEFT. The unlawful taking or stealing of property or articles of value without the use of violence or fraud (e.g., shoplifting, pickpocketing, purse-snatching, thefts from parked autos, and so on). The law differentiates between petit larceny and grand larceny, the former usually being limited to thefts where the value of property stolen is 50 dollars or less.

LAW ENFORCEMENT ASSISTANCE ADMINISTRATION (LEAA). The agency of the U.S. Department of Justice responsible for administering law enforcement grants and loans under terms of the Omnibus Crime Control and Safe Streets Act of 1968.

LINEUP. A police identification procedure by which the suspect in a crime is exhibited before the victim or witness to determine if he committed the offense. To be accepted as valid, the lineup must meet certain standards (e.g., the suspect cannot be the only one handcuffed, and so on).

Mala in se. The common-law term designating crimes "evil in themselves" (e.g., homicide, robbery, burglary, and so on). Many of these offenses are today referred to as "conventional" or "street" crimes.

Mala prohibita. The term designating crimes which are largely legislative creations (e.g., antitrust violations, income tax evasion, and other forms of white-collar crime).

Mens rea. This Latin term literally means a "guilty mind," and relates to criminal intent.

MIDDLE STAGES. The stages of the criminal justice process where formal charges are brought and innocence or guilt determined, and where convicted offenders are sentenced.

MISDEMEANOR. A criminal offense which is less serious than a felony, and which is usually punishable by no more than a year in a county jail, and/or a fine, restitution, or some other minor penalty. Also known as *delicta.*

Model Penal Code (MPC). The final draft in 1962 by the American Law Institute contains suggested revision of the substantive law of crime, and proposes a model sentencing structure.

Model Sentencing Act (MSA). Drafted in 1963 by the Advisory Council of

Judges of the National Council on Crime and Delinquency (NCCD), this 35-page document proposed model sentencing structures.

NATIONAL COUNCIL ON CRIME AND DELINQUENCY (NCCD). A private research corporation.

Nolle prosequi. The prosecutor's decision not to initiate prosecution even when there is sufficient evidence to do so. This accepted doctrine reflects the prosecutor's broad discretion.

Nolo contendere. The Latin term meaning, "I will not contest it." The name of a plea in a criminal action which has the same legal effect as a plea of guilty so far as it regards all proceedings on an indictment, and on which the defendant may be sentenced. Usually employed in corporate crimes, since it does not have the same repercussions in any subsequent civil suit, this plea is available in about half the states and in the federal jurisdiction.

NORM, SOCIAL. A rule or standard of behavior within a group or society which is defined by the shared expectations of the dominant members of that group or society. Social norms provide guidelines to the range of permissible behaviors which are appropriate in a given situation.

PAROLE. The conditional release of a prisoner from his uncompleted sentence of incarceration, to community supervision by state agents. The parole decision is made administratively, by a parole board, and is the dominant means by which convicts are released from prison.

PAROLE BOARD. The state administrative agency empowered to decide whether inmates shall be conditionally released from prison before completion of their sentences.

PAT DOWN. A physical search of the suspect's *outer* clothing (not inside pockets) which is conducted to protect the officer from a possible weapon.

Per curiam. Literally, "by the court." An opinion of the full court, as opposed to one with some judges affirming and others dissenting. Usually a brief decision, without detailed argument.

PLAINTIFF. The complaining party in any litigation, such as the state in a criminal case.

PLEA BARGAINING. The practice involving negotiation between prosecutor and defendant and/or his attorney, which often results in the defendant's entering of a guilty plea in exchange for the state's reduction of charges, or for the prosecutor's promise to recommend a more lenient sentence than the offender would ordinarily receive.

POLICE ADVISORY BOARD. A citizen's group organized to react to general police policy matters; sometimes organized on a neighborhood basis.

POLICE REVIEW BOARD. A citizen's group composed of representatives of particular ethnic, racial or other groups whose task is to investigate allegations of police misconduct.

PRELIMINARY HEARING. A court proceeding serving as the testing-ground for an information brought by a prosecutor against a criminal defendant. Unlike grand jury proceedings, it is open to the public and may be attended by the defendant and his attorney. At this hearing, the prosecutor seeks to convince the judge that there is probable cause to believe the defendant committed a crime and should be held over for trial; the defendant may challenge the state's evidence through cross-examination of witnesses.

PRESENTENCE INVESTIGATION. Investigation of the relevant background of a convicted offender, usually conducted by a probation officer attached to a court, designed to act as a sentencing guide for the sentencing judge. (See PRESENTENCE REPORT.)

PRESENTENCE REPORT. The report prepared from the presentence investigation, which is designed to assist the judge in passing sentence on a convicted defendant. Presentence reports vary in scope and focus, but most include information on the criminal history, employment and school background, and so on, of the defendant.

PRESENTMENT. A charge issued by a grand jury on its own motion, as opposed to an indictment which is a charge requested by a prosecutor.

PRETRIAL SCREENS. Stages in the criminal justice process which are designed to exert quality control over police arrests and prosecutor's charging decisions in order to reduce the chances of unwarranted and unnecessary trials.

PRISONIZATION. A process by which the prison inmate comes to strongly identify with and gain status within the inmate culture.

PROBABLE CAUSE. Reasonable cause, less than beyond a reasonable doubt and more than suspicion. This evidentiary standard requires enough reasonable trustworthy facts to justify a reasonably intelligent and prudent man in believing that an offense has been committed and that the accused person committed it.

PROBATION. A sentence served in the community without incarceration, under supervision of a probation officer and conditional upon adherence to rules established by the court.

PROJECT SEARCH. Launched in 1969, the System for Electronic Analysis and Retrieval of Criminal Histories (SEARCH) is a major, federally funded program designed to integrate the criminal statistical reporting system of all states. SEARCH was established to explore the potentialities and feasibility of an on-line system which would permit interstate exchange of offender history files maintained by state and local criminal justice agencies.

PROPRIETY. This basic principle, somewhat related to standards of fundamental fairness, asserts that law enforcement must conduct itself in proper fashion in obtaining confessions, guilty pleas, and so on, which are trustworthy and accurate, and in providing humane treatment to all suspects or defendants. The basic mandate for fairness and propriety rests in constitutional guarantees—protection against unreasonable search and seizure, freedom from self-incrimination, equal protection under the law, and due process of law.

PUBLIC DEFENDER. An attorney attached to a court jurisdiction whose job involves the defense of indigents.

RAP, RAP SHEET. "Rap" is slang for a conviction and sentence. "Rap sheet" is an offender's official criminal record listing prior arrests, convictions and sentences. "Rap partner" is a codefendant, convicted and sentenced for the same crime.

RAPE, FORCIBLE. The carnal knowledge of a female through the use of force or the threat of force.

RAPE, STATUTORY. Carnal knowledge of a female who has not yet reached a certain age, not requiring the use of force or lack of consent.

REFORMATORY. State incarcerative institution for young felons, usually those 18 to 21 years old, although many reformatories hold inmates up to age 30.

REINTEGRATION. A correctional goal or style which stresses the merging of correctional agencies with community resources and the necessity of on-the-street adjustment of offenders. The aim is to promote the offender's re-entry into the community, and to this end, both the offender and the community are viewed as change targets.

RELEASE-ON-OWN-RECOGNIZANCE (ROR). The pretrial release of an arrested person on his stated promise to appear for trial at a later date, and after a determination that he is likely to appear. Used primarily with indigent defendants as an alternative to monetary bail, ROR was initially developed in the 1960s by the Vera Institute of Justice in New York City.

RESEARCH, APPLIED. As opposed to pure research, this kind of inquiry is directed toward the formulation or discovery of scientific principles that can be used to solve some practical problem, to the *application* of scientific theories.

RESEARCH, PURE. As opposed to applied research, this kind of inquiry is conducted for the purpose of formulating scientific principles and theories, rather than for the purpose of solving a specific problem. Pure research seeks to lay an essential foundation for further scientific research.

RESTITUTION. The act of restoring, or making good; or giving equivalent for any loss, damage, or injury committed. Although seldom used as a dispositional alternative in the U.S. criminal justice system, it is primarily employed in minor property offenses and vandalism involving juveniles.

REVOCATION. Probation or parole may be revoked for commission of a new offense or for violation of any condition of the parole or probation. Revocation is decided by the same agency which grants the conditional release.

ROBBERY. A felony involving theft of property from a person by the use of force or the threat of force. Examples are mugging, holdups, yoking, and so on.

SEGREGATION. A secure unit in prison where inmates are held in solitary confinement as punishment for prison-rule infraction or for their own protection from other prisoners.

SELF-REPORT STUDIES. A modern survey technique designed to measure the number of criminals by asking respondents if they have committed crimes within a specific period. Although their validity may be somewhat suspect, even with firm pledges of confidentiality, as many as 91 percent of the respondents surveyed by some studies have admitted one or more criminal acts.

SENTENCE, FLAT (STRAIGHT). A fixed sentence without a maximum or minimum.

SENTENCE, INDETERMINATE. A sentence to incarceration with a spread of time between a minimum date of parole eligibility and a maximum discharge date. A completely indeterminate sentence has a minimum of one day and a maximum of natural life.

SENTENCE, MAXIMUM. A maximum sentence sets the outer limit beyond which a prisoner cannot be held in custody.

SENTENCE, MINIMUM. The time which an offender must spend in prison before becoming eligible for parole.

SENTENCE, SUSPENDED. Technically a "sentence," but involving unconditional, unsupervised release of the convicted defendant.

SENTENCING. The postconviction stage of the criminal justice process in which the defendant is brought before the court for imposition of sentence. Usually a trial judge imposes sentence, but in some jurisdictions sentencing is performed by jury or by sentencing councils.

SENTENCING COUNCILS. A panel of three or more judges which confers to determine a criminal sentence. Sentencing councils are not as commonly used as sentencing by a trial judge, though there appears to be a greater trend toward the council approach, in an effort to reduce sentence disparity.

SENTENCING JURIES. Trial juries attached to a court which impose sentence.

STAKEOUT. Hidden police keeping premises or vehicles under constant surveillance.

486

Stare decisis. Literally "let the decision stand." This judicial principle guides courts to consistently follow legal precedent from former cases.

SUBCULTURE. The culture of an identifiable segment or subgroup of a society, which is part of the larger culture but which differs in certain important respects (e.g., values, language, social norms, and so on). This sociological term is generally applied to subcultures of criminals, violence, delinquents, police, and so on.

SURVEILLANCE. Police investigative technique involving visual or electronic observation or listening directed at a person or place (e.g., stakeout, tailing suspects, wiretapping, and so on). Its objective is to gather evidence of a crime or merely to accumulate intelligence about suspected criminal activity.

TAIL. To follow a person, keeping him under hidden surveillance.

TOSS. To search.

TRACKING (See COHORT ANALYSIS). The following of an individual through the entire criminal justice process; this technique is still rarely employed. Also known as cohort analysis, which involves starting with a sample of persons at a specific point—all citizens questioned by police in a given period, for example—and tracking these persons as they flow through the system and are dropped or diverted from it, or carried further into it.

TRAINING SCHOOL. State institutions housing juvenile delinquents on court order; designed to offer educational and vocational training programs.

TRIAL, BENCH. A trial before a judge sitting without a jury.

TRIAL, JURY. The jury participating in the trial of a given case, which is ordinarily composed of 12 members; a petit jury as opposed to the larger, grand jury (23 members).

TYPOLOGY. A classification schema composed of two or more ideal types which provide abstract categories in terms of which individual or group phenomena are analyzed. A typology of criminal behavior, for example, seeks to organize data about different types of criminals for the purpose of aiding research efforts and developing general theories of criminal behavior. As a conceptual tool, typologies are potentially useful constructs.

Uniform Crime Reports (UCRs). National crime statistics maintained by the Federal Bureau of Investigation, they are based on data concerning seven "Index" offenses: willful homicide, forcible rape, aggravated assault, robbery, burglary, larceny over 50 dollars and motor vehicle theft. Their basic statistic is "crimes known to the police"; that is, those which are reported to the police or discovered by the police, but not necessarily solved. The UCRs are published annually by the U.S. Department of Justice.

VENUE. The place in which an alleged act from which a legal action arises takes place; place from which the jury is drawn and the trial takes place.

VICTIMIZATION SURVEYS. A technique for measuring crime more precisely than it is measured by official crimes known to the police, this survey method attempts to discover how many persons claim to have been victimized by a crime over a specific period of time. Some of the most famous victimization surveys conducted within recent years included studies performed for the President's Commission on Law Enforcement and Administration of Justice. Virtually all of these studies indicate that the incidence of crime is several times greater than reported by the police in the FBI's *Uniform Crime Reports*.

VICTIMLESS CRIMES. Crimes for which there is no nonofficial complainant or victim (e.g., drug law violations, prostitution, homosexuality between consenting adults, drunkenness, and so on). This class of offenses comprises the bulk of crimes handled by the criminal justice system.

Voir dire. The selection of jurors in court through examination by defense counsel and prosecutor, intended as a screening device to weed out persons who might be biased or otherwise incompetent to render a fair verdict. In addition to the judge's removal of jury candidates following the *voir dire*, the prosecutor and defense counsel each have the option to make a specific number of peremptory challenges which can result in the removal of jury candidates without demonstrated cause.

WARRANT, SEARCH. A warrant obtained from a judge empowering the police to search a specified premise on the belief that it contains criminal evidence.

WHITE-COLLAR CRIME. Introduced in 1939 by Edwin H. Sutherland, the late criminologist, this term usually signifies law violations by corporations or individuals including theft or fraud and other violations of trust committed in the course of the offender's occupation (e.g., embezzlement, price fixing, antitrust violations, and so on).

WIRETAPPING. A form of electronic eavesdropping where, upon court order, enforcement officials surreptitiously listen to phone calls.

WORK RELEASE. Correctional programs which allow an inmate to leave the institution for the purpose of continuing regular employment during the daytime, but reporting back to lockup nights and weekends.

WRIT OF *certiorari*. A method of obtaining review of a case by the U.S. Supreme Court; a writ issued by a superior court to an inferior court, directing that the record of a case be delivered for review.

WRIT OF *habeas corpus*. Literally, "You have the body." A common-law instrument designed to bring a person held in custody in a lockup, jail, prison, or other institution before a court or judge, to force the state to "show cause" why custody should continue; an instrument initiating an appeal of custody.

INDEX

References to figures and charts appear in italics;
following page numbers refers to footnotes